A COMPROMISE
OF PRINCIPLE

MICHAEL LES BENEDICT

A COMPROMISE
OF PRINCIPLE

Congressional Republicans and
Reconstruction 1863–1869

W · W · NORTON & COMPANY · INC ·

NEW YORK

FIRST EDITION

→》 *The text of this book is set in Linotype Times Roman. Composition,
printing, and binding are by the Vail-Ballou Press, Inc.* 《←

Library of Congress Cataloging in Publication Data
Benedict, Michael Les.
    A compromise of principle.
    Bibliography: p.
    1. Reconstruction. 2. United States—Politics and
government—1865–1869. 3. Johnson, Andrew, Pres. U.S.,
1808–1875. 4. Republican Party—History. I. Title.
E668.B46   973.8'1   74–10645

ISBN 0–393–05524–8

1 2 3 4 5 6 7 8 9 0

TO HAROLD
mentor and friend

Contents

Credits for illustrations following pages 170 and 300

With the exceptions noted below, the illustrations appearing in this book are United States Signal Corps photos, in the Brady Collection in the National Archives, and are reproduced by permission of the National Archives.

"Slavery Is Dead," *Harper's Weekly,* January 12, 1867. Reconstruction and How It Works, *Harper's Weekly,* September 1, 1866. "The First Vote," *Harper's Weekly,* November 9, 1867. The Senate as a Court of Impeachment for the Trial of Andrew Johnson, *Harper's Weekly,* April 11, 1974. Zachariah Chandler, Culver Pictures, Inc. Frederick Douglass, Schomburg Collection, New York Public Library. Senator Joseph F. Fowler of Tennessee, Historical Pictures Service, Chicago. Senator Jacob M. Howard of Michigan, Courtesy Chicago Historical Society. Hon. Edmund Gibson Ross of Kansas, Library of Congress. Wendell Phillips, Library of Congress.

*   *   *

Cartoons on the following pages are from *Harper's Weekly:* page 167, April 28, 1866; page 213, October 27, 1866; page 199, September 22, 1866; page 205, September 8, 1866; page 207, October 27, 1866; page 195, August 4, 1866; page 271, February 15, 1868.

Charts

Lists: Radicals and Conservatives in the 38–40 Congresses

12

Preface

THE "NEW WAVE" OF Reconstruction historiography has crested. Fifteen years ago most historians still considered the "Radical Republicans" the villains of the post-Civil War years, and Andrew Johnson the hero; Republican Reconstruction policy was an unmitigated disaster. When, without really knowing it, I began this book as a nervous college senior sitting in on Professor Harold M. Hyman's graduate seminar, the changes had just begun. A few years earlier, Eric L. McKitrick had published his reevaluation of the first years of Johnson's administration, for the first time presenting the origins of the Reconstruction struggle from the viewpoint of the Republican moderates. John Hope Franklin, Kenneth M. Stampp, and LaWanda and John H. Cox, inspired by the accelerating American civil rights movement, had just restored the question of racial accommodation to its central place in the conflict—"the issue of Reconstruction," the Coxes called it. By 1965 historians had slight respect for Johnson's conciliatory Reconstruction policy—a policy conciliating white southerners at the expense of blacks. The Republicans, who strove for legal and political equality for the newly freed slaves, emerged as the new heroes of the era.

Enthusiastically, I worked on the historiography of Andrew Johnson and then on the passage of the Civil Rights act of 1866. As a graduate student, still working under Professor Hyman, I thought I leapt to the forefront of historical interpretation of the Reconstruction era, for I had concluded that the so-called Radical Republicans had never been united on Reconstruction policy and that the truly radical among them had not controlled congressional legislation on the subject at all. But of course there were other historians, drawn by the same historiographical ferment, who have reached similar conclusions. As this book goes to press, historians are becoming more and more aware that "Radical Reconstruction" was not very radical after all.

In this study I have concentrated on the tensions and divisions among the "Radical Republicans," placing in the background the well-studied struggle between President Johnson and the party which elected him to office. But in centering upon the Republicans this way, the reader should remember that I am offering a somewhat distorted picture: the immense differences between Republicans and Andrew Johnson and his Democratic allies are intentionally left without major attention. Leading Republicans emerge as conservatives although neither President Johnson nor the Democrats (who were *truly* archconservatives) recognized them as such. Indeed, compared to the President and the Democrats, conservative and moderate Republicans like Henry L. Dawes, John Sherman, John A. Bingham, and William Pitt Fessenden emerge at least as men of liberal views, even if they were not the radicals that Democrats claimed they were. Nonetheless, radical Republicans knew that their conservative allies were not as committed as they to the racially egalitarian principles of the Republican party, and they were continually frustrated in their attempts to win what they conceived to be true security for the Union and its loyal southern adherents. They recognized the differences between what they called "radical Radicalism" and "conservative Radicalism." And it is to those differences and their consequences that I have directed my attention.

As part of that effort I have made modest use of techniques utilized by political scientists to analyze legislative bodies. But I have not used them in the same way as scholars in our sister discipline. They use these tools with maximum precision, obtaining results which may be accepted with confidence because they are valid according to the laws of statistics and probability. I have used these tools merely to explicate points that I intend to prove through more traditional historical analysis. My lists of radicals and conservatives are not intended precisely to define those groups; they are not the starting points for the analyses which follow them, although they have aided immeasurably in understanding the nature of radicalism and the development of Reconstruction legislation; they are intended primarily to give the reader a general statement of who radicals, moderates, and conservatives were individually, to answer the complaint that most studies of Reconstruction do not give that information. This is not to downgrade the importance of this statistical analysis. With corroborating historical evidence, this statistical work indicates that radicals never controlled the process of Reconstruction, that moderates and conservatives dominated the institutional mechanisms of Congress. But it does this only because the historical evidence supports it. Standing alone, it would not have the scientific precision that political scientists require.

Some portions of this book have already appeared in print. Chapter IX has been published in a different form in *Civil War History;* parts of chapters XII, XIII, and XV, and all of chapter XIV appeared in my *Impeachment and Trial of Andrew Johnson,* published in 1973. In completing this work I have been aided by the careful and forceful criticism of

Harold M. Hyman, William P. Hobby Professor of History at Rice University, and by the helpful suggestions from many of his graduate students. The Woodrow Wilson Foundation and the Center for Research in Social Change and Economic Development, located in Houston, Texas, provided essential financial support for my research, and the staffs of manuscript repositories throughout the country—especially those of the National Archives and the Library of Congress—offered invaluable assistance. Mr. Frederick Jones prepared the computer programs that made it possible for me to employ statistical techniques of analysis in addition to more conventional historical methods, and he gave freely of his time to guide me in their use. Finally, I must thank my wife, Karen, who gave up her own activities so often to help me in my work.

MICHAEL LES BENEDICT

Columbus, Ohio

I have been taught since I have been in public life to consider it a matter of proper statesmanship, when we aim at an object which we think is valuable and important, if that object . . . is unattainable, to get as much of it and come as near it as we may be able to do.

WILLIAM PITT FESSENDEN

A moral principle cannot be compromised.

CHARLES SUMNER

A COMPROMISE
OF PRINCIPLE

ONE

Radical Radicals and Conservative Radicals

————————————————— ✦ —————————————————

A "DARK AND BLOODY GROUND," Bernard Weisberger called it—this battle-field of Reconstruction history, on which scholars have so long contested the nature of the era's issues and the motivation and morality of its actors.[1] To one group of partisans—predominant from 1900 to the 1940s—the heroes were the suffering white southerners, who had to endure the rigors of "Radical Reconstruction." By the 1920s and 1930s, they painted in similar hues President Andrew Johnson, "plebeian and patriot," who fought for a mild restoration program to the point of his own impeachment. As villains they cast the "Radical Republicans," the northern "vindictives" led by the sinister Thaddeus Stevens and the zealot Charles Sumner, who imposed black suffrage and carpetbag-scalawag rule on the South.[2] Opposing scholars, triumphant in the 1960s and 1970s, have redeemed the Radical Republicans' reputations, finding in them the fore-bears of the modern civil rights movement, "Lincoln's vanguard for racial justice," while in Andrew Johnson and the southern whites that he tried to protect they discern the precursors of present-day segregationists and white racists.[3]

In the course of the historiographical conflict, historians have learned that the "Radical Republicans," described by earlier generations of schol-ars as a monolithic, overpowering unit welded by the fire of Thaddeus Stevens's will, the fanaticism of Charles Sumner, and the power of the party whip, were neither monolithic nor even very radical. Eric L. Mc-Kitrick rediscovered William Pitt Fessenden, the moderate Republican leader of the Senate, and suggested that the Fourteenth Amendment had not been framed by radicals after all. He, William R. Brock, David Donald, and Charles Fairman have recorded the furious wrangling over the final congressional plan of Reconstruction, demonstrating that it was not whipped through Congress by Stevens's lash, but rather was the result of last-minute compromise between bitterly contesting Republican factions.[4]

So the revisionists of the 1960s and 1970s have posed new questions: Was Reconstruction in any true sense radical? To what extent did it incorporate the ideas of those Republicans whom contemporaries identified with the radical wing of the party? Who really dominated Congress and the Republican party during the era historians have called "Radical Reconstruction"?

Indeed, who were the radicals?

For many years historians were only dimly aware that differences existed among "Radical Republicans" after 1865. Many factors contributed to their uncertainty. The first lay in the very appellation "Radical Republicans," for the fact is that contemporaries used that term not to elucidate but to obfuscate the real alignments in the Republican party. Originally "radical" seems to have come into wide use to describe those members of the Union party who believed that abolition should become one of the northern war aims, whether as a humanitarian gesture or an effort to weaken the southern aristocracy. Since President Lincoln, Secretary of State William Henry Seward, the Blair family, and most Democrats resisted this conclusion during the first years of the war, they became known as conservatives. As the Democratic party machinery revived, the term "conservative" came more and more to refer primarily to Union party members who resisted emancipation, rather than to Democrats. When the president endorsed emancipation, he removed the clear distinction which until then had prevailed. After 1862 radicalism was a rather foggy notion embodying an inclination to insist on more secure guarantees for freedom than the president's Emancipation Proclamation, a more vigorous prosecution of the war, and especially resistance to any hint of peace without northern victory.[5]

But by 1865 radicalism ceased to be defined in terms of war issues and instead related to questions of peace: the terms of Reconstruction. In particular, radicalism came to be identified with the insistence that black southerners be given a meaningful role in the political life of the restored states. In practical terms, this again brought radicals into sharp conflict with Lincoln's position, for he had committed himself to recognizing states reorganized by the action of white unionists alone. Conservative Republicans sustained the president's policy and pressed for an almost automatic congressional recognition of any reconstructed state government that Lincoln endorsed. Finally, as throughout the Reconstruction years, there were Republicans who took a position midway between the extremes. Often these "centrists" would act together, formulating their own compromise policies; on other occasions they would divide, some supporting more radical and others more conservative positions. (In the following pages, the term "nonradical" will denote conservative Republicans and those centrists who generally allied with them when centrists divided.)

During the summer and fall of 1865 differences between radicals and nonradicals were sharply delineated. The radicals insisted on the incorporation of black suffrage in any plan of Reconstruction, no matter what position Lincoln's successor, Andrew Johnson, might take, while nonradicals abandoned that requirement (which most of them had earlier come to accept) rather than alienate the president, and because they believed that Johnson's opposition rendered insistence upon Negro suffrage politically impractical. But despite this clear conflict, Johnson either failed or refused to recognize the differences. And when he would not acquiesce in the mild peace program nonradicals required, he and his Democratic and renegade Republican allies deliberately lumped all Republicans together as radicals, insisting that the entire congressional party had come under the domination of the "fanatics," Thaddeus Stevens and Charles Sumner.

From this time forward all anti-Johnson Republicans were called—and called themselves—Radical Republicans, and it was this journalistic and political convention which for so long submerged the incontestable fact that many "Radicals" were radical with a capital *R* only. For four years, the entire term of Andrew Johnson, the anomaly of what radical Senator Charles D. Drake called "conservative radicalism" persisted, and the failure to recognize this has subsequently plagued historical literature. Thus, more radical Radicals referred to "conservative Radicals," while the more conservative Radicals complained of "extreme Radicals" or "Radical-Radicals." Drake called himself "a representative, not of a conservative radicalism, but of a radical radicalism . . . which has a strange and new-fashioned way of shelving those who vacillate or stagger, as well as those who desert," while Stevens reminded the House of Representatives that the Senate as a whole was "several furlongs behind the House in the march of . . . radicalism." [6] To avoid problems of semantics, in this work Radical Republicans will be called simply Republicans and the term *radical* (in lower case) will refer only to those Republicans whom it accurately describes.

A second factor led historians to the conclusion that Republicans were in fact as united under radical leadership as their enemies insisted—their essential unanimity on the votes by which they passed their legislation and rejected Democratic and Johnsonite amendments to it. During the first session of the Thirty-ninth Congress, for example, the average index of cohesion of Republican senators was a high 68.01. [7] And of the sixty-four votes on Reconstruction-connected legislation, forty-six had indices of cohesion above the already high average. Only one of the eighteen votes below the average involved the actual passage of legislation.

But tensions between more extreme "Radical Republicans" and their

less radical allies flared into the open often enough to let investigators
know they existed. In February 1865 a small coterie of radicals joined
Democrats to prevent the restoration of Lincoln's reconstructed Louisiana
government. Conflict rekindled with the meeting of the Thirty-ninth Congress in December 1865, when in the Republican caucus Senate conservatives and centrists forced modification of the resolution creating the Joint
Committee on Reconstruction. Republican nonradicals defeated an attempt
by Sumner and Henry Wilson to void the southern black codes in the first
weeks of that Congress. In March radicals joined Democrats to defeat one
of the original versions of the Fourteenth Amendment, while conservative
and center Republicans joined Democrats to defeat an 1866 version of the
Tenure of Office bill. The following session witnessed a sharp struggle over
a new plan of Reconstruction. Continuing conflicts over the wisdom of
adjourning Congress for the summer and fall, leaving President Johnson
unwatched, culminated in the ill-fated impeachment, which led to the best-
known and most spectacular division of all.

Occasionally individual Republicans would grow exasperated at such
factionalism. After the defeat of his 1866 proposal to regulate tenure of
offices, Lyman Trumbull bitterly complained of the willingness of "a few
Republicans" to "unite with conservatives and Democrats to beat their
own friends." Two years later California's John Conness was still regretting
"that Senators here representing the great national, patriotic party of the
Union . . . so often differ upon questions of doctrine and policy." [8]

It was despite such disagreements that the "Radical Republicans"
maintained their astonishing unity on their most important legislation.
With the presidency occupied by a man whose position on Reconstruction
was unacceptable to even the most conservative among them, there was
no choice but to maintain such agreement as would enable them to control two thirds of the votes in each house of Congress. "Standing right
here in the ranks where our elbows as it were constantly touch, I can feel
the slightest symptom of faltering," Timothy Otis Howe wrote his niece.
"We count so much upon each other—and each man in a time like this
counts so much." [9] Republicans feared not only that they might be unable
to overturn Johnson's vetoes, but that intraparty differences might allow
Democrats and those few congressmen (usually called Conservatives) who
followed Johnson out of the Union party to seize the balance of power.
Even with the high level of Republican agreement on major legislation,
Conness complained, "Senators on this side of the Chamber allow them
[Democrats] often to dictate a policy to divide and distribute out forces,
while they never vote apart." [10]

To minimize this danger, Republicans resorted to various parliamentary tactics. In the House, the rules encouraged unity. A bill's manager
could move to commit his legislation to a committee immediately after it
came to the floor. While this motion was before the House, no representa-

tive could move amendments. After general discussion, the manager could withdraw his motion to commit and move that the House proceed to consider "the previous question." If the representatives agreed (that is, *seconded* the motion), amendments again would be foreclosed. Representatives would have to vote on the bill as it first came before them. Republicans would have to accept or reject the bill *in toto,* and as they usually accepted its fundamental principles, the legislation generally passed with overwhelming party support. Only on the rarest occasions did enough representatives oppose a bill so strongly that they defeated the previous question, opening it to amendment.

Second, both branches of Congress employed committees to frame or modify legislation. In the 1860s as now, these committees were the real working bodies in Congress. In the House they were appointed by the Speaker in a manner to reflect as accurately as possible the party, sectional, and philosophical makeup of all the representatives. In the Senate, committees were chosen by a special group of influential senators appointed by the caucus of the majority party. Here committee chairmen had more to say about the makeup of their committees, but still party, philosophical, and sectional balance was generally maintained. These committees were expected to report legislation that would win the approval of a broad spectrum of their parent bodies. And as they generally paralleled their houses in outlook, they usually did so. Conflict and debate usually arose on an issue when the committee was divided or when another committee which had studied a similar question challenged the first committee's decision. In these situations committee members would be the leading advocates—often the only speakers—on either side.[11]

In the House the prestige of these committees, combined with rules hostile to free debate and amendment, made their will almost irresistible and did much to force an almost artificial unity upon Republicans. Nonetheless, Reconstruction was an issue so controversial, on which so many representatives considered themselves expert although they sat on no committee with direct jurisdiction over it, of such fundamental importance for the nation's future, that even with these restraints on free and full debate Republican unity often disintegrated.

In the Senate, committees carried less weight. Sometimes they did not reflect the opinions of senators as accurately as they should have because of the greater influence of their chairmen in appointing members. Moreover, senators were (and are) more independent than representatives and more inclined to consider themselves expert in fields outside their committee jurisdictions. Nonetheless, here too committees served as harmonizing agents on Reconstruction legislation, although, without the benefit of the House's strict rules, they were less formidable to challenge.

Finally, when the normal procedures of Congress failed to secure harmony, Republicans took their differences to the caucus, not to enforce regularity on a harassed minority, but to settle upon some policy that would allow them to keep the initiative in the face of their resolute opponents. This was the case in May 1866, when Senate Republicans called a party conference to reconcile conflicting opinions on the constitutional amendment proposed by the Joint Committee on Reconstruction, and again in February 1867, when senators would not agree to the military government bill reported by the same committee.[12]

The result of these harmonizing institutions was what must be considered an artificial degree of unanimity on Reconstruction legislation, which has hampered efforts to determine radical-conservative alignments through analysis of voting patterns.[13] To overcome this problem as much as possible, I have studied the votes congressmen cast on Reconstruction and other issues through scale analysis. The advantage of this method is that it is not intended to determine representatives' voting behavior per se, but rather their *attitudes* towards an issue. Since House and Senate rules and customs limited the legislative alternatives with which congressmen were presented, the most extreme radicals might be able to demonstrate their differences with less radical colleagues on only one or two roll calls during each congressional session. Although these might involve apparently minor questions, in fact they often indicated fundamental differences in attitude and opinion—differences that could not receive legislative exposition due to the institutional structure of Congress. Scale analysis highlights these votes and thus proves far more illuminating for the purposes of this study than alternative statistical techniques.[14]

Such analysis discloses that radical-conservative lines were fluid during the Thirty-eighth, Thirty-ninth, and Fortieth Congresses. Not only did congressmen frequently display different attitudes in different sessions, but groups were not completely distinct in any given session, with numerous representatives and senators falling between one faction and another. Major shifts in alignment occurred between the first and second sessions of the Thirty-eighth Congress, when war issues gave way to those of peace and Reconstruction; between the second session of the Thirty-ninth Congress and the first session of the Fortieth, as questions of restoration gave way to those of impeachment and legislative-executive relations (in the Senate this shift occurred between the first and second sessions of the Thirty-ninth Congress); and between the second and third sessions of the Fortieth Congress, when—with most states restored to normal relations with the Union—congressmen began to consider the problem of permanent national government protection for citizens of fully equal states.[15]

Despite this chaotic inconsistency (and despite the fact that fewer congressmen were reelected in the 1860s than in later years), it is possible to compile a list of men who voted consistently as radicals, centrists, and conservatives during at least two Congresses from 1863 to 1869—the core of each group throughout these years. Significantly, the list includes most of the recognized leaders of each group, men like Stevens, Ashley, Dawes,

Butler, Bingham, Blaine, and Schenck in the House, and Sumner, Wade, Chandler, Fessenden, Trumbull, and Sherman in the Senate. They were the magnets to whom the floating material in each house was attracted, stronger in one session than another, but always there, beacons in a sea of shifting allegiances.

As Lists 1 and 2 suggest, the radical Republicans did not dominate Congress during the Reconstruction era. More Republican Senators scaled consistently conservative than radical, while in the House, where radicalism was stronger, consistent nonradicals (conservatives and centrists) still outnumbered radicals. The simplest index of radical strength, the percentage of Republicans voting for radical legislation from 1863 to 1869, reinforces the conclusion (see Charts 1 and 2). The groups that supported radical legislation never made up 50 per cent of either house of Congress, constituted the majority of the Republicans only half of the time, and never controlled an overwhelming majority of the Republican votes.

LIST 1

CONSISTENT REPUBLICAN FACTIONS IN THE HOUSE OF REPRESENTATIVES, 38–40 CONGRESSES

CONSISTENT RADICALS

Samuel M. Arnell, Tennessee
James M. Ashley, Ohio
Portus Baxter, Vermont
George S. Boutwell, Massachusetts
Henry P. H. Bromwell, Illinois
John M. Broomall, Pennsylvania
Benjamin F. Butler, Massachusetts
Henry L. Cake, Pennsylvania
Sidney Clarke, Kansas
Amasa Cobb, Wisconsin
John Covode, Pennsylvania
Shelby M. Cullom, Illinois
Jacob H. Ela, New Hampshire
Josiah B. Grinnell, Iowa
Abner C. Harding, Illinois
George W. Julian, Indiana
William D. Kelley, Pennsylvania
William H. Kelsey, New York
John Lynch, Maine
Horace Maynard, Tennessee
Joseph W. McClurg, Missouri
Ulysses Mercur, Pennsylvania
Charles O'Neill, Pennsylvania
Halbert E. Paine, Wisconsin
Robert C. Schenck, Ohio
John P. C. Shanks, Indiana
Ithamar C. Sloan, Wisconsin
Aaron F. Stevens, New Hampshire
Thaddeus Stevens, Pennsylvania
William B. Stokes, Tennessee

Rowland E. Trowbridge, Michigan
Charles Upson, Michigan
Robert T. Van Horn, Missouri
Charles H. Van Wyck, New York
Hamilton Ward, New York
Thomas Williams, Pennsylvania
William Williams, Indiana
Stephen F. Wilson, Pennsylvania

CONSISTENT CENTRISTS

Oakes Ames, Massachusetts
Nathaniel P. Banks, Massachusetts
James G. Blaine, Maine
John C. Churchill, New York
Reader W. Clarke, Ohio
Ebenezer Dumont, Indiana
Benjamin Eggleston, Ohio
Samuel Hooper, Massachusetts
George F. Miller, Pennsylvania
Burt Van Horn, New York
Martin Welker, Ohio

CONSISTENT CONSERVATIVES

John A. Bingham, Ohio
Henry T. Blow, Missouri
Ralph Buckland, Ohio
Thomas T. Davis, New York
Henry L. Dawes, Massachusetts
Henry C. Deming, Connecticut
Thomas W. Ferry, Michigan

John A. Griswold, New York
Isaac R. Hawkins, Tennessee
Chester D. Hubbard, West Virginia
John H. Ketcham, New York
Addison H. Laflin, New York
George V. Lawrence, Pennsylvania
James M. Marvin, New York

Charles E. Phelps, Maryland
   (Johnson Conservative)
Luke P. Poland, Vermont
Theodore M. Pomeroy, New York
William H. Randall, Kentucky
Worthington C. Smith, Vermont
Elihu B. Washburne, Illinois
Kellian V. Whaley, West Virginia

To qualify for each designation, a representative must have scaled in four sessions of Congress, and he must have scaled consistently three times for every divergence and then have diverged by no more than one group from his consistent pattern (e.g., from radical to centrist but not from radical to conservative). In a session in which a representative scaled in a joint group (e.g., radical-centrist), he was counted as having voted with one or the other, whichever was more consistent with his pattern in other sessions. Where a representative began his service in the Fortieth Congress, his record was investigated through the Forty-first. These standards were modified only in the cases of James G. Blaine, Amasa Cobb, William D. Kelley, Thaddeus Stevens, and Robert T. Van Horn. Cobb, Kelley, and Van Horn each voted with the conservatives in one congressional session but voted so consistently radical for at least six other sessions that it would be misleading to omit them from the list. Stevens voted with the conservatives in the second session of the Thirty-eighth Congress in order to defeat any program of Reconstruction that did not meet his radical standards. Blaine diverged from his centrist voting pattern on two occasions in the seven sessions in which he voted, but his record as Speaker of the House in the Forty-first and Forty-second Congresses was so cleary nonradical that he too belongs in the list.

LIST 2

CONSISTENT REPUBLICAN FACTIONS IN THE SENATE, 38–40 CONGRESSES

CONSISTENT RADICALS

Benjamin Gratz Brown, Missouri
Simon Cameron, Pennsylvania
Zachariah Chandler, Michigan
Aaron Cragin, New Hampshire
   (consistently radical-centrist)
Jacob M. Howard, Michigan
James W. Nye, Nevada
Charles Sumner, Massachusetts
John M. Thayer, Nebraska
Benjamin F. Wade, Ohio
Henry Wilson, Massachusetts
Richard Yates, Illinois

CONSISTENT CENTRISTS

Justin S. Morrill, Vermont
Lot M. Morrill, Maine
John Sherman, Ohio (leaning towards
   conservatives)
William Sprague, Rhode Island
Thomas W. Tipton, Nebraska

CONSISTENT CONSERVATIVES

Henry B. Anthony, Rhode Island
Roscoe Conkling, New York
Henry S. Corbett, Oregon
Edgar Cowan, Pennsylvania
   (Johnson Conservative)
James Dixon, Connecticut
   (Johnson Conservative)
James R. Doolittle, Wisconsin
   (Johnson Conservative)
George F. Edmunds, Vermont
William P. Fessenden, Maine
Ira Harris, New York
John B. Henderson, Missouri
Daniel S. Norton, Minnesota
   (Johnson Conservative)
Lyman Trumbull, Illinois
Peter G. Van Winkle, West Virginia
Waitman T. Willey, West Virginia
George H. Williams, Oregon
   (leaning towards centrists)

To qualify for each designation, a senator must have scaled in four sessions of Congress, and he must have scaled consistently three times for every divergence and then have diverged by no more than one group from his consistent pattern (e.g., from radical to centrist but not from radical to conservative). In a session in which a senator scaled in a joint group (e.g., radical-centrist), he was counted as having voted with one or the other, whichever was more consistent with his pattern in other sessions. Where a senator began his service in the Fortieth Congress, his record was investigated through the Forty-first. These standards were modified in only one case, that of Lyman Trumbull, who voted with radicals in the second session of the Thirty-ninth Congress, but who otherwise demonstrated so consistent a pattern of conservatism from the Thirty-eighth through the Forty-second Congresses that it appeared more misleading to omit him from the list than to include him.

Nor were radicals overrepresented among the congressional Republican elite, that small number in each house who dominated proceedings— who spoke most often, reported bills from committees, managed them through the House or Senate, and served on conference committees to compromise differences with the other branch of the legislature, and whose influence invariably arose directly from their positions as chairmen or

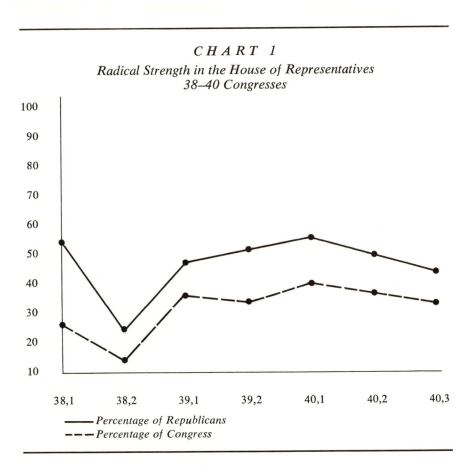

CHART 1

Radical Strength in the House of Representatives
38–40 Congresses

——— *Percentage of Republicans*
— — — *Percentage of Congress*

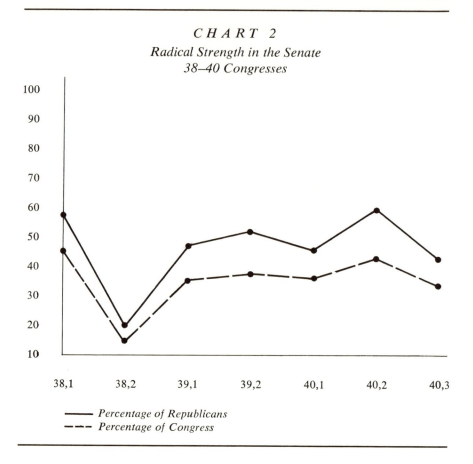

CHART 2

Radical Strength in the Senate
38–40 Congresses

——— Percentage of Republicans
– – – Percentage of Congress

senior members of important committees (see Lists 3 and 4). Nearly all of these seventeen most prestigious Republican representatives did support radical legislation in one session or another, but only four can be identified as consistent radicals, while seven clearly emerge as nonradicals. In fact, these leaders gave overwhelming support to radical legislation in only three of the seven sessions of Congress from 1863 to 1869: in the first session of the Thirty-eighth Congress, when they tried unsuccessfully to create a precedent for black suffrage in United States territory; in the first session of the Thirty-ninth Congress, when they enacted universal black suffrage in the District of Columbia; and in the first session of the Fortieth Congress, when they voted against adjourning over the summer and fall and leaving President Johnson unwatched in Washington. But during the critical second session of the Thirty-ninth Congress, when Republicans framed the Reconstruction act, the House leadership supported a conservative approach.[16]

LIST 3

PRESTIGIOUS REPUBLICAN MEMBERS OF THE HOUSE OF REPRESENTATIVES, 38–40 CONGRESSES

REPRESENTATIVES WITH PRE-EMINENT INFLUENCE *

NATHANIEL P. BANKS, 39–40 Congresses. Chairman of the Foreign Relations committee, 39–40 Congresses. Member of the Rules committee, 39–40 Congresses. Often chairman of the House Republican caucus. Sixteenth in seniority among Republicans by the 40 Congress. Former Speaker of the House. *Centrist.*

JOHN A. BINGHAM, 39–40 Congresses. Member of the Reconstruction committee, 39–40 Congresses, and chairman 40 Congress, third session. Impeachment manager, 40 Congress. Eighth Republican in seniority in the 40 Congress. *Conservative.*

JAMES G. BLAINE, 38–40 Congresses. Chairman of Military Affairs committee, 38–39 Congresses. Member of both the Appropriations and Rules committees during the 40 Congress. *Centrist.*

BENJAMIN F. BUTLER, 40 Congress. Member simultaneously of the Reconstruction and Appropriations committees during the 40 Congress. Impeachment manager, 40 Congress. *Radical.*

SCHUYLER COLFAX, 38–40 Congresses. As Speaker of the House, chairman of the Rules committee, 38–40 Congresses. Third in seniority. *Not voting.*

HENRY W. DAVIS, 38 Congress. Chairman of the Reconstruction committee and the Committee on Foreign Affairs simultaneously. Eighth in seniority. *Erratic.*

JUSTIN S. MORRILL, 38–39 Congresses. Chairman of the Ways and Means committee, 38 Congress. Chairman of the Republican caucus often in the 38–39 Congresses. Simultaneously a member of the Joint Committee on Reconstruction. Shared third and fourth seniority with Colfax. *Centrist.*

ROBERT C. SCHENCK, 38–40 Congresses. Chairman of the Military Affairs committee, 38–39 Congresses. Chairman of the Ways and Means committee, 40 Congress. Member of the Joint Committee on Retrenchment during the 39 Congress, while simultaneously chairman of Military Affairs. Same in seniority as Thaddeus Stevens, although as an earlier entrant into Congress, he was slightly senior. *Radical.*

THADDEUS STEVENS, 38–40 Congress, second session. Chairman of the Ways and Means committee, 38 Congress. Chairman of the Appropriations committee, 39–40 Congress, second session. As such, the recognized leader of the House. Shared sixth and seventh seniority among Republicans with Robert Schenck in the 38 Congress. By the 40 Congress, they shared fourth. Senior Republican on the Joint Committee on Reconstruction, 39 Congress, simultaneous with the Appropriations committee chairmanship. Also a member of the Pacific Railroad committee. Chairman of the Reconstruction committee, 40 Congress, first and second sessions, again simultaneously with the Appropriations committee chairmanship. Impeachment manager in the 40 Congress. *Radical.*

ELIHU B. WASHBURNE, 38–40 Congresses. Member of the Rules committee, 38–40 Congress. Chairman of the Commerce committee, 39 Congress, and the Appropriations committee in the 40 Congress. Candidate for Speaker of the House in the 38 Congress. Second in seniority. *Conservative.*

JAMES F. WILSON, 38–40 Congresses. Chairman of the Judiciary committee, 38–40 Congresses. Impeachment manager in the 40 Congress. *Erratic.*

OTHER INFLUENTIAL REPRESENTATIVES **

WILLIAM B. ALLISON, 38–40 Congresses. Member of the Ways and Means committee, 39–40 Congresses. *Radical* through the 39 Congress, first session. *Centrist* thereafter.

GEORGE S. BOUTWELL, 38–40 Congresses. Simultaneously on the Reconstruction and Judiciary committees, 38–40 Congresses. *Radical.*

ROSCOE CONKLING, 39 Congress. On the Joint Committee on Reconstruction and the Ways and Means committee simultaneously. *Centrist.*

JOHN F. FARNSWORTH, 38–40 Congresses. Chairman of the Post Office committee, 40 Congress; simultaneously a member of the Reconstruction committee. A member of the Appropriations committee in the 39 Congress. Shared fourth Republican seniority with Horace Maynard. *Erratic.*

JAMES A. GARFIELD, 38–40 Congresses. Member of the Military Affairs committee, 38 Congress. Member of the Ways and Means committee, 39 Congress. Chairman of Military Affairs in the 40 Congress. *Radical* through the 39 Congress, first session. *Conservative* and *Centrist* thereafter.

SAMUEL HOOPER, 38–40 Congresses. Member of the Ways and Means committee, 38–40 Congresses. Simultaneously a member of the Banking and Currency committee, 39–40 Congresses, second session. Chairman of the Ways and Means committee in the 40 Congress, third session. *Centrist.*

* *Speaker of the House, chairmen of the Committees on Ways and Means, Appropriations, Judiciary, and Reconstruction (in its various forms); members of two of these committees simultaneously or members of the Rules committee who also served in important positions on other committees.*
** *Members who fit in the above category except for having spent less time in important positions on other committees. Also senior members of the Ways and Means, Appropriations, Judiciary, and Reconstruction committees, and members of the above committees who also are chairmen of House policy committees.*

LIST 4

PRESTIGIOUS REPUBLICAN SENATORS
38–40 CONGRESSES

SENATORS WITH PRE-EMINENT INFLUENCE *

WILLIAM PITT FESSENDEN, 38–40 Congresses. Chairman of the Finance committee, 38–39 Congresses. Chairman of the Joint Reconstruction committee, 39 Congress. Member of the Foreign Relations committee, 40 Congress. Member once of the Committee on Committees. Secretary of the Treasury in early 1865. The only senator to leave Congress and return immediately to a previously held chairmanship. Shared third and fourth Republican seniority with Wilson. *Conservative.*

LAFAYETTE FOSTER, 38–39 Congresses. Member of the Foreign Relations and the Judiciary committees simultaneously in the 38 Congress. President *pro tem* of the Senate in the 39 Congress. Member three times of the Committee on Committees. Shared sixth through eighth seniority. *Centrist* in the 38 Congress, *Conservative* in the 39 Congress.

LOT M. MORRILL, 38–40 Congresses. Chairman of the Appropriations committee, 38 Congress, second session, through the 40 Congress. Chairman of the D.C. committee in the 39 Congress. *Centrist.*

JOHN SHERMAN, 38–40 Congresses. Chairman of the Finance committee, 38 Congress, second session, through the 40 Congress, and chairman of the Committee on Agriculture, 38 Congress, first session. Member four times of the Committee on Committees. Chairman of the Select Committee on Promoting Commerce Among the States in the 40 Congress, second and third sessions. *Centrist.*

CHARLES SUMNER, 38–40 Congresses. Chairman of the Committee on Foreign Relations, 38–40 Congresses. Chairman of the Committee on Slavery and Freedmen, 38 Congress. Member of the Committee on the Revision of Laws in the 40 Congress, third session. Shared first and second Republican seniority. *Radical.*

LYMAN TRUMBULL, 38–40 Congresses. Chairman of the Judiciary committee, 38–40 Congresses. Member three times of the Committee on Committees. Fifth in seniority in the 40 Congress. *Conservative.*

HENRY WILSON, 38–40 Congresses. Chairman of the Military Affairs committee, 38–40 Congresses, and a member of the Appropriations committee in the 40 Congress while chairman of Military Affairs. Member once of the Committee on Committees. Shared with Fessenden third and fourth seniority. *Radical.*

OTHER INFLUENTIAL SENATORS **

ROSCOE CONKLING, 40 Congress. As a freshman senator, simultaneously a member of the Appropriations and Judiciary committees. *Conservative.*

JAMES W. GRIMES, 38–40 Congresses. Chairman of the Naval Affairs committee in the 38–40 Congresses and of the Committee on the District of Columbia in the 38 Congress, first session. Simultaneously a member of the Appropriations committee, 40 Congress. Twice a member of the Committee on Committees. *Erratic.*

IRA HARRIS, 38–39 Congresses. Member of the Judiciary committee, 38 Congress, and simultaneously a member of the Foreign Relations committee and the Joint Committee on Reconstruction in the 39 Congress. Three times a member of the Committee on Committees. *Conservative.*

BENJAMIN F. WADE, 38–40 Congresses. Chairman of the Committee on Territories, 38–39 Congresses, and simultaneously on the Foreign Relations committee in the 39 Congress. President *pro tempore* of the Senate, 40 Congress. Member once of the Committee on Committees. Shared first and second seniority with Sumner. *Radical.*

GEORGE H. WILLIAMS, 39–40 Congresses. Member of the Finance committee and the Reconstruction committee simultaneously in the 39 Congress as a freshman. Member of the Finance committee through the 40 Congress. Once on the Committee on Committees. *Conservative.*

* *Chairmen of the Finance, Appropriations, Judiciary, or Foreign Relations committees.*
** *Members of two of the above committees simultaneously, or chairman of a major Senate standing committee and member of one of the above committees simultaneously.*

It was well understood by Americans in the 1860s that the United States Senate was more conservative than the House of Representatives. In fact, only three of the twelve most prestigious senators of the Thirty-eighth through Fortieth Congresses consistently acted with the radicals.[17] Moreover, after 1865, the radicals only once won the support of a majority of them (a narrow majority in the second session of the Fortieth Congress).

Although the elites of the House and Senate set the tone of Congress from 1863 to 1869, Reconstruction policy was set primarily by several congressional committees. (Of the twenty-two major Reconstruction-connected bills and resolutions that passed both Houses, all but three were reported from committees of the house that first considered them.) The

House delegated some specific Reconstruction-connected responsibilities to a number of rather minor committees, but the real Reconstruction policy-making committees in the House were the Committee on the Judiciary and the select, joint, and standing committees on Reconstruction that the House raised in various sessions of Congress. The Reconstruction committees had primary responsibility, framing most of the Reconstruction acts, the Restoration acts, and the Fourteenth Amendment, and the speaker carefully balanced them in their various forms. From 1863 to 1869 Republican man/sessions of support and opposition for radical legislation were almost equal (twenty-five and twenty-two, respectively).[18] Moreover, during the Thirty-ninth Congress, when congressional Republicans devised their basic Reconstruction program, the Senate and House created a *joint committee* on Reconstruction, on which nonradical Republicans clearly outnumbered radicals. In the House Judiciary committee too—the committee that reported the Civil Rights bill of 1866 and framed the Fifteenth Amendment and in general represented the legal expertise of the House—radical and nonradical Republicans carried nearly equal weight, its Republican members offering twenty-four man/sessions of support for radical legislation and nineteen of opposition.

The leading members of these Reconstruction-connected committees shared with the general Republican elite the major influence in the development of Republican Reconstruction policy in the House. The two groups together included the great actors in the Reconstruction drama. Pre-eminent among them stood Thaddeus Stevens, the leader of the House by virtue of his position as chairman of its most important committees— first the Committee on Ways and Means and then the Committee on Appropriations. Too feeble in his seventies to limp any longer on his clubfoot, Stevens had to be carried in a special chair to his seat in the center of the chamber. His eyes glowing from their cavernous sockets as if his body exuded the burning power of his will, he ruled, Alexander K. McClure remembered, "in grim and relentless mastery."[19] But Stevens's reputation as a tyrant rested more on his personality than on his power. His scathing wit and scornful invective were most effective when he spoke as party leader, defending decisions made by its policy-making institutions—the caucus or congressional committees. Then, as Ben Perley Poore, the Boston *Evening Journal*'s Washington correspondent, recalled, "rising by degrees, as a telescope is pulled out . . . , he would lecture the offender against party discipline, sweeping at him with his large, bony right hand, in uncouth gestures, as if he would clutch him and shake him."[20] His wit was utterly humorless. "When his sharp sallies would set the entire House in uproar," Blaine wrote, "he was as impassive, his visage as solemn, as if he were pronouncing a funeral oration."[21]

But the decisions Stevens enforced so despotically in matters of Reconstruction were all too rarely his own. Upon his death the editors of the

Boston *Daily Advertiser* observed, "While he held his position as 'Leader of the House' no man was oftener outvoted. Very few of the measures he originated came to maturity; or if they came, they were so far changed as to have lost much of the distinctive character he gave them." His efforts to territorialize the South, to confiscate and redistribute its great estates, his inflationary financial proposals were all aborted. As he died, he declared his life a failure. "When some admiring newspaper would speak of him as 'the Leader of the House,' he would bitterly smile—sometimes in scorn of his cowardly followers, and sometimes in contempt of his feeble self." Theodore Tilton eulogized in his New York weekly newspaper, *The Independent:* "Hopelessness—a half despair—was the prevailing mood of his mind. . . . It was always touching . . . to find how little expectation he entertained that his cherished measures would be carried." [22] Even in the great days of 1866, when congressional Republicans surprised him by standing up to Andrew Johnson, the *New York Tribune* refuted those who believed him to be the evil genius responsible for the trouble.

Mr. Stevens . . . is followed no further than his views are identical with those cherished originally and independently by the great body of his associates. There are few men on his side of the House whom that House is less reluctant to vote down when he is wrong. . . . His strength grows out of the fact that he is generally right, and that, whenever he errs, he errs through devotion to Justice and Equal Rights.[23]

Entering Congress only in 1867, Benjamin F. Butler rose to leadership of the radical forces as Stevens's health failed, his undisputed heir after the great leader's death in 1868. Sharing Stevens's audacity and his talent for invective, he was, Poore wrote, "more feared on the Republican side of the House than on the Democratic." He had what Blaine called "a talent for turbulence," but Butler did not have Stevens's long history of commitment to humanitarian causes to soften the resentment of his colleagues.[24] A proslavery Democrat who supported Jefferson Davis for his party's presidential nomination in 1860, the chairman of the bolting southern Democratic convention that nominated John C. Breckenridge, a man who appeared to his critics to be devoid of personal integrity, Butler was vulnerable to his enemies' charges that his radicalism was born of ambition rather than idealism.

Beyond Stevens and Butler, often grumbling that even these stalwarts were too willing to compromise fundamental principles, were less influential radical representatives—the "impracticables," like James M. Ashley and George W. Julian. More important were more practical politicians, not so conspicuous as Stevens or Butler, men like Ohio's Samuel Shellabarger, who was largely responsible for the final compromise on the Reconstruction act, and George S. Boutwell, the second-ranking Republican on the Judiciary committee, who laid the legal groundwork for the impeachment movement and managed the Fifteenth Amendment through the House.

John A. Bingham, second-ranking Republican on the Reconstruction committee, former chairman of the Judiciary committee, led the Republican nonradicals in the House. Slender and blond, with vapid blue eyes, he diverged as much from Stevens in appearance as he did in his views. The sharpness of his features belied the hint of fraility in his slight frame: one reporter wrote that he looked "like a steel scythe, with a flash of forelight in it." [25] Inflexible, as quick to anger as Stevens, he braved Stevens's and Butler's wrath, ultimately having a greater influence on the course of Reconstruction than the radical leaders themselves.

Even more conservative was the popular Henry L. Dawes, chairman of the Committee on Elections, more warmly loved by his colleagues than any other representative. Dawes would barely lose the speakership to Blaine in the Forty-first Congress, emerging as chairman of the Appropriations committee and two years later of the Ways and Means committee. He would thus fill the position later formally called "majority leader." But during the Reconstruction controversy his opinions differed so greatly from those of the majority of the party that in the Thirty-ninth Congress he arranged to have jurisdiction over the question removed from his Elections committee rather than risk losing its chairmanship.

Blaine himself, almost as popular as Dawes and more respected, generally allied with Bingham. Personally sympathetic to the claims of racial justice, Blaine's first commitment was always to the Republican party, through whose ranks he rose to Speaker of the House, senator, secretary of state, and presidential candidate. Not a member of committees with direct jurisdiction over the problem, he was the author of the most important provision of the Reconstruction act, the so-called "Blaine amendment," which marked the final defeat of the radical program.

Although senators often paid less attention to their committees than did representatives, those committees were still the most important influence in the development of Senate Reconstruction policy. (Twenty-three of the twenty-four major Reconstruction-connected bills and resolutions that passed the Senate from 1863 to 1869 were first reported from Senate or joint Senate–House committees.) Here one can see a critical shift in 1865 from radical to nonradical predominance in Reconstruction matters. During the Thirty-eighth Congress (1863–65), Benjamin F. Wade's radical Committee on Territories held jurisdiction over Reconstruction and reported the Wade-Davis Reconstruction bill to the Senate with an amendment enfranchising blacks in the South. The Select Committee on Slavery and Freedmen, chaired by Charles Sumner and on which radicals held the outright majority of places, reported and managed through the Senate legislation creating the Freedmen's Bureau. The conservative Judiciary committee limited itself to framing the Thirteenth Amendment to the Constitution. So during the Thirty-eighth Congress, radicals—especially Wade and Sumner, as committee chairmen—held strong institutional positions from which to influence the development of Reconstruction policy.

But that influence was already curtailed by the second session of the Thirty-eighth Congress, early in 1865. With President Lincoln opposed to the Wade-Davis bill, the Judiciary committee took over jurisdiction of Reconstruction, reporting a bill to the Senate which restored Lincoln's reconstructed Louisiana state government to normal relations in the Union. At the same time that Sumner managed to win passage of the Freedmen's Bureau bill, he proved barely able to filibuster to death the Louisiana Restoration bill.

In the Thirty-ninth Congress the Senate stripped the radicals of their strength in the Senate committees. Jurisdiction over Reconstruction was taken from the Committee on Territories and shared by the Judiciary committee and a new Joint Committee on Reconstruction. Logic and custom dictated the appointment to that committee of senators who already had experience with Reconstruction questions, but to Sumner and Wade's chagrin, the Senate caucus named only one member of either the Committee on Territories or the now-defunct Select Committee on Slavery and Freedmen to serve on it. Senate Reconstruction policy after 1865 was framed by a nonradical Joint Committee on Reconstruction and a conservative Judiciary committee that killed so many of his measures that Sumner called it "a receiving tomb." [26] Neither Sumner nor Wade would ever again chair a committee with influence over Reconstruction, nor did radicals ever again gain a majority of the seats on a major Reconstruction-connected Senate committee.

The senior Senate members of the Joint Committee on Reconstruction and the senior members of the Judiciary committee shared with the Senate leadership of List 2 the major influence in setting Reconstruction policy in the upper chamber. Towering above the radicals among them stood Charles Sumner. With a noble visage, dignified demeanor, and deep, rich voice, Sumner looked every inch a classical Roman senator. But he wielded far greater influence with the American public than with his colleagues. "He had no genius for detail," his friend Representative George F. Hoar recalled. "He lacked that quality which enables the practical statesman to adjust the mechanism of complicated statutes." [27] Lacking wit, unable to find the humor in others' jokes, he could not compete with his colleagues in extemporaneous debate or repartee; he was often bested by opponents in unrehearsed contests. Even his prepared speeches were often "laborious essays," Blaine remembered. But in print "they were the anti-slavery classics of the day, and they were read more eagerly than speeches which produced greater effect on the hearer." While many congressmen directed their speeches only to the few hundred who heard them, forgetting about the million who might read them, Blaine noted that "Mr. Sumner never made that mistake. His argument went to the million." [28] Again and again in those great speech-essays, he hammered at the same theme, winning a firm hold on the intellectual and moral opinion-makers of the North, no matter what impression he made upon senators. His greatness, wrote Henry Cabot Lodge, remembering the Sumner of his youth, "rest[ed] securely on the fact that he was the representative of an idea. He stood for human freedom." [29]

Like so many men who devote their lives to humanity as a whole, Sumner rarely seemed able to develop intimate relations with his contemporaries. Lodge wrote, "As I look back on that vanished time I see now, that which I vaguely felt then, what a pathetic, almost tragic figure he was. He was singularly lonely." [30] His fellow senators bitterly resented his assumption of moral superiority and his persistent efforts to force them to live up to their own principles—what Carl Schurz called "a sort of intellectual and moral dragooning." [31] When many thought him at the pinnacle of power, Sumner confided to one of his few intimates, "How few here sympathize with me! I sometimes feel that I am alone in the Senate." [32] Even his marriage, the Washington social event of the 1860s, ended in failure and humiliation. Through all this he pursued "with absolute singleness of purpose and unwavering courage" his goal of complete freedom for men of all colors, "serene," his one-time private secretary, Moorfield Storey, wrote, in his "confidence of ultimate success." He seemed not even to notice the obstacles. "His gaze was fixed on a distant goal, and he did not stoop to look at what lay in the path." [33]

Presenting sharp contrasts to Sumner were the tough, blunt radical politicians Benjamin F. Wade and Zachariah Chandler. As impatient with Sumner's everlasting erudition as with the timidity of their more conservative colleagues, they boldly advocated stern solutions to the problem of restoration and excoriated Republicans who disagreed with them as mercilessly as they did Democrats. More influential were Sumner's colleague from Massachusetts, Henry Wilson, and Chandler's fellow Michigan senator, Jacob M. Howard. More moderate in temperament if not in principle, they had the confidence of more conservative Republican Senators and thus had larger impact on Reconstruction legislation than their more belligerent allies.

Pre-eminent among the nonradical Senate leadership were William Pitt Fessenden and Lyman Trumbull. As chairman of the Committee on Finance and the Joint Committee on Reconstruction, Fessenden was the acknowledged leader of the Senate majority. Thin, almost pinched, complaining continually of his physical infirmities, he was, as Blaine wrote, "above all things practical; he was unwilling at any time to engage in legislation that was not effective and direct." [34] Impatient with Sumner's brand of intellectualizing, he insisted, "My constituents did not send me here to philosophize. They sent me here to act." [35] But although respected as Senate leader, he was flawed by a prodigious capacity for personal hatred. ("What a strange compound he is," Senator Timothy Otis Howe wrote his niece. "He is capable of such noble things and is constantly doing such ignoble things.") [36] He was contemptuous of Wade and Chandler, who publicly attacked his conservatism in 1867, but his animosity focused on his New England rival, Sumner. Scornful of Sumner's legislative ineffectiveness and "impracticality," he bitterly resented standing in his shadow. His hatred bordered on the pathological; after 1865 he seemed unable to write his family without some ill-tempered reference to the radical leader, "the meanest and most cowardly dog in the parish." As one Washington correspondent put it, Fessenden had "Sumner on the brain." [37]

Fairly radical during the war years, Fessenden announced at the restoration of peace that he would "act upon different principles now and hereafter . . . from those which I adopted and defended before," [38] and although he favored qualified black suffrage, he used his immense influence to try to prevent the rupture with the president in 1866, to abort the Reconstruction bill of 1867, and to protect the president from impeachment and removal in 1867–68. There may have been some truth in California's Senator John Conness's evaluation of the two great leaders in 1865 —"Sumner has been a Republican because he loves human freedom; Fessenden has been a Republican because he comes from New England." [39]

Trumbull exercised even greater influence over Senate Reconstruction policy than Fessenden. As chairman of the Judiciary committee, he managed fourteen Reconstruction-related bills through the Senate, thirteen successfully. (No other senator managed more than two.) He continually opposed radical legislation, leading the effort to restore Louisiana in 1865, leading the movement to weaken the disqualification section of the Fourteenth Amendment in 1866, opposing black suffrage in the same year, voting against remaining in Washington to watch Johnson in 1867, voting to acquit Johnson on the impeachment in 1868, and opposing efforts to sustain southern Republican governments after 1868. But when in 1870 Sumner accused Trumbull of having been out of sympathy with Republican Reconstruction policy, the acerbic Illinois senator, who disliked Sumner nearly as much as Fessenden did, could reply truthfully:

All your reconstruction measures . . . with the exception of the first act . . . have passed through the hands of the Judiciary committee . . . ; and I have had charge in the Senate of nearly every one of them . . . . [I]t has been over the idiosyncracies, over the unreasonable propositions, over the impractical measures of the Senator from Massachusetts that freedom has been proclaimed and established. His impracticable, unreasonable, unconstitutional and ineffectual measures would never have accomplished the object.[40]

Sustaining Fessenden and Trumbull were the young, rising John Sherman, whose influence in the Senate already exceeded that of all but

a handful of his seniors; George F. Edmunds, who warmly sustained racial
political and legal equality but whose constitutional conservatism impelled
him constantly to object to the means for achieving it ("Edmunds was
always contrary-minded," Hoar remembered. "I once told him . . . that
if George Edmunds were the only man in the world, George would object
to everything Edmunds proposed."); [41] and the charismatic Roscoe
Conkling, who entered the Senate only in 1867 but who so quickly
amassed influence that Poore pronounced him its real leader. [42]

Historians of Reconstruction who wrote from the 1890s to the 1930s
were convinced that the radicals had forced a tragic policy on the nation
after the war. But they never doubted that radical Republicans agreed
on one basic principle—that political power must be transferred from the
men who went into rebellion to those who had remained loyal. The greatest
of these historians—James Ford Rhodes, John W. Burgess, and William
A. Dunning—never suggested that this determination was inherently wrong
or immoral. In their opinion the tragedy was that the Republicans, in
Rhodes's words, "showed no appreciation of the great fact of race." [43]
Firmly grounded in the racist science of their times, these historians concluded that black suffrage was not a viable alternative to continued white,
rebel rule. [44] By the 1920s and 1930s historians had added to this conception of the radicals that imputation of vengefulness which culminated
when James G. Randall in his widely used text on the Civil War and
Reconstruction ceased referring to "Radical Republicans" at all, instead
denominating them "Vindictives." [45]

A second interpretation of radicalism originated in the assumption, so
fundamental to progressive historians, that men's actions are dictated by
economic considerations. This interpretation suggested that the radicals
were the political spokesmen of northeastern businessmen, hoping for a
Reconstruction that would open the South to economic development and
exploitation and would minimize the power of agrarian and anti-industrial
interests. Although expressed primarily in one major work on Reconstruction, Howard K. Beale's The Critical Year, this interpretation swept the
field and in an incredibly short time became the new orthodoxy. [46] Robert
P. Sharkey, studying the economic issues during the Civil War and Reconstruction, arrived at a third conclusion, diametrically opposed to Beale's.
He determined that radical Republicans were generally united by an egalitarian economic as well as racial ideology which led them to support high
tariffs and soft money. [47]

In recent years historians have returned to a position more similar
to that forwarded by the first group of Reconstruction historians led by
Dunning, Rhodes, and Burgess. Once again matters of race and security
for the Union and its southern partisans have come to the fore, although
the early historians' racial notions have been rejected. If Reconstruction
was a tragic era, they insist, its tragedy lay in the reluctance of Republi-

cans to press harder for racial justice rather than in their decision to press at all. But with the new revisionism has come real confusion over what radicalism was. Dunning, Rhodes, Bowers, Beale, Randall, and Sharkey all seemed confident of what constituted radicalism. McKitrick, Donald, Brock, and the Coxes seem less certain. They point to numerous convictions and attitudes that radical and nonradical Republicans held in common, but have more trouble trying to determine differences. Trefousse has called the radicals a "vanguard for racial justice," and historians tend to agree, but the amount of study being devoted to the subject reveals the depth of their perplexity.[48]

As historians have abandoned the Progressives' assumption that economic interest dictates political ideology, Beale's thesis that economic considerations underlay radicalism has come under sharp attack. Beginning with Stanley Coben's seminal discussion of the divisive economic questions of the Reconstruction era, continuing with Peter Kolchin's analysis of the attitude of the business press and Glenn M. Linden's analyses of Republican voting patterns on economic issues, rejection of Beale's assumption has become a new orthodoxy. Sharkey's conclusions, though less widely challenged, simply have not been accepted.

Indeed, it is almost fruitless to look for non-Reconstruction issues on which radicals united. Beale's suggestion that they spoke for northeastern interests is palpably wrong (see Charts 3 and 4). If anything, proportionally more Westerners supported radical legislation than any other group, but in fact there seems to have been no association of any significance between section and radicalism. Linden searched in vain for any correlation between radicalism and voting patterns on issues generally involving the economy.[49] In preparing this work I too analyzed roll calls involving a broad range of non-Reconstruction issues and found slight evidence of correlation between voting patterns on those issues and voting patterns on Reconstruction questions.[50]

In light of recent work on Republican ideology, it seems most appropriate to begin an assessment of radicalism by suggesting that by 1865 congressional Republicans were united primarily by shared convictions about racial justice, slavery, and the restoration of the Union. Certainly their voting patterns differed from Democrats most distinctly on those issues. (Charts 5 and 6 give the Rice indices of likeness for key votes on the most important legislation in several areas).[51]

Moreover, as early as 1864 twenty-two Republican senators voted to extend the franchise to any black man who might live in Montana. Among them were such consistent conservatives and centrists as James Dixon, who supported Andrew Johnson throughout his term, Fessenden, Ira Harris, and Lot M. Morrill.[52] Fifty-four Republican representatives voted for black suffrage in Montana, including conservatives and centrists Oakes Ames, Blaine, Dawes, Ebenezer Dumont, Samuel Hooper, and James M. Marvin.[53] In the summer of 1865 nearly the entire Republican

CHART 3
Factions and Sections in the House of Representatives
38–40 Congresses

	CONSISTENT CONSERVATIVES	CONSISTENT CENTRISTS	CONSISTENT RADICALS
NEW ENGLAND STATES	4	4	6
ATLANTIC STATES (*N.J., N.Y., Pa.*)	7	3	12
BORDER STATES (*Del., Ky., Md., Mo., Tenn., W.Va.*)	6	0	5
WESTERN STATES (*Ill., Ind., Iowa, Kans., Mich., Minn., Neb., Ohio, Wis.*)	4	4	14
FAR WESTERN STATES (*Cal., Nev., Ore.*)	0	0	0

CHART 4
Factions and Sections in the Senate
38–40 Congresses

	CONSISTENT CONSERVATIVES	CONSISTENT CENTRISTS	CONSISTENT RADICALS
NEW ENGLAND STATES	4	3	3
ATLANTIC STATES	3	0	1
BORDER STATES	3	0	1
WESTERN STATES	3	2	5
FAR WESTERN STATES	2	0	1

party was prepared to endorse black suffrage as an element of Reconstruction in the South, until President Johnson's opposition persuaded the more conservative to abandon the measure, not because they believed it wrong but because they believed it impolitic (see pp. 110–16). Even after the president made his position on the suffrage question clear, two thirds to three quarters of the Republicans in Connecticut, Minnesota, and Wisconsin voted in favor of enfranchising black men in their states. It is likely that the proportion favoring suffrage extension in the South was greater.[54]

CHART 5

*Comparison of Republican and Democratic
Voting Patterns in the House of Representatives
38–40 Congresses*

	RICE INDEX OF PARTY LIKENESS
CURRENCY CIRCULATION	
Currency Circulation bill	
40 Congress, third session, 1325 (Feb. 17, 1869) *	97.83
40 Congress, third session, 1333 (Feb. 18, 1869)	90.94
LABOR	
Eight-hour day for government workers	
40 Congress, first session, 425 (March 28, 1867)	93.01
CONTRACTING AND INFLATING THE CURRENCY	
Currency bills	
39 Congress, first session, 75 (Dec. 18, 1865)	98.72
39 Congress, first session, 1467 (March 16, 1866)	52.36
39 Congress, second session, 49 (Dec. 10, 1866)	55.32
39 Congress, second session, 150 (Dec. 17, 1866)	70.02
39 Congress, second session, 992 (Feb. 4, 1867)	57.85
39 Congress, second session, 1424 (Feb. 21, 1867)	83.85
39 Congress, second session, 1735 (March 2, 1867)	94.65
40 Congress, second session, 70 (Dec. 7, 1867)	71.98
40 Congress, second session, 1761 (March 9, 1868)	58.42
40 Congress, third session, 1332 (Feb. 18, 1869)	72.88
BANKRUPTCY BILL	
Bankruptcy bill	
38 Congress, first session, 2835 (June 9, 1864)	52.32
38 Congress, second session, 24 (Dec. 13, 1865)	60.36
39 Congress, second session, 1708 (Feb. 22, 1867)	94.97
39 Congress, second session, 1708 (Feb. 22, 1867)	94.06
FUNDING AND PAYMENTS OF THE NATIONAL DEBT	
Funding bills	
39 Congress, first session, 1468 (March 16, 1866)	39.12
39 Congress, first session, 1614 (March 23, 1866)	54.06
39 Congress, second session, 49 (Dec. 10, 1866)	55.32
39 Congress, second session, 1424 (Feb. 21, 1867)	91.60

* *Page numbers refer to the appropriate volumes of the* Congressional Globe.

	RICE INDEX OF PARTY LIKENESS
FUNDING AND PAYMENTS OF THE NATIONAL DEBT	
39 Congress, second session, 1424 (Feb. 21, 1867)	83.85
39 Congress, second session, 1735 (March 2, 1867)	94.65
40 Congress, third session, 1538 (Feb. 24, 1869)	60.76
AID TO TRANSPORTATION	
Northern Pacific Railroad bill	
38 Congress, first session, 2297 (May 16, 1864)	77.71
Niagara Ship Canal—motion to lay on table	
39 Congress, first session, 2330 (May 2, 1866)	27.19
Union Pacific Railroad bill	
39 Congress, first session, 3424 (June 26, 1866)	81.27
Land grant for the Atlantic & Pacific Railroad	
39 Congress, first session, 4183 (July 26, 1866)	57.34
Resolution that financial condition of the country should prevent further land-grant legislation	
40 Congress, first session, 797 (Nov. 26, 1867)	87.17
Niagara Ship Canal—tabling; motion to refer to the Committee of the whole on the state of the Union	
40 Congress, second session, 402 (Jan. 15, 1869)	89.70
40 Congress, second session, 405 (Jan. 15, 1869)	94.34
ANTIMONOPOLY RAILROAD LEGISLATION	
Bill to regulate commerce	
38 Congress, first session, 2264 (May 13, 1864)	19.49
New York–D.C. Railroad resolution	
38 Congress, first session, 108 (Jan. 6, 1864)	41.52
Airline Railroad bill	
39 Congress, first session, 4263 (July 27, 1866)	24.01
Regulation of Pacific Railroad rates	
40 Congress, second session, 1218 (Feb. 17, 1868)	74.94
40 Congress, second session, 1861 (March 12, 1868)	80.83
40 Congress, second session, 2130 (March 26, 1868)	93.14
40 Congress, second session, 2428 (May 12, 1868)	86.11
TARIFF	
Tariff bill	
39 Congress, second session, 1658 (Feb. 28, 1867)	35.22
FINANCES AND BANKING	
Taxing state banks	
38 Congress, first session, 1695 (April 18, 1864)	5.90
38 Congress, first session, 1941 (April 28, 1864)	78.47
38 Congress, second session, 906 (Feb. 18, 1865)	13.17
RECONSTRUCTION AND RACIAL ISSUES	
Military Government resolution	
38 Congress, first session, 22 (Dec. 14, 1863)	38.95
Resolution for restoration without disturbance of internal state institutions	
38 Congress, first session, 258 (Jan. 18, 1864)	2.59
38 Congress, first session, 2289 (May 16, 1864)	8.51
Freedmen's Bureau bill	
38 Congress, first session, 895 (March 1, 1864)	12.66

	RICE INDEX OF PARTY LIKENESS
RECONSTRUCTION AND RACIAL ISSUES	
Black suffrage in Montana territory	
38 Congress, first session, 1652 (April 15, 1864)	7.03
Reconstruction bill	
38 Congress, first session, 2108 (May 4, 1864)	9.76
Thirteenth Amendment	
38 Congress, first session, 3014 (June 15, 1864)	8.26
38 Congress, second session, 531 (Jan. 31, 1865)	23.15
Reconstruction bill	
38 Congress, second session, 1002 (Feb. 22, 1865)	19.51
Creation of the Joint Committee on Reconstruction	
39 Congress, first session, 6 (Dec. 4, 1865)	0.00
D.C. black suffrage bill	
39 Congress, first session, 311 (Jan. 18, 1866)	10.00
Apportionment constitutional amendment	
39 Congress, first session, 538 (Jan. 31, 1866)	8.40
Freedmen's Bureau bill	
39 Congress, first session, 688 (Feb. 6, 1866)	0.73
Civil Rights bill	
39 Congress, first session, 1367 (March 13, 1866)	5.13
Civil Rights bill veto	
39 Congress, first session, 1861 (April 9, 1866)	5.88
Second Freedmen's Bureau bill	
39 Congress, first session, 2878 (May 29, 1866)	5.88
Fourteenth Amendment	
39 Congress, first session, 3149 (June 13, 1866)	0.00
Tennessee restoration bill	
39 Congress, first session, 3980 (July 20, 1866)	80.68
Resolution to investigate the conduct of President Johnson	
39 Congress, second session, 321 (Jan. 7, 1867)	10.09
Louisiana Reconstruction bill	
39 Congress, second session, 1175 (Feb. 12, 1867)	8.13
Reconstruction bill	
39 Congress, second session, 1215 (Feb. 13, 1867)	12.80
Supplementary Reconstruction bill	
40 Congress, first session, 67 (March 11, 1867)	0.00
Impeachment	
40 Congress, second session, 68 (Dec. 7, 1867)	52.71
Supplementary Reconstruction bill	
40 Congress, second session, 664 (Jan. 21, 1868)	0.78
Impeachment	
40 Congress, second session, 1400 (Feb. 24, 1868)	0.73
Arkansas restoration	
40 Congress, second session, 2399 (May, 8, 1868)	3.42
Southern state restoration bill	
40 Congress, second session, 2465 (May 14, 1868)	2.61
Fifteenth Amendment	
40 Congress, third session, 745 (Jan. 30, 1869)	1.36
Louisiana electoral vote count resolution	
40 Congress, third session, 1057 (Feb. 10, 1869)	61.39

CHART 6

Comparison of Republican and Democratic Voting Patterns in the Senate
38–40 Congresses

	RICE INDEX OF PARTY LIKENESS
LABOR	
Eight-hour day for government workers	
40 Congress, second session, 3429 (June 24, 1868)	88.75
BANKRUPTCY LEGISLATION	
Bankruptcy bill	
39 Congress, second session, 1012 (Feb. 5, 1867)	81.69
ANTIMONOPOLY LEGISLATION	
Rate regulation amendment to the International Ocean Telegraph bill	
39 Congress, first session, 1539 (March 21, 1866)	73.18
Interstate Transportation and Commerce bill	
39 Congress, first session, 2870 (May 29, 1866)	58.84
39 Congress, first session, 2876 (May 29, 1866)	38.24
Rate regulation amendment to the Niagara Ship Canal bill	
39 Congress, first session, 3480 (June 29, 1866)	75.86
National incorporation of railroads bill	
40 Congress, third session, 472 (Jan. 20, 1869)	95.45
AID TO TRANSPORTATION	
Pacific Railroad land grant	
38 Congress, first session, 2424 (May 23, 1864)	59.01
Mail subsidy for steamer transportation to Brazil	
38 Congress, first session, 2485–86 (May 24, 1864)	80.48
Intercontinental telegraph subsidy	
38 Congress, first session, 3126 (June 21, 1864)	88.88
Subsidy for steamer transportation to China	
38 Congress, second session, 766 (Feb. 13, 1865)	42.58
Niagara Ship Canal bill	
39 Congress, first session, 3792 (July 13, 1866)	56.66
Denver Pacific Railroad land grant	
40 Congress, second session, 4442 (July 25, 1868)	31.76
Western Pacific Railroad land grant	
40 Congress, second session, 3681 (July 2, 1868)	86.87
Central Branch of the Union Pacific Railroad land grant	
40 Congress, third session, 635 (Jan. 27, 1869)	62.01
TARIFF	
Tariff bills	
38 Congress, first session, 3053 (June 17, 1864)	0.00
39 Congress, second session, 828 (Jan. 29, 1867)	50.00
39 Congress, second session, 931 (Jan. 31, 1867)	71.87
RECONSTRUCTION AND RACIAL ISSUES	
Test Oath for Senators	
38 Congress, first session, 54 (Dec. 18, 1863)	12.50
Thirteenth Amendment	
38 Congress, first session, 352 (April 8, 1864)	22.22

	RICE INDEX OF PARTY LIKENESS

RECONSTRUCTION AND RACIAL ISSUES

Black suffrage in D.C.
38 Congress, first session, 2545 (May 28, 1864) — 70.27

Recognition of the reconstructed government of Arkansas
38 Congress, first session, 2906 (June 13, 1864) — 76.29

Repeal of the fugitive slave law
38 Congress, first session, 3191 (June 23, 1864) — 18.18

Freedmen's Bureau bill
38 Congress, first session, 3350 (June 28, 1864) — 8.70

Black suffrage amendment to the Reconstruction bill
38 Congress, first session, 3449 (July 1, 1864) — 77.73

Reconstruction bill
38 Congress, first session, 3461 (July 1, 1864) — 33.33

Electoral vote count resolution
38 Congress, second session, 595 (Feb. 4, 1865) — 99.19

Recognition of the reconstructed government of Louisiana
38 Congress, second session, 1107 (Feb. 25, 1865) — 60.60

Creation of the Joint Committee on Reconstruction
39 Congress, first session, 30 (Dec. 12, 1865) — 9.17

Freedmen's Bureau bill
39 Congress, first session, 421 (Jan. 25, 1866) — 0.00

Civil Rights bill
39 Congress, first session, 606–607 (Feb. 2, 1866) — 8.33

Freedman's Bureau bill veto
39 Congress, first session, 943 (Feb. 20, 1866) — 21.05

Black suffrage amendment to the Apportionment Amendment to the Constitution
39 Congress, first session, 1284 (March 9, 1866) — 73.66

Civil Rights bill veto
39 Congress, first session, 1809 (April 9, 1866) — 15.38

Disqualification section of the Fourteenth Amendment
39 Congress, first session, 2921 (May 31, 1866) — 10.81

Apportionment section of the Fourteenth Amendment
39 Congress, first session, 3042 (June 8, 1866) — 10.81

Second Freedman's Bureau bill veto
39 Congress, first session, 3842 (July 16, 1866) — 8.33

Black suffrage amendment to the Tennessee Restoration bill
39 Congress, first session, 4000 (July 21, 1866) — 87.50

Tennessee Restoration bill
39 Congress, first session, 4001 (July 21, 1866) — 73.66

D.C. black suffrage bill
39 Congress, second session, 109 (Dec. 13, 1866) — 8.57

Black suffrage in the territories
39 Congress, second session, 382 (Jan. 10, 1867) — 4.00

Reconstruction bill
39 Congress, second session, 1469 (Feb. 16, 1867) — 0.00

Reconstruction bill veto
39 Congress, second session, 1976 (March 2, 1867) — 14.29

Supplementary Reconstruction bill
40 Congress, first session, 171 (March 16, 1867) — 33.33

	RICE INDEX OF PARTY LIKENESS
RECONSTRUCTION AND RACIAL ISSUES	
Supplementary Reconstruction bill	
40 Congress, first session, 586 (July 11, 1867)	12.50
Arkansas Restoration bill	
40 Congress, second session, 2749 (June 1, 1868)	12.50
Southern state restoration bill	
40 Congress, second session, 3029 (June 10, 1868)	0.00
Electoral vote count resolution	
40 Congress, second session, 3926 (July 10, 1868)	3.45
Georgia electoral vote count resolution	
40 Congress, third session, 978 (Feb. 8, 1869)	5.56
Fifteenth Amendment	
40 Congress, third session, 1044 (Feb. 9, 1869)	13.33
40 Congress, third session, 1318 (Feb. 17, 1869)	10.00
Louisiana electoral vote count resolution	
40 Congress, third session, 1050 (Feb. 10, 1869)	85.11

Their common antislavery heritage, their shared desire to guarantee the security of southern loyalists, their determination to realize a Reconstruction that would firmly and permanently cement the Union, and their united wish to see justice done the freedmen enabled Republicans to act in fundamental harmony under great pressure, despite disagreements that rose out of the interaction of other factors with the Reconstruction problem. Agreeing on fundamentals, Republican nonradicals rarely attacked radical proposals as wrong but merely as "impractical"; radicals did not look upon nonradicals as irreconcilable enemies, but rather as men who believed "that it is wrong to follow right, unless with extreme moderation, and at almost geological intervals." "The spirit of conservatism," they averred, "is but a preeminent admission of a want of courage and hope." [55]

The radicals, then, were the men who acted upon the essentially radical principles of the Republican party unalloyed by other considerations. They were, the conservative Boston *Evening Journal* conceded, the "exponents of a feeling, an underlying sentiment of their party," its "great and characteristic principles"—the men, as a Minnesota party warhorse put it, "that *'believe in it.'* " [56]

"The Republican party is called radical, and it is radical in sentiments," radical representative Job E. Stevenson of Ohio once affirmed during a campaign, "but it is exceedingly conservative in action. You can never get the Republican party to take one radical step until it can't help it." [57] For despite their abstract commitment to legal equality and a thorough restructuring of southern political institutions, other factors led many Republicans to hesitate when it came to putting those convictions into law. Among the most important of these considerations seems to have been congressmen's positions on the second most controversial issue of the Reconstruction era—how fast to contract the United States' inflated paper currency or whether to expand it further. As Charts 7 and 8 indicate, most Republicans who consistently urged contraction of the currency opposed radical legislation from 1863 to 1869, while most who favored further expansion sustained it. The correlation becomes even more obvious if conservative, border state Republicans (Representative Hawkins and Senators Willey, Van Winkle, and Henderson) are eliminated from consideration, with γ (gamma) then equaling 0.701 in the case of the Senate and 0.788 in the case of the House.[58]

CHART 7

Radicalism and the Money Question in the House of Representatives 39–40 Congresses

	CONTRACTIONISTS	SUSPENSIONISTS AND MODERATE INFLATIONISTS	INFLATIONISTS
CONSISTENT RADICALS	Broomall, Pa. Mercur, Pa.	Clarke, Kans. Julian, Ind.	Butler, Mass. Cobb, Wis. Paine, Wis. Trowbridge, Mich.
	3	2	4
CONSISTENT CENTRISTS	Ames, Mass. Banks, Mass. Churchill, N.Y. B. Van Horn, N.Y.	Clarke, Ohio Welker, Ohio	
	4	2	0
CONSISTENT CONSERVATIVES	Dawes, Mass. Griswold, N.Y. Ketcham, N.Y. Laflin, N.Y. Lawrence, Pa. Marvin, N.Y. Poland, Vt. Pomeroy, N.Y.	Bingham, Ohio Ferry, Mich.	Hawkins, Tenn.
	8	2	1

Only consistent factionists who voted consistently on the money question in at least two Congresses are included. They may have been unscalable during one Congress. Where subscales existed, the representatives must have scaled on them consistently with the major scale.

For citations to roll calls on the money question, see Appendix II.

CHART 8

Radicalism and the Money Question in the Senate
40–41 Congresses

	EXTREME AND IMMEDIATE CONTRACTIONISTS	STEADY CONTRACTIONISTS	SUSPENSIONISTS	INFLATIONISTS
CONSISTENT RADICALS		Sumner, Mass. Wilson, Mass.	Cameron, Pa. Howard, Mich. Nye, Nev. Yates, Ill.	Wade, Ohio
			Cragin, N.H.	
	0	2 1 *	4	1
CONSISTENT CENTRISTS	Morrill, Vt.	Morrill, Me.	Sherman, Ohio Tipton, Neb.	
	1	1	2	0
CONSISTENT CONSERVATIVES	Conkling, N.Y. Corbett, N.Y. Edmunds, Vt. Fessenden, Me.	Trumbull, Ill.	Henderson, Mo. Willey, W.Va. Williams, Ore.	
			Anthony, R.I.	Van Winkle, W. Va.
	4	1 1 *	3	1 *

* *Senators falling between groups.*
Senators must have scaled consistently on currency questions in both Congresses.
For roll calls on the money question in the Senate, see Appendix III.

This identification of such well-known radicals as Thaddeus Stevens, Benjamin F. Wade, and Benjamin F. Butler with "soft-money" views led Sharkey to his conclusion that Republicans who favored a radical Reconstruction policy also advocated a common economic program of currency expansion and high tariffs which grew out of "a fairly consistent social philosophy." [59] But several consideratons militate against his interpretation. Most important, the soft-money radicals—Stevens, Butler, Wade, and others—rarely and possibly never connected the two issues themselves. [60] Unless one suggests, as some historians have, that the radicals wanted to keep their real objectives secret, such omissions are inexplicable. Second, there seems to have been no meaningful correlation between radicalism and support for high tariffs in the only Congress from 1863 to 1869 that voted on a general tariff bill (see Chart 9 for the vote in the House). Of the seven senators who voted against the tariff bill of 1867, one was a consistent radical and one a consistent conservative.[61]

Finally, the relationship between radicalism and positions on currency questions was not constant. Representatives who sustained or opposed inflation in the first session of the Thirty-ninth Congress manifested no particular pattern in their votes on Reconstruction (see Chart 10). During the second session of the Forty-first Congress those who opposed inflation advocated radical measures more firmly than those who urged it (see Chart 11). The correlation between the money question and radicalism was clearest during the first and second sessions of the Fortieth Congress (see Charts 12 and 13), and the reason is plain: by the first session of the Fortieth Congress the issue that divided radical from nonradical Republicans was impeachment, and President Johnson's secretary of the treasury, Hugh McCulloch, was a militant contractionist, who had put his beliefs into practice as soon as the war had ended. Benjamin F. Wade, who as president *pro tempore* of the Senate would succeed Johnson if he were removed, was an equally militant inflationist. As the radical issue shifted to impeachment, contractionists shifted towards conservatism. With that issue removed by the Forty-first Congress, the association disappeared.

Although the prospect of a Wade administration was the primary reason contractionists moved towards conservatism, less practical considerations also impelled them in that direction. Americans identified Republican radicalism with Thaddeus Stevens, Ben Butler, William D. Kelley, George S. Boutwell, Ben Wade, and Charles Sumner. Of these only Sumner was a firm contractionist. Boutwell wavered, and the others were the lead-

---

CHART 9

*Consistent Republican Factionists and the Tariff
in the House of Representatives
39th Congress, 2nd Session*

	ANTI-PROTECTIONISTS	MODERATE PROTECTIONISTS	HIGH PROTECTIONISTS
RADICALS	6	2	18
CENTRISTS	2	0	7
CONSERVATIVES	1	3	14

For a list of the roll calls upon which this chart is based, see Appendix III.

CHART 10
Radicalism and the Money Question in the House of Representatives
39 Congress, first session

	NONRADICALS (CONSERVATIVES AND CENTRISTS)		RADICALS (RADICALS AND RADICAL CENTRISTS)
CONTRACTIONISTS 0		16	15
SUSPENSIONISTS 1		10	7
SUSPENSIONISTS 2		5	8
EXPANSIONISTS 3–4		9	10

For citations to individual roll calls, see Appendix II.

CHART 11
Radicalism and the Money Question in the House
of Representatives, 41 Congress, second session

	NONRADICALS (CONSERVATIVES AND CENTRISTS)	RADICALS (RADICALS AND RADICAL CENTRISTS)
ANTI-EXPANSIONISTS	14	23
MODERATE EXPANSIONISTS	8	10
EXTREME EXPANSIONISTS	10	9

For citations to individual roll calls, see Appendix II.

C H A R T 12

*Radicalism and the Money Question in the House of Representatives
40 Congress, first and second sessions*

		NONRADICALS (CONSERVA-TIVES AND CENTRISTS)	RADICALS (RADICALS AND RADICAL CENTRISTS)
CONTRACTIONISTS	0	25	10
MODERATE INFLATIONISTS	1	6	17
INFLATIONISTS	2	6	15

*Representatives must not have deviated from a consistently radical or nonradical
voting pattern in any session.*
   For citations to individual roll calls, see Appendix II.

C H A R T 13

*Radicalism and the Money Question in the Senate
40 Congress, first and second sessions*

	IMMEDIATE CONTRACTIONISTS	STEADY CONTRACTIONISTS	SUSPENSIONISTS	INFLATIONISTS
RADICALS		Harlan, Iowa Sumner, Mass. Thayer, Neb. Wilson, Mass.	Cameron, Pa. Cole, Calif. Nye, Nev. Pomeroy, Kans. Ramsey, Minn. Yates, Ill.	Wade, Ohio Howe, Wis.
		Howard, Mich.		
	0	4 1 *	6	2

NONRADICALS	Corbett, Ore.
	Ferry, Conn.
	Fessenden, Me.
	   Edmunds, Vt.
	   Patterson, N.H.
		Frelinghuysen, N.J.
		Trumbull, Ill.
		   Anthony, R.I.
			Willey, W.Va.
			Williams, Ore.
			   Henderson, Mo.
			   Van Winkle, W.Va.	

	3 2 *	2 1 *	2 2 *	0

* Senators falling between groups.
   *Senators must have voted consistently radical or nonradical in both sessions, with
one nonscaling session permissible.*
   For citations to individual roll calls, see Appendix III.

ing spokesmen for currency expansion in Congress. Contractionists could not help but connect the two issues. By summer 1867, they feared that southern radicals—owing so much to Stevens and Butler—might follow their lead in financial matters.[62]

Other legislative issues also inclined men away from radicalism, though not so dramatically. The tariff question appears to have been one of these. It is difficult to pinpoint this issue's effect to the same extent as that of the money question. The Fortieth Congress considered no general tariff bill; when the Thirty-ninth Congress did consider one, antitariff sentiment was just budding and few Republicans in Congress opposed its passage. But many hard-money men were also freetraders, and the well-known high-tariff views of Stevens, Kelley, Zachariah Chandler, Wade, and other radicals could only have added to their determination to oppose radicalism. All the remaining Republican senators who had opposed the tariff bill of 1867 voted to acquit President Johnson on the impeachment charges in 1868, precluding the elevation of the pro-high-tariff Wade to the presidency.

Another question that may have affected radicalism, especially after 1868, was the issue of aiding railroad construction through grants of land. Before the Fortieth Congress Republicans supported or opposed individual grants on the merits of each case, taking into special account the effect of each upon their constituents. But the Fortieth Congress witnessed continuing efforts to end the land-grant system as it related to railroads. In some respects this movement related to financial and tariff questions. Contractionists were urging retrenchment of government expenditures to aid redemption of the currency. The iron interest, perhaps the most important soft-money, high-tariff lobby, naturally supported government aid to the railroads, which were among their best customers. Reformers blamed logrolling by railroad lobbyists for much of the corruption they believed pervaded Washington. And these reformers, "the best men," as they thought of themselves, generally adhered to the hard-money, free-trade doctrines of nineteenth-century liberalism.

When opponents of railroad land grants first brought a resolution opposing any further grants before the House, in the first session of the Fortieth Congress, more consistent radicals than conservatives favored it. But as the movement to end the practice gained momentum, radicals proved the land grants' most tenacious supporters. By the third session (1869) all but two of the consistent nonradicals voting opposed further grants. Nearly all those who had not converted to opposition were radicals (see Chart 14). Moreover, of the fifty-four Republicans most inclined to favor land-grant aid in the third session, twenty-eight represented southern constituencies (including the border states Missouri, Kentucky, Tennessee, and West Virginia). Of the ninety-one Republicans who opposed it, only fourteen came from the South.[63] Southerners were also overrepresented among

CHART 14

Radicalism and Aid to the Railroads in the House of Representatives
40 Congress

	ANTI-AID	GENERALLY AGAINST BUT IN FAVOR DURING 40 c., 2 s.	AGAINST AID BY 40 c., 3 s.	PRO-AID THROUGHOUT
CONSISTENT RADICALS	Boutwell, Mass. Broomall, Pa. Cullom, Ill. Harding, Ill. Mercur, Pa. Shanks, Ind. Ward, N.Y. Williams, Pa.	Ela, N.H. Julian, Ind. Kelsey, N.Y. Paine, Wis. Wilson, Pa.	Bromwell, Ill. Butler, Mass. Covode, Pa. Williams, Ind.	Arnell, Tenn. Cake, Pa. Clarke, Kans. Kelley, Pa. Maynard, Tenn. O'Neill, Pa. Schenck, Ohio Stokes, Tenn.
		Van Wyck, N.Y.	Ashley, Ohio Lynch, Me. McClurg, Mo. Stevens, N.H. Van Horn, Mo.	
	9	1 * 5	4 5 *	8
CONSISTENT CENTRISTS	Clarke, Ohio 1 *	Miller, Pa. 1 *	Blaine, Me. 1 *	Banks, Mass. 1
CONSISTENT CONSERVATIVES	Washburne, Ill.	Bingham, Ohio Buckland, Ohio Ferry, Mich. Laflin, N.Y. Lawrence, Pa. Pomeroy, N.Y.	Hubbard, W.Va.	Smith, Vt.
		Hawkins, Tenn.	Ketcham, N.Y. Marvin, N.Y.	Griswold, N.Y. Poland, Vt.
	1	1 * 6	2 * 1	2 * 1

* *Representatives falling between groups.*
  For the roll calls on which this chart is based, see Appendix VI.

Republicans who pressed for an increased circulation of currency after 1869. Republicans from other regions divided almost evenly on currency expansion, fifty-four opposing and fifty favoring it. Of thirty-four southern Republicans taking a clear position during the Forty-first Congress, thirty favored expansion. Although they joined their northern allies in opposing efforts to pay United States bonds with greenbacks rather than gold (the second key financial issue of the times), southern Republicans' "pro-corruption," "pro-logrolling," support of national aid to railroads and their soft-money sympathies help explain why orthodox, hard-money Republicans so quickly agreed to the "carpetbagger" and "scalawag" labels Democrats fastened upon them.[64]

David Donald has suggested yet another factor which he believed influenced some Republicans to modify their radicalism. Investigating the majorities by which constituents elected Republican representatives who voted with radicals, moderates, and conservatives in the second session of the Thirty-ninth Congress, he found that within states radicals generally enjoyed greater majorities than nonradicals.[65] But I have found no similar pattern among representatives who voted consistently with one group or another from 1863 through 1869.

There may be several explanations for the inconsistency. Donald evaluated only those representatives voting in one session of Congress, and he used a somewhat unrefined statistical method to determine his groups, so that his characterizations and mine do not always agree. Perhaps there was something in the issue of the second session of the Thirty-ninth Congress (passage of the Reconstruction act) that forced Republicans to consider political expediency more than they did when voting on other issues.[66]

Donald suggested that Republicans from close districts had to appeal to Democratic voters to secure election and therefore were forced to moderate their radicalism. Actually, the danger was slightly different. The political customs of the times made crossing of party lines rare. The traditional way to signify disapproval of the candidate or the course of one's party was to stay away from the polls or to "scratch" one of the names from the party ticket before depositing it in the ballot box. A Republican congressman in a close district might well conclude that his radical constituents would prefer him to a Democrat in any case, while conservative voters might prove less firm. If conservatives refused to vote, their absence might mean defeat, and this consideration might moderate the legislative position of a careful Republican.

But the decision to conciliate conservatives was not so easily made: when one nervous Republican complained to radical Representative "Long John" Wentworth that a vote to enfranchise blacks in the nation's capital would cost him his reelection, Wentworth growled, "Reelection? You'd better get your nomination first. Haven't you learnt that it is the Radicals who do that job nowadays?" [67] So before a congressman could adopt a course designed to satisfy his conservative constituents, he had to make quite certain that the local workers, who made the nominations, agreed with his assessment. But despite the dangers, it is likely that many Republicans from strongly contested districts feared legislation framed with eyes open only to the principles of the party and not to its political necessities.

Many Republicans who enjoyed safe seats also worried over the political effect of adhering too rigidly to its principles. Fessenden, Blaine, Grimes, Morrill, and others feared the people were not yet ready to accept those principles if carried to their fullest extent. James A. Garfield in 1866 warned of "those who . . . are right in their practical wishes and intentions yet [who] . . . give a club to our enemies to break us to pieces." [68] Their concern was not primarily for their own safe seats but for the success of the organization as a whole. Radicals like George Julian sometimes referred to these stalwart party loyalists as "the mercenary element," but that was hardly fair. They considered the continued success of the party the only way to secure the ultimate supremacy of its principles. They would have agreed with Blaine when he answered Wendell Phillips's accusation in 1879 that the party failed its mission by not insisting on more secure guarantees for black men's rights. Phillips's policy would have led to political disaster, Blaine retorted. And this would have led to an immediate restoration of the Union

without the imposition of a single condition, without the exaction of a single guarantee. All the inestimable provisions of the Fourteenth Amendment would have been lost: its broad and comprehensive basis of citizenship; its clause regulating representation in Congress and coercing the States into granting suffrage to the negro . . . . These great achievements for liberty, in addition to the Fifteenth Amendment, would have been put to hazard and probably lost, could Mr. Phillips have had his way.[69]

When Republicans entered this area of "practicality," they demonstrated that something more than the mere size of majorities or positions on non-reconstruction issues influenced individuals towards or away from radicalism. Radicalism related to temperament as well—to how different men *perceived* practicality. Their contemporaries understood there was something different in the patterns of thought of conservatives like Fessenden, Sherman, Bingham, and Dawes and radicals like Stevens, Butler, Sumner, and Wade. Concerned with the political repercussions of their actions, their undefinable differences of attitude led to opposing conclusions. For instance, the conservative Rufus P. Spalding (who was once known as the "Great Radical from Ohio," but who lost that designation after the war) worried, "I have been a partisan long enough to know that extreme measures will not always promote the interests of a party. . . . What will our people at home think of . . . rank and radical measures? . . . Will not these matters react?" But the radical Josiah B. Grinnell warned, "Yielding a principle . . . through fear, [the party] . . . disgusts the moralist, and dampens the ardor of the young and heroic whose service has been determined by the nature of our boldness, constancy, and trust in the Almighty Ruler." [70]

Those who, like Spalding, believed the electorate basically unsympathetic to Republican principles argued it was a political necessity to move slowly in enacting those principles into law. Radicals argued that timidity lost votes. This was the key to radical-conservative differences, commented a radical observer. "Policy is the rule of the one, Principle is the only guide for the other." [71] The conservative Fessenden did not dispute the moral mission of the Republican party. But in pursuing its principles, he insisted, "we ought to be practical." Later he explained, "I have been taught since I have been in public life to consider it a matter of proper statesmanship, when we aim at an object which we think is valuable and important, if that object . . . is unattainable, to get as much of it and come as near it as we may be able to do." To this the radical Sumner answered, "Ample experience shows that [compromise] . . . is the least practical mode of settling questions involving moral principles. A moral principle cannot be compromised." [72]

T W O

The Politics of Radicalism

————————— ✦ ✦ —————————

THERE WERE TWO ASPECTS to radical Republicanism during the Civil War and Reconstruction: political and legislative. Republicans became identified as radicals or conservatives as a result of political as well as intellectual commitment. So there were actually two radical factions working on different planes. The first consisted of men committed to a legislative program for change in southern society, a program with implications of increasing magnitude for northern society as well. The factions acting on this level are those that may be identified by voting analysis. The second stratum of Republican radicalism related to the hard-nosed business of politics. Men who desired to gain or maintain power in the party proclaimed their adherence to the amorphous radical or conservative ideologies, using such commitments as weapons to battle their adversaries.

One of the greatest obstacles to understanding Republican radicalism and conservatism during the Civil War period has been the tendency of historians to confuse political and legislative radicalism. This confusion is not surprising. Contemporaries did not differentiate between the two aspects of radicalism either. But because they did not, they were equally perplexed by the ideological somersaults of Salmon P. Chase, Horace Greeley, George Julian, and a host of lesser lights. To understand how a Chase could be the radical candidate for the Republican presidential nomination in 1864 and then aspire to the Democratic nomination four years later, one must perceive the factional nature of American politics.

Traditionally, the United States has been a two-party democracy; in many states there has been only one viable political party. Yet, for nearly every position in American national and state government there have been more than one or two aspirants. These rivals have had to fight their battles within one or another of the parties. Often ideological similarities, personal friendships, or pure self-interest have spurred groups of aspirants to office to ally themselves against their rivals. Sometimes these factions are short-lived; often they persist for many years, and this is the genesis of factional politics.

Intraparty factional battles often have been fought on the basis of personality alone, but it has been more common for contesting factions to seize upon issues that they believe will obtain the support of their constituencies. From the outbreak of the Civil War until 1868, legislative radicalism held wide appeal for Republicans. Advocating bold action to carry into effect principles most Republicans held in common, radicalism could not help but win the adherence of broad segments of the party. In certain areas, conservatism too could exert wide appeal. In states with nearly even balances between the parties, conservatism might offer greater promise of success in general elections, and consequently a greater likelihood of office and patronage. Not as important as ideological purity to the rank and file, perhaps, these considerations might carry great weight with local workers, the muscle and sinew of the party, who determined congressional nominations and local appointments. The tendency of Republican factions to adopt radicalism or conservatism as an organizing issue was what gave both concepts their real political power. After 1868, when other issues—civil service and revenue reform, antimonopolism, and money questions—displaced the radical-conservative dichotomy as the basis of factional organization, radicalism went into a swift and fatal decline.

Perhaps the best-known factional rivalry in the Republican party during the 1860s was that in New York between the friends of William Henry Seward, governor, senator, and then United States secretary of state, and Thurlow Weed, Whig and Republican political manager and editor of the Albany *Evening Journal,* and those of Horace Greeley, editor of the *New York Tribune,* the most powerful Republican newspaper of the East. Originally allies in the liberal faction of the New York Whig party, Greeley had drifted away from Seward and Weed over mild disagreements regarding Whig political strategy and Greeley's own ambitions for office. Greeley preceded his former allies into the newly forming Republican party. When they too entered Republican ranks, he cooperated with them uneasily until 1860. The feud broke into bitter warfare that year, when Seward and Weed blamed Greeley for Seward's failure to win the Republican presidential nomination—Seward had been the radical candidate at the Chicago Convention. Greeley had favored the archconservative Missouri Whig, Edward Bates.

Weed repaid Greeley for his anti-Seward activities in 1861, defeating Greeley's drive for the Republican nomination to the United States Senate. During the secession winter, as Weed advocated concessions to slavery to preserve the Union, Greeley opposed compromises, preferring to allow the South to secede peacefully. Strife continued as both factions tried to win Lincoln's favor and control of the national patronage. Lincoln gave control of the customs house in New York City to former Democrats, who generally disliked Seward and allied loosely with Greeley, but the Seward-Weed forces generally received the choicer appointments in the rest of the state.

In 1862 anti-Weed forces, made up of Greeley's friends and the allies of independent-minded former Democrats such as William Cullen Bryant of the New York *Evening Post,* David Dudley Field, Daniel S. Dickinson, Daniel E. Sickles, and Lyman Tremain, controlled the Republican nominations. Weed, advocating a strong appeal to Union Democrats, left the state convention disgruntled and did little to elect the ticket. When the Republicans lost the canvass, Greeley and his allies charged him with sabotage. But with the only patronage now available to Republicans in the state emanating from the national government, Weed slowly regained control of the state organization.

By 1864 Weed, who first worked for Lincoln's renomination and then threatened to sit out the campaign unless Lincoln acceded to his ever-growing patronage demands, had won control of every important national appointment in the state. Lincoln had replaced the former Democrat Chase as secretary of the treasury and soon thereafter turned out Chase's formerly Democratic friends in the New York customs house, substituting for them allies of Weed. At the same time he named a Seward-Weed partisan city postmaster. Given this political situation, it is little wonder that Greeley opposed Lincoln's renomination and that many leading former Democrats—David Dudley Field, Lyman Tremain, Parke Godwin, and John Cochrane, among others—actively promoted the Frémont third-party movement. When Lincoln died, the Seward-Weed wing of the New York party had almost total control of the national patronage in New York City, while the radicals, who had managed to elect Reuben E. Fenton governor in 1864, dominated the state's.

LaWanda and John H. Cox have shown how Weed and Seward hoped to use Andrew Johnson to gain complete control of the Union party in 1865 and early 1866 by driving the radicals out of the organization on the issue of Negro suffrage. Seward and Weed failed because Johnson went too far, making the issue civil instead of political rights and denying the North virtually any guarantees for the South's future conduct. By adhering to the president's policy too long, Seward and Weed discredited themselves with the party, and Fenton and Greeley used the state patronage to perfect their control of the Republican organization. But former members of the Seward-Weed machine—Representatives Henry J. Raymond, James M. Marvin, Addison H. Laflin, Robert S. Hale, William A. Darling, William E. Dodge, and senators Edwin D. Morgan and Ira Harris—remained among the most conservative Republicans in Congress.

Weed made a last effort to restore his political fortunes in 1867, trying to generate and dominate a presidential boom for General Ulysses S. Grant, but events brought nearly all Republicans to Grant's support, and Weed's effort to become the general's special advocate failed. Grant did name a political ally, former governor Hamilton Fish, secretary of state, but this did not revive Weed's fortunes, and the old politician's influence continued to fade.

As the Seward-Weed versus Greeley struggle developed, contemporaries began to refer to the Weed forces as "conservatives" and to Greeley's allies as "radicals," primarily because Greeley favored emancipation early in the war while Seward and Weed opposed it. As opposition to Lincoln's renomination came to be identified with radicalism, Greeley's position in 1864 reinforced the identification. Yet there can be no doubt Greeley's reputation as a radical stemmed more from his political position than ideological commitment. In 1860 and 1861, as noted, Greeley favored the presidential aspirations of an extreme conservative—Bates—and opposed coercion of the South. In the winter of 1862–63 he began to hint at acceptance of peace without reunion, and his party rivals accused him of defeatism. In early 1865 his newspaper endorsed Lincoln's mode of Reconstruction in Louisiana, and at the same time the erratic editor-politician arranged the Niagara peace conference.

In the summer of 1865, with Seward and Weed apparently enjoying the confidence of the new president, Greeley endorsed black suffrage and with moderation questioned Johnson's Reconstruction program. But after Johnson's desertion threatened the defeat of the Republican party, Greeley acquiesced in the abandonment of Negro suffrage and endorsed the proposed Fourteenth Amendment. By 1867 Greeley generally opposed disfranchisement of southern whites, repudiated confiscation, aided conservative Republicans in the South against radicals, and raised money to bail Jefferson Davis, for which he was attacked by Wendell Phillips, Stevens, and the Union Club of New York. But despite his conservatism on these essentially ideological and legislative questions, Greeley vigorously opposed the movement to nominate Grant, favoring Chase instead. Since Grant was considered a conservative Republican candidate in 1867 and Chase a radical, Greeley's inconsistency is patent. Yet it is also easily explained when one remembers that the Seward-Weed organization was Grant's most active backer in New York.

The essentially factional nature of Greeley's politics became even more apparent after 1868. Between 1866 and 1869, the "radical" faction of the New York Republican party, led by Greeley and Governor Fenton, held complete sway over the party organization. But in 1868 Fenton determined to win the Senate seat Morgan occupied. Traditionally, New Yorkers agreed that one Senate seat should go to an upstater and one to a man from New York City. In 1868 the seats were so arranged—Roscoe Conkling being the upstate senator and Morgan residing in the metropolis. If Fenton, an upstater, succeeded in displacing Morgan, he would create an imbalance that four years later would imperil Conkling's seat. Therefore Conkling bent every effort to reelect Morgan, beginning a new factional dispute. Fenton's efforts succeeded—he took his seat in March 1869—and Conkling decided he must challenge Fenton's control of the party to make his own reelection certain. He did this by attacking the legitimacy of Greeley's radical New York City organization, accusing it of maintaining ties with the Tammany Democrats (which was true) and advocating the creation of a new city organization in which the old Seward-Weed faction would share control. The "radicals" steadfastly refused to disband, and after two extremely hard fought convention battles in 1870 and 1871, Conkling succeeded in wresting control of the state party from the Greeley-Fenton coalition.

When Grant recognized Conkling's primary voice in patronage matters, Greeley and Fenton began to oppose efforts to renominate him. By 1871 the old "radical" organization (minus those who deserted to their triumphant opponents) was in full revolt against the regular party. But when Greeley and Fenton adopted issues on which to attack their enemies, they turned to civil service reform, retrenchment, and an end to "centralization" (particularly with reference to national enforcement of the Fifteenth Amendment). Traveling through the South in May 1871, Greeley denounced "carpetbaggers" and Republican corruption. He developed contacts in the region that would influence southern leaders to prefer him to all other dissident Republicans when the anti-Grant forces determined to nominate a coalition presidential candidate.

In the spring of 1871, Greeley and his intimates began conferring with other disgruntled Republicans, who would form the nucleus of the "Liberal Republican" movement. Yet as late as October 1871, Greeley was attempting to devise means to maintain the unity of the New York party (and, of course, to restore his own access to power and patronage).[1] Not until winter 1871–72 did Greeley finally decide to bolt the party completely. When he did so, he confessed it was not due to philosophical disagreements alone, but because "General Grant has seen fit to make especial war on my friends in this State . . . repeatedly, and without excuse. . . . [Grant] proscribed all who were formerly known as radicals, lately as 'Fenton' men. . . . It is now too late for reconciliation. We must go to the wall, or he must."[2]

Greeley's contemporaries generally considered him a radical, but to understand the twists and turns of his political career and his abandonment of radicalism, one must recognize that his was essentially a "political radicalism." He no doubt fully believed in his radical convictions while he held them, but his mind was elastic enough to adjust to new political necessities. When it became necessary, he could believe just as passionately in a new program, elements of which were diametrically opposed to the one to which he had adhered for so long.[3]

The course of the former Democrats in New York's Union party offers an even better example of factional politics. Although they had allied themselves loosely with Greeley during the war and spearheaded the anti-Lincoln radical third-party movement in 1864, when Johnson, a fellow War Democrat, became president they recognized immediately an opportunity to take the leadership of a new, revitalized, loyal Democratic party based on opposition to radicalism. During the summer and fall of 1865, such former radicals as Dickinson and Cochrane (who had been vice-presidential candidate on the radical Frémont ticket) busily tried to win Johnson's support for their project. The New York *Evening Post,* edited by Bryant and Godwin, who had been extremely radical during the war, endorsed Johnson's conservative Reconstruction program and supported him vigorously until he vetoed the Civil Rights bill in March 1866. Lucius Robinson, a close ally of Greeley during the war, accepted the Democratic-Soldiers' Convention nomination for state comptroller, the position to which he had been elected in 1864 as a Republican. David Dudley Field was prominent among Johnson's supporters throughout his administration.[4]

Similar factional alignments existed in the Republican and Union parties of nearly every state. In Maine the friends of former Democrat Hannibal Hamlin vied for control of the Republican machinery with those of James G. Blaine, Lot M. Morrill, and William Pitt Fessenden. In Massachusetts the radical "Bird Club" battled the conservative "Banks Club" before 1860. During the war Richard Henry Dana, Jr., fired by the ambition to replace Sumner in the Senate, outspokenly supported the conservative measures of the Lincoln administration against radical criticisms. From 1865 to his death in 1867, former Governor John A. Andrew staked out a more conservative position than Sumner's, preparing for a run for the presidency or Sumner's Senate seat. The feud between Simon Cameron and Andrew G. Curtin rent Pennsylvania's Republican party for fifteen years. Curtin allied himself closely with Lincoln during the war, becoming one of the leaders of the "moderate" group of northern war governors. In 1865 Cameron, returning from a diplomatic post in Russia, attempted to cultivate friendly relations with President Johnson, and Curtin followed suit. Cameron then swung towards radicalism, while Curtin continued to urge conciliation with the president until the summer of 1866. Cameron defeated Curtin for the Republican Senate nomination in 1866–67 when Thaddeus Stevens's friends swung their support to him to prevent the election of the more conservative man. By 1871 Curtin, like Greeley, was a Liberal Republican.

In Indiana, George W. Julian and Oliver P. Morton fought a long and bitter battle for control of the party. During the war and until 1871, Julian attacked Morton's conservatism. Morton challenged Julian to leave the party on the issue of black suffrage in 1865 and distinguished himself as one of President Johnson's most zealous defenders. Abandoning Johnson after he vetoed the Civil Rights bill in 1866, Morton adopted a policy more closely attuned to the centrist element of his party, but with a partisanship and anti-Johnson fervor which satisfied many radicals. In 1867 he managed to defeat Julian in a contest for the Republican Senate nomination. Continuing to dominate the state party, Morton's allies finally redrew Indiana's congressional districts in such a way as to deprive Julian of his overwhelming local majorities. Reelected to Congress by a narrow margin in 1868, Julian failed to win renomination in 1870. By 1872 he too assailed his enemies as a Liberal Republican.

Similar factional strife—though sometimes with less emphasis on national issues—obtained in Wisconsin between former Whig Timothy Otis Howe and former Democrat James R. Doolittle, both senators; in Minnesota between Representative Ignatius Donnelly and former Governor and Senator Alexander Ramsey; and in Iowa between the forces of Representatives Grenville Dodge and William Boyd Allison and those of Senator James Harlan.[5]

Some struggles were particularly noteworthy for the inconsistencies they produced. In Connecticut, for instance, the major factional division was between former Whig and American party members, led by Senator James Dixon, Nehemiah D. Sperry, and the Hartford *Courant,* and former Democrats and Free-Soilers, led by James R. Hawley, the editor of the Hartford *Press,* and William S. Buckingham. As they organized about war issues, the Dixon faction became known as "conservative" and the Hawley faction as "radical." Yet Gideon Welles, Lincoln and Johnson's archconservative secretary of the navy, belonged to the "radical" faction and used Navy Department patronage to support it whenever possible. Moreover, in 1865 the "conservative" faction joined the "radicals" in endorsing an amendment to Connecticut's constitution enfranchising black men, and both groups worked diligently for it despite President Johnson's known oppositon. As in New York, the conservative faction controlled the national patronage, while the radical faction controlled that of the state, through Buckingham and then Hawley, state governors from 1864 to 1867. In 1865–66, Dixon allied with Johnson, hoping, like the New York conservatives, to drive the radicals from the party. Instead he lost his influence. His colleague, Senator Lafayette S. Foster, president *pro tempore* of the Senate, remained loyal to the regular party on the national level but cooperated with the Dixon forces in Connecticut. Despite efforts by Johnson men, Dixon's friends, and the conservative Senator William Pitt Fessenden of Maine, Foster lost his Senate seat in 1867.[6]

Perhaps the most explicit interaction between political and legislative radicalism occurred in Kansas. There James H. Lane, first governor and then senator, for years battled Charles Robinson for control of Kansas's Republican party. In the course of this long rivalry the Robinson adherents became identified with conservatism and Lane's supporters with radicalism. Lane's voting record as senator justified the appellation. Committed to vigorous prosecution of the war, emancipation, the use of black troops, and by 1864 Negro suffrage, Lane far outdistanced his colleague Samuel C. Pomeroy in claims to radical credentials. But in 1863 Lane found himself in serious trouble back home. Governor Thomas Carney, Robinson, and Pomeroy had joined forces in an attempt to strip Lane of power. With the state legislature also arrayed against him, Lane's position was critical. To save himself, Lane became Lincoln's most outspoken supporter in the state. Gaining control of the national patronage in Kansas through this maneuver, he soon regained his pre-eminent place in the party. Pomeroy, his power waning, became one of the leaders of the drive to replace Lincoln with Chase as the Republican presidential candidate in 1864, authoring the famous attack on Lincoln, the Pomeroy Circular. Despite his relatively conservative voting record in the Senate up to this time, Pomeroy became in the eyes of contemporaries and historians one of the leading wartime radicals.

As the gulf between President Johnson and the party widened, Lane was loath to risk his control of the national patronage in Kansas. Supporting the congressional leadership at first, he altered his course and endorsed the president, sustaining Johnson's veto of the Civil Rights bill despite cautionings from his allies in Kansas that they feared the consequences. The day of the vote Lane received a telegram warning him that he would make the mistake of his life if he sustained the veto. "The mistake has been made," he lamented despondently. "I would give all I possess if it were undone." [7]

As Lane hesitated, his enemy Pomeroy veered sharply toward radicalism. Lane's friends were forced to abandon him, and when both radicals and Democrats charged him with corruption, the former radical, isolated and depressed, committed suicide.[8]

Perhaps the state in which legislative and political radicalism were most confused was Ohio. Historians have generally identified radicalism with support of the presidential ambitions of Salmon P. Chase in 1864 and in 1867 (before he precipitately converted to conservatism). This is accurate. Chase's supporters were looked upon as radicals by conservatives. The mistake is in assuming that such political radicalism necessarily implied legislative radicalism. Ohio's politics were nearly as faction-ridden as New York's, and less organized. But the Republicans with the most numerous followings in Ohio during the Civil War were Chase, Benjamin F. Wade, and Columbus Delano. Delano had challenged Chase for the Republican Senate nomination in 1859–60, worked to defeat his presidential nomination in 1860, and opposed him again in 1864. Between Delano's adherents and Chase's, there was a true radical-conservative dichotomy.

But no such philosophical division separated the Chase and Wade factions. Wade's opposition to Chase's ambitions was no less thorough than Delano's. He too opposed Chase for the 1860 presidential nomination, and Chase blamed him rather than Delano for his defeat. In 1862 Chase tried to repay Wade, first by trying to replace him as senator himself and then by supporting Rufus P. Spalding, at this time known as "the Great Radical from Ohio," for the place. Spalding also enjoyed the support of the conservative wing of the Cleveland Republican party, in his home district. When Wade allied himself with Spalding's more radical local enemies, Chase aided Spalding, who steadily became more conservative in legislative as well as political terms.

To add to the confusion, the conservative Delano also challenged Wade. He quickly developed into a more dangerous opponent than Spalding, but opponents in his legislative district prevented his renomination to the state legislature, effectively destroying his prestige. With Wade's prospects improving, Chase tried to gain the support of the conservative War Democrat element of the Union party through an alliance with William S. Groesbeck, while at the same time he tried to patch his quarrel with Wade. When the Republican caucus of the state legislature met in January 1863, to settle the Senate question, the ex-Democratic element refused to be bound by its decision and bolted the meeting, perhaps intending to nominate Chase or Groesbeck. But Delano, evidently deciding that he disliked Chase more than Wade, threw his support to the latter. The Unionists then coalesced, all but sixteen of them voting for Wade in the state legislature; fifteen—die-hard conservatives—voted for Thomas Ewing and one for Robert C. Schenck.

Naturally these enmities had an impact on Chase's drive for the 1864 nomination. Wade, an enemy to both Lincoln and Chase, aided neither. Delano's forces became Lincoln's primary supporters in Ohio, but their conservatism did not prevent Chase from trying to reach a modus vivendi with them. After negotiations, the Delano men agreed to relax their pressure for Lincoln's renomination and to close the 1864 session of the state legislature without bringing a resolution endorsing Lincoln before the Republican caucus. But the furor over the premature Pomeroy Circular convinced Delano and his friends that they stood to gain more by continuing their alliance with Lincoln than by deserting to Chase, and they forced passage of the endorsement shortly thereafter.

Once again political radicalism did not always run parallel to legislative radicalism. Among Chase's most important allies in Ohio was John Sherman, whose voting record in the Senate was very conservative. He served on the committee that framed the Pomeroy Circular and circulated denunciations of Lincoln under his frank. Robert C. Schenck, on the other hand, displayed a very radical voting record in the Thirty-eighth Congress. Despite his legislative radicalism, however, Schenck had been a conservative Whig, allying with the Republicans' conservative wing only in 1859. Although Lincoln had urged his election to the Senate seat Chase had vacated to become secretary of the treasury in 1861, Chase's supporters had opposed him and elected Sherman instead. In 1864, while the conservative (in legislative terms) Sherman worked for Chase in Ohio, the radical Schenck became Lincoln's most vociferous defender in the southern part of the state.

In 1866, Schenck once more challenged Sherman, then running for reelection. He attacked Sherman's conservatism, pointing especially to his vote in the Senate against repealing the 1793 Fugitive Slave act. Once again Chase supported Sherman, and Schenck was defeated.

By 1867 Chase, though considered a radical candidate for president by most observers, was the more conservative aspirant in Ohio, where Wade worked to forward similar ambitions. To secure the state's support for his presidential nomination, Chase and his allies tried to force the nomination of Benjamin Cowen for governor in 1867. When this failed, they determined to renominate the extremely conservative Governor Jacob D. Cox. But the Wade forces, under the leadership of William Henry Smith, forced the nomination of Rutherford B. Hayes, winning a crucial victory over Chase. After the Republican losses in the ensuing election, however, the prospects of both candidates were irreparably damaged. Given the background of Chase's political maneuverings, it is not surprising to find him trying to win the Democratic nomination instead.[9]

Factional rivalries ran to the local level also. Schenck's leading opponent within the Republican party in his congressional district was Lewis D. Campbell, also a former Whig, who had supported Bell and Everett in 1860. Campbell was intensely jealous of Schenck, who, he complained, "seems to act on the idea that he is the only man entitled to consideration in this section." [10] In 1864, as Schenck supported Lincoln for renomination, Campbell supported Chase. In 1866, though disenchanted with Chase, Campbell supported Sherman's campaign for reelection against Schenck's challenge. As soon as he saw President Johnson was not in sympathy with Schenck's ideas of Reconstruction, Campbell offered him advice and support, exaggerating his part in opposing radical schemes in the state. For his services, Johnson rewarded him with the ministry to Mexico. Using his patronage lever, Campbell tried unsuccessfully to pry his district's Republicans from their allegiance to Schenck. But in 1870 he finally succeeded in replacing his old antagonist, running as an independent Republican with Democratic support.

Similar hostilities obtained in many local areas. They are not easily detailed, because historians have not studied local politics as thoroughly as the subject warrants, but they probably existed in many more localities than those for which evidence exists. Felice A. Bonadio alludes to several in Ohio: between Schenck and Campbell; between James M. Ashley and conservative opponents in Toledo; between the editors of the Cleveland *Herald* and Cleveland *Leader;* between Samuel F. Cary and Richard Smith in Cincinnati; and between John Hutchins and James Garfield in the Nineteenth Congressional District.[11] The Trumbull papers in the Library of Congress offer detailed insights into factional struggles on the local level in Illinois. And published materials by and about George W. Julian give some indication of the depth of the antagonism between him and General Solomon Meredith, his local Republican rival.[12]

Historians have accepted contemporary assessments that Johnson did not use his patronage power wisely. Yet there is evidence that he wielded it in such a way as to make use of these factional rivalries. He named Meredith district tax assessor in Julian's congressional district, for instance.[13] He nominated A.G. Clark, one of Ashley's long-standing rivals in Toledo, for city postmaster.[14] In 1865 Rush R. Sloan, a close friend of Sherman and a conservative, succeeded in winning a presidential appointment as special agent of the Post Office in Ohio. His chief competitor had been S.M. Penn, a radical. When Sloan refused to endorse the president in the summer of 1866, Johnson removed him and named Penn to his old position. Penn changed his politics.[15] The Trumbull papers also indicate that wherever he could Johnson used his patronage to aid preexisting factions of the Republican party in Illinois.[16]

Legislative and political radicalism, then, were not necessarily identical. The two facets of radicalism were often closely related, but political necessities often explain the legislative inconsistencies that men like Lane, Pomeroy, Morton, Chase, and Julian displayed. Moreover, radicalism must be understood as a potent political weapon in the hands of bitter personal and political enemies within the Republican party. Finally, the events leading to Andrew Johnson's desertion of the party must be understood in light of the bitter factional rivalries tearing at its organization at the state level. With such rivalries threatening the party, Johnson should have had—and at first did have—ready-made allies hoping to gain control of national patronage by supporting him. That he failed to carry the party organization with him indicates how unacceptable his position became to Republicans as it evolved.

THREE

The Wade-Davis Bill

+ + +

RECONSTRUCTION BEGAN shortly after the firing on Fort Sumter. As Union forces occupied territory once held by rebels, northern generals and then civilian policy makers were forced to cope with the problem of how to govern conquered areas and what their relations to the national government should be. By 1862 the Sea Islands of South Carolina and Georgia, the New Orleans area, and parts of Tennessee, Arkansas, and Virginia were under the control of national forces. But Congress was deep in the process of financing a gigantic war, increasing the size of the military establishment, and regulating the treatment of property of the disloyal. At the same time the lawmakers were reordering the nation's financial institutions and developing new policies towards public land, education, and taxation. These efforts took precedence over what appeared to be the more remote question of Reconstruction.

Nonetheless, Congress grappled diligently with the sinewy problems Reconstruction presented for the American constitutional system. More radical Republicans as early as 1861 argued that the rebellious states should be held as territories after the war, with territorial governments operating under the direct authority and supervision of Congress. By 1862 the majority of Republicans in Congress appeared to endorse this proposition, but the minority joined Democrats to prevent the enactment of any legislation. Radicals could not have suspected that their program of territorialization had won more Republican support in 1862 than it ever would receive again.[1]

Receiving no positive guidance from Congress, the people of reconquered areas were left to develop Reconstruction movements of their own. With Lincoln's prodding, provisional governors encouraged local citizens to resume the obligations and privileges of loyalty. But the results of such unaided "self-Reconstruction" were disappointing, and by the winter of 1863–64 changed conditions required the government to articulate some policy. As the conviction grew among Unionists in the wake of Gettysburg and victories in the West that the nation would emerge victorious from its struggle, as federal troops occupied increasing amounts of territory, the articulation of some program for restoring loyal government became a necessity. And the possible anti-Republican political repercussions of continuing the war without an established plan for the restoration of peace rendered that necessity urgent.

In response, Lincoln decided to promulgate more concrete guidelines for Reconstruction. Still relying in theory on voluntary action by the people, Lincoln suggested to southerners in his Amnesty Proclamation of December 8, 1863, "a mode in and by which the national authority and loyal State governments may be reestablished." He announced that he would pardon all rebels who took a specified oath to support the Constitution and to obey all laws of Congress and presidential proclamations promulgated during the war, unless modified or voided by the Supreme Court. If 10 percent or more of the number of electors of any state who cast votes in 1860 should organize a state government "not inconsistent" with the oath, "such shall be recognized as the true government of the State." [2]

Lincoln Plan

Lincoln enclosed a copy of the proclamation with his annual message to Congress, delivered shortly after the opening of the first session of the Thirty-eighth Congress. With Lincoln committed by his proclamation to accepting only state governments "not inconsistent" with oaths recognizing the abolition of slavery, radical as well as conservative Republicans in Congress acquiesced in its promulgation.[3] But this acquiescence did not mean that congressional Republicans were prepared to leave Reconstruction solely under the control of the president. After seven months of discussion and confusion, Congress finally passed a Reconstruction bill, which historians have described as the measure through which radicals "openly challenged Lincoln to battle on the issue of reconstruction." [4] In particular, they have argued that it was the radical response to Lincoln's conservative policy of Reconstruction as manifested in Louisiana.[5]

Several facts militate against such an interpretation, however. The situation in Louisiana was not all that clear in the spring of 1864, as Congress considered the bill. All that most congressmen knew at this time was that Nathaniel Banks, Lincoln's commanding general in Louisiana, had organized elections for civil officers in the state and also for delegates to a constitutional convention. Some Republicans were wary of Banks's intentions because of warnings and complaints voiced by dissident Unionist elements in Louisiana. A faction, led by Benjamin F. Flanders and Thomas J. Durant, claimed to represent radical opinion there, and Durant persistently dunned radical congressmen, urging them "to procure the action of Congress, to regulate the whole matter by proper legislation, and not to permit this military commander to usurp the powers which belong to Congress alone." But while Henry Winter Davis ultimately responded to Durant's importunings, Durant complained that none of his letters to other Republican leaders "have been acknowledged." They must have been intercepted, he added archly, for if the letters had been received, "I suppose those Gentlemen would have let me know it." [6] Many Republicans, accustomed to factional carping, apparently dismissed the charges.

Other Republicans were concerned that Banks had not shown enough sympathy in his dealings with black Louisianans, but a large proportion of those who supported the Wade-Davis Reconstruction bill were not overly sympathetic to black aspirations either, as their reactions to various measures in the Thirty-eighth Congress involving racial attitudes would demonstrate. Uncertain as to Congress's feelings, Banks's local opponents did not challenge his conservatism on racial matters in their attacks upon him. James McKaye's damning report on the Louisiana labor system under Banks, which was sponsored by the Freedmen's Inquiry Commission and finally aroused widespread concern in antislavery circles, would not be published until July.[7] With the Louisiana constitutional convention not scheduled to meet until the same month, the situation there was murky.

So while some Republican leaders no doubt distrusted the sincerity of the men emerging as leaders of the restoration movement in Louisiana, that concern was not universal among the Reconstruction bill's supporters. Henry Winter Davis, William Darrah Kelley, and Nathaniel B. Smithers all explicitly or implicitly attacked Lincoln's efforts at Reconstruction in Arkansas and Louisiana, but other representatives, whose voting records proved them no less radical than Lincoln's critics, seconded radical-centrist Representative Fernando C. Beaman's avowal of "the utmost confidence in the ability and purity of intention of the present Commander-in-Chief." [8] Even Kansas Senator James H. Lane, the most zealous advocate of quick restoration of Arkansas to representation in the Union and one of Lincoln's closest political allies, voted consistently for the Reconstruction bill. In fact, the unanimity with which Republicans sustained this legislation, dealing as it did with so controversial a subject, is remarkable. Only six Republican representatives and five senators opposed the Wade-Davis bill when it finally passed July 2, 1864, and none of the senators opposed a more general affirmation of Congress's authority over Reconstruction.[9]

Historians have suggested that opposition to Banks's program in Louisiana was stiffened by radicals' resolve to replace Lincoln with Chase in the presidential election of 1864. There is some evidence to support this view. Francis Preston Blair, Jr., made this charge on the floor of the House of Representatives, and one of Chase's adherents in Louisiana, John Hutchins, wrote the Secretary that "if Gen. Banks' plan . . . shall be approved by Congress, I am fearful it will materially prejudice your prospects." But in fact Chase had come to the conclusion that he was more likely to further his presidential aspirations by conciliating Banks than by irritating him. Informed by more reliable sources that Banks was not inimical to his interests, Chase endeavored to win his friendship and informed his Louisiana allies that he regretted the opposition to Banks's efforts. And in Congress

Blair's charges were vigorously denied.[10] As Lists 5 and 6 indicate, Republican divisions were reflected most clearly in the controversy over imposing black suffrage in the Montana territory. It was that issue, not reaction to Lincoln's Reconstruction program, which divided radical Republican from conservative.

In reality, Republicans—whether they supported or opposed Banks's policy in Louisiana, whether they favored or deprecated Lincoln's renomination to the presidency—desired the passage of a Reconstruction measure for practical reasons relating primarily to law and what they believed to be the proper principles of government.

The idea that the president alone must judge when the southern states should be restored to normal relations with the national government was so foreign to American political thought that few Republicans in Congress —radical, centrist, or conservative—believed Lincoln had meant to preclude congressional action on Reconstruction when he promulgated his Amnesty Proclamation. In it Lincoln himself acknowledged that admission of any state's representatives to Congress would rest "exclusively with the respective Houses, and not to any extent with the Executive." Republicans in Congress were reassured that the executive intended no infringement on congressional powers by the opinions of William Whiting, the solicitor of the War Department and Lincoln's chief "constitutionalist in residence." From Whiting's prolific pen came what were considered the official constitutional justifications for Lincoln's broad use of the war power. When radical James M. Ashley prepared a Reconstruction bill in December 1863 —after the appearance of the president's Amnesty Proclamation—he asked Stanton for his suggestions, or those of Whiting. In answer Whiting published a treatise on military government. Taking an extremely broad view of Lincoln's right to authorize local governments under the war power, Whiting averred nonetheless that "although the President may, while engaged in hostilities, and in the absence of laws restricting his authority, enforce belligerent rights against a public enemy, Congress also may establish rules and regulations which, without interfering with his powers as commander of the army, it will be his duty to administer." Though the governments the president might erect in conquered areas were essentially military, and therefore under his control, "yet the President is bound to execute all laws which Congress has a right to make; and so far as the Legislature has the *authority* to interfere with or control the President by laws or by regulations, or by imposing upon him the machinery of provisional governments, so far he is bound to administer them according to statute."

Whiting carefully refrained from drawing the exact limits to which Congress could interfere, saying only that the question would "require careful consideration," but he had explicitly recognized some degree of congressional control. Moreover, once peace was restored, he emphasized, "there can exist no reason why the President should not obey and enforce the rules and statutes of Congress, regulating his own conduct and the military governments and military tribunals established by him. . . . His refusal to do so would subject him to impeachment." [11] Ashley may have been referring to Whiting's opinions or to private conversations with Lincoln when he informed the House of Representatives, "I can speak authoritatively when I say the President does not intend to [recognize governments formed under his proclamation] . . . without the concurrence of Congress." [12]

Republicans, then, did not really conceive that the president might interpret passage of Reconstruction legislation as an attack upon himself. Representative John Broomall declared:

The proclamation is simply an invitation to the people to organize governments, and a promise to protect them in so doing by the war power. If the plan be accepted and carried out, the next step will be an act of Congress ratifying the action of the people and admitting the State. . . .

It is not pretended that the proclamation of the President can admit a State . . . . That document expressly guards against such construction, by denying all attempt [sic] to give the State organized under it any right to participate in the law-making power.[13]

Indeed, where congressmen divided was not over *Congress's* power to legislate on Reconstruction, but the *president's*. Despite the growing power of the president as a political force, legal theory held that, except for the veto power, his office was divorced from legislation. American statesmen had grown up with the conviction that all government had three functions—judicial, legislative, and administrative—and, as Francis Lieber, the most influential political theoretician in America, insisted, "A principle and guarantee of liberty . . . of really organic and fundamental importance, is . . . the keeping of these functions clearly apart." "The union of these functions," they agreed, "is absolutism." [14]

Many presidential activities during the war contravened this axiom of political philosophy. Lincoln and Whiting had discerned in the president's war powers as commander in chief a source of authority for acts that in peacetime would have been clearly legislative. Lincoln or his subordinates in the executive branch had suspended the privilege of the writ of habeas corpus, established martial law, emancipated slaves, issued rules to govern the armed forces, and promulgated regulations governing trade with the enemy. But not all congressmen—even Republicans—conceded the legitimacy of these activities.[15] So while Sumner, Broomall, and others conceded some power over Reconstruction to the president in the absence of congressional legislation, Henry Winter Davis saw in his Amnesty Proclamation "a grave usurpation of the legislative authority of the people." And John W. Longyear, conceding that the "proclamation of amnesty, as a general plan or outline for organizing new State governments . . . will ever stand as a bright and glorious page in the history of the present Administration," insisted that it was "incomplete for lack of constitutional power." That power "can be conferred by Congress alone." [16]

But if Republicans in Congress disagreed as to the propriety of Lincoln's Amnesty Proclamation, nearly all of them—conservative as well as radical—agreed that of itself the proclamation was insufficient. Again the source of their concern could be traced to the concept of separation of powers. The simple fact was that the proclamation was not *law.* It was not the binding, sovereign will of the nation as expressed through its legislative channels; instead, the proclamation rested on the temporary military power of the executive, the branch of government that according to political theory was charged only with enforcing laws, not making them.

Only by law could national action on Reconstruction be rendered stable and uniform. By the decision of *Luther* v. *Borden,* congressmen believed, the judicial department had already conceded that it was bound to follow the decision of the other departments in recognizing state governments.[17] But only the passage of a law could bind both the executive and legislative departments. For through the veto power, the president too had a part in the legislative process. By requiring that restored governments be "recognized by Congress," Ashley explained, "I mean by the concurrent action of the Senate, House, and President." [18] Davis made the same point:

If we recognize a government in Arkansas and the President refuse to recognize it, in what condition are we? If the Senate recognize a government and we fail to recognize it here, in what condition are we? Or . . . if the President . . . shall see fit to recognize [Arkansas's provisional government] as the government of a State . . . , and if this House or both Houses of Congress refuse to recognize it, where are we? Can there be a recognition of a State government which does not unite the suffrages of all three political departments?

Recognition "must be done by the concurrence of the legislative and executive powers, and without that, it is nothing," he concluded.[19] Representative Ignatius Donnelly warned: "The plan of the President, unsupported by any action on our part, hangs upon too many contingencies. It may be repealed by his successor; it may be resisted by Congress; it may be annulled by the Supreme Court. It rests the welfare of the nation upon the mind of one man; it rests the whole structure of social order upon the unstable foundation of individual oaths." [20]

Concern that Reconstruction proceed by a law binding on all branches of the government prompted the House at the beginning of the session (December 15, 1863) to create a special committee to "report the bills necessary and proper for carrying into execution" the clause of the Constitution guaranteeing republican forms of government to the states, instead

of agreeing to the Republican leadership's proposal to name a committee
merely to study the matter without requiring it to do more than make a
general report. (This became the Select Committee on the Rebellious
States that Davis chaired and which finally reported the Wade-Davis
Reconstruction bill.) [21] The same consideration impelled Davis to oppose
referring the credentials of Arkansas representatives-elect to Henry L.
Dawes's Committee on Elections. Historians have suggested that Davis's
effort to lay the credentials on the table illustrated radical hostility
towards Lincoln's Reconstruction program. But Davis's real apprehension
was that the Elections committee might report in favor of seating the
representatives without first reporting a bill to recognize the Arkansas
government by law. "It is not a mere question of election law which would
be involved" in the committee's deliberations, he argued, "but a question
of the recognition or refusal to recognize the organization of a State government." He would be happy to refer the credentials to Dawes's committee
if it would agree "to consider whether there exists a State government of
the State of Arkansas, making it a direct and substantive topic of examination." [22]

The Senate too made its position clear, when Kansas Senator Lane
and Vermont's Solomon Foot tried to present the credentials of Arkansas's
Senators-elect. Senate Republicans quickly showed themselves unwilling
to admit senators without first recognizing Arkansas's new government by
law. Lane was forced to propose a resolution to that effect and to move
that both it and the credentials be referred to the Judiciary committee.[23]

While trying to maintain uniformity of action in Reconstruction,
Republicans also wanted to proceed by law for a second reason. By his
Emancipation Proclamation Lincoln had freed the slaves in areas in
rebellion against the United States on January 1, 1863, but there were
grave doubts as to the proclamation's legality. Issued by virtue of the
President's war powers, the proclamation, Republicans feared, might not
withstand peacetime litigation, especially given the proslavery record of
the Supreme Court. Though Lincoln's Amnesty Proclamation required
southerners returning to their allegiance to organize governments that did
not recognize slavery, Davis reminded his colleagues that none of the old
state constitutions or the United States Constitution had specifically recognized slavery either. Beaman agreed. "I fail to perceive that any one of
[Lincoln's proclamations] . . . has vacated the constitution or laws under
which the institution of slavery is protected and sustained," he worried.
Those who did not take the amnesty oath or who violated it might still
restrain blacks from their freedom, and they would have to turn for relief
to the courts.[24] There was only one way to bind the judiciary to enforce
emancipation: "I do not desire to argue the legality of the proclamation of
freedom [that is, the Emancipation Proclamation]," Winter Davis insisted.
"I think it safer to *make it law*." [25]

Davis proposed that Congress in a Reconstruction law require re-organized state governments to incorporate provisions specifically prohibiting slavery in their constitutions. Since the Supreme Court had already acknowledged it was bound to recognize state governments previously recognized by the legislative and executive branches, the courts would be obligated to honor the abolition provisions of their constitutions. And not only the federal courts would have to uphold the legality of abolition—state courts, bound by the constitutions of their states, would have to do the same. In this way Congress could "preclude the *judicial* question of the validity and effect of the President's proclamation by the decision of the *political* authority in reorganizing the State governments," Davis explained. "It makes the rule of decision the State constitutions, which, when recognized by Congress, can be questioned in no court." [26]

The Wade-Davis bill, then, was the result of these convictions and apprehensions, and practical legal considerations had far more to do with the nearly unanimous support Republicans gave it than partisan and anti-Lincoln politics. In fact, the nearly universal conviction that some congressional enactment on Reconstruction, almost *any* enactment, was a legal and practical necessity far overshadowed any controversy over its actual provisions. Moreover, although historians have called the Wade-Davis bill radical, the fact was that the radicals really did not know how to secure a safe Reconstruction. Insofar as the mechanics of restoration were concerned—the appointment of governors, the framing of oaths, the rules for holding elections, etc.—the Reconstruction bill was not very different from the program followed in Arkansas and Louisiana pursuant to the Amnesty Proclamation and under Lincoln's watchful prodding. And although it received the support of most conservative Republicans, the bill did not differ much from the earlier one proposed by the radical James M. Ashley either.[27] Where it did differ from Ashley's bill was in its stipulations as to who could vote. And if representatives of southern states were to return to Congress, their attitude toward the Union would depend on who elected them, no matter what the mechanics of restoration were. The Ashley bill had enfranchised all men; the Wade-Davis bill limited the ballots to whites. In this, it resembled Lincoln's policy more closely than the one that most radicals favored. It was not a concession ungrudgingly granted.

Davis's Committee on the Rebellious States reported its proposed Reconstruction bill to the House in February 1864, with the white suffrage provision that radicals opposed. Not until April 19 would Davis allow action on the bill to proceed, and in the intervening two months Congress fought its battle over black suffrage, not in the course of considering a measure directly related to Reconstruction, but while it was organizing a government for the territory of Montana.

The House of Representatives passed a bill to organize a territorial government in Montana on March 17, 1864. But after a sharp fight, the Senate amended the bill to eliminate the word "white" from the qualifications for voting on the motion of the radical Morton S. Wilkinson. Twenty-two of the thirty-one Republicans who voted supported the change. The Senate then passed the bill itself 29 to 8, with only two Republicans voting against it.[28]

When House Democrats discovered what the Senate had done, they exploded, arguing against even appointing a conference committee to meet with the Senate to solve the differences. But with the bill's manager implying the House conferees would not accede to the Senate's black suffrage amendment, House Republicans overcame Democratic objections and appointed the committee. Following tradition, Colfax appointed the measure's manager and the chairman of the committee reporting the bill to the conference committee. In this case, the men were Fernando C. Beaman and James M. Ashley, both at least tending toward radicalism and strong proponents of black suffrage. The two representatives decided to accept the Senate amendment and see if the House would concur.

When the clerk read the conference committee report on April 15, the House was thrown into turmoil. A Democratic motion to table the entire bill failed only by the casting vote of the speaker, but the motion to concur in the report was decisively defeated, 54 to 85. Twenty Republicans joined the united Democrats in opposition; another thirty did not vote.[29] The Democrats then moved to order the House conferees to agree to no report that enfranchised anyone other than white citizens. This went too far for many of the Republicans who had opposed outright concurrence in the Senate amendments, but the motion passed 75 to 67. Ten Republicans—including Winter Davis—voted even for this.[30]

Faced with the unprecedented prospect of House conferees (now Democrats, replacing Ashley and Beaman) under instructions not to compromise the sole point at issue, the Senate refused to appoint a conference committee to meet them. The House then retreated, rescinding its instructions but maintaining the Democratic majority in its conference delegation. Now Senate opponents of Negro suffrage mounted a powerful counterattack. More conservative Republicans warned of the political consequences of endorsing black suffrage. "The tendency is to alienate and divide loyal men and to help the rebellion," Lyman Trumbull complained. "You give men who are really opposed to the Government something to go to the people upon, and get up divisions and distractions, when we want no divisions. . . . [T]he effect of such a proposition is evil, and only evil." [31] Nonetheless, the senators did not recede from their amendment and appointed conferees who favored black suffrage. Deadlocked for three weeks, the conference committee finally abandoned Negro suffrage after one of the Senate members, Lot M. Morrill, deferred to the House's opinions.

Morrill defended his decision in the Senate and immediately received the support not only of conservatives but several radicals, including Benjamin F. Wade, who, noting that no black men resided in Montana, averred, "I never legislate or act in reference to shadows." Other radicals refused to accede, but the Senate concurred in the report, 26 to 13.[32]

But there is no question that the Senate acted reluctantly, conceding principle to expediency. When Senator Morrill was "really in earnest, when his heart and his voice and his judgment and his impulses are all in unison, all sympathetic on the same chord, he thunders his convictions," Wilkinson observed. "But, sir, it was not so to-day. The Senator spoke well, but not loud enough." [33]

The battle over black suffrage in Montana killed the possibility for black suffrage in the South under the Wade-Davis bill. If Congress would not impose Negro suffrage in Montana, where its constitutional right to do so was unquestioned, there was no hope of imposing it on the South, where its constitutional power was in doubt.

Davis held back debate on his Reconstruction bill until April 19, four days after the House so emphatically rejected the Senate's Negro suffrage proposition. The decision probably stiffened his resolve to exclude blacks from any part in his process of restoration, and in this radicals had to acquiesce, but, as Boutwell said, "only in deference to what I suppose is the present judgment of this House and of the country." The radicals had hoped the House would recognize the right of black men to the franchise. "The vote upon the amendment of the Senate to the bill establishing the Territory of Montana dissipated at once for the present this hope. The country will speedily revise our proceedings in this particular," Boutwell prophesied. "Mark the progress of events!" [34] Parliamentary procedures allowed Davis to prevent representatives from offering amendments to his bill, and when John H. Rice of Maine tried to amend the bill to eliminate white-only voting restrictions, Davis rudely cut him off.[35]

In the Senate the Reconstruction bill was referred to Wade's radical Committee on Territories. With the Senate evincing some inclination to support Negro suffrage during the Montana controversy, the committee voted to amend the measure to enfranchise the freedmen. But on June 15 an attempt to pass a constitutional amendment abolishing slavery in the United States failed in the House. This meant that the only way to provide a legislative basis for emancipation was to pass the Reconstruction bill. The passage of the measure was now more important than ever, so when the Senate voted July 1 on whether to agree to the committee's amendment, Wade explained, "Although I agreed to this amendment in committee I would rather it should not be adopted, because, in my judgment it will sacrifice the bill." Two other Republican members of the committee joined Wade in abandoning the suffrage provision, Wilkinson abstaining and John P. Hale sadly announcing he was compelled to "waive my conscientious scruples and go for expediency." Only Lane remained firm, and the amendment lost, 5 to 24.[36] On this most fundamental and controversial of all Reconstruction issues, the terms of Lincoln's Amnesty Proclamation and the Wade-Davis bill agreed.

But there were some variations. Once Republican congressmen had determined that a Reconstruction bill was necessary, it was inevitable that it should differ in some respects from Lincoln's proclamation and the policies military commanders in occupied areas were developing under his surveillance. One important difference arose from the desire of congressmen to postpone the whole question as much as possible. Republicans were really torn in opposite directions by the Reconstruction issue. Nearly all of them agreed that there was an urgent necessity for a general statement of policy which, in Lane's words, "will advertise the loyal people as to what course they are to pursue." [37] But at the same time, the Republicans, whether radical or conservative, did not really feel that they were yet prepared to define specific regulations for Reconstruction. This reluctance was most pronounced in the Senate, where on July 1 a group of Republicans joined Democrats to amend the bill in such a way as to put off the whole question. The substitute resolution, proposed by Missouri Republican Senator B. Gratz Brown, stated simply that the representatives of a state in rebellion would be admitted into neither Congress nor the Electoral College until its people were declared to be in obedience to the United States government. This declaration was to be made in the form of a presidential proclamation issued by virtue of a law of Congress to be passed at a later date. The Brown resolution did not question the necessity for a law, but left its specific terms to be worked out later.[38] Brown's proposal was defeated the next day as Wade, with the aid of absentees of the day before, persuaded the Senate to recede from its amendment in the absence of five senators who supported it—including Brown himself.[39]

But the desire of Republicans to postpone Reconstruction was still manifest in the bill as it passed. When Davis's special committee first reported the bill, it had authorized restoration processes to begin in a state when 10 percent of the number of voters in the 1860 presidential election had taken Lincoln's amnesty oath. In this it had corresponded exactly to the terms of Lincoln's proclamation. But before the bill passed the House, the committee suggested increasing the required number to 50 percent of the state's population, effectively delaying Reconstruction until war's end (and sweeping away the possibility of restoring government in the areas where such efforts had already begun). Since the amnesty oath would be relatively meaningless with the war over (instead of a voluntary resumption of loyalty while war continued, the sponsors feared it would become a grudging submission of defeated rebels trying to avoid punishment), only those who could swear they had never voluntarily aided the rebellion would be permitted to participate in the political process leading to restoration.

The second variance resulted directly from the Republicans' concern

that abolition have a firm basis in law. To accomplish this the bill required
that a provision guaranteeing freedom be incorporated in the restored
states' new constitutions.[40] Except for these provisions, the Reconstruction
procedure enunciated in the Wade-Davis bill was very similar to that
developed by the military governors in Louisiana and Arkansas. Even the
requirement that abolition be incorporated into state constitutions was not
inconsistent with developments where provisional governments had been
established by Lincoln's authority. Both Louisiana and Arkansas had already adopted new constitutions abolishing slavery. Moreover, the bill left
local government in the hands of a provisional governor appointed by the
president with the advice and consent of the Senate. There was no reason
to believe, therefore, that the actual political control of the states in which
civil governments had been partially restored would pass from the hands
of the men many radicals so distrusted.

The manifest importance of passing some bill had led the special
House committee to frame legislation that could command the assent of
men of all shades of radicalism and conservatism. The committee itself
had consisted primarily of Republicans who generally voted with centrists
and conservatives and they had endorsed the bill unanimously. "The committee have sought to avoid the adoption of any especial theory in the
bill which they have presented," Ashley explained. "As a member of the
committee, . . . I have sought to secure the best bill I possibly could." [41]

But congressional Republicans had altered the bill in precisely the
ways Lincoln would not accept. First, the Wade-Davis bill was a peace
bill; its effect was to delay Reconstruction until hostilities ceased. Lincoln's
suggested mode of restoration was a war plan. It was designed to weaken
support for the rebellion by providing a "rallying point" for those willing
to abandon it and resume loyalty. As a war measure, the Amnesty
Proclamation was not nearly so lenient as some historians have believed.
Lincoln offered amnesty only to those who made a conscious decision to
abandon the insurrection while it still had a chance of success. As Carl
Schurz later pointed out, "so long as the rebellion continued in any form
and to any extent, the State governments he contemplated would have
been substantially in the control of really loyal men who had been on the
side of the Union during the war." [42] Lincoln evidently did not intend to
be bound indefinitely by this proclamation. In his annual message to Congress he had affirmed his commitment to reconstructing the Union only
on the basis of loyalty. It was obvious that once Union armies were victorious the amnesty oath would no longer be, in Lincoln's words, "a test
by which to separate the opposing elements, so as to build only from the
sound." [43] As a wartime measure, Lincoln's program was a safe and logical
tactic. By delaying the possibility of Reconstruction until war's end, congressional Republicans were depriving London of what he hoped would
be a potent weapon for shortening the conflict.

The second point of collision originated from that very concern for legality which prompted the Wade-Davis bill's passage. For despite Lincoln's active encouragement of restoration movements in Tennessee, Arkansas, and Louisiana, it became apparent that he still considered these movements to emanate "voluntarily" from the people. Lincoln's constitutional justification for Reconstruction had not progressed to the same degree as his activities. In retrospect, this could be seen from his proclamation and message of December. "On examination of this proclamation," Lincoln had pointed out, "it will appear, as is believed, that nothing will be attempted beyond what is amply justified by the Constitution. True, the form of an oath is given, but no man is coerced to take it." And in the proclamation itself Lincoln carefully avoided any hint of compulsion. Provisions for the care, education, and freedom of former slaves "will not be objected to by the National Executive." Maintenance of old boundaries, old constitutions, legal codes, and subdivisions were "suggested as not improper." And although the mode of restoration suggested in the proclamation was acceptable, "it must not be understood that no other possible mode would be acceptable." [44] Behind the scenes, Lincoln was much more active in getting his "suggestions" enacted than his modest words indicated, but evidently he did not believe these activities really to be coercive.

But the Wade-Davis bill compelled the people of the southern states to include an emancipation provision in their new constitutions, as well as prohibitions on office-holding by high-ranking Confederates and a repudiation of the rebel war debt. The Republicans had not recognized Lincoln's objections to such coercion. Indeed, they believed their bill to be based on the same constitutional groundwork as the president's proclamation. "The bill goes somewhat further," explained Beaman, "but the principle upon which the authority is assumed is the same in each." The president required test oaths and dictated who should control the restored state governments. "If you can impose one condition you may insist upon others. . . . Conceding, then, the competency of the proclamation, it is clear that the difference between that instrument and the bill does not arise out of the question of constitutional authority." [45] Lincoln made no objection to the bill while it was debated. Since the bill, reported with unanimous Republican support from House and Senate committees, was clearly going to pass unless the president intervened, such silence could only be taken for acquiescence.

The Republicans, then, were unprepared for what ensued. Sumner and Boutwell waited in the president's room as he signed bills Congress passed at the last minute. But when he came to the Reconstruction bill, he set it aside and went on signing other measures. Sumner and Boutwell stood in nervous silence. Zachariah Chandler, the blunt, radical senator from Michigan, then entered and asked—apparently in all innocence—whether Lincoln had signed the bill yet. "No," came the answer. Agitated, Chandler pointed to the bill's raison d'être, the provision assuring the permanence of emancipation. "The important point is that one prohibiting slavery in the reconstructed states," he said.

"That is the point on which I doubt the authority of Congress to act," Lincoln answered.

"It is no more than you have done yourself," Chandler urged. But Lincoln responded, "I conceive that I may in an emergency do things on military grounds which cannot be done constitutionally by Congress." Lincoln did not sign the bill before Congress adjourned, killing it by a "pocket veto." [46]

But Lincoln's veto was also motivated by other considerations. True, Lincoln wanted to allay possible Democratic criticism that Republicans were pursuing a war of conquest without a plan for Reconstruction and to create that "rallying point" for rebels willing to return to their allegiances, but in encouraging Banks's activities in Louisiana, he was also building a political alliance. Although Secretary of the Treasury Chase had made overtures to Banks regarding political cooperation, by July 1864, when the Reconstruction bill passed, Banks and his supporters were Lincoln's steadfast political friends. The president could hardly aid in dismantling the fruits of their efforts.[47]

Lincoln's actions finally divided Republicans in Congress along radical-conservative lines on the Reconstruction issue. Some—like Wade, Davis, Chandler, and Sumner—were prepared to stand firm and would so demonstrate during the next session, but others already began to regret their support for the congressional bill. Fessenden, the Senate Republican leader, had abstained from voting on the measure and now informed Lincoln that he had doubted its constitutionality all along.[48]

Despite their unhappiness, most radicals kept silent under the pressure of the 1864 presidential election. Nonetheless, Wade and Davis, the bill's Senate and House managers, penned an address "To the supporters of the government." Once again emphasizing the necessity of a legal basis for Reconstruction, the two radicals excoriated the president's policies in Louisiana and Arkansas, accused him of intending to use the electoral votes of the two "states" to maintain himself in power should he lose the election, and bitterly but conclusively demonstrated the inconsistency of the president's constitutional scruples over emancipation where Congress was concerned as compared to his own assumption of war powers on the subject. But Wade and Davis stood alone. Republicans of all shades of opinion joined to denounce their manifesto, so rashly conceived during a hot campaign.[49]

FOUR

The Radicals on the Defensive

✦✦✦✦

WITH GRANT'S ARMY slogging towards Richmond and Sherman's slicing through rebel territory further south, Reconstruction became the primary war-connected concern of the second session of the Thirty-eighth Congress. No longer were enrollment bills, habeas corpus acts, and confiscation measures the chief centers of congressional controversy. Now the question was restoration and the place of black men in American society, and in the winter of 1864–65 the position of congressmen on the question of recognizing the governments reconstructed under Lincoln's authority in Louisiana and Arkansas became the new test of radicalism, precipitating a major shift in the radical-conservative alignment in Congress. Since radicals and conservatives fought the most clear-cut battle in the Senate, the shift was especially noticeable there. Radical and conservative lines broke and re-formed with considerable change in personnel and a significant decline in radical power (see List 8).[1]

Not only did individual congressmen shift to more conservative groups, but the groups themselves took more conservative positions on Reconstruction than they had in previous sessions. Only the most radical Republicans still spoke of "territorializing" the South. Furthermore, although nearly all Republicans had cooperated in passing the Wade-Davis bill a few months earlier, during the second session sponsors of a similar Reconstruction measure could make little headway. Conservative and center Republicans united to press instead for recognition of the government erected in Louisiana under Lincoln's authority. Suddenly conservative Republicans found, as Davis bitterly observed, that the Reconstruction bill "violates the principles of republican government." Nothing better demonstrates that most Republicans had not passed the Wade-Davis bill as a challenge to Lincoln than Davis's sardonic comment:

Gentlemen who at the last session voted for this bill . . . in the quiet and repose of the intervening period have criticised in detail the language, and not stopping there, have found in its substance that it essentially violates the principles of republican government . . . . That these discoveries should have been made since the vote of last session is quite as remarkable as that they should have been overlooked before that vote. But they were neither overlooked before nor discovered since. . . . It is the will of the President which has been discovered since.[2]

Lincoln's growing power within the party induced Republicans to accede to his now manifest desires regarding Reconstruction. He had demonstrated surprising strength among Republicans in the election of 1864. Easily defeating Chase's opposition candidacy, Lincoln was nominated by the overwhelming decision of the local politicians who attended the Republican national convention in Baltimore. Though many congressmen, both radical and conservative, opposed him for his apparent incapacities and vacillation on questions of principle, the local politicians, interested in winning elections, believed him to be the only Republican candidate who promised victory.

An attempt to create a radical third party, frustrated by appeals for party unity and Democratic ineptitude (Democrats framed a peace platform that literally forced leading radicals to support Lincoln rather than risk disunion), served only to weaken radicalism's appeal and reduce radicals' prestige. Republicans expected Lincoln, the first president since Jackson to be reelected, to appoint new, deserving supporters to government office. The four-year terms of numerous government officials expired with the president's second inauguration. They would be reappointed or replaced. In the faction-ridden Republican party, Lincoln's favor would be indispensable to ambitious local politicians who needed access to patronage to build solid support.[3]

This power was more than most Republicans could resist. Kansas's Senator Pomeroy, bloodied in his struggle against Lincoln and Lane, became one of the Senate's leading advocates of Lincoln's Reconstruction program. Horace Greeley had been identified with the anti-Lincoln radicals during the nomination fight. Although his allies had won control of the New York state government, Greeley's enemies, Weed and Seward, had consolidated their hold on the national patronage in the state. Greeley, perhaps trying to restore his diminished influence with the president, began vociferously to support the administration and its Reconstruction policy.[4] When Wendell Phillips and George Luther Stearns went to Washington to lobby against recognizing Lincoln's restored state governments, they found themselves "critically situated." Radical congressmen informed them that "A.L. has just now all the great offices to give afresh & cant [sic] be successfully resisted. He is dictator." [5]

Other factors also influenced Republicans to favor Louisiana's restoration and to oppose legislation that put in doubt the status of the governments in Louisiana, Arkansas, and Tennessee. When Republican congressmen had considered the Wade-Davis Reconstruction bill, the situation in Louisiana had been murky. Now it was clearer, and most

Republicans were satisfied with Lincoln's policy there. Louisiana's government was controlled by moderately conservative unionists who were opposed to slavery but indisposed to champion black men's political or civil rights.

Because Louisiana was the state in which wartime Reconstruction progressed farthest, Republicans formulated their positions on Reconstruction with reference to it. Therefore developments there require detailed examination: In December 1863, Lincoln, impatient for signs of progress in Louisiana's restoration movement, had instructed the commanding general, Nathaniel P. Banks, to "give us a free State reorganization of Louisiana in the shortest possible time" and had given him complete authority to fulfill that assignment.[6] With this Lincoln put a political general in absolute control of Louisiana's restoration process. Banks was a politician rather than a professional soldier, a volunteer general with presidential aspirations who intended to return to politics after the war. During his nimble political career in Massachusetts, he had been successively an antislavery Democrat, an American (or Know-Nothing), and finally a Republican. By 1857 Banks had been the acknowledged leader of the conservative wing of the Massachusetts Republican party, called after him the "Banks Club." Elected governor that year, he had served three terms from 1858 through 1860, during which he had battled the radical wing of his party.[7]

Replacing the fiery, radical Benjamin F. Butler in Louisiana, Banks had determined to pursue a conservative, conciliatory policy. In the process he had modified Butler's orders and framed a labor policy which had been denounced by leading abolitionists, because although it recognized the freedom of former slaves, it forced them to work on plantations for only a small share of the profit from crops they raised. Moreover, the Banks labor code applied strict punishments for freedmen who would not work under its restrictive provisions.[8]

Searching for materials with which to build his free state government, Banks turned to Michael Hahn and his adherents, one of the Unionist factions fighting for control of the state. Withdrawing patronage from another faction which Butler had favored, Banks had distributed it to the Hahn group and created, in the words of his biographer, "a personal political machine, run in the interests of Banks, Hahn, and their lieutenants." [9] The displaced group, cut off by Banks from Lincoln's support and patronage, attacked Banks and Hahn, veered towards radicalism, and allied itself with the interests of then Secretary of the Treasury Chase. Led by Benjamin F. Flanders and Thomas J. Durant, these radicals urged their allies in Congress not to recognize the Banks-Hahn regime and warned them Reconstruction could not be secure under the control of such conservative elements. By December 1864, as Congress reassembled, Hahn had been elected governor of Louisiana, his allies occupied the other state offices, Louisianans had adopted a new state constitution which abolished slavery, and representatives and senators-elect were ready to claim seats in Congress.[10]

During the summer and fall of 1864, Banks and his allies launched a broad campaign to win approval for his policy in the North. Private emissaries wooed the Massachusetts congressional delegation, while Banks's Superintendent of Negro Labor, Thomas W. Conway, and Benjamin Rush Plumly, a radical opponent converted to Banks's cause, tried to offset the damage done by the McKaye report on the Louisiana labor system. In late fall, Banks came North himself to defend his program. By November 1864, Banks had divided the opposition, winning over William Lloyd Garrison and his influential newspaper, *The Liberator*.[11]

Despite the opposition of Louisiana radicals and the impassioned eloquence of Wendell Phillips, who excoriated Lincoln and Banks for "sacrificing the very essence of the negro's liberty to the desire for a prompt reconstruction," most Republicans were willing to recognize the new Louisiana government.[12] After all, as Banks had convinced them, Hahn's regime was controlled by loyal Union men, committed to emancipation. The Hahn-Banks policy was to appeal to white Louisianans to resume their loyalty and to govern with the support only of those who did so. Most Republicans preferred this to the policy pursued by Hahn's and Banks's radical rivals, who advocated rigid proscription of former Confederates and therefore were forced to turn more and more to black men in their search for a constituency upon which to base a government.

At the same time, congressional developments reduced Republicans' fears that Louisiana's restoration would adversely affect the freedom of black men. On January 31, 1865, Congress finally passed a constitutional amendment abolishing slavery in the United States. With prospects good that the amendment would be swiftly ratified, the danger that slavery might persist in restored southern states seemed to recede.

Of similar importance was the apparent intention of Congress to pass legislation establishing a national bureau to protect black men's interests during the transition from slave to free labor in the South. The Senate and House had passed differing versions of the bill during the first session of Congress, with only two Republicans opposing the Senate bill and only nine defections in the House, although a significant number of conservative Republican representatives had abstained. The House vote was close, but although they feared constituents' reactions, most of the conservatives favored the bill. It was clear the measure would have enough support to pass, and that those who had abstained would vote for it if necessary.[13]

The passage of this measure was the first in a series of Republican attempts in effect to separate the race problem from that of restoration. By creating a *national* agency to protect the interests of black men, Republicans made it less critical that local restored governments should be responsive to their needs. The Freedmen's Bureau, as envisioned by its sponsors, would secure forty acres of land to each black family and provide food, shelter, and clothing for freedmen and refugees during the war and for a year thereafter. The result would be a black yeomanry, many of whom had served in the Union's armed forces, numerous, independent—possibly strong enough to persuade restored loyal governments to extend political privileges to them, and at least powerful enough to make it impossible to tamper with their civil rights.[14] It was these expectations that would enable the radical Thomas D. Eliot, chairman of the House committee which reported the Freedman's Bureau bill, also to be one of the leading proponents of quick recognition of the loyal Louisiana regime.

Although a majority of Republicans were willing to recognize the Louisiana government, all but the most conservative still insisted that this recognition required a law of Congress. So on December 13 Eliot submitted to the House a joint resolution declaring the state of Louisiana entitled to resume normal relations with the government. This resolution Eliot proposed to refer to the Judiciary committee, leading to a conflict of jurisdiction between it and Davis's more radical Reconstruction committee.[15] At first Eliot succeeded in referring his proposition to the more moderate committee, but many Democrats then reversed themselves, joining with radicals to reconsider the original vote and send the recognition measure to the Reconstruction committee, where they hoped it would die.[16] But although the radicals won this skirmish, they did so only with Democratic aid. It was clear that the majority of Republicans had lost confidence in their Reconstruction committee, led by Davis; three quarters of them voted to send the Eliot resolution to the Judiciary committee instead.

The radicals' position was desperate. The credentials of the Louisiana representatives already had been referred to Dawes's conservative Elections committee. Banks was in Washington lobbying strenuously for the recognition of the government he had helped to create. On December 13 he testified before the Elections committee. Shortly thereafter he delivered a written opinion to the Senate Judiciary committee to which the credentials of the Louisiana senators-elect had been referred. In both cases he avowed that the new state constitution embodied the freely ascertained will of Louisianans and that two thirds to three quarters of all Louisianans resided behind Union lines. Louisiana's loyalty was assured, Banks insisted. It was secured by a radical reform "of all the elements of power which effect public opinion." And before Dawes's committee he emphasized that had the Wade-Davis bill passed, the result in Louisiana would have been the same. "In fact, in the measures taken to reorganize a government they have anticipated it," he argued. The Wade-Davis bill's "provisions were adopted by the people of Louisiana without knowing anything that was in the bill." [17]

The general's urgency was dictated by events in Louisiana. While Banks was away, things had not gone as well there as he had hoped. His allies urgently informed him that the military authorities under Banks's new superior, General E.R.S. Canby, were Democrats aiding the Hahn group's enemies. Worse, Banks's temporary replacement as commander of the Gulf Department, General Stephen A. Hurlbut, was demanding the right to appoint civil officials, despite Hahn's protests, thus depriving Hahn of the state patronage. Relations between Hahn and Hurlbut quickly degenerated.[18]

Banks received another jolt when the new Louisiana state legislature elected R. King Cutler and Charles Smith to the United States Senate over the Hahn-Banks candidates, E.H. Durrell and Cuthbert Bullitt. It had been understood that Bullitt would serve only the short term and that Banks would replace him the following year. The state legislature's decision to send Cutler and Smith instead destroyed that plan.[19] Banks won permission to write Lincoln directly, outside of military channels, on Louisiana's civil affairs, but when he used this privilege to urge Canby's replacement it was revoked.[20]

Only by winning recognition for Louisiana could Banks's political allies there regain complete control over the state patronage, and he put all his skill into the effort. Going beyond the testimony he gave the committees, Banks privately assured concerned Republicans that black people's interests in Louisiana would be protected. He informed Chase, now chief justice of the United States and still influential with his fellow radicals, that he personally favored black suffrage. Banks probably told Thomas D. Eliot, whom he knew from his Massachusetts days, that the state legislature would enfranchise at least some of the black population.[21]

Banks exerted his personal influence with the Massachusetts delegation, especially Samuel Hooper, with whom Banks had worked closely in Massachusetts politics, and the all-important Dawes, who had been a member of the "Banks Club" and had been Banks's candidate for governor in 1860, only to lose the Republican nomination to the radical John A. Andrew.[22] In his endeavors Banks had the aid of the entire Louisiana delegation. To them Banks left the task of discrediting the opposition of Louisiana radicals, and A.P. Field, the Louisiana delegation's most articulate spokesman, accepted the assignment with relish.[23] To make their admission still more appealing to Republicans, the Louisiana claimants gave Banks a written promise that they would act with the Republicans in Congress and—most important—vote for the emancipation amendment to the Constitution, which at this time still appeared to be short a handful of votes.[24] Banks no doubt paraded this letter before wavering Republicans.

Lincoln too joined the campaign. In mid-December he informed a delegation of congressmen that he would sign no Reconstruction bill unless Louisiana was recognized.[25] "The President is exerting every force to bring

Congress to receive Louisiana under the Banks government," Sumner wrote the English reformer John Bright.[26] On January 8, when Senate Judiciary committee chairman Trumbull brought a copy of Banks's testimony to the president for his comment, Lincoln showed him correspondence from Louisiana that urged recognition and pledged loyalty. The next day Lincoln sent Trumbull a note endorsing Banks's views and asked, "If I neither take sides or argue, will it be out of place for me to make what I think is the true statement of your question as the proposed Louisiana Senators?

" 'Can Louisiana be brought into proper relations with the Union *sooner* by *admitting* or by *rejecting* the proposed Senators?' " [27] Lincoln did not issue his proposed statement until April 11, when it was the nucleus of his last public address, but everyone knew where the president stood.[28]

Against all this the most the Louisiana radicals could muster was a memorial to Congress opposing the admission of the Louisiana delegation because the military power had dominated the elections; the elections themselves had been held without the authorization of law; and neither one half of Louisiana's voting population nor one half of its territory had participated in them. Evidently the radicals felt it unwise even to mention Negro suffrage.[29]

Radicals outside Congress joined their Louisiana allies in protesting against recognizing the Louisiana government. Wendell Phillips, Frederick Douglass, William M. Grosvenor, James Miller McKim, and the Boston *Commonwealth* denounced Banks's government and urged congressional radicals to remain firm, but to no avail. When Phillips and George Luther Stearns traveled to Washington to confer with radicals there, they found their friends convinced that opposition was hopeless.[30]

The radicals had no alternative but to bend in the face of this pressure. Ashley, though antagonistic to the Banks-Hahn regime in Louisiana, framed a Reconstruction bill which recognized the Louisiana government but which in return enfranchised all black men in other southern states. He submitted it to the House on December 15, 1864.[31] Eagerly prodded by Banks, Lincoln agreed to the Ashley measure as a compromise, although it included nearly all the features to which he had objected in the Wade-Davis bill. But he insisted that the black suffrage provision be stricken, and Banks concurred, despite his assurances to radicals that he favored black enfranchisement, agreeing it "would be a fatal objection to the Bill. It would simply throw the Government into the hands of the blacks, as the white people under that arrangement would refuse to vote." Moreover, Lincoln appears to have agreed with Banks's soothing advice that passage of the measure would not preclude his continued recognition of governments organized by methods other than those the bill prescribed. If he intended to act on that interpretation, Lincoln was very close to an act of betrayal which might have alienated the radicals from him forever.[32]

In response to Lincoln's objections, Ashley and Winter Davis grudgingly modified Ashley's legislation so it enfranchised only black veterans of the Union armed forces and reported the measure from the Reconstruction committee on December 20. "Banks has been pressing his Louisiana govt.," Davis lamented. "All Mass. took his part & the Prest. joined. It was plainly a combination not be resisted so I had to let La. in under Banks' govt. on condition of it going in the Bill defeated by the Prest. last year." The *New York Times*'s Washington correspondent sanguinely reported that Ashley's bill now met the views of conservative Republicans. "It will pass Congress at once and receive the signature of the President. Louisiana will be admitted . . . and the delegation now here will be at once admitted to seats in Congress." [33]

But Ashley found it impossible to satisfy both radicals and conservatives. Wendell Phillips and other radicals, including Stevens and Julian in the House, objected to any measure that recognized Louisiana, fearing the precedent no matter what provisions the bill might make with regard to other states in rebellion. William D. Kelley—and others, no doubt—objected to any restriction on the enfranchisement of black men. "We are to shape the future," Kelley insisted. "We cannot escape the duty. And 'conciliation, compromise, and concession' are not the methods we are to use." [34] In his effort to pass some bill acceptable to both his radical friends and Republican conservatives, Ashley modified his legislation seven times. Each time conservatives in particular found something objectionable and forced him to begin again.

Meanwhile, centrist Republican representatives, no longer willing to sustain the Wade-Davis bill, divided. Some favored quick restoration of Louisiana, differing with more conservative Republicans, however, in their insistence that admission of southern representatives to Congress required a prior congressional declaration recognizing the restoration of the state to normal relations. Representing this group, Eliot moved to amend Ashley's Reconstruction bill to substitute a simple resolution declaring Louisiana entitled to resume political relations with the United States government. Judiciary committee chairman Wilson, articulating the wishes of other centrists, proposed yet another substitute, designed to delay the entire divisive question and to define Congress's general position: "Senators and Representatives shall not be received from any State heretofore declared in rebellion . . . until by an act or joint resolution of Congress . . . such State shall have been first declared to have organized a just local government, republican in form, and to be entitled to representation in the respective houses of Congress." [35]

On January 17, 1865, despite Davis's passionately stated objection that a vote to postpone was equivalent to a vote to kill the bill, the House agreed to a two-week delay in considering Ashley's measure. After the two weeks elapsed, Ashley himself moved a temporary postponement to enable the Reconstruction committee to modify the bill once more in light of the passage of the proposed Thirteenth Amendment and continuing conservative objections. Finally, on February 18, Ashley again brought an amended bill to the floor of the House. The new version enfranchised all black men in the states without loyal governments, but recognized the restoration of Louisiana, Tennessee, and Arkansas to normal relations in the Union. It was a true compromise, acquiescing in the president's policy of Reconstruction where it had begun and adding new provisions to the Reconstruction program where it had not. Nonetheless, it met a tremendous barrage of criticism.[36]

Dawes made the most devastating attack. Affirming that he personally favored black suffrage, Dawes denied that Congress had the power to require it. He insisted that southerners did not require national authority to begin the process of restoration. They could—and should—begin reorganizing their governments themselves, untrammeled by congressional requirements. Dawes objected to provisions that gave the president the right to fill all state offices until regular state authority was restored, charging that "these rebel states may thus be converted into asylums for broken-down politicians." By continuing in force all state laws of 1860 not inconsistent with emancipation, Dawes warned, the Reconstruction measure would countenance the southern black codes which regulated free blacks. There was no time limit to the bill, he complained: it was in the discretion of the provisional governor appointed by the president under the bill to determine when a subdued state was loyal enough to begin organizing a state government.[37]

Stung by the criticism, Ashley withdrew the bill the next day and offered yet another version, abandoning efforts to win the support of conservatives like Dawes. To conciliate radicals he eliminated the provisions recognizing the Lincoln governments; answering Dawes's criticism of provisions confirming southern state laws as they stood in 1860, he added a section requiring the governments organized under his bill to guarantee equal civil rights to all citizens, regardless of race; and finally, to avoid alienating too many moderate Republicans, he restricted voting rights to white loyalists and black veterans. "It has been my earnest desire to conciliate all gentlemen on this side of the House . . . ," Ashley told his fellow Republicans. "For that purpose I consented to what might properly be called a compromise, in providing for the readmission or recognition of the new governments of Louisiana, Arkansas, and Tennessee . . . in order to secure what I thought of paramount importance—universal suffrage to the liberated black men of the South." But, he continued angrily "disappointed in my efforts to secure the cooperation of gentlemen who profess to entertain . . . practically the same opinions which I do in favor of securing universal suffrage to the colored men . . . , I now decline to offer my substitute." [38]

Kelley immediately moved his radical amendment to enfranchise all blacks, Eliot moved his substitute recognizing Louisiana, and Wilson again proposed his delaying resolution. In the confusion and rancor, Democrats moved to lay the bill on the table; conservative Republicans joined them, and the motion passed. [39]

The defeat meant Lincoln would remain free to pursue any Reconstruction program he saw fit during the recess of Congress between March and December 1865. "Sir, when I came into Congress ten years ago, this was a Government of law," Davis mourned. "I have lived to see it a Government of personal will. Congress has dwindled from a power to dictate law and the policy of the Government to a commission to audit accounts and appropriate moneys to enable the Executive to execute his will and not ours." [40]

With the radical Reconstruction bill scuttled, conservative Republicans went on the offensive. On January 17, Dawes's Committee on Elections voted to seat two of the five Louisianans claiming seats in the House, Field and M.F. Bonzano, without waiting for the formality of a congressional recognition resolution. Dawes expressed the conservative Republican position on Reconstruction in his report on the Bonzano case:

Congress cannot pass an enabling act for a State. It is neither one of the powers granted by the several States to the general government, nor necessary to the carrying out of any of those powers . . . . [Therefore] it follows that the power to restore a lost State government in Louisiana existed in "the people," the original source of all political power in this country. The people, in the exercise of that power, cannot be required to conform to any particular mode. [41]

Dawes spoke for four of the six Republicans on his committee. But of tremendous importance for the future was the acceptance of Dawes's formulation of the constitutional question by its two Democratic members. They would support the immediate admission of representatives from restored southern state governments and deny any power to Congress to dictate requirements. [42] In February the committee voted to seat two of the three claimants from Arkansas and another from Louisiana, Dawes reporting resolutions to this effect on February 11 and 17. [43] They remained on the speaker's table, privileged questions waiting to be taken up at any time, but Dawes decided against pressing them.

Instead, conservative Republicans made their strongest effort in the Senate, in a struggle to count the electoral votes Louisiana had cast for Lincoln. If a joint resolution were required to recognize the restoration of normal relations with a rebel state, as most Republicans insisted, then in the absence of such a resolution Louisiana's electoral vote obviously could not be counted. For that reason Wilson's House Judiciary committee passed a joint resolution that no electoral votes from states in rebellion be counted when Congress opened the ballots of the Electoral College on March 1865.[44] Unwilling to imply that the southern states were out of the Union, the Senate Judiciary committee modified the resolution to read simply that because of the rebellion "no valid election" was held in the southern states. Trumbull informed the Senate that his committee had purposely avoided deciding whether Louisiana should be considered a state entitled to a voice in the Electoral College in the absence of a congressional resolution recognizing its government.[45]

But Senator Robert C. Ten Eyck, the most conservative Republican on the Judiciary committee, determined to force the issue by moving to strike Louisiana from the list of rebel states. Conservatives argued that Louisiana was in the Union; it had never been out. When the people erected a loyal state government the state automatically resumed its normal functions and reacquired all its privileges. Moreover, they argued, Congress could not refuse to count electoral votes; to hold otherwise would enable a political majority in Congress to exclude the electoral votes cast for the candidate of the opposing party. But unlike their House counterparts, Senate Democrats refused to support the conservative Republican position. In fact, they took essentially the same position on Louisiana as the radicals. Both argued that Louisianans could not express their free determinations while occupied by the military, and centrists insisted on postponing the entire question by accepting the Judiciary committee's version of the resolution. With Democrats, radicals, and center Republicans united against them, the conservative offensive failed. Ten Eyck's motion to exempt Louisiana from the joint resolution's operation lost 16 to 22. Six Democrats joined the Republican centrists and radicals in opposition. Had the Democrats followed the lead of their brethren in the House, the conservatives would have won by the same margin by which they had lost.[46]

Lincoln, conceding that "the two Houses of Congress . . . have complete power to exclude from counting all electoral votes deemed by them to be illegal," decided that "it is not competent for the Executive to defeat or obstruct that power by a veto, as would be the case if his action were at all essential in the matter." But if he accepted congress' *right* to refuse to recognize his reconstructed states, he made clear his dissatisfaction with its decision to do so, adding pointedly, "He disclaims that, by signing said resolution, he has expressed any opinion on the . . . subject of the resolution." [47]

Lincoln's position was becoming clearer. He would resist efforts to limit his alternatives on specific measures of Reconstruction, which he considered so intimately connected with the prosecution of the war that they came within the scope of his wartime powers as commander in chief of the armed forces. At the same time, he would not deny powers that the Constitution expressly delegated to Congress. The power to determine the legality of electoral votes was one of these; the power to seat congressmen-elect patently would be another. But he would use all his legitimate influence to persuade Congress to reach decisions in these areas of undoubted congressional jurisdiction which would recognize the results of his Reconstruction initiatives.

With Lincoln exerting all his efforts to that end, center Republicans determined to affirm their position that congressional recognition of reconstructed state governments must precede admission of representatives to Congress and to satisfy their president at the same time: they would recognize the reorganized government of Louisiana through the joint resolution that they believed necessary.

On February 18, Trumbull reported such a resolution from his Senate Judiciary committee. On February 23, shortly after the House shelved Ashley's Reconstruction bill, he began his drive to pass his joint resolution. Sumner attempted to derail the movement by proposing a substitute similar to Wilson's delaying measure in the House, but he was brushed aside by a vote of 8 to 29, and it became apparent that a large majority of Republicans was prepared to follow the Judiciary committee's lead.[48] Again Democrats joined radicals in opposing recognition, but the conservatives, having failed in their attempt to win recognition for Louisiana without first passing a law, now supported the Republican center group. Hopelessly outnumbered, the radicals determined to filibuster.

On February 25, after two days of debate, Trumbull, still unaware of the radicals' purpose, suggested an evening session to conclude consideration of the bill. Late that evening the radicals launched their operation. Wade moved to postpone consideration of the resolution until the following December and demanded a roll-call vote. The clerk called out the name of each senator. After each responded or was recorded as absent, the vote stood 12 to 17 against postponement. Jacob M. Howard then moved that the Senate adjourn. Again the Senate had to endure the tedious business of a roll-call vote. The motion lost 12 to 19. Howard then moved to postpone the bill to the following Monday, February 27, when there would be only four days left in the life of the Thirty-eighth Congress. Another roll call. And another on a dilatory motion by Sumner. One roll call later Trumbull was on his feet.

It is manifest now by the course being pursued by the Senator from Massachusetts, . . . that he is in a combination here of a fraction of the Senate to delay the important business of the country. . . .

Does he hold in his hand the Senate of the United States, that, in his omnipotence, he is to say when votes shall be taken and public measures shall be passed? Has it come to this? Is he charged with the administration of the Government . . . ? Sir, there can be no excuse for such action.[49]

Sumner remained adamant:

I would counsel the Senator . . . to look at the clock. He will see that it is twenty-five minutes of eleven; that it is approaching Sunday morning. Then let him think we have been here all day; and then I would counsel him to ask himself whether, all things considered, it is advisable to press this revolutionary measure after this protracted session, and at this late hour . . . . At any rate . . . all his efforts will be fruitless.

He moved to adjourn.[50]

Desperately, Trumbull tried to arrange a compromise. He would agree to adjourn to Monday if the vote were taken that day, with no more dilatory motions. Sumner refused and assailed Trumbull with the carefully chosen invective that alienated so many of his colleagues:

There was a Senator from Illinois once in this Chamber. His name was Douglas. He, too, brought forward a proposition calculated to bring discord upon the country [the Kansas-Nebraska bill, the measure which the Republican party was first organized to oppose]. He brought that proposition in precisely as my friend from Illinois now brings this in, proudly, confidently, almost menacingly, saying he was to pass it—was it not in twenty-four hours? . . .

The Senator from Illinois tears a leaf out of that hateful book. . . . He is going to cram his resolution down the throats of the Senate, and he appeals to us to enter into some compact or understanding that we will allow the operation to proceed without the least resistance.[51]

Shocked and furious, Trumbull had no alternative but to let the Senate adjourn without conditions. The radicals knew they had won.[52] When the Louisiana resolution came up on Monday, John Sherman, chairman of the Finance committee, moved to take up the tax bill instead. With only four days left before the final adjournment of the Thirty-eighth Congress, there was too much business yet undone to permit long debate on the question of recognizing Louisiana, and the Senate agreed to Sherman's motion 34 to 12, with only the most conservative Republicans standing firm.[53]

The radicals had managed to prevent the recognition of Louisiana during the Thirty-eighth Congress, but they had been put on the defensive. Their ranks had broken. They had been forced to rely on Democrats for support. The Reconstruction question remained under the jurisdiction of the two most conservative committees of the respective houses of Congress, while the radicals' base of power—the House's Select Committee on the Rebellious States—automatically expired with the Thirty-eighth Congress. To revive it would require the assent of the whole House, and even then the speaker might feel obligated to name a conservative-center Republican majority to it.

Conservative and center Republicans, on the other hand, could be confident. With Congress adjourned until December and no Reconstruction bill passed, Lincoln would be free to reconstruct the southern states according to his desires. Judging from his past policy, this meant the restoration process there would be placed in the hands of loyal, antislavery unionists, conciliatory towards the conquered and anxious to persuade them to return to their former allegiance and to accept the finality of abolition. When the Thirty-ninth Congress assembled, recognition would be under the jurisdiction of the conservative House Elections committee and the Senate and House Judiciary committees. With nine months or more in which to act during the next session, no filibuster by radicals or Democrats could prevent recognition.

Still, to Sumner the radicals' successful holding action meant opportunity. "In rejecting the application of [Louisiana] . . . during this session we obtain the vacation for the discussion of the question & the appeal to the sober 2d thought of the people," he wrote. "We shall insist upon the Decltn of Indep. as the foundation of the new state govt., & the argt. will be presented, not merely on the grounds of human right, but of self-interest. It will be shown that we shall need the vote of the negroes to sustain the Union." Basking in the gratitude of his radical friends outside of Congress, Sunmer was optimistic about the future. "Believe me, all this will be done. To this consummation everything tends." [54]

But other radicals were less certain. Wendell Phillips believed "Negro suffrage ripens rapidly," and exhorted Sumner, "That needs only *reputable* leadership to open almost every press & every class with favor. Your indorsement of it will lift it forward as much as years could do." But at the same time he feared that this public enthusiasm might not be translated into power. "The trouble is neither the Senate or House has a Head—as Clay or Webster was," he wrote. "Sumner leads ten; Trumbull twenty. Fessenden some. *But the three quarrel.* . . . [In] the House Boutwell makes good speeches, but no one follows him. Stevens is the only approach to a leader. In fact Congress is a mob—the Admt. a *unit.* Hence its success." [55]

With the war drawing to a close, no Reconstruction policy had yet been established. Unwilling to commit the government to a rigid program, Lincoln found he had no program at all. The amnesty oath would hardly separate the loyal from the disloyal once the war ended. At the same time he was extremely worried lest southerners resort to guerilla tactics. It would be a difficult task to restore complete peace in the South and still limit control of Reconstruction to loyalists.

Lincoln remained committed to his reorganized governments in Louisiana, Arkansas, and Tennessee, but he seemed to flounder in his efforts to create a policy for the other rebel states. On February 6 he suggested to the cabinet that the government pay $400,000,000 to the southern states in exchange for peace. The money could be used to recompense former slaveholders or for any other purpose. The Cabinet's frosty reception of that proposal persuaded the president to abandon it.[56] Early in April Lincoln offered to allow the rebel Virginia legislature to meet with the protection of Union forces if it would call for peace. In exchange the president would exercise his pardoning power to exempt Virginians from confiscation of all but slave property.[57] Lincoln believed this to be the most certain way to convince southerners to cease resistance. The southern state legislatures were, after all, organizations that southern soldiers recognized as legitimate voices of authority. An appeal to end the fighting might well carry more weight if it emanated from them rather than from the northern enemy.[58]

Lincoln did not intend to recognize the rebel legislature or negotiate with it. He wanted them "to do a specific thing, to wit, 'withdraw the Virginia troops and other support from resistance to the general government,' for which I promised . . . a remission to the people of the State . . . of the confiscation of their property. I meant this, and no more." [59] But most Republicans were appalled. They believed Lincoln meant to treat with the rebels, recognizing the Virginia legislature, and they urged him to reconsider.

In the midst of this confusion, Lincoln delivered a formal address on Reconstruction. He had been pressed to speak on April 10 by boisterous crowds celebrating Lee's surrender the day before. Preoccupied by other duties, he had declined but promised to say a few words the next evening at a more formal demonstration. Lincoln decided to make the plea for Louisiana recognition which he had suggested to Trumbull three months earlier. In January Lincoln had wanted to make a statement of the question as he saw it. Now he did so: "The question is . . . 'Can Louisiana be brought into proper practical relation with the Union *sooner* by *sustaining,* or by *discarding* her new State Government?'" Having asked the question in the form he preferred, the president found little difficulty answering it likewise. He hinted similar policies might be applied to other rebel states. But again inveighing against setting rigid policies, Lincoln announced no "exclusive and inflexible plan" would be prescribed. He informed his audience he should be pleased if Louisiana enfranchised at least its literate black citizens and those who bore arms for the Union, but he refused to make this a condition for restoration. And he closed with the tantalizing suggestion that "In the present *'situation,'* as the phrase goes, it may be my duty to make some new announcement to the people of the South. I am considering, and shall not fail to act, when satisfied that action will be proper." [60]

Some historians of Reconstruction have suggested that Lincoln's final statement indicated that he was about to move in a more radical direction. But at the time he spoke, Lincoln was still holding open his offer to the Virginia legislature, and radicals might just as easily assume that his reference to "a new announcement" referred to a proclamation extending his offer to other state legislatures. Sumner certainly did not believe that the president had signaled growing radicalism. "The President's speech and other things [Sumner had just learned of the Virginia negotiations] augur confusion and uncertainty in the future, with hot controversy," he wrote Francis Lieber. The Marquis de Chambrun, an acute observer whose company Sumner enjoyed, recorded in his diary that the address "called forth violent reactions" against the president. By April 13, the marquis noted, "a veritable campaign against him was launched." [61] But faced with the opposition of his cabinet, led by Stanton and his newly appointed attorney general, James Speed, Lincoln discarded his Virginia initiative.[62]

To combat what he believed to be Lincoln's desire to employ southern rebel legislatures to stabilize the southern situation, Secretary of War Edwin M. Stanton drafted a plan to provide temporary military government in Virginia and North Carolina. Under Stanton's proposal the president would appoint a military governor who would issue regulations to restore order. The temporary government's authority would be founded upon martial law, and a provost marshal corps would enforce its decrees. Under the protective shield of military authority, the national government could reestablish its presence, reopening federal courts, revenue offices, post offices, and land offices. Lincoln concurred when Welles objected to combining Virginia and North Carolina under one military governor, and he ordered Stanton to redraft his plan and present it again at a future cabinet meeting.[63] At the same time other Republicans were trying to convince Lincoln to adopt their views of Reconstruction. Chief Justice Chase ardently championed the cause of black suffrage. House Speaker Colfax discussed Reconstruction matters with Lincoln on the day of his death. Several senators visited him the same day. But before he arrived at any conclusions—or at least before he told anyone of them—Lincoln lay assassinated.[64]

Like other Americans, radicals were shocked and stunned by the news of Lincoln's death. But though they mourned the man, they did not mourn his policies. "God had graciously withheld him from any fatal mistep in the great advance," Phillips said. With the war ended, "the nation needed a sterner hand for the work God gives it to do." Most radicals shared the mixed feelings of radical representative John B. Alley. "The decease of Mr. Lincoln is a great national bereavement," he wrote Sumner, "but I am not so clear that it is so much of a national loss." Still, he continued, "I feel his death personally very much. He was very *kind to me.*" [65]

FIVE

The Radicals on the Offensive

—————————— ✦✦✦✦✦ ——————————

"JOHNSON, WE HAVE FAITH IN YOU. By the Gods, there will be no trouble now in running the Government," tough Benjamin Wade enthused when he first visited the new President after Lincoln's death.[1] From this and other evidence, historians have recognized that during the first month of Johnson's administration radicals considered him an ally. Rarely devoting more than a paragraph or two to this "aberration," they have not delved into just what this meant to the radicals and to the Republican party. Furthermore, historians never have offered a clear picture of the developments during the crucial six months that preceded the meeting of the Thirty-ninth Congress in December 1865—a period of confusion, with growing distrust of the president and increasing conviction that the South was not yet ready for restoration. Within this confusion historians have been unable to separate radical from conservative satisfactorily. Nor have they recognized how profoundly President Johnson's course altered the program of a Republican party on the verge of endorsing black suffrage, or how close nonradical Republicans believed they were to a complete understanding with him—an understanding that would have left the radicals isolated and nearly powerless within the party or bolters outside it.[2]

Radicals appear to have had good reason to believe Johnson sympathetic to them. He evinced an inclination to hold rebels strictly accountable for their activities. Whereas Lincoln, during the war at least, had been willing to treat former rebels as allies if they would just take the simple amnesty oath swearing future loyalty, Johnson seemed more disposed to demand strict justice. "Robbery is a crime; rape is a crime; murder is a crime; *treason* is a crime; and *crime* must be punished," he said. Radicals had feared Lincoln intended to work through recognized southern leaders to establish peace (especially when his Virginia initiative became known); there seemed to be no reason to apprehend Johnson's following a similar policy. Furthermore, as Julian noted happily, "The conservatives are not here [in Washington]." But the radical Joint Committee on the Conduct of the War, on which Wade, Chandler, Julian, and other radicals sat, had been authorized to meet during the congressional recess. Julian expected that the "influence of the War Committee with Johnson, who is an ex-member, will powerfully aid the new administration in getting onto the right track." [3]

Although Johnson denied that he sought vengeance against southern leaders, he reiterated his "treason is a crime" theme several times in the early days of his administration. He seemed to advocate large-scale criminal prosecutions and the death penalty for rebel leaders.[4] As the new president repeated these opinions, many northerners, including radicals, began to grow apprehensive. Sumner acknowledged that Johnson's position on the treatment of rebels was far more radical than his and continued to hope that rebel leaders would be driven into exile rather than executed. Wade, who on general principle was not nearly so reluctant as Sumner to shed rebel blood, also believed Johnson's oft-expressed determination unwise. He told Johnson, "I should either force into exile or hang about ten or twelve of the worst of those fellows."

"But how are you going to pick out so small a number and show them to be guiltier than the rest?" Johnson asked, surprised that Wade was willing to allow leading secessionists to escape so easily. Wade left Johnson fearing that his bitter policy would lead to a reaction in the North against radicalism.[5] He needn't have worried. In his final Reconstruction policy Johnson would abandon any effort to hold leading rebels strictly accountable for their crimes.

Violent denunciations of rebels leaders and assurances that their treason would be punished showed the state of the new president's temper, but they were not a Reconstruction policy. As the Marquis de Chambrun wrote, "To punish traitors may be the order of the day, but afterwards what? [Johnson] . . . is a radical to be sure, no one denies that, but what sort of radical is he?" [6]

Johnson indicated at least one program he would *not* follow. This was the policy enunciated in a peace convention agreed to by General William Tecumseh Sherman and rebel General Joseph E. Johnston. Sherman's terms were incredibly liberal—recognizing the Confederate state organizations as legal governments (although not conceding their secession); providing for Supreme Court adjudication of any claims of rival state governments; guaranteeing to rebels peaceful possession of their property, possibly including slaves and certainly precluding confiscation of anything else; and granting a universal amnesty.

Sherman believed these provisions consistent with Lincoln's desire, expressed to him shortly before his death, to restore order in the South quickly. To Sherman they seemed not much different from the abortive policy Lincoln had attempted in Virginia. Nonetheless, the cabinet unanimously rejected the terms, and Johnson concurred. Stanton, fearing Sherman's terms might win wide public approval, launched a bitter attack on the general's action and motives, which, though alienating the Sherman brothers and the powerful Ewing family (the general's wife was Ellen Ewing), demolished any possibility of the plan's acceptance or the approval of one like it.[7]

Johnson was slow in coming to final conclusions regarding Reconstruction. The subject arose in cabinet on April 21 but only in regard to the Sherman-Johnson convention, which was roundly condemned. Not until the first week of May did Johnson tell Stanton to send cabinet members copies of his plan to reestablish national authority in North Carolina, as modified by Lincoln's instructions to preserve the state's territorial integrity. Not until May 9 would it be considered.[8]

Meanwhile, the radicals lobbied for their program. The recent session of Congress had demonstrated the weakness of their influence on legislation. The radicals were well aware of what lay ahead. George Luther Stearns, the influential abolitionist, wrote Sumner, "You I understand are to have a 'fight' with Trumbull & Co. next winter. Today when the events of the past month have softened mens [sic] hearts and disposed them to listen to the voice of God, is the time to prepare the public mind for it." If Andrew Johnson could be persuaded to endorse black suffrage, Sumner knew, the battle would be virtually won. The radicals needed time. "There are some who have supposed that Congress would be convened at once. I hope not," Sumner wrote. "We are not ready for the discussion of domestic policy." [9]

The radical campaign for Negro suffrage had been gaining momentum since January. Phillips and Douglass had called abolitionists to the standard at the Massachusetts Anti-Slavery Society meeting January 26. Stearns had collected their speeches, the speech Kelley had delivered in Congress in support of his Negro suffrage amendment to the Reconstruction bill, and several letters, in a pamphlet which radicals distributed throughout the country.[10] The radical New York *Independent,* the *National Anti-Slavery Standard,* the *Liberator,* and the Boston *Commonwealth* took up the cause.[11]

Stearns opened a correspondence with antislavery men throughout the country, and by mid-February had a list of 5000 names and expected to get up to 15,000. On February 16 he called together a few Boston radicals to decide what to do with it. "Our general idea was that between the sessions of Congress, public opinion should be molded to demand no readmission of rebel states without securing equal rights," wrote Edward Atkinson, the radical Boston textile manufacturer. As a result Stearns, Atkinson, Charles Eliot Norton, and others founded the New York weekly newspaper, the *Nation,* with Edwin L. Godkin as editor. When that journal emerged less radical than Stearns had hoped (it did espouse black suffrage, however), he withdrew his money and began another paper, this time in Boston, *The Right Way,* which he circulated throughout the country without charge. Chase, of course, also had been working hard to develop public opinion on the suffrage question, urging his friends actively to aid the cause.[12]

Lincoln's death had given a strong impetus to the demand for Negro suffrage. In the eulogies and analyses which followed the assassination, opinion began to swing in the radicals' direction.[13] In May, Wendell Phillips joyfully wrote Sumner, "Public opinion surprises me by the rapidity with which it crystallizes on this point. *Every* one hastens. From Blake the banker & Ames the Probate Judge all around to clergymen small & great & to the rank & file here, literally *no dissent.*

"But if you wish an expression," Phillips continued, " . . . come home . . . assemble forty of your personal & political friends & give them their cue. Start the thing thus—the harvest is ripe." The people "only wish a leader whom they feel *it safe to follow* . . . ," he urged. He himself was too controversial a radical; Sumner was the man for the job. "Come & unseal their lips. Have one or two large conventions & the work is done. The Ball will roll itself onward." [14]

But Sumner knew Andrew Johnson would be a better and "safer" leader yet.

The radicals worked hard to convince Johnson that Negro suffrage was necessary. For though he had been a radical during the war and was radical still in his desire to punish rebel leaders, this did not mean he would be radical on Reconstruction questions. Many of the Republicans who had voted against the Reconstruction bill in the House and in favor of recognizing Louisiana in the Senate also had been radical on war issues. More than this kind of radicalism was needed. Chambrun observed that many Republicans now believed that "to hang Davis won't do any good; we have no guarantee against the South, who gave him up as a holocaust, hoping thereby to get themselves out of trouble with no other sacrifice demanded of them." They insisted that "what we want now is Negro suffrage." [15]

On April 18, Chase urged the president to delay any invitation to the people of North Carolina to reorganize their government. "Would it not be far better to make Florida and Louisiana really free States with universal suffrage, and then let other States follow?" he asked. Johnson must consider carefully. "Everything now, under God, must depend on you." On the 22nd, Chase and Sumner visited Johnson together to argue for requiring Negro suffrage in the South. "He is well disposed, and sees the rights and necessities of the case, all of which I urged earnestly," Sumner wrote. "Both of us left him light-hearted. . . . I am confident that our ideas will prevail."

A week later Sumner saw Johnson again. He seemed even more in agreement than before. The president "deprecates haste," Sumner found, "is unwilling that States should be precipitated back; thinks there must

be a period of probation, but that meanwhile all loyal people, without distinction of color, must be treated as citizens, and must take part in any
proceedings for reorganization." Sumner left Johnson elated, the President's words that "there is no difference between us" on the black suffrage
question echoing in his ears. "As I walked away from the President on
that evening the battle of my life seemed to be ended," he recalled, "while
the Republic rose before me, refulgent in the blaze of assured Freedom, an
example to the nations." [16]

But other Republicans exerted pressure in the opposite direction. On
April 22, conservative Indiana Governor Oliver P. Morton led a state
delegation to an interview with the president. In his address, Morton expounded an extremely conservative view of the power of the national government in Reconstruction. He concluded:

The powers of the state government . . . [should] be in abeyance only until
new men [can] . . . be called to the exercise of those powers. There is in
every rebel state a loyal element of greater or less strength, and to its hands
should be confided the power and duty of reorganizing the state government,
giving to it military protection until such time as it can, by convention or otherwise, so regulate the right of suffrage that this right will be intrusted only to
safe and loyal hands.

Morton publicly opposed Negro suffrage and by his last sentence advocated not extension of suffrage to blacks but restrictions against disloyal
whites.

Johnson, in a brilliantly vague answer, agreed with all Morton's main
points—Rebellion was an individual matter, but it could reach such proportions as to overthrow the state authorities and paralyze its activities.
When this happened, the national government had the duty to resuscitate
it, and it must be done through the medium of its friends, that is loyalists.
But Johnson did not define the color of its "friends." He did close, however, by assuring the delegation that he opposed centralization of power
in the national government. Morton left satisfied. Julian, who had accompanied the delegation, was "mortified" and left believing the radicals'
confidence entirely unwarranted.[17]

There was also a latent conservatism on the Reconstruction question in the executive department as Johnson found it. Throughout the war
Lincoln had endeavored to leave restoration to the voluntary action of the
southern people. This desire for voluntarism, or at least the illusion of it,
had colored his whole policy of Reconstruction insofar as Lincoln had developed one. In particular it had been important in Tennessee, where Johnson, as military governor, had been left largely to his own devices in encouraging the people of the state to resume loyal relations with the Union.
To a large extent, past experience limited future policy.

Johnson was committed to preserving this illusion of voluntarism. He told Sumner that for political reasons he wanted the black suffrage movement to "appear to proceed from the people." To encourage this voluntary extension of suffrage to the newly freed black men, Johnson decided to send Chief Justice Chase on a tour of the southern states and authorized him privately to urge Negro suffrage in the president's name. Sumner doubted southerners would agree to such a step voluntarily, but affirmed that he "regarded the *modus operandi* as an inferior question." [18]

Chase's travels fulfilled Sumner's pessimistic expectations. The chief justice wrote Johnson that southern whites would not themselves enfranchise the freed blacks, but added that they would not resist if the president required it.[19] Now Johnson would have to make the distasteful decision of whether to abandon all pretense of voluntarism and require southerners to enfranchise black men, or to acquiesce in the southerners' refusal.

Although his conviction that Negro suffrage could come only through pressure seemed to have been verified, Sumner remained sanguine. Radical fortunes had soared. In February he and a handful of others had barely prevented recognition of Louisiana with its discriminatory suffrage regulations. President Lincoln had seemed adamant. A hard fight had lain ahead. Now Sumner wrote,

I said during this winter that the rebel States could not come back, except on the footing of the Declaration of Independence and the complete recognition of human rights. I feel more than ever confident that all this will be fulfilled. And then what a regenerated land! I had looked for a bitter contest on this question; but with the President on our side, it will be carried by simple avoirdupois.[20]

But on May 8, Johnson recognized the government of Francis H. Pierpont in Virginia, a government that had not enfranchised its black citizens. This loyalist regime had maintained a tenuous existence throughout the war and Lincoln had felt obligated to sustain it. He evidently had intended to recognize Pierpont's government, and Johnson's cabinet agreed to this early in May. The executive order pointedly referred to Pierpont as "Governor of Virginia" rather than provisional governor, and left his government in unrestricted control of the state's domestic affairs.[21]

Many radicals were alarmed. Stevens wrote Sumner, "I see the President is precipitating things. Virginia is recognized! I fear before Congress meets he will have so bedeviled matters as to render them [incurable?]. It would be well if he would call an extra session of Congress." [22]

But Sumner and other radicals still in Washington remained calm. They had known of the prospective Virginia order—on April 16 Sumner, Colfax, Dawes, and several other congressmen had met with Stanton to discuss Reconstruction. Stanton had already altered his tentative plan of military occupation to exclude Virginia and recognize its loyal government.

The plan now applied only to North Carolina, but it was a prototype for all the rebel states. The men had acquiesced in the Virginia recognition and turned their attention to Stanton's occupation plan.

Stanton's original draft, placed before the cabinet the day before Lincoln died, had provided primarily for military government. Now he modified it, either himself or at the suggestion of his visitors, to include a plan for reorganizing the state governments. Following the pattern set by Lincoln and the proposed congressional Reconstruction bills, Stanton's program added to the provisional governor's duties that of organizing elections for a constitutional convention, which would alter the state constitutions to conform to the new situation. Finding Stanton had left the vote in the hands of whites alone, Sumner argued the necessity of its extension. Stanton had resisted, fearing its divisive effect on the party, but after a long discussion Sumner and Colfax convinced the secretary that all loyal men, irrespective of color, should participate in the election of delegates to the state constitutional conventions.[23]

Sumner, Colfax, and others knew that on May 9, the day after Johnson promulgated his executive order recognizing Virginia, the cabinet had discussed the amended North Carolina occupation plan. The cabinet had agreed unanimously to all but its suffrage provision. On this Johnson's advisors had divided evenly: Stanton, Postmaster General William Dennison, and Attorney General James Speed favoring it, and Navy Secretary Gideon Welles, Treasury Secretary McCulloch, and outgoing Secretary of the Interior John P. Usher opposed. The president withheld his opinion and took the matter under consideration.[24] Sumner and Wade, knowing Johnson favored Negro suffrage, remained certain of the result.

On May 12 the radicals met in the National Hotel in Washington. Those who called the meeting feared Johnson was falling under conservative influence, but the two radical leaders convinced them that their alarm was groundless. Even the skeptical Julian wrote, "Radicalism will not be expelled from the Cabinet, but will rule the Administration." [25] But Stevens remained dissatisfied. He wrote Johnson, attempting—but failing in his agitation—to be tactful. The last Congress, Stevens insisted, had considered Reconstruction "a question for the Legislative power exclusively. While I think we should agree with you almost unanimously as to the main objects you have in view I fear we may differ as to the manner of affecting [sic] them." Complaining specifically of the Virginia order, Stevens asked Johnson to suspend further Reconstruction activity. "Better call an extra session," he argued, "than to allow many to think that the executive was approaching usurpation." [26] Such language could hardly increase radical influence.

Nearly three weeks passed before Johnson made his decision known. On May 29 he issued two proclamations. One offered amnesty to most southerners; the other announced a Reconstruction plan for North Carolina. The plan was substantially Stanton's. But in its key provision it limited the vote for delegates to the constitutional convention to those "qualified and prescribed by the constitution and laws of the State of North Carolina in force immediately before the 20th day of May, A.D. 1861, the date of the so-called ordinance of secession." The constitutional convention would then prescribe any new qualifications for suffrage. The radicals were shocked. Sumner wrote Bright of his "immense disappointment." "This is madness," he lamented. "But it is also inconsistent with his sayings to the chief-justice and myself." [27]

What had happened? There are virtually no clues to the processes of Andrew Johnson's mind in the last ten days of May. Contemporaries suspected that the influence of the Blairs or of Secretary of State Seward had intervened. Others have pointed to the blandishments of returning former rebels. But the former Confederates did not rally to Andrew Johnson's support until *after* he had enunciated his policy. Seward had been disabled by the attempt on his life and had just returned to his duties in mid-May. Indeed, radicals had as easy access to the president as conservatives. They had clearly had the inside track. If Andrew Johnson was swayed by conservatives, it could only have been because he was more susceptible to their arguments.

Some historians have emphasized Johnson's intense Negrophobia. Certainly Andrew Johnson was a racist, but so were many radicals. The argument for black suffrage was not based only on Negrophilism. Many Republicans believed Negro suffrage necessary to protect *white* southern unionists. Benjamin F. Wade's personal anti-Negro prejudice, for example, probably matched the president's.[28]

The most plausible explanation is that Andrew Johnson had not changed his mind at all. He had told the radicals he favored black suffrage but wanted it to emanate voluntarily from southerners themselves. He manifested his sincerity when he sent Chase south, authorized to inform southerners of the president's desire. In August Johnson telegraphed Mississippi's provisional governor, W.L. Sharkey, urging that the state's constitutional convention "extend the elective franchise to all persons of color who can read the Constitution of the United States in English and write their names, and to all persons of color who own real estate valued at not less than two hundred and fifty dollars, and pay taxes thereon." This would make Mississippi's voting provisions similar to those of several free states, and more liberal than most, disarming radical criticism. Johnson showed this telegram to Missouri's Senator John B. Henderson in October and authorized him to inform others that this was his position, although he withheld permission to quote the telegram directly.[29]

On October 3 Johnson told Stearns, who had obtained an interview with him, that were he in Tennessee, "I should try to introduce negro suffrage gradually; first those who had served in the army; those who could read and write; and perhaps a property qualification for others, say $200 or $250." Johnson again authorized the publication of his views.[30] He never again endorsed Negro suffrage after October. This hardening position probably resulted from some radicals' bitter attacks upon him, the cordial support antiblack elements began to give, and—probably most important—the unwillingness of northern states to accept Negro suffrage in their own constitutions, as expressed in elections during the fall.

Moreover, Johnson's reluctance to require black suffrage had been based on more than political expediency. Johnson apparently had decided he had no constitutional power to force certain voting qualifications on the people of the southern states. This was "a power the people of the several States composing the Federal Union have rightfully exercised from the origin of the Government to the present time," he explained in his proclamation.[31]

Johnson was dead wrong in his constitutional interpretation. He was in no way obligated to adhere to old constitutional provisions in providing election rules for a new constitutional convention. "There is not a single state constitution which defines the qualifications of voters at an election of a state *convention*," an unidentified New York lawyer pointed out in the *Independent*. "The qualifications of voters for *governors* and *legislators* are carefully stated, but nothing is said about *conventions*. Delegates to a convention are not 'officers' under the constitution of a state. They do not swear to support it. On the contrary, they usually meet for the very purpose of abrogating it." This was so plain that radicals evidently never had conceived the president might have constitutional objections to ordering Negro suffrage. Sumner concluded simply, "The Federal Power, whether Prest or Congress, that undertakes to the State machine a-going can say who shall take part in the meetings to organize & thus at the outset fix the suffrage."[32]

Radicals were astounded at Johnson's misguided scruples. "How easy it was to be right!" Sumner lamented. "The President seems to have made an effort to be wrong."[33]

Radicals were despondent. They had placed great hopes on Johnson's conversion. Now, Sumner mourned, "We have before us controversy & an agony of strife." And they had to rely on Congress, where they had barely staved off defeated a few months earlier. "I almost despair of resisting Executive influence," Stevens had written after Johnson recognized Virginia. Now he wrote, "[the president's] North Carolina proclamation sickens me. . . . By the time congress meets all will be passed [*sic*] remedy I fear. Yet what can we do? The excitement and self complacency of power will give but little heed to reason. I write merely to vent my mortification. I do not know that I can suggest anything . . . ." The experience of the previous session weighed heavily upon him. "Is there any hope that Congress will overrule the Prest?" he asked Sumner. "I fear we are [lost?], for I have little faith in Congress." [34]

Other radicals shared Stevens's anguish. If Johnson was firmly committed to his Reconstruction policy, Wendell Phillips believed, "he will *sway* Congress as he pleases." Henry Winter Davis and Wade shared his conviction. Almost in despair, Wade raged to Gideon Welles that "the Executive has the control of the government, that Congress and the Judiciary are subordinate and mere instruments in his hands; . . . our form of government was on the whole a failure; that there are not three distinct and independent departments but one great controlling one with two others as assistants." [35]

But the radicals, some angry and all apprehensive, zealously continued to agitate for black suffrage. Many believed Johnson not yet firmly committed to the policy enunciated in the North Carolina proclamation. "Let me warn impulsive Republicans against hasty judgment of the President in this matter," wrote the *Independent*'s radical Washington correspondent, David W. Bartlett. "Personally, he favors negro suffrage. He has said so repeatedly of late. He is in doubt of the means to be used. Probably he has a little of the old prejudice against the negro. . . . Give Mr. Johnson a little time to watch events," he urged.[36] Attorney General Speed wrote Boutwell that the proclamation related only to North Carolina and did not preclude a different rule for other states. Johnson himself sent Carl Schurz, who had criticized his proclamation, on a tour of the southern states to report how well his plan actually was operating. From the rebel states Schurz sent a barrage of reports, most discouraging.[37]

Encouraged, Sumner urgently wrote Chase that he was needed in Washington. "I hope it is not too late to arrest this fatal policy. I have reason to believe that the President has lately shown a disposition to treat what he has done as an experiment," he added hopefully. Sumner tried to influence Johnson through his cabinet. But McCulloch vigorously defended Johnson's program, and the new secretary of the interior, James Harlan, though he assured Sumner that he personally favored black suffrage, said flatly, "I do not doubt that the 'North Carolina Proclamation' will be followed substantially in the proposed re-organization of the other Rebel States." He conceded that Congress could refuse to readmit southern congressmen until their states adopted Negro suffrage, but such a course, he warned, "would lay the foundation of a certain and inevitable division of the Union organization, which I am inclined to think would result in the triumph of the President's policy." Sumner soon realized that his efforts were futile.[38]

After reading the North Carolina proclamation, Boutwell hastened to Washington, where he and Representative Justin Morrill saw the president. Johnson assured them that his program was experimental; if it failed, a new proclamation would be forthcoming. Boutwell then visited

McCulloch and urged him to work for a change in policy. John Murray Forbes, who shared a warm friendship with McCulloch; Joseph Medill, coeditor of the *Chicago Tribune;* Whitelaw Reid, Horace Greeley's conservative lieutenant on the *New York Tribune;* and Edward Atkinson all wrote McCulloch that support for Negro suffrage was growing and urged him to intercede with the president. "I don't believe that five republican members of Congress in the ten Western States approve of the President's clause excluding the loyal blacks from voting in the reorganization, nor that five percent of the republican party endorse his course," Medill wrote. "People try to be quiet on the question but they are growing very restive and alarmed. The President ought to be informed."

McCulloch forwarded at least one of the letters (Forbes's) to the president, yet in August the secretary insisted that he did not believe "one man in an hundred of the intelligent men of this country" favored immediate Negro suffrage. Instead of warning the president of impending danger, he urged moderation upon his correspondents.[39]

Still, many radicals believed Johnson personally committed to black suffrage. Even as they expressed their distaste for his program, they assured audiences that the president would accept a popular verdict in favor of suffrage extension and would insist on blacks' voting if southerners displayed disloyalty. This impression remained current through July and even August.[40] But the radicals' faith began to wane as other aspects of the president's policy became apparent. McCulloch began to appoint treasury agents in the South who could not take the test oath required by law. When Sumner complained to McCulloch, the secretary answered that he did not believe the law was intended to apply to the new situation. Attorney-General Speed began to dilute the application of the Confiscation act. And the president ordered the Freedmen's Bureau to begin returning the property of all rebels receiving executive pardon.[41] By August Republicans began to concede that Johnson's policy seemed final.[42]

Throughout these critical months popular support for Negro suffrage had continued to grow. In May Henry Winter Davis, no longer limited by the prejudices of his constituents since his defeat for reelection to Congress, had announced in favor of extending the franchise. In June New York City's Union League club joined the campaign. The *Independent, National Anti-Slavery Standard,* and *Liberator* continued their radical campaign for Negro suffrage, joined by the *New York Tribune,* the *Nation,* the Boston *Evening Journal* and Boston *Daily Advertiser,* and the *Chicago Tribune.*[43]

Boston had become the center for the movement, due to the efforts of Sumner, Stearns, and others. The agitation there culminated in a massive meeting at Faneuil Hall on June 21, as conservative and radical Bostonians united in support for suffrage extension. Richard Henry Dana, Henry Ward Beecher, and Theophilus Parsons spoke, and Governor

Andrew endorsed their position in a long, carefully drawn letter. The meeting appointed a committee of nine, consisting of Boston's most illustrious citizens, radicals and conservatives, to prepare an address to the people of the United States in support of Negro suffrage.[44] As an outgrowth of the meeting, John Murray Forbes and others decided to form "an association to mould public opinion, against [i.e., in anticipation of] the meeting of Congress." Members contributed $50 to $500 each. In August Forbes, Dana, Parsons and others persuaded more than two hundred Boston businessmen and professionals to sign a letter to President Johnson, urging him to enfranchise southern blacks.[45]

The movement had spread nationwide. In Ohio, the conservative John Sherman argued simply, "If we can put negro regiments there [in the South] and give them bayonets, why can't we give them votes? Both are weapons of offense and defense. Votes are cheaper and better." [46] July Fourth brought a flood of pro–Negro suffrage oratory. Garfield, Winter Davis, Edwin Channing Larned, Senator Richard Yates, Boutwell, Phillips, Stearns, John B. Alley, Henry Wilson, and even Banks endorsed the measure in speeches given around the nation.[47]

Many conservative and centrist Republicans also decided Negro suffrage should be part of Reconstruction. Besides Sherman and Banks, their number included Edwin D. Morgan, Fessenden, and James Dixon. During the summer, Republican party conventions in Iowa, Minnesota, Vermont, Maine, and Massachusetts all endorsed suffrage extension. As early as June, Joseph Medill discovered that nearly all those attending the Northwest Sanitary Fair in Chicago favored Negro suffrage; Boutwell discerned a similar feeling among western congressmen. With such pressure growing, even the *New York Times,* the conservative organ of the Seward-Weed faction of the New York Republican party, suggested a constitutional amendment to give the ballot to all male adults who could read.[48]

Sumner took the lead in trying to convert this public opinion into political power. He barraged his fellow senators with letters, sounding out their positions on the great issue. In general the prospects seemed uncertain. Michigan's Senator Jacob M. Howard and his colleague, Zachariah Chandler, were sound. Sumner believed he could rely on both of Maine's senators and Missouri's B. Gratz Brown. Howard counted on Sherman, Wade, Pomeroy, Lane of Kansas, Yates, and Alexander Ramsey of Minnesota. But other senators might waver. John Conness doubted Congress's power to demand black suffrage. Morgan, though favoring the measure in the abstract, was Seward's ally and clearly desired to avoid any difficulty with the president. The Connecticut and Vermont senators were conservative. Doolittle opposed Negro suffrage, as did James W. Grimes. Trumbull had privately given Johnson his support.[49]

It is apparent that as pressure for Negro suffrage grew, politicians close to the president and the president himself concluded that the radicals had become political enemies. By June 25 McCulloch already foresaw a party division. Welles concluded after the Maine and Pennsylvania conventions "that extensive operations are on foot for an organization hostile to the Administration in the Republican or Union party." [50] By mid-August the president too spoke of the radicals, "who are wild upon negro franchise," as "the adversary." [51]

As the president's opposition to black suffrage hardened, more and more leading Republicans began to back away from the measure. John W. Forney, editor of the Philadelphia *Press* and owner of the Washington *Daily Morning Chronicle,* which was considered the administration's organ while Lincoln was in office, vigorously supported the president's policy, despite his earlier pro-Negro suffrage avowals to Sumner. Morgan urged Sumner to "be cautious and conciliatory with the President," and wrote Lieber urging him to use his influence to moderate the Massachusetts radical. Charles A. Dana, founding a new newspaper in Chicago, told Sumner that while he favored black suffrage with a literacy test, "I am quite willing to see what will come of Mr. Johnson's experiment. And I think it is desirable to keep with him as far & as much as possible. I don't want to see the Democrats coming back into power through any unnecessary quarrel among ourselves." [52]

Phillips was thoroughly alarmed.

Most if not *all* of those *high in office* & *near* [Johnson] who in *May* professed to go for unconditional negro suff. as *preliminary* to admitting rebel States *now* write that *they've changed their minds*. The *dodge* is to be not to strike us radicals square in the face but evade & then say "oh yes, we go for negro suff: but it is a *State matter*—the States are alive with all their rights & they *ought* to grant it but we *cant* [sic] interfere. My fear is we are to be sacrificed. The States will be admitted . . . next winter—that will reinstate the old Democ & Slave Power alliance.[53]

The hesitation afflicted many of the newspapers that supported black suffrage as a general principle. Most urged Republicans to conciliate the president; many outspokenly supported him. The Democrats were hoping for a Republican division over Negro suffrage, wrote David L. Phillips, editor of the Springfield *Illinois State Journal.* If a division occurred they could win the day for their real issues, state sovereignty and Democratic control of southern states. They might even prevent abolition. "It is for the Union or Republican party to prevent so fatal a catastrophe," Phillips urged, "and that only can be done by the force of *united action.* Whatever differences of opinion may exist among individual members of the party on the question of colored suffrage, they must be reserved and not allowed to interfere with the greater issue of *universal freedom,* which is at stake." [54]

As the reaction gained strength, factions of local Republican parties began to use the suffrage issue as weapons. In Indiana, Governor Morton's supporters bitterly assailed his radical enemy, George Julian, as "bent on destroying the supremacy of the Union party" by insisting on Negro suffrage. The radicals, the Indianapolis *Daily Journal* charged, were the "Would-be Dictators to the Union Party." By November the Morton forces suggested, "Mr. Julian and his satellites may be ready to forsake the Union party." The battle between Morton and Julian raged through the fall, culminating in a physical attack on Julian which he always blamed on his adversary.[55]

A similar struggle developed in New York. Conservatives dropped unsubtle hints that the radicals were about to leave the party. The Seward-Weed organ, the *New York Times,* forecast a reorganization of parties around the question of Reconstruction, with conservative Republicans and Democrats joining against radicals. Though the *Times* usually referred to the radicals as "Sumner, Stevens & Co.," the attacks were primarily aimed at the so-called radical faction of the New York party, led by Horace Greeley and the *Tribune.*[56] The New York struggle culminated in the state convention held in Syracuse in September. The radicals claimed a majority of the delegates, but adroit maneuvering by Weed and the reluctance of some radicals to force a confrontation gave the conservatives control of the meeting. Conservatives received most of the nominations and the *Times*'s editor, Henry J. Raymond, was named chairman of the Committee on Resolutions, where he smothered attempts to endorse Negro suffrage and forced through a resolution supporting the president.[57]

At the same time War Democrats attempted to wrest control of the New York Democratic organization from those who had controlled it during the war. Led by John Van Buren, John A. Dix, and John Cochrane (who had been Frémont's vice-presidential candidate on the Radical Democratic ticket in 1864), these Democrats—aided by the Blairs—urged party leaders to endorse President Johnson warmly and support his policy. The Democrats followed their advice and named a unionist ticket. Challenged by the Democrats, the Republicans coalesced. Conservatives ceased their bitter attacks on radicals, and the radicals urged their followers to support the party despite their dissatisfaction. Circumstances had forced the New York radicals to moderate their position for the sake of harmony.[58]

Similar patterns appeared in other states. In Wisconsin radical efforts to pass a pro–black suffrage resolution in the state convention were defeated by conservative and center Republicans, led by Doolittle. Instead the convention endorsed the president. Disgruntled radicals met in a counterconvention in Jaynesville, Wisconsin, where the formerly conservative Timothy Otis Howe announced his conversion to black suffrage. But the Madison *Wisconsin State Journal,* voice of the dominant "Madison regency," and the gubernatorial candidate, Lucius Fairchild, steered a middle-of-the-road course. The *Journal,* while endorsing Negro suffrage, argued that it was not a party question; Fairchild refused to commit himself to suffrage extension at all.[59]

Ohio Republicans met in late June to nominate a candidate for governor. Radical efforts to pass a black suffrage resolution failed here too, conservatives preventing a vote on the question. "The overthrow and eradication of slavery was felt to be a paramount consideration of the hour; and no expression of opinion that might embarrass or prevent this consummation was permitted," Ohio Secretary of State William Henry Smith recalled. Richard P.L. Baber, who was to support President Johnson faithfully throughout his term, happily wrote Seward that "our State Committee was so organized . . . as to exclude all the opponents (but four or five) of the President's policy." [60] The radicals tried to force the issue into the open by publishing a letter asking Jacob Dolson Cox, the gubernatorial candidate, to declare his position. Cox responded to the "Oberlin letter," as it was called, by repudiating black suffrage and calling for complete physical separation of the races.[61] The radicals were furious, many of them attacking their candidate, while conservatives attacked the radicals. One of Chase's local allies, Dwight Bannister, wrote him, "The politics of this State is [*sic*] getting daily more unsatisfactory. I do not see how it is possible for the present Union party to remain together much longer." Other observers agreed.[62]

Cox became one of Johnson's most outspoken supporters. "We must not only ask ourselves what we would desire to do with the Southern States," he urged his friend Garfield, "but what we *can* do." The people would support the president's policy, he warned, and to oppose it meant division and the ruin of the party.[63] Opinion in Ohio was too much divided on the suffrage question for the Republicans to commit themselves to it. Even Robert C. Schenck, who was contending with Sherman for the senatorial nomination, found he was forced to abandon radical ground. In August he announced the president's restrictions against black voting in the South "did not trouble him in the least." Instead of Negro suffrage, he suggested a change in the basis of congressional representation: seats should be apportioned according to the number of *voters* in each state rather than *inhabitants,* he suggested.[64] The radical Ohio correspondent of the New York *Independent* lamented that the suffrage question had "been dodged in the platform . . . [and] dodged by nearly all the public speakers." Many disgruntled Republicans, especially in the radical Western Reserve area, refused to vote, but Cox was elected anyway.[65]

At the same time in Pennsylvania, the old enemies Curtin and Cameron renewed their factional strife, each striving for the president's support.[66] In Kansas the erratic James H. Lane's faction controlled the party, and he adhered to President Johnson rather than risk throwing the patronage to his opponents.[67] In California, Iowa, and Illinois, Republicans divided over the Negro suffrage question, with both sides about evenly balanced.[68]

The reaction reached even into Massachusetts. In June Governor John A. Andrew had written the Faneuil Hall meeting endorsing black suffrage, but he had also urged "temperate, philosophical and statesmanlike treatment" of the question and expressed his confidence in the president.[69] Hoping that the president and Bostonians might be brought closer by the experience, Andrew urged Johnson to visit New England to attend Harvard's Day of Commemoration in honor of the college's war dead. But Johnson politely declined.

As Andrew continued to urge moderation, the distance between him and Sumner, opened during Andrew's campaign for a cabinet position months earlier, grew wider. In November, Andrew wrote the senator urging him to cooperate with Johnson so far as possible and clearly signified his abandonment of Negro suffrage as a necessary measure of Reconstruction. Sumner answered coldly,

Mr. S. hopes that the Governor will not cease that watchfulness which has done him so much honor. He ventures to suggest that first & foremost "among the arts & methods of peace," which the Govr now wishes to cultivate, is justice to the oppressed, & he entreats the Govr not to allow any negro-hater, with his sympathizers, to believe him, at this crisis, indifferent to the guarantees of Human Rights or disposed to postpone his efforts in their behalf.[70]

Clearly the tide was running against the radicals. "Every Republican convention has indorsed President JOHNSON, and . . . the party, as a party, does not include negro suffrage among its issues," the *New York Times* announced with pleasure. "The more the subject has been discussed, the more has it been seen to be encompassed with difficulties, and the more hearty has been the acquiescence in the wise conclusion of President JOHNSON to begin at least the work of reconstruction without any definite judgment upon it.[71] The Radical drive was sputtering.

But the deathblow to the radical campaign for Negro suffrage came from Connecticut. There the people were to vote on a proposition to amend the state constitution to enfranchise blacks. All understood the necessity of its success. Local Republican leaders worked hard to pass it. New York's radical newspapers directed their editorials to their northern neighbors. The *Independent* pleaded for victory. "On Monday next Connecticut is to decide whether her Christianity and Republicanism, being brought to the test, mean anything. She will decide that day if she believes in the Bible of Christianity or the Slave Code of Carolina; whether in the Declaration of Independence of the Montgomery Constitution," Tilton exhorted.

But all pleadings failed; the voters of Connecticut rejected the Negro suffrage amendment, although Connecticut had only two thousand black citizens. "This unmanly vote is like the act of a strong man striking a lame child," wrote the disgusted Tilton. Connecticut, mourned Greeley, "has committed wrong from pure love of it." [72]

The effect of Connecticut's vote was predictable. It meant there was no longer any possibility that Republicans would make Negro suffrage a party question. Conservatives pointed to the returns as justification for their reluctance. Similar amendments met defeat in elections held in November in Minnesota and Wisconsin. Yet in all three states well over half the voters who cast ballots for the Republican ticket (in Wisconsin, about three fourths) also supported Negro suffrage. And most of the Republicans who had not endorsed the proposition has abstained rather than vote against it.[73] As Tilton complained, "If the Administration had chosen a policy of justice, instead of injustice, and asked from the people a verdict in favor of equal suffrage as a basis of permanent peace, the response would have been a sweeping approval throughout the North. On the contrary, the President virtually invited Connecticut to join with Alabama in denying the negro his rights." [74]

The radical Republicans had failed to force a shift in the party. The conservative Indiana Republican Jonathan D. Defrees wrote Doolittle,

> A few months ago I feared there might be men enough among us so short-sighted as to commit us to the fatal dogma of negro suffrage as a condition precedent to a recognition of the rebel States. I have no such fear now. There is a healthy reaction taking place among our friends. . . .
>
> Before the adjournment of Congress Sumner, Thad Stevens, Phillips and Anna Dickenson [sic] will be about all that is left of the State-Suicide, negro suffrage party.[75]

To Welles also prospects seemed bright. "Things are working very well. . . . Some of the extreme Republicans of the Sumner school are dissatisfied, but I think their numbers are growing less. . . . I think the policy of the Administration is growing in favor." [76]

The radicals were forced to alter their tactics. Lieber warned Sumner that insisting on Negro suffrage in the present situation "would weaken you and our side altogether." Casting about for a new issue, Garfield wrote Chase, "If we shall not be able to maintain the fight on the suffrage question alone, should we not make a preliminary resistance to immediate restoration and thereby gain time?" [77]

But it was not certain that this tactic could succeed either. Only by the most strenuous effort had Senate radicals prevented recognition of Louisiana without requiring Negro suffrage a few months before. The House Elections committee had reported in favor of seating representatives from Louisiana and Arkansas. If the president succeeded in reconstructing civil government in the South around loyal elements, it seemed he need not worry about congressional resistance.

SIX

The Center Republicans Change Their Minds

— ✦✦✦✦✦ —

BY OCTOBER 1865, the radical offensive had failed. Unwilling to divide the party, conservative and center Republicans refused to make commitment to Negro suffrage a test of party loyalty. They might favor suffrage extension personally, but they were not going to force their preference on the president or that minority of Republicans who opposed it. Given the course these Republicans had taken during the previous session of Congress, the future should have been bright for early readmission of reconstructed southern states. In the Senate recognition of southern states would come under the jurisdiction of the Committee on the Judiciary, which had led the fight for Louisiana restoration a few months earlier and whose chairman, Lyman Trumbull, had confided to Gideon Welles that he supported the president's policy. Moreover, Senate Democrats, who in the previous session had joined radicals to filibuster Louisiana recognition to death, now vociferously supported presidential Reconstruction. In the House the conservative Elections committee had control of the question, and it had already reported in favor of seating Louisiana representatives. Both Dawes and Thomas D. Eliot, the most important proponents of quick restoration in the Thirty-eighth Congress, would be returning in the Thirty-ninth. Furthermore, the conservatives could expect to receive important additional support, for General Banks was returning to Congress, elected from his old Massachusetts congressional district. Experienced and influential, Banks would receive an important committee assignment and carry great weight among his colleagues.

But even as the radical drive for Negro suffrage collapsed, events were altering the more conservative Republicans' position. The most important developments occurred in Louisiana.

Louisiana in large measure provides the link between wartime and peacetime Reconstruction. This was the state in which Reconstruction had advanced furthest during the war; Republicans had hammered out their conception of Reconstruction in reference to it. Banks's and Lincoln's policy there had been to place the state in the hands of moderate unionist elements, opposed to slavery but conciliatory toward the sensibilities of white southerners and allied with the moderate-conservative elements of the Republican party. Most Republicans had decided that this was the correct policy and in the spring of 1865 attempted to recognize the Louisiana government over the opposition of radicals who demanded the enfranchisement of black Louisianans. During the spring and summer of 1865 the Louisiana situation changed so radically that the conservative and centrist Republicans changed their minds and decided that it—and all the other southern states—must remain in the cold.

The Banks-Hahn political machine in Louisiana had begun to sputter as soon as Banks left Louisiana in 1864 to campaign for the state's restoration. Banks's replacement, General Stephen A. Hurlbut, had been a Democratic lawyer and politician in Illinois. With ambitions of his own, he had little use for the New Orleans municipal authorities who had been the backbone of Banks's political organization. The new commander announced that he regarded the Hahn government as merely provisional and subject to military power. Rejecting Hahn's political appointments, he substituted his own from among the old, proslavery Conservative Unionists, threatening Hahn's control of the patronage. That Hahn's control was slipping became apparent when the state legislature defeated his candidates to fill Louisiana's vacant seats in the United States Senate. By late 1864, Banks's Louisiana allies already were appealing for his aid.[1] When Banks's efforts to persuade Congress to recognize the restored Louisiana government failed, Hahn realized that his power was crumbling. With Louisiana due to elect a new senator to the Thirty-ninth Congress, Hahn repudiated an earlier understanding promising the seat to Banks and determined to take it for himself, hoping to secure a six-year term in the Senate before his political machine failed completely. The outraged Banks condemned Hahn for "vacating the power which had been put into his hands at the cost of such outlays of treasure and blood." [2]

With Hahn resigning to take the Senate seat, Lieutenant Governor J. Madison Wells ascended to the governorship. Unquestionably one of the most unattractive figures of the Civil War era, Wells was to fight on nearly every side in its political battles, and betray them all. He began by abandoning Louisiana's Unionists. Recognizing the imminent collapse of the Banks machine, Wells allied himself with Hurlbut and the Conservative Unionists. He removed the loyal municipal authorities, replacing them with former Confederates, put his allies in control of the police department, and removed Banks's close friend, A.P. Dostie, as state auditor and replaced him with the man Dostie had defeated at the polls.

When Banks returned to his Louisiana command late in April he reversed most of Wells's decisions, restoring his moderate supporters to power, but Wells traveled to Washington to appeal Banks's orders directly to Johnson. Banks too informed the president of the situation, both directly and through intermediaries. Louisiana loyalists sent letters and delegations attacking Wells's course, but the governor responded by accusing his accusers—charging that they sought power so they could defraud the state. Johnson hesitated, but Wells finally emerged victorious, and on May 17, Johnson ordered a reorganization of the Military Department of the Southwest. Banks lost his command but was to remain in New Orleans without any position or power. Recognizing defeat, he resigned.[3]

With the war over, returning Confederates hurried to take the loyalty oath required by the president for amnesty. Wells decided to win these elements to his support and make himself the master of Louisiana politics. Discarding the voting register prepared under his predecessor, Wells announced new elections for the fall, declaring eligible to vote all white male citizens who had resided in the state for the previous twelve months and had taken the president's amnesty oath. Only the exceptions listed in Johnson's Amnesty Proclamation were ineligible, unless they had already received their pardons from the president. In the election Wells was nominated both by the Democrats, made up of returned Confederates, and the Conservative Unionists, although the rest of their candidates differed.[4] Banks and his supporters, now completely powerless in the state, coalesced with their old radical enemies in July to form the National Republican Association. At the organizational meeting they passed a resolution calling upon the president to remove Wells, name a provisional governor, and reorganize the state "upon the basis of universal freedom and suffrage." [5]

Louisiana Republicans did not despair of convincing President Johnson of his error. In July Banks still believed the president would change his course when he realized the situation.[6] Their hopes were buoyed by evidence that the administration was striving to acquire the true facts. Late in May, Stanton commissioned Congressman John Covode to investigate Louisiana affairs for the War Department. Covode reported that the situation was deteriorating. He concluded that those in control of Louisiana's government were out of harmony with the policy of the national government, and that if the situation continued, the entire South would be influenced to array itself against the government. Although "unwilling to urge upon the Government the adoption of radical measures," Covode reluctantly concluded that only the extension of suffrage to black men could restore Louisiana to the control of loyalists.[7]

In September the Louisiana Republicans received another opportunity to appeal to the president, when Carl Schurz, touring the South at the president's request, arrived in New Orleans. Purposely ignoring the radical element led by Flanders, Durant, and Henry C. Warmoth, Schurz asked the conservative Republicans to give their views in writing. These he forwarded to the president with a covering letter agreeing with their conclusions. The protests came from Hahn, Banks, Thomas W. Conway, and others of the Banks-Hahn faction. Even General Canby and the archconservative senator-elect R. King Cutler joined in the effort. All agreed that Unionists could control the state if Johnson removed Wells. But "if things continue and as they are now, they feel powerless and despondent," Schurz wrote.[8] Johnson again hesitated, telegraphing Wells of the accusations September 18. But the governor again responded by impugning the honesty of his detractors, dismissing them as "unscrupulous and tainted opponents of your policy." Wells sent two of his lieutenants to confer with the president, and evidently they removed Johnson's doubts.[9]

Even the most conservative Unionist elements in Louisiana were thoroughly alarmed. James G. Taliaferro, one of the claimants for a seat in the House of Representatives in the previous Congress and the Conservative Unionist candidate for lieutenant governor, complained that the rebels were regaining control of the state. "Their affrontery [sic] is astonishing," he exclaimed. A.P. Field confided to Schurz that only the frantic efforts of the Conservative Unionists had deterred Wells from abrogating the 1864 Free-State constitution and reinstating the aristocratic constitution of 1852 as Democrats had wanted. He appealed to Schurz to persuade the president to order the military to prevent the registration of former rebels.[10]

When the Democrats elected their state ticket in November, receiving four fifths of the vote, the Conservative Unionists joined the Republican protest; the men who had been most active in lobbying for recognition nine months earlier now opposed it. Field wrote Banks, "Hatred of the Government and to the Union men is now more intense than it was in 1860 & 1861, and were we without the Protection of the Federal troops in this State the union men would be persecuted and driven out of the country." Field, who had spent four months in the winter of 1864–65 trying to win recognition for Louisiana, came to what must have been an unpalatable conclusion: "If Congress recognises . . . the late election as valid and admits the members under it the union men of this State will be forced to leave here." [11] In an effort to build united Republican opposition to recognition, the aristocratic conservative even wrote his old antagonist Thaddeus Stevens expressing the same opinions.[12]

By October Louisiana's conservative Republicans were on the stump. In Massachusetts Banks told his audiences,

The death of President Lincoln . . . has led, momentarily only, I think, to a suspension of [Banks's and Lincoln's] . . . generous policy of organizing a Government of the Union men, excluding our enemies. . . . A change has come over the spirit of the people, and now the entire political power is given to the men who were prominent in the . . . rebel government. The Union men are disappointed; they are discouraged. . . . The true course to be pursued in Louisiana, and in every other of the rebel States, in my judgment is the same that has been pursued there before. *Put the government of the States into the hands of loyal men.*

Speaking before the National Equal Suffrage Association in Washington, Hahn called for congressional legislation prohibiting apprenticeship laws, requiring free schools, and guaranteeing legal equality. Finally, he endorsed an extension of the franchise to black soldiers and a literacy requirement for voters of both races.[13]

The Louisiana Republicans made their influence felt privately also. Banks, of course, had many friends in Congress, among them his colleague and old political ally Henry Laurens Dawes, the conservative chairman of the House Elections committee. Louisiana's Senator-elect R. King Cutler had worked closely with Lyman Trumbull in trying to win recognition for Louisiana during the Thirty-eighth Congress. Now he wrote his friend, "Rebels reign supreme here. . . . If Congress would admit La. reserving the right to regulate the franchise of her people White and Black, there would be no danger in the future." [14]

Republican disquiet grew as evidence mounted that southerners were not prepared to protect the rights of black and white Unionists or reward their faithfulness to the nation with political office. Newspapers carried disquieting accounts of brutality toward blacks and threats against white loyalists. The reluctance of many of the southern state conventions to repudiate the rebel debt and the new state legislatures' hesitation at ratifying the Thirteenth Amendment added to northerners' fears. Even more convincing were the new "Black Codes" southern legislatures passed in the winter of 1865–66 to regulate their black populations.

Men who had led the fight for Louisiana recognition during the Thirty-eighth Congress slowly concluded that recognition would be premature, after all. The most important of the centrist Republican converts probably was Trumbull, since his committee would exert large influence over Reconstruction legislation. But other conservative and moderate Republicans received similar information from Louisiana and other states and arrived at corresponding conclusions. William Pitt Fessenden, the most influential Republican in the Senate, expressed his doubts to his best friend, Senator James W. Grimes of Iowa. Senator Lot M. Morrill echoed his colleague's fears. Massachusetts Governor Andrew, in the same letter in which he urged moderation on Sumner, acknowledged that he too had received discouraging reports from the South, and affirmed that something had to be done.[15]

Republican disquiet grew as conventions organized in other states under the president's authority manifested their reluctance to conform to the new national order. Even Henry J. Raymond, editor of the *New York Times* and spokesman for the Seward-Weed faction, worried privately, "Public matters are getting *foggy*. . . . The general opinion is that [the president] . . . is going too fast in his policy of reconstruction and that the rebel States must rest awhile longer under military rule." [16] In his newspaper Raymond, who was expected to be the administration spokesman in the next Congress, wrote, "With much regret we confess our disappointment. Admitting many honorable exceptions, we conclude (from every source of information within our reach) that public sentiment [in the South] is still as bitter and unloyal as in 1861." Raymond pointed out that the people and press of the North, "with the exception of a few extreme theorists . . . have been guided by most generous sentiments; they have had no words of malice; they have forborne the discussion of irritating topics; they have sought every feasible occasion to assure the Southern people of a willingness to forgive and forget . . . .

"And how are we met? . . . [E]very indication of their policy . . . seems to be in the wrong direction." Raymond admonished southerners that they were provoking a powerful reaction. "Already we are conscious of a decided change of feeling in this section," he warned.[17]

As more Republicans concluded that Reconstruction was going badly, sentiment grew to delay readmission of southern representatives into Congress. Of course, Republicans feared that as matters now stood southern congressmen would unite with northern Democrats on most issues, restoring the prewar coalition that had dominated the national government, but more important yet inforcing the change was the constitutional framework in which Republicans viewed the war and Reconstruction. During the war, most Republicans had justified extraordinary measures by arguing that the conflict had forced a suspension of peacetime constitutional provisions. Unionists reached this conclusion by two different routes. Francis Lieber, the leading student of government in mid-nineteenth-century America, for example, espoused the first interpretation: "The whole Rebellion is beyond the Constitution," he insisted. "The Constitution was not made for such a state of things . . . . [T]he life of a nation is the first substantial thing and far above the formulas [for government] which . . . have been adopted." The Constitution had been intended to serve a *nation* which had been forged by a common heritage and experience before and during the War of Independence. That nation had to be preserved, even if the Constitution were violated. Thaddeus Stevens was the most important American statesman to accept this view.[18] A second school argued that the Constitution itself incorporated virtually unlimited war powers through the clause vesting in Congress the power to prosecute war. These powers were as much a part of the Constitution as its peacetime provisions, but in a state of war the war powers naturally became more prominent while other provisions receded into the background.[19]

By justifying the massive wartime expansion of the national government's power in this way, Republicans believed they had preserved the Constitution from contamination. With war's end, the occasion for using the war powers—whether under the Constitution's authority or outside it —would cease. The limitations of the peacetime fundamental law would regain their sway.

A second important conviction Republicans developed during the war was that only the people of the southern states could reorganize civil governments there. Lincoln and the Republicans in Congress shared this commitment to voluntarism, although they sometimes interpreted it rather loosely. Both presidential Reconstruction under Lincoln and the congressional Reconstruction bills during the war were essentially enabling acts. Under either program the president appointed a provisional governor to administer the state temporarily while the people themselves framed new constitutions and elected new officers. The provisional governors might regulate the election of delegates to the constitutional convention, and either the president or Congress might make it clear that they would withdraw military control from no state that did not meet certain conditions, but the people were not ordered to comply with those conditions. They could refuse and remain under military government. At some point, of course, this kind of "voluntarism" becomes coercion. But in constitutional theory, at least, the new civil governments of the South were to spring from the authority of the southern people themselves.[20]

As Republicans reluctantly concluded during the summer and fall of 1865 that they had to take some action to preserve the fruits of victory in the South, they found themselves limited by their wartime constitutional doctrines. By strictly differentiating between national powers during war and peace, they had preserved federal relations as they had existed antebellum. If the war were truly over, if Republicans restored the southern states to normal relations within the Union, then the national government would have no more power over those states' domestic affairs than it had before the war, except insofar as the Thirteenth Amendment might authorize Congress to legislate to prevent reintroduction of slavery. As Wendell Phillips said, once restore a state and "we have put a fence between the Federal Government and the State Government. . . . Put up the fence and the [national] law runs to it, not over it, except in two or three specified cases." [21] The implications were clear. "The time is to come when each southern State is to take its own local affairs into its own hands," the Boston *Evening Journal* pointed out, "and the only security we can have that it will then move on in a loyal orbit is to be found in the permanent forces we shall have previously implanted in it." [22] The fruits of victory had to be secured *before* the southern states were restored to proper relations in the Union.[23]

Before Andrew Johnson's position had hardened, many Republicans had decided the best internal force they could implant in the rebel states would be black suffrage, forcing southern politicians to appeal for black votes for election, votes that one could hardly expect to win by advocating violations of black men's rights. For several reasons, Negro suffrage in the South had appealed to conservative Republicans as well as radicals. It would have given black men protection within their states without requiring a broad expansion of national government power. As James Russell Lowell pointed out, the ballot would give the freedmen "that power of self-protection which no interference of governments can so safely, cheaply, and surely exercise in their behalf." [24] Also, Negro suffrage could have been instituted at the outset of the restoration process without doing violence to Republicans' constitutional scruples. Since, the new civil governments in the South had to be organized by the southern people themselves, it would have been an easy matter to allow *all* southerners, black and white, to vote in the first elections for delegates to constitutional conventions. (Republicans assumed that delegates elected in part by black votes would not restrict the franchise to whites in the new constitution.) But the president had refused to allow blacks to vote in those elections, and with civil governments in the process of organization under presidential authority, the constitutional problem had grown knottier.

Some of the radicals forwarded a bold solution: the president had usurped the power of Congress by beginning the restoration process in the first place, they argued; Congress should overturn Johnson's work and treat the southern states as conquered territory. The southern state governments were overthrown, but the people and territory of the South still owed allegiance to the United States. Congress should give them territorial governments. In this way the president could appoint the territorial governor and the judiciary (only federal courts operated in United States territories) with the Senate's advice and consent, while the people could govern themselves through a territorial legislature and elected local officials, all under the supervisory power of Congress. Since Congress determines voting requirements in territories, blacks could be enfranchised by congressional action. As in any territory, the people could frame a state constitution and petition Congress for statehood. Again this constitution making would be voluntary, but Congress could refuse the petition until the state presented a constitution that protected the rights of southern loyalists.[25]

This program still protected the old balance between the state and national government in the federal system. Once southern territories were granted statehood, they would have all the rights of other states, and the national government could no longer interfere in their internal affairs.

This alternative provided a way for the national government to retain its power over the South for a long period under peacetime constitutional provisions, but was still conservative in protecting the old federal system.[25] The territorialization scheme was radical *politically,* however. Congress not only would refuse admission to the reorganized southern states but would overthrow their governments completely, forcing the entire process to begin anew. Territorialization, therefore, meant a complete repudiation of the president's program.

Conservative and center Republicans would not accept a policy that so manifestly would alienate the president and divide the party. Determined to conciliate President Johnson, they wanted to accept his work as the basis for Reconstruction. But if Reconstruction were not to begin anew, they had to find a way to persuade the reorganized southern governments to protect the rights of southern unionists and preserve the victory won on the battlefield. What emerged was a new justification for Reconstruction which seemed to fit the situation perfectly and which also seemed consistent with past Republican constitutional doctrine.

The natural assumption had been that peace would restore the sway of peacetime constitutional limitations to the power of the national government. But some legal writers had suggested that it was up to the national government to decide precisely when peace had arrived. In that case the government might demand certain concessions in return for recognition that peace was restored. This view had been forwarded in the *Atlantic Monthly* as early as August 1863: "The Rebel States will not cease to be enemies by being defeated . . . . They have invoked the laws of war, and they must abide the decision of the tribunal to which they have appealed. We may hold them as enemies until they submit to such reasonable terms of peace as we may demand." [26] This doctrine had been popularized by Richard Henry Dana in the speech he had delivered to the Faneuil Hall black suffrage meeting on June 21. "The conquering party may hold the other in the grasp of war until it has secured whatever it has a right to acquire," he maintained.[27] Under this theory the national government still held great leverage over the reorganized states, without having to remand them to the status of territories or overturning their new governments. Dana advocated that Congress insist upon Negro suffrage as the main condition for the formal restoration of peace, but the theory justified alternative requirements—the ratification of new constitutional amendments, for instance. The "grasp of war" theory received immediate and wide support. Collis P. Huntington, the railroad financier, wrote McCulloch that the doctrine met with favor in Boston. Ohio's conservative new governor, Jacob D. Cox, House Speaker Schuyler Colfax, William Pitt Fessenden, George S. Boutwell, Chief Justice Chase, John Sherman, William Lawrence, and Carl Schurz all expressed views similar to Dana's.[28]

The influence of the "grasp of war" theory would be manifest in the policy Congress finally adopted. The first congressional Reconstruction program would promise restoration of political privileges to the southern states upon ratification of the guarantees embodied in the Fourteenth Amendment. The second combined the enabling act approach with the "grasp of war" doctrine. Congress would require southerners to begin anew to reorganize their state governments, allowing blacks to participate in the process, and also would formulate conditions the new governments would have to meet before Congress accepted their constitutions and released them from "the grasp of war." [29]

The "grasp of war" doctrine, like the territorialization plan, gave no permanent power to Congress. Once released from military control, southern states regained all their old prerogatives. Dana meant his program to preserve prewar federal balance between the state and national governments. "It would do irreparable mischief for Congress to assume civil and political authority in state matters," he wrote his friend Charles Francis Adams, Jr. immediately after his speech, "but it is not an irreparable mischief for the general government to continue the exercise of such war powers as are necessary until the people of these States do what we in conscience think necessary for the reasonable security of the republic." [30] Moreover, the guarantees would be given through voluntary state action, rather than national imposition. This might be done only under the pressure of continued exclusion from the Union, but again the states were not forced to do anything. They might choose to remain under military control if they preferred.

There was one more reason conservative and center Republicans felt it safe to adopt the "grasp of war" approach, with its continued exclusion of southern states. It seemed that President Johnson had adopted it too.

President Johnson's proclamations appointing provisional governors in the southern states and instructing them to call constitutional conventions had said nothing about any requirements the states would have to meet before restoration to normal relations with the United States. The provisional governors were to exercise any power necessary "to present such a republican form of State government as will entitle the State to the guarantee of the United States therefor," Johnson said. He had given no indication of what provisions if any he considered necessary to "a republican form of State government." This led the Boston *Daily Advertiser* to conclude that the president believed that as soon as he started the wheels of state government moving again the states automatically resumed their places in the Union.[31] This was the precise doctrine that Andrew Johnson would later insist he had acted upon, but in fact he had privately informed his provisional governors that he wished the state conventions to declare the secession ordinances null and void, repudiate the rebel debt, and abolish slavery within their states. Furthermore, he wanted the conventions or the new state legislatures to ratify the Thirteenth Amendment. At first these appeared to be no more than suggestions, consistent in theory with Lincoln's "suggestions" to Unionists reconstructing Tennessee, Arkansas, and Louisiana during the war.

Democrats took advantage of the ambiguity of Johnson's policy. Adopting the position of the Democratic members of the House Committee on Elections during the second session of the Thirty-eighth Congress, leading Democrats argued for immediate restoration of the reorganized southern state governments to normal relations in the Union. Pointing to the president's original Reconstruction proclamations, they interpreted his position to be that once civil governments in the states were reinstituted, they automatically resumed all the privileges and duties of statehood. The national government—whether president or Congress or courts—immediately lost any war power they may have once held over southern territory. Democrats vociferously supported the president and what they proclaimed to be "his policy," privately offering him the political support of the Democratic organization and urging the appointment of a Democratic cabinet.[32]

But as conservative and moderate northern Republicans became alarmed at events in the South, reports multiplied that the president too was dissatisfied.[33] The political ascendancy of the returned rebels in many of the southern states became manifest in the actions of the constitutional conventions. In North Carolina, South Carolina, and Georgia the conventions refused to repudiate the rebel debt. Many of the new state legislatures hesitated to ratify the Thirteenth Amendment. Johnson reacted by ending his policy of noninvolvement. Bluntly, he wrote the governors that he would recognize no restored state government that did not meet his "suggested" requirements. His letters, immediately made public, fit exactly into the mold of the "grasp of war" doctrine. The southern state governments would have to meet his conditions before he would recognize them as having resumed loyal relations to the Union.[34]

The *New York Times,* the opinions of which took on added importance because of editor Raymond's intimacy with Secretary of State Seward, pointed to Johnson's actions as demonstrating the difference between the president's Reconstruction policy and that of the Democrats, who so vigorously proclaimed their support for him. The Democratic theory, Raymond argued

is that the close of the war of itself revives the relations of the rebel States to the Union, and that the practical restoration consists only in the civil reorganization of the States by the Southern people themselves, in accordance with their own will. On the other hand President JOHNSON's principle is, that the abeyance of constitutional rights does not pass away with the mere close of the war; that it must terminate only at the discretion of the government against

which the rebellion was directed, and that the first duty of the government is
to see that it continues until all obligations are fulfilled and safeguards established. The Democratic party considers that the Southern States have a right
to a restoration immediate and unconditional. President JOHNSON, on the other
hand, deems it to be both his right and his duty to impose conditions.[35]

At the same time Johnson began to inform leading Republicans that
he considered his policy an experiment. He authorized Missouri's Senator
John B. Henderson to tell audiences that he personally favored limited
Negro suffrage and repeated his conviction in a published interview with
George Luther Stearns. He told Ohio congressman Robert C. Schenck that
he would intervene in the southern states if his experimental policy failed
to secure the ascendancy of Unionists, and in a two-hour interview convinced the influential Fessenden that he was in complete agreement with
the party on all issues but the imposition of black suffrage.[36]

His cabinet joined in the campaign. McCulloch assured the doubting
Sumner that the president's policy was "but an experiment."

If it fails, it will not be the fault of the President; and he will then be at liberty
to pursue a sterner policy, and the country will sustain him in it. Rebels and
enemies will not be permitted to take possession of the Southern States, or to
occupy seats in Congress, or to form coalitions with the Northern Democracy
for the repudiation of the National Debt or a restoration of Slavery. . . . No
action of his is *final*.

And he added, "If he makes mistakes and does not rectify them, Congress
has the power to do it." [37]

But Secretary of State Seward played the most important role.
Recognizing that the Democrats were making a strenuous effort to win
the president's support, he launched a campaign to commit Johnson to a
course that would insure harmony with the conservative and moderate
Republicans and alienate the Democrats.[38] One element in his strategy was
to highlight the differences between the Reconstruction policy of the president and the Democrats. Raymond's editorial in the *New York Times* was
part of that effort.[39] A second was to assure Republicans that the president
intended to leave final disposition of Reconstruction questions to Congress.

Seward began his effort to commit the administration to this course
when Mississippi's provisional governor, William L. Sharkey, asked President
Johnson to order the military authorities to release an accused murderer
into civil custody. Seward answered, "The President sees no reason to
interfere with General Slocum's proceedings. The government of the State
will be provisional only[,] until the civil authorities shall be restored, with
the approval of Congress. Meanwhile, military authority cannot be withdrawn." [40] Seward followed this with a communication to the provisional
governor of Florida, William Marvin. Commenting on Marvin's proclamation calling for the election of delegates to the required state convention,

Seward—indicating that he spoke for the president—admonished, "It must . . . be distinctly understood that the restoration to which your proclamation refers will be subject to the decision of Congress." [41]

Seward determined to press his campaign in the cabinet. Late in September he read the draft of a letter to one of the provisional governors informing him that the president intended to continue the provisional governments in power until Congress decided whether to recognize the civil governments founded under the new state constitutions. But Welles immediately objected, and Johnson ordered Seward to omit any reference to Congress from any of his communications.[42]

Despite this rebuff the *Times* continued to assure Republicans that the president would defer to Congress's decision in the recognition of the southern regimes he had organized. Furthermore, the *Times* emphasized the point Seward had pressed on the cabinet:

All the late insurrectionary States are still under a military government. The Provisional Governors who are at their head were appointed by the National Executive by virtue of his war powers. By virtue of these same powers they are still retained at their posts, even in those States in which the people have elected new Governors. . . . It still rests absolutely with the government to determine in its own high discretion, whether the late insurrectionary States have done all that can reasonably be required of them . . . . Until that decision is reached and acted upon, the insurrectionary States must remain as they are, under military law.

That decision would be Congress's, Raymond assured his readers. "The military government of the States will be removed as soon as their representative functions are revived." [43]

As the *Times* publicized what many believed to be the administration policy, many Republicans gained confidence in the president. "The events of each day make it clearer and clearer that he means to do right," Godkin concluded.[44] Conservative and moderate Republican organs happily predicted harmony would prevail in Republican ranks.[45] Even radical Jacob M. Howard took heart. "I still have . . . confidence that Mr. Johnson will stand with us," he wrote Sumner hopefully. "His policy, that of Lincoln, has been liberal, indulgent to a fault. I cannot believe he will fail to see that he has been warming a viper. I think his late dispatches & notes indicate his distrust of the experiment, & his resolution to be more rigid & exacting." And although he still favored black suffrage, Howard urged, "We ought to do all in our power to avoid a break with him & to keep him with us . . . . We must not suffer our strength to be divided." [46]

Johnson encouraged this optimism as he himself raised the conditions required for restoration. As the new southern state legislatures demonstrated their inclination to limit as much as possible the rights of the freed slaves, Johnson informed Mississippi's governor-elect, Benjamin G. Humphreys, that before he would withdraw military authority he required "loyal compliance with the laws and Constitution of the United States *and the adoption of . . . measures giving protection to all freedmen or freemen in persons and property without regard to color."* [47]

As the meeting date of the Thirty-ninth Congress approached, Speaker of the House Schuyler Colfax decided to take advantage of the growing optimism to voice the opinions of moderate Republicans and outline their program. Responding to a serenade in Washington on November 18, he warmly endorsed the president's decision to begin the restoration process in the absence of congressional legislation. This was preferable to leaving the southern people under purely martial law, he said. He endorsed the minimum conditions the president had set for restoration, and he went on to list several more conditions on which he believed all Union men would agree. First, the freedmen's civil rights must be protected (the president's letter to Humphreys had not yet been published); they must be guaranteed equality before the law. Second, Colfax wanted the southern people to ratify by referendum the amendments to their state constitutions, adopted by their conventions so reluctantly under presidential pressure. Finally, he urged caution in restoring privileges to the rebellious states. "Let us rather make haste slowly," Colfax suggested, until the southerners showed a more tractable spirit.[48] The address received the immediate endorsement of the conservative and moderate Republican journals that had been supporting the president. Morton's organ, the Indianapolis *Daily Journal,* agreed that Colfax "spoke the determination of his party." [49]

Colfax's speech clearly indicated that the moderate and conservative Republicans had abandoned Negro suffrage as a guarantee of Reconstruction. If the *New York Times* had accurately gauged the president's position, if his communications to the provisional governors meant what they implied—that the president believed the national government could hold the southern states under military control until they met certain conditions—then harmony between the president and the majority of Republicans in Congress was assured. Even if the president had been wavering between the policy advocated by the Democrats and that advocated by his Republican confidantes, Colfax's speech and the immense enthusiasm it aroused among even the most conservative Republicans had to bring the president over to the Republican position. "You have spoken 'the word in season,' " James G. Blaine congratulated Colfax. "The omens are bright now for the future—and the President sees them!!!" [50]

As if in response to the Republicans' bubbling optimism, the president on November 27 advised South Carolina's provisional governor, Benjamin F. Perry, not to send the state's congressmen-elect to Washington immediately. "On the contrary," he wrote, "it will be better policy to present their certificates of election after the two Houses are organized." [51] The president was vague about just what Congress's rights in the matter were ("it will . . . be a simple question under the Constitution of the members taking their seats," he wrote), but he clearly rejected the Democratic contention that the southern states had already resumed all their rights and privileges in the Union and that the names of their representatives must be called upon the organization of the House, subject to challenge if any of them could not take the required oaths. And once again he urged the adoption "of a code in reference to free persons of color that will be acceptable to the country, at the same time doing justice to the white and colored population." [52]

Johnson wrote his provisional governor of North Carolina, William W. Holden, who had just been defeated in his state's gubernatorial election by a rebel-supported candidate, that the election had "greatly damaged the prospects of the State in the restoration of its governmental relations." He warned, "Should the action and spirit of the legislature be in the same direction, it will greatly increase the mischief already done and might be fatal." [53]

Even Sumner was somewhat mollified. Since he had deemphasized Negro suffrage in favor of delay in restoration, many Republicans believed even he might remain in harmony with the administration. Fessenden said his views had "modified down to *just* the right point," and George Bancroft wrote Johnson that he had succeeded in calming the Senator during a three-hour visit. Sumner remained firm in his resolution to deliver speeches in the Senate critical of southern conditions, Bancroft wrote, but was "resolved to cultivate friendly relations with you." On his arrival in the capital, Sumner immediately went to visit the president. But he was profoundly disappointed with the result. "He does not understand the case," he wrote. "Much that he said was painful, from its prejudice, ignorance, and perversity." [54]

But other Republicans remained enthusiastic. Senator Henry S. Lane, just arrived in Washington, found that "there is good feeling here & less excitement on the subject of reconstruction . . . then [*sic*] in Indiana." Happily, the *New York Times* recorded the disappointment of those who had looked for the disruption of the party. "Indeed the Union party seems to be quite as thoroughly united upon all cardinal points of national policy, and quite as harmonious in support of the President, as any party, equally strong in numbers and popular support, has ever been before," the *Times* noted. The radicals had little support for their policies, few Republicans insisted on Negro suffrage as a condition for restoration, and the remaining minor differences would "be harmonized without difficulty." [55]

The first session of the Thirty-ninth Congress opened December 4, 1865. As expected, the secretaries of the House and Senate listed none of the southern claimants' names on the roll of the houses, and the congressmen settled back to await the annual message of the president.[56] Here would be the great test; here the president would inform the country whether the Republicans' optimism had been well-founded.

Seward had been hard at work. He had written a draft of the president's message as he hoped Johnson would deliver it. It marked the culmination of his efforts. The power to admit southern representatives, Seward wanted Johnson to say, "belongs, not to the executive department of the government, but to Congress. I leave it there with entire confidence." He hoped the president would remain flexible:

I have not at any time fixed, and it is not my purpose now to insist upon . . . a detailed scheme to be applied in all cases for the restoration of their [the southern states'] political connection with the Union. On the contrary, I have held, and with the sanction of Congress shall for the present continue to hold . . . such control therein as would be sure to prevent anarchy.[57]

But the president rejected such explicit language. Instead he turned to George Bancroft, the great historian, to prepare a message brilliant in its ambiguity. Had Republican conservatives and moderates known that the president had rejected Seward's clear enunciation of policy, they might have been less pleased with the final product. But they were ignorant of the maneuvering behind the scenes. The conservative editor of the *Wisconsin State Journal* happily reported "the hearty satisfaction which glowed upon the faces of the members of the Union side as they listened." The message appeared to be all the conservative and centrist Republicans could desire.

The president, as expected, explicitly rejected black suffrage for the South, but he explained his decision to begin the restoration process in the South in precisely the same terms Colfax had employed, emphasizing the preferability of civil to military government. The president affirmed his commitment to securing to the freedmen "their liberty and their property, their right to labor, and their right to claim the just return of their labor." On the question of recognition, Johnson wrote:

it would remain for the States whose powers have been so long in abeyance to resume their places in the two branches of the National Legislature, and thereby complete the work of restoration. Here it is for you, fellow-citizens of the Senate, and for you, fellow-citizens of the House of Representatives, to judge, each of you for yourselves, of the elections, returns, and qualifications of your own members.[58]

Later, Republicans could look back upon this message and recognize that the president had conceded nothing, that the careful language left him uncommitted on all essential points.[59] But in light of Johnson's activities, his communications to his provisional governors, his assurances to Republican leaders, and the simple fact that he was the titular leader of their party, Republicans could only interpret the message as they did: a clear statement by the president that though he desired speedy restoration, he recognized Congress as the final judge of Reconstruction, a clear indication that he shared their concern for the safety of southern loyalists. Banks confidently informed a happy audience that "all fear of dissensions between the different branches of the Government representing the loyal people is removed. The country will be relieved of its apprehensions, the friends of the Government encouraged and its enemies depressed." Virtually all Republicans concurred, but as the *Nation*'s correspondent observed, "The message . . . is praised most loudly by the most moderate." [60] Morton and Bancroft congratulated Johnson that the conciliatory tone of the message put the radicals in an untenable position. "In less than twenty days the extreme radical opposition will be over," Bancroft predicted.[61]

The Thirty-ninth Congress had opened auspiciously for the conservative and centrist Republicans. But radicals' feelings were mixed. Many were happy at the prospect of harmony; others feared that Congress might concede too much to the president's desire for haste. Stevens fretted, "We shall be betrayed by the Senate I fear—Fessenden! Trumbull Doolittle et al. are all weak kneed, or trimming. . . . The House I believe will be right, if not over-ruled by the Senate." [62] The opening days would indicate the direction of Congress, as it turned its attention to the great questions before it.

SEVEN

Conservative Reconstruction — Part One

———————————— ✦✦✦✦✦✦ ————————————

WITH THE PROSPECTS improving for harmony between the president and conservative and center Republicans, Congress began to formulate Reconstruction policy. Despite radical resistance, conservatives and centrists took the lead in the endeavor. Pursuing a conservative policy early in the session in order to conciliate the president, they would continue it after his desertion, fearing that to do otherwise would insure the disruption and defeat of the party.

As indicated in Chapter I, radicalism depended in large part on Republicans' perceptions of political practicality rather than differences in principle. At no time was this more evident than from August 1865, when Andrew Johnson made clear his opposition to black suffrage in the South, to December 1866, when the second session of the Thirty-ninth Congress opened. Most conservatives did not differ widely from radicals in their views of abstract justice; they differed in the strength of their commitment to carrying out those principles when balanced against other considerations. Although many conservative and center Republicans earlier had endorsed black suffrage, they had by now (December 1865) decided not to press the issue in the face of Johnson's unyielding opposition. They based their decision not merely on deference to the president's wishes, but on the conviction that without his support black suffrage was unattainable. This reluctant abandonment of Negro suffrage by those who once espoused it brought them closer to the positions of those Republicans, like Doolittle, Grimes, Trumbull, Morton, and Governor Cox of Ohio, who had never endorsed suffrage extension at all, and widened the gap between them and the radicals.

Still, most Republicans shared the conviction that the southern states should be restored by the joint action of both houses of Congress and the executive—by law. Until that was done no legal governments existed in the

South; the Johnson governments were provisional. As the lawmaking power, Congress had final authority over those governments. Fessenden said:

I assert the power in its fullest extent. I assert that by the civil war . . . [the rebel states] lost all . . . rights [of states in the Union] . . . . I assert that they have many things to do in order to regain that position. I assert that in the mean time we have a right to govern them . . . ; and I assert, moreover, that they cannot come back here to occupy these seats or seats in the other House until we . . . be satisfied ourselves and decide that they are entitled to occupy these seats again; and that we have a right to take all the time necessary in order to give ourselves entire satisfaction on that subject.[1]

Only a small, conservative minority denied that Congress had any right to exclude loyal representatives and senators from states restored under presidential authority, as long as their credentials were in order.

But the differences between these ultraconservatives and other non-radical Republicans were not so great as they might appear. For while *radical* Republicans might propose the employment of Congress's power over the southern states to require black suffrage, to institute territorial governments, and to exclude them from normal relations in the Union for an indefinite time, *conservatives* and *centrists* had no such intention. Agreeing with radicals that Congress had plenary power over the southern states, nonradicals like Fessenden continued, "It is another question about what we should do; I have been talking about the right. Now I hold that the good of this country requires that these States should be admitted . . . just as soon as it can be done consistently with the safety of the people of this country." To do otherwise, Fessenden warned, would "demoralize" the nation. "We are teaching ourselves to exercise a power which the Constitution did not contemplate." [2]

Left unsaid, but just as important, was the patent fact that to abolish Johnson's state governments, to govern them by law of Congress, meant to alienate the president completely and to risk the failure of the party of the Union. These considerations carried little weight with the radicals. Wade affirmed with pride,

I have ever had one polar star to guide my action, and to that I adhere whether I am in the majority or the minority, and I never intend to be tempted from it one single inch. I fix my eye upon the great principle of eternal justice . . . . Talk not to me about unpopular doctrines, and endeavor not to intimidate me by the intimation that I shall be found in a minority among the people! . . . I know that I tread in the great path of rectitude and right, and I care not who opposes me.[3]

With such differences in temperament and attitude rather than principle, radicals and conservatives inevitably developed differing programs for Reconstruction.

The conservatives and centrists (see Lists 9 and 10 for the approximate makeup of these groups in this session of Congress) predicated their entire program upon the assumption that Negro suffrage would not be at the basis of Reconstruction, and that the governments created under presidential authority in the South would be the ones eventually restored to normal relations in the Union. For this reason their policy consisted not so much of reconstructing the political, social, or economic institutions within the states as trying to protect northern and freedmen's interests from a potentially hostile restored South. Therefore the first element in the conservative-centrist program was a constitutional amendment to change the basis of representation in Congress.

Under the Constitution only three-fifths of the slave population in southern states were counted in determining each state's proper representation in the House of Representatives. With abolition, the entire population would be counted, increasing the number of congressional seats to which southern states would be entitled. If blacks did not vote, the ballot of a white man in South Carolina, where blacks made up more than one-half the population, would count twice as heavily in congressional and presidential elections as the ballot of a northerner. To remedy the inequity, conservative and centrist Republicans favored an amendment to the Constitution which somehow would make congressional representation more consistent with the number of voters in a state. It was a measure necessary only if Republicans did not intend to force black suffrage on the reluctant South.

Conservatives and centrists further insisted that the Constitution be amended to prohibit the assumption of the Confederate debt or the repudiation of that incurred by the Union in subjugating the South. Again the amendment was necessary because Republicans feared and expected that power in the South would be wielded by those who had led and aided the rebellion. Third, Republicans insisted that only men who could take the "ironclad" test oath be admitted to Congress. Fourth, Republicans demanded equal *civil* rights for freedmen with whites. This vague term included rights of property and physical security, and equal access to the courts which protected them. Whatever else "civil rights" did include, it emphatically did not include political privileges. Finally, conservative and centrist Republicans endorsed the conditions required by the president: the ratification of the Thirteenth Amendment, repudiation of the rebel debt, and the nullification of secession ordinances. Individual conservatives or moderates might phrase their demands differently or demand something more; many desired a constitutional amendment clearly rejecting the right of secession and nullification, for instance. Some desired to enfranchise blacks in the District of Columbia, where Congress has absolute jurisdiction under the Constitution. Others were willing to restore Tennessee and perhaps Arkansas immediately. But nearly all agreed to the terms outlined above. Even those conservatives who denied Congress's power to exclude the southern states from representation generally agreed to the propriety of the conservative-center program and would vote for legislation to carry it out.

Radicals did not oppose the policy advocated by more conservative Republicans; they demanded more. Yet radicals seemed less unified than nonradicals in determining what they believed to be the proper course. One common denominator was a continued insistence on black suffrage. Radical George Luther Stearns observed, "There are many ways of human government in the world, but there is only one right way, and that is the way of a democratic republic, or a representative democracy, in which every person unconvicted of crime, of mature age and sound mind, without respect to color or pecuniary condition, enjoys the right to voting for and selecting the makers and executors of the laws of the community in which the voter may reside." No adequate Reconstruction was possible unless it rested on the democratic principle. "Equal manhood suffrage for all men in the South," Stearns insisted, "is the right way, and the only right way." [4]

By advocating black suffrage, radicals already risked the displeasure of the president, but even more likely to alienate him was the mode by which they proposed to secure it. They were willing if necessary to proceed by constitutional amendment—a course that even some conservatives supported—but most radicals desired to reorganize the southern states completely on the basis of equal suffrage, overthrowing the Johnson governments and beginning the Reconstruction process anew. Many, probably a large majority, hoped to erect territorial governments in the South. Southerners, black and white, could elect territorial legislatures and officials; they would enact their own laws. But Congress would retain ultimate jurisdiction. In this way southerners, especially black southerners, would be educated in the processes of democratic government. These radicals wanted southern states to undergo "a probationary training, looking to their restoration when they should prove their fitness for civil government as independent states," Julian explained later. They knew, he wrote, "that no theories of democracy could avail unless adequately supported by a healthy and intelligent public opinion. They saw that States must grow, and could not be suddenly constructed where materials were wanting." [5]

Many radicals further insisted on a national guarantee for the education of the newly freed black men. Like the probation they envisaged, education would render black men fit for the responsibilities of democratic government. Others, like Stevens and Julian, urged that the national government endow the freedmen with the confiscated and abandoned lands of their former owners.[6] But with so many Republicans reluctant even to stand on the demand for black enfranchisement, radicals were forced to concentrate on that great, fundamental, minimum requirement, without which they believed Reconstruction would be but a sham. During the first session of the Thirty-ninth Congress, questions of education, confiscation, land reform, and territorialization remained in the background.

The radicals' attitude toward the president seemed to be mixed. They insisted that they desired no split with the chief executive, but they did not intend to let his conservatism sway them from their course. No letters or speeches exist to prove they wanted the president to break with the party; but they must have realized that so long as Republicans determined to conciliate the president, radical policies had slight chances of adoption. The final rupture could not have occasioned much grief.[7]

The conservatives and centrists, on the other hand, had every reason to believe that the president would cooperate with their program. They had rejected the two proposals calculated to antagonize him: black suffrage and a new reorganization of the southern states. It seemed inconceivable he should object to the constitutional amendments they had suggested—they seemed so eminently just and uncontroversial. Johnson himself had called for the protection of freedmen's rights in his annual message, and his commissioner of the Freedmen's Bureau had called for such legislation in his report to Congress. If they could secure such protection for freedmen and northern interests, the nonradicals would make no issue with the president over Negro suffrage. The radicals must acquiesce or bolt the party. The president, then, was in a strong position as the Thirty-ninth Congress met.[8]

It is extremely difficult to understand the processes through which Andrew Johnson arrived at his conclusions and formulated his policy, but it is patent that the president seriously misunderstood the nature of the differences within the Republican party. Johnson came to power two and a half months after the great struggle over the recognition of Louisiana, which pitted Lincoln and conservative and center Republicans against a handful of radicals. Those radicals had given two reasons for opposing the Republican majority: Louisiana had been reconstructed by military force rather than voluntary action, and black Louisianans were denied the vote. Observers agreed that black suffrage had been the key issue. Then, after Johnson promulgated his North Carolina proclamation, outlining the restoration process he instituted in the southern states, the radicals had attacked one element of that policy alone: he had restricted political power in the process to whites. During 1865, when conservative and moderate Republicans backed away from Negro suffrage, Johnson's closest Republican advisers informed him that this was a swing toward his policy. So by this time confidantes like Gideon Welles, Doolittle, and James Dixon began to identify opposition to the president's policy solely with Republicans of the Sumner-Stevens ilk and their advocacy of prolonged national control of the South and black enfranchisement.[9] As far as these Republicans, and probably the president, were concerned, the only opposition to Johnson's policy emanated from those who demanded black suffrage.

Therefore they seem completely to have misunderstood the reasons that conservatives and moderates changed their positions on immediate recognition during the fall of 1865. In the opinion of Johnson and his advisers, a Republican who opposed the speedy admission of loyal representatives from reconstructed states could only have one objection—the absence of black suffrage. This misunderstanding continued even after the Reconstruction committee proposed a constitutional amendment virtually conceding a state's right to discriminate against blacks in suffrage regulations. Witness the confusion and frustration of a pro-Johnson politician in Ohio: "I . . . found the whole game of the radicals was to misrepresent the issue, and deny that negro suffrage was the issue, which was at the *bottom* of their whole opposition of the President's plan. Why do not our friends in Congress compel them to tear off this mask and come plainly on the record?" [10] The reason was that the Republicans whom this observer called "radicals" (all who opposed the president) did *not* "bottom" their opposition to the president's plan on black suffrage. There was no mask to tear off.[11]

It is an open question whether the president's advisers really misunderstood the position of conservative and moderate Republicans or purposely misled him. There can be no doubt that the Democrats intentionally mislabeled all Republicans as "Radicals" for party purposes. But men like Doolittle, Morton, and Dixon should have known better. However, all three were involved in bitter factional struggles with rival Republicans who did indeed advocate black suffrage. Their oft-proclaimed support for the president was based at least in part on their desire to gain control of the patronage in their states. They may consciously have determined to pander to Johnson's prejudices and, by misrepresenting others, bind him more closely to themselves.[12] If so, they were indirectly aided by other Republicans. Surprisingly, and perhaps disastrously for nonradical Republicans in 1865–66, there is a nearly total lack of correspondence between moderate Republicans and the president during the critical months before the meeting of the Thirty-ninth Congress. One looks in vain for letters from Fessenden or Trumbull or Sherman or Grimes. Perhaps they believed that the president would learn the true situation easily enough by reading the Republican newspapers, which supported him and at the some time agreed that Congress should ultimately decide Reconstruction questions. If that is what these men believed, they were wrong. Johnson remained convinced that only radical Negro suffragists would seek to delay recognition of his restored governments. Alexander K. McClure, a Pennsylvania politician of conservative leanings, recalled that Johnson "was amazed when I expressed grave doubts about Congress recognizing his reconstructed authority in the States and admitting their Representatives to Congress." [13] The president was so confident of support that he did not insist that southern representatives be included by the clerk of the House of Representatives on the roll of the House before it organized, as claimants from recognized states customarily were. "It will be better policy to present their certificates after the two Houses are organized," he wrote an inquirer.[14] Johnson was convinced that Congress would quickly admit representatives from Tennessee at least, and thus set a precedent for the other states.[15]

Pro-Johnson newspapers insisted that the president conceded Congress's right to admit or not admit southern states to representation in Congress, and Johnson had not publicly contradicted these reports. But his refusal to incorporate Seward's distinct avowal of this policy in his annual message, unbeknown to Republicans in Congress, indicates his reservations. It seems reasonable to believe that he would have made no issue if Congress had acted speedily in admitting loyal representatives. When Republicans delayed, he would demonstrate that Republicans had misjudged his position as badly as he had misjudged theirs.

As the Thirty-ninth Congress opened, conservative and center Republicans quickly demonstrated that they could check the radicals. The first test of strength came over a resolution to create a joint committee on Reconstruction, to consist of nine representatives and six senators, to whom all pertinent documents and papers from either house of Congress would be referred without debate. By the resolution's terms no southern claimant could be admitted to a seat in the Senate or House until this committee reported its findings on conditions in the southern states. Originally authored by the conservative Dawes, who feared he might lose the chairmanship of the House Elections committee if it retained jurisdiction over admission of southern representatives, it was taken over by Thaddeus Stevens, who gained the approval of the House Republican caucus for it on December 2. The House passed it on December 4, with only one Republican in opposition.[16]

But in the Senate, several elements of the resolution inclined conservative and centrist Republicans to vote against it. First, the House passed the measure as a *joint* resolution, which required the signature of the president. Usually joint committees were created by *concurrent* resolution, which did not go to the president for approval. Although conservative Republican senators believed that the president would acquiesce in a congressional decision to delay admission of loyal representatives from his restored state governments, they feared he would refuse to take an active part in their exclusion by signing a joint resolution. They did not want to set the stage for an early veto and collision on Reconstruction matters. Moreover, the resolution in effect gave the House a veto over the action of the Senate, as the House contributed nine of the sixteen members of the committee and neither house could seat a southern claimant until the committee reported. Leading senators decided the measure must be modified. The conciliatory tone of the president's message reinforced their determination.

In a caucus of Senate Republicans December 11, conservatives and many centrists, led by Fessenden, Trumbull, Doolittle, Dixon, and Morgan, succeeded in amending the resolution over the opposition of Sumner, Chandler, Wilson, and Wade by a close 16-to-14 vote. Changing the measure to a *concurrent* resolution and eliminating the prohibition against seating southern claimants until the committee reported, senators agreed to pass a resolution simply creating a joint committee on Reconstruction. This passed the Senate with only three Republicans dissenting. In the House Stevens advised agreement to the Senate amendments, and the representatives acquiesced.[17]

As Speaker Colfax pondered his appointments to the joint committee, the lines between House factions became more definite. Henry J. Raymond, considered the administration spokesman in the House, presented the credentials of the representatives-elect from Tennessee and moved that they be referred to the joint committee when named. The House agreed, with only six Republicans voting in the negative, among them Dawes. Stevens then moved that the House allow the claimants to occupy seats on the floor. But the radicals objected, separating as they often would during this session of Congress from the man so many considered their leader. Center and radical Republicans joined to table a resolution that would have granted the claimants the privileges of the House as appearing "to have been elected by the people of Tennessee." They objected to the implication that this was an ordinary election case merely involving the credentials of claimants from a recognized state of the Union. But a resolution simply to seat the representatives-elect, without the offending language, passed over radical objections, with Stevens voting with the majority.[18] The Tennessee claimants were confident of quick admission. Observers reported a strong disposition among Republicans to recognize the restored government without requiring further conditions. Judging by the votes, radical opponents could muster the support of only one-third of their party.[19] Seward told visitors the House action made a breach with the president impossible. "Small favor this!" Sumner grumbled.[20]

The weakness of both the radical and the extreme conservative Republican position in the House was further demonstrated by the reaction to the first oratorical passage at arms between radical and conservative ideologists. Stevens expounded on his radical ideas for the first time during the session on December 18. Denying the authority of the president to reconstruct the dead states, he insisted that Congress should create territorial governments for them, allowing both blacks and whites to vote for territorial legislators and local officeholders under the supervision of Congress. But even as he spoke, the powerful radical acknowledged his isolation. "I trust the Republican party will not be alarmed at what I am saying," he said. "I do not profess to speak their sentiments, nor must they be held responsible for them. I speak for myself, and take the responsibility, and will settle with my intelligent constituents." [21]

Raymond enunciated the extreme conservative position December 21. He supported legislation to protect freedmen and constitutional amendments to alter the basis of representation in the House and guarantee the national debt; in general, he agreed to the entire nonradical program. But he denied that Congress could demand acquiescence in it from the reconstructed states *as a condition for restoration*. The United States government had a right to require guarantees from the defeated rebel states, but only on questions arising directly out of the war. The president had already demanded and received acquiesence in those conditions. They were the ratification of the Thirteenth Amendment, the repudiation of the secession ordinances, and the repudiation of the rebel debt. Congress could ask no more; there was no point, therefore, in delaying final restoration.[22] Republicans had assumed that if the president had acted on the "grasp of war" theory of Reconstuction—holding southern states under military government until they gave securities for the future—he would concede Congress the same right. Now Raymond had denied that proposition. It boded ill for the future.

Stevens's program was too radical. "No party, however strong, could stand a year on this platform," commented Forney's Washington *Chronicle*. It meant certain collision with the president and division of the party. Raymond's position was patently absurd. His distinctions as to what conditions the government could ask in return for peace were completely artificial. If the government could legitimately demand agreement to an abolition amendment to the Constitution as a necessary result of the war, why should a civil rights amendment to protect abolition be impermissible? If the president could require repudiation of the rebel debt in state constitutions as a legitimate result of the war, why could Congress not require the southern states to ratify the same provision in the national constitution? The entire argument was self-serving. Neither Raymond nor Stevens found much support.[23]

In the Senate too radicals displayed surprising weakness. When Republican senators had considered Stevens's proposed joint resolution in the privacy of the caucus, Sumner, Wade, and Chandler had criticized the president. But in open session only Sumner went on the attack. He labeled President Johnson's report on conditions in the South a "whitewash." He urged immediate passage of a bill by Henry Wilson to nullify the discriminatory laws regulating freedmen in the southern states, the "black codes." In a long speech the Massachusetts radical overwhelmed the Senate with evidence of white southerners' brutality toward the freedmen and their determination to institute a system of quasi-slavery. Sumner insisted that the Thirteenth Amendment had already been ratified without the action of the rebel states. They were out of the Union and should have no part in the ratification process.

But the senator received virtually no support. Trumbull and Sherman implicitly rejected his argument as to the ratification of the Thirteenth Amendment. Wilson, while urging passage of his bill, went out of his way to praise the president. After Sumner's speech, immediate passage of the bill would have signified Senate approval of his sentiments. Under Sherman's and Trumbull's prodding the Senate instead referred it to the Judiciary committee.[24] In the midst of the controversy, Sumner wrote the beautiful widow Alice Hooper—daughter of Representative Samuel Hooper—of his gloom and told her Fessenden was "cross & perverse." [25]

Radicals might praise Sumner's "whitewashing" speech ("Glorious— just the truth & just the time & place to speak it," Wendell Phillips wrote), but most Republicans determined to work for harmony and remained convinced that division was not inevitable.[26] To these Republicans speeches such as Sumner's and Stevens's constituted threats. These radicals were trying to manufacture issues on which to attack the President, complained David L. Phillips, an important southern Illinois politician. "There is no reason for it," he insisted. The pro-black-suffrage New York *Nation* termed Sumner's speech an "unseemly . . . outburst," making "slapdash charges." [27]

So while Sumner and most radicals grumbled, the moderate and conservative majority—and many radicals—continued to urge conciliation in private letters, newspapers, and official speeches. Of especial importance were the addresses delivered by Republican governors, nearly all of which were moderate in tone. Outgoing Massachusetts Governor Andrew took occasion to widen the growing gulf between himself and Sumner, abandoning black suffrage as an element of Reconstruction and outlining a program similar to that advocated by nonradicals. "It is well that Stevens and Sumner show their hands," Thurlow Weed wrote Morgan optimistically. "So far, the President gains strength with the People." [28]

With Republicans so clearly manifesting their desire for harmonious relations with the President, Speaker Colfax and the president *pro tempore* of the Senate, Lafayette S. Foster, chose the members of the joint committee carefully. Colfax announced the names of the House members December 14, after the meaningful votes on the privileges of the Tennessee representatives. The Speaker appointed two Democrats, Henry Grider and Andrew J. Rogers; one Republican who had voted with the conservatives to admit the Tennessee claimants as appearing "to have been elected by the people of Tennessee," Henry T. Blow; one Republican who had abstained on that vote, Roscoe Conkling; four who had voted only to seat the claimants without mentioning Tennessee—Stevens, John A. Bingham, Elihu B. Washburne, and Justin Morrill; and only one who had joined the radicals in opposing any seating, George S. Boutwell.

In the Senate, the most important contest was between Fessenden and Sumner for the chairmanship of the committee. The differences between the men were clear. Fessenden had openly avowed his conviction that the time for radical measures was over. He had suggested that he would "act upon different principles now and hereafter in a state of peace, from those which I adopted and defended before." [29] On December 21, Foster announced that Fessenden would chair the committee. To serve with him Foster appointed Fessenden's friend Grimes, who had been one of the few centrists publicly to oppose black suffrage before President Johnson made his opposition clear; Ira Harris, who the same day informed Gideon Welles that he agreed with the administration's views on Reconstruction; George H. Williams; Jacob M. Howard, the lone radical; and Reverdy Johnson, the most respected Democrat in the Senate. [30]

All in all, Fesseden wrote, the committee consisted "of a large majority of thorough men, who are resolved that ample security shall attend any restoration of the insurgent States, come what will—while they desire to avoid, if possible, a division between Congress and the Executive which would only result in unmixed evil." [31] Voting analysis shows that the committee consisted of three Democrats, two conservative Republicans, six centrists of varying degrees of radicalism, three radicals, and one Republican who did not vote regularly. The centrists would have control. [32]

But the president received advice from men bent on fomenting discord. Advisers like Dixon, Doolittle, and Welles lumped the conservatives and moderates, who insisted that formal recognition by Congress was necessary for readmission of southern states, together with the radicals, who were demanding black suffrage and a reorganization of the civil governments Johnson had instituted. Welles blindly viewed Sumner and Stevens as the Republican leaders. Instead of recognizing that centrists controlled congress, he believed they were "under the discipline of party, which is cunningly kept up with almost despotic power." [33] Welles, Doolittle, and Dixon joined in urging the president to admit the irreconcilability of his differences with the "radicals," who—as Welles, Doolittle, and Dixon defined them—made up virtually the entire party. Seward, Welles noted with disgust, deprecated the suggestion. [34]

As he received such advice, the president determined to increase the pressure for quick admission of the southern states. Seward had hoped that Johnson would maintain military control in the southern states until Congress recognized them. [35] But Johnson determined to follow a different course. On December 4, he ordered Seward to notify William W. Holden, the provisional governor of North Carolina, that he should now remit the control of local affairs "to the constitutional authorities chosen by the people" under their new constitution. [36] This should have served as a clear indication to Republicans of the president's intentions. It meant that political power in the rebel states would be turned over to Johnson's restored governments whether Congress admitted them to representation or not. And in mid-nineteenth-century America, state governments were far more active than the national government and affected citizens' lives far more intimately. The citizens of the United States were among the least governed in the world, but what government there was, was state government. The southern states might have to await congressional action for readmission into the national legislature, but in the meantime they would control the government that really counted—local government.

The *New York Times* quickly recognized the importance of the president's decision. "After all," it concluded, "we think Congress will find its action decided, if not forestalled, substantially by the course of events and the action of the President." Congress would never supplant the authorities recognized by the president. "It is possible for Congress to embarrass the President somewhat in acting upon this question, but it cannot defeat him." [37] As radicals, centrists, and conservatives maneuvered for position in Congress, Johnson terminated the activities of his provisional governors in Alabama, Georgia, North Carolina, and South Carolina. The *Times* observed confidently that it would take a law of Congress to alter the president's action, and that it would require a two-thirds majority to pass such a law over a veto. "Even if any conflict of opinion or of purpose, therefore, should exist or arise between the President and Congress on this subject, the President is clearly 'master of the situation.' " [38]

When Congress reconvened after the Christmas holiday, many recognized what the *Chicago Tribune*'s Washington correspondent called "the changed situation." A Congress that faced the "cautious non-committalism of the message," he wrote, "has now to confront an Executive pledged beyond hope of recall to the speediest possible restoration of the rebel States." [39]

In light of the president's new belligerence it is remarkable that Republican conservatives and moderates remained optimistic about prospects for harmony, but they did. They pointed out that the president had not revoked the authority of the Freedmen's Bureau, which continued to supervise and protect state citizens, and that national troops still kept the peace. If the president intended to restore the states to all their old rights, he could not have continued the exercise of such military authority within their boundaries.

Shortly after Congress convened, Fessenden, Washburne, and Reverdy Johnson visited the president on behalf of the Joint Committee on Reconstruction. They assured him that they desired to avoid all controversies, and asked him to suspend any future Reconstruction activities. Johnson responded "very well indeed," wrote Washburne; he left reassured that there would be no division. Most Republicans shared his belief.[40]

With the political situation muddled, the House of Representatives early in January turned its attention to the explosive issue of black suffrage in the District of Columbia. Since the Constitution gives Congress direct authority to govern the district, no constitutional objection based on state rights clouded the issue. In voting on the District suffrage bill, Republicans would declare their principles pure and simple.

On December 18, the House Judiciary committee had reported a bill to strike the word *white* from the district's voting qualifications. The bill was made the special order for January 10. During the intervening three weeks, resistance to it among Republicans had grown. Friends of the president and western Republicans, fearful of their constituents' reactions, urged its modification. After a day of debate on January 10, House Republicans caucused on the measure. Angry with the Judiciary committee for trying to prevent amendments, hesitant Republican representatives demanded that the bill be modified to allow a literacy test. The radicals resisted, arguing that such a test would effectively disfranchise most blacks. If extended to the South, enfranchisement on such a basis would provide virtually no security at all. The caucus appointed a special committee to revise the bill, but with differences so fundamental, Republicans could arrive at no compromise. As a confrontation neared in the House, both sides believed they had the votes to secure their versions of the bill.

The final test came on January 18. The Republicans who favored qualified suffrage—some of them radicals with anti-black-suffrage constituencies—moved to recommit the bill to the Judiciary committee with instructions to require a literacy test for all new voters except those who had served in the armed forces. Fifty-three Republicans favored the recommittal, but Democrats and anti-Negro-suffrage Republicans joined radicals to defeat it. The Democrats and anti-black-suffrage Republicans hoped in this way to kill the measure, but they had misjudged. The angry moderates joined radicals to pass the bill without any restrictions. Only sixteen Republicans dissented.[41]

Again more moderate Republicans expressed their irritation. The president had been prepared to sign the qualified black suffrage measure, Ben Perley Poore reported; the radicals and Democrats had spoiled that chance for harmony.[42] But in the Senate, the radical Committee on the District of Columbia prudently held the bill back pending further developments. So died the *only* radical legislation of the first session of the Thirty-ninth Congress.

Meanwhile the center Republicans busily formulated a Reconstruction program upon which both they and the president could stand. It was no easy task, Fessenden wrote. "In addition to all other difficulties, the work of keeping the peace between the President & those who wish to quarrel with him, aided as they are by those who wish him to quarrel with us, is a most difficult undertaking. The fools are not all dead, you know." [43] The centrists' work centered in two committees: Fessenden's Joint Committee on Reconstruction and Trumbull's Senate Judiciary committee. Between them they fashioned the conservative Reconstruction program of the Thirty-ninth Congress.

From the Judiciary committee came two bills that put the freedmen under national protection: the Freedmen's Bureau bill and the Civil Rights bill. Trumbull reported both bills from his committee January 12. Trumbull, John W. Forney wrote later, was "distinguished for his frequently manifested desire to sustain the President, and known for his opposition to some of Mr. Sumner's particular theories." [44] His opposition to black suffrage was well known. "The most sovereign remedy . . . since the days of Townsend's Sasparilla," he called it.[45] Newspapers taking a proadministration stance in January 1866 identified the conservative senator as an administration ally. Even the suspicious Welles had recognized as much.[46]

Trumbull authored the bills, he explained later, in light of the president's call for protection for the freedmen in his annual message and in response to the report of the Freedmen's Bureau commissioner. He hoped to separate the issue of protection for the blacks from restoration. Protect the blacks by national action, he believed, and black suffrage and well-disposed southern governments became less critical. "One great cause of apprehension on the part of the loyal men of the country would be removed, and I believe[d] the work of restoration would go on," Trumbull explained. Later, he told Welles that if the president had signed his bills, Tennessee, Louisiana, and Arkansas would have been recognized immediately. Trumbull visited Commissioner Oliver Otis Howard at the Freedmen's Bureau office to get his help in framing the bills. He visited the president several times and believed he had won his approval. There can be little doubt that he informed his colleagues of this, and that this information played a large part in the prevalent optimism among center and conservative Republicans.[47]

Trumbull's Freedmen's Bureau bill promised to be less controversial than his Civil Rights bill. The primary purpose of the Freedmen's Bureau bill was to extend the agency's life. The original legislation creating the bureau had specified that it could continue operations during the war and for one year thereafter. The new legislation allowed the bureau to continue indefinitely. Trumbull modified the original legislation in several other ways. His bill authorized the bureau to protect freedmen "in all parts of the United States," instead of limiting its jurisdiction to the states in rebellion. It authorized the president to set aside large tracts of the public lands in Florida, Mississippi, and Arkansas for the use of freedmen and "loyal refugees," and directed the commissioner to parcel these out in forty-acre tracts to be rented and then purchased by the bureau's wards. The bill authorized a national appropriation to fund the bureau instead of forcing it to rely entirely on private donations and income from abandoned lands as it had before. It extended military jurisdiction over freedmen in any state that discriminated against them in its laws, and protected them against involuntary servitude except for violation of laws.[48]

As peacetime legislation the bill would have been incredibly radical, but Republicans justified it under the war powers. The bureau would not be a permanent institution. Its necessity arose out of the direct results of the war; it would serve only to aid in the transition from slave to free labor in the South. Nonetheless, so important a senator as Fessenden had trouble determining its constitutionality. Only after private talks with Trumbull did Fessenden concede that legislation of this sort could be passed, as a necessity under the war powers of Congress.[49]

Trumbull's second measure, the Civil Rights bill, was a peacetime measure, to be passed by virtue of Congress's power under the second section of the Thirteenth Amendment to enforce emancipation by appropriate legislation. The bill, as originally presented, declared the inhabitants of every state and territory entitled to equal privileges and immunities. Specifically it mentioned the rights "to make and enforce contracts, to sue, be parties, and give evidence, to inherit, purchase, lease, sell, hold, and convey real and personal property, and to full and equal benefit of all laws and proceedings for the security of person and property, and . . . [to] be subject to like punishment, pains, and penalties, and to none other" irrespective of race, color, or previous condition of servitude. The proposed measure made it a crime for anyone to deny these rights under the cover of law. All violations of the bill were to be tried in United States district courts. Most important, any person who could not secure the rights guaranteed them under the bill in state or local courts could transfer his case to the United States district or circuit courts in his locality. Other sections outlined enforcement procedures.[50] When Trumbull brought the bill up again two weeks later, he moved an addition to the first section, declaring all persons of African descent born in the United States citizens.[51]

On its face the Civil Rights bill radically expanded national power. For the first time the national government accepted the responsibility for protecting the rights of its citizens. National courts might try cases of every description, civil and criminal, wherever state and local courts did not grant all citizens equal protection in the rights guaranteed by the bill. This broad, apparently radical bill was patently inconsistent with Trumbull's political conservatism on Reconstruction matters and his constitutional conservatism generally.[52] But in fact Trumbull had found a way to *preserve* rather than alter the old federal system.

Although theoretically Trumbull's bill vastly expanded the duties of the national government, in fact these new duties would not be permanent. Court jurisdiction was the key to the bill's real purpose. Jurisdiction would be taken from the state courts only so long as state law required them to discriminate in the rights guaranteed to all inhabitants by the first section of the bill. Once the states enforced these rights equally, there could be no removal of jurisdiction from state to national courts. Thus there would be great pressure on states to change their laws to give equal rights to blacks in order to regain their old spheres of jurisdiction. There would be no point in resisting: retain unequal law and blacks would simply take their cases into the federal courts.

It was a brilliant piece of legislation. Trumbull had found a way to force the states themselves to alter their discriminatory laws. Once they did so, they would regain jurisdiction over all their citizens, and the balance of power between the state and national governments would remain unchanged. Trumbull emphasized this in his defense of the measure:

[The bill] may be assailed as drawing to the Federal Government powers that properly belong to "States"; but I apprehend, rightly considered, it is not obnoxious to that objection. It will have no operation in any State where the laws are equal, where all persons have the same civil rights without regard to color or race.[53]

Trumbull's measures won immediate approval from the proadministration press and congressmen. Doolittle, one of the president's leading defenders in the Senate and an ultraconservative, had himself prepared a Freedmen's Bureau bill similar to Trumbull's.[54] The Wisconsin conservative now supported Trumbull's measure. Observers predicted the bills, along with a constitutional amendment to change the basis of representation, would be the basis for harmonious action by the president and Congress.[55] But radicals were only lukewarm. "The measure itself was not particularly acceptable to the radicals," Forney wrote, "but was accepted by them as an expedient, preparatory to the adoption of a more drastic and permanent system." [56]

The Freedmen's Bureau bill sped through the Senate with virtually no Republican opposition, passing January 25. Not one Republican voted against the bill on its passage. Two did not vote. One of them, Cowan, had signified his opposition on earlier roll calls.[57]

In the House the bill came under attack not only from Democrats but radicals. Ignatius Donnelly urged the House to adopt an amendment requiring the bureau commissioner to provide free education to all black children. Only education would eradicate the effects of slavery. Congress's decision on this question would be "the great test, . . . the crucial test, of our institutions and the popular judgment." [58]

Stevens emphasized the necessity of providing land for the freedmen. During the war ex-slaves had been allowed to work the land of their former owners in the Sea Islands of South Carolina and Florida. General Sherman had confirmed the blacks' titles to the land by a general field order, but President Johnson had begun returning it to former owners. Trumbull had confirmed the blacks' possession of the land for only three years in his Freedmen's Bureau bill. Sumner had objected, but the Senate overwhelmingly approved the provision. Stevens now moved to strike the three-year limitation. The bill also authorized the president and the commissioner to lease or sell small homesteads to blacks from the public lands; Stevens moved to add to this the lands confiscated from rebels and limit the rent to two cents per acre per year. Finally he added Donnelly's education amendment to his own amendments.

Stevens bitterly attacked the landholding provisions of the Trumbull bill. Under it the poverty-stricken freedmen would have to rent the public land at the same fee all men had rented them for before the war. And the only public lands available were everglades, Stevens insisted. (He was wrong.) "What boon is that to a freedman?" he asked. The Trumbull bill recognized the power of the president to restore seized land to rebels by his pardon. The freedmen had built villages and schoolhouses and churches on those lands. And they "now receive notice to turn out, and reeking rebels are to be brought back and take their places, under the pretense that a pardon can restore to them lands which belonged to us and which we have given to these freedmen. God forbid that I should ever vote for such a bill as that." Even the emperor of Russia gave land to the serfs when he freed them. "But, by this bill, we propose to sell our land at not less than the Government price, or to rent it at prices which these poor people can never pay."

But Stevens pleaded in vain. His amendment received only thirty-seven votes. Thirty-one Democrats and ninety-five Republicans defeated it. Seven more abstained. On its passage, only two Unionists voted against the Freedmen's Bureau bill. The president's staunchest friends signified their approval.[59]

As soon as the Senate had passed the Freedmen's Bureau bill, it had taken up Trumbull's Civil Rights bill. With as much alacrity as possible in a body with no limitations on debate, this bill too passed the Senate. The final vote came on February 2, with only three Republicans dissenting. The president's "special friends," Dixon and Doolittle, favored the bill throughout.[60] The House referred the bill to its Judiciary committee, where it remained as the representatives concentrated on appropriations bills.

With action on Trumbull's bills concluded, the Senate turned its attention to the third element of the centrist program—a constitutional amendment to alter the basis of state representation in Congress. This proposed amendment had been hammered out with difficulty by the Reconstruction committee and passed by the House after a tough fight. When Stevens, as senior House member of the committee, reported it to that branch of Congress, the measure had read:

Representatives and direct taxes shall be apportioned among the several States . . . according to their respective numbers, counting the whole number of citizens of the United States in each State, excluding Indians not taxed: *Provided* that, whenever the elective franchise shall be denied or abridged in any State on account of race, creed or color, all persons of such race, creed or color shall be excluded from the basis of representation.[61]

The committee had proposed the amendment in this form rather than merely basing representation on voters, because under the alternative form New England, with proportionately more women than the western states, would have lost representation.

The Reconstruction committee's proposed constitutional amendment had met a hail of Republican criticism in the House. Kelley and other radicals had immediately announced their opposition. Many western Republicans had demanded that representation be apportioned according to the number of voters in each state. Despite Stevens's determination to force the amendment through the House the same day that he reported it, the representatives had debated the proposition for six days. Democrats insisted that the Constitution was being too much amended; western Republicans complained that the committee had framed the measure to please New England; radicals worried that the amendment in effect recognized the states' right to discriminate in voting on the basis of color. By January 30 all knew that the proposal could not win the two-thirds vote needed to pass a constitutional amendment. The House had recommitted the measure to the Reconstruction committee.

But on the same day, Washington newspapers reported an interview between the president and Senator Dixon. The president had denounced black suffrage and complained of the number of constitutional amendments pending in Congress. He had opposed any more amendments but affirmed that if one had to be passed it should base representation on voters. Furious, Stevens had reported the constitutional amendment back to the House. The House had agreed to vote immediately. An amalgam of radicals and western Republicans failed in an attempt to modify the amendment to base representation on voters, and then the House passed the original amendment—less the taxation provision—by a vote of 120 to 46. Only two radicals had withstood the party's pressure. They had been joined by the Democrats and only ten conservative Republicans.[62] But to radicals outside Congress the centrist program was betrayal. "We are now . . . invited to cement the Union with the blood of the negro," Moncure Conway wrote.[63]

Fessenden took the responsibility of steering the apportionment amendment through the Senate. It would be no easy job, he wrote. "Mr. Sumner says he shall put his foot on it and crush." [64] Many radicals would rise in the Senate to oppose the amendment or espouse black suffrage. Sumner would have the public support of Tilton's *Independent* and black lobbyists, led by Frederick Douglass and George T. Downing; he would have the private support of numerous important radicals like Schurz, Gerritt Smith, William Lloyd Garrison, George Bailey Loring, Parker

Pillsbury, and Wendell Phillips. But in essence the battle over the proposed constitutional amendment was fought by two men, the great titans of the Senate, Sumner and Fessenden, in a bitter, personal contest. In the Senate Sumner stood virtually alone. "You are the keystone of our arch," Smith wrote him later. "If you fail all falls." [65]

Fessenden and Sumner each spoke twice on the apportionment amendment. Sumner opened the debate February 5 and 6. Fessenden followed the next day. Sumner spoke again March 7, and Fessenden closed the debate March 9. Numerous other senators joined the discussions: Henderson, who offered an enfranchising amendment, Wilson, Henry S. Lane— but the nation concentrated on the two giants. They debated not just the amendment but two different approaches to politics, two different approaches to political morality.

Speaking on February 5 and 6, Sumner proposed an alternative to the committee measure. He suggested a simple act of Congress to guarantee republican forms of government in the states and to enforce the constitutional amendment prohibiting slavery: "That there shall be no Oligarchy, Aristocracy, Caste, or Monopoly invested with peculiar privileges and powers, and there shall be no denial of rights, civil or political, on account of color or race anywhere within the limits of the United States or the jurisdiction thereof." [66] Sumner found four justifications for such legislation—necessity, the power of Congress over areas under United States jurisdiction where no legal governments exist, the right under the laws of war to demand conditions from defeated enemies, and Congress's power to guarantee republican forms of government in the states. Sumner devoted most of his attention to the last source of power. Under it, he argued, Congress had a duty to provide the southern states with republican governments. In defining republican government, Sumner turned to the principles espoused by the American revolutionaries before and during the Revolution, the public acts of the states, and the precedents of Republican France.

Universal suffrage, Sumner insisted, was a right subject only "to such regulations as the safety of society may require." These included qualifications of age, character, registration, and residence. Conspicuously absent from his list were property and educational requirements. The ballot would be a peacemaker, forcing former masters to respect erstwhile slaves. The ballot would encourage reconciliation between black and white, forcing each to treat the other with respect. It would educate black men to responsibilities of free manhood. Most important, the right of suffrage would protect the freedmen, obviating the dangers which were impelling Republicans to seek guarantees for their security. "When the master knows that he may be voted down, he will know that he must be just." [67]

But Sumner best illustrated his temperament, the temperament of the radical in politics, in his denunciation of the committee amendment. It was "nothing else than another Compromise of Human Rights, as if the country had not already paid enough in costly treasure and more costly blood for such compromises in the past." [68] He expanded on this in his second speech, with some of the most brilliant and bitter invective ever delivered in Congress.

The present Compromise, like all other compromises, has two sides; in other words, it is a concession for a consideration. On one side it is conceded that the States may, under the Constitution, exclude citizens counted by the million from the body-politic and practice the tyranny of taxation without representation, provided, on the other side, that there is a corresponding diminution of representative power in the lower House of Congress . . . .

It was, said Sumner, "the most utterly reprehensible and unpardonable" proposition ever set before Congress.

The attempt now is on a larger scale and is more essentially bad than the Crime against Kansas or the Fugitive Slave Bill. Such a measure, so obnoxious to every argument of reason, justice, and feeling, so perilous to the national peace and to the good name of the Republic, must be encountered as we encounter a public enemy. . . .

Adopt it, and you will put millions of fellow-citizens under the ban of excommunication; you will hand them over to a new anathema maranatha; you will declare that they have no political rights which white men are bound to respect . . . . Adopt it, and you will stimulate anew the war of race upon race. . . . The proposition is as hardy as it is gigantic; for it takes no account of the moral sense of mankind, which is the same as if in rearing a monument we took no account of the law of gravitation. It is the paragon and master-piece of ingratitude, showing more than any other act of history what is so often charged and we so fondly deny, that republics are ungrateful. The freedmen ask for bread, and you send them a stone. With piteous voice they ask for protection. You thrust them back unprotected into the cruel den of their former masters. . . . Adopt it, and you will cover the country with dishonor. Adopt it, and you will fix a stigma upon the very name of Republic. . . . As to the imagination there are mountains of light, so are there mountains of darkness; and this is one of them. It is the very Koh-i-noor of blackness. [69]

At least, Sumner urged, change the proposed amendment to base representation on the number of voters alone. This would not incorporate into the Constitution itself the right to discriminate in voting qualifications. Henderson proposed a constitutional amendment to prohibit discrimination in voting rights on account of race or color. (Eventually, this would become the Fifteenth Amendment to the Constitution.) Other senators endorsed it.

If Sumner displayed the uncompromising devotion to absolute justice that characterized radicalism, Fessenden demonstrated the devotion to practicality that characterized its Republican opponents. He too favored black suffrage, Fessenden confessed, though not as immediately and unqualifiedly as did Sumner. Suffrage was not a right but a trust. Nonetheless, it "should be extended just as fast and as far as the public good will allow."

"But," Fessenden continued, "the argument that addressed itself to the committee was, what can be accomplished? What can pass?" If the committee reported a constitutional amendment enfranchising blacks, "is there the slightest probability that it will be adopted by the States . . . ? It is perfectly evident that there would be no hope." The votes in Wisconsin and Connecticut the previous fall had shown that. "We must take men as we find them." If Republicans could not win a constitutional amendment to give blacks the vote, they must do something else. Aiming his shaft directly at Sumner, Fessenden averred, "I do not think it my duty as a legislator in this Hall to trouble myself much about what are called abstractions. My constituents did not send me here to philosophize. They sent me here to act . . . . I speak to those who are willing to do something." [70]

Of the two practical alternatives—the committee's amendment or the amendment Sumner desired, simply to base representation on the number of voters in each state—Fessenden favored the first. Sumner's alternative would be unfair to the eastern states; it might encourage a race among the states to enfranchise more people—aliens, women, children—in order to gain representation; and it would encourage southern and border states to enfranchise rebels. Besides, Fessenden sighed, despite Sumner's pretensions, there really was no difference in principle between the two alternatives. Each recognized the states' right to determine voting qualifications. Sumner was splitting hairs. The committee bill was no compromise. It punished discrimination; it did not sanction it.

What lawyer in the world ever heard that a denial is an admission? What lawyer ever heard that a penalty is permission? By this proposition we say simply this: "If in the exercise of the power that you have under the Constitution you make an inequality of rights, then you are to suffer such and such consequences." What sane man could ever pretend that that was saying, "Make an inequality of rights and we will sanction it?" [71]

But in his very example, Fessenden had conceded what Sumner was so desperately trying to deny—that the states had the absolute right to discriminate in their voting regulations.

Sumner answered wearily,

There is a familiar story of a shield with inscriptions on it which was suspended in a highway. Two travelers approached it from opposite quarters, and standing face to face, each read the inscription as he saw it. Straightway there was a difference and a contest. Each insisted that the inscription was as he read it. At last on looking at both sides it was ascertained that each was right, as the inscriptions on the two sides were different. So it is on the present occasion. The Senator from Maine, as he approaches it, sees only the side which limits the representation. As I approach it I see the recognition of a caste and the disfranchisement of a race. He defends it; I condemn it. But he defends only what he sees. I condemn only what I see. It is the misfortune of the measure that it has two sides with two opposite inscriptions. [72]

As the Senate approached a vote on the controversial amendment, the president precipitated a change in all political calculations. Congress had sent Trumbull's Freedmen's Bureau bill to the president on February 13. Earlier Republicans had been certain that Johnson intended to sign it. They had looked forward eagerly to Democratic reaction, predicting that the president's approval would put an end to the Democratic courtship.[73] But by early February many were more uncertain. The president had denounced black suffrage in such uncompromising, inflammatory terms to the delegation of black lobbyists that had visited him that Count Adam Gurowski told friends that "he felt ashamed of belonging to the white race." [74] Poore and David W. Bartlett, another leading Washington correspondent, predicted an open rupture. Garfield, still striving for harmony, acknowledged that if Johnson went much further, "We shall make the open issue and abide the results." [75]

Many conservatives and moderates blamed the radicals for the disintegrating situation. Fessenden complained of Sumner, "with his impracticable notions, his vanity, his hatred of the President, coupled with his power over public opinion."

"There are a few who are determined to have a quarrel with the President," Dawes wrote grimly, "and he is not disposed to disappoint them." [76]

In fact, the president had already on February 13 intimated to Welles his intention of vetoing the Freedmen's Bureau bill, just before he officially received it. He confided his apprehension that the radicals meant to depose him by declaring Tennessee out of the Union and then to administer the government through a central directory (he probably meant the Reconstruction committee). Nothing could better demonstrate how out of touch Johnson was with the reality of Republican politics. Recognizing the president's drift, Seward tried desperately to persuade him to cooperate with the party; he "greatly embarrassed" Johnson, Welles wrote, with his advice of "compromise and concession." [77]

Johnson turned to his advisers for aid in preparing a veto message. Again Seward wrote a conciliatory draft, avowing the responsibility of the national government to protect the freedmen but questioning the necessity of the specific legislation. Extolling the bureau's usefulness, Seward argued in his draft that technically the war was not yet over and reminded Congress that the bureau would run for one year *after* the formal proclamation of peace. Seward's message assured Congress that the president would sign a bill to extend the bureau's life if it proved necessary.[78]

By February 17, Republicans knew the president intended to veto the bill, but they hoped that he would approve its principles if not its specific terms—they hoped for a veto like the one Seward had prepared. Instead, the president chose to send in broad objections. His message, sent to Congress February 19, denied Congress's power to pass any such bill in peacetime. More ominous yet, Johnson questioned whether peace had not yet arrived. He indicated that he would approve no such legislation unless Congress admitted loyal representatives from the southern states.[79]

As the Boston *Daily Advertiser* observed, "Mr. Johnson, had he chosen, could have so vetoed that measure as to cause hardly a ripple on the surface of affairs." Instead he had argued that the rebellion was at an end and Congress was derelict in not admitting the southern state representatives. "These points . . . are the special features which give sorrow to those who have heretofore been his supporters," wrote the *Advertiser*'s Washington correspondent.[80]

The next evening, Johnson responded to a Washington's Birthday serenade offered by enthusiastic supporters. His pugnacity aroused, the president lashed the radicals as disunionists, naming not only Stevens and Sumner but John W. Forney, secretary of the Senate, whose two newspapers, the Philadelphia *Press* and the Washington *Daily Morning Chronicle,* had supported him until the veto. Disillusioned by both the veto and Johnson's speech, most of the newspapers that had supported him began to criticize his course.[81]

To Republican conservatives and centrists, the president's veto bordered on betrayal. He had said in his annual message that the freedmen must be protected. In private conversations and published interviews he had announced his determination to cooperate with the Republican party. He had indicated to Trumbull, and possibly others, his approval of Trumbull's bills. But most important of all, he had seemed to be acting on the same assumptions as the nonradical Republican majority. Both had recognized a constructive state of war. As Trumbull urged the Senate to pass the Freedmen's Bureau bill over the veto, he cited instance after instance in which the president had interfered with southern state institutions through the military. Military courts in the South tried civilians; they prohibited the publication of rebellious sentiments in southern newspapers; the privilege of the writ of habeas corpus was still suspended throughout the South. Where was the authority for all this if the war was over? [82]

Fessenden pointed to the disparity between the president's sentiments in his annual message and in the veto. In the annual message he had recognized Congress's absolute right to determine for itself whether to admit southern representatives; in his veto he denied that right. He had demanded conditions of the southerners before he would recognize them. "He undertook to tell them that he would have nothing to do with their governments unless they made specific provisions in their new constitutions. . . . If he had the right to do it, have we not? If he could impose conditions with reference to what he would do, have we not the power to impose conditions with reference to what we are called upon to do?" [83]

The Republicans had abandoned black suffrage to please the president. They had been willing eventually to recognize governments restored under his authority, dominated as they were by former Confederates. They had passed legislation they knew to be acceptable to him and had held back that which would have been disagreeable. They were rewarded by the veto of their first Reconstruction legislation and denial of their jurisdiction.

Since 1864, Congress had proceeded upon the conviction that the political departments of the government must recognize the restoration of the rebel states concurrently, that is through an act of Congress requiring the president's signature. This had been the basis for the Wade-Davis bill. With this understanding the Senate Judiciary committee had pressed its joint resolution recognizing Louisiana in early 1865. The joint resolution creating the Reconstruction committee and forbidding the seating of claimants until it reported and carried a restoration resolution was grounded on the same idea. Although the Senate had refused to concur in the prohibition, fearing it might alienate the president and encourage radicalism in the House, they had not discarded the principle. By arguing that each house of Congress was obligated to admit loyal representatives from state governments created and recognized by presidential authority alone, President Johnson was challenging the established congressional position.

The Reconstruction committee decided to clarify it, proposing a concurrent resolution to both houses declaring that "no senator or representative shall be admitted into either branch of Congress from any of said states until Congress shall have declared such state entitled to representation." [84] The House passed the resolution February 20, with only seven Unionists in opposition. Eleven more conservatives had absented themselves. The House defeated a motion to reconsider the vote the next day. Three of the conservatives not voting the day before joined the minority; three more voted with the majority.[85] In all, only ten Unionists sustained the presidential position.

Fessenden managed the resolution in the Senate. He assured his colleagues that the resolution did not deny the *right* of each house of Congress to proceed separately in admitting southern claimants; it merely declared the opinion of the Senate that the houses should act concurrently. He himself would join in admitting southern senators if the House delayed action unreasonably. With such assurances from its leader, the Senate agreed to the resolution by a vote of 29 to 18. Eight Republicans voted with the minority.[86]

Although the Republicans were angry, not all despaired of bringing the president to his senses. "The only way to prevent his going over," Timothy Otis Howe wrote, "is to convince him he must go alone. He now thinks the crowd is going with him"—in practical terms, that meant they had to pass the Freedmen's Bureau bill over the veto.[87] But on the vote, eight Republicans joined the Democrats to sustain the president. The vote was 30 to 18, two short of the two-thirds majority that the Republicans needed. One more Republican joined the conservative minority six days later.[88] In the House, Republicans determined to pass several test resolutions to clarify representatives' positions on the issues of Reconstruction. Here Republican ranks held firmly; no more than ten Unionists voted against any of them, with perhaps ten more abstaining.[89]

In the House Republicans commanded a solid two-thirds majority. In the Senate they were two or three votes short. The situation would be touch and go. Outside Congress the same uncertainty prevailed. In the Indiana state Republican convention, held February 23, conservatives and radicals fought to a standstill. The convention passed a resolution endorsing both Congress and the president.[90] In New York City, Johnson supporters organized a large rally, attended by Seward, Morgan, Weed, William M. Evarts, Hamilton Fish, and other members of the Seward-Weed faction of the Republican party, and War Democrats such as Daniel S. Dickinson, David Dudley Field, and William Cullen Bryant. The *Times, Evening Post,* and *Herald* lent Johnson their support.[91] In Massachusetts, Andrew exerted his influence to delay resolutions supporting Congress in the state legislature. Montgomery Blair was so impressed with Andrew's position that he urged the ex-governor to take the leadership of proadministration forces in New England, but Andrew declined, urging forbearance instead.[92]

But the Republican split threatened the greatest damage in Ohio, always a swing state. There Governor Jacob D. Cox openly sustained the president, joined by, among others, Rush R. Sloan, John Sherman's campaign manager. It was natural, therefore, for Ohio Republicans to lead efforts to effect a reconciliation between the president and the party. Sherman led the movement with a long, prepared speech on February 26, in which he defended the president's motives and intentions, arguing that Johnson was justified in adopting a presidential Reconstruction policy when Congress had through its own dereliction failed to pass one of its own. The president, Sherman pointed out, had incorporated into his program nearly all the features of the Wade-Davis bill. Moreover, he had insisted that the southern states meet certain conditions before he would remit them to local self-government. Sherman defended Johnson's decision not to enfranchise blacks, pointing out that nearly all the northern states made the same discrimination and that Congress had not yet enfranchised black men in the District of Columbia.

Pointing to the resolutions passed by the Indiana Union convention and other by the Ohio state legislature, Sherman urged, "The people of the United States now demand of us wisdom and moderation. This is not the time for extreme counsels. It is not the time to attempt great reforms and works." Poore reported that Sherman's effort made a strong impression on the Senate.[93]

The same day that newspapers reported Sherman's speech, they published a letter from Governor Cox to the chairman of the Ohio Union party central committee. Cox wrote that he had seen the president and was convinced that no split need occur. Johnson wished to cooperate with the Union party. He wanted military government in the South to cease as soon as possible, fearing its effect on the nation, but he would admit into Congress only representatives who had been completely loyal throughout the war. Most important, the president assured Cox that he would endorse purely civil legislation to protect the freedmen, implying approval of the Civil Rights bill. That evening Cox visited Welles, Postmaster Dennison, and Doolittle. Welles clearly believed him an ally.[94]

By late February and early March, Republicans spoke hopefully of "better signs." Conservative Massachusetts Representative John D. Baldwin, Representative Leonard Myers of Pennsylvania, and Grimes assured Welles that radicals were losing influence. Welles recorded that Grimes "guessed we were nearer now than some apprehended. This he said with a smile and manner that impressed me as coming from one who thinks his associates have the reins in their hands and intend to guide the government car safely." [95]

Grimes was confident, no doubt, because he knew that the Reconstruction committee had decided to demonstrate Republicans' desire for harmony to the president by recognizing Tennessee's restoration to normal relations with the United States. The Reconstruction committee had been debating the form of such a resolution since February 15. Significantly, Grimes had chaired the conservative subcommittee that decided Tennessee was ready for admission.[96] On February 20 the Joint Committee had rejected by a 5-to-6 vote Boutwell's motion to require the state to grant impartial suffrage without regard to race—Howard, Stevens, Washburne, Morrill, and Boutwell in favor and Harris, Williams, Bingham, Conkling, Grider, and Rogers opposed. Fessenden had abstained. On March 5 the committee voted to report a resolution recognizing Tennessee, with the fundamental conditions that it maintain for five years the provisions of its constitution disfranchising former rebels and never pay the debt incurred during the rebellion or compensate former slaveowners for the loss of their slave property. With these conditions, the committee voted to report the resolution over the objections of the Democrats and Washburne and Boutwell, who alone held out for the imposition of black suffrage.

Radicals were disgusted. They had hoped that once the president's hostility to even a mild congressional Reconstruction program became clear, Republicans would ease their opposition to black suffrage and relax pressure for recognition of southern states without it. The conservative and centrist majority on the committee, complained the radical Washington correspondent of the *Chicago Tribune* "have furnished the insidious organizer at the White House an entering wedge, that will enable him, sooner or later, to enlarge the split already made in the body of the Union party to a disintegrating extent. Adopted or not it will . . . prove the point upon which the faithless political Archimedes will rest his lever to lift the congressional opposition to his usurpation from the ground it has heretofore held so firmly." [97]

Instead of allowing the party to move to the left, Johnson's apparent desertion had forced it to the right. In the House a second proposition from the Reconstruction committee—a constitutional amendment giving Congress power to guarantee all citizens of the United States equal protection in life, liberty, and property—met strong opposition. Its supporters were forced to agree to postpone its consideration to mid-April.[98] The Civil Rights bill met a similar reception when reported from the House Judiciary committee. A coalition of Democrats and conservative and centrist Republicans led by Bingham forced the bill's recommittal on March 9.[99]

On the same day the Senate finally voted on the proposed apportionment amendment. Here too Johnson had forced a shift toward conservatism. Men who openly had espoused black suffrage now opposed Henderson's proposition to prohibit racial discrimination in voting regulations. The Senate defeated his amendment to substitute this for the committee measure by a vote of 37 to 10. Other black suffrage proposals garnered still less support.[100] Party pressure upon radicals to support the committee proposal grew. Stevens and Chase urged Sumner to cease his opposition. Stevens hoped, he wrote Sumner, "that if we are to be slain it will not be by accident." But as some who might have opposed the amendment out of radicalism swung to its support as a result of Johnson's course, conservatives who would have supported it earlier now joined the opposition. On the final roll call the proposed constitutional amendment received only twenty-five votes. A coalition of five holdouts for black suffrage, eight Johnson-supporting conservatives, and nine Democrats prevented its passage.[101]

Republicans were furious. The constitutional amendment had "been slaughtered by a puerile and pedantic criticism," Stevens fumed, " . . . by the united forces of self-righteous Republicans and unrighteous Republicans." Fessenden wrote bitterly of "Sumner's folly and wickedness." He scorned Sumner's professions that his course was dictated by principle. "The only ground of his opposition was mortified vanity," Fessenden insisted. "He was not made chairman of the Reconstruction Committee." [102]

The Republican situation was critical. Every radical and centrist Reconstruction measure had been defeated. Congress had no policy at all. The *Chicago Tribune* correspondent wrote:

Nothing has been gained but further evidence of the great, apparently increasing diversity of opinion among the members of the majority. . . . Indeed the fatality of disagreement, that has been hanging over the majority ever since the opening of the session, preventing all substantial legislative achievements . . . threatens to become a chronic, insuperable obstacle to the success of Congress in conflict with the President.

"The President has gone over to the enemy," Washburne wrote home gloomily, "and our friends are all split up among themselves." [103]

EIGHT

Conservative Reconstruction— Part Two

$\leftarrow\leftarrow\leftarrow\leftarrow\leftarrow\leftarrow\leftarrow$

UNWILLING to endorse the president's policy without modification, unable to unite on an alternative, congressional Republicans recognized that they stood at the edge of political catastrophe. "Our great victory I fear has turned to ashes," Chicago congressman John Wentworth wrote home in despair.[1]

With pressure intense to do *something,* the House Judiciary committee reported the Civil Rights bill back to the floor only four days after it had been recommitted, with only minor changes. In its most important amendment, the committee proposed to eliminate from the bill the general provision barring discrimination in civil rights and immunities. Primarily designed to reassure congressmen that the bill could not be construed to enfranchise blacks, the amendment limited the rights black men could claim under the law to those specifically listed. Then, to meet the constitutional objections of conservative Republicans, the committee incorporated a provision specifically inviting the statute's appeal before the Supreme Court.

Over Bingham's continued objections that the bill could find no warrant in the Constitution, Judiciary committee chairman Wilson rammed it through the House. At last Republicans of all stripes united. Forty-three Republicans who had voted to recommit the bill four days earlier now voted to pass it, including three who agreed with the president's views on restoration. Only five Republicans joined Bingham in dissent. The Senate agreed to the House amendments with the barest of opposition. On the one roll call vote demanded by Senate Democrats, the Republicans were unanimous, including even those who had sustained the veto of the Freedmen's Bureau bill.[2]

Republicans anxiously awaited the president's reaction. They had high hopes. After all, Johnson had indicated to Trumbull that he approved the

Civil Rights bill. He had told Ohio Governor Cox that he favored protection of freedmen's rights by a civil rather than military process (see p. 159 above). The president's leading supporters in the Senate had voted for the legislation. Moreover, the Reconstruction committee had indicated its willingness to recognize Tennessee's restoration to the Union as a peace offering. According to Welles's *Diary,* Republican conservatives and centrists bombarded him with hints and suggestions for accommodation (see p. 159 above). It is likely that other cabinet members were approached in the same way.

Cabinet members too desired a reconciliation. McCulloch urged Senator Henry Wilson to arrange a conference between congressmen and loyal southern conservatives like Alabama's provisional governor, Lewis Parsons. Postmaster Dennison tried to persuade Welles to accompany himself and McCulloch on a visit to the president to work out some means to preserve harmony.[3] In Congress a desire for harmony seemed to prevail among Johnson's adherents. Not only did they endorse the Civil Rights bill, but Doolittle, Kansas's Senator Lane, and William M. Stewart, all Johnson supporters, attended a Republican caucus called in an effort to unite on a new constitutional amendment.[4]

By March 17, Sherman told Republicans that he believed that Johnson would sign the Civil Rights bill. Newspapermen learned that senators "likely to be advised" agreed.[5] But an editorial in the *National Intelligencer* of March 21, now believed to reflect the thinking of the administration, signaled that Republican hopes had been misplaced. By March 25 nearly all Republicans realized that Johnson would veto the bill. Once again the question became how far he would go. Would he merely object to some of the enforcement provision. or would he again question Congress's jurisdiction and oppose any national protection of the freedmen's civil rights? [6]

Although the president had retained a fair amount of Republican support after his Freedmen's Bureau bill veto, it soon became clear that reaction would be different if he disapproved the Civil Rights bill as well. From Ohio Sherman learned,

The general feeling here & all over the country is much more united in sustaining the action of Congress than it was soon after the [Freedmen's Bureau bill] veto message. . . . We all feel that the most *important interests* are at stake. We are ready to do anything for harmony in the Union party that will not lead to a sacrifice of right or endanger our safety as a people. If the President vetoes the Civil Rights bill, I believe we shall be obliged to draw our swords for a fight and throw away the scabbard.[7]

With public opinion strongly in favor of the bill, Johnson's supporters began to grow uneasy. Governor Cox and Indiana's ex-Governor Morton urged the president to sign it. In the cabinet, Stanton and Dennison offered the same advice. McCulloch and Harlan, more tentative, told Johnson they hoped he could endorse it. Seward opposed the enforcement provisions but urged approval of some measure declaring black men citizens. Only Welles remained in adamant opposition.[8] But Johnson determined to veto the bill despite his friends' apprehensions. Learning of this, Doolittle prepared a new civil rights bill, which he hoped would overcome the president's objections. Probably hoping that Johnson's veto message would endorse the principle of protecting freedmen's civil rights, objecting only to specific provisions in Trumbull's bill, Doolittle intended to propose his measure in the Senate, perhaps drawing off enough votes from the majority to sustain the veto. Thus he might force Republicans to unite in favor of his measure. But Welles objected to Doolittle's proposition on the same grounds as Trumbull's, a bad omen.[9]

Once more Johnson turned to his friends to help frame a veto message. For the last time Seward tried to moderate Johnson's opinions to preserve the possibility of Republican harmony. In his draft, Seward elaborately defended Congress's constitutional power to legislate in protection of the freedmen's civil rights, objecting only to specific provisions of the bill. He virtually asked Congress to modify the bill and resubmit it. As Johnson prepared his message, Seward scrawled a hasty note appealing to the President "to intimate that *you are not opposed to the policy of the bill but only to its detailed provisions.*"[10] It was to no avail. The president sent in a broad, uncompromising veto the same day.

"In all our history, in all our experience as a people living under the Federal and State law, no such system as that contemplated by the details of this bill has ever before been proposed or adopted," Johnson objected. His constitutional objections to the bill were so fundamental that he seemed to leave no room for national legislation to protect civil rights.[11] Still, a few Senate conservatives and centrists wished to make absolutely certain, and on April 3, Morgan and Fessenden visited the president in an effort to agree upon a compromise bill. But Johnson adamantly opposed any legislation by Congress to declare black men citizens, and the effort collapsed. Morgan, who had sustained the president up to this time, told his allies in the Seward-Weed faction that he would vote to override the veto.[12]

As the breadth of the president's veto became known, local Republican support of Congress began to solidify. "The last veto hits harder than the first and has fewer friends by far," an Ohio correspondent wrote Sherman. The president had thrown away his great opportunity for reconciliation, and newspaper correspondents found that "those who formerly defended him are now readiest in his condemnation."[13]

The Civil Rights bill's essential conservatism served it well in the struggle for Republican support. In urging the president to sign the measure, Governor Cox had drawn his attention to this:

If the Southern people will . . . do right themselves, by legislation of their own which shall break down distinctions between classes in the matters specified in the bill, as I hope they will do, the law itself would become of little practical moment . . . and a very short time would make it a practically dead letter.

Another administration supporter, Senator William M. Stewart, decided to support the bill on the same grounds. "When I reflect how very easy it is for the States to avoid the operation of this bill, how very little they have to do to avoid the operation of the bill entirely, I think that it is robbed of its coercive features," he said. If the southern states would only modify their laws to do right, "this civil rights bill . . . will simply be a nullity." [14]

Still, the result was in doubt as the Senate prepared to vote April 6. Ailing Senator Dixon was not in his seat. All expected him to support the veto; his absence might be critical. Morgan remained silent, not informing the bill's supporters of his intention to vote for it. Messenger after messenger went to summon Dixon, but he did not come. Finally, as Garrett Davis droned through an attack on the bill, Doolittle took Morgan's carriage to find the absent senator. He returned alone, but he and Morgan both anxiously looked at the clock as more Democrats spoke. Finally the vote commenced. One by one the senators answered the call. Dixon did not appear. When the clerk called Morgan's name, he voted "Aye," and the galleries broke into cheers. Even if Dixon arrived, the bill would pass over the veto. President *pro tempore* Foster gaveled the galleries into silence and the vote continued. Finally the clerk announced the final tally, thirty-three Senators in favor of overriding the veto and fifteen against.[15] "And then you ought to have heard the galleries," Howe wrote his niece. "They sprang to their feet clapping hands, stamping, shouting, yelling, waving handkerchiefs." The radical editor of the *Independent,* Theodore Tilton, stood in those galleries as the Senate overrode the veto. "Senators shook hands, old friends clapped each other's shoulders, women shed tears, and joy reigned!" he wrote. "O Gentle Reader, it was good to be there." [16]

The House passed the bill over the veto April 9 by a vote of 122 to 41. Eight Unionists, including Raymond, joined the minority. Bingham was absent but a collague announced he would have voted against the bill. Three more who had previously supported the president rejoined the majority.[17] It was "a glorious day . . . . A day of days!" wrote Colfax.[18]

"The demand of the President," explained the Philadelphia *North American,* which had supported him until the Freedmen's Bureau bill veto, ". . . is that the Republican party shall to suit him, stultify itself and its whole past career and principles. By this simple process he has managed to make the term radical synonymous with the entire mass of the dominant party." [19] The president had made an issue not on policy favored by the radicals alone, but on legislation framed and passed by the conservatives and centrists. He would have to fight a united Republican party.

For radicals like Sumner, the future seemed bright, difficult as a struggle with the president might be. A year before, he and a handful of radicals had barely fought off the restoration of Louisiana, a measure supported by the president and the nearly united Republican force in the Senate, led by the same man who now led the fight for the Civil Rights bill. Sumner had prepared a speech in defense of the bill, but he had determined not to deliver it. "If I were disposed to despair on other questions," Sumner had intended to say, "I should take heart, when I see how Senators once lukewarm, indifferent, or perhaps hostile, now generously unite in securing protection to the freedmen by Act of Congress." [20] The Democratic press began referring to men like Trumbull and Fessenden as "Radicals," and they accepted the label proudly. If they accepted the label, might they not accept the program?

Radicals recognized the opportunity. "Remember these are no times of ordinary politics," Phillips admonished Sumner.

They are formative hours: the national purpose & thought grows and ripens in thirty days as much as ordinary years bring it forward. We *radicals* have all the elements of national education in our hands—pressure of a vast debt—uncertainty of it—capital unwilling to risk itself in the South but *longing* to do so—vigilant masses—every returned soldier a witness—every defeated emigrant to the truth a witness & weight.

Breathing radical fire, Phillips urged Sumner to stand firm.

Plant yourselves on the base claim no state readmitted without impartial suffrage—live & die by that, vote alone, if necessary against everything short of it . . . . *Three years* will justify the position. *You* can afford to wait that verdict. Disclaim all coming down to the level of dead Whiggery (Fessenden) cowardly Republicans (Wilson) disguised copperhead (Doolittle) unadulterated treason (Raymond) stolid ignorance . . . (Trumbull) & stand for what every clearsighted man sees and confesses as indispensible for safe settlement . . . . Secure as many "civil rights" as you can, bolster up as many Bureaux as you please but never open your doors to *any* State unless on [the] avowed principle of negro suffrage.[21]

Others offered similar advice to Republicans as a whole. "Congress has demoralized itself in the effort to find some middle ground so moderate, so 'conservative' . . . , that they and the President can stand on it together," the *Chicago Tribune* noted. "We hope the veto of the Civil Rights bill . . . will end all such futile attempts." [22]

But other Republicans, angry as they were with the president, were not disposed to embark on a new career of radicalism. Many of the most conservative Republicans blamed the radicals for the split as much as they did the president. Dawes was disgusted, "A few of our people are in their element now—perfectly happy," he wrote his wife. "They can cry and howl and . . . alarm the country at the terrible crisis the President has

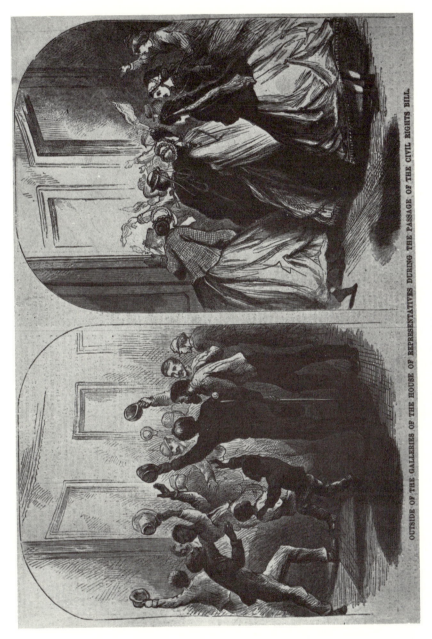

OUTSIDE OF THE GALLERIES OF THE HOUSE OF REPRESENTATIVES DURING THE PASSAGE OF THE CIVIL RIGHTS BILL.

Harper's Weekly, April 28, 1866

involved us in, and he is fool enough, or wicked enough . . . to furnish them with material fuel for the flame, depriving every friend he has of the least ground upon which to stand and defend him." [23]

Several leading Ohio politicians warned Sherman of the situation. There was a strong desire for unity among Ohio Republicans, as a necessity to survive the president's possible defection. "But to this end there is a most serious difficulty in the way," they wrote. Although Ohio Republicans generally opposed the president's policy,

it is in vain . . . to secure their united support to Congress or even to maintain the ascendance of the Union party in Ohio unless Congress shall pursue a course more temperate. If it is to be carried along the furious tide with Stevens & Sumner . . . I assure you that the power of the Union party will die with the present Congress.

As Warner Bateman cautioned,

The controversies between the President and Congress has [sic] not so much divided [the people] . . . among themselves as it has separated them from both you and Johnson. The great body of the people are entirely harmonious as to their general aims and the one that leaves them is lost be it the President or Congress.[24]

Congressional Republicans understood the situation. Speaker Colfax determined that Congress should adopt "some plan which, obtaining the needed security for the future from the rebel States, shall not take on any loads of popular prejudice that can be avoided." The Illinois, New York, and Ohio Republican delegations caucused and concluded to oppose black suffrage in deference to the prejudices of their constituents. Trumbull told Welles that no more than eight senators and perhaps sixteen representatives favored black suffrage. Even Boutwell, who had held out for black enfranchisement in the Reconstruction committee, now recognized that it was unattainable and joined his colleagues in framing a "practical" plan.[25]

Moreover, the president appeared to have stopped for a second look after the passage of the Civil Rights bill over his veto. The overwhelming Republican support for the measure, William Cullen Bryant wrote, seemed to have "stunned him." Rumors circulated that Johnson desired a rapprochement. This too inclined Republicans to moderation.[26]

The first test of Republican sentiment came in the Senate April 25, as the Senate voted on admitting Colorado to statehood. Sumner proposed to require the territory to enfranchise blacks as a condition for admission, but his amendment was overwhelmed, receiving only seven votes, two or three of which came from senators more interested in defeating the legislation than securing black suffrage. Following Phillips's advice, Sumner then joined the Democratic opposition to Colorado statehood. In the House a similar amendment garnered only thirty-seven votes—here Boutwell, Eliot, Kelley, Julian, Stevens, Elihu B. Washburne, and other Republicans joined the opposition in a futile effort to defeat passage.[27]

In the Reconstruction committee, Republicans took cognizance of their colleagues' opinions. The committee accepted as its basis of action a proposal that Robert Dale Owen had suggested to Stevens, incorporating into one constitutional amendment nearly all the elements of the centrist program. Among its other provisions the amendment prohibited racial discrimination in voting regulations after July 4, 1876. On April 28, two days after Ohio's Republican congressional delegation had voted to oppose Negro suffrage, Stevens moved to eliminate even this mild black *en*franchisement provision; instead the committee recommended a limited rebel *dis*franchisement—disqualifying men who had voluntarily aided the rebellion from the right to vote in national elections until July 4, 1870.[28]

On April 30, Stevens reported the joint committee's Reconstruction plan to Congress. It consisted of two parts. The first was the proposed (Fourteenth) amendment to the constitution, with five sections. The first section—a modification of the amendment Bingham had proposed to the House in February—forbade states from abridging the privileges or immunities of United States citizens or depriving them of life, liberty, or property without due process of law, or denying them the equal protection of the law. The second section was based on the rejected apportionment amendment, excluding from the basis of congressional representation any class of people whose adult males were denied the right of suffrage, excepting those excluded for participation in the rebellion or for other crimes. The third section contained the voting disqualification, and the fourth forbade the state and national governments to pay the rebel debt or compensation for freed slaves. The final section gave Congress power to enforce the amendment by appropriate legislation.

The second part of the committee's plan was a bill to provide for the restoration of the rebel states to the Union. Under its provisions the representatives of any southern state which ratified the Fourteenth Amendment and altered its laws to conform to it would be admitted to Congress, but only after the amendment became part of the United States Constitution. Furthermore, any state that did ratify the amendment could defer payment of direct taxes uncollected during the war for ten years.[29]

The Reconstruction committee plan was the culmination during the first session of the Thirty-ninth Congress of the "grasp of war" doctrine on which so many conservatives and centrists based their constitutional justifications for Reconstruction. This became plain when the committee submitted its report a month later. Holding that "the conquered rebels were at the mercy of the conquerors," the Reconstruction committee offered the constitutional amendment under "a most perfect right to exact indemnity for the injuries done and security against the recurrence of such outrages in the future." To be entitled to restoration, the committee insisted, the southern states

must prove that they have established with the consent of the people, republican forms of government in harmony with the Constitution and laws of the United States, that all hostile purposes have ceased, and should give adequate guarantees against future treason and rebellion—guarantees which shall prove satisfactory to the government against which they rebelled, and by whose arms they were subdued.[30]

At the same time, the proposed amendment again demonstrated Republicans' reluctance radically to expand the national government's jurisdiction over its citizens. The amendment in no way challenged the tradition that states had primary jurisdiction over citizens in matters of police regulation, the regulation of conduct for the protection of the community. Instead, its first and fifth sections gave Congress power to assure that these police regulations would not discriminate against citizens on account of race, color, or previous condition of slavery where the regulation involved some "fundamental right" of United States citizens. It limited states' alternatives in framing and enforcing laws involving these rights; it did not transfer to the national government the power to frame all laws touching on these rights. National jurisdiction could arise only through the states' prior wrongdoing. It was the expedient of the Civil Rights bill employed once again. As the archconservative Governor Cox of Ohio explained in endorsing the amendment

If these rights are in good faith protected by State authorities, there will be no need of federal legislation on the subject, and the power will remain in abeyance; but if they are systematically violated, those who violate them will be themselves responsible for all the necessary interference of the central government.[31]

In framing their plan, the committee members had not divided along purely ideological lines. They had agreed that some plan was necessary for the political survival of the Republican party, and they had determined to hammer one out. The differences that had arisen among Republican committeemen were over what provisions were most likely to guarantee the security of the Union and of black men. Each member had his favorite measure. All the Republicans and Democrat Reverdy Johnson had insisted on the section of the proposed amendment repudiating the rebel debt. Only the two House Democrats had resisted. Bingham had been most insistent on a broad national guarantee of United States citizens' "privileges and immunities." He had insisted on the phrase. "It's euphony and indefiniteness of meaning were a charm to him," Boutwell remembered.[32] On the other hand, Howard and Washburne had been the only Republicans to hold out for black suffrage to the end; all the others proved willing to

ANDREW JOHNSON
Seventeenth President of the United States

The Great New England Rivals

WILLIAM PITT FESSENDEN

CHARLES SUMNER

(*On the facing page*)

The President's Republican Supporters

WILLIAM H. SEWARD
Secretary of State

GIDEON WELLES
Secretary of the Navy

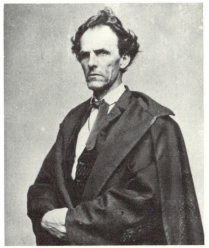

JAMES H. LANE
Senator

HUGH McCULLOCH
Secretary of the Treasury

JAMES R. DOOLITTLE
Senator

HENRY J. RAYMOND, *Representative; Editor,* New York Times

JAMES M. ASHLEY

Radical Leaders

in the House of Representatives

GEORGE S. BOUTWELL

BENJAMIN F. BUTLER

GEORGE W. JULIAN

ROBERT C. SCHENCK

THADDEUS STEVENS

HENRY WINTER DAVIS   WILLIAM D. KELLEY   SAMUEL SHELLABARGER

Conservative and Centrist Leaders

RUFUS P. SPALDING

JOHN A. BINGHAM

JAMES G. BLAINE

HENRY L. DAWES

of the House of Representatives

SCHUYLER COLFAX

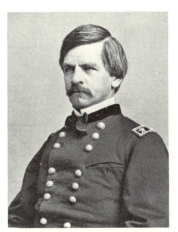

NATHANIEL P. BANKS

. . . And a Few Who Shifted

ELIHU B. WASHBURNE

JAMES F. WILSON

JAMES A. GARFIELD

Radical Leaders of the Senate

ZACHARIAH CHANDLER

HENRY WILSON

JACOB M. HOWARD

BENJAMIN F. WADE

Conservative and Centrist Leaders
of the Senate

ROSCOE CONKLING

OLIVER P. MORTON

JOHN SHERMAN

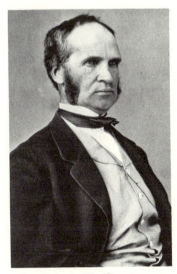

JAMES W. GRIMES

LYMAN TRUMBULL

"(?) Slavery Is Dead (?)." Republican reaction to continued Southern resistance.
Harper's Weekly, January 12, 1867.

"Andrew Johnson's Reconstruction . . . and How It Works." President
Johnson's Professed solicitude for the freedmen, as seen by Republicans.
Harper's Weekly, *September 1, 1866.*

abandon it. Stevens, Conkling, and Washburne pressed for the most stringent possible disqualification of rebels from voting and office holding privileges; Bingham, Blow, Williams, and Fessenden worked to minimize it.

In framing the Reconstruction bill, Williams, Bingham, and Blow wanted to admit southern states' representatives and senators to the Fortieth Congress if their states ratified the proposed constitutional amendment and altered their laws to conform with it, without forcing them to wait until the amendment became part of the Constitution. The other Republicans had insisted on the more stringent requirement.[33]

So the Republican committee members had eschewed ideology in favor of practicality. And in so doing, the radicals among them had, in effect, acted as moderates. They were aware of this and defended their actions vigorously. Note Stevens's explanation:

This proposition is not all that the committee desired. It falls far short of my wishes . . . I believe it is all that can be obtained in the present state of public opinion. . . . I shall not be driven by clamor or denunciation to throw away a great good because it is not perfect. I will take all I can get in the cause of humanity and leave it to be perfected by better men in better times.

Fessenden could not have said it better.[34]

Radicals outside Congress were shocked at the plan's conservatism. "Its surrender is total," Wendell Phillips lamented. He urged Sumner to raise his voice against it. "Seven years will show that this settlement allows the South to carry off the . . . best part of the victory." Phillips publicly hoped that the Republicans would be defeated in the upcoming elections if they adhered to the committee platform.[35] The *Chicago Tribune* complained that conservatism had "undue weight" with the committee, but accepted the program. Privately, however, coeditor Joseph Medill informed Trumbull that Republicans received the plan coldly. "I regard it as the offspring of cowardice—want of faith in the people," he wrote. Frederick Douglass, Benjamin F. Butler, and other radicals, including important southern Unionists, echoed the negative opinions and reluctant endorsements.[36]

But from Washington Republicans urged toleration upon the radicals. The *Independent*'s correspondent, David W. Bartlett, pleaded with his radical readers to "remember that it was extremely difficult to secure a two-thirds vote for any proposition disapproved by President Johnson. . . . The emergency is great. In the opinion of the leaders of Congress, it is absolutely necessary that a fair plan of restoration be submitted to the South at once." Colfax wrote a friend on the staff of the *New York Tribune* in the same vein: "I wish the Tribune was more cordial in its indorsement of Congress. I know, with the difficulties around us, we can't quite reach its standard of choice as to legislation and terms; but . . .

[w]e cannot go further than we can command a two-thirds vote in both Houses. . . . So we agreed on the best we could do . . . —just as John Bright takes what he can get in Parliament, not what he wants." [37]

In fact, many Republicans in Congress attacked the proposed Fourteenth Amendment for being too *restrictive,* rather than too conservative. Radicals found themselves defending against conservative attacks the one real restriction in it: the five-year prohibition on voting by those who had joined the rebellion voluntarily. The insertion of this disfranchisement had made the abandonment of black suffrage at least palatable to the radicals. Now *Republicans* were insisting that men who had committed treason should vote in national elections, while those who had remained loyal but were born black should not! Moreover, even as it stood the third section of the amendment was quite liberal. It disfranchised only those who had joined the rebellion voluntarily, excluding the hundreds of thousands who had been drafted. It allowed all whites to vote in state and local elections, electing lawmakers whose activities would have far more influence on their daily lives than those in Washington. But it still seemed too strict to many Republicans, and not only conservatives.

James A. Garfield announced his disappointment that the amendment did not guarantee impartial suffrage; he also opposed the disqualification of rebels. Whereas the radicals on the Reconstruction committee believed that the denial of the franchise to blacks made it imperative to disfranchise rebels, men like Garfield believed the opposite. If blacks should continue unenfranchised, rebels *must* continue to vote. To do otherwise left one-tenth or less of the population in each southern state with the right to vote. "Will nine tenths of the population consent to stay at home and let one tenth do the voting? Will not every ballot-box be the scene of strife and bloodshed?" he asked. To enforce this policy would require a large standing army in the South, and this he could not support. Yet he conceded his willingness to accept the amendment without this section. He would not carry his views to their logical conclusion and insist on black enfranchisement.[38] Dictated perhaps by political necessity, the willingness of Garfield and men like him to entrust political power to southern Confederates while excluding southern blacks from sharing it marked a definite shift away from the radicalism they once pronounced and still professed.

As Bingham, Blaine, and Raymond added their voices to Garfield's, Stevens, Boutwell, Eliot, and other radicals defended the restriction. The test came May 10: Republicans who wanted to modify or eliminate the disqualification section opposed the seconding of the previous question. If their opposition succeeded they could move amendments; if they failed they could not.

The final speeches before the vote brought the first of the great confrontations between the two great House leaders of the Reconstruction committee, Thaddeus Stevens and John A. Bingham, which would mark

Reconstruction during the Johnson administration. The third section could not be enforced, Bingham insisted. He was not unalterably opposed to its inclusion in the amendment, but he did not like adding an unenforceable provision to the fundamental law. If representatives insisted on such a measure, let them embody it in ordinary legislation. Stevens answered with controlled fury. "Give us the third section or give us nothing," he retorted.

Gentlemen tell us it is too strong—too strong for what? Too strong for their stomachs, but not for the people. Some say it is too lenient. It is to lenient for my hard heart. Not only to 1870, but to 18070, every rebel who shed the blood of loyal men should be prevented from exercising any power in this Government. That, even, would be too mild a punishment for them.

Ordinary criminals did not vote, Stevens noted acidly. "They have done nothing but err. There is no blood on their hands; they have only erred in committing such little acts as arson and larceny." Stevens remembered the scene six years earlier when

every southern member . . . came forth in one yelling body, because a speech for freedom was being made here; when weapons were drawn, and Barksdale's bowie-knife gleamed before our eyes. Would you have these men back again so soon as to reenact those scenes? Wait until I am gone, I pray you. I want not to go through it again. It will be but a short time for my colleague to wait. I hope he will not put us to that test.[39]

Stevens won; the motion to second the previous question passed 84 to 79. Bingham, Blaine, Garfield, Dawes, Hayes, and James M. Ashley were among the sixty-two Republicans voting in the opposition. Fourteen Democrats and the archconservative Unionist Lovell R. Rousseau had joined the radicals, hoping the more conservative Republicans would then vote against the entire amendment. They had miscalculated; Republicans united to pass the measure 128 to 37. Even Raymond voted for it, and the galleries applauded him. Only five Unionists voted with the opposition.[40] But more conservative Republicans were fairly certain the Senate would remove the objectionable provision. "We shall then adopt it solid," Hayes informed Bateman. "There is now almost perfect harmony in the Party here. Negro suffrage is not to be insisted upon, but difference of opinion over that allowed." [41]

The expectations of those representatives who wanted to modify the proposed amendment's disfranchising section proved justified. Trumbull, Grimes, and others criticized it before the measure even reached the Senate. Once there, Jacob M. Howard, the respected, radical member of the Reconstruction committee, who managed the amendment through the Senate when Fessenden pleaded illness, immediately abandoned the controversial section, arguing instead for an officeholding disqualification.

Such a position, taken by the amendment's Senate manager, signaled the death knell of disfranchisement.[42] Again a leading radical member of the committee, this time Howard, urged moderation on his radical colleagues. He too desired black suffrage, he conceded.

But . . . it is not the question here what we will do; it is not the question what, you, or I, or half a dozen other members of the Senate may prefer in respect to colored suffrage; it is not entirely the question what measure we can pass through the two Houses; but the question really is, what will the legislatures of the various States to whom these amendments are to be submitted do in the premises; what is it likely will meet the general approbation of the people who are to elect the Legislatures . . . ? [43]

As senators discussed what to do, pressure increased for a reconciliation between President Johnson and the party. On May 22, Seward delivered a carefully prepared address in his home town of Auburn, New York. Carefully treading a tortuous path between the president and Congress, he argued that Johnson and the party were not so widely separated. He insisted that the southern states had been reorganized on a loyal basis and that reconciliation between sections was the nation's prime necessity, but he indicated that the president favored protection for freedom and a change in the basis of congressional representation. Despite Seward's efforts, however, his speech was not nearly so conciliatory in tone as the drafts he had prepared of the president's messages. Stanton too informed audiences that he saw "a steady and encouraging advance towards practical adjustment" in Congress's rejection of radical solutions to the problem of Reconstruction.[44] Rumors of reconciliation filled the press.[45]

With hope rising that the Republican party might present a united front in the next elections, Senate Republicans on Trumbull's suggestion met in caucus to modify the proposed amendment in such a way that all could approve it. On May 25, in what the correspondent of the Washington *National Intelligencer* reported "is understood to be a tender of reconciliation between [the President] . . . and Congress," they agreed to eliminate the third section as it stood.[46] Meeting again on May 28, the senators wrangled for several futile hours, finally deciding to let Fessenden, Grimes, and Howard alter the amendment in light of the opinions senators had expressed. The three senators reported the next day. Most of the changes they suggested were minor, but they proposed important alterations in the third section: instead of disfranchising rebels in national elections, they proposed to disqualify from the right to hold office any former Confederate who had taken an oath to support the United States Constitution in order to hold office before the rebellion. Congress could remove the disability by a two-thirds vote of each house. The changed provision left rebels with the vote. Although only men who had never held major government positions or who had remained loyal might hold office in the South, they would be responsible to rebel constituents. Despite its effect, the caucus agreed to the modification and the other alterations that the committee recommended with little debate.

But the caucus's other decisions aroused greater controversy. After long debate the caucus decided to restore Tennessee immediately, since loyalists controlled its government and already had modified its laws to disfranchise rebels, to secure civil rights to blacks, and to repudiate the rebel debt. Moreover, the Republicans agreed to modify the Reconstruction bill reported by the Reconstruction committee to provide for restoration of each southern state upon its ratification of the constitutional amendment rather than upon the amendment's incorporation into the Constitution. The radicals' defeat was total.[47]

Because its rules allowed unlimited debate, it took the Senate over a week to amend the proposed constitutional amendment in accordance with the caucus decision. Not until June 8 was the process completed and the amendment passed, only four Republicans voting against it. Stewart, Morgan, and Lane of Kansas, all of whom had once supported the president, voted with the majority.[48] The House agreed to the Senate amendments without change. The Senate modifications had so far eliminated the vestiges of radicalism from the measure that not one Republican voted against it. Raymond, Delano, Hale, George R. Latham, Kuykendall, Charles E. Phelps, Green Clay Smith, Kellian V. Whaley, and Thomas N. Stilwell—almost the entire corp of the president's Unionist supporters—joined their former allies to pass it. Rousseau and Thomas E. Noell, who had drifted farthest from their Unionist moorings, abstained rather than register opposition.[49]

It was no day of triumph, Tilton observed. Again he had traveled to Washington to watch history being made. As he sat in the galleries he saw the ghosts of the cheering throng who had witnessed the passage of the Civil Rights bill over the president's veto. But on this day, "There was not a cheer, not a murmur of applause, not even a ripple of enthusiasm." [50]

Before the vote, Stevens had surveyed the scene.

In my youth, in my manhood, in my old age, I had fondly dreamed that when any fortunate chance should have broken up for a while the foundation of our institutions, and released us from obligations the most tyrannical that ever men imposed in the name of freedom, that the intelligent, pure and just men of this Republic, true to their professions and their consciences, would have so remodeled all our institutions as to have freed them from every vestige of human oppression, of inequality of rights, of the recognized degradation of the poor, and the superior caste of the rich. In short, that no distinction would be tolerated in this purified Republic but what arose from merit and conduct. This bright dream has vanished "like the baseless fabric of a vision." I find that we shall be obliged to be content with patching up the worst portions of the ancient edifice, and leaving it, in many of its parts, to be swept through by the tempests, the frosts, and the storms of despotism.

Tilton lamented, "If there had been a few more minds like his own in the party into whose hands the government of the country has fallen, his dream of political justice would have been a reality. It is tormenting to think of what might have been." [51]

NINE

The Elections of 1866

————————— ✦✦✦✦✦✦✦✦ —————————

WITH CONGRESS COMMITTED to a conservative Reconstruction program, Republicans hoped that the president would retrace his steps rather than oppose the party in the upcoming 1866 congressional elections. After all, Trumbull wrote his wife, "there is really nothing in it, which he hasn't approved one time or another." [1] Conservative Republicans, who had been waiting to see what Congress would do after its split with the president, pronounced themselves satisfied. Jacob D. Cox, the archconservative Governor of Ohio, still disliked the officeholding disqualification, mild as it was, but he informed Garfield, "Since the party has made undoubted progress in my direction within the past year, I can afford to be easily suited." [2] Stephen J. Field, one of the most conservative justices of the Supreme Court, wrote Chase, "The proposed amendments to the Constitution . . . appear to me to be just what we need. I think we members of the Union Party can unite cordially in their support. If the President withholds his approval he will sever all connections with the Union Party." Chase, who unknown to the radicals had great sympathy for the president, agreed. In general, Republicans agreed with David Ross Locke, the editor of the Toledo *Blade:* "There is nothing in these propositions which the most conservative Unionist can object to—nothing which he ought not to heartily endorse." [3]

Through mid-June rumors that Johnson might decide to fight out his disagreements within the party multiplied. Radicals and already burned Republicans like Trumbull remained skeptical ("I have no faith in his good intentions," Trumbull wrote home. "How could I after he so deceived me about the Civil Rights bill and Freedmen's Bureau bill?"). But conservative senators with links to the administration through Seward visited Johnson's advisers to urge reconciliation. [4] As the cautious courtship developed, Raymond noted "a more openly avowed desire on both sides for harmony of action," while other Republican congressmen agreed that Johnson seemed "more friendly with his old friends than usual." Cautiously optimistic, many Republicans concluded that "the President . . . has determined to cease hostilities." [5]

Indeed, Johnson was hesitating. Privately, some of his leading Republican allies urged him not to make the breach final. In Ohio, Johnson's friends, Governor Cox, Rush R. Sloane, and M.P. Gaddis, cooperated with Senator Sherman and Postmaster General William Dennison to check efforts to condemn the president at the state Republican convention. The resolutions, drawn in Washington by Sherman and Dennison, paralleled the decision in Congress, merely endorsing the proposed Fourteenth Amendment and avoiding the question of whether southern states should have to ratify it before restoration. Pleased with his success, Cox urged Johnson to show restraint. "The action of the Convention . . . strengthens my belief that with a little further exercise of patience we shall see the logic of events bring the whole Union party to the support of the true theory and practice of restoration," he wrote.[6]

Within the president's official family, Seward worked to commit Johnson to a moderate policy. In fact, it was his efforts more than anything else that created June's optimism. In Congress all of Seward's New York allies, Representatives Raymond, Robert S. Hale, Addison H. Laflin, James M. Marvin, William A. Darling, John Ketchum, and Thomas T. Davis and Senator Morgan—many of whom were standing by the president—had joined the Republican majority to pass the constitutional amendment.[7] The *New York Times,* the leading organ of Seward's wing of the party, encouraged harmony, while Seward himself in a major political address suggested that Congress and the president "differ only with regard to non-essentials." Carefully withholding endorsement of the Fourteenth Amendment as a *precondition* for restoration, Seward emphasized that the president had endorsed similar proposals.[8] When the House Committee on Enrolled Bills delivered the official resolution proposing the amendment to the secretary of state's office on June 16, Seward speedily sent copies to the state governors, although it was Saturday and he might have delayed. More belligerent presidential advisors, like Gideon Welles, grumbled, "Representations are sent out that Congress has made great concessions . . . , that they have yielded about everything, and that the President is pretty well satisfied with the question as now presented. There is design in all this, and some professed friends of the President are among the most active in it. . . . All looks to me like a systematic plan to absorb the President, or to destroy him." [9]

As prospects for reconciliation grew brighter, Republicans in Congress fragmented over the last elements of the conservative Reconstruction policy. Many nonradicals, led by Bingham, determined to complete their program by passing the joint committee's Reconstruction bill, which guaranteed admission to southern states upon ratification of the Fourteenth

Amendment and its incorporation into the Constitution. But even this was not lenient enough for Bingham, and he worked to moderate it further, moving to eliminate the requirement that the amendment be incorporated into the Constitution before southern states might be restored. He wanted restoration to be contingent on each state's ratification of the amendment alone.[10]

But radicals, having already conceded so much, finally determined to resist. "We must never permit the passage of an act pledging the country to the admission of rebel states when amendments are ratified," Boutwell urged Sumner. "Better that Tennessee be admitted at once, which, however, I hope will not happen." [11] One after another radicals proposed alternatives to the nonradical scheme. Boutwell proposed to substitute a measure restoring only Tennessee and Arkansas, and even those states only they after they instituted impartial suffrage; Judiciary committee chairman Wilson offered a modification of the Reconstruction committee's measure, providing that states which enfranchised blacks would not be required to wait for restoration until the amendment became a part of the Constitution; Ashley suggested an amendment requiring a new election for state officers in all the rebel states but Tennessee and Arkansas before they could be restored under the committee's program.[12]

But Stevens introduced the most radical proposal, perhaps in an effort to make the other radical suggestions appear more attractive to centrists. Stevens's measure declared the Johnson-authorized state governments valid for municipal purposes only and authorized them to call new constitutional conventions to be elected by all adult, male citizens. It disfranchised all Confederates for five years after they signified their intentions to resume allegiance to the United States. Finally, the bill would have forbidden the submission to Congress of any new state constitution which made any racial discrimination in citizens' rights. The gruff old radical ignored the constitutional amendment altogether.[13]

Despite the radical opposition, however, it was apparent that most Republicans favored Bingham's program. When the Reconstruction bill first came before the House as the regular order of business on May 15, Bingham violated an informal agreement among Reconstruction committee members to delay consideration of the measure by objecting to Stevens's motion to postpone the bill for two weeks. Suddenly, the growing hostility between the two Republican leaders flared into the open. The radical members of the Reconstruction committee had agreed to abandon black suffrage; they had supported the constitutional amendment in good faith, restraining their desire to offer radical amendments. But while the radical members of the Reconstruction committee had sustained even those provisions of the amendment they believed too lenient, Bingham had not adhered to the committee's proposal where he felt it too stringent. He had joined the attempt to modify the section disfranchising rebels and had helped create the climate in which the Senate eliminated that section; he proposed an amendment to the committee's Reconstruction bill to allow the readmission of southern states before the final adoption of the constitutional amendment. Now he opposed the bill's postponement.

"I must say that I do not understand what the gentleman from Ohio means," Stevens complained. "I thought it was understood that the bill should take the course I have indicated, but it so happens that my friend from Ohio never agrees long to what he and the rest of the committee may agree to at any time upon any particular point." Stung, Bingham denied that he had agreed to the postponement. Stevens was hardly satisfied. Recognizing that some delay was inevitable, Bingham moved that it be for one week only, but a combination of radicals and Democrats hoping to kill any legislation defeated him. Nonetheless, Bingham had carried a majority of the Republicans with him, a clear indication that most Republican congressmen would vote for his version of the bill.[14]

But when Bingham's measure came before the House again on May 29, after its two-week postponement, Seward's allies warned their colleagues that while the Fourteenth Amendment itself on the whole was consistent with Johnson's policy, a bill making it a formal precondition for restoration would destroy the budding prospects for reconciliation. Southerners' right to representation in Congress without further conditions was the only issue still separating the president from the party majority, Raymond warned, and "the only way to secure harmony of action is to avoid the issue altogether." [15]

But if Republican nonradicals, beguiled by Raymond's tempting proffer of unity, believed that Seward and his friends intended cordial cooperation in the future, they were probably wrong. Although evidence is not conclusive, it appears that Johnson's allies intended to continue the battle within the party, to use the president's restored party influence and congressional Republicans' failure to complete their own alternative Reconstruction policy to attack radicals and regain ascendancy, especially in New York. When Republican leaders in the House, faced with radical attacks on one side and Seward and Raymond's flirtation on the other, finally abandoned the Reconstruction bill, Raymond wrote to Weed exultantly, "The Radicals *feel beaten*. They cannot agree and will *drop* the Reconstruction bill altogether! Stevens told me yesterday he thought they had better do so, & Boutwell, Banks, Garfield, & the rest are today urging it. They can't help themselves." [16]

With success in sight, Raymond and Seward prepared to foster a movement for a national convention of Republicans, which they would control, to provide a new platform on which the party could expand its organization into the South. Raymond hinted at it in a speech delivered in the House on June 18, and several days later his newspaper, the *New York Times,* called upon the Union party's national executive committee (of which Raymond was chairman) to announce such a convocation.[17]

As Democrats and intransigent Conservatives realized "that the insidious advice of Mr. Raymond—or rather of Mr. Seward of whom Mr. Raymond is the mouth-piece—will be accepted" by Republicans, they began bitterly to assail their competitors for Johnson's allegiance, the archconservative Washington *National Intelligencer* proclaiming the New York editor-congressman a "renegade and recreant." [18] Shaken Democrats angrily demanded that Johnson clarify his position. Johnson's intimate, Montgomery Blair, and the New York *World,* organ of the "Albany Regency," which dominated the New York Democratic party, persistently urged the president to "unify" his cabinet with the ouster of Seward, Stanton, and others who hoped to maintain the Union party organization. After a particularly heated confrontation with congressional Democrats, one of their leaders, Samuel J. Randall, had to assure Johnson, "Do not despair. . . . Success shall come to you and us." [19]

Fearing Seward's machinations, Doolittle and Welles agreed that "the game of the Radicals and of certain conspicuously professed friends of the President, that the Republican party must be sustained and kept up at any sacrifice . . . must be checked, and the opposition to any such policy made clearly manifest." The best way to accomplish that goal, they decided, was to call a national convention of men who sustained Johnson's policy and opposed the legislation of Congress.[20] So two bitterly hostile wings of Johnson's supporters had arrived at similar plans for opposite reasons.

Trying to harmonize the action of both groups, other Johnsonians—possibly the president himself—urged Doolittle to frame his call for a meeting in such a way as to insure the cooperation of Seward's friends. Taking a rough draft to Raymond, Doolittle found him still hoping for an essentially Republican gathering, objecting that Doolittle's draft "would admit all who had been in rebellion against the Government and all whose political sympathies had been with them, while it would exclude many who stood by the Government, but who now desired action on the national questions resulting from the war." [21] When Welles saw Doolittle's rewritten draft several days later, shorn of its most militantly anticongressional phrases, he believed his fears verified: the call had been "perverted to an intrigue in behalf of the old Whig Party, on which Seward and Weed rely," he wrote. "Seward . . . expects to control the convention by aid of Weed and Raymond. . . . They mean to rule the President, and I fear he will let them." [22]

Desperately, Welles, McCulloch, and Montgomery Blair argued with Johnson, but although the president seemed to share their fears, the final version of the call for a National Union Convention, issued June 25, left out all references to the legislation of Congress, opening the convocation (to meet in Philadelphia August 14) to all who "sustain the Administration in maintaining unbroken the Union of the States under the Constitution" and "loyally accept the national situation." Welles recorded gloomily in his diary that it was "a Seward call; the party is to be Seward's party." [23]

But Seward's victory was short-lived. Responding to Democratic pressure, Johnson determined to make clear his opposition to the constitutional amendment, and Seward, finally forced to choose between the president and the party in which he had once held so much influence, chose the president. In an official message, Johnson notified Congress that Seward's quick transmittal of the proposed amendment to the state governors a week earlier was

purely ministerial, and in no sense whatever committ[ed] the Executive to an approval or a recommendation of the amendment to the State legislatures or to the people. On the contrary, a proper appreciation of the letter and spirit of the Constitution, as well as of the interests of national order, harmony, and union . . . may at this time well suggest a doubt whether any amendment to the Constitution ought to be proposed by Congress upon the legislatures of the several States for final decision until after the admission of such loyal Senators and Representatives of the now unrepresented States.[24]

The New York *World* recognized happily that "the wily scheme of Secretary Seward and Mr. Raymond for hushing up, or smoothing over, the quarrel between Congress and the President, proves signally unsuccessful. . . . The message . . . shows that President Johnson does not fall in with Mr. Seward's party strategy." [25]

With the president's refusal to cooperate with congressional Republicans at last manifest, Democrats openly endorsed the "National Union" movement. Congressional Democrats offered their public support in an open address to their constituents, while Montgomery Blair, Seward's leading rival in the Johnson camp, won the agreement of the convention's sponsors to a supplementary call, inviting Johnson's northern adherents to send four delegates to the meeting from each congressional district, two Democrats and two Unionists.[26]

As Raymond's hopes for using the convention to shore up the political position of himself and his allies faded, he began to disengage from the Johnsonian program. "I fear that giving the Democrats half the delegates has damaged the movement," he wrote Weed. "It allows the opposition to charge that the Convention is designed to throw everything into Democratic hands." [27] But both Seward and Weed considered Raymond's presence, as chairman of the Union party's national committee, essential to the convention's success. Raymond noted that when he complained to Seward that the meeting "seemed likely to be in the hands of the former rebels and their Copperhead associates," his friend cajoled, "Of course the Convention would fall into the hands of Copperheads if all our friends deserted it. What he wanted me to go into it for was to *prevent* that result. If it could not be prevented, then would be time enough to bolt." Enlisting the aid of the president himself, who assured his reluctant champion of "his wish to have this matter settled within the Union party," Seward confided to Raymond that he had arranged "the Philadelphia Convention [in such a way] that they could *go into it* if it was a success and *go out of it* if it should prove a failure." [28]

Even as Weed cooperated with Dean Richmond, leader of the Albany Regency and the most influential Democratic wirepuller in New York, to coordinate efforts in the upcoming congressional campaign, Raymond's *Times* and the Regency's *World* battled over the character of the convention.[29]

But despite Raymond's efforts and those of the Johnson-supporting, independently Democratic New York *Herald,* by mid-July it became obvious that Democrats would provide the muscle for the National Union movement and that the convention, in the *World*'s words, would not be "engaged in regarding the small phobias of Mr. Weed, nor the clever balancings on Mr. Raymond's rope." [30] With the Johnson movement becoming more and more a Democratic concern, conservative Republicans recoiled. "If you are determined that we should choose between Radicalism and Copperheadism," a leading Indiana conservative Republican explained, "I fear there is danger of making Radicals of us all." [31] Three members of Johnson's cabinet—Secretary of the Interior Harlan, Postmaster General Dennison, and Attorney General Speed—resigned rather than abandon their party. Secretary of War Edwin M. Stanton, torn between conflicting loyalties but disagreeing with Johnson's policies, heeded pleas to remain from Republicans and army officers, who urged him to serve as a buffer between the president and the army.[32]

The cabinet's desertion probably mirrored the decisions of thousands of lesser Republicans. The New York *Evening Post,* which originally had been friendly to the proposed convention, finally gave up: "It is no use. This is not the way to do it. The country is not blind; the people . . . feel that many of the Republican leaders are blunderers; but they remember that they are at least faithful to the Union . . . ; and if there is no other choice, the country will stick to them rather than go with such company as is now on the way to Philadelphia." [33]

By the time the National Union convention met on August 14, few Republicans of note endorsed it; Raymond almost alone still struggled to maintain its Union character. Influential in drawing resolutions and the convention's address to the people, Raymond largely surrendered his earlier position. When he read his proposed address to the Committee on Resolutions, its members struck all his references to the evils of slavery and his defense of Congress's right to propose constitutional amendments.

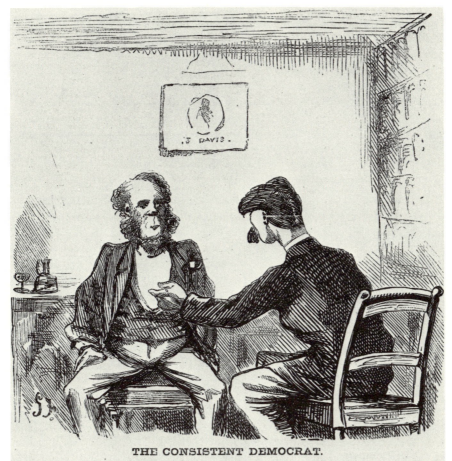

THE CONSISTENT DEMOCRAT.

MANAGING MAN. "You must be a Delegate to this Philadelphia Convention!"
CONSISTENT DEMOCRAT. "Is it on the basis of the Constitution as it was?"
MANAGING MAN. "Yes, and on the principle of love and cherish your enemies; and, what's more, BEN WOOD and VALLANDIGHAM will be there."
CONSISTENT DEMOCRAT. "Then I am with you!"

A Republican attack on the Philadelphia Convention.
Harper's Weekly, August 4, 1866

The resolutions themselves directly repudiated Raymond's suggestions. They attacked the legitimacy of the proposed amendment, insisting that "all the States of the Union have an equal and an indefeasible right to a voice and a vote" in proposing them.[34]

The final blows to the Democratic-conservative Republican coalition came with the actual nomination of candidates to Congress and state offices. Throughout the North, the Democrats determined the candidates. Although they occasionally named conservative Republicans, especially in close congressional districts, where they had to appeal to Republicans to win, as a whole the Democracy relied on its old party stalwarts. The New York nominations were an especially bitter blow to the Seward-Weed-Raymond Republicans. With Weed, Raymond, the New York *Herald,* and Johnson himself pressing for the nomination of John A. Dix, a Democrat who had cooperated closely with the Union party (Weed also worked for Henry C. Murphy, the candidate he and Dean Richmond had agreed upon before Richmond's untimely death, shortly before the convention), the state Union convention, dominated by Democrats, instead nominated the Tammany Hall candidate, John T. Hoffman.[35]

Disgusted, much of the lingering Republican remnant in the Johnson movement deserted or gave up the struggle. "With the failure of the Philadelphia . . . Convention to organize a new national party from the conservative Republicans and the remains of the old broken down democratic party," the *Herald* explained, "these fall elections are but a repetition of those between the Union war party and the copperhead peace party." [36] Even Raymond at last withdrew his support from the Johnson party. "The Democratic Party has pushed itself into the foreground of the President's supporters, and has seized the occasion to reconstruct and strengthen its own organization, rather than sustain the President upon the principles which he asserts . . . ," he charged in the *New York Times.* "We have no hesitation whatever in saying that this policy is fatal . . . and will end in its own defeat. *The people of the Northern States will not hand over the control of the Government to the control of the Democratic Party.*" [37]

Even before the Johnson movement crumbled, nonradical Republicans worked to make their party as comfortable for conservatives as possible. With Johnson clearly opposing them in the 1866 elections, they insisted that Congress dared not adjourn without giving some indication that the constitutional amendment embodied an actual alternative to the president's plans for restoration, that Republicans did not intend to keep the southern states in limbo indefinitely. So when the Tennessee state legislature ratified the amendment, Bingham and other conservative and centrist Republicans immediately moved to restore the state to normal relations in the Union. In effect, they were adopting Bingham's amendment to the Reconstruction bill, admitting a southern state that ratified the constitutional amendment *before* the amendment became part of the Constitution.

Brushing aside Stevens's efforts to delay the matter's consideration, Republicans evidenced their determination to finish their work.[38] In a desperate effort to turn the tide, Boutwell emphasized the implications of Bingham's Tennessee resolution. Its preamble affirmed that Tennessee had framed a republican form of government, he pointed out. Pass that preamble and admit Tennessee on its affirmations, and Congress would recognize that black disfranchisement and republican government were consistent. Pass the resolution, and the other southern states would be admitted under the same precedent. Congress would acquiesce in the creation of a dissatisfied, disfranchised class of over four million people. And to the loyal white men of the South it offered "only submission, degradation, or expatriation. . . . I speak under the impression, the firm conviction, that we to-day here surrender up the cause of justice, the cause of the country, in the vain hope that the admission of. Tennessee may work somewhat for the advantage of the party which has controlled the country during these last six years." [39] But Boutwell's objections failed to deter his colleagues, faced as they were with a bitter election campaign in which the opposition would have the power of the presidency and the patronage. The radical opposition fragmented, over half of those who had voted with Stevens earlier now joining the majority, Stevens himself among them. Only thirteen radicals held out against the combined weight of the Democrats and nearly all the Republicans as the resolution passed.[40]

In the yet more conservative Senate, even fewer Republicans opposed the recognition resolution. An attempt by Sumner to require impartial suffrage as a further condition was defeated, garnering only four radical votes.[41] After a stiff fight over the proper wording of the preamble, the Senate passed the resolution 28 to 4. Only two Republicans voted against it: Sumner and B. Gratz Brown.[42]

In the effort to undercut the president's appeal to conservative members of the party, Republicans had virtually adopted his program. The Johnson-supporting New York *Herald* observed happily that Tennessee's restoration "amounts to a surrender by the radicals [i.e., Republicans] of the points for which they have been contending so long . . . . Congress thus adopts the President's policy in substance, and only differs with him about the form." Outside Congress, many radicals agreed. "The flag of the nation ought to hang at half-mast over the halls of the National Capitol," the *Standard* mourned, "in commenoration of the dead courage of Congress." Dejected, Tilton lamented, "The Republican majority . . . abandoned for the sake of party a principle which they ought to have maintained for the sake of mankind." [43]

Despite the misgivings of many radicals, Republican leaders worked to demonstrate the conservatism of the party position throughout the campaign of 1866, emphasizing "the inability of the extreme men in Congress to rule the majority when the question of moderation or fanaticism is brought to a direct vote." [44] Outright glorifications of radicalism, such as that of retiring Indiana Senator Henry S. Lane in a speech at Indianapolis, were so rare as to shock the researcher. ("I am a radical member of the most radical Congress that ever assembled in the United States, and any man who has honest convictions, who listens to his own conscience and to the teaching of Providence, if he is worth a single cent for any human purpose, he is a radical," Lane avowed. It may be significant that he had already announced his decision not to seek reelection to the Senate.) [45] Instead Republicans regularly insisted that little or nothing in their policy was inconsistent with the president's original policy. As John Sherman informed his audiences, "Everything that was radical which he [Johnson] objected to . . . was stricken out." [46] James G. Blaine claimed, "I have never met a supporter of Mr. Lincoln's Administration, even of those most conservative, who was not ready to declare that the system of Reconstruction thus proposed is not only just to the white population of the South, but generous." [47] Even most radicals cooperated in Republican efforts to calm the fears of conservatives who might bolt to Johnson. Although many complained "that as a general plan of reconstruction . . . , this Constitutional amendment never appeared broad enough," they generally avowed their commitment to more stringent measures in such a way as to illustrate the conservatism of the actual Republican program. Few of them openly denied its finality.[48]

Concentrating on the proposed Fourteenth Amendment as the platform for their campaign, Republicans denied charges persistently leveled by Johnson's adherents that they intended to impose black suffrage upon the South and the nation.[49] The constitutional amendment at least implicitly embodied an offer of a final settlement to the South. Although the Reconstruction committee's bill guaranteeing restoration to states that ratified the amendment had not passed, the national executive committee of the Republican party in its official address announced that "under it, the State of Tennessee has been formally restored to all the privileges she forfeited by rebellion . . . . And the door thus passed through stands invitingly open to all who still linger without." Despite the insistence of some radicals that still more securities must be required, the centrist New York *Nation* concluded, "It is not difficult to see that the Republican party is substantially committed" to the conservative program.[50]

So powerful was the force of the Republican campaign that many of Johnson's adherents urged the president to deprive the opposition of the issue by endorsing the amendment himself. As the *Times* and *Herald* prepared to abandon the president, Weed and a leader of the New York Democrats, Edwin Croswell, added their weight to the pressure for a changed course, warning Johnson that newspapers would bolt unless he agreed. But such a shift in position would have alienated the president's Democratic supporters. Trapped, Johnson refused. The conservative New York papers returned to the Republican fold, endorsing the amendment as they did so. "There is nothing, after all, so very objectionable in this amendment—nothing which President Johnson himself has not, at one time or another, recommended . . . ," the *Herald* admitted as it deserted Johnson. "It is not the platform of Thaddeus Stevens, Sumner, or any of the noisy radicals in Congress. They can do nothing. It was adopted against all their remonstrances and in spite of their threats." [51]

Not all radicals were willing to mute their dissatisfaction with the congressional program. Tilton charged that the national executive committee's

SCENE UPON THE ASSEMBLING OF THE SOUTHERN LOYALISTS' CONVENTION AT THE "NATIONAL HALL" IN PHILADELPHIA, SEPTEMBER 3, 1866

Harper's Weekly, September 22, 1866

address amounted to "the white feather" of surrender on principles of political equality that the vast majority of Republicans shared. "God grant that
the great Party of Liberty shall prove braver than its half-hearted leaders!"
he prayed.[52] Bitterly, Wendell Phillips denounced "The Swindling Congress," which "having passed through the war sustained by four millions
of allies, sat down and swindled those allies out of their rights, forfeited
their own pledges to the world, and called it a *compromise*." [53]

Only once could dissatisfied Republicans make their views known
through more or less official channels, however, when a Republican-
sponsored convention of "Southern Loyalists" met in Philadelphia during
the first week of September. Originally designed to counter the Johnsonian
National Union convention of a month earlier, in which northerners and
southerners entered the hall arm in arm, the prestigious northern delegations quickly abandoned plans to join their southern allies in the meeting
when it became apparent that they intended to publicly advocate black
suffrage. Intensively lobbying the delegates in support of objections of
representatives from the border states, who outnumbered delegates from
farther south, Republican leaders desperately tried to stifle the opinions
of the southern radicals. "I speak for the delegations of my State," future
Senator Arthur I. Boreman of West Virginia announced, "when I say we
did not come here to commit suicide; we did not come here to destroy the
Union party." [54]

Led by Maryland's Senator John A.J. Creswell, Tennessee Governor
William G. Brownlow, and former Attorney General Speed of Kentucky,
the convention's presiding officer, the border-state men for three days held
back their southern brethren. Stacking the committee on resolutions, they
reported a platform with no mention of the great issue, promising the dissenters that the convention managers would appoint a special committee of
representatives from the unreconstructed states to frame special resolutions
and an address. But after the milkwater resolutions passed, Brownlow
moved to adjourn the meeting *sine die*, insisting that any further resolutions emanate from an informal meeting of delegates from the Deep South,
so that the convention itself—and especially border-state Republicans—
would escape responsibility. To tumultuous applause Andrew J. Hamilton,
who had served Johnson as provisional governor of Texas, denounced the
efforts to gag radical southerners.

We have yielded much, very much to these gentlemen. Yea, sir, we have yielded
too much to them. The cry has come up to us that they are in [political] danger.
Why, sir, the very object of calling the convention was to place before the
intelligent millions of the people of the United States the true condition . . .
of the reconstructed States. We did not come here to study how one more or
less Republican representative from Maryland in the next Congress was to be
secured . . . ; but to acquaint the people with solid truths . . . . It is time
the truth should be known. . . . If you want to escape the responsibility of what

we may say in that connection, no one asks you to endorse it, and you need not be compelled to remain here with us. But you want the moral effect of saying to your constituencies . . . "the convention had adjourned *sine die* before that was done, and we are not responsible for what the poor whites from the nonreconstructed States have said." I declare you shall not do this.

With the applause roaring as he spoke, Hamilton warned, "I can go before your constituencies as well as you." If the adjournment resolution proved successful, "all that is left to us is to remain and give that statement to the country nevertheless, and at the same time to state to the country the manner in which we have been treated." [55]

Unintimidated, Boreman insisted, "Sir, we have all got to be sustained or we have got to go down together; and I feel that if this convention . . . shall adopt the dogma of negro suffrage, . . . we are gone, irretrievably gone, and gone forever." But from throughout the southern delegations representatives called, "Then let us go." [56]

With bitterness increasing, the delegates reached a sour compromise: the convention did not adjourn *sine die,* but only delegates from unreconstructed states discussed and voted upon the report from their special committee. Speed, Boreman, Creswell, Brownlow, and most of their delegations withdrew. The next day the sullen remainder finally endorsed universal suffrage over the objections of scattered conservatives, and authorized leading members to travel through the North to enlighten public opinion.[57] Ecstatic at the opportunity to brush Republicans in the radical colors they had avoided so successfullly, the New York *World* gleefully dubbed the southern speakers the "Torch-and-Turpentine Brigade."

But despite pressure from the Southern Loyalist convention, Republicans adhered to their conservative campaign. Even the Massachusetts Republican state convention resolved only that the delegates "were fully prepared to believe the declaration of Southern Unionists that there can be no safety to the country until the national birthright of impartial suffrage and equality before the law shall be conferred upon every citizen of the States they represent." [58] A second Republican-sponsored national convention, this one of members of the Union armed forces, which James G. Blaine remembered as the most influential of the canvass, proceeded smoothly. Its managers frustrated radical Benjamin F. Butler's efforts to be named presiding officer, electing conservative Governor Cox of Ohio (formerly a major general on Sherman's staff) instead. The convention's mild resolutions endorsed the proposed constitutional amendment and criticized the president, but went no further.[59]

Sadly, the radical editor of *The Right Way* conceded that "it seems to be determined that impartial suffrage is not to be an issue in the election this season," while the *New York Times,* newly returned to the Republican fold, welcomed the "more moderate, conservative and pacific tone" of its party. As Johnsonians tried to capitalize on the radicalism of southern loyalists and fear of black suffrage, Republicans manifested an "unalterable determination" to make the Fourteenth Amendment "the leading feature of the campaign," Blaine remembered, "to enforce it in every party convention, to urge it through the press, to present it on the stump, to proclaim it through every authorized exponent of public opinion." [60] As the first elections indicated Republican victory, the *Times* wrote happily, "Seldom, indeed, has a contest been conducted with so exclusive reference to a single issue." In sustaining Republican candidates, the people were endorsing "not negro suffrage—not confiscation—not harsh vindictive penalties; but the plan of restoration dictated by Congress, and designed to be a final adjustment of our national difficulties." Those who still adhered to Johnson also recognized the success of the Republican appeal to conservatives, but they could not believe the sincerity of Republicans' conservative professions. "There never was a canvass conducted by any party so entirely upon false pretenses as the one just concluded . . . ," complained the *National Intelligencer*. "By the obscurities of the much-talked-of constitutional amendment, they conceal[ed] the real objects of the congressional faction." [61]

Ironically, as efforts by Johnson and his Democratic and Conservative supporters to taint Republicans with radicalism seemed to fail, ever more conservative Americans began to identify the president as the real threat to national stability. To a large extent such fears were inevitable, given the president's constitutional position on the great issues of the campaign. For Democrats, the central question involved the status of the southern states. Again and again they insisted that those states had never left the union and were now entitled to all the rights and privileges accorded to loyal states. As Johnson's National Union convention resolved: "Representation in the Congress of the United States and in the electoral college is a right recognized by the Constitution as abiding in every State, . . . and neither Congress nor the General Government has any authority or power to deny this right to any State or to withhold its enjoyment under the Constitution from the people thereof." [62]

Generally, Johnson's adherents remained silent on what these doctrines implied about the status of the present Congress and what legal recourse might be had to remedy its "usurpation," but as the campaign grew hotter they waxed ever more eloquent—and extreme—in their denunciations. Johnson's influential advisor Montgomery Blair and the New York *World* referred to the "rump Congress" throughout the canvass, and Johnson, his invective growing progressively more bitter, declaimed, "We have seen hanging upon the verge of the Government, as it were, a body called, or which assumes to be, the Congress of the United States." [63] As Johnson made his disastrous campaign "Swing Around the Circle" from Washington to Chicago and back, he attacked Congress over and over.

Shouting over the boos and hisses of his turbulent audiences, trying to ignore the reaction, he compared its "disunionist" policies to the treason of Jefferson Davis.[64] Regularly, Democrats and Conservatives charged that Congress's exclusion of southern representatives was "revolutionary," that the contest of 1866 was "a conflict between Union, freedom, and liberty, on the side of the President, and disunion, treason, despotism, and tyranny, on the side of Congress." [65] Such open belligerence on the part of leading Johnsonians tinged even calm statements of the anti-Republican position with an implicit threat.

A few Democrats averred that Johnson might hold the remedy in his hand if his supporters made even minor gains in the 1866 congressional elections.

There is no plainer principle of constitutional law than that the President has the right to ascertain what body of men is the Senate and what the House of Representatives when there are two bodies of men claiming to be each. . . .

Kentucky's belligerent Senator Garrett Davis warned his colleagues,

Whenever Andrew Johnson chooses to exercise his high function, his constitutional right to say to the southern Senators, "Get together with the Democrats and Conservatives of the Senate, and if you constitute a majority I will recognize you as the Senate of the United States," what then will become of you gentlemen? You will quietly come in and form a part of that Senate.[66]

As the *World* queried, "Is the Rump a Congress?" and another leading presidential advisor, Thomas Ewing, Sr., referred to "the illegal constitution of the two Houses of Congress," Johnson's allies issued vague warnings that "it is more than probable that, in the event of the success of the Radicals [in the elections], we shall have another and perhaps a still more bloody civil war." [67]

As some leading Johnsonians—including Montgomery Blair and the *New York Times* (before it deserted to the Republicans)—endorsed Davis's argument that the president could recognize a counter-Congress if his adherents and southern claimants together constituted more than a majority of the entire body, more and more Republicans became convinced that the president intended to carry out the threat.[68] Calling a secret Republican caucus in mid-July, leading congressmen—George S. Boutwell, John F. Farnsworth, Garfield, Kelley, and others—warned of the danger and urged their colleagues to remain in permanent session over the summer and fall of 1866, both to guard against Johnson's rumored coup and to forestall any massive removal of Republican officeholders. Shocked conservatives, discounting the danger, reacted with fury. "We had a caucus last night and nothing short of the wild ravings of the Girondists before the French Revolution would parallel our proceedings," Dawes wrote his wife. "If the Insane Asylum was not full I should advise that they hold their sessions there." [69]

Moving quickly, conservative Republicans seized control of a second caucus. Opposing the recommendations of a specially appointed caucus committee, Elihu B. Washburne, Lot Morrill (senator from Maine), and John Sherman insisted upon normal adjournment, cautioning that the Senate would not agree to anything less. Despite Stevens's determined efforts, in Dawes's words, "the bedlamites who ruled the caucus were in a decided minority," and conservatives carried an adjournment resolution by a vote of 64 to 40.[70] Carrying the fight to the floor of the House, radicals were beaten again, and Congress adjourned July 28.[71]

But even as Congress adjourned, Johnson reinforced Republican fears by intervening in an embroglio in Louisiana which to some degree paralleled the crisis that might develop in Washington after the elections.

Flung from authority by resurgent Confederates, conservative Louisiana Unionists—Hahn, Cutler, Field, A.P. Dostie, and other members of the old Banks-Hahn machine—joined with their estwhile radical enemies in a desperate attempt to regain power. Meeting secretly, the newly cooperating leaders tried to persuade Judge Edmund H. Durell to reconvene the constitutional convention, over which he had presided in 1864 and which had never adjourned *sine die*. When Durell refused, a secret caucus of convention members appointed Judge Rufus K. Howell to replace Durell as presiding officer. Encouraged by Banks and congressional radicals, the Louisiana loyalists intended when the delegates met to call elections to fill the seats of absent members; amend the state constitution to enfranchise blacks, disfranchise rebels, or both; submit it for ratification to the people, both black and white; and, if ratified, send it to Washington, where several congressmen had promised to try to get Congress to approve it and restore the state to normal relations in the Union. Suspecting that his Confederate former-allies intended to dump him, Governor Wells assented to the loyalist plan, calling elections for September 1866 to fill vacant convention seats.

But as the governor endorsed the loyalist movement, Lieutenant Governor Albert Voorhies, Attorney General Andrew S. Herron, and New Orleans Mayor John T. Monroe moved to thwart it. Determining to indict the convention leaders for unlawful assembly, Voorhies, Herron, and Monroe found the local federal military commander, General Absalom Baird, unwilling to permit their arrest. Both he and his commander, General Philip Sheridan, insisted that convening the assembly was no crime and that the validity of its proceedings should be tested in the courts. Moreover, a decision to disperse the delegates should emanate from the governor, Baird insisted, not subordinate state officials. Informed by their private contact with Johnson that the president would sustain their aggressive course, the anticonventionists adamantly pressed the unhappy General Baird, finally persuading him to refer the question to Washington for

A cartooned editorial on the New Orleans Massacre.
Harper's Weekly, September 8, 1866

final action. Until a decision was forthcoming, they assured the general, they would not attempt to arrest the loyalists.

But as about thirty delegates and several hundred primarily black supporters gathered at Mechanics' Institute on July 30, Johnson, responding to Voorhies's and Herron's claim that the loyalists intended a black insurrection, telegraphed them directly—without going through Secretary of War Stanton or General Grant—that he would expect the military authorities to sustain them in dispersing the convention. Publishing the message in the newspapers and passing out copies on the street, Voorhies, Herron, and Monroe ordered the police to arrest the delegates. The police and white Louisianans, in a paroxysm of hatred and fear, mobbed the delegates. Ignoring white handkerchiefs that Cutler, Hahn, Dostie, and others ran up the flagpole and waved from the windows of the Institute, the mob fired into the building, shot loyalists as they emerged, and pursued them through the streets, clubbing, beating, and shooting all they caught. Forty of the delegates and their supporters were killed, another one hundred and thirty-six wounded. Hahn was brought to jail bloody and lacerated; Dostie had been cornered and shot to death. When Sheridan and Baird imposed martial law to prevent renewal of violence, Johnson once more answered Voorhies's and Herron's pleas to intervene on their behalf, instructing his officers "not to interpose any obstacle in the way of the civil authorities, but render whatever aid may be required by them for the preservation of the public peace." [72]

Johnson's activity in the Louisiana crisis was probably the most important factor in his abandonment by the state-rights-oriented Democratic wing of the Republican party represented by the editors of the New York *Evening Post,* who had sustained him until July because they shared his aversion to "centralization" of power in the federal government. The *Post* asked.

Are we to understand that a state of this Union cannot hold a convention without the permission of the President of the United States? The President . . . has done an act contrary to all his written and spoken policy. We shall expose his action, and point out its illegality . . . just as faithfully as we denounced Congress for refusing to admit those southern representatives who were qualified and could take the test oath.[73]

Not only had Johnson brought into question his own commitment to state rights and his oft-stated position that the southern states had been restored to the Union, but he had demonstrated his willingness to disperse a political body of questionable legality with force. The implications were not lost on Republicans. Over and over they warned that Johnson would follow a similar course if the people elected enough of his northern adherents to form a counter-Congress with southerners. A majority of the whole House consisted of one hundred and twenty-one members, they

President Johnson's "Swing 'Round the Circle."
Harper's Weekly, October 27, 1866

warned. A Johnsonian gain of only twenty or thirty seats would bring on the crisis. As some Johnson-supporters urged Congress to avert the danger by admitting southern representatives, Republicans urged northern voters to "secure the all-important point, *the election of at least 122 Republicans to the next House of Representatives,* the only way . . . by which the country can be saved from an outbreak of violence." [74] But even as they grew more fearful of the possibilities, Republicans turned the danger into a campaign advantage. Republican candidates challenged their opponents to declare "what Congress are you a a candidate for? If you are a candidate for the Congress to be composed of Northern Copperheads and Southern rebels . . . , then I desire to say that I am not a candidate for any such Congress." [75] Throughout the nation Republican candidates and newspapers insisted to conservative members of their own party that an overwhelming Republican victory "is now the only practicable road to peace." [76]

The issue came to a head in October, when the Washington correspondent of the Democratic Philadelphia *Ledger* reported that Johnson had asked his new attorney general, Henry S. Stanbery, for an opinion on the constitutionality of Congress. Immediately repudiated by both Johnson and Stanbery, the report led Johnson's adherents openly to disavow such intentions. The only remedy for the usurpations of Congress, the New York *World* announced, "rests in the hands of the people. . . . Argument and agitation are the only resource in a case which neither executive nor judicial action can reach. . . . The true theory of the Rump Congress is, that it is a constitutional body which has perpetrated some outrageously unconstitutional acts." [77] Orville Browning, Johnson's new secretary of the interior, urged his political allies to remain calm. "I trust it will be the pride and glory of the friends of the Administration, in the threatening contest through which we are passing, to keep their passions in subjection to reason, and to do no act not fully warranted by the Constitution and the laws," he wrote.[78]

But the damage was already done. To most northerners, the party of Andrew Johnson, the party that had rested its appeal on a promise immediately to restore the Union and with it peace, had become identified as a threat to peace instead. In the words of the *Evening Post,* which once supported him, "Mr. Johnson has to thank his own intemperate language that he thus falls under suspicion of intending an act of usurpation." [79]

Republicans could barely believe the election returns—a victory as great as that of 1864, a majority of over three quarters of each branch of Congress. Cox, one of the Republicans who had sustained Johnson longest, both from principle and because he had been so desperately concerned about the consequences of a party split, tried to explain the unbelievability of events:

> The fact stared us in the face that to suffer any *interruption* in our control of the government, even for a single session of Congress, would result in such a "reconstruction" as would lose to us all we had been struggling to attain. . . . It was impossible for us to foresee that the unspeakable folly of the President himself would be the cure for the evils of a rupture with him. . . .

Had Mr. Johnson used the most ordinary discretion . . . , we should have been in a most critical condition during the late canvass . . . ; but he succeeded in doing, with an absolutely incredible fortuity, the very things which were sure to ruin his plans, and the only things which could place our success beyond doubt.[80]

TEN

"Radical" Reconstruction — Part One

++++++++++

As victorious Republicans returned to Washington for the second session of the Thirty-ninth Congress, they knew intraparty strife was not yet over. The differences between radical and nonradical Republicans during the first session had been deep. The nonradicals had enacted their program with the sullen acquiescence of some radicals and over the open opposition of many. Although most radicals had muted their dissatisfaction during the campaign and nearly all had endorsed the Fourteenth Amendment, many of them had carefully avoided any commitment to it as the *final* solution to the Reconstruction problem. Ominously, their most outspoken leaders had rejected that notion.

Stevens had publicly announced his intention to renew pressure to pass his Reconstruction bill and again endorsed confiscation and land redistribution. Sumner proposed a complete Reconstruction program, including creation of new provisional governments, land redistribution, guaranteed education for all races, and black suffrage. Boutwell, emphasizing that Congress had not passed the Reconstruction committee's bill promising restoration upon ratification of the constitutional amendment, insisted that "it would be in the highest degree unwise and unsafe . . . to accept these States." Succinctly, he explained the radicals' objection: "Like the President's policy, the amendment turns over the ten States to the control of of the rebels. The amendment itself only by indirection obtains security for the recognition of the negroes." [1]

Other radicals, like Butler, conceded that they had felt bound to accept the finality of the proposed amendment when Congress had adjourned, but that southern outrages in New Orleans and other places had relieved them of that obligation. [2] At the same time, the campaigners appointed by the Southern Loyalist convention traveled throughout the North, urging more thorough Reconstruction measures than those of 1866. Grimly, Republicans prepared for the renewal of the struggle, which would inevitably follow southern ratification of the constitutional amendment.

Preparing for the battle he expected, Stevens suggested to his Pennsylvania colleague and friend, John M. Broomall, that fifteen or twenty leading radical senators and representatives form their own caucus. Broomall's answer illustrated the seriousness with which radicals viewed the coming confrontation. "A caucus of the entire party would result in nothing, as we both well know," he wrote. "Bingham and myself would agree upon nothing. You would help me to disagree. I take it that the inevitable question whether all the adult males of the South are to be consulted in the reconstruction will find you the leader on one side and Bingham on the other. This question will make the coming political parties and I think it will divide our party in the coming session." Moreover, Broomall was a witness to how badly the radicals had fragmented during the previous session in the face of conservative and centrist pressure and political necessity: "Now if we could get together those who would be upon *our* side of that question alone I would like it very much, but after the first dozen who can tell who they are[?] Would it not be better . . . for us to communicate by letter with Boutwell, Kelley, Williams, Wilson of Iowa and such others as we feel sure of?" [3]

But there could be little doubt as to the ultimate result of the battle. Ohio Republicans had won the election on the pledge that the ratification of the constitutional amendment was the quid pro quo for restoration. Even Wade owned that he felt obligated to restore southern states ratifying it. The more conservative Sherman naturally expressed the same sentiments. Zachariah Chandler, another radical champion, conceded that he too felt bound by Michigan Republicans' commitment to the finality of the amendment. The New York state Republican convention had resolved "that when any of the late insurgent States shall adopt that amendment, such State shall, at once . . . be permitted to resume its place in Congress." Most New York representatives would honor that declaration. Years later Blaine opined that "if the Southern States had accepted the broad invitation thus given, there is little doubt that before the close of the year [1866] they might have been restored to the enjoyment of every power and privilege under the National Constitution." "There would have been opposition to it," he conceded, "but the weight of public influence and the majority in both branches of Congress would have been sure to secure this result." [4] In the House, it is likely that the Democrats, Johnson Conservatives, and at least the conservative and conservative-centrist Republicans who would vote to kill Thaddeus Stevens's Reconstruction bill in January 1867 (see List 11) would have pressed for restoration. That number included 102 of the 174 voting representatives. The opposition probably would have been even weaker in the Senate.

As the conservative New York *Herald* recognized, southerners held the future in their own hands.

The future struggle is to be between the conservative republicans who have triumphed in these elections . . . and the radical republicans who . . . are now contending against [the constitutional amendment's] acceptance as a final settlement of the national difficulties. . . .

[On] this rock the party must sooner or later split. In this condition of affairs all that is necessary is for the South to come forward and accept the amendment . . . , and they will secure their early admission into Congress and so strengthen the hands of the moderate republicans that they will be able to defeat all the efforts of the radicals in requiring new guarantees.[5]

The major Republican and independent journals that had sustained Johnson until the summer of 1866—the *Herald, Evening Post,* and *Times*—all urged southerners to ratify the amendment without delay. Even the self-consciously apolitical General Grant warned southern visitors to adopt the amendment to avoid harsher treatment.[6]

As this pressure grew, Republican optimists, this time spearheaded by Chief Justice Salmon P. Chase, again tried to fashion a compromise with the erstwhile head of their party. As Chase and Johnson conferred, rumors spread that the administration intended a major shift in policy—an endorsement of the amendment or a combination of universal suffrage for blacks and universal amnesty for rebels. Eagerly, the *Herald* and *New York Tribune* ran up the universal-amnesty–universal-suffrage standard. The president hesitated, even preparing a conciliatory annual message to Congress embodying Chase's views, but he decided not to send it and determined to reiterate his old views instead. By mid-November Chase's hopes collapsed. The president remained stolid, and the chief justice wrote Horace Greeley that he retained "little or no hope except in the Providence of God & in the constancy of the people & their representatives."[7]

Johnson had listened to other advisers, who still enticed him with the prospect of ultimate victory. Their views may be garnered from a letter Doolittle sent Secretary of the Interior Browning: if southerners killed the constitutional amendment by refusing to ratify it, he wrote, "the extreme Rads will go for Stevens['s] Bill for reorganizing the southern States on negro suffrage. . . . That will present the issue squarely of forcing negro suffrage upon the South, and upon that we can beat them at the next Presidential Election."[8]

Once again the attitude of Andrew Johnson and the defiance that his position bred in the South rescued Republicans from impending division. One by one the southern states rejected the constitutional amendment. Texas, Florida, and Georgia did so before the second session of the Thirty-ninth Congress began. In South Carolina, Alabama, and Virginia, sentiment for ratification grew, but Johnson's personal intervention stiffened resistance.[9] By February 6 the process of rejection would be complete, and Republicans would ponder what to do next. The result was a new program,

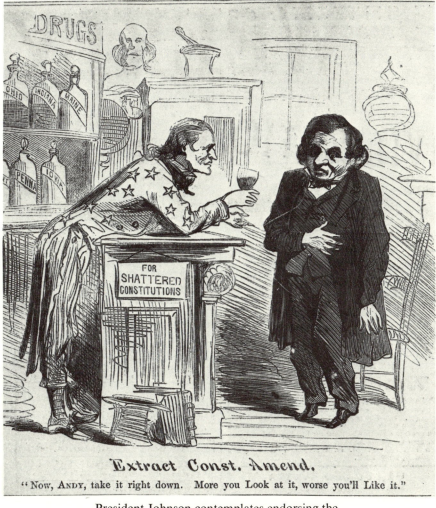

Extract Const. Amend.

"Now, ANDY, take it right down. More you Look at it, worse you'll Like it."

President Johnson contemplates endorsing the
Fourteenth Amendment.
Harper's Weekly, October 27, 1866

considerably more radical than the first.

For many years historians viewed the result of these new deliberations —the Reconstruction acts of 1867—as the final victory of radicalism. But recently scholars have concluded that this is an oversimplified view, and that the program of radical Reconstruction emerged only after furious tugging and hauling among various Republican factions.[10] In fact, the Reconstruction acts fell short of what the radicals originally had wanted. Studying the events of the Thirty-ninth Congress's second session separately from radical opinion of a year earlier, taking as a starting point radical opinion in December 1866, rather than December 1865, many scholars have suggested that the radicals held their own if they did not win a complete victory in the struggle over the Reconstruction acts. But men like George W. Julian, Wendell Phillips, Zachariah Chandler, and Josiah B. Grinnell did not see in the passage of those acts the enactment of the program they had advocated. Most of the radicals originally had favored territorial governments for the southern states, but they were forced to give that program up as impractical even before the second session of the Thirty-ninth Congress convened—the struggle with the president had forced public opinion too far to the right. Johnson had forced the public to debate the proper mode of *restoring* the rebel states, not governing them. Republicans could urge stringent policies for restoration, but they could not hope to retain power if they appeared to advocate no restoration at all, or a program of long delay. Radicals knew there was no prospect that a territorialization program could win enough support to pass Congress, much less survive a presidential veto. In a large sense, the radicals had been beaten before the battle had begun.[11]

Having abandoned the program they believed best suited to the emergency, radicals cast about for another. One conclusion they arrived at quickly: the attempt to protect black southerners by national action while leaving southern state governments under the control of former rebels could not work. The influence of local government on the lives of Americans was too powerful for the national government to counteract, even when the national government was represented by the Freedmen's Bureau. The prospect for national protection through the courts and national civil officers alone was even less promising.

Radicals cited the reports of the assistant commissioners of the Freedmen's Bureau to support their arguments. They pointed to the race riots in which organized mobs, aided by white southern police, brutalized and murdered black citizens. Civil Rights bills and constitutional enactments could not do the job. "Everything there is organized against the black man, from the judge upon the bench to the constable with his process," New York's radical representative, Hamilton Ward, observed. "[E]very officer, State, legislative, judicial, county, town, and municipal, who is called upon in any manner to enforce those laws and carry out those sacred guarantees of the Constitution are the enemies of the loyal men and freedmen, and opposed to the execution of those laws and guarantees." [12] The only answer, radicals insisted, was totally to reorganize the southern states, completely displacing the governments erected under President Johnson's authority.

Southern loyalists pleaded for such action. "Our present State Government is a *curse* to us," they lamented.[13] Loyalists, white and black, suffering under the rule of former rebels, understood the true political complexion of Congress better than its Democratic and pro-Johnson critics.

"We talk of some of the members [of Congress] as being radical," one of them observed. "They are not. They have but a faint glimmering of the facts, else they could not be so slow in looking up the measures for the relief of the country." In Washington, the southern Unionists who had toured the North during the summer and fall campaigns organized the Southern Loyalist Association, with Thomas J. Durant, the wartime radical leader in Louisiana, as president, to lobby for a truly radical Reconstruction.[14]

Any such reorganization, radicals insisted, must be based on universal suffrage for loyal men and, furthermore, the disfranchisement at least of rebels who held civil or military office under Confederate state or national authority. Most important, radicals generally wanted Congress to create loyal civil governments to administer the southern states until they adopted new constitutions and elected new officers. They proposed different modes of doing this—appointment of new provisional governors by the president with the advice and consent of the Senate, similar selections by the chief justice, or appointment of committees of public safety by new state conventions—but they agreed that southerners should be governed by civil administrations under the control of unionists, who would in good faith protect the rights of all citizens and use their influence and power to secure constitutions consistent with the radicals' conception of a republican form of government. In the process, no doubt, these unionists would use the patronage of their offices to nurture new, Republican political organizations, just as Johnson's appointees had nurtured conservative organizations.

Radicals justified plans to reorganize southern state governments by citing the national government's obligation to guarantee republican forms of government to the states or Congress's power to govern United States territories. The president had no authority to organize civil governments in the South in the absence of congressional law, they argued. Therefore southerners were without legal governments, and it was in Congress's power to provide temporary administrations until the people could organize their own by constitutional convention.

Finally, to render Reconstruction completely secure, the radicals desired the impeachment and removal of the president. This was essential to any plan, Boutwell argued. Congress "is powerless to execute. It has no hand by which it can wield or control the vast powers of this government." So long as Johnson remained in office, he could obstruct any Republican effort.[15]

On the other hand, the conservative and center Republicans for all practical purposes no longer had a program. They had enacted their Reconstruction policy during the first session, proceeding on the "grasp of war" theory by which southern state governments remained unrecognized by Congress until they "voluntarily" agreed to the conditions embodied in the proposed constitutional amendment. Now conservatives and centrists watched those states reject their terms. Few alternatives remained. They could surrender to the president and admit the southern states without requiring further conditions. They could adopt a policy of nonaction, maintaining the status quo until the recalcitrant southerners decided to ratify the amendment. They could acquiesce in a radical plan to replace the Johnson governments completely. Eventually most were driven to add a single further condition to ratification of the constitutional amendment—the acceptance of Negro suffrage. But although most conservative and moderate Republicans accepted the abstract justice of equal suffrage, they only reluctantly accepted it as one of the bases for Reconstruction. They adhered, as long as they could, to the proposed constitutional amendment alone. Even after every southern state rejected it, some conservatives, like Fessenden, Sherman, and Bingham, still regarded the constitutional amendment as the most important element in Reconstruction. Many nonradicals simply feared the political consequences of going further. ("Is it not better thus to secure reconstruction upon a safe basis approved by the people rather than endanger *all* by compelling organization of new State governments?" Sherman wrote Cox.) But other Republicans, certainly Bingham, Fessenden, and Trumbull, frankly doubted what many of their colleagues so ardently believed—that the ballot was the citizen's ultimate and best protection. "My opinion," Fessenden recalled, "was that, once recognized, the wealth and intelligence of the State would rule them [the freedmen]." [16] Doubting the wisdom and practicality of rebel disfranchisement, Fessenden, Bingham, and other more conservative Republicans expected the old southern leadership to retain power, and they deeply believed that the constitutional amendment would prove the only protection for southern black and white loyalists.

The struggle over Reconstruction legislation began January 3, 1867, when the joint committee's Reconstruction bill, left in limbo during the previous session, came before the House as the regular order of business. Stevens immediately proposed to substitute the more radical measure that he had suggested during the first session. Stevens's proposition was essentially an enabling act, detailing the steps southerners must take to form valid state governments. It recognized the Johnson state governments as valid "for municipal purposes" until replaced by the process outlined in the bill. The Supreme Court of the District of Columbia would appoint a commission for each state to organize an election for delegates to a constitutional convention. All adult male citizens meeting certain residence requirements would be entitled to vote. But the bill declared that men over twenty-one when Lincoln was inaugurated president who held civil or military office under the Confederacy, or who swore allegiance to it, had forfeited their American citizenship. They could only resume it five years after swearing allegiance to the United States anew. However, anyone who swore he favored peace by March 4, 1864, and who did not voluntarily aid the rebellion thereafter, would be exempted from the forfeiture.

Finally, the bill announced that no constitution could be presented to Congress if it denied equal rights, privileges, and immunities to all citizens; all laws had to be impartial, "without regard to language, race, or former condition." These provisions must be irrevocable. If any state reorganized under the act violated them after its restoration, it would lose its right to congressional representation once again.[17]

Stevens's proposition abandoned any notion of territorialization, but most radicals realized there was no choice. However, they did object to the section recognizing the Johnson governments, even if only for "municipal purposes." So long as rebels administered those states, radicals feared, they would obstruct any plan of reorganization and in that way retain control "for municipal purposes" indefinitely. Stevens acceded to radicals' demands and eliminated the objectionable provision.[18]

Knowing that Bingham and Fessenden were hostile to further Reconstruction legislation (Fessenden, as chairman of the Senate Finance committee, was busy framing the difficult, complex tariff bill; even if he were sympathetic to Stevens's measure, he would have difficulty scheduling Reconstruction committee meetings), Stevens believed he could win the bill's passage only if he brought it before the House without referring it to the Reconstruction committee. He knew this would be risky. Without the prestige of a committee behind the bill, representatives would give it a thorough going-over. But it was his only chance. Offering to allow representatives free rein to perfect the measure on the floor, the Republican leader gingerly refrained from calling the previous question, which would have barred amendments.

Immediately, James M. Ashley, who had labored so long on Reconstruction legislation during the Thirty-eighth Congress, proposed a substitute. Much longer and more complex than Stevens's proposition, Ashley's measure too was essentially an enabling act, providing, however, for the election of two conventions. The first would appoint a committee of public safety which would elect a provisional governor. He would administer the government while the committee arranged an election for the second convention, which would appoint a new governor, all state officers, and frame a new state constitution "not repugnant to the Constitution of the United States and the principles of the Declaration of Independence." Moreover, the convention would pass ordinances, irrevocable without the consent of Congress, guaranteeing equality before the law, repudiating the rebel debt and forbidding compensation for slaves, guaranteeing the establishment of free public schools for all children between six and twenty without regard to race, disqualifying Confederate officeholders from holding state office unless the state legislature removed the disability by a two-thirds vote, and conceding the national government's right to exclude state representatives from Congress in case of rebellion by state authorities.

Like Stevens, Ashley extended the franchise to black men, but he did not revoke the citizenship of rebels. Still, he did restrict the ballot to men who swore an oath similar to Stevens's, and only men who never voluntarily bore arms or aided the rebellion could serve in the conventions. Ashley's substitute went on to enact further regulations in great detail.[19]

Neither proposition satisfied all the radicals, much less the conservatives and centrists. Stevens's went further than Ashley's in revoking the citizenship (and therefore the right to vote or hold office) of all men who would not swear they had opposed the rebellion after Lincoln's second inauguration. Ashley disfranchised the same men in the original elections for convention delegates, but nothing in his proposal prohibited those conventions from enfranchising them in the new state constitutions. On the other hand, Ashley's measure swept away the Johnson governments completely, even declaring laws passed and acts done under their authority null and void unless ratified by the new authorities. Both measures embodied primarily the radicals' program and went much too far for their more moderate colleagues.

The press of other business and Stevens's decision to return to Pennsylvania, where he was a candidate for the Republican senatorial nomination, delayed consideration of the proposed Reconstruction measures until January 16, but on that day Bingham launched a slashing attack. Moving to refer the bill to the Reconstruction committee, the conservative Ohioan urged Congress to adhere to the constitutional amendment as the basis of Reconstruction. It was conciliatory, an "act of general forgiveness and amnesty, securing to each, however guilty, the equal protection of the laws by the combined power of the nation, in a sublime humanity which challenges a parallel since man was upon the earth." [20] Stevens's proposed bill, in contrast, was

framed in the spirit of the utterances of a distinguished man of this country [Wendell Phillips] who has been waging war on this amendment and this Congress, denouncing both as a "swindle." . . . I submit with all confidence that what is contemplated by the gentleman's bill is to patch up a restoration by the usurpation of powers which do not belong to the Congress of the United States, induce the people to fling aside the constitutional amendment, and thereby subject the future of this Republic to all those dread calamities which have darkened its recent past.[21]

Bingham denied that Congress could revoke citizenship in the United States. He denied that it could force irrevocable, nonamendable provisions into state constitutions. He complained that the proposal, by dictating the conditions for restoration, denied southern citizens the right to petition freely for admission under other plans. In sum, Bingham wanted to maintain that illusion of voluntarism (which could be more than illusion, as southern rejection of the constitutional amendment proved) which characterized Reconstruction under the "grasp of war" theory; he objected to the direct imposition of northern will justified by radicals under the power to guarantee republican forms of government or to govern territories.[22]

Representatives debated the Reconstruction measures for nearly two weeks. Most Republicans offered qualified approval; only three (Bingham, Raymond, and William E. Dodge) argued for outright rejection. On January 21 Stevens, who must have felt confident, announced that he would press for a vote the next day.[23] But instead the House swept into a wild debate and filibuster (in those days this was possible in the House as well as Senate) on a bill to bar former rebels from practicing law before United States courts. When the Reconstruction bills came before the House once more January 24, the situation had changed. Radicals, especially, seemed to feel that Stevens's measure did not go far enough. Stevens decided not to force a vote and instead announced, "I see such diversity of opinion on this side of the House that if I do not change my mind I shall to-morrow relieve the House from any question upon the merits of this bill by moving to lay it on the table." [24] It was a bold, dangerous ploy, designed to force the radicals to give up special objections and projects and unite behind the bill or face a complete conservative and Democratic victory.

Two days later Stevens announced his intentions. He would ask Ashley to withdraw his amendment and Bingham to withdraw his motion to recommit the bill to the Reconstruction committee. The House would then, Stevens hoped, go under the five-minute rule (allowing each speaker only that amount of time), and he would open the bill for amendment, not calling the previous question until the House modified it into an acceptable form. This, radicals now agreed, was the only hope for passage. Ashley, withdrawing his substitute, urged Bingham and the House to acquiesce in Stevens's suggestion. The Reconstruction committee had not yet met during the second session, despite the large number of Reconstruction bills referred to it, he observed. If it did meet, its members were not likely to agree. "I fear that if this bill goes to that committee it will go to its grave, and that it will not during the life of the Thirty-Ninth Congress see the light," Ashley warned. "If I were opposed to these bills I would vote to send them to that committee as sending them to their tomb." [25]

The test came January 28. In an effort to win support, Stevens accepted several amendments to his substitute and struck out the section requiring irrevocable provisions in the new state constitutions. He then appealed to Bingham to withdraw his motion to recommit the bill so that the House could amend it. He promised he would give his antagonist an opportunity to renew his motion afterwards. But Bingham would not bend. It could mean only one thing: he did not want the House to modify Stevens's bill; he wanted no Reconstruction bill at all.

Grimly, Stevens reiterated his conviction that recommittal meant the death of the measure. Bingham denied it. Angrily, Stevens turned on his rival. "The gentleman will recollect that I did not ask his concurrence. In all this contest about reconstruction I do not propose either to take his counsel, recognize his authority, or believe a word he says." [26]

As the anguished old radical watched helplessly, the House agreed to Bingham's motion, 88 to 65. Bingham carried fifty-three Republicans and Unionists with him, including three supporters of the administration. Thirty-five Democratic votes provided his victory.[27] "You need not fear rash measures from Congress," Sherman had reassured Cox as debate in the House began. "We feel that while courage is the first attribute of soldiers—prudence is now needed in law makers." The House's decision appeared to prove the cautious senator right. Sentiment was growing to continue exclusion of the southern states until they reconsidered the proposed amendment. As the *New York Times* editorialized with satisfaction, Congress seemed to be "in no haste to throw overboard the terms of restoration adopted last session." [28]

But Stevens had not lost all. He had won the support of over half the Republicans, indicating a significant shift to the left over the previous session, when the fragmented radicals had been unable to carry any of their points. As a comparison of Lists 9 and 18 indicates, Republican centrists divided, with one third of them joining radicals on key votes, while each group voted for more radical measures than it had one year earlier.

As Republicans fought and floundered over Reconstruction legislation in Congress, conservatives continued to send the president signals of their hope for compromise. Despite the evident stolidity of Johnson's annual message to Congress, the ambitious Banks called on Orville H. Browning, one of the president's closest advisors, to express his "great gratification" at its "tone and temper." Furthermore, Banks assured Browning that there was no danger of impeachment or "revolutionary measures." [29] Banks's assurances and possibly his services (Banks played a leading role in some of the conservative efforts to obstruct the Reconstruction bill) did not go unrewarded. He received access to government patronage once more and succeeded in getting an ally named port collector in Boston, the most important patronage position in Massachusetts.[30]

Republican moderates and conservatives sent Johnson another clear signal of their willingness to compromise when they rejected radical efforts to force Raymond out of the Republican caucus. Raymond's *New York Times* had been the leading Republican paper to support Johnson's Philadelphia "Arm-in-Arm Convention." Raymond himself had attended it and delivered the keynote address. He was, therefore, a surrogate for Johnson. When the caucus refused to expel him and then refused even to declare that no man who still adhered to the Philadelphia platform could participate in the caucus with honor, they were in effect telling Johnson he was welcome to rejoin the fold. He need do only what Raymond did: avow his adherence to the party and acquiesce in the adoption of the constitutional amendment.[31]

Under these circumstances, some of President Johnson's less intransigent supporters determined to take advantage of the deadlock in Congress. James L. Orr, governor of South Carolina, proposed a new Reconstruction plan. Southern states would amend their constitutions to extend the ballot to all men who could read the Declaration of Independence and the Constitution in English and write their names, or who owned $250 of taxable property. However, no one entitled to vote under state laws before the adoption of the amendment would be disfranchised. The southern states would also pledge to ratify a new constitutional amendment if passed by Congress. This would declare the Union perpetual, guarantee the national debt and repudiate the debt incurred in support of the rebellion, declare all persons born in the United States and subject to its jurisdiction citizens and guarantee them equal protection of the laws, and deduct classes excluded from the ballot from the basis of representation in Congress.

Late in January, Orr presented this plan to leading Republicans and became satisfied it would win the support of conservatives. On January 31 he, former provisional governors Parsons of Alabama and Marvin of Florida, and two North Carolina representatives-elect proposed the plan to the president, who signified his cautious approval in the belief that if southern states adopted it, radical and nonradical Republicans would split irrevocably over their restoration. Published in many newspapers, the plan caused a great stir, frightening radicals and those moderates who believed something had to be done to protect southern loyalists.[32]

However, despite Orr's apparent conviction to the contrary, most Republicans, even conservatives, could not accept his proposal.[33] It eliminated the proposed constitutional amendment's mild disqualification clause and weakened its civil rights section, alienating nonradicals. It displeased radicals because (and this was its manifest purpose) it confirmed the presently constituted state governments, dominated by former rebels, and left the enforcement of its slight guarantees to them. Finally, it permitted all whites to vote, including rebels, while enfranchising only literate blacks or those with $250 worth of property. And there was no guarantee southerners would institute free public schools to educate their black fellow citizens.

This new political offensive, designed to convince the public that while Congress presented no Reconstruction plan southerners were willing to compromise, forced a Republican response. The hopes of conservative and centrist Republicans like Bingham that southerners would eventually ratify the Fourteenth Amendment if Congress insisted on that alone were no longer viable. The Orr plan threatened not only the party but the cherished Amendment as well. All Republicans now agreed that something had to be done.[34]

Unwilling simply to acquiesce in radical proposals, nonradicals determined to keep the proposed constitutional amendment at the center of new Reconstruction legislation. But at the same time southerners' intransigence forced them to conclude that rebel-dominated state governments would not themselves enforce its provisions. Faced at last with the clear realization that reliance on the Fourteenth Amendment alone would require continual national protection of citizens' rights, non-radical Republicans finally recognized the essential conservatism of black suffrage. As Carl Schurz put it in his *Reminiscences,* conservative Republicans, "after a faithful and somewhat perplexed wrestle with the complicated problem of reconstruction, finally landed—or it might almost be said, were stranded —at the conclusion that, to enable the negro to protect his own rights as a free man by the exercise of the ballot was after all the simplest way out of the tangle." [35] But they would not endorse schemes for territorial government, disfranchisement, or impeachment.

The conservative and center Republicans' decision to add black suffrage to their Reconstruction program guaranteed that the measure would be part of any final Reconstruction legislation. Radicals no doubt derived great satisfaction from this, but it certainly represented no great radical victory. Nonradicals endorsed it as an *alternative* to a permanent, or even long-term, alteration in the balance of power between state and national government. The same constitutional conservatism which impelled them to adopt the "grasp of war" theory of Reconstruction persuaded them that the primary protection for citizens' rights must come from the states themselves—from a reconstruction of power within the states rather than a reconstruction of the federal system with a vast increase in the powers of the national government. E.L. Godkin, the ever more conservative editor of the *Nation,* explained this new conservative position succinctly:

Our government owes to those who can get it no other way the one thing for which all governments exist . . .—security for person and property. This . . . we can supply either by a good police or by the admission of the blacks to such a share in the management of state affairs that they can provide a police for themselves. The former of these courses is not strictly in accordance with the spirit of our institutions; the latter is.[36]

So in the Reconstruction bill that would finally pass, black suffrage would be an alternative to a radical Reconstruction program that embodied much more.

ELEVEN

"Radical" Reconstruction —
Part Two

— ✦✦✦✦✦✦✦✦✦✦ —

WITH REPUBLICAN congressmen now demanding new Reconstruction legislation, the overworked Fessenden was forced to call together his Joint Committee on Reconstruction once more, to wrestle with the measures the House had referred to it.

The conflict between Stevens and Bingham flared immediately. Stevens pressed for his plan completely to reorganize the southern state governments, requiring at least universal male suffrage in the reorganization process; Bingham countered with a more moderate proposal. Resurrecting the committee's original Reconstruction bill, which promised restoration to states ratifying the constitutional amendment, Bingham moved to amend it to require the states to enact impartial (as distinct from *universal*) suffrage in addition. Battle lines appeared set: a radical plan requiring total reorganization of the South on a loyal basis versus a non-radical plan to restore the existing Confederate-dominated state governments upon their agreement to the Fourteenth Amendment and impartial suffrage, with the present state authorities setting the "nondiscriminatory" voting standards, which might include literacy or property requirement that few blacks could meet.[1]

Stevens and Bingham wrangled for two hours before the divided committee.[2] Finally, at a second meeting, the committee attempted to end the impasse by postponing consideration of both proposals, turning its attention at Conkling's suggestion to a new measure, submitted in the Senate by the centrist committee member, George H. Williams, two days earlier. Bypassing the controversies of Reconstruction, Williams's bill proposed simply to place the southern states under military authority. Military commanders were empowered to protect southerners in rights of person and property and to punish criminals and those who disturbed the peace. They could employ military commissions to do this, but the bill also authorized the use of the civil tribunals of the Johnson state governments. While pronouncing those governments "of no constitutional validity," the measure did not eliminate them, providing only that any attempts by them to interfere with the military authorities would be null and void.[3] Conkling led the committee in making minor amendments, while Bingham tried and failed to eliminate language he believed questioned the existence of the states. Bingham then again tried to persuade the committee to report their original Reconstruction bill. If both measures passed, the military occupation bill would remain in force only until the southern states met the conditions of the Reconstruction bill: ratification of the constitutional amendment and conformation of state laws and constitutions to it. But the committee, unwilling to renew the controversy over actual Reconstruction terms, defeated Bingham's motion.[4]

Williams's bill, reported to the House February 6, was not a radical measure, nor even a measure for Reconstruction. It was, as Williams explained in the Senate later, "proposed simply to enforce good order in these so-called States until loyal and republican State governments can be legally established." [5]

In proposing the measure Conkling and Williams no doubt expected the support of nonradical Republicans. Their bill did not stiffen the terms for readmission nor erase the governments already organized by presidential authority, although it denied their legitimacy. It did not foreclose those southern governments from acting on their own initiative to alter their laws or state constitutions in such a way as might satisfy Congress. It did not, in fact, do anything more than instill vigor into the "grasp of war" theory upon which the congressional reconstruction policy had been based. The measure did not proceed from a broad authority in Congress to guarantee southerners republican forms of government. It imposed no solutions. As Connecticut representative Augustus Brandegee observed, "It holds those communities in the grasp of war until the rebellion shall have laid down its spirit as two years ago it formally lay down its arms," until, in Bingham's words, "those people return to their loyalty and fealty in such a manner as shall satisfy the people of the United States, . . . represented in Congress, of their fitness to be restored to their full constitutional relations." [6]

On its face, the joint committee's proposition was a temporary measure to protect loyal men's lives and property, justified by Congress's war powers, and leaving southerners free to demonstrate their loyalty and good faith voluntarily and without coercion. But Stevens, managing the bill as senior House member of the Reconstruction committee, presented it in a way that immediately eroded nonradicals' faith in its moderation. As Stevens interpreted the measure it was "a bill for the purpose of putting under governments ten States now without governments." Viewed from Stevens's standpoint, the bill appeared to erect formal governments, military governments. And he said nothing indicating that those governments would be temporary.[7] Moreover, he justified the action on his theory that the confederacy of southern states had reached the status of a foreign power, that the United States held them as conquered provinces to be administered in any manner decreed by the conqueror and consistent with the customary laws and usages of war. Stevens had found in the new bill, originally suggested as a compromise, an opportunity to enact his theory of Reconstruction into law, an opportunity to hold southerners indefinitely under national power, an opportunity to enact a program closer to his original scheme than he had believed possible only a month earlier, when he had been willing to settle for an enabling act that would assure quick restoration. From the time of Stevens's speech, the measure would be known as the Military Government bill.[8]

When Stevens reported the bill February 6, he immediately moved to recommit it, a parliamentary tactic that foreclosed amendments. The following day he announced his determination to press for a vote the next afternoon.[9]

Shocked by Stevens's explanation of the committee's bill, conservative and moderate Republicans announced their opposition. But, for different reasons, so did many radicals. The dissident radicals might not have objected to temporary military government over the South, but southern loyalists who had traveled to Washington wanted above all to gain control of their state governments. Permanent military rule held no charm for them. It would "prove a delusion & a snare," worried Judge John C. Underwood, one of the leaders of the radical wing of Virginia's fledgling Republican party. "The leading rebels would by their frauds and flatteries manage to control the military authorities as effectually as they did President Johnson." It represented, complained the Louisiana radical Thomas J. Durant, "the sheer desperation of incapacity or unfaithfulness." [10] Julian, writing for his brother's newspaper, avowed his opposition to military Reconstruction and commented on the plight of the southern lobbyists, who "with anxious and weary looks are still daily watching the action of Congress while despair begins to write itself in their faces." [11]

More conservative Republicans objected as strenuously. Once more Bingham took the lead. Endorsing the bill in principle (another indication of its essential conservatism), Bingham denounced Stevens's justification for it. He proposed to eliminate all wording that indicated that the southern states had ceased to exist, that southerners whether loyal or disloyal had become alien enemies subject to the will of the conqueror without the rights and protection due American citizens. In particular, he demanded a new preamble, because Stevens interpreted the one reported by the committee "as a solemn declaration on the part of this House that those States are foreign conquered territories." Denying that the bill proceeded upon Stevens's theory of conquered provinces, he insisted it was based simply

on Congress's duty to administer the South and would remain in force only
until its citizens reorganized their governments in a fashion acceptable to
the national government. To make this clear, he proposed to include in his
version of the preamble the assurance that the military administration was
intended only to enforce "peace and good order . . . until said States
respectively shall be fully restored to their constitutional relations to the
United States." [12]

He wanted this amendment in the preamble, Bingham explained,

to notify in the most solemn form the men who constitute . . . the majority
of the people in those ten lately insurgent States, and who themselves were in
open and armed rebellion, that . . . all they have to do, in order to get rid of
military rule and military government, is to present to the Congress of the
United States a constitutional form of State government in accord with the
letter and spirit of the Constitution and laws of the United States, together with
a ratification of the pending constitutional amendment.[13]

One by one radicals like Shellabarger and Lawrence, conservatives
like Griswold and Raymond, avowed their dislike of military government,
threatened to vote against the bill, or announced they would support it
only with the understanding that it was temporary. Finally on February 8,
as he had promised, Stevens demanded the previous question. If the House
agreed to it, the vote would take place one hour later and again no amendments would be in order. Banks took the floor to oppose the motion. He
urged the House to abandon the committee's temporary, inconclusive bill
and try to reach a final solution to the Reconstruction problem. He hinted
that the president might now be willing to come to an understanding with
the party. The aspiring politician, whose career had become so entwined
with the great issue, suggested that no Reconstruction program could be
effective without the president's cooperation. Republicans should make a
final effort to reach an agreement with him. If they failed, he indicated,
impeachment was the only solution.[14]

Stevens would have none of it. Once again the old radical felt success
slipping through his clutching fingers; he could feel the representatives
waver, feel them balk. "I have seen enough in this House, and have heretofore noted its demoralization, to doubt if there is enough left of the spirit
of the party that sent us here to carry out the will of the people and perfect
the legislation they expect from us," he said. In an effort to gain support, he
backed away from his implication that the bill was more than a short-term
expedient. He acknowledged that it was designed only to protect loyalists
"until we can have time to frame civil governments more in conformity
with the genius of our institutions."

For Stevens, it was the critical moment.

I know not whether it is the desire of this House to pass any such bill or
whether they prefer to go home and leave the President triumphant. I am

quite sure that much of the opposition . . . comes from a modification of views coinciding with the President . . . . I have yet to learn to what extent this has prevailed, and after the previous question has been voted upon I shall be more satisfied whether it is worth while to proceed further in this attempt by Congress to resist the power of the President, or whether it is our duty . . . to submit to the powers which have conquered us and allow the southern States to remain in their present condition.[15]

But all Steven's venom and will could not prevail. The House refused to second the previous question by a vote of 61 to 98, and it became clear the bill could not pass without amendment.[16] By February 12, amendments by Bingham, Lawrence, Kasson, Ashley, Blaine, and Isaac R. Hawkins lay before the House. It did not seem possible to amend and pass any Reconstruction bill in time to prevent a pocket veto.[17]

The most conservative proposals, not offered formally until February 12, came from Bingham and James G. Blaine. Bingham proposed to combine the original Reconstruction bill reported by the joint committee during the first session with the Military Government bill. Announcing that the southern states would be restored after they ratified the proposed constitutional amendment, conformed their laws and constitutions to it, and enacted impartial suffrage laws, Bingham's measure went on to enact the provisions of the Military Government bill—minus language which might suggest a recognition of Stevens's conquered provinces theory—until those conditions were met. Furthermore, any state that ratified the amendment could postpone for ten years payment of direct taxes not collected during the rebellion.[18]

Blaine suggested simply adding one more section to the Military Government bill, embodying the same conditions for restoration as Bingham and using nearly the same language, except that Blaine would allow provisions in the new state constitutions disfranchising participants in the rebellion, and would require southerners to ratify their constitutions as amended by popular vote. Ashley, abandoning the radical measure he had proposed earlier in the session, presented amendments similar to Bingham's and Blaine's.[19] Occupying a sort of middle ground were proposals by Kasson and Lawrence, but these did not play an important role in the upcoming struggle.[20]

Then on February 11, as the Military Government bill floundered, a new Reconstruction bill came before the House—a radical alternative—in what promised to be an important radical parliamentary coup. Since the reference to the joint committee of Stevens's substitute for the original Reconstruction bill, radicals had been unable to bring a proposition embodying their program to the floor. House rules required that all Reconstruction measures be referred to the joint committee without debate. The committee had not even considered any of these propositions, and its well-balanced membership made the report of a truly radical proposition virtually impossible. But early in the session the House had appointed a special committee to investigate the New Orleans riot of the summer of 1866 and empowered it to report appropriate legislation. Radical Thomas D. Eliot, who suggested the committee, was named chairman; Samuel Shellabarger, another radical, was the second Republican member, with William B. Campbell representing the Democrats.

Taking the testimony and advice from military officers assigned to the South and from the southern loyalist lobby, which urged a territorial government for Louisiana, Eliot and Shellabarger framed a bill to re-establish civil government there and reported it to the House. The bill required Johnson to name a new provisional governor and a nine-member provisional council for the state. The consent of the Senate was required for both confirmation and removal, rendering the appointees relatively independent of the president for their tenure. The new governor and council had to be citizens of Louisiana who never indicated approval of secession or support for the rebellion. They would have complete legislative power in the state and would appoint all state officers provided for under the existing state constitution. These state officers would be required to take the test oath that they never voluntarily aided the rebellion (as distinguished from the governor and council, who must not have aided the rebellion under any circumstances).

In June the voters would elect a provisional government, with the same officers as existed under the constitution of the Johnson government, all of whom, however, would have to meet the tests of loyalty required of the presidential appointees they were to replace. The bill enfranchised every adult male United States citizen living in Louisiana for a year who could take the test oath. Furthermore, any former rebel who swore he had not voluntarily aided the rebellion and had held no rank higher than private in the rebel armed forces could vote if a person who never aided the rebellion at all would swear the petitioner opposed it after March 4, 1864. The Eliot-Shellabarger bill then ordered an election for delegates to a constitutional convention, all of whom must never have supported secession nor aided the rebellion. They would frame a constitution forbidding legal distinctions among men on grounds of color or race, and that constitution had to be ratified by the voters. All elections would be conducted under regulations issued by the secretary of war. The president was required to appoint a military commander over the state, who would protect the rights of citizens and enforce the laws whenever local authorities were unable or unwilling to do so, or whenever they requested aid. Finally, Congress had to approve all laws passed by the provisional government.[21]

The differences between the three alternatives—the Military Government bill, the bill as amended by Bingham or Blaine, and the Louisiana Reconstruction bill—were patent. The military bill itself was but a stop-gap, designed to protect loyal southerners from the outrages condoned if not perpetrated by the Johnson state governments. Although it pronounced the Johnson governments illegal, it did not actually displace them, merely declaring void any attempts they might make to interfere with the military authority. Moreover, the bill authorized the military to utilize local courts (and this meant all the officials which made up the courts—not only judges but sheriffs and constables who served judicial processes). Given the proven reluctance of military men at this time to substitute military for civil authority, under the Military Government bill most of the state administration might very well remain in the hands of the very governments the bill declared illegal. Moreover, the military was not known for its sympathy for the aspirations of southern blacks. And finally, Andrew Johnson as president also was the armed forces' commander in chief. Although the military bill at first vested the power to appoint military commanders in General Grant (whose radicalism was thoroughly suspect anyway), Congress reconsidered, and left this power in the hands of the president.[22]

As a compromise measure, the Military Government bill remained silent on the conditions for restoration. These might be prescribed in a future Reconstruction bill, or southerners might be left free to frame their own constitutions and submit them to Congress, which would decide if they met satisfactory standards of republicanism and offered such security as the safety of the nation required. If Republicans chose the second alternative, then there would be a great chance that former rebels, having at their command the administrative machinery of the states and their patronage, as well as the patronage of the national government, would dominate the new Reconstruction process as they did the old. They might frame new constitutions guaranteeing impartial, certainly not universal, suffrage, they might guarantee equality before the law and ratify the constitutional amendment (many had offered to do all these things anyway, in the compromise proposed by Governor Orr), but as the best-organized force in each state, they would retain control of the administration. If the Republicans in Congress did not approve, southerners, Johnsonites, and Democrats could portray them as vindicative radicals refusing honest petitions of loyalty.

The Bingham and Blaine amendments merely spelled out in detail the conditions southerners must meet for restoration. They created no machinery to oversee the process of their acceptance. Blaine, trying to secure maximum support for this amendment, assured his colleagues that Congress could erect such machinery if it wished, but Bingham made no such concession. "The formation of a State government must be the voluntary act of the people themselves," he insisted. The state authorities recognized by Johnson would submit constitutional amendments meeting Congress's requirements to the people for ratification.[23] As soon as those governments met Congress's requirements, Congress would recognize their legitimacy.

Under this process, former rebels were certain to be the dominant influence in "reorganization." Bingham recognized this. Indeed, this was what he desired—for the rebels themselves to accede to the conditions Congress laid down, for the rebels themselves to demonstrate their loyalty.[24]

The Louisiana bill, of course, differed completely from the Bingham-Blaine alternative, dispersing the Louisiana government recognized by the president and replacing it with a provisional government controlled by loyal unionists. The people would reorganize their government under the surveillance of this provisional government and the military, under regulations framed by the secretary of war. The radical measure also took a far different approach to voting than the more conservative one. The Bingham-Blaine alternative required merely *impartial* suffrage, allowing any voting qualifications other than those based on race or color. This meant, as Senator Wilson observed later, "nothing more nor less than the exclusion of nearly all the colored persons from the polls." [25] All white southerners need do was require literacy, property, or educational qualifications. Second, although Blaine's amendment would allow the disfranchisement of rebels, it did not require or encourage it. In fact, Bingham accepted Blaine's language into his own amendment and denounced disfranchisement moments later.[26] The Louisiana bill, it was true, required no permanent disfranchisement and only insisted upon impartial suffrage in the state constitution, but by disfranchising nearly every rebel in the reorganization process and enfranchising every black man, the bill virtually guaranteed universal suffrage for blacks and encouraged some measure of disfranchisement of whites, as well as strict loyalty qualifications for officeholders. Bingham bitterly attacked these provisions. "Has it, indeed, come to this," he asked, "that gentlemen are not content to secure the emancipated citizens of the Republic the elective franchise, and all the rights of citizens and men, but by act of Congress insists farther . . . to secure to them even in a minority the whole power of the State, . . . and compel the majority of white citizens to be their subjects for life?" [27]

The House voted on the Louisiana Reconstruction bill first. When Eliot reported it to the House, Bingham suggested that he wait until the House disposed of the Military Government bill before pressing his measure, but the press of business was so great that Eliot feared his bill would be lost if he agreed. Desperately both men scrounged for some parliamentary maneuver that would assure Eliot that his bill would come back to the floor later if he acceded to Bingham's request, which was, after all, a logical one. But none availed. There was no alternative. "Let him show his pluck," a representative challenged, "and call the previous question on it at once." This would bar amendments and allow only one hour for debate.

Eliot decided to try it.[28] Although debate on the general merits of the bill was not in order, most representatives knew where they stood. On the first vote Republican disagreement was manifest as the House refused to second the previous question, 66 to 68. But Eliot called for a vote by tellers, and this time he won 79 to 70. An effort to reconsider the decision failed 64 to 66. Eliot had shown his pluck; he had won.[29] Now he moved to proceed to the main question, the last step before final debate and a vote, and most Republicans united behind the bill rather than give the Democrats and Johnsonites the victory. But high-power representatives committed to the Blaine or Bingham amendments joined the Democratic opposition, among them Bingham, Dawes, and Robert C. Schenck. Others abstained. The next day, after Eliot steered his bill through more treacherous parliamentary shoals, the House passed it, nearly all Republicans finally acquiescing; Bingham was the only Republican leader to hold out.[30]

Radicals were elated. Radical senators hoped to substitute the Louisiana bill for any military bill that might pass the House. Julian predicted that Congress would enforce similar provisions in North Carolina and Arkansas, where there were enough loyalists to support them, while it put Virginia, South Carolina, and other states with few white loyalists under purely military control. Southern Republican lobbyists urged Congress to reorganize all the rebel states upon the same principles.[31] But when Republicans returned to the consideration of the military government bill on February 12, conservatives and moderates were more determined than ever to modify its provisions. That determination increased as nonradicals made one final attempt to compromise with the president.

At the center of the last Republican effort to compromise their differences with the president were two of Johnson's intimate supporters, W.W. Warden and General George P. Este, who had been urging the president to reach some agreement with more conservative Republicans to bring the Reconstruction controversy to a close. If he cooperated, they assured Johnson, a majority of Republicans would settle for ratification of the constitutional amendment and black suffrage as a basis for Reconstruction without overthrowing his state governments. After long hesitation, the pugnacious president agreed to make the effort.

Informing conservative Republicans—Raymond, Dodge, Delano, Bingham, Banks, Blow, Dawes, and others—of Johnson's new tractability, Warden convinced a few of them to meet him and Este in their rooms at the Metropolitan Hotel the evening of February 12. There about fifteen Republicans listened as Warden and Este reiterated their convictions that Johnson was willing to rejoin the party and restore its control over patronage if they could reach a compromise on Reconstruction. The Republicans, assuring the two men that seventy to eighty of their colleagues would agree to a compromise if one could be reached, appointed Representatives Addison H. Laflin and Alexander H. Rice to meet Johnson. At the same time Banks visited the president and urged him to name Horace Greeley postmaster general. Johnson mused to his private secretary that if he named a new cabinet including Greeley, Grant, Farragut, and Charles Francis Adams, the Reconstruction question would be settled in two hours. Laflin anxiously kept Greeley abreast of the negotiations.[32]

With the movement for compromise gaining momentum, Blaine determined to force a vote on his amendment to the Military Government bill. In a sharp parliamentary maneuver, Blaine circumvented the rule that no amendment is in order pending a motion to recommit (Stevens had never withdrawn that motion) by moving to commit the bill to the Judiciary committee with instructions to report it back immediately with his amendments. Then he moved that the House vote immediately upon his motion. The Democrats, aware of the backstage compromise efforts and torn between conflicting desires to modify the bill and to obstruct Republican efforts to harmonize with the president, split evenly as the House agreed by an 85 to 78 margin to Blaine's motion to vote at once. Sixty-nine Republicans, including all the conservatives meeting with Este and Warden, voted with Blaine. Also joining Blaine were at least eight radicals who had been assured by Judiciary committee chairman Wilson that he would attempt to add a provision disfranchising leading rebels, among them Ashley, Donnelly, Hayes, and Broomall (see Group 5 of List 11). Only sixty-two Republicans voted with Stevens.

Once again Stevens took the floor, in an effort, he believed, to avert disaster.

For the last few months Congress has been sitting here, and while the South has been bleeding at every pore, Congress has done nothing . . . . Although we are insensible to it, the whole country is alive to the effect of the supineness with which Congress has conducted itself. . . . We are enjoying ourselves . . . while the South is covered all over with anarchy and murder and rapine.

Angrily, he attacked Bingham for preventing passage of his first Reconstruction bill earlier in the session "in a most unparliamentary and discourteous manner."

I do not know whether that bill was good or bad. I thought it was a good bill; I had labored upon it in conjunction with several committees of loyal men from the South for four months, I had altered and realtered it, written and rewritten it four several times . . . . It was, therefore, not altogether my fault if it was not so good a bill as might be found; but I did think that, after all, it was uncivil, unjust, indecent not to attempt to amend it and make it better, to see whether we could do something to enable our friends in the southern States to establish institutions according to the principles of republican government.

When the joint committee reported the Military Government bill, "it came here with a perfect understanding that if it was to pass and become a law it must pass without amendment. . . . But . . . this bill encounters precisely the same obstacles as the other, and is met in precisely the same spirit." Then Stevens made a final, impassioned appeal to the radicals who had joined Blaine out of dissatisfaction with the military bill, his voice so weak that his listeners left their seats to gather around him.

If, sir, I might presume upon my age, without claiming any of the wisdom of Nestor, I would suggest to the young gentlemen around me, that the deeds of this burning crisis, of this solemn day, of this thrilling moment, will cast their shadows far into the future and will make their impress upon the annals of our history, and that we shall appear upon the bright pages of that history, just in so far as we cordially, without guile, without bickering, without small criticisms, lend our aid to promote the great cause of humanity and universal liberty.

When he closed, the House defeated Blaine's motion, 69 to 94. Seventeen Republicans (the radicals and the centrists listed in Group 3 of List 11) switched sides.

The conservatives, angry at the Democrats who had joined the radicals, now united with their allies to pass the bill without the Blaine amendment. Only nineteen Republicans dissented. Gratefully, Stevens turned to Colfax. "I wish to inquire, Mr. Speaker," he said, "if it is in order for me now to say that we indorse the language of good old Laertes, that Heaven rules as yet and there are gods above." [33]

Yet the battle was not ended. The House sent two bills to the Senate —the Louisiana Reconstruction bill and the Military Government bill. In the form they arrived, the measures were complementary, and yet radicals understood the danger. The House nearly had accepted the Blaine amendment to the military bill, which would have outlined terms for Reconstruction far milder than those incorporated in the other Reconstruction bill. Pressure might prove even greater in the more conservative Senate. If the Senate did adopt provisions similar to those Blaine proposed, the two measures would be arrayed in open hostility to one another. Southern Republican lobbyists, therefore, began a campaign to persuade the Senate to extend the Louisiana bill's provisions to other southern states and abandon the military bill. Wade, Sumner, Wilson, Conness, and other radical senators expressed their preference for the Louisiana measure.[34]

Still, Senate radicals announced their willingness to support both measures, but they emphasized that the two bills served different functions. "One is the beginning of a true reconstruction; the other is the beginning of a true protection . . . ," Sumner explained. "Both must be had, and neither must be antagonized with the other. The two should go on side by side the guardian angels of this Republic." [35] But Fessenden took a different view. Denigrating the Louisiana bill as merely experimental and of narrow application, he insisted that the Military Government bill, with the Blaine amendment, would make "as complete a system . . . as could possibly be offered now." [36]

The Louisiana Reconstruction bill, passed first by the House, came up in the Senate before its companion measure, and Wade, its Senate manager, hoped to pass it with an amendment applying its provisions to all the rebel states. But Fessenden and Sherman urged the Senate to consider the Military Government bill first. Despite his announced preference for the bill under his control, Wade agreed (over Sunmer's objections), with the understanding that the military bill's manager, Williams, would persevere in the fight until his bill passed, allowing no delays which might jeopardize both measures.[37]

Wade believed he had been assured that Fessenden and other conservatives would oppose all amendments to that bill, and the Blaine amendment in particular.[38] This provides the only explanation for his decision to give up the Louisiana bill's preferred place. It is not conceivable that he would have done so had he expected the Senate to adopt any amendment which would convert the "protection" bill into a "Reconstruction" bill with provisions completely inconsistent with those of the measure he preferred. Indeed, Williams, who originally intended to propose an amendment similar to Blaine's, withdrew it and opposed all amendments from that time forward.[39]

When Williams brought the Military Government bill before the Senate, Friday, February 15, it met the same hail of criticism that had greeted it in the House. But in the upper chamber, where there was no way to cut off amendments, the criticism degenerated into confusion. Conservative senators objected to unlimited military rule, demanding some provision for the return to civil government. The Maryland Democrat, Reverdy Johnson, proposed the Blaine-like amendment Williams had decided to abandon, and senator after senator moved amendments to it.[40] Conservative and centrist Republicans like Stewart, Kirkwood, Lane, and Cragin announced their support for the modification, as did the radical Yates.[41] But most radicals opposed it vigorously, despite its acceptance of universal suffrage. The amendment was inconsistent with the bill, they pointed out. The measure itself pronounced the Johnson governments illegal, but the amendment recognized their power to amend their constitutions. With accurate prescience, Howard predicted "a collision between the Federal military authorities and the State authorities which we thus recognize by this amendment." Sumner worried over the same problem. "This whole proposition is . . . thoroughly vicious in every line and in every word from the first to the last," he insisted. In response to these criticisms, the Senate amended the amendment to require the states to alter their constitutions by conventions rather than through legislative action.[42] But Sumner objected to other provisions also.

As Friday night wore into Saturday morning, senators fought over amendments to require only impartial suffrage, more certainly to require universal suffrage, to require free public education for children of all races, to guarantee equal rights to pursue professions, and to declare the number of states necessary to ratify the constitutional amendment. Democrats moved adjournment time and again, but Williams fought them off. Finally, shortly before 3:00 A.M., Wade and Henderson moved to substitute the Louisiana bill for the entire mess. This was too much for Williams; he himself called for an adjournment and his colleagues gratefully agreed.[43]

The next morning, only a few hours after they had adjourned, the weary and irritable Republican senators caucused and after some discussion decided to appoint a seven-member committee to hammer out a bill. They named Sherman chairman and Fessenden, Sumner, Trumbull, Howard, Ira Harris, and Frederick T. Frelinghuysen members. It was a distinctly conservative group.

The caucus committee had a wide range of propositions to choose from—from the Bingham and Blaine amendments on the right to the Louisiana bill on the left—and after acrimonious debate, it reported an amendment to the Military Government bill incorporating elements of all three. In the most important concession to the radicals, the committee proposition required southerners to hold new state constitutional conventions. As nearly all Republicans demanded, delegates to them would be elected by all adult male voters meeting certain residency requirements, except those who might be disfranchised for their parts in the rebellion. The rest of the proposal embodied primarily the Blaine-Bingham program. The conventions would frame constitutions organizing republican governments and submit them to the voters for ratification. If these constitutions met the approval of Congress and the state legislatures organized under them ratified the constitutional amendment, the states would be restored to normal relations with the United States and the other provisions of the Military Government bill would become inoperative.

The radicals remained dissatisfied. The committee had refused to disperse the Johnson state governments declared illegal in the military bill's preamble. It had not provided new governments under southern unionist control. It had abandoned the election machinery of the Louisiana bill, leaving the present state governments in a position possibly to organize and administer the election of convention delegates. Adhering to that all-important illusion of voluntarism, the committee proposal required the incorporation of no specific provisions in the new state constitutions—it did not insist upon universal suffrage, nor upon a guarantee of free and equal public education, nor upon the disfranchisement of rebels. It effected no land redistribution. Many senators no doubt argued that Congress could refuse to approve the state constitutions until such provisions were made, but this would mean new battles, with Republicans perhaps in a weaker position than now numerically, with the public impatient for an end to crisis. Further requirements would almost certainly be more difficult to effect later.

In the full caucus, Sumner and Wilson led a fight to require at least universal suffrage in the state constitutions. After a long and impassioned debate, the full caucus overruled the committee decision by one vote. Wilson was so elated that he grabbed senators and danced with them, but Sunmer, still unsatisfied, left the Senate in a rage and refused to vote on the bill. "Rarely have good and evil been mixed on such a scale," he said later. "Look at the good and you are full of grateful admiration. Look at the evil and you are impatient at such an abandonment of duty. You have done much; but you have not done enough." In the absence of detailed machinery and disfranchisement, the rebels could inaugurate the reconstruction process and dominate the elections. "With their experience, craft, and determined purpose, there is too much reason to fear that all your safeguards would be overthrown, and the Unionist would continue the victim of rebel power." [44]

Sherman proposed the caucus measure to the exhausted and short-tempered senators that night. At six o'clock Sunday morning they finally passed the bill. Sumner and Wilson tried to take up the Louisiana bill the following day, but conservatives forced an adjournment, and the bill was lost in the press of business during the session's closing days.[45]

The Senate had reversed Stevens' victory in the House. "The savage recital is changed to a legal proposition," Sherman wrote Cox with gratification, and Republican conservatives and centrists in the House labored to force acceptance of that reversal.[46] President Johnson strengthened that determination by indicating that he might sign the Reconstruction bill if it included the Blaine amendment. Playing a double game (he assured anxious Democrats that he would veto the measure) he led the representatives appointed to confer with him at the Metropolitan Hotel meeting of February 12 to believe that he hoped to cooperate with Republican conservatives and centrists. At a second meeting, held in the rooms of Representative William E. Dodge, the conservatives decided to bend all their efforts on behalf of the Senate bill.[47] But as Raymond and Banks assured Republican representatives of Johnson's good intentions, Democratic leaders gave similar assurances to their followers. "Somebody is sure to be cheated," [48] the Springfield *Republican*'s correspondent observed.

As the House struggled over Stevens's motion to refuse to concur in the Senate amendment and instead to appoint a conference committee to iron out the differences, radicals warned that "by the bill as now amended you transfer the reorganization of these ten States to the rebels; you give to rebels the chief places in the work of reconstruction, possessing as they do for the time being, the means of influence, of trust . . . ." But Blaine argued that this was all "mere bugaboo and scarecrow." Congress retained the right, "plenary and absolute," to disapprove of any constitution brought before it.[49]

The conservatives brought forward their most powerful men—Blaine,

Bingham, and Garfield—and representatives who earlier had cooperated with radicals—Schenck and Wilson. Practical legislators, well inside what modern analysts would call the House "establishment," they bitterly denounced impractical idealists, who, in Garfield's words, "live among the eagles on the highest mountain peaks, beyond the line of perpetual frost," and who denounced every reasonable effort to secure freedom as "poor and mean and a surrender of liberty." [50] It was one of those battles again highlighting an essential difference between radicals and nonradicals—the unwillingness of radicals to settle for the politically practical when it appeared to put in jeopardy the goals shared by all Republicans.

As the vote approached, the nonradicals appeared to possess the greater strength. But southern Republican lobbyists worked hard to prevent concurrence, and Fessenden, who had endorsed the Blaine amendment in the Senate, now urged representatives to reject it, hoping to deadlock the two houses and thus defeat all efforts to go beyond the constitutional amendment as a basis for Reconstruction. Finally, many Democrats refused to cooperate with the Republican conservatives, instead deciding to vote with radicals. By helping radicals to defeat the Senate's moderate amendments, Democrats hoped to force conservative Republicans to kill the measure entirely or pass it in a form that would preclude any compromise between the president and his party. As representatives recorded their votes, other less Machiavellian Democrats held back, trying to determine whether their votes could carry the motion to concur. When it became apparent that they could not, they voted with the radical-Democratic coalition, swelling its margin of victory to twenty-five votes. But Stevens had carried only a minority of Republican congressmen with him; the radicals owed their success to the Democrats.[51] The House then agreed to request a conference, and Colfax named a tough committee, Stevens and Shellabarger representing the radical-Democratic majority and Blaine the minority.

Radical unity broke down completely in the Senate when word arrived of the House's action. Sumner, hoping for radical modification, urged senators to agree to the conference. Wade, hoping to kill the bill and begin anew in the Fortieth Congress, tried to persuade his colleagues to refuse. Others feared that if the bill died or if Congress passed only Stevens's Military Government bill, the southern state legislatures might reconsider their rejections of the Fourteenth Amendment. If they ratified that proposition, pressure could well be irresistible to restore southern representation without requiring the suffrage extension for which radicals had struggled so hard.

But what aggravated and confused radicals most was Fessenden's course. They knew that he had urged representatives to reject the Senate amendments, and many of his colleagues were outraged. Fessenden had never indicated his opposition to the bill or its amendments in the Senate.

He had served on the caucus committee that had framed the compromise modification. He had partaken in that caucus debate and under the accepted custom was bound by its decision. He had not announced his objections or voted against the bill on its passage, instead going home while other senators sweated through the debates until early Sunday morning. Now he had employed his immense influence as Republican leader in the Senate to persuade representatives to resist the Senate's version of the bill. Radicals feared that if Fessenden had such secret doubts, then Sherman and Williams, who were almost certain to represent Senate Republicans in a conference committee and who had both favored milder amendments to the bill than those the Senate finally adopted, might share similar misgivings.[52]

Attempting to justify his course by claiming he objected to the bill's conservatism, Fessenden pointed out that he and Stevens were in agreement, observing smugly that "if gentlemen who glory in the name of radical are not quite so radical on that subject as I am, that is all the difference between us." Wade could not bear it. "He tells us that the fault we find with him is his radicalism," he exploded. "Well, sir, if he has become radical I shall be compensated for all that has happened here today." Referring to Fessenden's role in the caucus debate, he observed archly, "If I were permitted to speak of what transpired in other places, I should say that I was entirely convinced it was not its radicalism that troubled him then." [53] Unwilling to risk the concessions they had won, most radicals joined more conservative allies in refusing a conference.[54]

When the bill returned to the House with the Senate's refusal to appoint conferees, disgruntled radicals cooperated with Democrats to delay its passage at least for one day, enabling the president to kill it with a pocket veto.[55] But as radicals caucused privately the next morning, James F. Wilson, in a final attempt to save the bill, offered them a compromise on behalf of the nonradical Republicans with whom he had been cooperating—an amendment disfranchising all men disqualified from office under the constitutional amendment, the same disfranchising amendment that had persuaded some radicals to vote for Blaine's motion to recommit the bill to the Judiciary committee a week earlier. But the radicals insisted on a further minimum condition for their support: an amendment by Stevens and Shellabarger specifically declaring the Johnson state governments provisional and subject to the authority of the military. The commanders were empowered to modify or abolish those governments, men disqualified from holding office under the constitutional amendment were not to be allowed to hold office in them, and universal suffrage was required in any elections to fill vacancies. Blaine refused to accede to this amendment, however, and when the bill came before the House once more, he moved the previous question to prevent its submission. The House refused to support him by only four votes and then, over Democratic and conservative opposition, accepted the radical amendment and returned the bill to the Senate.[56] There Wilson made a brief effort to amend the bill to require the dispersal of the Johnson governments, but he made no headway, and the Senate concurred in the House amendment, with all the Republicans present and one Democrat (Johnson) in the majority.[57]

The bill had passed at last. "We have cast loose from the whole dead past and have cast our anchor out a hundred years ahead and now have to pull our civilization up to it . . . ," Howe wrote home. "Does it not seem grand? Alas! there was nothing grand about it. Congress has never seemed . . . more querulous, distracted, incoherent and ignoble than when undergoing this very transformation." [58]

Passed on February 20, the Military Government bill (since its amendment called the Reconstruction bill) could not be enrolled and signed by the Speaker of the House and president *pro tempore* of the Senate until the next day. By not returning it to the Senate, the president could pocket veto it. But some observers, pointing to the negotiations in which he had engaged with conservative Republicans and to Reverdy Johnson's vote in favor of the measure, predicted that he would sign it. Fearful of the consequences of a rapprochement, radicals hoped for a veto. But Este reported to Johnson "that all the more moderate Radicals [i.e., Republicans] desire you to sign the bill. I mean those who dont [*sic*] wish to follow the lead of Stevens, Boutwell & Co. *They* say your signing the bill will forever kill the extreme wing of the party and give you control of the situation." Greeley, Grant, and Charles Nordhoff, one of *Evening Post* editor William Cullen Bryant's protégés, urged the president to sign. A veto "would merely give strength to Stevens, . . . while it would cripple the sensible republicans," Nordhoff warned. If Johnson signed the bill, "the southern leaders would give up, & accept it, & all their troubles would be ended."

But Nordhoff found Johnson bitter even at Republican moderates, convinced (as Nordhoff wrote another *Post* editor, Parke Godwin) "that the people of the south, . . . quiet[,] unoffending, harmless, were to be trodden underfoot 'to protect niggers.' " Angrily, the young journalist, who like his newspaper had earlier sustained the president's policy, reported "that he is a pig-headed man, with only one idea, & that is bitter opposition to universal suffrage, & a determination to secure the political ascendancy of the old Southern leaders. . . . I think it was a great mistake on our part," he admitted, "that some of us did not last winter visit Washington, so as to comprehend the real facts." [59]

By signing the Reconstruction bill, Johnson could have put the Republican coalition under terrific stress. With the Fortieth Congress scheduled to meet immediately upon the dissolution of the Thirty-ninth, radicals were already preparing to press for a supplementary Reconstruction bill to remedy the weaknesses of the measure just passed. Sumner announced his intention of bringing the Louisiana bill to a vote.[60] Impeachment efforts were under way (see pp. 244–45). With the president evincing an inclination to return to the fold, the tensions between more conservative Republicans who would welcome such a development and the radicals who abhorred it would have intensified tremendously. At minimum the president would have been in a strong position to modify future legislation.

Despite the political advantages that would have accrued to him had he signed the bill, Johnson decided to veto it. But having decided this, his decision to send a veto to Congress rather than just pocket the bill is simply inexplicable.[61] Stevens, Sumner, Wade, Ashley, Julian, and their radical cohorts would not have settled for a simple repassage of the Reconstruction bill they had fought so bitterly. The whole divisive contest would have been fought again, with congressmen anxious to return home, tempers shorter, recriminations greater. Again the stubborn Johnson had come to his enemies' rescue. The veto arrived March 2, and both houses promptly overrode it.[62]

Johnson's veto and his continued hostility to all Republicans and their program persuaded conservatives and centrists to endorse a supplementary Reconstruction bill. The quid quo pro that conservatives who hoped for a new understanding with Johnson had offered him was the continued existence of his state authorities as provisional governments. Under the Reconstruction act as it passed, those governments might have called the required constitutional conventions, organized the elections, and generally exercised a great influence in the process of reorganization. When Johnson signified his continued opposition, these Republicans could not help but fear that if his southern governments did initiate the Reconstruction process, they would do so in bad faith. Therefore, they endorsed a second law, giving the military the sole authority to administer the registration and elections. Although some historians believe this a radical measure, driving home the advantage radicals won when Congress agreed to declare the state governments provisional only, in fact it was framed by a House Judiciary committee whose Republican membership was evenly balanced between those who had generally cooperated with the Bingham-Blaine forces and those who had cooperated with Stevens. The bill went no further than the original law. Republicans intended it, as Blaine explained, simply "to secure to everybody entitled to vote at all an even start in the race." [63]

Misconstruing the nature of the supplementary Reconstruction bill, W.R. Brock has remarked upon "the collapse of moderate opposition" which allowed its easy passage. But in fact there was no collapse of moderate opposition. In the House, where the Judiciary committee chairman moved the previous question to cut off amendments to the bill, it was the radical opposition which collapsed, recognizing the futility of opposing swift passage of the measure with congressmen anxious to adjourn the session and go home.

But radicals and conservatives continued their battle in the Senate. As petitions continued to arrive from southern Republicans asking Congress to disperse the Johnson state governments completely and erect territorial governments over their states, Sumner proposed a detailed new Reconstruction bill. Although it was never published and is no longer in the Senate bill file in the National Archives, its general outline may be gathered by resolutions Sumner presented in the Senate on March 11. Pronouncing the passage of the Reconstruction act only a beginning, Sumner's resolutions called for the complete overthrow of the present southern governments, the creation of provisional governments, further measures to minimize rebel influence in the Reconstruction process (meaning further disfranchisement and officeholding disqualifications), the establishment of free and equal systems of public education in the South, and the guarantee of a homestead to the head of every family of freed slaves. But after a full, occasionally acrimonius discussion, the Senate laid the resolutions on the table, only ten Republicans dissenting.[64]

Sumner, already burdened by the disintegration of his short marriage, was crushed. In his loneliness he scrawled a note to his intimate friend, Edward L. Pierce: "How few here sympathize with me! I sometimes feel that I am alone in the Senate.

"God bless you." [65]

The most important conflict over the supplementary Reconstruction bill itself emanated from the fear of many Republicans, primarily radicals, that Congress was in too great haste for final restoration. This anxiety manifested itself momentarily in the House when Benjamin F. Butler, entering Congress for his first term, proposed to eliminate provisions setting dates for the commencement of the Reconstruction process. This would allow the military commanders to decide when the states were ready to begin. But Judiciary committee chairman Wilson, the bill's manager, refused to give Butler the floor and persuaded the House to second his motion for the previous question without even a roll call vote.[66]

In the Senate the battle was joined over the question of whether to require an absolute majority of the registered voters to assent to the calling of conventions and to the ratification of proposed constitutions, or to allow a simply majority of the votes cast to suffice. More divisive and confusing was an amendment proposed by Fessenden to require the Johnson state legislatures to agree to call a convention before the reorganization process could begin. The radicals of the Thirty-ninth Congress divided on these questions. Some, like Howe, Pomeroy, and Wilson, wanted to bring southern Unionists into power as soon as possible and joined nonradicals in urging speed. Taking the opposite view were radicals like Howard, Sumner, and Nye, who had never desired quick restoration and now saw a chance to let white southerners delay it by their own inaction. Some conservative Republicans like Fessenden and possibly Morgan, Anthony, and Frelinghuysen, secretly convinced that former rebels inevitably would control the southern states, joined the radicals in a simple effort to delay this inevitable evil. After prolonged wrangling, the advocates of delay won a minimal concession: a majority of all registered voters would have to vote in the election to ratify the new state constitutions.[67]

Radicals agreed on two further amendments to the bill. First, they wanted to require irrevocable provisions in the new constitutions for voting by closed ballot rather than viva voce. The importance of such a security for blacks where whites held overwhelming economic power was patent. But Fessenden, still clinging to that illusion of voluntarism, objected to dictating the contents of the constitutions, and Roscoe Conkling and Oliver P. Morton, just elected senators, denied Congress's power over subjects within state jurisdiction. A Democratic-conservative-centrist coalition defeated the radical amendment, as its sponsor, freshman senator Charles D. Drake, grumbled at discovering what veterans had long known, "that there is such a thing on the floor of this Senate as conservative radicalism." [68]

Second, the radicals joined to support Sumner's effort to require constitutional provisions for free public education open to children of all races. But New Jersey's conservative new senator, Frederick T. Frelinghuysen, denied that Congress had the constitutional power to legislate for public education, and men like Trumbull, Sherman, Fessenden, and Williams, who had vehemently announced their opposition to *any* further conditions, joined him. Again a Democratic-conservative Republican coalition defeated the radicals.[69]

With the passage of the supplementary Reconstruction bill and its repassage over the inevitable veto, Republican Reconstruction policy was fixed. This was "Radical Reconstruction." But was it radical? Sumner publicly announced that he voted for it "not because it is what I desire, but because it is all that Congress is disposed to enact at the present time." [70] Stevens expressed similar sentiments, and Ben Perley Poore, the knowledgeable Washington correspondent for the Boston *Evening Journal,* wrote that other radicals felt the same way. Timothy Otis Howe felt more strongly. In his opinion the program was a "monstrous blunder." [71]

Compare congressional Reconstruction with the program envisaged by radicals at the beginning of the Thirty-ninth Congress. The radicals had insisted upon the complete dispersal of the Johnson state authorities; the Reconstruction acts recognized them as provisional governments. The radicals had advocated the creation of territorial governments in the South, through which southerners would govern themselves with congressional supervision until educated in the processes of democracy; the Reconstruction acts left most administration in the hands of governments dominated by rebels, placed paramount authority in military commanders, and encouraged virtually immediate restoration. Many radicals had wanted guarantees for black education, confiscation, and land reform; the Reconstruction acts embodied none of these. Radicals had wanted a rather widespread disfranchisement; the Reconstruction act disfranchised only rebels who had held state or national office prior to the rebellion and then joined it. The radicals had wanted to proceed upon the broad authority to reinstitute civil government in the South implicit in Congress's power to govern territories or guarantee republican forms of government; the Reconstruction acts proceeded on the more restrictive "grasp of war" theory, which relied on voluntary acceptance of peace conditions by southerners, leaving them free, for instance, to refuse to hold constitutional conventions by voting against them, or to refuse to ratify the constitutions they framed.[72] Moreover, that theory left Congress without power to enforce the conditions southerners accepted once normal relations were restored.

Nor did the Reconstruction acts correspond to the program radicals espoused when the second session began. It did not put Republicans in control of the restoration process as congressional and southern radicals pleaded; it minimized disfranchisement; it left officials of the Johnson state governments in office and in control of the state patronage; it encouraged speedier restoration than radicals wanted; it ignored necessities of education and land reform. Its radicalism lay in one provision: black suffrage. But by ignoring the other elements of the radical program, Republicans would learn that they had minimized the effectiveness of the one element they had accepted.

Finally, by propelling the southern states into quick restoration, the Reconstruction act prevented that slow maturation of healthy public opinion and democratic capabilities that radicals had hoped to nurture in the South through territorialization. Radicals, dissatisfied with the Reconstruction acts when enacted, grew more so as years passed. They blamed Reconstruction's failure on this untoward haste to end it before it had barely begun. The Reconstruction acts, Julian insisted, were responsible for "the horrors of carpet-bag government, Ku Klux outrages, and a system of pro-consular tyranny as inconsistent with the rights of these States as it has been disgraceful to the very idea of free government and fatal to the best interests of the colored race."

"It was," the disillusioned carpetbagger Albion Tourgee wrote, "cheap patriotism, cheap philanthropy, cheap success!" [73]

TWELVE

The Impeachment Movement and Presidential Obstruction

———————————— ✦✦✦✦✦✦✦✦✦✦✦✦ ————————————

IF RADICALS were unsatisfied by the Reconstruction act's provisions for the security of white and black loyalists in the South, they had another, more short-term reason to fear its practical effects, for the law designated the United States Army as the agency responsible for enforcing it, and so long as he remained in office, President Johnson would be the commander in chief of the armed forces. "As well commission a lunatic to superintend a lunatic asylum, or a thief to govern a penitentiary!" the *Anti-Slavery Standard* exclaimed. It was "an act of folly which no language can fitly describe." [1]

The passage of the Reconstruction bill really marked the end of the battle for a fundamental reorganization of southern political and economic institutions. Radicals would continue to demand more—to call for confiscation, land redistribution, and guaranteed equal education—but their efforts would prove futile, receiving only slight attention after the fatal elections of 1867. Instead, radicals and nonradicals would divide over the new issue of impeachment as a measure to ensure restoration under the Reconstruction laws. As they did so, many congressmen who had cooperated with one faction drifted to another—men like Representatives Francis Thomas and Schenck and Senator Stewart moving towards radicalism and Representatives James F. Wilson and Thomas D. Eliot away.

More radical and more conservative Republicans had already joined battle over impeachment during the second session of the Thirty-ninth Congress. Outside of Congress, the radical newspapers, Benjamin F. Butler, George Wilkes, editor of the radical *Wilkes' Spirit of the Times,* and Ebon B. Ward, president of the pro-soft-money, high-tariff Iron and Steel Association, led the movement. Inside Congress, Boutwell, Stevens, and James M. Ashley spearheaded efforts.[2]

Bingham and Rufus P. Spalding led the opposition. Moving quickly after Ashley announced his intention to present resolutions calling for an investigation of Johnson's activities, Spalding called a caucus of House Republicans. To check Ashley's designs, Spalding moved that no measure of impeachment be presented in the House unless first approved by the caucus. Elihu B. Washburne proposed to add the further requirement that the caucus itself not approve any actual impeachment unless sanctioned by the House Judiciary committee. Over the objections of Stevens and Ashley, the Republicans agreed to the proposals overwhelmingly. But Ashley refused to be bound by the caucus decision and offered his resolution anyway. Two Missouri Republicans moved similar resolutions, which despite the efforts of Bingham and Speaker Colfax came to the floor. However, although this handful of radicals had thwarted the will of the Republican majority, the Republicans acted on the second branch of their caucus decision and referred the resolutions to the Judiciary committee, which began the long and tedious job of collecting evidence and taking testimony.[3]

After the passage of the unsatisfactory Reconstruction bill, radicals concluded that the president's removal was a necessity. Impatient with the Judiciary committee's slow progress, Butler called a secret caucus of radicals to prepare a resolution appointing a special committee to investigate Johnson in its place. Advocated by Butler, John A. Logan (just entering Congress), and Schenck, the resolution was defeated in caucus March 6 through the efforts of Bingham, Blaine, and Judiciary committee chairman Wilson, who promised all possible dispatch in his committee's investigation.[4]

Fearing what Johnson might do during a long congressional recess, and hoping to pressure the Judiciary committee into an early report on the impeachment resolutions, radicals determined to prevent the customary adjournment to the following December. Over both radical and conservative objections, centrist Republicans in the same caucus carried resolutions to adjourn, but only until May 8.[5]

In the Senate, however, the conviction grew that impeachment was not a viable possibility. In a Senate Republican caucus, only Chandler endorsed the measure. Grimes wrote home, "We have very successfully and thoroughly tied his [Johnson's] hands, and, if we had not, we had better submit to two years of misrule . . . than subject the country, its institutions, and its credit, to the shock of an impeachment. I have always thought so, and everybody is now apparently coming to my conclusion." [6]

A hard-fought struggle ensued. Radicals, led by Stevens, Butler, Ashley, Schenck, and Ignatius Donnelly in the House and Sumner and Drake in the Senate, fought for a short adjournment to be followed by a reconvened session which would settle the impeachment question. Conservatives, led by Representatives Bingham and Blaine and Senators Trumbull and Fessenden, tried to force an adjournment to November or December. After these rival forces battled to a stalemate, conservatives joined centrists to pass an adjournment resolution providing that Congress might reconvene the first Wednesday in July if a quorum was present. If no quorum could be found, Congress would reconvene the first Wednesday of November. Behind the scenes, radical Representative Schenck and conservative Senator Morgan, the co-chairmen of the Congressional Campaign Committee, were delegated the responsibility of deciding whether it would be necessary to meet. All agreed a July meeting was unlikely; the radicals had received another setback.[7]

A correspondent of the *New York Times* had gauged the sentiment in Congress correctly in February. Impeachment was dead, he wrote. But

there is one qualification to be made. . . . If the President persistently stands in the way . . . ; if he fails to execute the laws in their spirit as well as in their letter, if he will forget nothing, if he will learn nothing; if, holding the South in his hand, either by direct advice or personal example he shall encourage them to such resistance to progress as may tend to defeat the public will—in such event . . . the President may, after all, come to be regarded as an "obstacle" which must be "deposed." [8]

Radicals had good reason to suppose that the president would not execute the provisions of the Reconstruction act in good faith. In the first place, Andrew Johnson was no compromiser. His private secretary, William G. Moore, noted in his diary that at the time so many observers urged him to sign the Reconstruction bill, Johnson mused admiringly, "Cato was a man . . . who would not compromise with wrong but being right, died before he would yield."

"Without directly expressing the thought in words," Moore recorded, "he intimated a parallel between his own position and that of Cato." [9]

Certain of his rectitude, Johnson seemed able to rationalize actions that others believed bordered on dishonesty. His on-again, off-again promises to sign a nonradical Reconstruction bill in February 1867 were a case in point. Both John Sherman and Lyman Trumbull, who had tried to cooperate with him in 1866, privately complained that Johnson had "deceived and misled" them.[10] Governor Cox of Ohio, who had stood by the president longer than most of his Republican allies, marveled, "He is obstinate without being firm, self-opinionated without being capable of systematic thinking, combative and pugnacious without being courageous. He is always *worse* than you expect." [11]

Moreover, Johnson had already demonstrated his willingness to ignore and even contravene laws of Congress in the pursuit of his Reconstruction policy: Republican congressmen had not passed a Reconstruction law before the rebel armies lay down their arms in April and May of 1865, but they had passed a series of measures that should have had a large impact on the reorganization of the southern political, social, and economic institutions after the war. The "ironclad" test oath, required of all elected and appointed officers in United States public service, effectually barred former rebels from national office. The Confiscation act of July 17, 1862, made the prohibition explicit but was less effective than the law requiring the oath, because its disqualification provision referred only to those *convicted* of treasonable activities.[12]

The Confiscation act provided for the seizure of all the real and personal property of major rebel officeholders and all rebels who did not return to their allegiances within sixty days of a presidential warning proclamation. Title would be secured to the government through proceedings *in rem,* before federal courts, and the property would be used in prosecuting the war or the proceeds of its disposal would be paid into the United States Treasury.[13] An explanatory resolution limited the forfeiture to the life of the rebel, minimizing the law's utility.[14]

The concept of confiscation had been fundamentally altered when Republicans passed the Freedmen's Bureau bill during the second session of the Thirty-eighth Congress, in early 1865. By that act southern lands abandoned by their owners, which were subject to confiscation under the Confiscation act, were put under the administration of a new Bureau of Refugees, Freedmen, and Abandoned Lands. The commissioner of the bureau was to use the abandoned land to aid black men in the transition from slavery to freedom. He was specifically empowered, under the direction of the president, to set aside for the use of the freedmen and refugees abandoned land and land to which the government had acquired title through confiscation proceedings. The land was to be divided into forty-acre plots or less and rented to individual freedmen and refugees for three years. At the end of the three years, or any time earlier, the occupants could purchase the land they were working, receiving from the government "such title thereto as the United States can convey." [15]

The peculiar limitation Congress set upon the title which the freedmen could purchase indicates one of the problems the bill raised. Because federal courts were not yet operating in most areas conquered from the rebels, the national government had secured the title to hardly any land at all through confiscation proceedings. Of course, land liable to confiscation that lay behind rebel lines remained untouched. Most rebel land in government hands, therefore, was classified as "seized" or "abandoned." When it passed the Freedmen's Bureau bill, Congress evidently intended that government officers institute confiscation proceedings while freedmen worked the land. But the bill required no one to do so. Under the Confiscation act, treasury agents had spurred the small number of confiscation proceedings instituted, since it was the Treasury department which gained from them. With that spur removed, it was not clear who would accept the burden of litigation.

Nonetheless, the landholding provisions of the Freedmen's Bureau bill clearly demonstrated a desire on the part of Republicans to provide an economic foundation for black men's new freedom. Republicans further evidenced their intentions when each house of Congress passed legislation repealing the resolution that limited forfeiture under the Confiscation act to the lifetime of the rebel. Since no single resolution to this effect passed both houses, however, the limiting resolution remained law.[16]

Congress, therefore, had set rather specific parameters to the Reconstruction process when the Thirty-eighth Congress had adjourned. If Lincoln, and later Johnson, intended to continue the policy of administering conquered areas through provisional governors, those provisional governors, as officers of the United States, would have to take the ironclad test oath. They would be thoroughly loyal men who had never endorsed or encouraged secession or resistance to national authority. Moreover, although former rebels could take part in state reorganization after taking the amnesty oath, national patronage could go only to those who could take the test oath. Republicans believed that the best security for a loyal reconstruction would be a government politically allied to the Republican party, even if former rebels served in it. With national patronage by law required to be put in the hands of loyalists, with the all-important provisional governors required always to have been loyal Union men, Republicans could expect their allies to control the Reconstruction process in the South. Certainly this had been true in Tennessee, Arkansas, and Louisiana.

Furthermore, a strong start had been made in solving the problem of transition from slave to free labor. The Freedmen's Bureau, funded by the income of abandoned, seized, and confiscated lands, would cooperate with missionary organizations in educating black people, guard freedmen's interests in the unaccustomed process of contracting for wages, and begin the process of distributing land to establish black homesteads.

But within a year of Andrew Johnson's elevation to the presidency, the preliminary Reconstruction program enacted by Congress lay in utter ruin; Johnson had destroyed it without violating a law, using only his constitutional powers as president of the United States. Ignoring the Test Oath law of Congress, he appointed former rebels provisional governors in several southern states. He himself had excepted leading Confederates from his Amnesty Proclamation (a somewhat more stringent measure than Lincoln's on the surface, but incredibly mild as a peacetime proposal), but he willingly pardoned virtually any rebel upon the recommendation of his provisional governors. The provisional governors were politicians, interested in political power, and they knew that their political futures would be more promising if they conciliated white southern leaders. When Johnson made it obvious that he would support such a policy by pardoning rebel leaders, and when he made alternatives impossible by opposing black suffrage, most of the provisional governors began to work with former Confederates and to proscribe former Unionists who refused to cooperate. By December 1865 nearly every southern state had returned to Confederate leadership.[17]

The Johnson administration also had ignored the congressional oath requirement in making ordinary appointments to the national civil service in the South. Postmaster General Dennison and Attorney General Speed found it possible to obey the law (although with difficulty), but Treasury Secretary McCulloch, encouraged by Secretary of the Navy Welles, had abandoned the oath requirement in August 1865, staffing the southern Treasury Department network with former rebels. After the Post Office Department, the Treasury Department was the largest single source of national patronage within the states, and its positions were far more lucrative and sought-after. In ignoring the oath requirement enacted by Congress, McCulloch's policy complemented the pro-rebel policy established at the state level by most of Johnson's provisional governors.[18]

Johnson's decisions had been as disastrous to Republican race and labor policy as they had been to their protean Reconstruction program. These decisions centered about enforcement of the Confiscation act and the president's absolute right of pardon under the Constitution.

By late July, Attorney General Speed began to restrict the enforcement of the Confiscation act. It is not clear if he did so at the direct order of the president, but there can be no doubt that the decision was part of a uniform administration program to restore the Union by conciliating white southerners. At the urging of the provisional governor of Florida, Speed ordered the United States attorney for the northern district of Florida to halt proceedings for the sale of confiscated lands there, and to cease proceedings to confiscate railroads. The officer protested the individual case, but agreed that no new confiscation proceedings should be instituted lest such a course "make desperadoes of ninety-nine in every hundred of the property holders of this country." [19] In September Speed ordered the cessation of all confiscation proceedings in Virginia and ruled that the law could not be invoked to seize corporate property.[20] From September 1865 to December 1867, the Attorney General's office repeatedly ordered local officers to cease or suspend confiscation proceedings, bringing to a standstill nearly all the activity in this area.[21]

By fall and winter of 1865, Speed was informing his subordinates "that it is not the wish of the Government to harass or impoverish any of the citizens who desire in good faith to return to their allegiance and duty." Confiscation proceedings should be carried out only against "those who are still rebellious and contumacious." [22] Both Speed and his successor, Henry Stanbery, finally decided confiscation was illegal in peacetime. In June 1866, Speed ordered a complete end to all proceedings.[23]

At the same time the attorney general acted to minimize enforcement of the confiscation law, Johnson had effectively destroyed the capacity of the Freedmen's Bureau to fulfill its congressional mandate. Former Confederates pardoned under the Amnesty Proclamation or by special presidential action immediately began to demand the return of their abandoned and seized property. When bureau officials refused to accede to their demands, the pardoned rebels appealed to the president. Commissioner Howard argued that acquiescence in the rebels' demands would completely disrupt the bureau's activities and urged Johnson to consider property already condemned by the government beyond the reach of pardon. Instead, the president held that only confiscated land *already sold to third parties* should remain unreturned. Even land to which the government had received title under the confiscation law would be restored to its former owners. Since little land had been subject to confiscation proceedings before war's end due to the absence of courts, and since even land to which the government had received title had been turned over to the Freedmen's Bureau rather than sold, Johnson's order effectually nullified both the confiscation and the Freedmen's Bureau laws.

Howard then asked Johnson to add a stipulation to the pardons he was granting former Confederates to require them to transfer five to ten acres of land to the head of each slave family living on their property. The president did not act on the proposal.[24] After the fall of 1865, one of the Freedmen's Bureau's primary functions was to administer the restoration of seized and abandoned property to pardoned rebels. The Freedmen's Bureau held roughly 800,000 acres of land in September 1865. It never gained control of any more. By April 1866, 414,652 acres had been restored to former owners, including almost 15,000 acres that had been already turned over to freedmen.[25]

As the conflict between Johnson and Congress grew in intensity, the president became progressively more hostile to the Freedmen's Bureau, its agents, and its commissioner. After May 1866 he began a program of harassment, authorizing political allies to "investigate" operations, removing and reassigning key bureau personnel, and holding the threat of dismissal over Howard.[26]

Johnson used his presidential powers to moderate Reconstruction in other ways also. One of the principal objects of his attacks was the army's use of military tribunals to punish wrongdoers in the South when state courts would take no action. One type of military tribunal, the Freedmen's Bureau court, was an integral part of the bureau's operation. Other military commissions occasionally were organized in the South due to the unwillingness of state courts to protect Union soldiers, loyal whites, or blacks. To put an end to such tribunals' jurisdiction over civilians, Johnson had issued a proclamation on April 2, 1866, formally declaring an end to the insurrection and cleary intended to restore in all states the privilege of the writ of habeas corpus. The proclamation wrought chaos in the southern military establishment, as commanders urgently sought instructions.

To circumvent the president's decree, Secretary of War Stanton and General Grant had been forced to issue a secret circular reminding commanders in the South that military courts were authorized under the Freedmen's Bureau law, which continued in force during peace. In

response to direct queries, Grant stolidly insisted that he did not interpret the Peace Proclamation as abrogating martial law.[27] But on May 1,
1866, Johnson had forced the circulation of an order requiring an end to
all trials of civilians by military tribunal wherever civil courts were open.
In July he had delivered yet another blow, ordering the release of all
prisoners sentenced by military courts who had served six months, except
those held for murder, rape, arson, and those in the Tortugas.[28] On August
20, Johnson issued a second Peace Proclamation, this one applying specifically to Texas, which had been excluded from the last, and affirming that
"peace, order, tranquillity, and civil authority now exist in and throughout
the whole of the United States of America." But after some hesitation,
Grant continued to insist that the proclamations did not abrogate martial
law.[29]

By May 1866, Johnson's interference on behalf of the South had become so blatant that many Republicans had feared the president might attempt a coup d'état. This apprehension, fanned by Johnson's intemperate
language and by the open advocacy of such a course by southern and
northern Democratic organs, continued until the impeachment.[30]

The president's course, none of the elements of which clearly violated
law, had a staggering effect on the South. He converted a conquered
people, bitter but ready to accept the consequences of defeat, into a hostile,
aggressive, uncooperative unit. He restored to them political and economic
power, and through these domination of the men and women they recently
had held as slaves. He set back the work of Reconstruction, as it turned
out, two full years and insured that southerners would resist the process
instead of cooperate. To a large degree, the failure of Reconstruction
could be blamed on Andrew Johnson's abuse of his presidential powers.[31]

The Republicans' response to the president's activities had been remarkably slow and unbelievably mild. In the attempt to conciliate Johnson
before he vetoed the Freedmen's Bureau and Civil Rights bills, Republicans virtually ratified his dismantling of their Reconstruction and race
policies. In his Freedmen's Bureau bill Trumbull had confirmed for only
three years black men's rights to the land they had been promised in the
Sea Islands. He had recognized the end to hopes of land reform based on
confiscation by authorizing the bureau to procure homesteads for black
families in the public lands alone. Trumbull accepted Johnson's elimination
of the bureau's independent financial support, which originally was to
come from the income of confiscated and abandoned lands, by authorizing
a specific appropriation. House Republicans roundly defeated Stevens's
attempt to restore the freedmen's rights to homestead on confiscated
property.[32]

Moreover, Republicans made no legal objections to the governments
reorganized under Johnson's authority through provisional governors, none
of whom had taken the test oath and several of whom could not have taken

it, even though those governments had been controlled by the very elements Republicans had wanted to proscribe. On the contrary, Republicans
had implicitly offered to recognize those governments should they ratify
the mild Fourteenth Amendment. Even when enacting the Reconstruction
law most Republicans had not intended to disperse Johnson's governments,
only at the last minute acquiescing in radical demands to disqualify from
office under them those classes of men disqualified by the Fourteenth
Amendment.

Republicans were only slightly more insistent that the test oath law
be adhered to in the national civil service. They did not comply with
McCulloch's and Johnson's requests to repeal or modify the Test Oath act,
but Sumner's opposition to paying men who had accepted government
positions contrary to the law failed to impress his Senate colleagues. Only
the House's resistance prevented Congress from appropriating money to
pay the former rebels' salaries.[33]

After radical efforts failed to prevent adjournment of Congress in
spring 1867, Johnson fulfilled their expectations by again using his presidential powers to obstruct congressional Reconstruction in every way he
could. When Sheridan, commander of the military district comprising
Louisiana and Texas, removed the state and local officials responsible for
the New Orleans massacre, Johnson demanded an explanation, making his
displeasure manifest. Stung, Sheridan answered, "I did not deem it necessary to give any reason for the removal of these men, especially after the
investigations made by the Military Board on the massacre of July 30th,
1866, and the report of the Congressional Committee," but he sent the
information.[34] Johnson then ordered Sheridan to defer the removals, asking
his conservative attorney general, Stanbery, for an opinion on Sheridan's
power in the premises.[35]

When other commanders indicated that they too had decided it was
necessary to remove officials in the states under their command, Johnson
and Stanbery hurried the opinion. Stanbery read it to the cabinet on May
14 and 21, and it appeared officially on June 12, 1867. Stanbery's interpretation virtually emasculated the Reconstruction law. Holding that all
new laws should be narrowly construed, the attorney general insisted that
the military commanders had power only to keep the peace, to punish
criminal acts. The Johnsonian provisional governments and the United
States courts retained all other jurisdictions, and therefore the military
authorities could not intervene to protect the rights enumerated in the
Civil Rights act. They had no jurisdiction over crimes committed before
Congress passed the Reconstruction act, and none over acts not in violation of state or national law. Commanders could not remove the officials
of the provisional governments, Stanbery insisted. Registration boards had
to accept southerners' oaths that they were not disqualified by law from
voting; they had no power to investigate whether the swearer had perjured

himself. Finally, Stanbery affirmed that the president retained supervisory power over the enforcement of the Reconstruction acts, "to see that all 'the laws are faithfully executed.' " [36]

Welles, although despairing of its practical effect, agreed that the attorney general "had done more for popular rights, under a law which despotically deprived the people of the undoubted guaranteed rights, than I had supposed possible." But General Sickles, whose acts in the Carolinas Stanbery had specifically denounced as illegal, angrily requested to be relieved from duty so he could defend his conduct before a court of inquiry. "The declaration of the Attorney General that Military authority has not superceded [the provisional governments] . . . prevents the execution of the Reconstruction acts, disarms me of means to protect life, property, or the rights of citizens and menaces all interests in these States with ruin," he wrote.[37] Sheridan and Pope hurriedly asked Grant if they must consider the circular notifying them of the attorney general's opinion a direct order. The general of the army told them to enforce their own constructions of the law until ordered otherwise.[38]

As rumors circulated that Johnson would order the military commanders in the South to restore to office all officials they had removed, even conservative Republican congressmen and newspapers recognized that a July session of Congress would be necessary after all. But they worried lest radicals use the occasion to press for a more stringent Reconstruction law or impeachment of the president. They determined to limit the business of the session to repairing the damage Johnson and his law officer had done to the Reconstruction act, and assurances from Washington that Johnson did not intend to interfere further with the law's enforcement reinforced that determination. "I am disgusted with Johnson for giving [the radicals] such a pretense," Fessenden wrote Grimes. "God only know what mischief will be done if we get together." [39]

When congressmen gathered in Washington, nonradicals seized control of the session. In caucus senators agreed to Conkling's proposed resolution to limit the business of the session to amendments of the Reconstruction act. A similar resolution passed the House on July 5, with radicals making only ineffectual opposition.[40] In the Senate Sumner opposed the resolution on the floor, despite the caucus decision, but only nine senators sustained him.[41]

By July 6 radicals realized that they could not hope to persuade their reluctant allies to remain in Washington's summer heat to impeach the president. Instead they decided to press for an October session for the purpose. "They are determined to ruin the Republican party," Dawes complained. But like Fessenden, he lamented, "The President . . . *does* continue to do the most provoking things. If he isn't impeached it wont [*sic*] be his fault." [42]

On July 10, Boutwell proposed a resolution in the House to adjourn

until October 16. In the course of the discussion Judiciary committee
chairman Wilson announced that the committee at the moment opposed
impeachment by a five to four margin. From the acrimonious debate it
became clear that Wilson himself led the opposition to impeachment, sustained by two Democrats and Representatives Woodbridge and Churchill.
Boutwell, William Lawrence, Williams, and Francis Thomas advocated the
measure. As opposition to an October "impeachment" session continued to
mount, radicals warned their colleagues of the effect of timidity. The
people were becoming impatient. "We want peace and quiet," Illinois
Representative Lewis Ross implored. "We want this disturbing element removed." [43] But despite the earnest entreaties of radicals and those centrists who agreed with them, a Republican-Democratic coalition succeeded
in amending Boutwell's resolution to provide for reconvening Congress in
mid-November.[44]

Even this was too much for Senate conservatives. Sherman amended
the House resolution to provide for reassembly the first day of December,
and again a conservative Republican-Democratic coalition passed this
amended resolution over the radicals' objections.[45]

But Senate radicals had seen enough. On July 20, Chandler launched
a bitter attack on Fessenden, contemptuously referring to him as "the
Conservative Senator from Maine." He and conservative allies had steadily
opposed provisions for a July session; now they were following the same
course in regard to an October session. Yet the president had for all practical purposes announced his intention not to execute the law, Chandler
insisted.

When we first captured this monster there was one thing for us to do, and only
one; but instead of doing that we undertook to surround him with nets, to hem
him in, to bind him with nets of zephyr. The very moment we left he thrust
his paw through. . . . Now we have met here and what have we done? We
have patched up the net. It is the same net; but we have mended up the hole.
. . . And now this Congress seems to hope that the same animal that thrust
his paw through the net when it was new will not thrust it through again when
it is merely a patched net.[46]

As Fessenden defended himself, naming the senators who had voted with
him, it was evident that the gap separating radicals and conservatives was
widening.[47]

But the conservatives would not weaken. In the conference committee to iron out differences, the House was represented by nonradicals
who had forced adjournment until November 13, and the Senate by nonradicals who had insisted on adjournment to December. They compromised on November 21. The radicals had been routed.[48]

While Congress debated the date to which it should adjourn, it also
passed another Reconstruction measure. Both the Senate Judiciary com-

as usual

mittee and the House Reconstruction committee had reported bills patching, as Chandler said, the torn netting of the previous law. Radicals in both houses tried and failed once more completely to disperse the Johnsonian provisional governments, and the Senate ruled Sumner's proposed amendment to require free and equal systems of public education out of order under the rule limiting business to remedying defects in the Reconstruction act alone.[49] The bill as passed did no more than restore the authority of the military commanders and voting registration boards to what it had been when Congress passed the original Reconstruction acts. Once again Congress had refused to take the steps radicals considered essential: the dispersal of the Johnson governments and impeachment. "This is the third bill of reconstruction on which we have been called to act," Sumner lamented. "We ought never to have acted on more than one; and if the Senate had been sufficiently radical, . . . there would have been no occasion for more than one." [50]

As soon as Congress adjourned, Johnson proved that the radicals had been right. Betraying the conservatives, who had believed his interference ended, on August 5 he asked for Stanton's resignation. The secretary of war, encouraged by Republican friends, refused, and on August 12 Johnson ordered his suspension and named Grant secretary of war *ad interim.* Johnson followed this by ordering the removal of Sheridan from his southern command, against the advice of Grant and his entire cabinet, except the irrepressible Welles.[51] Republicans reacted with stunned outrage. Even Grant, who had not yet publicly questioned Johnson's policy or motives, wrote that Johnson's course would embolden rebels to oppose the Reconstruction laws and oppress loyal men. It would "be regarded as an effort to defeat the laws of Congress," he warned.[52] The conservative publisher of the Boston *Daily Advertiser* wrote Sumner, "Is the President crazy, or only drunk? I am afraid his doings will make us all favor impeachment." The *Chicago Tribune*'s editor, Horace White, now decided that impeachment was necessary. Congressional leaders Colfax, Elihu B. Washburne, and Henry Wilson reached the same conclusion. Such conservative newspapers as the *New York Times,* Boston *Daily Advertiser,* Boston *Evening Journal,* Indianapolis *Daily Journal,* and *Providence Journal* began to threaten impeachment, as did the *Chicago Tribune,* which previously had opposed it.[53]

But despite Republicans' violent reactions, Johnson continued the offensive, removing Sickles on August 27 and threatening the removal of General Pope from his command in Georgia, Alabama, and Florida.[54] As Johnson's rampage continued, Republicans began to worry more than ever that he might finally transcend the bounds of reason. "What does Johnson mean to do?" former Attorney General Speed begged Sumner. "Does he mean to have another rebellion on the question of Executive powers & duties?" The *Times* uneasily worried, "Mr. JOHNSON has said and done so much that is wild and wanton that people have ceased to judge of the probabilities of his action according to any received standard of right or duty." [55]

Radicals blamed conservatives for the destruction and the danger. "For every broken heart and desolate home in the South, for every murdered black there, we hold Fessenden, Wilson, Edmunds, Conklin [*sic*], and their clan, responsible," the *Anti-Slavery Standard* railed.[56]

One fact clearly emerged from the confusion: the conservative Republican policy had failed. As the observant French correspondent, Clemenceau, explained to the readers of *Le Monde:*

> Congress may, when it pleases, take the President by the ear and lead him down from his high seat, and he can do nothing about it except to struggle and shout. But that is an extreme measure, and the radicals [i.e., the Republicans generally] are limiting themselves . . . to binding Andrew Johnson firmly with good brand-new laws. At each session they add a shackle to his bonds, tighten the bit in a different place, file a claw or draw a tooth, and then when he is well bound up, fastened, and caught in an inextricable net of laws and decrees, more or less contradicting each other, they tie him to the stake of the Constitution and take a good look at him, feeling quite sure he cannot move this time.
>
> But then . . . Samson summons all his strength, and bursts his cords and bonds with a mighty effort, and the Philistines (I mean the radicals) flee in disorder to the Capitol to set to work making new laws stronger than the old, which will break in their turn at the first test.[57]

Confused constituents turned to their congressmen: "Is it possible that there can be a wrong without a remedy . . . ?" one asked Trumbull. "Must the great people who patriotically saved the Republic remain chained by an arbitrary rule until a usurper at Washington overthrows our liberties?" [58] Many congressional Republicans were finally prepared to answer the question by removing the obstacle to peace. But they could not do so until Congress reconvened on November 21. And before that the people would be able to indicate their feelings in the elections of fall, 1867.

THIRTEEN

The Critical Year: The Elections of 1867

————————— ✦✦✦✦✦✦✦✦✦✦✦ —————————

HOWARD K. BEALE closed his influential book *The Critical Year* with a detailed account of the elections of 1866. Those elections, he argued, marked the culmination of the critical year of conflict between the president and Congress. The people endorsed Congress and radical Reconstruction over the president and reconciliation.[1] But he and other historians have ignored the elections of the next year, elections perhaps as important to the future of Reconstruction and the nation as those which have received so much attention. For the elections from March to November 1867 marked the turning point in the battle between radical and nonradical Republicans. The Republican reverses of 1867 led to the defeat of radical hopes to impeach Andrew Johnson, stiffen the Reconstruction laws, and elect a radical president upon a radical platform in 1868.

The victories Republicans won in 1866 had demonstrated popular support not for the radical Republican program but for that of the conservatives and centrists. Refusing to make black suffrage an issue, bridling the radicalism of southern loyalists, and implying that the constitutional amendment embodied the final settlement of war issues, the moderates had won their crushing victory.

In 1867 the situation was different; the radicals once more were on the offensive. Not only were Republican campaigners pointing to their recent legislation, with its imposition of black suffrage in the South, but radicals were promoting those elements of their program more conservative Republicans had excluded from the Reconstruction act. The impeachment issue had become completely entwined with the campaign by the end of the July session of Congress. Despite opposition from conservatives like Trumbull, radicals increased pressure for Sumner's proposal to enfranchise black citizens in all the states by congressional enactment.[2] Sumner still argued that Congress should insist on the establishment of a free public school program in each state as a precondition for readmission. Some radicals still wanted southern states to undergo an indefinite period of probation before they returned to their normal places in the Union. When asked whether he would support the restoration of southern states that enfranchised blacks, guaranteed their rights and education, and sent men who could take the test oath to Congress, Stevens, "without a moment's pause," answered, "No." Durant opposed restoration "until an amendment to the National Constitution be adopted establishing irrevocable universal suffrage . . . in every state of the Union." [3] Stevens also continued to agitate for confiscation. Wendell Phillips articulated the program many radicals favored at the annual meeting of the American Anti-Slavery Society in New York City early in May. Antislavery men, he said, "will believe the negro safe when we see him with 40 acres under his feet, a schoolhouse behind him, a ballot in his right hand, the sceptre of the Federal Government over his head, and no State Government to interfere with him, until more than one-half of the white men of the Southern States are in their graves." [4]

In May, Stevens fueled the radical campaign for confiscation with a widely published letter to the Gettysburg (Pa.) *Star and Herald,* edited by his friend Edward M. McPherson, clerk of the House of Representatives. Stevens deemphasized arguments of justice to blacks and appealed instead to the appetites of northern whites. Stevens argued that southerners should be required to pay reparations to loyalists whose property was damaged or lost because of the war. This could most easily be accomplished, Stevens suggested, by "the confiscation of a small portion of the property of the wealthy rebels." Benjamin Butler joined the drive. In a letter to a Republican campaign meeting in the capital, he argued that landed aristocracy was inconsistent with republican institutions, and insisted that land reform in the South was necessary "as the very base of reconstruction." [5]

With pressure for confiscation apparently growing in the North, southern blacks and their white radical allies renewed hopes for meaningful land redistribution. Newspaper correspondents touring the South informed northern readers that "the confiscation humbug has taken hold of the negro mind, especially in the towns, and . . . confidently they look to being presented with a neat farm and stocks 'when Congress meets.' " [6]

The implications of confiscation were not lost upon more conservative Republicans. The moderate Boston *Daily Advertiser* conceded that confiscation was "bottomed . . . on a just and praiseworthy and eminently republican aspiration," but fretted,

"General Butler . . . says that a landed aristocracy is fatal to the advance of the cause of liberty and equal rights. Why a *landed* aristocracy? This mode of argument is two-edged. For there are socialists who hold that *any* aristocracy is "fatal to the advance of the cause of liberty and equal rights"—socialists who would not hesitate to say that General Butler's large income places him in the ranks of an aristocracy whose existence is essentially hostile to progress.

As the *Advertiser* concluded, "It is dangerous to prove too much." The conservative Cincinnati *Commercial* began to refer to Butler and Stevens as "The Red Rads." [7]

Moreover, conservative Republicans feared the impact of the confiscation issue on southern politics. The *New York Times* charged,

The ultraists . . . are determined to build up a party in the Southern States fully in accord with themselves. They scout and reject the moderation and tolerance of Senator WILSON, and hold such Senators as SHERMAN, FESSENDEN, and others of kindred temper, in quite as much disfavor as Democrats themselves. Their plan is to consolidate the negro vote with that of the "original Union men" of the South. . . . And they rely upon *confiscation* to secure this result. A promise of a homestead . . . will be a most formidable weapon for the accomplishment of their object. [8]

This prospect ran counter to the wishes of many Republican politicians. Southern whites, they hoped, were tired of relying on northern Democrats. Whether or not to comply with the congressional Reconstruction acts had become the new organizing issue in southern politics. Those former Confederates who argued for compliance to avoid harsher conditions, like Georgia's ex-Governor Joseph E. Brown and General James W. Longstreet of Louisiana, were bitterly attacked by those more intransigent. As the battle lines developed, men like Brown and Longstreet began cooperating with Republicans. These men and their friends, conservative Republicans hoped, would form the nucleus of a southern Republican party appealing to both races. Talk of confiscation or delay in readmission could only drive them back to the Democrats.

Republican efforts to nurture this new party centered about Senator Henry Wilson. His enthusiasm was the chief catalyst of Republican hopes for the South. He had discovered new southern flexibility while on an extended speaking tour of the unreconstructed states. In letters and published interviews he urged northern Republicans to turn their attention southwards. [9] Other Republicans caught his optimism. "The harvest is white," exclaimed the Boston *Evening Journal,* "and we trust that our sagacious men will see that it is not neglected." [10]

The whites, Wilson found, suspected that compliance with the Reconstruction laws would not guarantee immediate restoration. They were anxious about Republican intentions regarding matters of race. Wilson decided to reassure them by admonishing southern blacks. "I do not want to see a white man's party nor a black man's party," he told a black audience in New Orleans. "I warn you to-night, as I do the black men of this country everywhere, to remember this: that while a black man is as good as a white man, a white man is as good as a black man. See to it while you are striving to lift yourselves up, that you do not strive to pull anybody else down." Going further, Wilson implicitly but clearly criticized southern radicals. "I sometimes hear men . . . adopt the language of a bloody contest, and not the language of two years of peace, and the mighty future which we hope will be peace," he complained. "He who causes alienation and distrust between the white men and the black men of this country is an enemy of the white man and of the black man alike." The Massachusetts senator acknowledged that "prejudices still existing . . . may keep you for a little time out of the full possession of all your privileges." But, he insisted, "the way to win a complete triumph is for you to be consistent, steady, inflexible, but loving, tender, kind to everybody, obedient to the law, never undertaking by lawless violence to right your wrongs." Finally, Wilson tacitly repudiated confiscation. "Millions of acres of land, which can be bought low, will be in the market for some time to come; and the first thing the colored men of the Southern country should do is to get land. Money will do it." [11]

Wilson returned North far more conservative than he had left. On his return he denounced confiscation and "the extreme measures proposed by Sumner, Stevens and others." Wade, receiving complaints from southern radicals, scrawled a note to Chandler: Wilson "is a ———— fool!" [12]

The erratic Horace Greeley shared Wilson's enthusiasm for building the new southern party. Speaking in Richmond, he too urged blacks to forgo hopes of confiscation, advocating that they turn their attention instead to the public lands. [13] To further demonstrate Republican desire to conciliate the South, Greeley joined in raising money to bail Jefferson Davis. Greeley had consistently opposed punishment for leading rebels, but he was well aware of the political implications of this action. It "has immensely contributed to the acceptance and triumph of Republican principles in the South," his newspaper boasted. [14]

But it also fired the controversy between radicals and conservatives in the North. Phillips criticized Greeley's endeavor, and Greeley hotly replied that Phillips "panders to mob passions for the gratification of his own." The Union League, the backbone of New York radicalism, called a special meeting to consider expelling the reformer, but Greeley issued a scathing reply to the league's invitation to attend the meeting, and the effort to oust him failed. [15]

Trying to capitalize on good will Wilson and Greeley had won in the South, the Union Congressional Republican Committee issued a conciliatory address to southerners. The committee argued that no fundamental conflict of interest existed between laboring men. Although black men's rights had been secured, Republicans did not intend to invade the rights of whites. While the politicians adhered to the congressional Reconstruction program, they clearly implied that no further measures were contemplated. If southerners complied with the Reconstruction acts, they averred, restoration would immediately follow. [16] As the Boston *Daily Advertiser* pointed out, the congressional campaign committee represented all shades of Republican opinion in Congress. If it stood upon the platform of Recon-struction as it was and rejected further requirements, dissatisfied radicals could hope to accomplish little. "It appears that an end is made of Mr. Stevens' querulous objections," the *Advertiser* announced happily.[17]

The conservative counteroffensive infuriated the radicals. Stevens bit-terly attacked Wilson, Greeley, and their supporters, "a few Republican meteors, always erratic in their course, . . . flitting and exploding in the Republican atmosphere." Phillips accused Sherman and Fessenden of "bartering principle for patronage." The *Anti-Slavery Standard* predicted the disruption of the party.[18]

After the conservatives successfully prevented radical legislation in the July session of Congress, Sumner joined the public criticism. In a well-publicized interview with the radical Boston journalist James Redpath, Sumner launched a broadside against his Senate opponents. He complained of the positions taken by Conkling and other newcomers. Edmunds was "a prodigy of obstructiveness and technicality," but "of all these, Fessen-den is the Captain . . . ," Sumner concluded. "He is the head of the obstructives. If any person calling himself a Republican, takes the side of the President, it will be Mr. Fessenden." [19]

With tempers beginning to fray, the *Nation* warned that if many rad-icals endorsed Stevens's position, the Republicans might very easily lose the upcoming elections. Other Republicans agreed.[20] Nonetheless, radicals continued the assault. Opening Republican disharmony to full public view, Chandler accused the conservatives of responsibility for President John-son's ability to impede Reconstruction. Incapable of decisive action, they had prevented the total dissolution of Johnson's provisional southern gov-ernments, and had opposed the radicals' determination to remain in session to watch the president. "These Conservatives had fixed it so they supposed we could not get together, and Mr. Johnson so understood it," Chandler charged.

But at the very last moment, when the session was given up as hopeless, and there was no intention of coming together, out came that opinion of Stan-bery's, and the people rose up in their might and said Congress must get together, and watch this bad man. . . . And, fellow citizens, your Conserva-tives dare not disobey their master's will, and the very men who had been most opposed to the meeting of Congress, were there on the 3d of July, at 12 o'clock. They did not dare to be a quarter of a second behind.[21]

As this agitation continued, the breach in the party widened. Fessen-den professed to find Sumner's attack "exquisitely funny." "All the world . . . is laughing at him for making such an ass of himself," he wrote his friend Grimes. The Iowa senator was just as disgusted. "The truth is . . . we have some terrible '*scalawags*' in our party & they will be sure to send us to the d——l as a party & I believe that we are in imminent danger of suffering them to send the country there to[o]." Oliver P. Morton's organ, the Indianapolis *Daily Journal,* again locked in deadly combat with his radical rival, Julian, blasted "radicals, fanatics, one idea men," who "demand that the train shall move without looking to see if the track is clear." [22]

The dispute clearly weakened the party. Those who had not realized the degree of the breach began to choose sides. Campaign contributions lagged. Popular campaigners decided to restrict their activities. Garfield worried to his close friend Burke Hinsdale that the political, economic, and social revolution inaugurated by the rebellion might not be arrested. He predicted that "unless our party could soon come to a stand-still the greatest of disasters must overtake us." [23]

Yet another issue was developing to add to Republican divisions: the money question. When the Thirty-ninth Congress had assembled, nearly all congressmen had approved Secretary of the Treasury Hugh McCulloch's general policy of contracting the currency as quickly as possible by withdrawing legal tender notes from circulation. Only six representatives had voted against a House resolution endorsing the program.[24] When it came to specifics, however, unanimity broke down. McCulloch proposed to take the greenbacks out of circulation by exchanging interest-bearing bonds for them. This meant a quick contraction likely to lead to economic recession. When Congress considered a loan bill specifically authorizing McCulloch to pursue his program at a rate left to his personal discretion, many Republicans balked, and the measure lost 65 to 70. A second measure similar to the first but limiting the amount of legal tender McCulloch could withdraw from circulation passed. There was about a forty-vote majority in the House during the first session of the Thirty-ninth Congress in favor of limited, cautious currency contraction.[25]

But by fall 1866, even the slower contraction McCulloch enforced under the Loan act began to affect the economy. Business slowed and prices fell in the winter of 1866–67 and throughout 1867. The depression continued until 1868. Businessmen, especially manufacturers, reacted by demanding an end to contraction. Between the adjournment of the first session of the Thirty-ninth Congress and the meeting of the second, the controversy over fiscal policy led a large number of congressmen to alter their positions. The group of representatives who had refused to give McCulloch a completely free hand in contraction but agreed to his program with limitations now joined anticontractionists to repeal the authority they had delegated.[26] Not only did the middle-of-the-road group vote to suspend contraction during the second session, but a large number of individual congressmen left the groups they had been voting with entirely and joined others. Thirteen Republicans and eight Democrats swung toward the position of currency expansionists. In a parallel shift, six Republicans became more firmly committed to contraction.[27]

The shift toward inflationary monetary policies thoroughly alarmed those who held orthodox financial views. As noted in Chapter One, hard-money men, recognizing Stevens, Butler, Kelley, and Wade as the leaders of the movement for currency expansion, began to tend towards conservatism and to worry what the effect of Johnson's removal by impeachment would be.

Among those most committed to eventual return to a specie standard was Edward Atkinson, a New England textile manufacturer. An abolitionist, radical Republican, and genteel reformer, Atkinson had been among the leading advocates of free labor on southern cotton plantations, in which he had a direct interest due to his profession. Though never an officeholder, Atkinson enjoyed politics. He particularly took pleasure in exercising behind-the-scenes influence. During the war he had traveled often to Washington to lobby for black men's rights and to offer his expertise in developing fiscal and tariff policy. No dogmatist, Atkinson opposed precipitate contraction as impractical, but an eventual return to a specie standard was his unwavering goal. To combat growing support for inflation, Atkinson enthusiastically began to create an informal but powerful propaganda organization.[28]

As McCulloch pursued a vigorous contractionist policy, hard-money men offered him cordial support. As early as fall 1866, Atkinson, then radical, had written him, "Much as I differ from you [on Reconstruction], I thank God you hold your present views and are thereby enabled to remain in the present cabinet." [29] In the spring of 1867, Atkinson launched his accelerated campaign in defense of hard money with a carefully staged invitation to McCulloch to attend a dinner in his honor in Boston. Engineered by Atkinson, the call was signed by such Massachusetts luminaries as Richard Henry Dana, Theophilus Parsons, Alexander H. Rice, Amos A. Lawrence, William Whiting, and Peleg Chandler. As arranged, McCulloch courteously declined the invitation but defended his monetary policy in a letter published and broadcast by the Boston group.[30]

As Atkinson turned his attention more and more to the money question, his radicalism became less and less ardent. Although he had been intimately involved with the Sea Islands experiment, which had demonstrated the potential of black men when given their own land to work, Atkinson now warned Sumner that confiscation "would about ruin the freedmen." [31] He informed McCulloch that he and his friends were trying to "prevent the creation of an exclusive black men's party and also to kill the scheme of confiscation in the South." The increasingly conservative reformer feared that the new Republican delegations from the reconstructed South would follow Thaddeus Stevens's lead not only on Reconstruction matters but on tariff and currency questions. In an effort to obviate the danger he helped hard-money Boston men found the Massachusetts Reconstruction Association. Designed to raise funds and send political speakers and organizers South, its implicit goal was to educate southern Republicans in sound financial and tariff policy.[32]

Free-traders as well as hard-money men, Atkinson and his friends looked forward to the end of the Reconstruction problem. Then, he wrote McCulloch, "the fight between Protection and Free Trade will be upon us, and Free-Trade views will win." He urged the secretary of the treasury to divorce himself from President Johnson's continued opposition to congressional Reconstruction, and to accept the Reconstruction acts as a finality without specifically giving them his approval. "Only give the Republicans who hold sound views on financial questions a chance to support you as the Secy. of the United States Treasury and not as a member of the present cabinet and you can almost dictate the future policy," he argued.[33]

McCulloch, meanwhile, had also maintained close relations with Fessenden and was well aware of the attitude held by the senator and his friends toward the radicals. If Atkinson felt that McCulloch could be weaned from Johnson, McCulloch believed Atkinson, Fessenden, and other conservatives might now divide from the radicals. McCulloch, seconded by Secretary of the Interior Orville H. Browning, urged Johnson not to force the Republicans to close ranks by removing Sheridan. The administration, McCulloch argued, should let the Republicans go on fighting among themselves. "It would break them down. The better portion of them were already sick of their measures." He told them that no less an authority than James F. Wilson, embittered by the battles over impeachment in his Judiciary committee, had assured him that if the president did nothing rash, the "extreme Radicals" would be defeated and the Republicans would divide. But the unbending and bigoted Welles took a hard line, emphasizing to Johnson his duty to stand by the southerners, and Johnson evidently agreed with him. On August 3, McCulloch visited Welles and pleaded with him to prevent Johnson from taking hasty action against Sheridan, but Welles remained stolid. He wrote in his diary that McCulloch had "been intimate with . . . conservative and timid Republicans." They had "impressed him with their cowardly, shrinking views." [34]

McCulloch's influence was weakened by his own tenuous position in the cabinet. Widespread rumors held that the secretary was about to leave Johnson's official family, along with Seward. Democrats pressured Johnson to name a Democratic cabinet, Johnsonians complained McCulloch protected anti-Johnson Republicans in the Treasury Department, and newspapers reported rumors of impending change.[35] Finally, McCulloch himself had to write the president to repel the attack. "In the discharge of my duties . . . I have no other aim, than to sustain your administration and promote the interests of the people," he wrote. "The charge, in whatever form it may be put, that I have sought to serve myself, at your expense, or at the expense of the political opinions of which you are the representative is false if not malicious." McCulloch remained in the cabinet, but he was so situated that further suggestions of restraint might be interpreted as disloyalty.[36]

Other friends of Johnson saw the possibilities of the situation. Henry A. Smythe, collector of the port of New York, urged the president to name a Republican cabinet to cut the ground from under the impeachers, suggesting Massachusetts' ex-Governor Andrew as secretary of state and Greeley as postmaster general. William Tecumseh Sherman offered similar advice. He suggested that the president name outgoing Governor Cox of Ohio secretary of war and urged him to make overtures to Fessenden, Trumbull, Sherman, Morgan, Morton, and other conservatives. But Johnson, though tempted, did not follow his advice, possibly because the election returns were to convince him that it was unnecessary.[37]

Nonetheless, Republicans were so badly divided that shrewd political observers believed that they were on the verge of disruption and that Andrew Johnson's own intransigence once again was the prime factor holding the party together. After the elections, John Sherman would describe the Republicans' situation: "A class of our people want Reconstruction, peace quiet and don't like Ben Butler and Ben Wade & the radicals, while another sett [sic] don't like Fessenden & the Conservatives, growled because we adjourned, and did not impeach the President. The truth is we were so strong that we quarreled among ourselves." [38]

Closely related to the substantive issues dividing radical from conservative Republican was the struggle for the Republican presidential nomination. Among the Republicans striving for that prize were Wade, Butler, Chase, Colfax, and Andrew. But their chief competitor was not even known as yet as Republican: Ulysses S. Grant.

Grant's past politics made him suspect in radical eyes. It was well known that the general had been apolitical prior to the war, and many considered him apolitical yet. In 1864, Republicans had feared that the Democrats might nominate him for president. From 1862 until late in 1864 radicals regarded his rising fortunes with misgivings. In the House leading radicals had opposed the recreation of the rank of lieutenant general of the army for him. Stevens, Boutwell, Garfield, Kelley, Julian, Ashley, and Winter Davis had tried to prevent it, but they had failed.[39]

During the war Grant had sought the removal of General Butler, who had won the radicals' respect and confidence. When Butler committed a military blunder in Virginia, Grant succeeded. Butler retaliated in speeches before his troops and in his home state, Massachusetts. He defended himself before the Joint Committee on the Conduct of the War, which exonerated him. But Grant's final report on the war cast grave doubts on

Butler's military ability. The radical leader, feeling deeply wronged, had broken off all social intercourse with Grant. His bitterness continued through 1867 and made him a powerful opponent of Grant's ambitions.[40]

When the Thirty-ninth Congress began its deliberations on Reconstruction, the Democrats and pro-Johnson Republicans had relied upon Grant's favorable report of conditions in the South; it had been Grant's report, as well as the president's accompanying message, which Sumner had called a "whitewash." There is not much direct evidence on Grant's political opinions at that time, but William B. Hesseltine has suggested that Grant generally supported Johnson's policies.[41] And there is no doubt as to the position of his staff. Adam Badeau and John A. Rawlins, his intimate friends and aides, both endorsed Johnson.[42]

During the 1866 election campaign, Grant had accompanied Johnson on his ill-fated "Swing 'Round the Circle." Although the general himself found the attentions of former Copperheads distasteful, he had allowed himself to be used on an obviously political junket. But it was at this time that some Republicans, hinting at future support for the presidency, began to unsettle him. By the end of the trip, Welles believed that he had deserted the president's camp, but Doolittle, evidently assured by Grant himself, had argued it was not so.[43] As late as August 1867, Montgomery Blair encouraged the nomination of Grant as a Conservative (i.e., Democratic-Johnsonian) candidate for president.[44]

Actually Grant appears to have been primarily interested in protecting the interests of the army. Grant believed those interests would best be served by maintaining a strict neutrality between president and Congress. But as the Reconstruction battle had developed, it became apparent that neutrality was impossible. Both Johnson and Congress determined that the army was the best available instrument for reconstructing the South. The president had used the armed forces to secure order during presidential Reconstruction and afterward had attempted a *fait accompli* by withdrawing its authority over the civil governments erected there. Congress had restored that authority and ordered the military to oversee a new Reconstruction process. The president had responded by trying to gain control of the army's activities in the South. The president's attempts to obstruct congressional Reconstruction had forced Grant to take sides, and by August 1867 he had privately aligned himself with the conservative Republicans in Congress.

But it was a slow process. As late as August, his friend General Sherman wrote his brother, "I don't think he has clearly defined political opinions." [45] Johnson's policies had not alienated Grant until the president forced Sheridan's removal from his command in Louisiana, and Johnson would not give up his attempts to win Grant's support until they broke completely in February 1868. Therefore, Grant was in no sense a committed Republican when his name first was pressed in the spring of 1867.

Many radicals were truly outraged and feared betrayal by those who urged his nomination. "I know this is not an anti-slavery speech on the model of the past two years," Wendell Phillips acknowledged before the American Anti-Slavery Society in May, "but when men tell me that they are going to nominate Gen. Grant for President, because if they don't take him, the Democrats will, it is time to talk as we used to in 1850." [46]

Despite Phillips's apprehensions, Grant was not yet conceded the nomination. Hoosier congressman Godlove S. Orth reported Indianans dissatisfied with the prospect. They asked "whether *Grant* is with us—and can be relied on &c. &c. Whether we must take him for the Presidency—or whether we have not the courage to speak right out and say we must have a true and tried civilian about whom there is no doubt or hesitancy." But already in Indiana, a pattern emerged that would reappear in other states. The conservative friends of ex-Governor (now Senator) Morton, Orth predicted, would "soon be found joining in the yelp for Grant." [47]

In Ohio the battle was between Wade and Chase. Both were Ohio men; each would have to control the Ohio delegation at the Republican national convention if he hoped to receive the nomination. Rutherford B. Hayes, a Wade man, succeeded in winning the Republican gubernatorial nomination in 1867 over the strong opposition of the Chase interest, led by a mixed group of radicals and conservatives.[48] Republican conservatives were disgusted. "I see that our V.P. is fairly in for the Presidency," Fessenden wrote Grimes. "I suppose he will divide the West with Colfax. Under which of these doughty champions will Iowa range itself? Were it not that the thing would look too sectional," he continued sarcastically, "I would suggest Chandler or Pomeroy for Vice." [49]

New York too was a center for presidential politics. Thurlow Weed, detecting an intention on the part of leading Democrats to nominate Grant, determined that "the adversary should not steal our thunder." He decided to organize a Grant movement in New York, launching the campaign in his New York *Commercial Advertiser* and arranging an endorsement of the general's candidacy by the Republican General Committee of New York City, his anti-Greeley organization. The old Seward-Weed organ, the *New York Times,* fell into line. Another old Whig stalwart, William Maxwell Evarts, endorsed the general at a Grant rally in Cooper Union in mid-October.[50] It was apparent that the discredited conservative faction intended to ride Grant back into respectability and power in the New York Republican party. "All that is fishy and mercenary in the Republican ranks combines with everything copperhead to escort Grant as the man destined to curb Radicalism and restore conservatives to power," Horace Greeley complained.[51]

In Pennsylvania radical politicians also remained cool or hostile to Grant. The conservative former governor, Andrew G. Curtin, who hoped a Republican state legislature would elect him to the Senate, linked his name with Grant's. He urged leading Republicans to endorse the general for president before the 1867 elections, but radicals and friends of other candidates combined to prevent it.[52]

Radicals especially complained of the general's reticence. Said Sumner:

> The great difficulty in his position is that we are left in harrowing uncertainty with regard to his opinions. Who could say that, as President, he would give to the freedmen, during the coming years, and through the processes of reconstruction, that kindly and sympathetic support which they need? Can we afford to be in any uncertainty on this point?
>
> I have from the beginning been insisting on "irreversible guarantees." Our next President must be in himself an "irreversible guarantee." Is Grant such? I wish I knew.[53]

Despite his growing dislike for Johnson and his policies, Grant had not publicly spoken out. "It is not proper that a subordinate should criticize the acts of his superior in a public manner," he wrote his close friend Congressman Elihu B. Washburne.[54] But Grant's chief of staff, General John A. Rawlins, determined to remedy the confusion Grant's silence occasioned. He prepared a speech endorsing congressional Reconstruction, which he proposed to deliver in Galena, Illinois, where he and Grant made their homes. Before delivering the speech Rawlins submitted it to two of northwestern Illinois's leading Republicans, friends of Grant, who after careful consideration endorsed it. Rawlins spoke on June 14, 1867, not mentioning Grant's name, but clearly intending to define the general's position.[55]

By July most Republicans were convinced that Grant was in the running. Washburne, vacationing in Europe, visited John W. Forney there. He told Forney that he was managing Grant's campaign for the presidential nomination, assuring him that Grant was as radical as Washburne himself and giving as evidence Rawlins's speech. But the publisher of the Philadelphia *Press* and Washington *Daily Morning Chronicle* told his visitor that "I shuddered at the idea of another doubtful man in that post and that many good and true Republicans had grave doubts as to General Grant &c." To Sumner Forney wrote, "I cannot tell you how this conversation has depressed me. If Genl Grant wants the nomination I presume with such agencies and his great military strength he will secure it. I fear his administration. God help us! Are we never to have the right man in that place?"[56]

Radicals' doubts seemed justified as reports circulated that sentiment was growing among Democrats to nominate Grant on a Union Democratic platform before the Republican convention.[57] The independent Democratic New York *Herald* began to promote Grant as a nonpartisan candidate. Pointing to the bitterness dividing Republicans, the *Herald* predicted,

> There will be a tremendous struggle in the republican camp for the Convention of 1868, between the radical Chase faction . . . and the republican conserva-

tives supporting General Grant. The result, in all probability, will be a split of the republican party into two distinct parties for the succession. In this event the Northern democracy will hold the balance of power, and by casting their weight into the scale of the Grant, or anti-radical party, they will carry the election.[58]

But after the July session of Congress demonstrated the radicals' weakness, the *Herald* concluded that few Republican politicians would risk opposing Grant. Moreover, the *Herald* observed, Johnson's continued obstruction "can only operate to hold the republican party of the North intact with Congress, and draw the radicals of both Houses in closer communion with the conservatives and General Grant, while Grant is drawn into closer relations with them all." The *Herald* prophesied that the southern states would emerge from Reconstruction firmly Republican, the Negro question would fade from politics—except for the agitation of a few radicals—and only a small splinter group led by Sumner and Butler would reject the Republican nomination of Grant. The paper urged Democrats to join in Grant's support, obliterating party lines and paving the way for new political organizations on new issues.[59]

Democratic courtship of the popular general worried Republicans, who feared he might be seduced. John Sherman tried through his brother to warn Grant against the siren song. "They would deaden any man they praise," he cautioned. He assured General Sherman that the political strength lay neither with the Democrats nor Republicans "of the Butler stripe, but with just that kind of men who would be satisfied with Grant." [60]

But radicals' fears redoubled in August when Grant agreed to become secretary of war ad interim after Johnson removed Stanton. Grant's acceptance made Stanton's removal far more palatable to the public than it would have been otherwise. "GEN. GRANT . . . ," Tilton worried, "appears to have become a cat's paw for the President." [61]

Grant's course gave Horace Greeley an issue on which to attack his candidacy and his New York supporters. "Does not every reasonable person know that had Gen. Grant declined the appointment—which being a civil office, he had a right to decline—the President would not have succeeded in removing the War Secretary?" the *Tribune* asked. "How is the conclusion to be avoided that the President sought and found in Gen. Grant the means by which he might break down Sheridan, and with him the spirit of the people." [62] Greeley recalled Grant's former opinions, reminding readers of his report on southern conditions in 1866 and his "swing 'round the circle" with Johnson during the 1866 elections. "It is suspicious," Greeley argued,

that the men who arranged [the Philadelphia National Union] Convention are now the busiest in "arranging" Grant. The *Times* and the *Post* are as loud now as they were then, and they follow the same tactics. . . . They are inherently treacherous, bad, anti-Republican. They tried to destroy us last year by the patronage and strength of Andrew Johnson's administration. They are trying the same game now with the dazzling and illustrious name of Grant.[63]

As the campaign summer wore on, radical attacks on conservatives became more and more entwined with presidential politics. Fessenden, smarting under the radicals' biting attacks, wrote, "They would do the same by Grant if they dared. . . . They don't want him if it can be avoided, and mean to dispose of me in case any happy accidents should kill off Grant. That's the story as I read it. . . . [T]he malice of these fellows is equalled only by their meanness & cowardice." [64]

Chicago Tribune editor Horace White warned Washburne of the effect of Grant's acceptance of the War Department. "It will confirm the impression which many people have that he is some sense tainted with Johnsonism. . . . Second, it will give a new impetus to the impeachment movement, which, you will learn, is an anti-Grant movement, the object being to get Wade into the Presidency long enough to give him prestige & patronage to control the next National Convention." If he had been Grant, White wrote, he would have refused the offer "even at the risk of Johnson's appointing Surratt Secretary of War. . . . [A]t the present the whole affair wears an unfavorable & unpromising aspect." [65]

Washburne hastened to repair the damage. He visited Grant and encouraged him to make his position plain. Grant did so in his bitter letter to Johnson protesting Sheridan's removal. Joyously published in Republican newspapers, the protest restored the faith at least of conservative Republicans. Grant further informed Johnson that he would not participate in cabinet meetings except to transact department business.[66] This was followed on September 4 by visits from several radical congressmen, Schenck, Burton C. Cook, and John P.C. Shanks. Grant assured them his views corresponded with the congressional majority's and that he would say so if the opportunity arose.[67]

Nonetheless, many radicals remained dissatisfied. The *Tribune* still insisted that Grant had allowed Johnson to use him. Tilton's *Independent* was disturbed that Grant finally acquiesced in Sheridan's removal. "GEN. GRANT has surrendered to the President," Tilton charged.[68]

Under these circumstances the elections of 1867 took on immense importance. They would exert a tremendous influence on the future of the Republican party, testing the political viability of radicalism. If the Republicans succeeded in an election in which radicals had taken such a prominent and unmuzzled part, conservative arguments of expediency would lose much of their force. This would affect both program and candidate in 1868. The conservatives were worried. James G. Blaine wrote afterwards, "I felt . . . that if we should carry everything with a whirl in '67 such knaves as Ben Butler would control our National Convention and

THE BABY THAT WON'T TALK AT PRESENT.

NURSE W——E. "Bless your souls, ladies, the child won't talk for several months yet."
DAME A. J. "Say 'My Policy!' that's a little dear."
MOTHER W. H. S——D. "Yes, Baby: say 'My—my—My Policy!' that's a nice 'ittle darling."
LADY BEN W——E. "Now, my Precious, put down that 'ittle horse one minute, and say 'Con-gress.'"
GRANNY HENRY W——N. "Yes, my Pet, say 'Re-con-struc-tion.'"
MADAME A. T. S——T. "Here's a penny for Baby: say 'Greenbacks,' darling—'Green-backs!'"

A spoof of General Grant's unwillingness to announce his political opinions.
Harper's Weekly, February 15, 1868

give us a nomination with which defeat would be inevitable *if not desirable."* [69]

In three states—Kansas, Minnesota, and Ohio—voters would decide whether to amend their state constitutions to enfranchise their black fellow citizens. The results, especially in the swing state of Ohio, would indicate the temper of the people toward extending blacks the vote in the North. The implications were plain for Sumner's proposal to do this by congressional enactment or other propositions to accomplish it by constitutional amendment.

The people of twenty states went to the polls from March to November 1867, and Republicans lost ground in nearly all of them. In March Connecticut had replaced its Republican governor with a Democrat and elected three Democratic congressmen and only one Republican. Republicans lost 12,000 votes in Maine. The Democrats swept California, with Republicans running 20,000 votes behind their 1864 pace. The Republican vote in New Jersey fell 16,000 short of that polled in 1865, with seven of the twelve counties that voted Republican that year returning Democratic majorities in 1867. In Maryland the Republican vote was reduced from 40 percent of the total to 25 percent. In Massachusetts Republicans had won 77 percent of the vote in 1866; one year later they received only 58 percent. Republican percentages were also reduced in Vermont, New Hampshire, Iowa, Minnesota, Rhode Island, and Wisconsin. Only in Michigan and Kentucky did the party improve upon its showings of a year earlier.

But most ominous were the losses Republicans sustained in Ohio, Pennsylvania, and New York, all three swing states, all three carrying great weight in the Electoral College. Republicans could not lose them in 1868 and still expect to carry the presidential election. The Ohio contest had been especially important. Benjamin Wade's reelection to the Senate was directly at stake there as Ohioans elected a Democratic state legislature. Unable to carry his own state, Wade was eliminated as a presidential possibility. Since Chase too was an Ohioan, his chances also had been seriously, probably irreparably, damaged. The correspondent of the *New York Times* had made the stakes perfectly clear before the election: Ohio "gives the key-note of the entire central West," he wrote.

If Ohio give a decided vote, you need not expect any of the ten States, west and north of it, including Missouri and Colorado to go otherwise. These States give about one hundred electoral votes in the Presidential election . . . . If Ohio carries the Constitutional Amendment [extending suffrage to blacks] . . . and gives the Radical candidate . . . a decided majority, you may rely upon it, that these one hundred electoral votes will be given to an uncompromising Republican candidate for the Presidency. By that I mean a Republican, and one whose principles on important questions cannot be mistaken. I say this by way of warning to those who think that any kind of machinery in New-York will be available to an amphibious candidate who is equally ready to walk on land or water.[70]

The Republicans had expected victory in Ohio. William Henry Smith had expected a two-to-one Republican majority in the state legislature, a 40,000 majority for the Republican candidate for governor, Hayes, and a 5000 to 10,000 majority for the Negro suffrage amendment. Instead the Democrats won the legislature, the black suffrage amendment lost by 38,000 votes, and Hayes squeezed into the governorship by only 3000 votes of 484,000 cast. The Republicans lost 13,000 votes from their 1866 total, while the Democrats gained 27,000. Twelve of the forty-five Republican counties returned majorities against Negro suffrage.[71]

In Pennsylvania the Republican state ticket lost by 1000 votes, although the party retained control of the legislature by a slim margin. The previous year the Republican statewide majority had been 17,000 votes. In New York, Republicans lost, the narrow 13,000-vote Republican majority of 1866 converted to a 50,000-vote deficit.

Francis Lieber wrote of "this sad day when the news from all quarters tells us that the party who ruined the country is returning to power," but actually Republicans had lost only a few major offices: the governorships of Connecticut and California and Wade's Senate seat. Conservatives were not despondent. "The truth is that the result of the election has had a suddenly sobering effect," the Springfield *Republican* recorded with equanimity, "like a bucket of cold water on the head of a drunken man, and the inclination now will be to moderate and reasonable counsels." As Blaine wrote, "[The losses] will be good discipline in many ways and will I am sure be 'blessed to us in the edification and building up of the true faith.' " [72]

But for the radicals the defeat was a disaster—"a crusher for the wild men," Banks wrote happily.[73] The causes were many. In Maine and Massachusetts referenda on the prohibition of liquor complicated the issues. In California a bitter factional dispute disrupted the party. In Minnesota and New Hampshire taxation of United States bonds became involved in the campaigns, and in Iowa and Wisconsin there was dissatisfaction among the Germans. In Ohio the money question had damaged Republicans. As Colfax had complained, "In nearly every State we have side issues weakening us." [74]

But as Sherman recognized, "The chief trouble no doubt, is the [Negro] suffrage question. It is clearly right that suffrage should be impartial without regard to color. It is easy to convince people so, but harder to make them feel it—and vote it. We will have to carry it because it is right but it will be a burden in every election." Ben Wade put it more simply: "We went in on principle, and got whipped." [75] The consequences were clear. The perceptive John Binney wrote hopefully, "The extreme

Radicals must now open their eyes to the palpable fact, that they must moderate their impetuosity so as to carry the prudent conservative Republicans along with them." But the unhappy Wade put it another way. "I fear its effect will be to make the timorous more timorous and the next session more inefficient than the last," he confided to Chandler.[76]

The defeats of 1867 signaled to conservatives that they must continue their opposition to the radical program. The *New York Times* declared the elections "a reaction against the extreme acts and measures of the Republican party" and particularly against unqualified suffrage, "the menace of confiscation, [and] the bullying influence which such men as WADE, CHANDLER, NYE, ASHLEY, and men of their stamp mistake for statesmanship." [77]

"Our friends Wade Chandler & Co. must feel particularly gratified with the result in Ohio," Fessenden wrote Grimes with grim pleasure. "Most of our influential journals . . . think it is owing to a general disgust with the leadership of Stevens and his drove . . . and such, I think, will be the general verdict. . . .

"But for the loss of Wade's invaluable service in the Senate," he continued drily, "you, I suppose would think no great harm had been done. If Chandler is saved, however, perhaps the Country can stand the loss of Wade." [78]

Radicals replied that the fault lay with conservatives. "The Republican party—notwithstanding its boasted high mettle, and not withstanding its more boasted high principle—even yet quakes at meeting a negro by day as at seeing a ghost by night," Theodore Tilton wrote disgustedly. "When Negro Suffrage is proposed for South Carolina . . . the Republican party uplifts a lion's paw, and magnificently enforces obedience; but when Negro Suffrage is at issue in Ohio . . . the Republican party borrows a hare's legs, and runs away from its own principles." In the frustration of defeat Stevens claimed he "thank[ed] God for our late defeat. The Republicans have been acting a coward's part and have met a coward's fate." But when he and Boutwell announced that they would still press for impeachment and a congressional equal suffrage law, the Springfield *Republican* suggested laconically, "These men had better endeavor to repair the damage they have already done, than to try how many new experiments the party can survive." [79]

Still, despite the attacks upon the radicals, most Republicans probably agreed with the Boston *Evening Journal*'s opinion. There was no necessity to drive radicals out of the party or attack them bitterly, the *Journal* insisted. But conservatives should once more exert their dominance in the field of practical legislation.

If we remain true to [great principles] . . . , extreme men will trouble us no more than a fantastic figure-head troubles a good ship—they will ever serve the uses of their day and generation. But their place is not among the masters and helmsmen, and pilots. These must be taken from our wisest and most discreet.[80]

Radical idealists should be honored but impotent.

The elections' practical effects were felt immediately. The *Independent*'s Washington correspondent found the change among congressmen "startling." "Our friends have an overwhelming majority," he wrote, "but with the people apparently against the Radical members, it will be impossible to secure Radical legislation." As the session opened, he gloomily assessed the prospects.

> First, the impeachment movement is dead . . . .
> Second, all confiscation bills will fail. . . .
> Third, Congress will not pass a national Equal Suffrage bill till after the presidential election. . . . It is barely possible that a bill relating merely to congressional and presidential elections will pass; but this is all that can be expected now.[81]

The elections of 1867 also gave a further impulse to the organization of the hard-money lobby, and this in turn weakened the position of radicals in Congress. The economic malaise that gripped the country led to stronger and more persistent calls from businessmen for an end to contraction of the currency. Centering especially in the Midwest and Pennsylvania, the financial issue had played an important role in the Ohio and Pennsylvania campaigns. Western Democrats accomplished a complete about-face, supporting during the 1867 elections what became known as the Pendleton plan. Ohio Democrat George H. Pendleton, its foremost exponent, proposed simply that as the war debt had been contracted in depreciated currency, it should be repaid in the same currency rather than in gold. Many Republicans interpreted this as a scheme of repudiation and attacked it vigorously. But since payment of the bonds in greenbacks meant an expansion of the currency, many Americans found the plan very attractive. The issue was in part responsible for Republican losses, and Republican congressmen and politicians began to urge their leaders to bow to public pressure.[82]

In response Atkinson increased his efforts to create a hard-money lobby. Through his friendship with Charles Eliot Norton, editor of the *North American Review,* Atkinson converted that journal into a mouthpiece for his views. With the cooperation of John Murray Forbes he reactivated the Loyal Publication Society, which had functioned so well during the war, and through its facilities broadcast hard-money arguments and propaganda. Together he and Norton enlisted the pen of the brilliant Charles Francis Adams, Jr. Atkinson used his personal influence with Sumner in an attempt to bring his powerful voice to the cause. He won to his views William Boyd Allison, then a young member of the House Ways and Means committee, maintained cordial relations with James A.

Garfield, already recognized as a future leader on financial questions, and corresponded with Horace White of the *Chicago Tribune* and David Ross Locke, editor of the Toledo *Blade* and creator of "Petroleum V. Nasby." [83]

Many Republicans felt as Grimes did, that "the great question in American politics today is the financial question, and [i]t must override all reconstruction and impeachment questions." [84] Hard-money Republicans continued to drift toward conservatism, and their distaste for the fiscal policies many radicals advocated began in some cases to turn almost to hatred. "There is not a man who fought against us in the rebellion in whom I have not more confidence & for whom I have not a greater respect that I have for Mr. B.F. Butler," Grimes wrote. And he added, "Thad. Stevens is no better." [85]

As contractionists and free-traders became more conservative, radicalism tended more and more to be limited to those who advocated expansion of the currency. This became more apparent with each session of the Fortieth Congress. Among representatives who remained consistently radical or nonradical throughout this Congress, the corresponding polarization on financial questions was nearly complete.[86] When fiscal conservatives like Henry D. Cooke, Jay's brother, insisted, "Such men as Butler and Stevens must be put down—or driven to associate with the Vallandighams and Pendletons of the . . . Democracy . . . ," this necessarily meant their Reconstruction policies would be "put down" with them. At the same time conservatives had to be sustained, for most fiscal conservatives agreed with Grimes, who warned, "Let Mr. Sumner's 'clogs & obstructions' be removed from Congress & Thad Stevens & Butler be in controul as they then would be with their revolutionary & repudiating ideas in the ascendancy & the government would not last 12 mos." [87]

The impact of the 1867 elections upon the race for the Republican presidential nomination proved as dramatic as its impact upon the issues of Reconstruction and the finances. "The real victims of the victory of the Democrats," Clemenceau observed, "are Mr. Wade and Mr. Chase." The weakness of the Republican organization meant it needed a candidate stronger than the party. The other candidates are "good men as we all know," a correspondent wrote Elihu B. Washburne, "but we can only win with Grant." [88] Other Republicans agreed. Washburne took the opportunity afforded by Republican apprehensions finally to lay at rest any lingering doubts about Grant's Republicanism. In a speech to an Illinois county party convention, Washburne announced Grant supported congressional Reconstruction and Negro suffrage. He had accepted control of the War Department after Stanton's ouster only to prevent presidential obstruction. Newspapers around the country reported the speech, and Republican conservatives expressed gratification.[89]

The conservatives held the whip hand. "These Republican defeats lay a good many men on the shelf who will be more useful *there* than they have been elsewhere," Raymond wrote McCulloch. "They will compel the nomination of Grant or split and defeat the party." He repeated his convictions in the *Times*. The Republicans "dare not nominate anybody else," he concluded.[90] Optimistic reports reached Washburne from leading Grant men in different states. From New York, where he was busily organizing a more broadly based Grant movement than Weed's, John Cochrane wrote, "I don't think Chase has a corporal's guard. Former Chase men have whipped off their livery, and the general cry is for Grant." Curtin informed Washburne from Pennsylvania, where he had met so little success in urging the general's name before the election, "Now everybody is for Grant and on the first opportunity our party will declare for him." The reason was patent: "Grant is the only man living who can carry this State next year on present issues." [91]

But many radicals remained unreconciled to their prospective standard-bearer, so recent a recruit. As the likelihood of Grant's nomination increased, the *Nation* observed, "complaints that nobody knows 'where he stands' seem to grow louder." Not only were true radicals uncertain of what the general's position would be on future Reconstruction issues, complained Tilton, but "that practiced soldier, but unpracticed civilian, could not even tell himself." And worse than the uncertainty was the class of men who supported him. "Out of every three Republicans whom one now meets," he continued, "two are chiefly anxious for the success of Negro suffrage, and the third for the success of Gen. Grant. On further inquiry the third Republican will most likely be found to have either refrained from voting at all in the late election, or to have voted for the Democrats." [92]

The "bread and butter" politicians and the conservatives were forcing on the radicals a candidate they did not want. Disheartened, Wade lamented, "It is very strange that when men talk of availability they always mean something squinting toward Copperheadism. They never think of consulting the Radicals, who are the only working men in the party. Oh, no; we must take what we get." [93]

But the radicals had one hope left. They might remove Johnson through impeachment and install Wade in the presidency, where he could, as White had feared, use his prestige and patronage to control the party. Furthermore, Johnson's removal would remedy the defective Reconstruction law, which left so much obstructive power in the president's hands. Perhaps it would resurrect the confiscation and education issues. With radical influence diminishing, impeachment was a last resort, and as the second session of the Fortieth Congress approached, radicals in the House feverishly worked to secure the majority needed to pass an impeachment resolution.

Conservatives, on the other hand, determined to stop them. Bingham warned Washburne of the radicals' intentions. They would try to remove the president, to disfranchise former Confederates, insuring black domination of the reconstructed states, to confiscate rebel's property, and to enfranchise black Americans in all states by congressional enactment. "Such is in short, the forthcoming project of Mr. Stevens & it will require some care to see that he does not commit a majority of our friends in the House to it," Bingham cautioned. Washburne agreed. "If Congress will only be half decent and half honest," he wrote, "we will be through like a whirlwind."

But it would not be easy. The radicals were bitter. "You must look out for squalls," Fessenden warned Grimes. Firmly, he contemplated the coming session. "There will be plenty of crimination and recrimination." [94]

FOURTEEN

Congress on the President's Hip

— ✦✦✦✦✦✦✦✦✦✦✦✦✦ —

DESPITE THE DEFEATS OF 1867, radicals determined to continue their campaign for impeachment. But they knew it would be more difficult now to win the majority needed to bring the impeachment before the Senate. For although the election reverses did not induce individual Republicans to break ranks—that is, most Republicans who had been radicals during the first session of the Fortieth Congress remained so in the second, and the same for centrists and conservatives—they did force each group to the right. The center groups, which might have favored impeachment had the elections demonstrated radical strength, now divided, most of them opposing impeachment. Confiscation, black enfranchisement by national law, and continued exclusion of southern states from the Union, all of which many radicals might have supported, now were out of the question. (For the factional composition of the second session of the Fortieth Congress, see Lists 15 and 16.)

Impeachment received a further blow when President Johnson refused to fulfill dire predictions that the Republican defeats would embolden him in obstructing Reconstruction. On the contrary, the president had acted with remarkable (for him) circumspection. He had removed no more military commanders in the South. He did not, as Republicans feared he would, recognize a rival Congress of southerners and northern Democrats. He had not even replaced his Johnson Republican cabinet with a Democratic one. In fact, he had been on his best behavior.

But the radicals did not believe that Johnson had turned over a new leaf. They surmised (accurately, it proved) that he had determined to add no more fuel to the impeachment controversy, but that he would act with vigor once that threat was removed. They had every reason to fear that in that case the congressional Reconstruction program would be defeated. The voters of the North clearly were growing tired of the controversy. If by use of the patronage and the army under docile commanders, Johnson and southern conservatives prevented ratification of the constitutions radical conventions were framing, Republicans would have to face the 1868 elections with a still unrestored Union. Exasperated northern voters might overwhelm them at the polls. Impeachment and removal would end that threat forever.

Presidential politics also played a role in the radicals' determination. The Grant movement was gaining strength rapidly, especially in New York, where leading conservative and apolitical businessmen, led by Hamilton Fish and Alexander T. Stewart, signed a call for a conservative, nonpartisan Grant meeting to be held December 4, 1867. Although Washburne had suggested the maneuver to his chief New York lieutenants, John Cochrane and Waldo Hutchins, both radicals, Thurlow Weed had infiltrated the movement and was personally responsible for many of the signatures. James Gordon Bennet, the editor of the New York *Herald,* and Parke Godwin, of the *Evening Post,* supported the campaign.

The Grant movement had become so manifestly the vehicle of Republican conservatism in New York that Washburne himself began to worry. Urgently he wrote Cochrane pressing him to secure radical support. With this a bitter struggle began between Washburne's forces and Weed's New York organization for control of the Grant campaign. The Weed faction tried to take over Grant meetings and clubs, calling leading conservatives to the rostrums and attacking radicals, in an effort, Cochrane wrote, "to use Grant as a banner to capture the Republican organization." The *New York Tribune*'s public endorsement of Chase for the presidency aided Weed's efforts, encouraging the *Tribune*-led radical faction of the New York Republican party to remain aloof from the Grant boom. Finally Weed attempted to induce Hutchins to betray Washburne and Cochrane. He secretly promised Hutchins his organization's aid in fulfilling any personal political ambitions if he would turn over control of the December 4 meeting to Weed partisans. At the same time, Cochrane wrote, Weed arranged with the Tammany faction of the Democratic party to bring Grant forward as a Democratic candidate. This would have created the broad-based, conservative party Weed had dreamed of for years, leaving radicals isolated. Although Cochrane and Hutchins managed to thwart Weed's machinations, the Committee of Twenty-Four appointed by the December 4 meeting to coordinate the Grant movement consisted entirely of rigidly nonpolitical businessmen. Washburne complained, but Cochrane explained there was nothing he could do. The businessmen had bitterly resisted all suggestions that they cooperate with mere politicians.[1]

Given this situation, radicals looked upon the prospect of Grant's nomination with something less than enthusiasm. Nonetheless the radical correspondent of the *Indiana True Republican* estimated that two thirds of the Republican congressmen believed the nomination inevitable. One of Benjamin F. Butler's most important local Massachusetts allies warned him, "The republican party in Massachusetts and New England are bound to have Grant for President," and urged him to come to terms with his enemy.[2] But as conservatives sensed, the radicals hoped to use impeachment against Grant. Wade, who would replace Johnson if he were removed, had publicly declared his preference for Chase rather than Grant. Many of Chase's partisans still remained in the Treasury Department, protected by McCulloch's reluctance to turn old Republicans out of office. Chase remained stronger than Grant with southern Republicans, who feared the general's conservatism. With Wade as president, Grant might be denied the nomination. At least the national convention would be certain to frame a radical platform which would commit Grant to radicalism or force him to withdraw his candidacy. As Chase's intimate friend and biographer, James W. Schuckers, wrote six years later, "The impeachment programme had . . . two motives; the first and most important was, of course, to get Andrew Johnson out of the presidency, and the second and hardly less important was, to keep General Grant from getting in." [3]

When Congress met, the impeachers appeared to be in a hopeless minority. The Judiciary committee had kept their proceedings strictly confidential, and most congressmen believed that the majority report would be against impeachment, as the June vote in the committee had indicated. Since the whole House customarily concurred in majority reports from committees, many Republicans planned to vote against impeachment but to aver they had simply endorsed a committee report, thus side-stepping the issue. The *Times*'s correspondent estimated that under these circumstances the impeachers could muster but fifty to fifty-five votes, with sixty Republicans and all forty-nine Democrats opposed, and fifteen undecided. But when the committee published its report November 25, Republicans learned that John C. Churchill had changed his mind as a result of Johnson's interference with the military. The majority report would favor impeachment. Churchill's reversal caused wild excitement, and radicals believed they could muster a fifteen- to thirty-vote majority. In the confusion both sides predicted victory.[4]

Conservatives were dismayed. "I have never been more than at this moment impressed with the peril of the Republican party," George G. Fogg, New Hampshire's just-retired senator, wrote Washburne. "I had hoped that the late elections had taught us something. I had hoped we would be allowed to breathe before being rushed forward into new disasters under the lead of men who are now little better than paroled prisoners of war." Washburne grimly agreed. Other conservative and moderate Republicans—and some radicals—echoed Fogg's forebodings and urged their representatives to abandon the impeachment issue and wrestle with the finances instead. But the impeachers remained adamant. Fessenden gloomily anticipated a radical victory. He confessed, "This I shall regard as ruin to our party—and it will be a just punishment for our cowardice and folly." [5]

Conservative and anti-Wade men determined to fight impeachment with all their resources. Garfield, Chase's chief supporter in the House; Washburne, Spalding, and Bingham, leading Grant men; Blaine, Dawes, James F. Wilson, and others worked hard to defeat the impeachment resolution proposed by the Judiciary committee majority. By December 5 they believed they had succeeded.[6]

Their work was made easier by the nature of the Judiciary committee's reports on impeachment. Republican members' disagreement centered about the law of impeachment, especially the nature of the offenses for which it was the appropriate remedy. The committee majority, in a report written by Representative Thomas Williams, argued that impeachment was designed to deal primarily with a broad range of official misconduct, including any malfeasance or misfeasance in carrying out official duties. In this case, the impeachers insisted, "the great salient point of accusation . . . is *usurpation of power.*"[7] By promulgating a complete program of Reconstruction, by appointing civil officials to administer states pursuant to no law and without sending their names to the Senate for confirmation, by ignoring the Test Oath and Confiscation acts and nullifying the law creating the Freedmen's Bureau, the president had usurped the powers of Congress, violating the Constitution. Moreover, the president had *abused* other powers rightfully his: pardoning rebels so as "to prevent not only the exaction of forfeitures, but the prosecution of crimes," reappointing to office nominees whom the Senate had rejected, and using the veto power in an unsuccessful attempt to bring "the [Reconstruction] legislation of the country to a dead stand."[8] These too were impeachable offenses, for even clearly presidential powers were not "without reasonable limitations altogether, . . . [to be] exercised without discrimination, to the great damage, and possibly to the entire destruction of the government."

"Every power granted by the Constitution is subject to such a qualification," the majority avowed, "and if susceptible to abuse, is only to be checked and controlled by the remedy of impeachment."[9] But though the reasoning was powerful and consonant with precedents and legal authority, the report was injudicious in language and violent in spirit, an inflammatory indictment of the president.[10] Conservatives pointed to it as evidence that the impeachers were motivated more out of hatred for Andrew Johnson than by a concern for the country.

In contrast, the Republican minority report, prepared by Chairman Wilson, assumed an air of moderation. Yet it too was more of a brief for the defense than a dispassionate analysis of the case. Deprecating "the temper and spirit" of the majority report, Wilson and Woodbridge insisted that "high crimes and misdemeanors"—which the Constitution defined along with treason and bribery as the sole grounds for impeachment— meant indictable violations of statutory or common law. They were used "as terms of art, and we have no authority for expounding them beyond their technical limits." [11] Johnson may have been guilty of many wrongs; "his contest with Congress has delayed reconstruction, and inflicted vast injury upon the people of the rebel States." But he had violated no laws in the process. His were political wrongs, and "political unfitness and incapacity must be tried at the ballot-box, not in the high court of impeachment." [12] The Democratic minority report, agreeing on the legal points with Wilson's, was of little importance.

As the Republicans prepared to vote on the impeachment question, they were shocked by the president's annual message. Ending his passivity, Johnson once again became defiant. Beginning with a conciliatory reaffirmation of his interpretation of the constitutional basis for Reconstruction, Johnson went on to denounce the constitutionality of the Reconstruction acts in less moderate terms. But he went further. Abandoning constitutional arguments, he proclaimed black suffrage "worse than the military despotism under which [the southern states] . . . are now suffering." Black men were inherently unable to govern themselves under republican institutions. They were "corrupt in principle and enemies of free institutions. . . . If the inferior [race] obtains the ascendency over the other, it will govern with reference only to its own interests—for it will recognize no common interest—and create such a tyranny as this continent has never yet witnessed."

But most ominous was the president's unsubtle threat:

How far the duty of the President "to preserve, protect, and defend the Constitution" requires him to go in opposing an unconstitutional act of Congress is a very serious and important question, on which I have deliberated much, and felt extremely anxious to reach a proper conclusion. Where an act has been passed according to the forms of the Constitution by the supreme legislative authority, and is regularly enrolled among the public statutes of the country, executive resistance to it . . . would be likely to produce violent collision between the respective adherents of the two branches of the Government. This would be simply civil war; and civil war must be resorted to only as the last remedy for the worst of evils. . . . The so-called reconstruction acts, though plainly unconstitutional as any that can be imagined, were not believed to be within the class last mentioned.[13]

For the first time the president had clearly indicated that he had considered forcible resistance to Congress. He had decided against it not because his action would have been illegal or unconstitutional, but because in the president's opinion, the Reconstruction acts did not justify it.[14]

The presidential message reinforced the radicals' opinion that his removal was a necessity. "The propositions which the President has laid down . . . will lead to certain difficulty if they are acted upon," Boutwell warned. The Constitution authorizes Congress to pass bills, subject to the president's veto. "If the House and Senate by a two-thirds vote pass a bill [over the veto] it becomes a law, and until it is repealed by the same authority or annulled by the Supreme Court the President has but one duty, and that is to obey it; and no consideration or opinion of his as to its constitutionality will defend or protect him in any degree." Moreover the president's vehement denunciation of black suffrage boded only evil. "Are we to leave this officer, if we judge him to be guilty of high crimes and misdemeanors, in control of the Army and the Navy, with his declaration upon the record that under certain circumstances he will not execute the laws?" Boutwell asked. "He has the control of the Army. Do you not suppose that next November a single soldier at each polling place in the southern country, aided by the whites, could prevent the entire negro population from voting: And if it is for the interest of the President to do so have we any reason to anticipate a different course of conduct?" [15] The tone of the president's message, Ben Perley Poore reported, had influenced eight to ten Republicans to vote for impeachment. But he believed that the impeachers still lacked the necessary votes.[16]

As the senior signer of the majority report, Boutwell opened debate on impeachment on December 5. He devoted his long address primarily to the legal question. The House, he knew, was well aware of the president's activities. The question would turn on whether they were impeachable, for, he acknowledged, "if the theory of the law submitted by the minority be in the judgment of this House a true theory, then the majority have no case whatever." He altered his address before it was published in the appendix of the *Congressional Globe,* but observers wrote that the House listened in rapt attention. As published, Boutwell's speech embodied a clear, eloquent, and convincing argument for a broad view of the impeachment power. Boutwell began by expressing his sympathy for those who feared the effects of an impeachment. He acknowledged that the House could decide impeachment inexpedient even if members believed the president liable to the process. He affirmed that he himself would be inclined to allow the president to finish his term if he did not believe evil consequences were sure to follow. Then, concisely and convincingly, he reiterated the legal propositions propounded in the majority report, that precedent and authority sustained the impeachers' view that the president could be impeached for abuse of power, and he riddled the logic of the minority position.

Then Boutwell turned to the facts. The president had taken upon himself the responsibility of reconstructing the southern states. The minority might argue that Congress had ratified that usurpation by acquiescing in the continued existence of his restored state governments. But, Boutwell reminded his listeners, the president had concealed his purposes. Congress had believed the president's plan temporary, to be annulled or approved when Congress met. "The public mind did not comprehend the character and extent of the usurpation." The president had vetoed all Congress's Reconstruction bills, urged the southern people to reject the Fourteenth Amendment, appointed to office men who could not take the test oath, surrendered the abandoned lands and confiscated railroad property, appointed and paid provisional governors in the southern states although Congress had neither created the office or appropriated money to reimburse its holders. The ultimate purpose of all this, Boutwell concluded, manifestly was to return the former rebels to power in the state and national governments despite Congress's judgment that this must not be done. "When you consider all these things, can there be any doubt as to his purpose, or doubt as to the criminality of his purpose and his responsibility under the Constitution?" Boutwell asked.

It may not be possible, by specific charge, to arraign him for this great crime, but is he therefore to escape? These offenses which I have enumerated . . . are the acts, the individual acts, the subordinate crimes, the tributary offenses to the accomplishment of the great object which he had in view. But if, upon the body of the testimony, you are satisfied of his purpose, and if you are satisfied that these tributary offenses were committed as the means of enabling him to accomplish this great crime, will you hesitate to try him and convict him upon those charges of which he is manifestly guilty, even if they appear to be of inferior importance, knowing . . . that in this way, and this way only, can you protect the State against the final consummation of his crime? [17]

Wilson followed Boutwell's effort on December 6. Boutwell's attack on the minority's legal argument was so powerful that Wilson immediately retreated from it. No member of the minority believed their legal doctrine "of the slightest importance so far as a correct determination of this case is concerned. . . . It is immaterial what opinion members may have of it." Nonetheless, Wilson devoted half of his speech to defending his position that impeachment lay only for indictable crimes and attacking its opponents. Ironically, Wilson turned the very superiority of Boutwell's argument against him. He pointed out the palpable fact that it was inconsistent with the committee report. In his speech Boutwell eschewed the value of English precedents as irrelevant to impeachment in American constitutional law; the report cited English cases. In his speech Boutwell pointed out that under the minority's view of the law, if an officer could commit murder in such a way as to be outside the jurisdiction of United States courts, he would be immune to impeachment; the report had stated that murder would not be an impeachable offense since it did not relate directly to office holding. Wilson's blunt analysis of the inconsistencies between Boutwell's brilliant speech and Williams's mediocre majority report did tremendous damage to the impeachers' case.

Wilson went on to emphasize the full implications of the majority position. Boutwell insisted that the impeachment power

is subject to no revision or control, and that its exercise is to be guided solely by the conscience of the House. Correctly interpreted, this doctrine, as it seems to me, comes to this: that whatever this House may declare on its conscience to be an impeachable offense, reduce to the form of articles, and carry to the Senate for trial, that body is only to be allowed to declare whether the officer impeached is guilty of the facts presented against him, but is not to be permitted to say that such facts do or do not constitute a crime or a misdemeanor. Does he desire us to intrust the character, extent, and uses of this power to the shifting fortunes of political parties? What could be more dangerous to the peace and safety of the Government than this?

Finally, Wilson discussed the individual charges. He pointed out that the report of the Joint Committee on Reconstruction, of which Boutwell was a member, assigned patriotic motives to the president when discussing his Reconstruction policy in June of 1866, long after Boutwell claimed to have discerned the president's master design to return power to the rebels. Testimony convinced him that the return of property to the rebels was done by advice of the cabinet and showed no evidence of criminal intent. But Wilson abruptly left this discussion and closed his address by returning to the legal issue.

Sir, we must be guided by some rule in the grave proceeding . . . . If we cannot arraign the President for a specific crime for what are we to proceed against him? For a bundle of generalities such as we have in the volume of testimony reported by the committee to the House in this case? If we cannot state upon paper a specific crime how are we to carry this case to the Senate for trial?

So despite his disclaimer, Wilson relied after all on his legal objections, and with that he moved that the impeachment resolution be laid on the table.[18]

The radicals were outraged. By moving to lay the resolution on the table, Wilson had cut off debate. Over forty radicals had prepared speeches on the question, many of them filled with vituperation toward the conservatives and their arguments, which the radicals so sincerely believed to be specious. Moreover Wilson's maneuver again opened the possibility of dodging the issue, enabling members to say they favored tabling to avoid a bitterly divisive argument which might disrupt the party.[19] Furious, the radicals, led by Logan and Schenck, began the difficult job of filibustering the House. With seven roll-call votes on adjournment the radicals delayed the vote into the dinner hour, mustering from fifty to sixty votes against the anti-impeachers' one hundred plus. But at five o'clock the anti-impeachers broke ranks, over twenty of them voting with the radicals to adjourn, giving them an 80 to 77 victory.

The next day the radicals began where they had left off, but they could not continue forever. Logan implored his opponents to allow the minority ten minutes to explain the reason for its filibuster. If the majority granted their request, Logan promised, the impeachers would agree to vote. But this would require unanimous consent, and although many of the anti-impeachers were willing, Rufus P. Spalding objected. "I will not give them a single minute now," he announced bitterly. Again the radicals moved an adjournment. Again the clerk read the name of each representative in turn. Again the effort failed.

Logan now asked Wilson to withdraw his tabling motion, promising to end the delay if the majority would agree to vote on the direct issue. Wilson agreed, and the House defeated the majority resolution 57 to 108. Three absent Republicans were announced in favor of impeachment and two against. All those who favored impeachment were Republicans; sixty-six Republicans voted against it; two more were so declared. The radicals had not been able to muster a majority even of their own party.[20] "You will see how Congress backed down on impeachment, & can guess the effect of it on the whole of the South, followed by such a message as the last," Julian wrote his wife. "It is pitiful!" [21]

The conservatives had betrayed the nation with their pettifogging lawyer's arguments, radicals believed. They would sacrifice southern loyalists rather than risk losing political power. Tilton exploded,

If the great culprit had robbed a till; if he fired a barn; if he had forged a check he would have been indicted, prosecuted, condemned, sentenced, and punished. But the evidence shows that he only oppressed the Negro; that he only conspired with the rebel; that he only betrayed the Union party; that he only attempted to overthrow the Republic—of course, he goes unwhipped of justice. . . . So a President of the United States begins by insulting, continues by bullying, and ends by conquering Congress. . . . At the last moment the brave men among them were denied even the right of opening their lips on the question. . . . [A] Republican majority of cowards gagged a Republican minority of statesmen. Thaddeus Stevens, George Boutwell, John Logan, and others of like heroic mold, stood by their country, and were throttled by their friends.[22]

It seemed too much for the radicals to bear. "It is no use disguising the fact," the *Anti-Slavery Standard*'s Washington correspondent wrote, *"The Republican Party is not now one. There are two distinct parties in its midst."* Butler bitterly informed a friend, "The party has lost its morale . . . it may as well break up or it will break down." [23] In the gall of defeat radicals met at Stevens's residence to find a way to bring impeachment up once more and keep the floor for speeches. They decided to meet again to perfect a parliamentary organization of radicals alone, to be led by Schenck and Stevens.[24]

A splinter group of radicals determined to meet in Washington on February 22, 1868, to adopt a platform of principles. If the Republicans nominated Grant on a watered-down platform, they would bolt. The *New York Times* jumped at the opportunity once again to call for a realignment of parties. "The true issue before the country to-day is between Radicalism and Constitutionalism—between a policy which recognizes and accepts the

Constitution as the paramount rule of action, and one which virtually discards it as inadequate to the emergency, and accepts the abstract doctrine and sentiments ascribed to the Declaration of Independence in its stead." Editor Raymond urged the radicals to act on their threat, organize a radical party, and nominate Butler and Wade for president and vice-president. "The people will understand what they have to do hereafter." [25]

If the radicals were furious, conservatives were elated. Republicans could turn to financial questions in peace now, Fessenden happily wrote. "It extinguishes the aspirations of the Radical-Radicals. . . . For once, Mr. Sumner cannot boast of the fulfillment of his prophecy, and his bitterness beats 'wormwood and gall,' " he exulted. "It is of no use, however. They are in a minority of their own party—and must stay there." [26]

The Democrats happily recognized that they now faced a party divided. Some Democrats determined to emphasize Grant's early statements against Negro suffrage and his friendliness to Johnson, rather than attacking him. "I shd be sorry to have assisted in overcoming Radical hostility to his nomination in the Republican convention by persuading them that he *is* in sympathy with them," the New York *World* editor, Manton Marble, wrote Doolittle.[27] But Andrew Johnson did not share such political wisdom. Freed, he thought, from the threat of impeachment, he now pursued a course which reunited the fragmented Republican party and nearly led to his removal.

The defeat of impeachment heartened Johnson's supporters. "It is generally thought that the President has Congress on the hip," Johnson's friend, Thomas Ewing, Sr., wrote optimistically.[28] In the South the anti-Republican forces stiffened their resistance to the Reconstruction acts. In Louisiana, Hancock determined to act. After Johnson had removed Sheridan, General Mower, Sheridan's second-in-command and temporary commander pending Hancock's arrival, had removed many officers of the Johnsonian provisional governments, appointing Republicans in their places. Now Hancock revoked the removals, restoring to office among others the Johnsonian state treasurer, auditor of public accounts, and several New Orleans police officials. On February 7 the conservative general removed the radical New Orleans city council that Sheridan had appointed. This was too much for Grant, and he ordered Hancock to suspend his removal order. Hancock protested, but Grant remained adamant, forcing his subordinate to rescind it. Bitterly, Hancock asked to be removed from his command.[29] Despite Grant's rebuffs Hancock continued to aid the anti-Reconstruction forces in Louisiana, removing the board of registrars appointed by the state constitutional convention to oversee the ratification election and appointing his own instead. The chairman of the board named by the convention complained they were "notorious rebels, and open enemies to reconstruction." [30]

In Virginia the conservative commander John M. Schofield continued his opposition to radical Republicans. He stolidly resisted radical pressure to remove officials of the provisional government whose terms had expired. He preferred to hold over the conservative and Democratic officers of the Johnson government rather than name radical Republicans. He was determined, he later wrote, to execute the Reconstruction acts in Virginia in such a way as "to save that State from the great evils suffered by sister States." [31] Hoping that Johnson would now act on their complaints, southerners renewed their attacks on the remaining strict military commanders in the South and increased their obstruction of the Reconstruction process. Disheartened with Johnson's failure to support him, Pope wrote Grant, "The indications now are that the managers of the disloyal faction in the South will succeed in breaking down every General who performs his duty." Pope suggested Johnson replace him with "some officer . . . whom the President will trust." [32]

On December 28, Johnson acted, relieving Pope, his subordinate, Wager Swayne, who had held command in Alabama, and General Edward O.C. Ord, commander in Mississippi and Arkansas. General George Meade replaced Pope and promptly instituted a more conservative policy, ordering the military to consider itself subordinate to the civil authority, forbidding interference with the Johnson government officials without his direct order, and allowing these officials to remain in office despite the expiration of their terms. He also allowed the state courts to exclude blacks from jury duty.[33] In Ord's place Johnson appointed conservative General Alvan C. Gillem.

Despairing, Oliver Otis Howard lamented, "The President . . . musters out all my officers . . . . Measures are on foot . . . which are doubtless intended to utterly defeat reconstruction." The angry, radical Washington correspondent of the Boston *Commonwealth* wrote, "Thus Johnson defeats Congress at every point. . . . While Congress is passing acts to reconstruct the South, the President is driving a carriage and six through them." [34]

Southern Republicans were desperate. Foster Blodgett, the chairman of the Central State Committee of the Georgia Republican party, pleaded with congressional Republicans for help. "The fact is that Reconstruction is now on a pivot . . . ," he warned. "The action of Congress for the next 10 or 15 days will decide whether the whole South will be Republican or Democratic." He concluded, "Our Northern friends seem to know nothing of the intense bitter hatred that is manifested towards us." Judge John C. Underwood, one of Virginia's leading radicals, appealed to Washburne to persuade Schofield to remove the Virginia provisional government. "Every State, city & county office with very few exceptions [is] in the hands of the rebels holding over," he complained.[35]

The chairman of the Alabama party joined the frantic appeal, as

Republicans there blamed their failure to win a majority for the new constitution on Swayne's removal. "Unfriendly military management has
killed us," one of them wrote. "The rebels have had all their own ways in
many counties. What next can we do?" From Georgia, Texas, Mississippi,
Arkansas, and Louisiana, Republicans urged their allies finally to erase the
Johnson state governments. They echoed Underwood's plea: "Can Congress save us from annihilation?" [36]

Even the *Chicago Tribune,* which had vigorously opposed impeachment, exploded, "Cannot Congress devise some means of checkmating the
villainous conspiracy of Johnson and Co. to defeat the restoration . . . of
the Southern States to the Union?" [37] Privately, the *Tribune*'s editor, Horace
White, wrote Washburne that he shared the "rather gloomy feeling you
express concerning the present phase of reconstruction." And he urged
that "inasmuch as Johnson carries all his points, by sheer audacity and
doggedness, it is necessary for Congress to meet him on the same ground,
and to be as audacious and obstinate as he is." [38]

The temporizing policies of the conservative and center Republicans
had allowed the president to take the offensive. To radicals this was patent.
"Our legislation on reconstruction was a monstrous blunder . . . ,"
Timothy Otis Howe fumed. "We declared those State organizations illegal
. . . . We asserted our complete authority over them & then instead of
abolishing them as we ought, we declared them provisional & subordinated
them to a military system at the head of which is Andrew Johnson." [39] The
entire congressional Reconstruction policy had been predicated on the hope
that the president would honestly enforce the law. He had not. But rather
than remove him, the conservatives and centrists had forced Congress to
amend its Reconstruction laws continually. "Congress enacts measure after
measure and adjourns in the pleasing delusion it has everything its own
way," the Boston *Commonwealth* lamented. "While Congress acts as if he
were an obstinate and stupid blockhead, [Johnson] . . . works quietly
and steadily in the White House, saying nothing, devoting himself with
an energy almost sublime to the accomplishment of his wicked ends." [40]

If only Congress had passed his Louisiana Reconstruction bill, Eliot
mourned. It rested "on a civil basis. . . . [I]ts provisions were such as
would . . . in the shortest period have restored civil government within
the confines of Louisiana; and under that bill loyal men would have presented themselves upon the floor of this House and would have represented,
in my judgment, a State loyal throughout." Now Congress must continually
amend its Reconstruction laws, although the original would have been suf-
ficient, if only it had been "fairly and *bona fide* carried out." [41]

In response to the crisis, Republicans prepared once again to pass a
supplementary Reconstruction bill. But they rejected a comprehensive bill
proposed by Ashley. That measure would have ended the military administration and authorized the constitutional conventions to elect a pro-

visional governor and a six-citizen executive committee to govern each state. They in turn were given the power to remove all present (Johnson) state officers who opposed Reconstruction or could not take the test oath. Finally, Ashley's bill repealed the requirement under the former Reconstruction laws that each constitution be ratified by an absolute majority of the registered voters.[42]

When Ashley brought his bill before the House on December 18, he agreed to let Stevens substitute a bill from the Reconstruction committee merely repealing the absolute majority requirement for ratification and authorizing each state to elect congressmen in the same election in which its citizens voted on ratifying the constitution. Calling the previous question, Stevens refused to allow radicals to offer an amendment authorizing the conventions to organize provisional governments, and the bill passed without Republican dissent.[43]

The Reconstruction committee then turned to the question of how to counteract the damage being done by Johnson's new military appointees in the South. Colfax had appointed an extremely radical Reconstruction committee, but despite this radical preponderance, Stevens alone—judging by later votes in the House—insisted on authorizing the conventions to organize provisional governments. On January 13, 1868, the number-two man on the committee, Bingham, reported a more modest proposal. This prohibited the president from appointing or removing military commanders in the South and placed the duty instead upon the general of the army, Grant. Furthermore, it authorized Grant personally to replace any official of the Johnson state governments. Finally—and pointedly—the bill declared any interference with its provisions a "high misdemeanor." [44] The conservatives and centrists had gone as far as they could go without impeaching the president or authorizing southern Republicans to take control of their states.

But why were many Republicans so disinclined to give control over the southern states to their allies? The answer lay in radical-conservative politics. In several of the southern states the Republican party was divided into factions. In Virginia the radicals, led by James W. Hunnicutt and John Hawxhurst, and supported by most blacks, were locked in a bitter duel with conservative Republicans, guided by General Schofield, Governor Francis H. Pierpont, James H. Gilmer, and John Minor Botts. But by December 1867, when the constitutional convention called pursuant to the Reconstruction acts met, the radicals had won overwhelming control of the party, despite Schofield's continued opposition. Pierpont and Botts were forced to acquiesce. In the convention itself, Schofield estimated, there were fifty-four radicals, twenty-two conservative and moderate Republicans, twelve Conservatives, and seventeen unreconstructed rebels.[45] Congressional Republicans expressed grave concern that the radical Virginia convention might propose measures that would damage Republicans in the

North. Republicans like Washburne—his fingers now in every pie—urged moderation.[46] If the convention were given control of the state, and its patronage, Schofield's restraining influence would be at an end, and radicalism would reign supreme in Virginia, bringing with it black officeholding and pressure for social reform which might embarrass northern Republicans in an election year.[47]

Similar divisions existed in Georgia, Louisiana, and Florida, with radical and conservative-center forces more evenly balanced, however. Nonetheless, many Republicans in Congress refused to risk disaster in the North by catering to their allies in the South.[48]

Most House radicals did not share this timidity. Led by Butler, they wanted to amend the bill to give the conventions control of the state governments. But Bingham prevented amendments by calling for the previous question. He then "graciously" yielded the floor. Acidly, Butler observed, "It is always an invidious task to argue a question after it has been virtually decided. . . .

"We are called radicals," he complained, "but by our legislation we only touch the topmost branches, never seeking to cut up the roots of all this trouble. We do not come to the trunk of the tree, much less at the root of the evil." [49] With Democratic support, Butler succeeded in forcing a reconsideration of the main question, allowing him to move his amendment. But on the amendment itself the Democrats deserted him, and Butler lost 53 to 112, with over seventy Republicans opposing him. Butler abstained as the bill passed.[50]

In the Senate the bill occasioned three weeks' debate between Democrats and Republicans, both trying to make a record for the upcoming elections. The endless debate wore on Republicans' nerves. Popular reaction to the "Military Dictator Bill," as Democrats labeled it, was not good. "We cannot be blind to the fact that a reaction has set in," Friedrich Hassaurek, the influential German Republican, warned Sherman. Hassaurek himself shared the feeling. "I [am] . . . not in favor of changing the American system of Government, merely because a certain individual happens to be in the Presidential chair," he informed Sherman bluntly. The Republicans must change their course. "We are losing ground daily. Men who have voted with us for many years, are going over to the opposition. The train-bands and camp-followers who scent the coming storm, are leaving us by hundreds, and, if the brakes are not put on in time, not even Gen. Grant's great popularity will be able to save us next October and November." The *Chicago Tribune,* impatient with delay and everlasting agitation, warned, "The people demand that the reconstruction imbroglio be brought to an end, and they will not go back to fight the battle ever again, *no matter how it is ended."* [51] Grant too opposed the bill, and Republicans decided to abandon it.[52] The conservative policy was no longer viable. Rather than take the politically radical step of removing Johnson, the conservatives and more conservative centrists had hedged him about with more and more restrictive laws, until these laws threatened a constitutionally radical alteration in the relations between Congress and the executive from which many Americans recoiled.

The political situation was unraveling. Gloomily, Boutwell predicted again that Johnson and his southern allies would succeed in preventing southern blacks from voting in the next presidential election.

In February, 1869, we shall receive [from the south] certificates of the election of electors who have given their votes to the candidates of the Opposition; and this country will be brought again to the extremity of civil war, or we shall be compelled to surrender . . . to the rebels, . . . who are yet struggling through their alliance with the Executive to destroy the Government.[53]

Republicans feared they stood at the edge of disaster, not only for themselves, but for the nation. And it was all unnecessary. The country would have been spared this "agony of strife" if only the president had remained true to his first Reconstruction policy. Even as they discussed their new legislation, Republicans knew the truth of Boutwell's conviction: "I know Andrew Johnson will thwart these measures as he has thwarted others." [54] And yet, from all their sources of information they knew the people would not support a new attempt at impeachment. There was no escape.

FIFTEEN

Impeachment and Trial

━━━━━━━━━━━━━━ ✦✦✦✦✦✦✦✦✦✦✦✦✦✦ ━━━━━━━━━━━━━━

WITH NORTHERN VOTERS growing ever more impatient with the intermi-
nable conflict over Reconstruction, Republican congressmen reeling from
the force of their own confrontations, and southern loyalists in despair,
Johnson in the early months of 1868 seemed on the verge of success in
his long struggle to defeat the congressional program. But he seemed un-
content to allow the stalemate simply to drift toward Republican disaster.
His secretary wrote that he was "very determined to pursue an aggressive
course." After a conference with Johnson, another Democratic confidant
left convinced that "he expects to crush his enemies, and he will." [1]

Intent on wrecking the Republican Reconstruction program irrevocably, Johnson determined finally to regain complete control of the armed
forces. But standing in his way was the redoubtable Edwin M. Stanton.
The previous August Johnson had suspended Stanton from his position as
secretary of war, evidently acting in conformity with a new congressional
law restricting the president's power to remove executive officers. That law,
the Tenure of Office act, had been designed primarily to protect Republican patronage appointees in the postal and revenue services, and it was
unclear whether cabinet members originally appointed by Lincoln were
covered by it: a murky provision required that the Senate agree to the
removal of department heads during the term of the president appointing
them and for one month thereafter. In the House, the bill's managers had
insisted that this protected Johnson's cabinet; the Senate managers had
held the opposite. [2] But Johnson had seemed to concede that the law applied to Stanton when he suspended him (as the law required during a
Senate recess) rather than removing him outright. Then, in December
1867, he sent to the Senate the justification for his action, again in conformity with the Tenure of Office law.

But Johnson had not intended to acquiesce if the Senate decided
adversely to his wishes. Shortly after his appointment as secretary of war
ad interim, Grant had agreed not to consent to his removal. Grant would

either remain or turn the office back to the president. Johnson later claimed that he believed this would force Stanton to go into the courts to press his claim to the office, thereby offering a test of the constitutionality of the Tenure of Office act. But Stanton's most recent biographers suggest that Johnson was far more interested in gaining control of the office of secretary of war than in testing Congress's law.[3]

Even if Johnson did desire a court test, this does not mean that he was merely an honest statesman trying to win a legal decision against a law he considered unconstitutional. The Tenure of Office act was part of a profound and bitter struggle over fundamental *political* questions. To ask the courts to decide the conflict, in which millions of Americans passionately adhered to one side or the other, was to risk the disaster that followed the Supreme Court's *Dred Scott* decision under similar circumstances a decade earlier. Johnson and his supporters were well aware of the true nature of the question. Widespread rumors held that five of the eight justices of the Supreme Court believed congressional Reconstruction unconstitutional. By appealing to these justices, Johnson hoped to win a victory against a policy he had been unable to defeat by appealing to the polls. If the Court ruled the Tenure of Office act unconstitutional, Johnson would perfect his control of the army. By retaining office, Grant would have signified his decision to support the president. If he returned the office to the president but did not retain it, Johnson could fill it with whomever he pleased and refill it with other friends if the Senate refused to confirm his first choice. When the Senate adjourned, he could appoint as secretary of war ad interim a supporter who would remain undisturbed until the Senate met again. With a loyal supporter as secretary of war, with Grant cooperating, with more conservative military officers in the South, Johnson might prevent the ratification of the new constitutions framed under the Reconstruction law, and frustrate Congress's program. In light of the aggressive southern policy Johnson inaugurated after the failure of the first attempt at impeachment, there is every reason to believe this was his intention. The Supreme Court was not to be a neutral arbiter; it would be the president's weapon.[4]

Grant could not help but understand the stakes involved. Even if he retained the secretaryship with every intention of seeing the Reconstruction acts faithfully executed, there would be nothing to prevent the president from removing him too if the Court ruled the Tenure of Office act unconstitutional. Moreover, such a course would certainly jeopardize his prospects for the Republican presidential nomination. Even if he were nominated, the radicals would be more inclined than ever to bolt. Finally, Grant learned that if the Court ruled that the Tenure of Office act *was* constitutional after all, he would be liable to a $10,000 fine and a five-year prison term. So when on January 10, 1868 the Military Affairs committee finally reported a resolution denying the Senate's advice and consent to Stanton's removal, Grant determined not to risk the consequences of resistance.

On January 11, Grant informed the president that he had decided that the law left him no alternative but to relinquish his office to Stanton if the Senate passed the committee's resolution. Johnson now offered Grant an argument he had not offered the Senate. He had suspended Stanton not under the provisions of the Tenure of Office act, he insisted, but under his presidential powers under the Constitution. He had appointed Grant by virtue of the same powers and not pursuant to the congressional law. In the heat of Johnson's personal plea that Grant honor his earlier commitment, the general must have tried to hedge. Johnson thought Grant had agreed. Grant later denied it, but there is no question as to the sincerity of Johnson's conviction that Grant had consented to fulfill the role he had assigned him.[5] But upon further consideration Grant became more and more dissatisfied with his position.

Hoping to ease the situation, Grant and General William T. Sherman, in Washington to help recodify the army's war regulations, suggested that the president name the conservative Republican former Governor of Ohio, Jacob D. Cox, to replace Stanton. This, Sherman believed, was "a mode practicable & easy to get rid of Stanton forever." Cox, though one of the most conservative of Republicans, had not deserted the party. Radicals might be disgrunted, but conservative and moderate Republicans would be likely to accede to the compromise, confident that Cox would enforce the law.[6]

But when Sherman proposed his idea to Johnson, he found the president uninterested. Sherman and Grant now realized that Johnson was intent on something more than ridding himself of an odious subordinate, that, as Sherman wrote, "there must be something behind the scenes." [7] On January 13, the Senate rejected Johnson's grounds for dismissal, and when Grant returned the keys to the secretary of war's office to Stanton, Johnson furiously accused the general of double-dealing. A bitter wrangle ensued, which wedded Grant firmly and finally to the Republicans and reconciled the grudging radicals to his nomination. "Now we will let him into the Church," Stevens announced.[8] Stanton returned to his office, an unyielding barrier between the president and the army.

With Grant lost to the enemy, Johnson turned to Sherman. Determined to remove Stanton in violation of the Tenure of Office act, Johnson intended either to force him out of the War Office building and order other government officials to ignore him, or to remove him and send Sherman's name to the Senate for confirmation. At the same time, Johnson determined to take the ominous step of creating a new army department, the Army of the Atlantic, with headquarters in Washington. Sherman would be placed in command. This, he told Secretary of the Navy Welles, was in preparation for the crisis when it came. He agreed with Welles that if an order went out for his arrest, as part of a radical "plot" to seize the government, Grant would take Congress's part. With Sherman the head of an army department centered in Washington, Johnson believed that he too would have access to military power. Sherman resisted the appointment, but on February 6, Johnson ordered Grant to issue an order creating the department and giving command to Sherman. At the same time, he acted to promote Sherman to general of the army—Grant's rank—sending the nomination to the Senate on February 13. "This would set some of them thinking," his private secretary quoted the president as saying.

Sherman was thunderstruck. He wrote the president that he did not want the command and hinted at his resignation. He telegraphed his brother, John Sherman, to oppose confirmation of his new rank in the Senate. "The President would make use of me to beget violence . . . ," he wrote. "He has no right to use us for such purposes, though he is Commander-in-Chief." On February 19, Johnson acceded to Sherman's pleas and rescinded his transfer to the new command. Despite the apparent collapse of his plans, however, on February 21 Johnson finally ordered Stanton's removal.[9]

The message appointing a new secretary of war ad interim in place of Stanton (the appointee was General Lorenzo Thomas, the nondescript adjutant general of the army) arrived at the Senate while it was debating the bill to repeal the absolute-majority requirement for ratifying new constitutions in the southern states. Chandler had casually gone to president pro tempore Wade's table to read the incoming message. When he realized what it meant, he dropped the papers and rushed to Alexander Ramsey, Jacob M. Howard, and Sumner. Senators ran up to Wade's place to see what had happened. As word spread through the chamber, representatives who had been on the floor rushed to their side of the Capitol to inform their colleagues, who had just received a message from Stanton telling them of the situation. Several senators hurried to Stanton's offices to urge him to hold on. Representatives broke into agitated groups—Wilson, Bingham, Williams, Halburt E. Paine, and Frederick A. Pike at one end of the House and Blaine, Butler, Dawes, and Lawrence at the other. John Covode rummaged through papers on his desk and found an old impeachment resolution. He jumped up to move its adoption, but other representatives shouted him down. Then Washburne moved the reference of Stanton's message to the Reconstruction committee, and Pike shouted, "Now all in favor of impeachment stand up." All the Republicans rose. Bingham was fuming. The president had not left well enough alone. He had revived "a contest which can exert no other than evil influence upon the welfare of the country," he said bitterly.[10]

At the War Office, Stanton did not know what to do. Radicals like Chandler, Sumner, and Boutwell were urging him to stay. Sumner sent a one-word telegram: "Stick." But if he were to risk defiance, Stanton wanted the support of the united party. He sent his son, Edwin L. Stanton, to get the advice of the conservatives. Nonradical Republican Senator George F. Edmunds told him that "Fessenden, Frelinghuysen, and all to whom he has spoken say you ought to hold on to the point of expulsion until the Senate acts." So Stanton determined to stay.[11]

As Stanton waited in the War Office, the Senate went into executive session. For seven hours senators argued over what to do. Edmunds proposed a resolution simply disapproving the president's action, but other senators moved amendments. Chandler tried to change Edmund's proposition by adding a provision that Johnson's act was disapproved "as a violation of the rights of the Senate and unauthorized by law." Radical Richard Yates suggested a resolution that Stanton's removal and the appointment of a replacement "is simple resistance to law and revolutionary in character." Both suggestions were defeated.

Instead, the Republicans turned to a substitute offered by Henry Wilson. Not as violent as Yate's proposal, Wilson's still averred: "That we do not concur in the action of the President . . . ; that we deny the right of the President so to act, under the existing laws, without the consent of the Senate." Its effect if passed was clear. The House had refused to impeach Andrew Johnson in December at least in part because many representatives did not believe he had committed a specific violation of law; the Senate—the body before which an impeachment would be tried— would now declare its solemn judgment that he had.

Fessenden, Edmunds, and probably others fought the resolution with all their resources. But nothing could alter the outcome. The case seemed too clear, the emergency too great. Wilson's resolution passed 28 to 6. Edmunds was the only Republican to vote against it. But a significant number of Republicans did not vote. These were mainly conservatives: John Conness, Henry W. Corbett, Fessenden, Joseph S. Fowler, Frelinghuysen, Grimes, Henderson, Edwin D. Morgan, and Sherman.[12] But other conservatives *had* voted. Van Winkle and Trumbull voted with the majority. So did Edmund G. Ross. All three would change their minds. But that night, when Illinois Representatives Shelby Moore Cullom and Burton C. Cook spoke to Trumbull, he was earnest for impeachment.[13]

In Fessenden's opinion, the worst had happened. The Senate had passed a resolution "upon the strength of which Mr. Johnson will probably be impeached—and that will end us," he prophesied gloomily. "I am utterly discouraged and out of spirits," he confessed. "Either I am very stupid, or my friends are acting like fools, and hurrying us to destruction." [14] But the radicals' anxiety was mixed with anticipation. The president had revived the radicals' sagging hopes for securing Reconstruction through his removal. "Even the weak kneed Republicans may find it impossible not to stand up to the work," Schenck wrote hopefully. And he seemed to be right. "He has thrown down the gauntlet to Congress," the archconservative Austin Blair conceded, "and says to us as plainly as words can speak it: 'Try this issue now betwixt me and you; either you go to the wall or I do.' And there is nothing left to Congress but to take it up." [15]

It seemed that Johnson had succeeded in uniting a party on the verge of disruption. "All the moderate and conservative Republicans are of one mind with the most radical," George Templeton Strong noted in his diary. Even Welles recognized Johnson's folly. "A little skillful management would have made a permanent break in that party," he wrote shortly afterward. "But the President had not tact himself to affect it, he consulted with no others, the opportunity passed away, and by a final hasty move, without preparation, without advising with anybody, he took a step which consolidated the Radicals of every stripe." [16] On February 24 a united party passed the impeachment resolution in the House of Representatives.[17] Now the Senate would hear the House's charges and evidence, and judge the president's guilt.

But it soon became clear that senators remained divided. Many of them pressed for speedy trial and conviction, but others, including most of the conservative leaders—Trumbull, Fessenden, Sherman, Anthony, Grimes, and others—urged deliberation and sought as much as possible to tie the Senate to judicial procedures and standards. They argued that the Senate heard impeachments as a "high court," and they worked to increase the influence of the Chief Justice Chase, who would preside over the Senate during the trial. After several hard-fought battles they succeeded: the Senate sat as the "high court of impeachment," and the proceedings, instead of lasting ten days as Sumner and other radicals had hoped, took two and a half months.[18] But by slowing the trial, by seeming to endorse the proposition that impeachments operated by the same rules and standards as ordinary trials, the conservatives—most of whom became firmly convinced of the president's guilt—set the stage for failure.

As the trial wore on, Republican confidence in ultimate success wilted. Grimes and Tennessee senator Joseph S. Fowler early signified their intention to sustain the president, Fowler scrupulously leaving his seat on the Republican side of the chamber and joining the Democrats each day as the Senate resolved itself into a "high court of impeachment." Time after time well over the one-third of the Senators required for acquittal voted against the majority, to exclude some piece of evidence that the House managers of impeachment wanted to present or to allow the president's counsel to offer evidence over the managers' objections.[19] Still, Republican hopes were not dead. Despite all their differences during preliminaries, Republican senators had always achieved near unanimity on final votes on Reconstruction legislation. The same might be true now, with so much depending on the outcome. As Ben Perley Poore wrote, "A Senator may have desired to elevate the trial above the proceedings in a Magistrate's Court, and yet have no desire to shield the great criminal." [20]

But the stresses were great, the differences deep. Personal animosities between leading radicals and conservatives played a part. While impeachment in the House had been the work of the entire party, with conservatives taking a leading part, in the Senate key Republicans seem never to have lost the conviction that the president's removal would represent primarily a *radical* victory. When the first impeachment resolution had failed in the House, Fessenden had crowed, "For once, Mr. Sumner cannot boast of the fulfillment of his prophecy, and his bitterness beats wormwood and gall." With Sumner's prophecy proved accurate after all, the bitterness seemed transferred to his rival. It was at this time that Fessenden referred to Sumner as "the most cowardly dog in the parish." The correspondent of the Boston *Traveller* attributed Fessenden's apparent unenthusiasm for conviction simply and solely to his hatred for the Massachusetts radical.[21] Moreover, the individual who stood to gain most from the impeachment's success was Benjamin F. Wade, who as president pro tempore of the Senate would succeed Johnson, virtually guaranteeing his nomination to the vice-presidency. Many conservative Republicans detested Wade nearly as much as they did Sumner. And Fessenden and Grimes had special worries. Each was faced with more radical factional rivals from his state whom Wade might favor in the redistribution of patronage sure to follow his elevation.[22] "If impeachment fails, be sure of one fact—dislike for Mr. Wade has done it," the *Independent*'s Washington correspondent informed his readers. "Certain Republican senators were determined that Mr. Wade should not be President." [23]

But far more than personal hostilities motivated several of the wavering senators' reluctance to place Wade in the presidency. As Hans L. Trefousse has pointed out, the character and politics of Johnson's would-be successor played a large role in the deliberations. He had delivered a speech in Lawrence, Kansas, a year before, which the Boston *Daily Advertiser* described as "simply and wholly . . . an avowal of agrarian sympathies." [24] He had expanded on it to question the fundamental value of freedom so long as workingmen were at the mercy of capitalists. But these opinions were merely vagaries. What really aroused powerful interests against him (and *for* him, it should be remembered) were his high-tariff, soft-money opinions. The tariff and financial questions were living issues, over which men fought passionately, and much more controversial than scattered musings over the rights of labor. These issues had already played a large part in the impeachment controversy and had helped to defeat the impeachment resolution of December 1867. The immediate threat apparent in Johnson's activities in February 1868 had persuaded Republican contractionists in the House to risk impeachment, but as time wore on many fiscal reformers, especially those outside the House, began

JOHN POPE

WILLIAM T. SHERMAN

OLIVER O. HOWARD

ULYSSES S. GRANT

Military Leaders

and the

Secretary of War

EDWIN M. STANTON

JOHN M. SCHOFIELD

PHILIP SHERIDAN

WINFIELD S. HANCOCK

SALMON P. CHASE
Chief Justice of the Supreme Court

THEODORE TILTON
Editor of The (*New York*) Independent

HORACE GREELEY
Editor of the New York Tribune

Radical Leaders

Outside Congress

FREDERICK DOUGLASS

WENDELL PHILLIPS

"The First Vote." A Republican view of the results of the reconstruction acts.
Harper's Weekly, *November 9, 1867.*

The Managers of Impeachment.
Top, left to right: James F. Wilson, George S. Boutwell, John A. Logan.
Bottom, left to right: Benjamin F. Butler, Thaddeus Stevens,
William Lawrence, John A. Bingham

"The Senate as a Court of Impeachment . . ." Harper's Weekly, April 11, 1868

THE SENATE AS A COURT OF IMPEACHMENT FOR THE TRIAL OF ANDREW JOHNSON.—SKETCHED BY THEODORE R. DAVIS.

The "Recreant" Republicans

They joined Fessenden, Grimes, and Trumbull to Acquit President Johnson.

PETER G. VAN WINKLE

EDMUND G. ROSS

JOSEPH S. FOWLER

JOHN B. HENDERSON

once more to worry about the effect of Wade's elevation to the presidency. When *Iron Age,* the organ of the protectionist iron industry, called for a meeting of high-tariff men to take advantage of Wade's prospective administration to pass a new tariff bill, the free-trade-oriented *Chicago Tribune* warned, "They are doing more to defeat the impeachment of Johnson than any other equal number of men in the country, and far more than the President's counsel." [25] The rumor (well founded, judging from Wade's correspondence) that he intended to name E.B. Ward, a leading opponent of contraction, secretary of the treasury worried the hard-money lobby.

Another rumor held that Wade intended to name Butler secretary of state. The controversial radical's intense hostility toward England was well known, and Republicans feared the damage he might do the delicate *Alabama* claims negotiations and the designs he might hold on Canada. By May 2, former Representative John B. Alley warned Butler that leading senators had determined to prevent anyone involved with impeachment, whether manager or senator, from going into Wade's cabinet.[26]

"I have a few words to whisper in your private ear, concerning what conservative Republicans think," Garfield wrote James Harrison Rhodes on May 7:

They say that "Conviction means a transfer to the Presidency of Mr. Wade, a man of violent passions, extreme opinions, and narrow views; . . . a grossly profane coarse nature who is surrounded by the worst and most violent elements in the Republican party . . . that already the worst class of political cormorants from Ohio and elsewhere are thronging the lobbies and filling the hotels in high hopes of plunder when Wade is sworn in." [27]

Johnson would be convicted for certain, the *Chicago Tribune* concluded, if Wade were not the man who would replace him. Before the vote, Fessenden called on the conservative Senator George F. Edmunds and virtually told him as much.[28]

These fears must be placed in perspective. When Republicans spoke fearfully of the calamity of a Wade administration, they referred to the effect his policies might have not only on the country but on the party. Naturally, free-traders believed high tariffs hurt the nation, and hard-money men believed the financial strength of the United States required a commitment to the resumption of specie payments. But these men, and others not strongly committed to one view or the other, knew that one of the strengths of the Republican party was that men of all economic opinions were united on the issues that now divided Republican from Democrat: security for northern and loyal southern interests in Reconstruction. The Republican party could—and did—mute its position on the other issues. So long as Andrew Johnson was president, men of such opposite tariff and financial views as Horace Greeley and Edward Atkinson, William D. Kelley and James A. Garfield, Richard Henry Dana and Benjamin F. Butler could share the same platform and vote the same ticket. But let Ben Wade become president, let high-tariff and soft-money interests begin a campaign to put their views into law, and many believed with Atkinson that "the Republican party would cease to exist." [29] The major political issue would shift from one on which Republicans were united, although with differing degrees of commitment, to one on which they were hopelessly divided. This was the real apprehension of the conservatives. As Richard Henry Dana, visiting Washington during the excitement, wrote home, he found many Republicans who worried "that it will lose us the election if we succeed. If the Pr. is convicted, we are responsible for Ben Wade, and all that happens." Or, as Fessenden put it, whether Johnson was finally removed or not, "the result is to be disastrous either way." [30]

Despite the considerations that inclined a substantial number of Republican senators against convicting Johnson on the impeachment, it is possible that they would have quickly voted to remove him had the House's case against him been as conclusive as Republicans first believed. But in fact, although it was far stronger than historians traditionally have conceded, Johnson's counsel, some of the foremost lawyers in the nation—Benjamin R. Curtis, William M. Evarts, and Henry Stanbery, and somewhat lesser lights William S. Groesbeck and Thomas A.R. Nelson—adroitly exploited its weaknesses. With consummate skill they turned the flexibility of the impeachment process against itself, highlighting its failure to provide the same rigid standards of procedure and evidence afforded in common law trials. They insisted that every allegation be proven, that senators forget things every American knew. They suggested, for example, that Johnson did not intend to violate the Tenure of Office act at all, that he did not believe that Stanton was covered by it, when all knew he had suspended Stanton in conformity to its provisions in August 1867 and sent his reasons for the suspension to the Senate as the law required the following December. He had done that, his lawyers averred, only in an effort to cooperate with Congress. That every senator knew the absurdity of such a suggestion did not matter; the president's evil intent had somehow to be proven. When the representatives appointed by the House to manage the impeachment—among them the conservative Bingham and Wilson, as well as the more radical Stevens, Butler, Boutwell, Williams, and Logan—insisted that such rigid standards did not apply in an impeachment, where punishment extended merely to removal from office but the alleged wrongdoing might involve "the life of a great state, and with it the liberties of a great people," Evarts answered that if the Senate swerved from a rigidly judicial proceeding, then a conviction would be no more than a bill of attainder—"a proceeding by the legislature, as a legislature, to enact crime, sentence, punishment, all in one." [31] Although the position taken by the House managers probably comported more closely with the law of impeachment as authorities had understood it before 1868, Johnson's defenders' eloquent appeals to the safeguards of common law standards made so powerful an impact on contemporary lawyers and subsequent historians that one recent investigator called the trial "Attainder by Impeachment." [32]

Even more damaging to the managers' case was the simple fact that Stanton probably was not covered by the law Johnson was accused of violating. The law declared that the terms of office of all department heads would run for the term of the president who had appointed them and for one month thereafter, and that during that period they could not be removed without Senate consent. But Stanton had been appointed by Lincoln. Was Johnson completing Lincoln's term? If so, Stanton's term continued through March 1869 and for a month thereafter, and Johnson could not remove him if the Senate objected. But Johnson's lawyers insisted that Lincoln's term had ended with his death; in that case, Stanton's term had ended one month later. Thus, he had been serving at Johnson's pleasure since May 15, 1865, and the president had violated no law in removing him against the Senate's wishes. So powerful was this attack that it soon became clear that there was no hope for conviction based on Johnson's violation of the Tenure of Office act alone.

But the impeachment managers were not without strong arguments for Johnson's removal. First, it was clear to anyone familiar with the events of 1867 and 1868 that the president had believed Stanton covered by the Tenure of Office act and had intended to violate it. If he had done nothing illegal, it was only because of the law's vague wording. Of course, few senators were willing to convict Johnson merely for intending to violate a law, but they could not have been sanguine at the prospect of a president remaining in office only because his attempt to break the law had been unsuccessful. And this no doubt inclined many of them to convict Johnson for a different violation alleged by the House's articles of impeachment —the appointment of a Secretary of War ad interim to replace Stanton without sending his name to the Senate for confirmation.

In the past, such temporary appointments had been made only when an incumbent had died, resigned, been taken ill, or left Washington, or during a recess of the Senate when confirmation of a successor was impossible. In the history of the Republic, the president had replaced an incumbent office holder while the Senate was in session without first obtaining its advice and consent fewer than ten times, and every time but one the president had resorted to such a procedure only because the incumbent had stolen funds. As the managers argued, if a president could remove officials and name replacements ad interim without going to the Senate for confirmation, then he need never ascertain the Senate's wishes; he could nullify the Senate's constitutional right to advise and consent to executive appointments by naming a string of such "ad interim" appointees. As the trial proceeded it became clear that the managers could obtain a conviction only on articles that included this offense.

But as the trial wore through April and into May, the likelihood that the managers could win Johnson's removal seemed to diminish. Grimes and Fowler were adhering to their positions. Several senators were voting to accept all defense testimony over the managers' objections—Ross, William Sprague, and Henry B. Anthony. (Sumner was following the same course, but no one doubted *him*.) Peter G. Van Winkle, Trumbull, and others were considered unreliable.[33] Still, it was questionable whether any but Trumbull, Grimes, and Fowler were strong enough to defy his united colleagues. But if they found more influential Senate allies to join them, Republicans feared that all but Sumner might vote to acquit. And by May it was clear that they had found such an ally, for by then all knew that the conservative leader, Fessenden, opposed conviction. As the Boston *Advertiser* put it,

It was not until he threw the weight of his great ability and acknowledged influence in the scale that the conviction and removal of the President became doubtful. . . . It might almost be said that he held the issue of this great trial in his hands, and took upon himself alone the responsibility of saying it should go no further.[34]

As their hopes rose, Johnson's defenders worked to encourage the Republican defectors. Fearful of what Johnson might do if he were acquitted, conservative Republicans (Welles later named Fessenden and Grimes) informed Evarts that they would feel freer to vote against conviction if they were assured that he did not intend to retaliate against Republicans or interfere with Reconstruction. They suggested that the president name the conservative military commander of Virginia, John M. Schofield, secretary of war. He had enforced the Reconstruction acts, but in such a way as to aid conservative Republicans against radicals. His presence in the War Department would reassure the people and the party. Evarts approached Schofield on Johnson's behalf and asked him to accept the office. The general agreed, on the condition that the president would enforce the Reconstruction laws. On April 23, Johnson prepared the nomination, and on April 24 sent it in to the Senate, where Johnson's secretary, who had delivered the message, wrote, "I could see it created considerable interest." [35]

On May 4, Senator Edmund G. Ross, another wavering Republican, informed acting Attorney General Orville H. Browning that he hoped the president would demonstrate his good intentions by forwarding to the Senate the new constitutions Arkansas and South Carolina had adopted under the Reconstruction laws. Browning and Stanbery urged the president to send the constitutions in, over the objections of the uncompromising Welles, and Johnson did so on May 5.[36] In a final maneuver, Reverdy Johnson arranged a meeting between Grimes and the president. Grimes told the president that senators inclined to acquit him were wavering out of fear of what Johnson might do after impeachment failed. Johnson assured him that he intended to do nothing in violation of the law or the Constitution, and Grimes, satisfied, relayed the message to other conservatives.[37]

Perhaps even more important than the president's assurances to conservative Republicans was the actual cessation of his interference while impeachment progressed. In explaining "What Has Happened During the Impeachment Trial," the *Chicago Tribune* wrote simply, "Andrew Johnson has been a changed man. The country has been at peace. The great obstruction to the law has been virtually suspended; the President . . . has been on his good behavior." [38]

The president's new docility enabled Republicans to recoup some of their losses in the South. In six of the unreconstructed states, Republicans were able to win ratification of the new constitutions framed under the Reconstruction laws, although by narrow margins in several. In Alabama, where the removal of General Swayned proved critical, Republicans failed to win the absolute majority of registered voters required to ratify the new constitutions. The opposition had refused to vote at all. But Congress decided to repeal the absolute-majority requirement to enable it to restore Alabama nonetheless. By the time senators voted on impeachment, it was clear that only Virginia, Mississippi, and Texas would remain unrestored and liable to presidential interference. It is remarkable how quickly the sense of crisis that gripped the capital a few months earlier eased.

To a large extent, therefore, impeachment had succeeded in its primary goal: to safeguard Reconstruction from presidential obstruction. Only after the political exigencies that in part had motivated impeachment were removed did Republican dissenters firm their opposition to conviction.

As the trial drew to a close, wavering Republicans urged delay of the final decision. Having won Schofield's appointment as secretary of war, they were now confident they could force the president to appoint a new, Republican cabinet. On May 7, in a closed meeting of the Senate, Fessenden urged the postponement of the final vote to allow him to study the case and especially Bingham's closing argument. Radicals suspected that he had motives beyond those he announced and demanded that the Senate open its doors and proceed to a final vote on the impeachment immediately. "This trial of impeachment, after that of Warren Hastings," Sumner complained, "ha[s] occupied more time than any other, more days and a shorter time each day. There ha[s] been postponement after postponement, and it [is] . . . now proposed to postpone the final question." But his motion to vote immediately was defeated, garnering the support of only sixteen members, and the Senate agreed to delay the final decision until the following week. Overcoming radical objections once more, the Senate decided to set aside May 11 for closed-door discussion of the articles and delivery of opinions.[39]

On that day, the seriousness of the Republican situation became apparent. Howe and Sherman declared their opinions that the Tenure of Office act as finally amended did not cover Stanton. Ignoring the managers' argument that in that case Stanton was protected under the law's general provisions, they announced that they would vote not guilty on the first article and all articles that relied on a violation of the Tenure of Office act. Since Sherman had been the chairman of the conference committee that had framed the amendment, his words carried great weight. Van Winkle, Fowler, Fessenden, and Grimes announced that they would sustain none of the articles, while Trumbull, without finally committing himself, indicated the same. Henderson declared against all but the eleventh. Nonetheless, the well-informed Poore believed that Johnson would be convicted on the second article, which alleged that he had violated the law by removing Stanton during a session of the Senate and appointing an ad interim replacement. Those senators who believed Stanton unprotected by the 1867 law would find Johnson guilty on this, Poore believed. Since the eleventh and third articles included this charge, senators hoped they could muster two thirds of their number to convict on these also. But the other articles were lost. Of the forty-two Republicans, at least seven would acquit on the seventh and eighth, eight on the first and fifth, nine on the fourth and sixth, ten on the tenth, and twelve on the ninth. And the doubtful senators, Anthony, Ross, Sprague, and Waitman T. Willey, had said nothing at all.[40]

As the vote neared, both sides turned their attention to the doubtful senators. Grimes won the president's promise not to take drastic action and used it to firm antiremoval sentiment. Katherine Chase Sprague, daughter of Chief Justice Chase, who opposed conviction, pressured her husband, Senator Sprague. Henderson was assured the support of Missouri Democrats in his campaign for reelection to the Senate if the state's Republicans should shunt him aside for voting to acquit. Pro-Johnson lobbyists and politicians touted a proposal to nominate Chase for the presidency, in an effort to give conservative Republicans an alternative to the regular party and the Democrats.[41]

Republicans, convinced that Johnson's acquittal would remove the last restraints on him, fearing that he might overturn the now forming reconstructed southern state governments entirely, worked desperately to apply political pressure to the uncertain senators. "Great danger to the peace of the country and the Republican cause if impeachment fails," Schenck telegraphed local leaders as chairman of the Republican Congressional Campaign Committee. "Send to your Senators before Saturday public opinion by resolutions, letters and delegations." [42] Letters, many of them harsh, poured in upon the recalcitrants. Fessenden's friend, Senator Justin Morrill of Vermont, urged, "The best legal learning of the Senate will sustain the 1st, 2d, & 3d article of Impeachment. My opinion is of no value but with a very close attention to the subject for two months I think there is no doubt about it." Morrill reminded Fessenden that, like himself, he was "not much in favor of this act nor of Impeachment as original questions, but I must do my duty at all hazards." Finally, he warned his friend of the consequences. "You could do nothing which would fulfill the ancient grudge of a certain clique of your foes sooner than a vote on your part in favor of Andrew Johnson." Within six months, Sumner, Chandler, Wade, and Fessenden's other enemies would drive him into the Johnson camp, Morrill predicted. But Fessenden would not budge.[43]

As the date set for the final vote, May 16, approached, the dissident senators wavered and urged delay. On May 12 and 13, Ross told his colleague Pomeroy that he would vote to convict on the first three articles and the eleventh. Anthony, Willey, and Frederick T. Frelinghuysen finally assured colleagues they would sustain the key articles. Henderson indicated that he would resign rather than cast the deciding vote for acquittal and held out the possibility that he would convict on the eleventh article. On May 12, the Missouri congressional delegation assured him that they did not want his resignation and suggested that he abstain on the articles on which he could not vote guilty. The senator seemed to agree but added that he would speak to Sprague, Van Winkle, Anthony, and Willey. If they intended to convict on the eleventh article, the president would be removed regardless of Henderson's vote.

On May 14, Ross, Henderson, Van Winkle, Willey, and Trumbull met in Van Winkle's rooms. When Pomeroy found them there, they urged another delay in the vote, assuring him it would bring a reorganization of the cabinet, with Massachusetts Republican Representative Samuel Hooper named secretary of the treasury, Evarts secretary of state, and Reverdy Johnson and Groesbeck in other positions. Republicans still believed that, despite their reluctance, Willey and Ross ultimately would cooperate with the party.[44]

But even as the pressure intensified, the dissident Republicans were fortified by demonstrations of support from within the party. Shocked by the sudden intrusion of overtly partisan pressure into the trial, many Republicans were repelled. The leading conservative Republican journals of the nation—the *New York Times, Evening Post, Nation,* and *Sun,* the Cincinnati *Commercial,* the Boston *Daily Advertiser,* Senator Anthony's *Providence* (Rhode Island) *Journal,* and Morton's Indianapolis *Daily Journal*—hastened to the defense of their long-time allies. The Republicans' unity was broken. As the *Evening Post* averred,

The hearings were full, and . . . impartial. The country regarded the trial as a calm and worthy judicial investigation . . . ; all parties were ready to acquiesce in the decision of the court. All this is suddenly changed, and that by the strenuous advocates of conviction. They have chosen to withdraw the case from the judicial and to bring it into the political arena. . . . These movements, made for the purpose of promoting the prosecution, have done more to bring it into discredit than all the shell of Mr. Johnson's advocates. Impeachment has struck a fatal blow at itself.[45]

On May 16, seven Republicans joined Democrats to acquit the president on the eleventh article of impeachment and then held firm on the other articles after a two-week recess. They were not the seven isolated "martyrs" so many historians have depicted. In fact, considering the stakes involved, Republican anger at the recusants was remarkably short-lived. Radicals continued to demand the dissidents' scalps, but Republican nonradicals immediately warned of the dangerous consequences of following such a policy with a presidential election approaching. "The impeachment trial is a failure," the conservative Cincinnati *Commercial* observed. "It need not be a disaster." [46] At the Republican national convention, meeting in Chicago on May 19 and 20, only a few days after the failure of impeachment, the efforts of radicals to persuade delegates to issue a formal repudiation of the seven recusants failed dismally.[47]

Republican congressmen remained bitter for a time. Wade, Chandler, James W. Nye, and a few other Republican senators left a Republican caucus on May 28 to protest the continued presence of Fessenden, Trumbull, and other acquitters. When Fessenden later met Nye, he fumed, "You had not the pluck to do as you thought right. You had not the courage to act conscientiously, and left seven of us to bear the whole brunt of the odium. It was a mean trick." Nye retorted that "at least he had not been animated by a malignant spirit and jealously." [48] But as Republicans swung into the campaign, the Boston *Evening Journal* noted, "It is surprising to see how far the whole subject of impeachment seems to have been thrown into the background and dwarfed in importance."

In the dissidents' states, Republicans quickly ceased attacks on their senators and concentrated upon the canvass.[49] The hard-money lobby, hoping to strengthen their conservative allies against radical atttacks, proposed a dinner in Fessenden's honor in Boston. Fessenden declined but in response penned a bitter denunciation of the radicals who had attacked him. "Unscrupulous, familiar with detraction, believers neither in public nor private virtue, or if believers, considering both as out of place in politics, they could not resist such an opportunity, nor fail to improve the occasion," he wrote.[50] By the next meeting of Congress, most of the dissenters had recovered their influence and Trumbull, Fessenden, and Grimes retained their immense prestige and power. "I am satisfied that I am stronger in the Senate in every respect . . . than I ever was before I was tried in the furnace of impeachment," Grimes wrote.[51]

The relations and balance of power between radical and nonradical Republicans had returned to normal.

SIXTEEN

Restoring the States... and State Rights

————————— ✦✦✦✦✦✦✦✦✦✦✦✦✦✦✦ —————————

THE PROCEEDINGS OF the spring of 1868, which restored all but three of the unreconstructed states to normal relations in the Union, marked the fundamental turning point in the history of congressional Reconstruction legislation. For although Republicans had been divided on specific programs, they had been united in their convictions that Congress had the power to secure some guarantees to insure future loyalty in the South and the safety of those who had supported the nation during its trial. They had attempted to accomplish that program despite the obstacles presented by their own traditional conceptions of the nature of federal government. Republicans had overcome those obstacles by denying that traditional limitations on the powers of the national government pertained to the crisis. They had argued that the states were out of normal relations with the Union, subject to the paramount control of the national government until they should be restored. By justifying themselves on these grounds such constitutional conservatives as Lyman Trumbull, John A. Bingham, James W. Grimes, Roscoe Conkling, and William Pitt Fessenden had been able to cooperate with Charles Sumner, Thaddeus Stevens, Zachariah Chandler, Benjamin F. Wade, and others who shared far less restrictive views of the proper role of the national government. But with the restoration of normal relations, that justification for "extraordinary" power in Congress no longer existed, and those Republicans who wished to preserve the old, narrow conception of national power began to draw apart from those who were willing to see the national government assume broad, new responsibilities for the protection of citizens' rights.

Because Republicans could maintain a united front only so long as conservative constitutionalists believed normal federal relations between the national government and the southern states did not exist, it had been apparent—most of all to the conservatives themselves—that the southern states must not be restored to normal relations in the Union until they were thoroughly reconstructed. For that reason many conservatives in the Senate had joined radicals in March 1867, in efforts to make it more difficult for southerners to qualify for restoration under the Reconstruction acts. After numerous defeats the coalition had succeeded in incorporating a minimum protection into the Supplementary Reconstruction act: the requirement that one-half the registered voters participate in the elections in which new state constitutions were to be ratified.[1]

But as the president launched his offensive in January 1868, as Democrats showed a resurgence in the elections of fall 1867, and spring 1868, as northern voters expressed their impatience with the continuing struggle, further delay in restoration seemed to threaten Republican political dominance. And if Republicans were vanquished in the congressional and presidential elections of 1868, the battles of the past two years would end in disaster. Yet Republicans received continuing evidence that loyalty was not yet secure in the southern states, that Reconstruction was not complete, that southern Republican organizations (the only loyal political organizations in the South, in Republicans' estimation) would be hard pressed to stand without the military presence provided by the Reconstruction acts.

In December the House reacted to the new situation by repealing the provision of the Reconstruction acts requiring majority participation in the ratification elections, but despite the House's proddings, the Senate Judiciary committee delayed action.[2]

The Republican dilemma became critical in February 1868, when Alabama Democrats waged a successful stay-at-home campaign against the new constitution drawn in conformity with the Reconstruction laws. Nearly 70,000 Alabamans voted to ratify the new fundamental law and only 1000 voted against it, but the combined total did not equal the one-half of the registered voters the law required for successful ratification.[3] Therefore, under the law Alabama remained unreconstructed, its pro-Johnson provisional government remaining in office. Similar Democratic campaigns in other southern states promised to be equally successful.

With the Alabama election bringing the crisis to a head, Senate Republicans apparently decided that repeal of the majority requirement was necessary, and on February 28 the measure passed.[4] Southern Democrats were forced to give up their nonparticipation strategy, and six states ratified new constitutions by June 1868. The *New York Tribune* proclaimed the results "The Triumph of Reconstruction," but congressional Republicans could hardly be so sanguine.[5] Despite the disfranchisement required in the Reconstruction act, had Congress not relaxed the ratification requirements at least one and possibly two of those constitutions would have been rejected. Five or six of the ten unreconstructed states would have remained out of normal relations with the Union.[6] Moreover, the people of Florida had ratified their new constitution over radical objections after a virtual coup d'état supported by Democrats, conservative Republicans, and the army.[7] If Republicans had insisted on complete demonstrations of loyalty (which they believed southerners could show only by offering clear Republican victories), only three states certainly would have been restored to the Union in 1868: Louisiana, North Carolina, and South Carolina.

Forced by political necessities to admit these southern states to normal relations with the national government, many Republicans expressed their apprehensions. "You are hastening back States where rebelism is pervading them from end to end," complained the radical Missouri Senator Charles D. Drake. And this reluctance to surrender authority over the South was not limited to radicals. Even Dawes, perhaps the most conservative Republican in the House, acknowledged,

I . . . have undergone some change of views during the years I have spent in this House touching the questions of granting representation in Congress to those portions of the country that have been under the control of the rebellion. . . . I have become satisfied that representation in Congress, instead of being the first thing to be secured to these States, should be the last thing; that the State should first be built up, personal rights should be secured, the damage done by rebellion should be repaired, the stability and securing of the State as an organized and peaceful community should be made certain; and representation in Congress should follow and grow out of that security.

These often hidden misgivings pervaded the Republican camp as Republicans reluctantly restored the Union. Despite the apparent unanimity by which the final restoration acts were passed, "there are not ten men . . . who believe it a safe thing to do at this time," Timothy Otis Howe concluded.[8]

When Congress first considered the situation in Alabama in March 1868, sentiment for delay wherever possible was still strong. The likelihood that President Johnson would be removed from office on the impeachment charges made the end of military control in the South less urgent. The impeachment had restored the morale of the Republican party. Nonetheless, on March 10 the House Reconstruction committee reported a bill recognizing the restoration of Alabama to the Union under the constitution that had failed of ratification at the polls. The committee justified its course with a catalogue of obstacles which had prevented the free expression of Alabamans' opinions on the ratification question. A violent storm had made polling places inaccessible to many voters, loyal men were deterred from voting by "the most atrocious and outrageous threats," "a system of ostracism, social and financial, prevailed," the committee insisted. Since Congress had already passed a law repealing the requirement that a majority of registered voters participate in the ratification election, "the committee could see no reason why Alabama should not have the benefit of that principle as well as the other States . . . ." [9]

But while the Reconstruction committee believed the succesful intimidation of loyal southerners justified Congress in restoring Alabama to its place in the Union under the constitution Alabamans had rejected, other Republicans pointedly asked, "What assurance [can] the gentlemen . . . give the House that if we admit the State of Alabama under these circumstances the next election will not find it in the hands of the rebel party?" [10] Under this pressure, the Reconstruction committee agreed to take the bill under advisement once again.

But with Alabama Republicans warning Stevens that they had polled their maximum strength in the ratification election and that they could not hope to ratify their constitution in a new one, Stevens's Reconstruction committee once again reported a restoration bill.[11] Torn between the apparent necessity to restore Alabama to normal relations in the Union and the clear indications that Reconstruction there was neither thorough nor secure, the committee proposed to require the state to agree to "fundamental conditions" as part of its readmission. The conditions stipulated that the state constitution could never be amended to restrict the vote of citizens which it now enfranchised (i.e., black Alabamans), nor to enfranchise any person disqualified from holding office under the Fourteenth Amendment. Congress would have the power to annul any law or amendment to Alabama's constitution which contravened the condition.[12] The fundamental conditions were a direct outgrowth of Republicans' fears that restoration was premature, that their Reconstruction policy was in jeopardy in the South. "We must try to shackle [the southern states] . . . in some way that while we are admitting these fraudulent white men we are securing the poor ignorant black man from their impositions," Stevens explained.[13]

The proposal of fundamental conditions to which Alabama (and presumably other southern states) would have to adhere after restoration was a radical departure from the theory of Reconstruction upon which Republicans had acted. Desperately trying to salvage some remedy for the dangers they foresaw from early restoration, Republicans for the first time attempted to preserve some congressional power over the southern states *after* they were restored to the Union. Stevens proposed an amendment that went even further. It provided that if Alabama reduced the right of suffrage below the standard required in the condition, the legislation restoring the state to the Union would be null and void. Implicitly, in that case Alabama would revert to direct congressional control and the national government might begin the Reconstruction process there anew.[14]

The proposal to impose fundamental conditions and through them to broaden the powers of the national government to protect the rights of citizens led to the first of a series of the intra-Republican confrontations on constitutional questions that would mark the Reconstruction legislation of the post-1868 era. Conservative constitutionalists in the Republican party, led by Bingham, were unprepared to cooperate in this new attempt to limit state prerogatives. By passing the Fourteenth Amendment Congress had conceded that it could interfere with states' rights to regulate the franchise only by amending the Constitution, Bingham argued. Urging the simple restoration of Alabama with no conditions whatever, Bingham insisted, "The American system of government is a total failure if the people cannot be intrusted with the right of altering and amending their constitutions of government at their pleasure, subject to the general limitations of the Federal Constitution." [15]

Other conservatives, also unwilling to acquiesce in the extension of national power implied by the fundamental conditions, were less willing to restore the state in its present condition. Instead they joined those radicals who opposed the state's restoration at all, urging that Congress replace the pro-Johnson provisional government with a new one consisting of the Republicans who would have been elected to state office had the constitution been ratified.[16] But many Republicans were rapidly losing patience with the entire Reconstruction question. They longed for peace and a return to traditional American governmental institutions. John F. Farnsworth, the Alabama restoration bill's manager, was one of them (he would join the Liberal Republican movement in 1872). "Things cannot drift along in this way forever," he warned his allies. "Those States must be admitted some time. There must be an end of the confusion, the anarchy now prevailing. We must have civil law and civil order. We cannot always control those States by the bayonet." [17]

When the House voted, the disunity in Republican ranks became apparent. A coalition of Republican constitutional conservatives and Democrats carried Bingham's amendment to strike the fundamental conditions from the bill. Stevens's version of the conditions failed without even a division of the House. With the conditions eliminated, most of those Republicans who had favored Alabama's admission with conditions joined those who had advocated continued exclusion to amend the bill to inaugurate a new provisional government instead.[18] Republicans circumvented the problem of extending the national government's power to protect citizens after restoration of the southern states by refusing to restore Alabama at all.

However, by May, as it became apparent that the president would not be convicted on the impeachment, Republicans almost unanimously agreed that the danger of leaving southern states unreconstructed far outweighed that of restoring them, even with rebel elements still strong. Johnson could be expected to exercise far greater control over the military commanders in the South with the threat of impeachment eliminated than he had before, when he had worked with remarkable diligence to disrupt the operation of the Reconstruction acts. Therefore, despite their doubts, even radicals made almost no resistance to speedily restoring the southern states that ratified their new constitutions between February and June 1868. In light of the record of the 1870s, forcing this precipitate restoration was Johnson's greatest victory of the Reconstruction struggle. It marked the utter demolition of radical hopes for a long Reconstruction in which loyalty and democracy would grow slowly and naturally in the South.

Key

Stevens reported a bill to restore the first of the rebel states, Arkansas, on May 7. Once again the bill included a fundamental condition:

that the constitution of Arkansas shall never be so amended or changed as to deprive any citizen or class of citizens of the United States of the right to vote who are entitled to vote by the constitution herein recognized, except as a punishment for such crimes as are now felonies at the common law, whereof they shall have been duly convicted.[19]

By this version of the condition, however, Congress did not reserve to itself the power to annul any changes made in contravention of the condition. The question of enforcement was never clarified, and many Republican congressmen announced their opinions that it would be unenforceable.[20] Moreover, the new condition did not include the provision disfranchising rebels disqualified from holding office by the Fourteenth Amendment and left the way open for the enfranchisement of all former rebels by the state governments.

Despite the modification, conservative Republican Representatives Jehu Baker and Rufus Spalding questioned the provision's constitutionality and opposed Stevens's effort to call the previous question, cutting off amendments. But other conservatives, notably the influential Blaine, urged Stevens to press on. "If there is any subject which has been talked to death in this country," Blaine complained, "it is the subject of reconstruction. What is wanted now is action." [21] With this clear indication that many conservatives were willing to acquiesce in the imposition of fundamental conditions on the returning southern states, the House seconded the previous question and quickly passed the bill.[22]

Several days later Stevens reported for the Reconstruction committee a bill recognizing the restoration of North Carolina, South Carolina, Louisiana, Georgia, and—signaling the end of all efforts to delay restoration in the House—Alabama. After minimal debate, the House passed the legislation with the same fundamental conditions included in the Arkansas bill.[23]

Like their allies in the House, Senate Republicans were unwilling to risk the consequences of delaying southern restoration. Howe's plea to reconsider went unheeded. ("I wish the Senate to answer the question to themselves whether they are entirely satisfied that this loyal constituency . . . is a constituency combining those numbers and that intelligence and that influence which will enable us to maintain this government in loyal

hands," he begged.) Howe's proposal to instruct the Senate Judiciary committee to report a bill organizing a provisional government in Arkansas
based on the new constitution was defeated without even a formal division.[24]

But in the Senate, with its unlimited freedom of debate, the concept of
fundamental conditions met its most powerful opposition. Despite the opposition of several of its most important members (including Chairman
Trumbull and the influential Conkling) to the imposition of fundamental
conditions, the Senate Judiciary committee reported the House bill restoring Arkansas—including the conditions—to the Senate without amendment.
Again constitutional conservatives refused to acquiesce in this effort to restrict state prerogatives permanently through national power. "While these
States were in their deranged and disordered condition, resulting from the
rebellion, their governments gone, we had a right to come in and reconstruct republican governments by any means that were necessary and
proper for that purpose," Oliver P. Morton conceded. "But when these States
are admitted, when they have complied with all our conditions and come
back and are received, then they stand upon the same platform with every
other State in the Union; they have every right and every power that belongs to every other State." [25]

Conkling and Trumbull echoed Morton's objections. Congress's power
over the South was only temporary, arising out of the war. It would cease
when southern states were restored to normal relations in the Union. "The
people of Arkansas will have the same right to change their constitution
when they are recognized . . . as the people of Wisconsin or the people
of Illinois," Trumbull averred.[26]

But such arguments had slight appeal to those who took a less restrictive view of the proper role of the national government in the protection
of civil and political rights. State rights had been a mere pretense in the
defense of slavery, Charles Sumner argued, and yet Republicans were
making similar arguments now. "Shall the pretension be allowed to prevail,
now that slavery has disappeared? The principal has fallen; why preserve
the incident? . . . [T]here can be no State Rights against Human Rights,"
he proclaimed.[27] But on May 30 the Senate defeated Orris S. Ferry's
amendment to strike out the House's fundamental condition by a bare 21
to 20 margin. Voting with the Democrats to eliminate the condition were
thirteen Republicans, including the architects of the Republican Reconstruction policy in the Senate, Fessenden and Trumbull (see List 18).[28]
Substituting a fundamental condition worded slightly differently than the
House version, the Senate passed the Arkansas restoration bill on June 1.[29]
After a conference both houses agreed to a fundamental condition somewhat modified again.[30]

Having completed action of the Arkansas admission bill, the Senate
turned its attention to the bill restoring North Carolina, South Carolina, Loui-

siana, and Georgia, in a debate that demonstrated how completely radicals had abandoned any hope of delaying readmission. The Senate Judiciary committee, to which the general restoration bill had been referred, had decided to strike Alabama from among the states restored while adding Florida, which had just ratified its new constitution. Now the radicals led the fight to restore Alabama to the bill, afraid to leave the state under the president's control. Only when several senators attacked the wisdom of the original legislation requiring one half of the registered voters to vote in the ratification elections did radical senators clearly evidence the agonizing position in which they had been placed. "That vote was given at a time when a different state of feeling prevailed from that which seems to prevail now," the radical Senator Yates retorted.

Those Senators who voted in favor of requiring the largest number of voters to sanction the new constitutions were in favor of more loyalty than is now contended for . . . . It may yet appear, sir, that that vote was right, and that those who cast that vote were more far-seeing than those who denounced it. Perhaps the time will come when the wisdom of it will be shown to those who now denounce it, when perhaps at the very first election these States shall send into the House of Representatives and into the Senate those rebel leaders who organized war, who sought and worked for their country's murder. When they come here, and, uniting with the Democratic party of the North, resume their former positions and power in this country to upset and to destroy our plan and policy of reconstruction which has cost us so much time and labor, it may then appear, sir, that those who required . . . the indication of the highest loyalty and of repentance on the part of these southern rebels, acted the part of statesmen.

But Yates too would vote for the admission of all the states. "There is danger either way," he acknowledged sadly.[31]

Overcoming conservative objections to including Alabama in the bill because it had not met the requirements set forth by the Reconstruction law as it stood when its citizens voted on the state constitution, Republican senators finally passed the bill after a long debate.[32] It included the fundamental condition both houses had agreed to in the Arkansas restoration bill. After an abortive attempt by a handful of House radicals to prevent the restoration of Florida under its conservative Republican–Democratic constitution, the House agreed to the bill as it passed the Senate.[33] Although three states in which conservative military commanders had obstructed Republican policy remained unreconstructed (Mississippi, Texas, and Virginia), as a practical matter Reconstruction was complete.

As Republicans waged the campaign of 1868, with their conservative presidential candidate, Ulysses S. Grant, on a platform that endorsed black suffrage only for the South ("an evasion of duty quite unworthy of the Republican party," Blaine admitted years later), it became even more apparent that the final Reconstruction policy had been set. Republican

CHART 15
Election of 1868

STATE	GRANT'S PERCENTAGE IN 1868	GENERAL TICKET'S PERCENTAGE IN 1868, IF RUNNING WITH GRANT	GENERAL TICKET'S PERCENTAGE IN 1867	GRANT'S TOTAL MAJORITY COMPARED TO 1868 STATE TICKET RUNNING WITH GRANT *
California	50.24	49.60 (Cong.)	47.81 (Sup. Ct.)	+1189
Connecticut	51.55		49.48 (Gov.)	
Delaware	41.06	41.06 (Cong.)		—32
Georgia	35.09 **			
Indiana	51.47	50.14 (Gov.)		8611
Illinois	55.69	55.28 (Cong.)		3772
Iowa	61.92	60.73 (Cong.)	60.66 (Judge)	4710
Kansas	68.80	66.00 (Gov.)		818
Kentucky	25.45		24.71 (Gov.)	
Louisiana	29.22 **			
Maine	62.42		55.60 (Gov.)	
Maryland	32.80		25.61 (Gov.)	
Massachusetts	69.67	67.62 (Gov.)	58.28 (Gov.)	8214
Michigan	56.98	56.87 (Gov.)	59.13 (Sup. Ct.)	720
Minnesota	58.80	60.74 (Cong.)	54.13 (Gov.)	74
Missouri	59.07	56.66 (Gov.)		6556
Nebraska	63.48	58.38 (Gov.)		1798
New Hampshire	55.01		43.02 (Co. Officers)	
New Jersey	49.12	48.58 (Gov.)	52.19 (Gov.)	1738
New York	49.45	48.40 (Gov.)	46.57 (Sec. State)	17946
North Carolina	55.57			
Ohio	54.01	51.68 (Sec. State)	50.30 (Gov.)	24045
Oregon	49.17	46.00 (Cong.)		1045
Pennsylvania	53.01	50.74 (Aud.-Genl.)	49.91 (Sup. Ct.)	19221
Rhode Island	66.46	64.33 (Gov.)		1045
South Carolina	57.93			
Tennessee	68.84		76.76 (Gov.)	
Vermont	78.57	73.60 (Gov.)	73.32 (Gov.)	4798
West Virginia	58.84	52.56 (Gov.)		4002
Wisconsin	56.23	55.71 (Cong.)	51.69 (Gov.)	2081
				112383
				— 32
				112351

* The difference between the number of votes by which Grant defeated Seymour or was defeated by him and the number of votes by which the Republican state ticket defeated the Democratic ticket or was defeated by it. Computed only where voters cast ballots for president and state officers at the same time.

** Allegations of widespread fraud render these percentages unreliable.

campaign orators promised "peace, . . . upon the basis of a restored Union, of results already accomplished and of a state of things already existing." [34] The Republicans were now the party of peace and moderation, the Democrats—who threatened to overturn the reconstructed southern governments—the party of extremism and war.

Grant's nomination and the conservative Republican platform not only reconciled to the party those most conservative Republicans, the seven senators who voted against convicting Johnson on the impeachment, it won the support of many Unionists and War Democrats who had endorsed Johnson's Reconstruction policy. Even Johnson's cabinet divided, Secretary of State Seward, Secretary of War Schofield, and Attorney General Evarts endorsing Grant. Throughout the nation Grant ran ahead of state candidates on Republican tickets, while thousands of Democrats scratched Seymour's name from theirs. Over all, Grant's majority exceeded by over 100,000 the majorities of state candidates running on the Republican ticket with him. Moreover, as Chart 15 indicates, those Republican state tickets bettered the Republican showings of 1867.

Yet as nonradicals enthused over what the *Chicago Tribune* called "the stampede of 'Conservatives' from the Democratic ranks," radicals worried. "There will . . . be a danger to the Republican party from this accession. Republican campaign managers will be tempted to lower the tone of Republican appeal to the level of Democratic applause. . . . That great party—which could be morally greater without being numerically less—is always ready to water the fine wine of Liberty, Justice, and Equality." [35] But, in fact, the victory of 1868 signified to most Republicans the end of the Reconstruction issue. "The triumph so glorious is for all time," declared the Chicago *Evening Journal*. "Reconstruction . . . can never again be brought into the area of popular politics as a vital issue." [36]

The opportunity for further nationally imposed social and political change in the South had ended. There would be no confiscation, no nationally enforced education policy, no long-term probation for southern states. The Reconstruction of the Union would rest upon a single pillar: the black man's right to vote. And many Republicans were already conceding that under the Constitution, the national government no longer had the power to guarantee that right once southern states were restored.

SEVENTEEN

Epilogue: The Fifteenth Amendment

✦✦✦✦✦✦✦✦✦✦✦✦✦✦✦

FOR MANY REPUBLICANS, the passage of the Fifteenth Amendment represented the real culmination of the quest for racial justice which had continued almost since the birth of the nation. But William Gillette has pointed out it was not really the culmination of the battle over Reconstruction. The Fifteenth Amendment would not offer any rights to southern blacks that they did not already possess under the new constitutions of their states and the fundamental conditions to which those states had to agree. The amendment's primary effect would be to enfranchise blacks in the North. However, Gillette argues that his grew out of the determination of Republicans to secure an accession of black votes in closely contested northern states, that the Fifteenth Amendment was a political expedient designed to secure Republican ascendancy in the North.

Recently, LaWanda and John H. Cox and Glenn M. Linden have challenged that interpretation, pointing out that Republicans had a long history of racially liberal legislation and that such legislation may well have lost rather than gained votes in the North. In fact, Gillette's evidence is critically weak, and in emphasizing the northern-centeredness of the amendment, he minimizes too much the losing struggle to broaden the amendment to make it more of a protection for southern, black Republicans.[1]

Gillette's conclusion is based almost entirely on inference. He lays special emphasis on the number of northern and border states in which the Democratic and Republican parties were evenly matched, arguing that the accession of loyally Republican black voters in those states would provide an important cushion for the party there. But, as the Coxes indicate, this is a rather naïve approach to American politics. No Republican could discount the danger that by enfranchising northern blacks the party might alienate that minority of its white adherents who still opposed black political participation in the North. As the amendment's author and House manager, George S. Boutwell, explained, "I doubt not that nine tenths of the Republican party of the country are in favor of manhood suffrage. One tenth of the party are not in favor of it, and they constitute the great obstacle in the way of perfecting this benign measure." [2]

The problem of the relation between Republican politics and the party's commitment to racial justice is far more complex than Gillette's simple analysis, or even the Coxes' more sophisticated answer, and it deserves an intensive discussion beyond the scope of this chapter. But an insight into the complexities of the question can be discerned in a colloquy on the subject between Senators Henry Wilson and Samuel C. Pomeroy, both radicals, but Wilson the more sensitive to conservative pressures. Wilson had answered Democratic Senator Davis's charge—similar to Gillette's—"that in proposing this [suffrage] amendment we are seeking to perpetuate power."

"A word to the Senator on that point," Wilson began.

He knows and I know that this whole struggle in this country to give equal rights and equal privileges to all citizens of the United States has been an unpopular one; that we have been forced to struggle against passions and prejudices engendered by generations of wrong and oppression . . . . I say to the Senator that the struggle of the last eight years to give freedom to four and a half millions of men who were held in slavery, to make them citizens of the United States, to clothe them with the right of suffrage, to give them the privilege to be voted for, to make them in all respects equal to the white citizens of the United States, has cost the party . . . a quarter of a million of votes. There is not to-day a square mile in the United States where the advocacy of the equal rights and privileges of those colored men has not been in the past and is not now unpopular.[3]

But if this view appears to support the Coxes' contention, Pomeroy's answer to it introduces yet another factor that must be considered. He conceded that Republicans may have lost votes by pursuing their crusade against racial discrimination in civil and political rights. But, he added,

let it be known in this country that the Republican party have abandoned the cause of the rights of man, of the rights of the colored men of this country, and . . . the party itself would not be worth preserving. The strength of the Republican party consists in its adherence to principle, and to that embodiment of its principles, equality of rights among men. . . . It was that for which it was organized; and instead of being a source of weakness it is, in my opinion, a source of strength and power.[4]

So, for many Republicans the essence of the party lay in its devotion to equal rights. In fact, when the party refused to endorse black suffrage extension throughout the Union in its platform for the presidential election of 1868, many Republicans had been outraged. "It is like most of the Republican platforms for the last six years—tame and cowardly," Stevens wrote. Butler predicted that the party would "go to pieces" if it did not espouse universal male suffrage in the North.[5] Only when the Democrats rejected suggestions that they nominate Chase on a platform acquiescing in Reconstruction and nominated instead men committed to overthrowing the reconstructed governments of the South had Republicans begun to work for their ticket enthusiastically.[6] If Republicans would not have pressed the Fifteenth Amendment, Pomeroy was implying, the resulting drop in morale might have destroyed the party. Most Republicans never had to choose between political expediency and political morality, for to a large extent the political fortunes of the Republican party were best served by fulfilling its liberal ideological commitments.[7]

The passage of the Fifteenth Amendment found Republicans divided once more on the issue of permanently expanding the power of the national government. Once again those Republicans who hoped to end the Reconstruction era with minimum possible alteration in the federal system resisted efforts to broaden the power of the national government to protect citizens' rights.

The events of 1868 amply justified Republicans' fears that Reconstruction advances were not secure in the South. So pervasive did he find terrorist activity during the campaign that Allen W. Trelease entitled part III of his study of the Ku Klux Klan during Reconstruction "The Klan Fails to Elect a President, 1868." In Tennessee Republicans received 20,000 fewer votes in the 1868 elections than they had in those of 1867. Only 4000 of those votes could be accounted for in Democratic gains. The larger portion of the decline, suggested John W. Patton, who studied Tennessee Reconstruction, was due to Ku Klux terrorism. The leading historian of Arkansas Reconstruction stated that Republicans managed to retain power in that state in the 1868 elections only through their control of the voting mechanisms. Had they not made fraudulent use of that power the Democrats would have carried the state through fraud and intimidation. In Florida, the Republicans were so uncertain of victory that they decided to have the state legislature name presidential electors rather than allow the people to vote. The election in Louisiana was marked by widespread violence, including several outright massacres of black men. The terrorists succeeded in frightening Republicans from the polls, and despite the black majority in the state the Democratic presidential candidate, Horatio Seymour, carried it by 45,000 votes.[8]

But by far the greatest disaster occurred in Georgia. There the Republicans had succeeded in ratifying the new constitution in spring 1868, and had won a narrow majority in the state legislature. Among the Conservatives (i.e., Democrats) elected were a large number who could not take the oath required of officeholders by the Reconstruction acts. Republicans had protested against seating these men in the legislature, but the

conservative General Meade had decided the Reconstruction acts' requirements did not apply to officers elected under the state constitution, which
required no such oaths. Grant had endorsed Meade's decision, and the
Conservatives were seated. They then challenged the right of the black
members of the legislature to hold office, arguing that the new Georgia
constitution did not specifically grant Negroes that privilege. Supported by
conservative, antiblack Republicans, the Conservatives proceeded to expel
their black colleagues, thus creating a Conservative majority in the legislature. In the 1868 presidential election the demoralized Republicans were
easily intimidated by an active and effective Ku Klux Klan, and here too
Seymour defeated Grant.[9]

The southern situation appeared so menacing to Republicans that on
January 5, 1869, Senator Stewart, the second-ranking Republican on the
powerful Judiciary committee, proposed a bill to repeal the restoration of
Alabama, Georgia, Florida, and North and South Carolina, continuing the
governments of those states as provisional only and subject to the Reconstruction laws.[10]

The critical conditions in the South put Republicans in an awkward
position. Constitutional conservatives among them believed Congress had
lost authority over the states once they had been restored to normal relations. They would be inclined to resist further interference as unconstitutional. The best solution was to secure the black political power on which
Reconstruction was based by constitutional amendment. Yet here too constitutional conservatives inclined to preserve the traditional balance of
power between state and national government. They would work to minimize the scope of any change in the fundamental law.

In the case of Georgia another alternative presented itself. The states'
senators and representatives had not arrived in time to be admitted to seats
in the second session of the Fortieth Congress, which adjourned in July
1868, before the crisis in the state arose. Republicans could argue that
Georgia's restoration was not yet complete, that the state remained under
the paramount authority of Congress. In the House the problem did not
arise when Congress reassembled in December 1868. Representatives from
Georgia were seated without challenge, and at the same time the House
agreed to a resolution instructing the Reconstruction committee to investigate affairs in the state.[11] But in the Senate, where Republican constitutional conservatism centered, radical senators objected to seating the
Georgia senator-elect, Joshua Hill. John Sherman, Hill's personal friend,
argued that Hill disapproved of the legislature's ejection of its black members, that he had been elected by the united vote of the Republican members, black and white, before that action had been taken. "It seems to me
it would be very hard indeed to make a gentleman duly elected by the
whole Legislature, and a Union man, . . . suffer for conduct which he

does not approve, and which he hopes, by having a seat here among us, to be able in part to correct." [12]

But the radical Charles D. Drake, fearing the implications of seating Hill, answered,

The question that is involved in the matter now before us is whether the power of the Senate over a reconstructed rebel State ends with the moment that that State may have been recognized as a State restored to her position in the Union. I contend not . . . . I hold, sir, that Congress has a continuing and undiminished power over those States, to preserve what was built up there in their reconstruction, and I do not intend to vote for the admission of any Senator from any one of those States that has attempted to undo the ascendancy there of loyal men and put rebels there into the ascendancy.[13]

At Hill's request, Sherman finally agreed to refer the Georgian's credentials to the Judiciary committee, which reported against seating him on January 25. But, signaling the deep division over the constitutional issue threatening Republicans, Chairman Trumbull disagreed with the decision and presented a minority report.[14]

Hoping to avoid a debate which would widen Republican differences, the party leaders decided not to take any action on the Georgia question during the remainder of the Fortieth Congress and the first session of the Forty-first, which would immediately follow it. They would leave the problem for the long second session in 1869–70. As part of this determination, Republicans decided to avoid the issue of whether Georgia's electoral vote for Seymour should be counted when Congress canvassed the official results of the presidential election in February 1869. On February 8, therefore, Congress passed a concurrent resolution providing that the results of balloting in the Electoral College would be announced as they stood both with and without the votes of the Georgia electors. Despite the conciliatory effort, Trumbull and Fowler in the Senate and Jehu Baker and Farnsworth in the House opposed the resolution's passage.[15]

But hearing of the Republicans' intentions, Georgia's Republican Governor Rufus Bullock wrote Butler, named chairman of the Reconstruction committee after Stevens's death in August 1868, that the rebels were "jubilant & defiant," expecting the conservative Grant to oppose congressional legislation on Georgia after his inauguration. Bullock urged Butler to take some action to circumvent the danger that Grant might follow in Johnson's footsteps, and Butler decided he would use the ceremony of counting the electoral vote to force the issue of Georgia's status.[16] Other House radicals determined to follow the same course with regard to Louisiana.

When the two houses met on February 10 to count the electoral vote, Representative James Mullins of Tennessee objected to counting the votes cast by the Louisiana electors, and Butler objected to counting those cast by Georgia's, despite the concurrent resolution passed only two days before. As the rules provided, each house met separately to consider the objections. In the Senate, Trumbull's motion to count the Louisiana vote passed over the objections of seven radicals.[17] The Senate then decided by a vote of 32 to 27 that Butler's objection to counting the Georgia vote was out of order under the terms of the concurrent resolution passed February 8. Twenty-two Republicans joined the Democrats in the majority.[18]

As in the Senate, a coalition of conservative Republicans and Democrats in the House overcame radical objections to counting Louisiana's electoral votes. But Republicans nearly unanimously deserted the concurrent resolution regarding Georgia's votes. By a margin of 150 to 41 the House sustained Butler's objection to counting the Georgia ballots.[19] When news of the Senate's position arrived, however, Republican lines began to waver, and conservative Republicans moved to reconsider the vote just taken. Butler and his allies succeeded in tabling the reconsideration, but this time twenty Republicans joined the opposition.[20]

With the Senate and House taking diametrically opposed positions on counting Georgia's electoral vote, president *pro tempore* of the Senate Benjamin Wade, who by law presided over the joint session, decided to enforce the Senate's decision and ordered the tellers to read the results both with and without Georgia's votes, as provided by the February 8 resolution. Butler, Schenck, and other radicals immediately objected, but Wade instructed the tellers to proceed. Over Butler's continued objections the tellers did as told. In the chaos, outraged radical representatives nearly assaulted the senators, and the anger and excitement "exceeded anything ever seen in that body, even during the years of the war." [21] After the Senate retired to its chamber, the furious Butler proposed a resolution protesting Wade's course as "a gross act of oppression and an invasion of the rights and privileges of the House." Although most representatives agreed, many Republicans joined Democrats to table the resolution out of deference to Wade, who they felt had meant to do right.[22]

"You cannot . . . imagine how the scene looked from the chair," the mortified Speaker of the House, Schuyler Colfax, wrote Elihu B. Washburne. It had been solely a Republican fiasco. "It was declaring the result of an election in which *our own party* had triumphed, by a V[ice] P[resident] pro tem of *our own party,* under a concurrent resolution passed by *nearly a party* vote in each branch." [23]

A clear confrontation on the Georgia question had been avoided and with it the issue of continuing congressional power over the reconstructed states. But the division was clear; it was reflected in the chaos on the floor of the House of Representatives. There were Republicans who would resist the further assumption of power by the national government. And there were Republicans determined to press for that same extension of power.

The constitutional amendment the House Judiciary committee proposed to the House on January 11, 1868, represented a clear effort to minimize the change in federal relations involved in enfranchising black Americans. Like the conservative Fourteenth Amendment, it was worded in the negative, limiting only the power of the state and national governments to deny citizens the ballot on grounds of race, color, or previous condition of slavery. The same was true of the version reported to the Senate, which differed primarily in guaranteeing citizens rights to hold office as well as to vote.[24] As the *New York Tribune* commented on a similar version of the amendment proposed earlier,

> The amendment . . . confers no power whatever on Congress, but only limits the power of the States. It does not give Congress the power to pass a national uniform Suffrage law, but, in effect, it *is* such a law embodied in the Constitution. It leaves the States free to make such changes in their Suffrage laws not affecting these points as may be called for.[25]

It did not remove the locus of power to regulate suffrage from the states. It merely prevented an *unjust* regulation. All Congress is saying is "that the States in regulating suffrage shall not destroy it," explained the conservative Republican Senator Frelinghuysen.[26]

Many Republicans, including some conservatives, objected to such a narrow protection for the right to vote, fearing that it would not offer adequate guarantees for the political rights of southern blacks. With support for the reconstructed Republican governments in the South eroding, they feared that resurgent Democrats would attempt to reverse black men's hard-won political advances. An amendment simply barring discrimination on account of race or former condition of slavery, they recognized, could be easily circumvented. "It does not determine who shall vote and hold office," Alabama Republican Senator Willard Warner complained of the Senate version.

> It does not protect any class of citizens against disfranchisement or disqualification. It simply and only provides that certain classes indicated shall not be disfranchised for certain reasons . . . . For any other reason any State may deprive any portion of its citizens of all share in the Government. . . . [U]nder it and without any violation of its letter or spirit, nine tenths [of the black men in the South] . . . might be prevented from voting and holding office by the requirement . . . of an intelligence or property qualification.

Such a proposition was worth virtually nothing at all. "Is this the Dead Sea fruit which we are to gather from the plantings of a hundred years?" Willard pleaded. "Is this to be the sum of the triumph of the grand struggle of a century past in this country for equal rights?"[27]

One group of radicals, led by Sumner, Wilson, and Yates in the Senate, met the difficulty by insisting that Congress already had the power to eliminate discriminatory state suffrage regulations. That position necessarily implied that Congress might overrule any state regulation that limited suffrage in such a way as to bring the state below the high standard of republicanism those radicals set. The House Judiciary committee reported a bill to enfranchise black men throughout the United States at the same time it reported the constitutional amendment, but Boutwell, its manager, quickly realized the bill could not pass and abandoned it. In the Senate Sumner's attempt to substitute such a universal suffrage bill for the constitutional amendment was overwhelmingly defeated; only eight senators joined him.[28] If radicals hoped to secure an "ironclad" guarantee of black men's right to vote, it would have to be through constitutional amendment.

Several Republicans proposed constitutional amendments designed to give Congress the positive right to regulate suffrage, but they won slight support in the committees studying the issue.[29] The only clear, concerted effort to alleviate radical objections to the limited proposals they reported came in the House when Samuel Shellabarger proposed a substitute on behalf of a large number of Ohio representatives. Specifically designed to make circumvention impossible, Shellabarger's proposition forbade states to pass "any law which shall deny or abridge to any male citizen of the United States of the age of twenty-one years or over . . . an equal vote at all elections in the State in which he shall have . . . actual residence . . . , except to such as have or may hereafter engage in insurrection or rebellion against the United States."[30] Shellabarger made an impassioned plea for his amendment: "I implore that we shall make no mistake here. Sir, a mistake here is absolutely fatal. Let it remain possible, under our amendment to still disfranchise the body of the colored race in the late rebel States and I tell you it will be done," he warned.[31]

But the mistake was made despite the radicals' warnings. Eighty-nine Republicans, including some radicals following the lead of the Judiciary committee, joined thirty-seven Democrats to defeat the proposed substitute.[32]

Republicans received one more opportunity to prevent the imposition of the literacy tests that one day would deprive black southerners of their right to vote when Henry Wilson offered a substitute for the proposed constitutional amendment that forbade any discrimination in suffrage or the right to hold office based on race, color, nativity, property, education, or creed. Although Wilson never indicated that his amendment was intended to secure stronger guarantees for southern blacks' political rights, the support Ohio representatives gave it in the House and southerners gave it in the Senate indicates that they may have had those considerations in mind. Defeated in the Senate at first, Wilson carried his proposal on a second vote February 9. Twelve southern and border-state Republicans voted for the substitute when it passed; only two opposed it. Northern Republicans divided almost evenly, eighteen in favor and seventeen against.[33]

In the House, Bingham, oddly out of character (the conservative Ohioan had actually voted *against* the constitutional amendment when it first had passed the House several weeks earlier), led the fight to concur in the Senate's broad version of the proposed amendment. Despite his efforts (or perhaps because many Republicans distrusted him), the House voted overwhelmingly to adhere to its own, narrow version.[34]

With this, the proceedings became more complex. The Senate had shelved its version of the constitutional amendment, passing the House version as amended by Wilson instead. When the House rejected it, the Senate had three courses open to it. It could recede from its amendment and agree to the House version; it could agree to a conference in an attempt to hammer out a compromise; or it could reject the House version entirely and pass its own amendment which it had shelved earlier.

The constitutional amendment's manager, Stewart, advocated the first course, but more radical Republicans offered bitter resistance. Abandoning hope for the broad, Wilson-sponsored version of the constitutional amendment (it was "too broad, too comprehensive, to generous, too liberal for the American people of to-day," Wilson commented bitterly), radicals determined at least to keep the provision protecting black men's rights to hold office, a right the House version omitted. With Georgians already denying their black fellow citizens that right, such an omission would be taken for acquiescence. It would encourage whites in other southern states to follow the same course.[35] But although they had the support of Democrats, who wanted to prevent the House and the Senate from agreeing on any measure at all, the radicals were unable to muster a majority. The Senate voted to recede from all its amendments to the House version.[36]

Having receded from their amendments, senators now had to muster a two-thirds majority to pass the House version of the amendment to the Constitution. But despite pressure from their more conservative allies, radicals refused to vote for it. "I do not feel bound here, to vote for an amendment to the Constitution which accomplishes nothing and under which any State may pass a law which shall disfranchise four fifths of the colored population without mentioning the word 'color,' " South Carolina's Senator Frederick A. Sawyer announced. "I had rather have nothing than to have this; and when I go back to my constituents they will say to me that I have voted right." [37] When the Senate voted on the House version of the constitutional amendment only thirty-one senators voted for it, and twenty-seven against.[38]

The House version of the proposed amendment defeated, Republicans wearily took up the Senate version and began anew the tedious business of discussing and voting on amendments to it. Through the night the exhausted men fought Democratic dilatory motions and defeated both

Democratic and Republican amendments to the proposition. Finally, after hours of grinding discussion, Republicans passed the Senate's proposed constitutional amendment, protecting both the right to vote and the right to hold office from discrimination on the grounds of color, race, or previous condition of servitude.[39]

On February 20, a fresh House of Representatives took up the Senate's proposition and wreaked havoc upon it. An amendment to delete the provision guaranteeing the right to hold office, sponsored by erstwhile radical John A. Logan in deference to his southern Illinois constituents, was defeated 70 to 95, thirty-six Republicans joining Democrats in the effort to narrow the amendment's scope. Then, reversing its decision of five days before which had precipitated the crisis, the House agreed to Bingham's amendment to ban discrimination in voting and officeholding based on race, color, nativity, property, creed, or previous condition of servitude. Conspicuously absent was a ban on educational requirements, but nonetheless, the House clearly had changed its position profoundly and radicals appeared on the verge of a major success.[40]

On February 23, with only eight Republicans in opposition—seven southerners and Ross—the Senate agreed to appoint a conference committee to meet with House representatives and compromise on the wording of the proposed amendment.[41] Logan, Boutwell, and Bingham represented the House in the conference, and Stewart, Conkling, and Edmunds represented the Senate. With both houses having indicated a preference for a broad amendment, at least protecting officeholding, radicals looked to the result with confidence. But when the committee reported, the shocked radicals found that it had eliminated not only the broad protections but also the guarantee of the right to hold office, even though both houses had agreed to that guarantee in the respective versions of the amendment which had been submitted to the conference. Logan had never favored the officeholding protection, but Boutwell, Bingham, Stewart, and Conkling had betrayed their friends. Edmunds refused to sign the report.

The House concurred in the report without debate on February 25, 1869, only one Republican in opposition, but in the Senate outraged radicals voiced their dismay.[42] Radicals assailed the committee's highhanded conduct. "Unparliamentary and almost unprecedented," Pomeroy complained. Without authority, the committee had altered "the substance, I may say because I feel it, the life of the text of the resolution," mourned Edmunds.[43]

But there was nothing the radicals could do. If this report were non-concurred in, the constitutional amendment would be dead. Republicans no longer had the heart to fight. "I have acted upon the idea that one step taken in the right direction made the next step easier to be taken," Wilson said sadly. "I suppose, sir, I must act upon that idea now; and I do so with more sincere regret than ever and with some degree of mortification." Southern Republicans were particularly bitter. "We have for two years been subject to the charge . . . that the Republican party of the northern States put the negro on one platform in the loyal States and upon another platform in the lately disloyal States," Sawyer complained. ". . . We have been constantly asserting that this could not properly be laid at the feet of the National Republican party, but that it was on account of some few weak-kneed Republicans . . . . Now, . . . we are asked to accept an amendment of the Constitution which pleads guilty to charge." [44]

On February 26 the Senate concurred in the House report. North Carolina Senator John Pool and Tennessee Senator Joseph Fowler joined the Democrats in opposition, Pool out of bitterness at the betrayal of his friends and Fowler because the amendment included no provision for amnesty. Seven Republican senators—including Edmunds, Pomeroy, Sawyer, and Sumner—did not have the heart to vote.[45]

The admission of most of the southern states to normal relations with the Union, the passage of the Fifteenth Amendment, the inauguration of Grant, and the retirement of Andrew Johnson combined to close an era. The justification for extraordinary legislation had disappeared. Except for three states, the federal Union was restored. Congressional legislation once again would be based on a peacetime Constitution, and in many ways this was the most significant change of all. For two convictions had unified Republicans in the face of Johnson's opposition between 1866 and 1869: they agreed, first, that the southern states were not in normal relations with the national government and, second, that those relations should not be renewed until the rights and well-being of loyal men in the South were secure. Republican differences had been important, but they had not been nearly so wide as the constitutional and moral chasm that separated even conservative Republicans from the president and the Democrats.

With restoration the gap separating the constitutional convictions of a Lyman Trumbull and the Democratic party would narrow rapidly. And the gap separating him from a Sumner or a Chandler would grow wider. With the impetus for harmony provided by Andrew Johnson no longer present, the personal animosities and differences of principle that marked a Bingham from a Butler would become more grating. The alliance between radical and conservative Republicans had been uneasy before 1869, it had often appeared on the verge of disintegration, but the chaos of the third session of the Fortieth Congress—the bitterness of the fight over the Georgia electoral vote, the confusion and mistrust engendered during the passage of the Fifteenth Amendment, the unwillingness of leading Republicans to continue to use national power to preserve Reconstruction—

portended the rupture of the party and the collapse of Republican Reconstruction policy.

But all this lay in an invisible, melancholy future. In the hopeful dawn of the Grant administration it seemed that a dismal era was ending, not beginning. As the *New York Tribune* exulted, "The last of the great issues—the social and political Reconstruction of the South, [is] . . . determined, and we may now look forward to a long era of peace and prosperity." [46]

LISTS
✦
APPENDICES
✦
NOTES
✦
BIBLIOGRAPHY
✦
INDEX
✦

Lists: Radicals and Conservatives in the 38–40 Congresses

LIST 1: Consistent Republican Factions in the House of Representatives, 38–40 Congresses, is on page 27 of the text.

LIST 2: Consistent Republican Factions in the Senate, 38–40 Congresses, is on page 28 of the text.

LIST 3: Prestigious Republican Members of the House of Representatives, 38–40 Congresses, is on page 31 of the text.

LIST 4: Prestigious Republican Senators, 38–40 Congresses, is on page 32 of the text.

*   *   *

CONGRESSMEN whose names appear in *italics* below, although falling within groups in which they are placed, displayed voting patterns approaching those of congressmen in the other groups nearest which they are placed.

LIST 5
RADICALISM IN THE HOUSE OF REPRESENTATIVES 38 CONGRESS, FIRST SESSION

GROUP 0 (EXTREME PEACE DEMOCRATS)

James C. Allen, Illinois
Sydenham E. Ancona, Pennsylvania
James Brooks, New York
John W. Chanler, New York
Alexander H. Coffroth, Pennsylvania
John L. Dawson, Pennsylvania
Charles Denison, Pennsylvania
John R. Eden, Illinois
Joseph K. Edgerton, Indiana
Charles A. Eldridge, Wisconsin
William E. Finck, Ohio
Benjamin G. Harris, Maryland
Charles M. Harris, Illinois
Anson Herrick, New York

Anthony L. Knapp, Illinois
John Law, Indiana
Jesse Lazear, Pennsylvania
Francis C. LeBlond, Ohio
Alexander Long, Ohio
Archibald McAllister, Pennsylvania
James F. McDowell, Indiana
John F. McKinney, Ohio
Daniel March, New Hampshire
William H. Miller, Pennsylvania
William R. Morrison, Illinois
Perry Noble, Missouri
John O'Neill, Ohio
George C. Pendleton, Ohio

John V.L. Pruyn, New York
Samuel J. Randall, Pennsylvania
James C. Robinson, Illinois
Lewis W. Ross, Illinois
John D. Stiles, Pennsylvania
Myer Strouse, Pennsylvania
Daniel W. Voorhees, Indiana
Chilton A. White, Ohio

Fernando Wood, New York
William J. Allen, Illinois
George Bliss, Ohio
Henry Grider, Kentucky
William A. Hall, Missouri
Phillip Johnson, Pennsylvania
James R. Morris, Ohio
Nehemiah Perry, New Jersey

—Amendment that no troops may be raised under the Conscription bill until the president offers an armistice, resolution that it is the moral duty of the people to crush the rebellion, censure of Benjamin G. Harris, resolution to appoint a peace commission to negotiate with the rebels.

GROUP 1 (MODERATE PEACE DEMOCRATS)

James S. Brown, Wisconsin
Samuel S. Cox, Ohio
James A. Cravens, Indiana
James E. English, Connecticut
Aaron Harding, Kentucky
Henry W. Harrington, Indiana
Wells A. Hutchins, Ohio
William Johnson, Ohio
Martin Kalbfleisch, New York
Francis Kernan, New York
Austin A. King, Missouri
Robert Mallory, New York
Homer A. Nelson, New York
William Radford, New York
Andrew J. Rogers, New Jersey

James S. Rollins, Missouri
John G. Scott, Missouri
William G. Steele, New Jersey
Lorenzo D. Sweat, Maine
William H. Wadsworth, Kentucky
    (Unionist)
Joseph W. White, Ohio
Charles H. Winfield, New York
Augustus C. Baldwin, Michigan
Brutus J. Clay, Kentucky
John Ganson, New York
John B. Steele, New York
John T. Stuart, Illinois
Elijah Ward, New York

—Tabling of the resolution to censure Benjamin G. Harris, resolution to reject negotiations with southerners on the grounds it amounts to recognition, final passage of the Conscription act as reported by a conference committee, motion to take up a bill to punish guerillas, resolution urging the president to continue negotiations for an exchange of prisoners and commending his past efforts, bill to aid enlistment of southern blacks, bill to amend the Conscription act, tabling of the bill to punish guerillas, tabling of the Emancipation Amendment to the Constitution, resolution censuring the administration for suspending the publication of the N.Y. *World* and the N.Y. *Journal of Commerce*, tabling of the resolution calling for continued war until all rebels are defeated.

GROUP 2 (WAR DEMOCRATS)

William S. Holman, Indiana
Ezra Wheeler, Wisconsin
George Middleton, New Jersey

Henry G. Stebbins, New York
George H. Yeaman, Kentucky

(ABOLITION DEMOCRATS)

John A. Griswold, New York

Benjamin B. Odell, New York

—Taking up, tabling, amendment, and passage of the Conscription bill, passage of the bill to punish guerillas, repeal of the Fugitive Slave law of 1799, tabling of the resolution promising no interference with slavery if rebel arms are laid down, tabling of the resolution requesting the president to appoint peace commissioners, postponement of the resolution asking the president to appoint a commission to report on Arkansas Reconstruction, resolution censuring the administration for banishing Vallandigham, resolution reaffirming the Tenth Amendment, passage of the Emancipation Amendment, postponement of the seating of the Louisiana representatives-elect, amendment to the black testimony section of the Civil Appropriations bill limiting the new right to those states which permit black testimony in their courts, resolution on emancipation, expulsion of Benjamin G. Harris, tabling of the resolution repudiating suggestions of military rule of the South after the war, expulsion of Alexander Long, passage of the Wade-Davis Reconstruction bill.

GROUP 3 (ABOLITION DEMOCRAT AND CONSERVATIVE BORDER-STATE UNIONISTS)

Joseph Baily, Pennsylvania
  (Democrat)
Francis P. Blair, Jr., Missouri
William G. Brown, West Virginia
Jacob B. Blair, West Virginia
James T. Hale, Pennsylvania

Francis Thomas, Maryland
Edwin H. Webster, Maryland
Kellian V. Whaley, West Virginia
William H. Randall, Pennsylvania
Green Clay Smith, Kentucky
Henry W. Tracy, Pennsylvania

—Joint Resolution explanatory of the Confiscation act, tabling and passage of the Freedmen's Bureau bill, creation of a special commission on the rebellious states, a bill to repeal the commutation and substitution provisions of the Conscription act, passage of the bill to organize the Montana territory without prohibiting black suffrage, printing of General McClellan's report, resolution instructing the House conferees on the Montana Territory bill to adhere to the House refusal to require black suffrage in Montana.

GROUP 4 (ANTI-NEGRO-SUFFRAGE REPUBLICANS)

Henry T. Blow, Missouri
John A.J. Creswell, Maryland
Thomas T. Davis, New York
Ignatius Donnelly, Minnesota
Reuben E. Fenton, New York
Nathaniel B. Smithers, Delaware

Glenni W. Scofield, Pennsylvania
Martin R. Thayer, Pennsylvania
Henry W. Davis, Maryland
John A. Kasson, Iowa
James M. Marvin, New York
John F. Starr, New Jersey

—Preamble to the Wade-Davis Reconstruction bill, agreeing to the conference committee report providing black suffrage for the Montana Territory.

GROUP 5 (CENTRIST REPUBLICANS—WILLING TO SUPPORT BLACK SUFFRAGE)

John R. McBride, Oregon
Daniel Morris, New York
James W. Patterson, New Hampshire
Frederick A. Pike, Maine
Frederick E. Woodbridge, Vermont
James M. Ashley, Ohio
John M. Broomall, Pennsylvania
Ebenezer Dumont, Indiana

Ephraim R. Eckley, Ohio
Augustus Frank, New York
Giles W. Hotchkiss, New York
Thomas A. Jenckes, Rhode Island
Samuel F. Miller, New York
Sidney Perham, Maine
John H. Rice, Maine
Thomas B. Shannon, California

—Motion to excuse Charles A. Eldridge's absence from the House, tabling of resolution which implies opposition to a radical Reconstruction.

GROUP 6 (RADICAL CENTRIST REPUBLICANS—WILLING TO ENDORSE WHITE-ONLY SUFFRAGE AFTER THE DEFEAT OF BLACK SUFFRAGE)

Portus Baxter, Vermont
Fernando C. Beaman, Michigan

James G. Blaine, Maine
Sempronius Boyd, Missouri

Augustus Brandegee, Connecticut
Freeman Clarke, New York
Henry C. Deming, Connecticut
John F. Driggs, Michigan
Samuel Hooper, Massachusetts
Francis W. Kellogg, Michigan
John W. Longyear, Michigan
Joseph W. McClurg, Missouri
Walter D. McIndoe, Wisconsin

Amos Myers, Pennsylvania
Jesse O. Norton, Illinois
Charles O'Neill, Pennsylvania
Godlove S. Orth, Indiana
Theodore Pomeroy, New York
Charles Upson, Michigan
Robert B. Van Valkenburg, New York
William B. Washburn, Massachusetts

(RADICAL REPUBLICANS)

Cornelius Cole, California
Nathan F. Dixon, Rhode Island
Daniel W. Gooch, Massachusetts
William D. Kelley, Pennsylvania
Samuel Knox, Missouri

Benjamin F. Loan, Missouri
Hiram Price, Iowa
Ithamar C. Sloan, Wisconsin
Thomas Williams, Pennsylvania

—Agreement to the conference committee report on the Montana Territory bill limiting suffrage to whites, resolution endorsing the vigorous prosecution of the war but vowing to do nothing "subversive" of the Constitution.

GROUP 7 (EXTREME RADICALS—UNWILLING
TO ENDORSE WHITE-ONLY SUFFRAGE)

William B. Allison, Iowa
Oakes Ames, Massachusetts
Lucian Anderson, Kentucky
George S. Boutwell, Massachusetts
Thomas D. Eliot, Massachusetts
James A. Garfield, Ohio
Josiah Grinnell, Iowa
Jonathan H. Hubbard, Connecticut

George W. Julian, Indiana
Dewitt C. Littlejohn, New York
James K. Moorhead, Pennsylvania
Robert C. Schenck, Ohio
Rufus P. Spalding, Ohio
Thaddeus Stevens, Pennsylvania
Able C. Wilder, Kansas

NONSCALAR: John B. Alley, Massachusetts; Issac Arnold, Illinois; John D. Baldwin, Massachusetts; Ambrose W. Clark, New York; Amasa Cobb, Wisconsin; Henry L. Dawes, Massachusetts; John F. Farnsworth, Illinois; William Higby, California; Asahel W. Hubbard, Iowa; Calvin T. Hulburd, New York; Orlando Kellogg, New York; Justin S. Morrill, Vermont; Alexander H. Rice, Massachusetts; Edward H. Rollins, New Hampshire; Elihu B. Washburne, Illinois; James F. Wilson, Iowa; William Windom, Minnesota (Republicans).

NOT VOTING: John W. Noell, Missouri; Benjamin Wood, New York (Democrats); Ebon C. Ingersoll, Illinois; Owen Lovejoy, Illinois; Henry G. Worthington, Nevada (Republicans).

For a list of the roll calls upon which this list is based, see Appendix VIII.

LIST 6

RADICALISM IN THE SENATE
38 CONGRESS, FIRST SESSION

GROUP 0 (ANTIABOLITIONIST DEMOCRATS)

Charles R. Buckalew, Pennsylvania
John S. Carlile, Virginia

Garrett Davis, Kentucky
Thomas A. Hendricks, Indiana

James A. McDougall, California
Lazarus W. Powell, Kentucky
William A. Richardson, Illinois

George R. Riddle, Delaware
Willard Saulsbury, Delaware

—Democratic amendments to the Emancipation Constitutional Amendment, passage of the Wade-Davis Reconstruction bill, passage of the Emancipation Amendment in the Senate, amendment to the Army Appropriations bill to require payment for the slaves of a loyal person recruited into the army, amendments to the Freedmen's Bureau bill to eliminate the commissioner's obligation to enforce military proclamations and to protect the rights of white men, resolution asking President Lincoln to rescind the order closing the Cincinnati *Enquirer,* motion to take up the bill to prohibit military interference with elections.

GROUP 1 (EXTREME CONSERVATIVE REPUBLICANS AND ABOLITIONIST DEMOCRATS)

Edgar A. Cowan, Pennsylvania
Reverdy Johnson, Maryland
    (Democrat)

James W. Nesmith, Oregon
    (Democrat)
Peter G. Van Winkle, West Virginia
Waitman T. Willey, West Virginia

—Dilatory motions, amendments, and passage of the Freedmen's Bureau bill in the Senate, amendment to the Civil Appropriations bill to permit black testimony in the national courts, dilatory motions on the bill to repeal the Fugitive Slave law, resolution to require test oaths of all Senators.

GROUP 2 (CONSERVATIVE REPUBLICANS)

Benjamin F. Harding, Oregon
Thomas H. Hicks, Maryland
James R. Doolittle, Wisconsin
John B. Henderson, Missouri
Henry S. Lane, Indiana

John Sherman, Ohio
Lyman Trumbull, Illinois
Ira Harris, New York
John C. Ten Eyck, New Jersey

—Amendment to the Freedmen's Bureau bill to repeal the proviso of the Confiscation act which limits confiscation to the lifetime of the rebel, amendments to the Civil Appropriations bill to permit black testimony in national courts and repealing the regulations for the coastal slave trade, reference of the bill to repeal the Fugitive Slave act, reference of the bill to prohibit military interference with elections to the Judiciary committee rather than to the Committee on Military Affairs.

GROUP 3 (CENTRIST REPUBLICANS)

Jacob Collamer, Vermont
Timothy O. Howe, Wisconsin

B. Gratz Brown, Missouri

—Amendment to the D.C. Registration bill to give suffrage to all soldiers, amendment to the bill to repeal the Fugitive Slave law to exempt the 1793 Fugitive Slave law, reference of the bill to prohibit military interference with elections to the Judiciary committee, amendment to the Wade-Davis bill to require exclusion of the southern states until restored by a presidential proclamation issued by virtue of congressional law, banning of the coastal slave trade.

GROUP 4 (CENTRIST AND RADICAL REPUBLICANS)

William P. Fessenden, Maine
John P. Hale, New Hampshire
Alexander Ramsey, Minnesota

John Conness, California
James Dixon, Connecticut
Solomon Foot, Vermont

Lafayette S. Foster, Connecticut   *Lot M. Morrill, Maine*
James Harlan, Iowa   *William Sprague, Rhode Island*
Jacob M. Howard, Michigan

—Motion to take up the Wade-Davis Reconstruction bill.

GROUP 5 (RADICAL REPUBLICANS)

James W. Grimes, Iowa   *Zachariah Chandler, Michigan*
Henry Wilson, Massachusetts   *Benjamin F. Wade, Ohio*

—Black suffrage amendment to the Wade-Davis bill.

GROUP 6 (PRO-BLACK SUFFRAGE RADICALS)

Henry B. Anthony, Rhode Island   Samuel C. Pomeroy, Kansas
Daniel Clark, New Hampshire   Charles Sumner, Massachusetts
James H. Lane, Kansas   Morton S. Wilkinson, Minnesota
Edwin D. Morgan, New York

NOT VOTING: William Wright, New Jersey (Democrat)

For a list of the roll calls upon which this list is based, see Appendix VII.

LIST 7

RADICALISM IN THE HOUSE OF REPRESENTATIVES
38 CONGRESS, SECOND SESSION

† *Republicans voting to guarantee civil trials to nonmilitary personnel.*
  NOTE: Democratic voting patterns did not correspond to those of Republicans and
therefore they were scaled separately.

GROUP 0 (EXTREME PEACE DEMOCRATS)

Harris, Maryland   *Long, Ohio*
C.A. White, Ohio   *Morris, Ohio*
Chanler, New York   *Perry, New Jersey*
Dawson, Pennsylvania   *Stiles, Pennsylvania*
Johnson, Ohio   *Ward, New York*
Law, Indiana

—Resolution of thanks to General Philip Sheridan.

GROUP 1 (ANTI-ABOLITION DEMOCRATS)

J.C. Allen, Illinois   Denison, Pennsylvania
W.J. Allen, Illinois   Eden, Illinois
Ancona, Pennsylvania   Edgerton, Indiana
Bliss, Ohio   Eldridge, Wisconsin
Brooks, New York   Finck, Ohio
Brown, Wisconsin   Grider, Kentucky
Clay, Kentucky (Unionist)   Hall, Missouri
Cox, Ohio   Harding, Kentucky
Cravens, Indiana   Harrington, Illinois

Holman, Indiana
Johnson, Pennsylvania
Kalbfleisch, New York
Kernan, New York
Knapp, Illinois
Mallory, Kentucky
Miller, Pennsylvania
Morrison, Illinois
Noble, Ohio
O'Neill, Ohio
Pendleton, Ohio
Pruyn, New York
Randall, Pennsylvania
Robinson, Illinois

Ross, Illinois
John G. Scott, Missouri
Steele, Ohio
Strouse, Pennsylvania
Stuart, Illinois
Sweat, Maine
Dwight Townsend, New York
Wadsworth, Kentucky (Unionist)
J.W. White, Ohio
Winfield, New York
B.F. Wood, New York
F. Wood, New York
Ganson, New York

—Tabling the resolution asking about prisoner-exchange conferences, the Emancipation Amendment.

GROUP 2 (ABOLITION DEMOCRATS)

Baldwin, Michigan
Coffroth, Pennsylvania
English, Connecticut
Herrick, New York
Hutchins, Ohio
King, Missouri

McAllister, Pennsylvania
Radford, New York
Rollins, Missouri
Steele, New York
Yeaman, Kentucky

—Conscription bill and amendment to end the draft, resolution to extend the life of the Joint Committee on the Conduct of the War.

GROUP 3 (STRONGLY PROWAR DEMOCRATS AND EXTREMELY CONSERVATIVE REPUBLICANS)

Baily, Pennsylvania (Democrat)
Blair, West Virginia
Griswold, New York (Democrat)
† Hale, Pennsylvania
Odell, New York (Democrat)
† Randall, Kentucky

Tracy, Pennsylvania
† Webster, Maryland
Whaley, West Virginia
Wheeler, Wisconsin (Democrat)
Smith, Kentucky
Thomas, Maryland

—Confiscation bill. Group #3 was derived from a separate scale involving votes on the Confiscation bill.

GROUP 4 (CONSERVATIVE REPUBLICANS)

Boyd, Missouri
Cobb, Wisconsin
Davis, New York
† Dawes, Massachusetts
† Deming, Connecticut
Eckley, Ohio
† Gooch, Massachusetts
Hulburd, New York
Littlejohn, New York
Marvin, New York
Pike, Maine

Pomeroy, New York
† Rice, Massachusetts
* Stevens, Pennsylvania
Van Valkenburg, New York
Washburn, Massachusetts
Clarke, New York
Farnsworth, Illinois
Frank, New York
Ingersoll, Illinois
Washburne, Illinois
Worthington, Nevada

* *Stevens voted with the conservatives to table the Reconstruction bill because of his opposition to any measure recognizing Louisiana.*

—Tabling the Reconstruction bill on February 22.

GROUP 5 (CENTRIST REPUBLICANS)

† Ames, Massachusetts
Arnold, Illinois
† Baxter, Vermont
Blaine, Maine
† Clark, New York
† Cole, California
† Dixon, Rhode Island
Donnelly, Minnesota
Driggs, Michigan
† Eliot, Massachusetts
† Higby, California
Hubbard, Iowa
Hubbard, Connecticut
† Kellogg, New York
† Miller, New York
† Morrill, Vermont
† A. Myers, Pennsylvania
† L. Myers, Pennsylvania

O'Neill, Pennsylvania
Orth, Indiana
Patterson, New Hampshire
† Perham, Maine
† Price, Iowa
Rice, Maine
Rollins, New Hampshire
Shannon, California
Thayer, Pennsylvania
Williams, Pennsylvania
Wilson, Iowa
† *Blow, Missouri*
Dumont, Indiana
Hooper, Massachusetts
† *Jenckes, Rhode Island*
Loan, Missouri
† *Moorhead, Pennsylvania*

—Tabling of the Reconstruction bill on January 17.

GROUP 6 (RADICAL REPUBLICANS)

† Allison, Iowa
Ashley, Ohio
† Baldwin, Massachusetts
† Beaman, Michigan
† Boutwell, Massachusetts
† Broomall, Pennsylvania
† Davis, Maryland
† Garfield, Ohio
Grinnell, Iowa
Kelley, Pennsylvania
Kellogg, Michigan
Knox, Missouri

Longyear, Michigan
McBride, Oregon
McClurg, Missouri
Morris, New York
Schenck, Ohio
Scofield, Ohio
Sloan, Wisconsin
† Smithers, Delaware
Starr, New Jersey
Upson, Michigan
Wilder, Kansas

NONSCALAR: †Brandegee, Connecticut; Norton, Illinois (Republicans).

NOT VOTING: Alley, Massachusetts; Anderson, Kentucky; Blair, Missouri; Brown, West Virginia; Colfax, Indiana; Creswell, Maryland; Hotchkiss, New York; Julian, Indiana; Kasson, Iowa; McIndoe, Wisconsin; Spalding, Ohio; Windom, Minnesota; Woodbridge, Vermont (Republicans). Lazear, Pennsylvania; LeBlond, Ohio; McDowell, Indiana; McKinney, Ohio; March, New Hampshire; Middleton, New Jersey; Rogers, New Jersey; Voorhees, Indiana (Democrats).

For a list of the roll calls upon which this list is based, see Appendix VIII.

LIST 8
RADICALISM IN THE SENATE
38 CONGRESS, SECOND SESSION

GROUP 0 (DEMOCRATS)

SUBGROUP A—Democrats voting with radical Republicans on the Electoral Count bill and the Louisiana Admission bill in order to prevent passage of any Republican legislation.

Buckalew, Pennsylvania
Carlile, Virginia
Davis, Kentucky

Powell, Kentucky
Riddle, Delaware
Wright, New Jersey

—Admission of the senator-elect from Virginia, dilatory motion on the Louisiana Admission bill.

SUBGROUP B—Democrat voting with radical Republicans on the Electoral Count bill and some votes on the Louisiana Admission bill

Hendricks, Indiana

—Dilatory motions on the Louisiana Admission bill, passage of the Electoral Count bill.

SUBGROUP C—Democrats voting with radical Republicans only on the Electoral Count bill.

Johnson, Maryland

Saulsbury, Delaware

—Amendments to the Electoral Count bill.

SUBGROUP D—Democrats voting with nonradical Republicans to recognize the Louisiana and Arkansas governments

McDougall, California

Nesmith, Oregon

—Democrats were ranked on a different scale than Republicans, as their voting patterns did not correspond.

GROUP 1 (CONSERVATIVE REPUBLICANS)

Cowan, Pennsylvania
Doolittle, Wisconsin
Harris, New York
Lane, Indiana
Lane, Kansas

Pomeroy, Kansas
Van Winkle, West Virginia
Willey, West Virginia
Howe, Wisconsin

—Tabling of the credentials of the senator-elect from Virginia; amendment to strike the preamble, which does not recognize Louisiana and Arkansas, from the Electoral Count bill; passage of the Electoral Count resolution.

GROUP 2 (CONSERVATIVE REPUBLICANS)

Nathan A. Farwell, Maine   Harlan, Iowa   Ten Eyck, New Jersey

—Amendment to the Electoral Count bill to recognize the validity of the governments in Arkansas and Louisiana but not to count their electoral votes, postponement of the Electoral Count resolution, amendment to the Electoral Count resolution to strike the preamble.

GROUP 3 (CONSERVATIVE CENTRIST REPUBLICANS)

Dixon, Connecticut   *Hale, New Hampshire*

—Amendment to remove Arkansas and Louisiana from the operation of the Electoral Count bill.

GROUP 4 (CENTRIST REPUBLICANS)

Foster, Connecticut   Trumbull, Illinois
Henderson, Montana   *Collamer, Vermont*
Morgan, New York   *Sprague, Rhode Island*

—Amendment to the Enrollment act to transfer trials for violations from military to civil courts.

GROUP 5 (CENTRIST REPUBLICANS)

Anthony, Rhode Island   Sherman, Ohio
Clark, New Hampshire   *Nye, Nevada*
Morrill, Maine   *Stewart, Nevada*

—Filibuster of the Louisiana Admission bill.

GROUP 6 (RADICAL REPUBLICANS)

Brown, Montana   Howard, Michigan
Chandler, Michigan   Sumner, Massachusetts
Conness, California   Wade, Ohio
Grimes, Iowa

NONSCALAR: Ramsey, Minnesota; Wilson, Massachusetts (Republicans).

NOT VOTING: Foot, Vermont; Harding, Oregon; Hicks, Maryland; Wilkinson, Minnesota (Republicans). Richardson, Illinois (Democrat).

For a list of the roll calls upon which this list is based, see Appendix VII.

LIST 9

RADICALISM IN THE HOUSE OF REPRESENTATIVES
39 CONGRESS, FIRST SESSION

† *Representatives voting against adjournment.*

GROUP 0 (DEMOCRATS)

Ancona, Pennsylvania   Grider, Kentucky
Benjamin M. Boyer, Pennsylvania   Harding, Kentucky
Eldridge, Wisconsin   Michael C. Kerr, Indiana
Finck, Ohio   William E. Niblack, Indiana
Charles Goodyear, New York   John A. Nicholson, Delaware

Thomas E. Noell, Missouri
Radford, New York
Randall, Pennsylvania
Rogers, New Jersey
George S. Shanklin, Kentucky
Charles Sitgreaves, New Jersey
Lawrence S. Trimble, Kentucky
Edwin R.V. Wright, New Jersey
Brooks, New York
Denison, Pennsylvania
Harris, Maryland

Edwin N. Hubbell, New York
James M. Humphrey, New York
Johnson, Pennsylvania
LeBlond, Ohio
Samuel S. Marshall, Illinois
Hiram McCullough, Maryland
Burwell C. Ritter, Kentucky
Strouse, Pennsylvania
Stephen Taber, New York
Nelson Taylor, New York
Winfield, New York

—Dilatory motions delaying the resolution that no southern representatives may be seated until the Reconstruction committee reports.

GROUP 1 (DEMOCRATS)

Teunis G. Bergen, New York
Chanler, New York
Coffroth, Pennsylvania
Dawson, Pennsylvania

Adam J. Glossbrenner, New Jersey
John Hogan, Missouri
Ross, Illinois
Anthony Thornton, Illinois

—Resolutions endorsing the suspension of habeas corpus and military occupation in the South, resolution calling for the trial of Jefferson Davis, resolution to discharge the Reconstruction committee, resolution to investigate the Memphis riot, resolution that the Test Oath law should be enforced, tabling of the Colorado statehood resolution, resolution creating the Joint Committee on Reconstruction, passage of the Fourteenth Amendment, concurring in the Senate amendments to the Tennessee Restoration bill, resolution endorsing Andrew Johnson's Reconstruction policy.

GROUP 2 (CONSERVATIVE [JOHNSON] UNIONISTS)

William A. Darling, New York
Robert S. Hale, New York
Andrew J. Kuykendall, Illinois
George R. Latham, West Virginia
Charles E. Phelps, Maryland
Henry J. Raymond, New York

Lovell H. Rousseau, Kentucky
Smith, Kentucky
Whaley, West Virginia
Thomas N. Stillwell, Indiana
Henry D. Washburn, Indiana

—Resolution to investigate the Freedmen's Bureau, motion to refer the credentials of Tennessee representatives-elect to the Judiciary committee, resolution that Congress has the power to prescribe governmental reorganization for southern states, second Freedmen's Bureau bill, passage of the Civil Rights bill, resolution asking the Judiciary committee to report on the expediency of banning suffrage discrimination in the territories, resolution that no southern representatives shall be admitted to Congress until the Reconstruction committee reports (February), resolution that the rebellion deprived southerners of civil government, resolution to admit Tennessee's Senator Patterson upon taking a modified oath, passage of the Civil Rights bill over the President's veto, tabling of the constitutional amendment giving Congress the power to enforce equal civil rights within states, D.C. black suffrage bill, resolution that no southern representative be seated until the Reconstruction committee reports (December).

GROUP 3 (CONSERVATIVE REPUBLICANS)

Randall, Kentucky
Ralph P. Buckland, Ohio
Davis, New York

Dawes, Massachusetts
Joseph H. Defrees, Indiana
John H. Farquhar, Indiana

Deming, Connecticut
Griswold, New York
Chester D. Hubbard, West Virginia
Kasson, Iowa
John H. Ketcham, New York
Addison H. Laflin, New York
George V. Lawrence, Pennsylvania
Marvin, New York
Tobias A. Plants, Ohio

† Robert T. Van Horn, Missouri
† George W. Anderson, Missouri
Blow, Missouri
Dumont, Indiana
† *Thomas W. Ferry, Michigan*
James R. Hubbell, Ohio
† *James Humphrey, New York*
William A. Newell, New Jersey
Orth, Indiana

—Resolution to grant the privileges of the floor to Arkansas representatives-elect (January), resolution to grant the privileges of the floor to Tennessee representatives-elect, postponement of the D.C. black suffrage bill, resolution authorizing presiding officers of Congress to call an emergency meeting of Congress, resolution to grant the privileges of the floor to Arkansas representatives-elect (February).

GROUP 4 (CENTRIST REPUBLICANS)

Benjamin Eggleston, Ohio
Rutherford B. Hayes, Ohio
George F. Miller, Pennsylvania
† *John L. Thomas, Maryland*
† *Nathaniel P. Banks, Massachusetts*
John A. Bingham, Ohio
Hezekiah S. Bundy, Ohio
Reader W. Clarke, Ohio
Columbus Delano, Ohio
Eckley, Ohio
John H.D. Henderson, Oregon
Hubbard, Connecticut
Hulburd, New York
William H. Koontz, Pennsylvania
† William Lawrence, Ohio
Longyear, Michigan

† Gilman Marston, New Hampshire
Morris, New York
† Myers, Pennsylvania
† O'Neill, Pennsylvania
† Rollins, New Hampshire
† Spalding, Ohio
† Burt Van Horn, New York
Samuel L. Warner, Connecticut
Washburn, Massachusetts
Stephen F. Wilson, Pennsylvania
† *Delos R. Ashley, Nevada*
† *Roscoe Conkling, New York*
† *Hooper, Massachusetts*
Moorhead, Pennsylvania
Thayer, Pennsylvania

—Motion to recommitt the Civil Rights bill to the House Judiciary committee, motion to recommit the D.C. black suffrage bill with instructions to add literacy qualifications, motion to set the date of adjournment (May), dilatory motions on the Tennessee Restoration bill.

GROUP 5 (RADICAL REPUBLICANS)

† Ames, Massachusetts
† Ashley, Ohio
† Jehu Baker, Illinois
Beaman, Michigan
† John F. Benjamin, Missouri
† John Bidwell, California
† Henry P.H. Bromwell, Illinois
† Cobb, Wisconsin
† Shelby M. Cullom, Illinois
† Farnsworth, Illinois
Roswell Hart, New York
Sidney T. Holmes, New York
† Hotchkiss, New York
Demas Hubbard, New York

Samuel McKee, Kentucky
Rice, Maine
† Schenck, Ohio
† Scofield, Pennsylvania
† Samuel Shellabarger, Ohio
† F. Thomas, Maryland
Upson, Michigan
† John Wentworth, Illinois
Alley, Massachusetts
† *Hubbard, Iowa*
† *Ingersoll, Illinois*
Ulysses Mercur, Pennsylvania
Philetus Sawyer, Wisconsin
Martin Welker, Ohio

—Tennessee Restoration bill, black suffrage amendment to the Colorado Admission bill, Nebraska admission without black suffrage.

GROUP 6 (RADICAL REPUBLICANS FAVORING BLACK
SUFFRAGE THROUGHOUT THE SESSION)

† Allison, Iowa
Baldwin, Massachusetts
Baxter, Vermont
Blaine, Maine
† Boutwell, Massachusetts
Broomall, Pennsylvania
† Sidney Clarke, Kansas
Burton C. Cook, Illinois
Dixon, Rhode Island
† Driggs, Michigan
Eliot, Massachusetts
Garfield, Ohio
Grinnell, Iowa
† Abner C. Harding, Illinois
† Higby, California
† Jenckes, Rhode Island
Julian, Indiana

† Kelley, Pennsylvania
† Loan, Missouri
† John Lynch, Maine
† McClurg, Maine
Morrill, Vermont
† Samuel W. Moulton, Illinois
† Halbert E. Paine, Wisconsin
† Perham, Maine
Price, Iowa
† Stevens, Pennsylvania
† Rowland E. Trowbridge, Michigan
Henry Van Aernam, New York
Hamilton Ward, New York
† Williams, Pennsylvania
† Wilson, Iowa
† Windom, Minnesota
Woodbridge, Vermont

NONSCALAR: Brandegee, Connecticut; † Donnelly, Minnesota; Ralph Hill, Indiana; John R. Kelso, Missouri; Donald C. McRuer, California; Pike, Maine; Rice, Massachusetts; Sloan, Wisconsin (Republicans).

NOT VOTING: Abraham A. Barker, Pennsylvania; Charles V. Culver, Pennsylvania; William E. Dodge, New York; McIndoe, Wisconsin; Horace Maynard, Tennessee; Patterson, New Hampshire; Pomeroy, New York; Starr, New Jersey; William B. Stokes, Tennessee; Washburne, Illinois (Republicans). Morgan Jones, New York; John W. Leftwich, Tennessee; Nathaniel G. Taylor, Tennessee (Democrats).

For a list of the roll calls upon which this list is based, see Appendix VIII.

LIST 10

RADICALISM IN THE SENATE
39 CONGRESS, FIRST SESSION

NOTE: Democrats and Johnson Conservatives were scaled separately from Republicans.

GROUP 0 (CONSERVATIVE DEMOCRATS AND
JOHNSON CONSERVATIVES)

Buckalew, Pennsylvania
Cowan, Pennsylvania (Johnson Conservative)
Davis, Kentucky
James Guthrie, Kentucky

Nesmith, Oregon
Riddle, Delaware
Saulsbury, Delaware
John P. Stockton, New Jersey

—Amendment to the Freedmen's Bureau bill to strike the authorization to buy schools and asylums for blacks, amendment to the Civil Rights bill adding a proviso that it does not authorize black suffrage, resolution authorizing West Virginia to annex two Virginia counties, amendment to the Freedmen's Bureau bill to set aside 3,000,000 acres of public land for blacks.

GROUP 1 (MODERATE DEMOCRATS)

Hendricks, Indiana   Johnson, Maryland   McDougall, California

—Amendments to the Freedmen's Bureau bill, vote to admit Colorado to statehood on reconsideration, amendment to the disqualification section of the constitutional amendment to apply it only to rebels holding office at the time of the rebellion, passage of the citizenship section of the Civil Rights bill, confirmation of V.L. Findlay.

GROUP 2 (JOHNSON CONSERVATIVES)

Dixon, Connecticut   Doolittle, Wisconsin

—Amendment to section 2 of the constitutional amendment to base representation on the number of voters, amendment to the Habeas Corpus Amendment of 1866 applying the law only to states where courts were closed and martial law proclaimed, admission of Colorado on reconsideration, amendment that constitutional amendments be ratified only by legislatures elected in 1866 or after rather than those currently sitting, concurrent resolution creating the Joint Committee on Reconstruction.

GROUP 3 (JOHNSON CONSERVATIVE)

Daniel S. Norton, Minnesota

—Seating of Arkansas Senators-elect, concurrent resolution on southern admission, constitutional amendment to disqualify from officeholding rebels who held U.S. office within ten years of the rebellion, Fourteenth Amendment, resolution asking the secretary of the treasury to report if he has hired agents unable to take the test oath, Freedmen's Bureau bill, Civil Rights bill, confirmations.

GROUP 4 (EXTREME CONSERVATIVE REPUBLICANS)

Van Winkle, West Virginia   Stewart, Nevada
Lane, Kansas   Willey, West Virginia
Morgan, New York

—Resolutions on seating southern representatives, seating the Arkansas delegation, Freedmen's Bureau bill veto, confirmation of F.P. Blair as the collector of internal revenue in Missouri, first vote on the tenure of office amendment to the Post Office Appropriations bill, confirmation of V.L. Findlay.

GROUP 5 (CONSERVATIVE REPUBLICANS)

Anthony, Rhode Island   Henderson, Missouri
Foster, Connecticut   Luke P. Poland, Vermont
Harris, New York   *George F. Edmunds, Vermont*

—Seating of New Jersey's Senator-elect Stockton.

GROUP 6 (CONSERVATIVE CENTRIST REPUBLICANS)

Fessenden, Maine   *Conness, California*
Sherman, Ohio   *Kirkwood, Iowa*
George H. Williams, Oregon

—Reconsideration of the tenure of office amendment to the Post Office Appropriations bill, admission of Tennessee's Senator Patterson with an unmodified oath.

GROUP 7 (RADICAL CENTRIST REPUBLICANS)

Clark, New Hampshire
Aaron H. Cragin, New Hampshire
John A.J. Creswell, Maryland
Grimes, Iowa
Howard, Michigan

Lane, Indiana
Morrill, Maine
Nye, Neveda
Ramsey, Minnesota
Sprague, Rhode Island

—Black suffrage amendments to the constitutional amendment on apportionment, confirmation of Green Clay Smith as governor of Montana.

GROUP 8 (RADICAL REPUBLICANS)

Chandler, Michigan
Howe, Wisconsin

Pomeroy, Kansas
Yates, Illinois

—Tennessee admission, black suffrage in Tennessee, admission of Tennessee Senator Patterson with a modified oath.

GROUP 9 (EXTREME RADICAL REPUBLICANS)

Brown, Missouri   Sumner, Massachusetts   Wade, Ohio

NONSCALAR: Trumbull, Illinois; Wilson, Massachusetts (Republicans).

NOT VOTING: Foot, Vermont; Joseph S. Fowler, Tennessee; Edmund G. Ross, Kansas (Republicans). Wright, New Jersey (Democrat).

For a list of the roll calls upon which this list is based, see Appendix VII.

LIST 11

RADICALISM IN THE HOUSE OF REPRESENTATIVES
39 CONGRESS, SECOND SESSION

GROUP 0 (DEMOCRATS AND JOHNSON CONSERVATIVES)

Ancona, Pennsylvania
Bergen, New York
William B. Campbell, Tennessee
Chanler, New York
Edmund Cooper, Tennessee (Johnson
    Conservative)
Dawson, Pennsylvania
Denison, Pennsylvania
Eldridge, Wisconsin
Finck, Ohio
Glossbrenner, Pennsylvania
Goodyear, New York
Hale, New York (Johnson Conserva-
    tive)
Harding, Kentucky
Harris, Maryland
Elijah Hise, Kentucky

Hogan, Missouri
Hubbell, New York
J.M. Humphrey, New York
Hunter, New York
Johnson, Pennsylvania
Jones, New York
Kerr, Indiana
Latham, West Virginia (Johnson Con-
    servative)
LeBlond, Ohio
Leftwich, Tennessee (Johnson Con-
    servative)
McCullough, Maryland
Marshall, Illinois
Niblack, Indiana
Nicholson, Delaware
Noell, Missouri

Phelps, Maryland (Johnson Conservative)
Radford, New York
Randall, Pennsylvania
Ritter, Kentucky
Rogers, New Jersey
Ross, Illinois
Rousseau, Kentucky
Shanklin, Kentucky
Sitgreaves, New Jersey
Stillwell, Indiana (Johnson Conservative)
Strouse, Pennsylvania
Taber, New York
Taylor, Tennessee (Johnson Conservative)
Taylor, New York
Thornton, Illinois
Trimble, Kentucky
Andrew H. Ward, Kentucky
Winfield, New York
Wright, New Jersey
Isaac R. Hawkins, Tennessee (Johnson Conservative)

—Passage of the Tenure of Office act, Indemnity act, repeal of presidential amnesty power conferred by the Confiscation act, resolutions relative to the Thirteenth and Fourteenth Amendments, bill to suspend payment for slaves taken into the army, passage of the Reconstruction act, motion to table the impeachment resolution, tabling of the resolution requiring the Judiciary committee to investigate Johnson.

GROUP 1 (CONSERVATIVE REPUBLICANS)

Kuykendall, Illinois (Johnson Conservative)
Whaley, West Virginia
Ashley, Nevada
Benjamin, Missouri
Bingham, Ohio
Darling, New York
Dawes, Massachusetts
Defrees, Indiana
Dodge, New York
Farnsworth, Illinois
Hubbard, West Virginia
Hubbell, Ohio
Jenckes, Rhode Island
Laflin, New York
Lawrence, Pennsylvania
Marvin, New York
Plants, Ohio
Pomeroy, New York
Randall, Kentucky
Raymond, New York
Rice, Maine
Schenck, Ohio
Thayer, Pennsylvania
Deming, Connecticut
Washburn, Massachusetts

—Louisiana Reconstruction, Shellabarger amendments to the Reconstruction bill, amendment to exclude department heads from Tenure of Office act coverage.

GROUP 2 (CONSERVATIVE CENTRIST REPUBLICANS)

Anderson, Missouri
Baldwin, Massachusetts
Banks, Massachusetts
Blaine, Maine
Blow, Missouri
Buckland, Ohio
Bundy, Ohio
Delano, Ohio
Ferry, Michigan
Garfield, Ohio
Griswold, New York
Hill, Indiana
Kelso, Missouri
Ketcham, New York
McIndoe, Wisconsin
McRuer, California
Patterson, New Hampshire
Rice, Massachusetts
Woodbridge, Vermont
Allison, Iowa
Ames, Massachusetts
Bidwell, California
Dumont, Indiana
Henderson, Oregon
Hooper, Massachusetts
Morrill, Vermont

—Amendment to limit the committee to investigate the Johnson-Conservative Republican negotiations on the Reconstruction bill to one member, motion to commit the Reconstruction bill to the Judiciary committee with instructions to add the "Blaine amendment," motion to refer the Reconstruction bill to the Reconstruction committee.

GROUP 3 (RADICAL CENTRIST REPUBLICANS)

Clarke, Ohio
Cook, Illinois
Dixon, Rhode Island
Eggleston, Ohio
Lawrence, Ohio
McClurg, Missouri
Miller, Pennsylvania

Moorhead, Pennsylvania
Price, Iowa
J.L. Thomas, Maryland
Hart, New York
J. Humphrey, New York
Welker, Ohio
Wilson, Iowa

—Main question on committing the Reconstruction bill to the Judiciary committee with instructions to add the Blaine amendment.

GROUP 4 (STEVENS RADICAL REPUBLICANS)

Alley, Massachusetts
Samuel M. Arnell, Tennessee
Barker, Pennsylvania
Beaman, Michigan
Cullom, Illinois
Driggs, Michigan
Eckley, Ohio
Eliot, Massachusetts
Grinnell, Iowa
Harding, Illinois
Higby, California
Holmes, New York
Hubbard, Connecticut
Hulburd, New York
Julian, Indiana
Kelley, Pennsylvania
Koontz, Pennsylvania
Loan, Missouri
Longyear, Michigan
Lynch, Maine

Marston, New Hampshire
Moulton, Illinois
Myers, Pennsylvania
Newell, New Jersey
O'Neill, Pennsylvania
Orth, Indiana
Perham, Maine
Rollins, New Hampshire
Scofield, Pennsylvania
Shellabarger, Ohio
Starr, New Jersey
Stevens, Pennsylvania
Stokes, Tennessee
Upson, Michigan
Van Aernam, New York
Van Horn, New York
Van Horn, Missouri
Ward, New York
Wilson, Pennsylvania

—Concurring in the Senate amendments to the Reconstruction bill.

GROUP 5 (RADICALS VOTING AGAINST STEVENS TO OPEN THE MILITARY GOVERNMENT BILL TO RADICAL AMENDMENT)

NOTE: This group is based on a subscale of two votes on concurring in the Senate amendments to the Reconstruction bill. On these votes radicals joined Democrats and Johnson Conservatives to vote against concurrence.

Ashley, Ohio
Baxter, Vermont
Boutwell, Massachusetts
Bromwell, Illinois
Broomall, Pennsylvania
Clarke, Kansas
Cobb, Wisconsin
Donnelly, Minnesota
Hayes, Ohio
Hotchkiss, New York

Hubbard, New York
Mercur, Pennsylvania
Paine, Wisconsin
Pike, Maine
Sawyer, Wisconsin
Sloan, Wisconsin
Trowbridge, Michigan
Wentworth, Illinois
Williams, Pennsylvania
Windom, Minnesota

NONSCALAR: Baker, Illinois; Davis, New York; Farquhar, Indiana; Ingersoll, Illinois; Kasson, Iowa; Maynard, Tennessee; McKee, Kentucky; Morris, New York; Spalding, Ohio; F. Thomas, Maryland; Warner, Connecticut (Republicans).

NOT VOTING: Brandegee, Connecticut; Conkling, New York; Culver, Pennsylvania; Hubbard, Iowa; Washburne, Illinois; Washburn, Indiana (Republicans).

For a list of the roll calls upon which this list is based, see Appendix VIII.

LIST 12

RADICALISM IN THE SENATE
39 CONGRESS, SECOND SESSION

NOTE: Democrats and Johnson Conservatives were ranked on a different scale than Republicans, as their voting patterns did not correspond to those of the Republicans.

GROUP 0 (DEMOCRATS AND JOHNSON CONSERVATIVES)

Buckalew, Pennsylvania
Cowan, Pennsylvania (Johnson Conservative)
Davis, Kentucky
Dixon, Connecticut (Johnson Conservative)
Doolittle, Wisconsin (Johnson Conservative)
Hendricks, Indiana
Johnson, Maryland
McDougall, California
Nesmith, Oregon
Norton, Minnesota (Johnson Conservative)
Patterson, Tennessee
Riddle, Delaware
Saulsbury, Delaware

GROUP 1 (EXTREME CONSERVATIVE REPUBLICANS)

Willey, West Virginia

—Repeal of presidential amnesty power conferred by the Confiscation act, resolution to set a meeting time for the 40 Congress, amendments to and passage of the Reconstruction bill, amendment to the Southern Claims bill to put the burden of proving loyalty on the claimant, amendment to the Pension bill to eliminate the section removing agents appointed after a specified date, Indemnity bill, Tenure of Office bill, bill regulating the reorganization of the House, amendment to the Army Appropriations bill to strike the section requiring the transmission of all orders through the General of the Army, bill extending suffrage to blacks in the territories, passage of the D.C. Suffrage bill.

GROUP 2 (CONSERVATIVE REPUBLICANS)

Fessenden, Maine
Foster, Connecticut
Henderson, Missouri
Sherman, Ohio
Van Winkle, West Virginia
Alexander G. Cattell, New Jersey
Edmunds, Vermont
Harris, New York

—Amendment to the Army Appropriations bill to disband the militias of the southern states.

GROUP 3 (CONSERVATIVE CENTRISTS)

Grimes, Iowa
Morgan, New York
Frederick T. Frelinghuysen, New Jersey
Poland, Vermont

—Amendment to the Pension bill to remove all agents appointed after July 1, 1865.

GROUP 4 (CENTRISTS)

Anthony, Rhode Island
Conness, California
Ross, Kansas

Williams, Oregon
Stewart, Nevada

—Amendment to the Consular and Diplomatic Appropriations bill to delegate the duties of the ambassador to Portugal to the ambassador to Spain, concurrence in the House amendments to the Tenure of Office bill, amendment to the Naval Appropriations bill to strike the section requiring Senate confirmation of new work supervisors, amendment to the Tenure of Office bill to bring department heads under its provisions.

GROUP 5 (RADICAL CENTRISTS)

Brown, Missouri
Cragin, New Hampshire
George G. Fogg, New Hampshire
Howe, Wisconsin
Kirkwood, Iowa

Morrill, Maine
Ramsey, Minnesota
Sprague, Rhode Island
Creswell, Maryland
Lane, Indiana

—Amendments to the Civil Appropriations bills to pay tax collectors in the South although they took office without taking the test oath, amendment to the Consular and Diplomatic Appropriations bill to give the duties of ambassador to Portugal to the ambassador to Spain, amendment to the Bankruptcy bill to limit its benefits to those who can take the test oath, confirmation of John A. Dix as ambassador to France, confirmation of Hugh Ewing as ambassador to Holland, amendment to the Reconstruction bill declaring that the Fourteenth Amendment will become part of the Constitution when ratified by three-fourths of the states represented in Congress.

GROUP 6 (RADICALS)

Fowler, Tennessee
Howard, Michigan
Nye, Nevada
Pomeroy, Kansas
Sumner, Massachusetts

Wade, Ohio
Trumbull, Illinois
Wilson, Massachusetts
Yates, Illinois

—Amendment to the Pension bill to remove agents named after October 1865.

GROUP 7 (ULTRA RADICALS)

Chandler, Michigan

NOT VOTING: Guthrie, Kentucky (Democrat).

For a list of the roll calls upon which this list is based, see Appendix VII.

LIST 13

RADICALISM IN THE HOUSE OF REPRESENTATIVES
40 CONGRESS, FIRST SESSION

GROUP 0 (DEMOCRATS AND JOHNSON CONSERVATIVES)

George M. Adams, Kentucky
Stevenson Archer, Maryland
Demas Barnes, New York
Boyer, Pennsylvania
Brooks, New York
Albert G. Burr, Illinois
Chanler, New York
Denison, Pennsylvania
Eldridge, Wisconsin
John Fox, New York
James L. Getz, Pennsylvania
Glossbrenner, Pennsylvania
Charles Haight, New Jersey
Holman, Indiana
Julius Hotchkiss, Connecticut
Humphrey, New York
Kerr, Indiana
McCullough, Maryland
Marshall, Illinois

George W. Morgan, Ohio
John Morrissey, New York
William Mungen, Ohio
Niblack, Indiana
Nicholson, Delaware
Noell, Missouri
Phelps, Maryland (Johnson Conservative)
Pruyn, New York
Randall, Pennsylvania
William E. Robinson, New York
Ross, Illinois
Sitgreaves, New Jersey
Frederick Stone, Maryland
Taber, New York
Daniel M. Van Auken, Pennsylvania
Philadelph Van Trump, Ohio
Fernando Wood, New York

—Resolution granting arms to Tennessee militia, resolution of thanks to Generals Sickles and Sheridan, Supplementary Reconstruction bill, second Supplementary Reconstruction bill, resolution instructing the Judiciary committee to report a Reconstruction bill, Reconstruction Appropriations bill, bill to reannex Alexandria to the District of Columbia, resolution authorizing the Judiciary committee to investigate articles of impeachment over the recess.

GROUP 1 (CONSERVATIVE REPUBLICANS)

Thomas E. Stewart, New York
Baldwin, Massachusetts
Beaman, Michigan
Bingham, Ohio
Blair, Michigan
Buckland, Ohio
Thomas Cornell, New York
Orange Ferriss, New York
Griswold, New York
Hubbard, West Virginia
Ketcham, New York

Laflin, New York
Marvin, New York
Luke P. Poland, Vermont
Spalding, Ohio
Ferry, Michigan
Bethuel M. Kitchen, West Virginia
Rufus Mallory, Oregon
Dennis McCarthy, New York
Worthington C. Smith, Vermont
Ginery Twichell, Massachusetts

—Resolution authorizing the investigation of the treatment of Union prisoners by the Confederates, resolution asking the Judiciary committee to report on impeachment immediately after the recess of Congress, compromise adjournment resolution.

GROUP 2 (CONSERVATIVE CENTRISTS)

Blaine, Maine
John C. Churchill, New York

Grenville M. Dodge, Iowa
George A. Halsey, New Jersey

Hayes, Ohio
John Hill, New Jersey
Koontz, Pennsylvania
William S. Lincoln, New York
William Loughridge, Iowa
Perham, Maine

William H. Robertson, New York
Thomas, Maryland
Wilson, Iowa
Hubbard, Iowa
John A. Peters, Maine

—Tabling of the resolution against adjournment over the summer, concurring in the Senate version of the adjournment resolution, adjournment to May.

GROUP 3 (CENTRISTS)

Ames, Massachusetts
Baker, Illinois
Clarke, Ohio
Hulburd, New York
Carman A. Newcomb, Missouri
Scofield, Pennsylvania

Cadwallader C. Washburn, Wisconsin
Washburn, Indiana
John T. Wilson, Ohio
Allison, Iowa
Dixon, Rhode Island
Sawyer, Wisconsin

—Tabling of the adjournment resolution.

GROUP 4 (RADICAL CENTRISTS)

Anderson, Missouri
Ashley, Ohio
Boutwell, Massachusetts
Driggs, Michigan
Jacob H. Ela, New Hampshire
William C. Fields, New York
Garfield, Ohio
Benjamin F. Hopkins, Wisconsin
Morton C. Hunter, Indiana
Ingersoll, Illinois
Lawrence, Ohio
Myers, Pennsylvania
Plants, Ohio
John P.C. Shanks, Indiana
Henry H. Starkweather, Connecticut

John Taffe, Nebraska
Caleb N. Taylor, Pennsylvania
Van Horn, New York
Welker, Ohio
Wilson, Pennsylvania
Windom, Minnesota
Ashley, Nevada
Banks, Massachusetts
Jacob Benton, New Hampshire
Henry L. Cake, Pennsylvania
Eckley, Ohio
Farnsworth, Illinois
Hooper, Massachusetts
Daniel J. Morrell, Pennsylvania

—Resolution directing the Judiciary committee to report on impeachment during the first session of the 40 Congress.

GROUP 5 (PRO-IMPEACHMENT RADICALS)

Broomall, Pennsylvania
Benjamin F. Butler, Massachusetts
Clarke, Kansas
Cobb, Wisconsin
John Coburn, Indiana
Cook, Illinois
John Covode, Pennsylvania
Cullom, Illinois
Donnelly, Minnesota
Darwin A. Finney, Pennsylvania
Joseph J. Gravely, Missouri
Norman B. Judd, Illinois
Kelley, Pennsylvania
John A. Logan, Illinois
Lynch, Maine

McClurg, Missouri
Miller, Pennsylvania
Loan, Missouri
O'Neill, Pennsylvania
Orth, Indiana
Daniel H. Polsley, West Virginia
Schenck, Ohio
Shellabarger, Ohio
Stevens, Pennsylvania
Upson, Michigan
Van Aernam, New York
Van Horn, Missouri
Ward, New York
Williams, Pennsylvania
William Williams, Indiana

NONSCALAR: Benjamin, Missouri; Eggleston, Ohio; Delano, Ohio; Cornelius S. Hamilton, Ohio; Jenckes, Rhode Island; Julian, Indiana; Mercur, Pennsylvania; William Moore, New Jersey; Paine, Wisconsin; William A. Pile, Missouri; Woodbridge, Vermont (Republicans).

NOT VOTING: Bromwell, Illinois; Dawes, Massachusetts; Eliot, Massachusetts; Harding, Illinois; William H. Kelsey, New York; Lawrence, Pennsylvania; Moorhead, Pennsylvania, Pike, Maine; Pomeroy, New York; Price, Iowa; Green B. Raum, Illinois; Lewis Selye, New York; Aaron F. Stevens, New Hampshire; Trowbridge, Michigan; Charles H. Van Wyck, New York; Washburn, Massachusetts (Republicans). William H. Barnum, Connecticut; Hubbard, Connecticut (Democrats).

For a list of the roll calls upon which this list is based, see Appendix VIII.

LIST 14

RADICALISM IN THE SENATE
40 CONGRESS, FIRST SESSION

MAIN SCALE AND DEMOCRATIC SCALE

NOTE: Democrats and Johnson Conservatives were scaled separately from Republicans.

GROUP 0 (DEMOCRATS AND JOHNSON CONSERVATIVES OPPOSED TO ANY COMPROMISE ON RECONSTRUCTION)

James A. Bayard, Delaware
Buckalew, Pennsylvania
Davis, Kentucky
Dixon, Connecticut (Johnson Conservative)

Doolittle, Wisconsin (Johnson Conservative)
Hendricks, Indiana
Norton, Minnesota (Johnson Conservative)
Patterson, Tennessee

—Arming the Tennessee militia, bill to pay contingent expenses of the Reconstruction act, passage of the Supplementary Reconstruction and the second Supplementary Reconstruction bills.

GROUP 1 (DEMOCRAT VOTING FOR THE RECONSTRUCTION BILLS)

Johnson, Maryland

—Arming the Tennessee militia, payment of contingent expenses of the Reconstruction act, bill to stop payment for slaves taken into the armed forces, confirmation of F.P. Blair as ambassador to Austria, confirmation of John P. Stockton as ambassador to Austria, bill to void officeholding restrictions against black residents of the District of Columbia.

GROUP 2 (CONSERVATIVE REPUBLICANS)

Edmunds, Vermont
Trumbull, Illinois
Van Winkle, West Virginia
Willey, West Virginia

Roscoe Conkling, New York
Conness, California
Henry W. Corbett, Oregon
Morgan, New York

Sherman, Ohio   *Stewart, Nevada*
Sprague, Rhode Island   *Williams, Oregon*

—Amendment to the Supplementary Reconstruction bill to ban racial discrimination in appointments to voter registration boards.

GROUP 3 (CONSERVATIVE REPUBLICANS)

Anthony, Rhode Island   Frelinghuysen, New Jersey
Cattell, New Jersey   *Ramsey, Minnesota*
Fessenden, Maine

—Amendments to the second Supplementary Reconstruction bill to ban racial discrimination in appointments to voter registration boards and requiring boards to explain why names are stricken from voting lists.

GROUP 4 (CONSERVATIVE CENTRIST REPUBLICANS)

Grimes, Iowa   Morrill, Maine
Henderson, Missouri

—Attempts to set a meeting of Congress before December 1867, amendment to the Supplementary Reconstruction bill to require voting by ballot, amendment to require free public schools for all in the South, motion to take up the national equal suffrage bill.

GROUP 5 (RADICAL CENTRIST REPUBLICANS)

Cragin, New Hampshire   Thomas W. Tipton, Nebraska
Justin S. Morrill, Vermont

—Attempts to water down the summer meeting resolution, amendment to the second Supplementary Reconstruction act to declare all southern state offices vacated, taking up the amendment to require free public schools in the South, amendment to make the violation of the Reconstruction act a misdemeanor.

GROUP 6 (RADICAL REPUBLICANS)

Cornelius Cole, California   *Chandler, Michigan*
Simon Cameron, Pennsylvania   *Charles D. Drake, Missouri*
James Harlan, Iowa   *Nye, Nevada*
Ross, Kansas

—Passage of the first adjournment resolution which provides for no summer meeting, resolutions declaring further guarantees are required for Reconstruction.

GROUP 7 (RADICAL REPUBLICANS)

Fowler, Tennessee   John M. Thayer, Nebraska
Howe, Wisconsin   Wade, Ohio
Pomeroy, Kansas   Wilson, Massachusetts
Sumner, Massachusetts   Yates, Illinois

NONSCALAR: Howard, Michigan; Oliver P. Morton, Indiana; James W. Patterson, New Hampshire (Republicans).

NOT VOTING: Guthrie, Kentucky; Riddle, Delaware; Saulsbury, Delaware (Democrats). Orris S. Ferry, Connecticut (Republican).

For a list of the roll calls upon which this list is based, see Appendix VII.

SUBSCALE—DELAY OF RESTORATION

GROUP 0 (REPUBLICANS UNCOMPROMISINGLY
COMMITTED TO SPEEDY RESTORATION)

Conness, California
Cragin, New Hampshire
Ferry, Connecticut
Frelinghuysen, New Jersey
Morton, Indiana
Pomeroy, Kansas
Ramsey, Minnesota

Ross, Kansas
Tipton, Nebraska
Trumbull, Illinois
Van Winkle, West Virginia
Willey, West Virginia
Wilson, Massachusetts
Cattell, New Jersey

—Amendment to the Supplementary Reconstruction bill to require one half of the
registered voters to vote in the election to ratify a new state constitution.

GROUP 1 (REPUBLICANS FAVORING SPEEDY RESTORATION)

Drake, Missouri
Howe, Wisconsin
Sherman, Ohio

Stewart, Nevada
Williams, Oregon

—Amendment to the Supplementary Reconstruction bill to require one half of the
registered voters of each state to vote on whether to hold a constitutional convention, amendment requiring ratification of the state constitutions in elections in which
a majority of registered voters participated, amendment to require three fifths of the
registered voters to vote in ratification elections, amendment to require ratification by
a majority of the "qualified" instead of "registered" voters.

GROUP 2 (REPUBLICANS FAVORING DELAY
IN RESTORATION)

Anthony, Rhode Island
Cameron, Pennsylvania
Chandler, Michigan
Cole, California
Fowler, Tennessee

Henderson, Missouri
Sumner, Massachusetts
Wade, Ohio
Morrill, Vermont

—Amendment to the Supplementary Reconstruction bill to require the southern provisional governments to call for constitutional conventions before they may be held.

GROUP 3 (REPUBLICANS FAVORING DELAY
OF RESTORATION)

Edmunds, Vermont
Fessenden, Maine
Howard, Michigan
Morgan, New York

Morrill, Maine
Nye, Nevada
Patterson, New Hampshire
Thayer, Nebraska

NONSCALAR: Conkling, New York; Corbett, Oregon; Harlan, Iowa (Republicans).

NOT VOTING: Grimes, Iowa; Sprague, Rhode Island (Republicans).

For a list of the roll calls upon which this list is based, see Appendix VII.

LIST 15

RADICALISM IN THE HOUSE OF REPRESENTATIVES
40 CONGRESS, SECOND SESSION

† *Radical Centrists, Radicals, Absentees, and Nonscaling Republicans who voted against impeachment in December 1867.*
†† *Conservatives, Centrists, Radical Centrists, Absentees, and Nonscaling Republicans who voted in favor of impeachment in December 1867.*

NOTE: Democrats were ranked on a different scale than Republicans, as their voting patterns did not correspond to those of the Republicans.

GROUP 0 (DEMOCRATS)

Adams, Kentucky
Archer, Maryland
Samuel B. Axtell, California
Barnes, New York
Barnum, Connecticut
James B. Beck, Kentucky
Boyer, Pennsylvania
Brooks, New York
Burr, Illinois
Samuel F. Cary, Ohio (Independent
    Republican)
Chanler, New York
Eldridge, Wisconsin
Fox, New York
Getz, Pennsylvania
Glossbrenner, Pennsylvania
Jacob S. Golladay, Kentucky
Asa P. Grover, Kentucky
Haight, New Jersey
Holman, Indiana
Hotchkiss, Connecticut
Hubbard, Connecticut
Humphrey, New York
James A. Johnson, California

Thomas L. Jones, Kentucky
Kerr, Indiana
Knott, Kentucky
James R. McCormick, Missouri
McCullough, Maryland
Marshall, Illinois
Morrissey, New York
Mungen, Ohio
Niblack, Indiana
Nicholson, Delaware
Phelps, Maryland (Johnson Conserva-
    tive)
Pruyn, New York
Randall, Pennsylvania
Robinson, New York
Ross, Illinois
Sitgreaves, New Jersey
Stone, Maryland
Taber, New York
Trimble, Kentucky
Van Auken, Pennsylvania
Van Trump, Ohio
Wood, New York

—Resolution that the Fourteenth Amendment is ratified, passage and amendment of the bill setting a quorum for the Supreme Court, tabling of the Freedmen's Bureau Continuation bill, resolution endorsing the congressional Reconstruction policy, resolution condemning the removal of Sheridan and commending Grant, resolution instructing the Reconstruction committee to investigate the expediency of authorizing state conventions to appoint temporary state officers, admission of Alabama representatives, tabling a resolution of thanks to General Hancock, February impeachment resolution, resolution censuring Fernando Wood, resolution to investigate corruption in impeachment, resolution to enlarge the Committee of Managers of Impeachment by adding Democrats.

GROUP 1 (EXTREME CONSERVATIVE REPUBLICANS)

Baker, Illinois
Hawkins, Tennessee

Ingersoll, Illinois
Spalding, Ohio

Stewart, New York
Baldwin, Massachusetts
Ferry, Michigan
Ketcham, New York

Lawrence, Pennsylvania
Marvin, New York
Poland, Vermont
Robertson, New York

—Motion to take up an impeachment resolution in July 1868.

GROUP 2 (CONSERVATIVE REPUBLICANS)

Blair, Michigan
Driggs, Michigan
Garfield, Ohio
†† Hopkins, Wisconsin
Jenckes, Rhode Island
†† Myers, Pennsylvania
†† Orth, Indiana
Pomeroy, New York
Sawyer, Wisconsin
Smith, Vermont
Taylor, Pennsylvania
Washburn, Massachusetts
Washburne, Illinois
Woodbridge, Vermont
Blaine, Maine
Cook, Illinois

Dawes, Massachusetts
Dixon, Rhode Island
Dodge, Iowa
Eggleston, Ohio
Eliot, Massachusetts
Griswold, New York
Halsey, New Jersey
Hooper, Massachusetts
Hubbard, Iowa
Hubbard, West Virginia
Moorhead, Pennsylvania
Starkweather, Connecticut
Van Aernam, New York
Washburn, Wisconsin
Wilson, Iowa
Wilson, Ohio

—Amendment to the Southern Restoration bill to strike Alabama from its provisions.

GROUP 3 (CENTRIST REPUBLICANS)

Ames, Massachusetts
Alexander H. Bailey, New York
Beaman, Michigan
Benjamin, Missouri
Benton, New Hampshire
Buckland, Ohio
Ferriss, New York
Hulburd, New York
Koontz, Pennsylvania
Lincoln, New York

Miller, Pennsylvania
Moore, New Jersey
Peters, Maine
Pike, Maine
Plants, Ohio
Polsley, West Virginia
Upson, Michigan
Van Horn, New York
Washburn, Indiana
Welker, Ohio

(RADICAL CENTRIST REPUBLICANS)

† *Allison, Iowa*
†† *Boutwell, Massachusetts*
†† *Bromwell, Illinois*
†† *Cullom, Illinois*
† *Fields, New York*
   Mallory, Oregon
†† *O'Neill, Pennsylvania*

†† *Paine, Wisconsin*
† *Perham, Maine*
†† *Scofield, Pennsylvania*
†† *Stevens, New Hampshire*
†† *Stevens, Pennsylvania*
†† *Trowbridge, Michigan*
† *Van Wyck, New York*

—December impeachment resolution, amendment to the third Supplementary Reconstruction bill to remove all officers of provisional governments and allow constitutional conventions to replace them.

GROUP 4 (RADICAL REPUBLICANS)

Anderson, Missouri
Broomall, Pennsylvania
Clarke, Ohio

Cobb, Wisconsin
Donnelly, Minnesota
Gravely, Missouri

Hunter, Indiana
Kelley, Pennsylvania
Kelsey, New York
Kitchen, West Virginia
Loughridge, Iowa
Mercur, Pennsylvania
Newcomb, Missouri
David A. Nunn, Tennessee
Raum, Illinois
Schenck, Ohio

Shanks, Indiana
Stokes, Tennessee
Thomas, Maryland
Wilson, Pennsylvania
Windom, Minnesota
Butler, Massachusetts
Churchill, New York
Eckley, Ohio
Ela, New Hampshire
Morrell, Pennsylvania

—Amendment to the Supreme Court Quorum bill to require a unanimous decision to overturn a law of the United States.

GROUP 5 (RADICAL REPUBLICANS)

Arnell, Tennessee
† Ashley, Nevada
Ashley, Ohio
John Beatty, Ohio
Cake, Pennsylvania
Clarke, Kansas
Covode, Pennsylvania
Farnsworth, Illinois
† Hamilton, Ohio
Harding, Illinois
Judd, Illinois
Lawrence, Ohio
Logan, Illinois

Loan, Missouri
Maynard, Tennessee
† McCarthy, New York
McClurg, Missouri
James Mullins, Tennessee
Pile, Missouri
Price, Iowa
Trimble, Tennessee
Van Horn, Missouri
Ward, New York
Williams, Pennsylvania
Williams, Indiana

NONSCALAR: † Bingham, Ohio; †† Coburn, Indiana; †† Higby, California; †† Julian, Indiana; †† Taffe, Nebraska; † Twichell, Massachusetts (Republicans).

NOT VOTING: †Banks, Massachusetts; † Cornell, New York; Delano, Ohio; † Hill, New Jersey; † Laflin, New York; McKee, Kentucky; †† Lynch, Maine; Selye, New York; Shellabarger, Ohio (Republicans).

For a list of the roll calls upon which this list is based, see Appendix VIII.

LIST 16

SENATORS AND IMPEACHMENT
40 CONGRESS, SECOND SESSION

MAIN SCALE—GENERAL IMPEACHMENT ISSUES

GROUP 0 (DEMOCRATS AND JOHNSON CONSERVATIVES)

Bayard, Delaware
Davis, Kentucky
Dixon, Connecticut (Johnson Conservative)
Doolittle, Wisconsin (Johnson Conservative)
Thomas C. McCreery, Kentucky
Patterson, Tennessee

Saulsbury, Delaware
George Vickers, Maryland
Buckalew, Pennsylvania
Hendricks, Indiana
Johnson, Maryland
Norton, Minnesota (Johnson Conservative)

—Motion declaring impeachment illegal without participation of senators from southern states, motion to adjourn *sine die* May 16, admissibility of hearsay evidence showing Johnson hoped only to test the constitutionality of the Tenure of Office act, motion to deny a defense request for delay, admissibility of report of Johnson speeches of 1866, motion to delay vote on articles, motion to adjourn *sine die* May 26.

GROUP 1 (REPUBLICANS VOTING AGAINST CONVICTION AND/OR TO SUSTAIN THE DEFENSE POSITION ON MOST QUESTIONS)

Fowler,, Tennessee   Henderson, Missouri
Ross, Kansas   Trumbull, Illinois
Fessenden, Maine   Van Winkle, West Virginia
Grimes, Iowa   *Anthony, Rhode Island*

—Motion to postpone vote on conviction, admissibility of evidence that Johnson hoped only to test the constitutionality of the Tenure of Office act, votes on the articles, motion to vote first on Article XI, motion to extend the hours of trial, motion to adjourn over the weekend, admissibility of testimony regarding cabinet discussions of the Tenure of Office act, admissibility of testimony that Johnson attempted to bring the Tenure of Office act before the courts, votes on defense requests for delays, admissibility of evidence of Johnson's intentions as expressed after he attempted to remove Stanton.

GROUP 2 (REPUBLICANS APPARENTLY UNCOMMITTED TO CONVICTION, FAVORING DELAY, AND NOT STRONGLY COMMITTED TO CONVICTION BY THE END OF THE TRIAL)

Edmunds, Vermont   Patterson, New Hampshire
Willey, West Virginia   Sherman, Ohio
Frelinghuysen, New Jersey   Sprague, Rhode Island
Morrill, Vermont   *Cole, California*
Morton, Indiana

—Motion to proceed with Article XI first, motion to adjourn after failure to convict on Article XI, admissibility of evidence of Johnson's intentions as expressed after his attempt to remove Stanton, motion to require the defense to respond to impeachment articles without delay, admissibility of General Sherman's evidence.

GROUP 3 (REPUBLICANS APPARENTLY UNCOMMITTED TO CONVICTION AS THE TRIAL BEGAN BUT OPPOSING DELAY AND COMMITTED TO CONVICTION BY ITS END)

Cattell, New Jersey   Howe, Wisconsin
Corbett, Oregon   Morrill, Maine
Cragin, New Hampshire   *Williams, Oregon*
Ferry, Connecticut   *Yates, Illinois*

—Motion to take up a resolution to investigate charges of intimidation of senators, motion to extend hours of trial, admissibility of evidence that Johnson sought to get a court test of the Tenure of Office act, motion to strip the chief justice of power to decide legal questions and to declare him not a member of the court of impeachment, motions to speed voting on articles.

GROUP 4 (REPUBLICANS STRONGLY COMMITTED TO CONVICTION)

Chandler, Michigan
Morgan, New York
Pomeroy, Kansas

Tipton, Nebraska
Wilson, Massachusetts

—Censure of defense counsel for impugning the Senate, admissibility of evidence of Johnson's intentions as expressed after he attempted to remove Stanton, motions to eliminate impeachment rules authorizing senators to file written opinions.

GROUP 5 (REPUBLICANS STRONGLY COMMITTED TO CONVICTION)

Cameron, Pennsylvania
Conkling, New York
Conness, California
Drake, Missouri
Harlan, Iowa
Howard, Massachusetts

Nye, Nevada
Ramsey, Minnesota
Stewart, Nevada
Sumner, Massachusetts
Thayer, Nebraska

NOT VOTING: Wade, Ohio (Republican).

For a list of the roll calls upon which this list is based, see Appendix IX.

SUBSCALE—DIVISIVE VOTES, PRIMARILY EARLY IN THE TRIAL

GROUP 0 (DEMOCRATS, JOHNSON CONSERVATIVES, AND REPUBLICANS NOT STRONGLY COMMITTED TO CONVICTION)

Anthony, Rhode Island (Republican)
Bayard, Delaware (Democrat)
Buckalew, Pennsylvania (Democrat)
Davis, Kentucky (Democrat)
Dixon, Connecticut (Johnson Conservative)
Doolittle, Wisconsin (Johnson Conservative)
Edmunds, Vermont (Republican)
Fessenden, Maine (Republican)
Fowler, Tennessee (Republican)
Frelinghuysen, New Jersey (Republican)
Grimes, Iowa (Republican)
Henderson, Missouri (Republican)
Hendricks, Indiana (Democrat)

Johnson, Maryland (Democrat)
McCreery, Kentucky (Democrat)
Norton, Minnesota (Johnson Conservative)
Patterson, Tennessee (Democrat)
Ross, Kansas (Republican)
Saulsbury, Delaware (Democrat)
Sherman, Ohio (Republican)
Sprague, Rhode Island (Republican)
Trumbull, Illinois (Republican)
Van Winkle, West Virginia (Republican)
Vickers, Maryland (Democrat)
Willey, West Virginia (Republican)
Williams, Oregon (Republican)

—Admissibility of General Sherman's testimony that Johnson intended only to test the Tenure of Office act's constitutionality, adjournment over the weekend, admissibility of testimony that Johnson illegally planned to gain control of the Treasury, motion to deny the chief justice's right to cast deciding votes in case of ties, motion to vote on Article XI by clause.

GROUP 1 (REPUBLICANS RELATIVELY COMMITTED TO CONVICTION)

Cattell, New Jersey
Conness, California
Corbett, Oregon

Cragin, New Hampshire
Drake, Missouri
Ferry, Connecticut

Howard, Michigan
Howe, Wisconsin
Morrill, Vermont
Morton, Indiana

Nye, Nevada
Patterson, New Hampshire
Wilson, Massachusetts

—Motion to lengthen the hours of the trial.

GROUP 2 (REPUBLICANS COMMITTED TO SPEEDY TRIAL AND CONVICTION)

Harlan, Iowa
Morgan, New York
Morrill, Maine

Ramsey, Minnesota
Tipton, Nebraska
Yates, Illinois

—Adjournment to allow the defense to prepare for trial.

GROUP 3 (REPUBLICANS COMMITTED TO SPEEDY TRIAL AND CONVICTION)

Cameron, Pennsylvania
Chandler, Michigan
Cole, California
Conkling, New York

Pomeroy, Kansas
Stewart, Nevada
Sumner, Massachusetts
Thayer, Nebraska

NOT VOTING: Wade, Ohio (Republican).

For a list of the roll calls upon which this list is based, see Appendix IX.

LIST 17

RADICALISM IN THE SENATE
40 CONGRESS, SECOND SESSION

GROUP 0 (DEMOCRATS, JOHNSON CONSERVATIVES, AND EXTREMELY CONSERVATIVE REPUBLICANS)

Bayard, Delaware
Buckalew, Pennsylvania
Davis, Kentucky
Dixon, Connecticut (Johnson
    Conservative
Doolittle, Wisconsin (Johnson
    Conservative)
Guthrie, Kentucky
Hendricks, Indiana

Johnson, Maryland
McCreery, Kentucky
Norton, Minnesota (Johnson
    Conservative)
Patterson, Tennessee
Saulsbury, Delaware
Vickers, Maryland
William P. Whyte, Maryland
Fowler, Tennessee (Republican)

—Arkansas Restoration bill passage, amendment to a disability removal bill to remove disabilities of all southerners, taking up the Freedmen's Bureau Continuation bill, passage of the Southern Restoration bill, passage of the second Supplementary Reconstruction bill, seating of Florida senator, Freedmen's Bureau Discontinuance bill, passage of the resolution counting electoral votes, removal of Alabama's Governor R.M. Patton's disabilities, resolution of thanks to Stanton.

GROUP 1 (CONSERVATIVE REPUBLICANS)

Anthony, Rhode Island	Van Winkle, West Virginia
Ferry, 'Connecticut	Willey, West Virginia
Patterson, New Hampshire	*William Pitt Kellogg, Louisiana*
Ross, Kansas	

—Credentials of Florida senators, amendments to the Arkansas Restoration bill to restore Arkansas without imposing fundamental conditions.

GROUP 2 (CONSERVATIVE CENTRIST REPUBLICANS)

Conkling, New York	Henderson, Missouri
Corbett, Oregon	Morton, Indiana
Drake, Missouri	Trumbull, Illinois
Fessenden, Maine	Williams, Oregon

—First amendment to the Arkansas Restoration bill to admit Arkansas without imposing fundamental conditions.

GROUP 3 (RADICAL CENTRIST REPUBLICANS)

Chandler, Michigan	Ramsey, Minnesota
Cole, California	Sherman, Ohio
Cragin, New Hampshire	Sprague, Rhode Island
Harlan, Iowa	*Cattell, New Jersey*
Morgan, New York	*Morrill, Maine*
Morrill, Vermont	*Wilson, Massachusetts*

—Motion to read the credentials of representatives both of the new Arkansas government and of the old Johnson government, motion to give the secretary of the treasury $1,000,000 to settle confiscation cases at his discretion.

GROUP 4 (RADICAL REPUBLICANS)

Yates, Illinois	*Pomeroy, Kansas*
Conness, California	*Stewart, Nevada*
Howe, Wisconsin	*Sumner, Massachusetts*
Nye, Nevada	*Tipton, Nebraska*

—Amendment to the Tenure of Office act to remove the secretary of state's authority to send department agents abroad at discretion, motion to omit the president's message from the documents to be printed.

GROUP 5 (RADICAL REPUBLICANS)

Cameron, Pennsylvania	Thayer, Nebraska
Howard, Michigan	Wade, Ohio

NONSCALAR: Edmunds, Vermont; Frelinghuysen, New Jersey (Republicans).

NOT VOTING: Joseph C. Abbott, North Carolina; Grimes, Iowa; John S. Harris, Louisiana; Alexander McDonald, Arkansas; Thomas W. Osborne, Florida; John Pool, North Carolina; Benjamin F. Rice, Arkansas; Thomas J. Robertson, South Carolina; Frederick A. Sawyer, South Carolina; George E. Spencer, Alabama; Willard Warner, Alabama; Adonijah S. Welch, Florida (Republicans).

For a list of the roll calls upon which this list is based, see Appendix VII.

LIST 18

REPUBLICANS AND "FUNDAMENTAL CONDITIONS" FOR SOUTHERN READMISSION
40 CONGRESS, SECOND SESSION

REPUBLICAN SENATORS VOTING FOR FUNDAMENTAL
CONDITIONS THROUGHOUT THE SESSION

Cameron, Pennsylvania	Morton, Indiana
Cattell, New Jersey	Nye, Nevada
Chandler, Michigan	Pomeroy, Kansas
Cole, California	Ramsey, Minnesota
Cragin, New Hampshire	Sherman, Ohio
Edmunds, Vermont	Sprague, Rhode Island
Harlan, Iowa	Stewart, Nevada
Howard, Michigan	Thayer, Nebraska
Howe, Wisconsin	Tipton, Nebraska
Morgan, New York	Wade, Ohio
Morrill, Vermont	Wilson, Massachusetts
Morrill, Maine	Yates, Illinois

REPUBLICAN SENATORS VOTING AGAINST
FUNDAMENTAL CONDITIONS

Anthony, Rhode Island	Henderson, Missouri
Conkling, New York	Patterson, New Hampshire
Corbett, Oregon	Ross, Kansas
Drake, Missouri*	Trumbull, Illinois
Ferry, Connecticut	Van Winkle, West Virginia
Fessenden, Maine	Willey, West Virginia
Fowler, Tennessee	Williams, Oregon
Frelinghuysen, New Jersey	

* Drake voted against the fundamental conditions as embodied in the House bill in an effort to add his own.

NOT VOTING: Conness, California; Grimes, Iowa.

This chart is based on roll calls found in the *Congressional Globe,* 40 Cong., 2 Sess., 2701–2702 (May 30, 1868), 2749–2750 (June 1, 1868).

LIST 19

RADICALISM IN THE HOUSE OF REPRESENTATIVES
40 CONGRESS, THIRD SESSION

GROUP 0 (DEMOCRATES AND EXTREME
CONSERVATIVE REPUBLICANS)

Adams, Kentucky	Axtell, California
Archer, Maryland	Baker, Illinois (Republican)

Barnes, New York
Barnum, Connecticut
Beck, Kentucky
Brooks, New York
Burr, Illinois
Cary, Ohio (Independent Republican)
Chanler, New York
Eldridge, Wisconsin
Fox, New York
Getz, Pennsylvania
Glossbrenner, Pennsylvania
Golladay, Kentucky
Grover, Kentucky
Haight, New Jersey
Hawkins, Tennessee (Republican)
Holman, Indiana
Hotchkiss, Connecticut
Hubbard, Connecticut
Humphrey, New York
Johnson, California
Jones, Kentucky
Kerr, Indiana
Knott, Kentucky
McCormick, Missouri

McCullough, Maryland
Marshall, Illinois
Morrissey, New York
Mungen, Ohio
Niblack, Indiana
Nicholson, Delaware
Phelps, Maryland (Johnson Conservative)
Pruyn, New York
Randall, Pennsylvania
Robinson, New York
Ross, Illinois
Sitgreaves, New Jersey
Stone, Maryland
Taber, New York
Nelson Tift, Georgia
Trimble, Kentucky
Van Auken, Pennsylvania
Van Trump, Ohio
Wood, New York
George W. Woodward, Pennsylvania
Pierce M.B. Young, Georgia
Spalding, Ohio (Republican)

—Passage of the Fifteenth Amendment, resolution authorizing the Reconstruction committee to investigate whether further Reconstruction legislation is necessary with respect to Georgia, tabling of the president's message.

GROUP 1 (CONSERVATIVE REPUBLICANS)

Beaman, Michigan
Beatty, Ohio
Bingham, Ohio
Nathaniel Boyden, North Carolina
Farnsworth, Illinois
Gravely, Missouri
Hopkins, Wisconsin
Hubbard, West Virginia
Jenckes, Rhode Island
Ketcham, New York
Kitchen, West Virginia
Koontz, Pennsylvania
Lawrence, Pennsylvania
Loan, Missouri
McKee, Kentucky
Moorhead, Pennsylvania
Pile, Missouri
Smith, Vermont
Sawyer, Wisconsin
Taylor, Pennsylvania
Trimble, Tennessee
Wilson, Iowa

Windom, Minnesota
Buckland, Ohio
Delano, Ohio
Oliver H. Dockery, North Carolina
James T. Elliott, Arkansas
Garfield, Ohio
Griswold, New York
David Heaton, North Carolina
Kelley, Pennsylvania
Francis W. Kellogg, Alabama
Lawrence, Ohio
Marvin, New York
Nunn, Tennessee
Peters, Maine
Pomeroy, New York
Price, Iowa
Shellabarger, Ohio
Thomas, Maryland
Washburn, Wisconsin
Washburne, Illinois
Wilson, Ohio

—Motion to reconsider the vote on counting the Georgia electoral vote.

GROUP 2 (CENTRIST REPUBLICANS)

Allison, Iowa
Ames, Massachusetts
Benjamin, Missouri
Blaine, Maine
Blair, Michigan
Broomall, Pennsylvania
Roderick R. Butler, Tennessee
Churchill, New York
Coburn, Indiana
John T. Deweese, North Carolina
Dixon, Rhode Island
Dodge, Iowa
Eggleston, Ohio
Ferriss, New York
Ferry, Michigan
Halsey, New Jersey
Higby, California
Hooper, Massachusetts
Alexander H. Jones, North Carolina
Judd, Illinois
Laflin, New York
Israel G. Lash, North Carolina
Lincoln, New York

Logan, Illinois
Loughridge, Iowa
Mallory, Oregon
McCarthy, New York
Miller, Pennsylvania
Moore, New Jersey
Newcomb, Missouri
Benjamin W. Norris, Alabama
Plants, Ohio
Poland, Vermont
Polsley, West Virginia
Raum, Illinois
Robertson, New York
Scofield, Pennsylvania
Selye, New York
Starkweather, Connecticut
Stewart, New York
Stokes, Tennessee
Twichell, Massachusetts
Van Horn, New York
Washburn, Massachusetts
Welker, Ohio
Woodbridge, Vermont

(RADICAL CENTRISTS)

Ashley, Ohio
Christopher C. Bowen, South Carolina
Bromwell, Illinois
Cake, Pennsylvania
John B. Callis, Alabama
Clarke, Ohio
Cobb, Wisconsin
Cullom, Illinois
Dawes, Massachusetts
Oliver J. Dickey, Pennsylvania
Eckley, Ohio
Samuel F. Gove, Georgia
Thomas Haughey, Alabama
Hill, New Jersey
Hulburd, New York

Hunter, Indiana
Ingersoll, Illinois
Morrell, Pennsylvania
Joseph P. Newsham, Lousiana
O'Neill, Pennsylvania
Orth, Indiana
Paine, Wisconsin
Perham, Maine
S. Newton Pettis, Pennsylvania
Pike, Maine
Schenck, Ohio
Trowbridge, Michigan
Upson, Michigan
Van Aernam, New York
Wilson, Pennsylvania

—Motion to count the Louisiana electoral vote, tabling of the protest against counting the Georgia electoral vote.

GROUP 3 (RADICAL REPUBLICANS)

Ashley, Nevada
Baldwin, Massachusetts
Banks, Massachusetts
Benton, New Hampshire
Thomas Boles, Arkansas
Boutwell, Massachusetts
Butler, Massachusetts
Clarke, Kansas
Joseph W. Clift, Georgia
Manuel S. Corley, South Carolina
Covode, Pennsylvania

Donnelly, Minnesota
Driggs, Michigan
Ela, New Hampshire
Eliot, Massachusetts
Fields, New York
John R. French, North Carolina
James H. Goss, South Carolina
Charles M. Hamilton, Florida
Harding, Illinois
Julian, Indiana
Kelsey, New York

Lynch, Maine
Maynard, Tennessee
Mullins, Tennessee
Charles W. Pierce, Alabama
Charles H. Prince, Georgia
Logan H. Roots, Arkansas
Shanks, Indiana
Stevens, New Hampshire
John H. Stover, Missouri
J. Hale Sypher, Louisiana

Van Horn, Missouri
Van Wyck, New York
Michel Vidal, Louisiana
Ward, New York
Washburn, Indiana
Benjamin F. Whittehorne, South
        Carolina
Williams, Pennsylvania
Williams, Indiana

NONSCALAR: Charles W. Buckley, Alabama; Taffe, Nebraska (Republicans).

NOT VOTING: Anderson, Missouri; Arnell, Tennessee; Bailey, New York; W. Jasper Blackburn, Louisiana; Colfax, Indiana; Cook, Illinois; Cornell, New York; William P. Edwards, Georgia; Hubbard, Iowa; Mercur, Pennsylvania; Myers, Pennsylvania (Republicans).

For a list of the roll calls upon which this list is based, see Appendix VIII.

LIST 20

SENATORS AND THE ELECTORAL VOTE COUNT
40 CONGRESS, THIRD SESSION

GROUP 0 (DEMOCRATS AND EXTREME CONSERVATIVE REPUBLICANS)

Bayard, Delaware
Buckalew, Pennsylvania
Davis, Kentucky
Dixon, Connecticut (Johnson
        Conservative)
Doolittle, Wisconsin (Johnson
        Conservative)
Fowler, Tennessee (Republican)
Hendricks, Indiana

McCreery, Kentucky
Norton, Minnesota (Johnson
        Conservative)
Patterson, Tennessee
Saulsbury, Delaware
Vickers, Maryland
Whyte, Maryland
Grimes, Iowa (Republican)
Sprague, Rhode Island (Republican)

—Concurrent resolution that Georgia Electoral Vote remain uncounted.

GROUP 1 (CONSERVATIVE REPUBLICANS)

Edmunds, Vermont
Anthony, Rhode Island
Corbett, Oregon
Cragin, New Hampshire

Ross, Kansas
Sherman, Ohio

—Amendment to the Fifteenth Amendment to enfranchise all men not convicted of crimes, including former rebels; passage of the Fifteenth Amendment.

GROUP 2 (CONSERVATIVE CENTRIST REPUBLICANS)

Abbott, North Carolina
Cattell, New Jersey
Conness, California
Ferry, Connecticut

Fessenden, Maine
Frelinghuysen, New Jersey
Morrill, Vermont
Morrill, Maine

Morton, Indiana
Patterson, New Hampshire
Sawyer, South Carolina

Tipton, Nebraska
Williams, Oregon

—Resolution that the House objections to counting the Louisiana electoral vote are out of order, resolution to refuse to count Georgia's electoral votes, amendment to the resolution to count Louisiana's electoral vote to add a preamble asserting that there are reliable reports of fraud in the Louisiana elections.

GROUP 3 (RADICAL CENTRIST REPUBLICANS)

Cameron, Pennsylvania
Cole, California
Conkling, New York
Drake, Missouri
Harlan, Iowa
Harris, Louisiana
Howe, Wisconsin
Kellogg, Louisiana
McDonald, Arkansas

Morgan, New York
Osborne, Florida
Pool, North Carolina
Ramsey, Minnesota
Rice, Arkansas
Spencer, Alabama
Warner, Alabama
Yates, Illinois

(RADICAL REPUBLICANS)

Chandler, Michigan
Howard, Michigan
Robertson, South Carolina

Stewart, Nevada
Sumner, Massachusetts
Wilson, Massachusetts

—Motion to count the Louisiana electoral count, joint resolution to pay claim of W. W. Corcoran if he will take the loyalty oath.

GROUP 4 (ULTRA RADICAL REPUBLICANS)

Nye, Nevada
Thayer, Nebraska

Wade, Ohio

NONSCALAR: Trumbull, Illinois; Van Winkle, West Virginia (Republicans).

NOT VOTING: Henderson, Missouri; Pomeroy, Kansas; Welch, Florida; Willey, West Virginia (Republicans).

For a list of the roll calls upon which this list is based, see Appendix VII.

LIST 21

SENATORS AND THE PASSAGE OF THE FIFTEENTH AMENDMENT, 40 CONGRESS, THIRD SESSION

GROUP 0 (DEMOCRATS AND EXTREME CONSERVATIVE REPUBLICANS)

Bayard, Delaware
Buckalew, Pennsylvania
Davis, Kentucky
Dixon, Connecticut (Johnson
    Conservative)
Doolittle, Wisconsin (Johnson
    Conservative)
Hendricks, Indiana

McCreery, Kentucky
Norton, Minnesota (Johnson
    Conservative)
Patterson, Tennessee
Saulsbury, Delaware
Vickers, Maryland
Whyte, Maryland
Fowler, Tennessee (Republican)

—Amendments to weaken the Fifteenth Amendment, removal of political disabilities of Franklin J. Moses, removal of political disabilities of South Carolina citizens, concurring in the conference committee report on the Fifteenth Amendment, motion to take up the Fifteenth Amendment, amendment to prohibit disfranchisement for crimes unless duly convicted.

GROUP 1 (CONSERVATIVE REPUBLICANS)

Anthony, Rhode Island	Williams, Oregon
Conkling, New York	*Chandler, Michigan*
Corbett, Oregon	*Pool, North Carolina*
Howard, Michigan	*Ramsey, Minnesota*
Trumbull, Illinois	*Robertson, South Carolina*
Van Winkle, West Virginia	

—Dilatory motions on the Fifteenth Amendment, amendment to the Fifteenth Amendment to bar discrimination in voting on the grounds of participation in the rebellion, amendment to the Fifteenth Amendment applying it only to the states, not the United States.

GROUP 2 (CENTRIST AND RADICAL REPUBLICANS)

Abbott, North Carolina	Morton, Indiana
Cameron, Pennsylvania	Nye, Nevada
Cattell, New Jersey	Osborne, Florida
Cole, Californiia	Patterson, New Hampshire
Conness, California	Pomeroy, Kansas
Cragin, New Hampshire	Rice, Arkansas
Drake, Missouri	Ross, Kansas
Edmunds, Vermont	Sawyer, South Carolina
Ferry, Connecticut	Sherman, Ohio
Fessenden, Maine	Spencer, Alabama
Frelinghuysen, New Jersey	Stewart, Nevada
Grimes, Iowa	Sumner, Massachusetts
Harlan, Iowa	Thayer, Nebraska
Harris, Louisiana	Tipton, Nebraska
Howe, Wisconsin	Wade, Ohio
Kellogg, Louisiana	Warner, Alabama
McDonald, Arkansas	Welch, Florida
Morgan, New York	Willey, West Virginia
Morrill, Vermont	Wilson, Massachusetts
Morrill, Maine	Yates, Illinois

NOT VOTING: Henderson, Missouri; Sprague, Rhode Island (Republicans).

For a list of the roll calls upon which this list is based, see Appendix VII.

LIST 22

REPUBLICAN SENATORS ON EXPANDING FIFTEENTH AMENDMENT COVERAGE 40 CONGRESS, THIRD SESSION

GROUP 0 (CONSERVATIVE AND CENTRIST REPUBLICANS)

Anthony, Rhode Island	Morrill, Vermont
Chandler, Michigan	Morrill, Maine
Cole, California	Nye, Nevada
Conkling, New York	Patterson, New Hampshire
Corbett, Oregon	Ramsey, Minnesota
Edmunds, Vermont	Sprague, Rhode Island
Fessenden, Maine	Stewart, Nevada
Frelinghuysen, New Jersey	Trumbull, Illinois
Morgan, New York	*Howard, Michigan*

—Amendment to the Fifteenth Amendment to bar discrimination in voting on account of race, color, nativity, property, education, or religion.

GROUP 1 (CENTRIST REPUBLICANS)

Cameron, Pennsylvania	Yates, Illinois
Cattell, New Jersey	*Howe, Wisconsin*
Ferry, Connecticut	*Tipton, Nebraska*
Williams, Oregon	*Willey, West Virginia*

—Motion to reconsider the Senate's recession from its version of the Fifteenth Amendment banning voting discrimination in a broad area.

GROUP 2 (RADICAL CENTRIST REPUBLICANS)

Cragin, New Hampshire	Van Winkle, West Virginia
Grimes, Iowa	Welch, Florida
Harris, Louisiana	*Harlan, Iowa*
McDonald, Arkansas	*Osborne, Florida*
Morton, Indiana	*Robertson, South Carolina*
Pomeroy, Kansas	*Sherman, Ohio*
Sumner, Massachusetts	*Wilson, Massachusetts*
Thayer, Nebraska	

—Recession from the Senate version of the Fifteenth Amendment, dilatory motion on the Fifteenth Amendment.

GROUP 3 (RADICAL REPUBLICANS)

Rice, Arkansas	*Abbott, North Carolina*
Wade, Ohio	*Ross, Kansas*
Warner, Alabama	*Sawyer, South Carolina*

—Motion to set the Fifteenth Amendment aside and take up the Tenure of Office act repeal.

GROUP 4 (EXTREME RADICAL REPUBLICANS)

Fowler, Tennessee *   Pool, North Carolina

*Voted with the Democrats to set aside the Fifteenth Amendment to take up the repeal of the Tenure of Office act.

NONSCALAR: Drake, Missouri; Kellogg, Louisiana; Spencer, Alabama (Republicans).

NOT VOTING: Conness, California; Henderson, Missouri (Republicans).

For a list of the roll calls upon which this list is based, see Appendix VII.

Appendices

APPENDIX A
REPRESENTATIVES AND THE MONEY QUESTION

For a list of the roll calls upon which this compilation is based, see Appendix II.

* *Inconsistent on subscale.*

■ 39 Congress

GROUP 0 (CONTRACTIONISTS): Alley, Mass.; Ames, Mass.; Baldwin, Mass.; Banks, Mass.; Baxter, Vt.; Bidwell, Calif.; Blaine, Me.; Brandegee, Conn.; Broomall, Pa.; Conkling, N.Y.; Darling, N.Y.; Davis, N.Y.; Dawes, Mass.; Deming, Conn.; Dodge, N.Y.; Garfield, Ohio; Hooper, Mass.; * Jenckes, R.I.; Kasson, Iowa; Ketcham, N.Y.; Laflin, N.Y.; Lawrence, Pa.; McRuer, Calif.; Marvin, N.Y.; Mercur, Pa.; Moorhead, Pa.; Morrill, Vt.; Patterson, N.H.; Perham, Me.; Pomeroy, N.Y.; Raymond, N.Y.; Rollins, N.H.; Scofield, Pa.; Spalding, Ohio; Van Horn, N.Y.; Ward, N.Y.; Washburn, Mass.; Washburne. Ill.; Wentworth, Ill.; Woodbridge, Vt.; *Griswold, Iowa* (Republicans)

Ancona, Pa.; Boyer, Pa.; Campbell, Tenn.; Chanler, N.Y.; Coffroth, Pa.; Cooper, Tenn.; Dawson, Pa.; Denison, Pa.; Eldridge, Wis.; Finck, Ohio; Glossbrenner, Pa.; * Hale, N.Y.; Harding, Ky.; Hunter, N.Y.; Hogan, Mo.; J.M. Humphrey, N.Y.; Latham, W. Va.; LeBlond, Ohio; Nicholson, Del.; Randall, N.Y.; * Ritter, Ky.; * Rogers, N.J.; Strouse, Pa.; Taber, N.Y.; Winfield, N.Y.; *Bergen, N.Y.; Brooks, N.Y.; Grider, Ky.; Sitgreaves, NJ.* (Democrats and Conservatives)

GROUP 1 (SUSPENSIONISTS): *Hubbard, Conn.;* Allison, Iowa; Ashley, Ohio; Clarke, Kans.; Cullom, Ill.; Delano, Ohio; Donnelly, Minn.; Dumont, Ind.; Marston, N.H.; Morris, N.Y.; Rice, Me.; Sawyer, Wis.; Upson, Mich.; Van Horn, Mo.; Warner, Conn.; Whaley, W. Va.; *Randall, Ky* (Republicans)

Jones, N.Y.; Kerr, Ind.; * Ross, Ill.; Taylor, N.Y.; * Thornton, Ill. (Democrats)

GROUP 2 (SUSPENSIONISTS): *Boutwell, Mass.; Farquhar, Ind.; Moulton, Ill.;* Barker, Pa.; Bromwell, Ill.; Buckland, Ohio; Clarke, Ohio; Defrees, Ind.; Grinnell, Iowa; Hubbard, Iowa; Ingersoll, Ill.; Julian, Ind.; Orth, Ind.; Plants, Ind.; Shellabarger, Ohio; *Cook, Ill.; Hubbard, W.Va.; Kelley, Pa.; Longyear, Mich.; Lynch, Me.; Maynard, Tenn.; McKee, Ky.; Rice, Mass.; Van Aernam, N.Y.* (Republicans)

Goodyear, N.Y.; * Hubbell, N.Y.; Johnson, Pa.; Marshall, Ill.; * Trimble, Ky. (Democrats)

GROUP 3 (EXPANSIONISTS): *Myers, Pa.; Price, Iowa;* * Anderson, Mo.; * Beaman, Mich.; * Bingham, Ohio; Blow, Mo.; Bundy, Ohio; * Ferry, Mich.; * Harding, Ill.; Hayes, Ohio; Higby, Calif.; Hubbell, Ohio; Kelso, Mo.; * Lawrence, Ohio; Loan, Mo.; McClurg, Mo.; Miller, Pa.; * O'Neill, Pa.; Paine, Wis.; Sloan, Wis.; Starr, N.J.; Thomas, Md.; Trowbridge, Mich.; * Welker, Ohio; * Williams, Pa.; * Wilson, Iowa; Wilson, Pa.; Windom, Minn.; *Eckley, Ohio; Stevens, Pa.* (Republicans)
Kuykendall, Ill. (Johnson Conservative)

GROUP 4 (EXPANSIONISTS): Baker, Ill.; Cobb, Wis.; * Thayer, Pa. (Republicans)

NONSCALAR: Arnell, Tenn.; Ashley, Nev.; Benjamin, Mo.; Dixon, R.I.; Eliot, Mass.; Farnsworth, Ill.; Hart, N.Y.; Holmes, N.Y.; Hotchkiss, N.Y.; Hubbard, N.Y.; Hulburd, N.Y.; Koontz, Pa; Newell, N.J.; Pike, Me.; Schenck, Ohio; Stokes, Tenn.; Taylor, Tenn.; Washburn, Ind. (Republicans)
Hawkins, Tenn.; Hise, Ky.; Leftwich, Tenn.; Niblack, Ind.; Noell, Mo.; Phelps, Md.; Shanklin, Ky.; Stillwell, Ohio (Democrats and Johnson Conservatives)

NOT VOTING: Colfax, Ind.; Culver, Pa.; Driggs, Mich.; J. Humphrey, N.Y.; McIndoe, Wis.; J.L. Thomas, Md. (Republicans)
Harris, Md.; McCullough, Md.; Radford, N.Y.; Rousseau, Ky.; Smith, Ky.; Ward, Ky.; Wright, N.J.; Voorhees, Ind. (Democrats and Conservatives)

■ 40 Congress

GROUP 0 (CONTRACTIONISTS): Ames, Mass.; Ashley, Ohio; Baldwin, Mass.; Banks, Mass.; Benton, N.H.; Boutwell, Mass.; Broomall, Pa.; Buckley, Ala.; Churchill, N.Y.; * Cornell, N.Y.; Covode, Pa.; Dawes, Mass.; * Dickey, Pa.; Dixon, R.I.; Eliot, Mass.; * Ferris, N.Y.; Fields, N.Y.; Garfield, Ohio; Griswold, N.Y.; Halsey, N.J.; Hill, Ohio; Hulburd, N.Y.; Jenckes, R.I.; * Kelsey, N.Y.; Ketcham, N.Y.; * Koontz, Pa.; Laflin, N.Y.; Lawrence, Pa.; * Lynch, Me.; McCarthy, N.Y.; Marvin, N.Y.; Mercur, Pa.; * Miller, Pa.; Moore, N.J.; Moorhead, Pa.; * Morrell, Pa.; * Myers, Pa.; * O'Neill, Pa.; Perham, Me.; * Peters, Me.; Pettis, Pa.; Poland, Vt.; Pomeroy, N.Y.; Price, Iowa; * Robertson, N.Y.; Scofield, Pa; Selye, N.Y.; * Smith, Vt.; Spalding, Ohio; Starkweather, Conn.; Stewart, N.Y.; Taylor, Pa.; Twitchell, Mass.; * Upson, Mich.; Van Aernam, N.Y.; Van Horn, N.Y.; Van Wyck, N.Y.; Ward, N.Y.; Washburn, Wis.; Washburn, Mass.; * Williams, Pa.; Wilson, Iowa; Woodbridge, Vt.; *Hooper, Mass.; Hubbard, W.Va.; Kelley, Pa.* (Republicans)
Axtell, Calif.; Barnum, Conn.; Brooks, N.Y.; Chanler, N.Y.; Hotchkiss, Conn.; Hubbard, Conn.; Robinson, N.Y.; Taber, N. Y.; *Barnes, N.Y.* (Democrats)

GROUP 1 (MODERATE EXPANSIONISTS): *Beaman, Mich.; Bingham, Ohio; Eckley, Ohio; Higby, Calif.; Mallory, Ore.; Trowbridge, Mich.;* Allison, Iowa; Anderson, Mo.; * Ashley, Nev.; Benjamin, Mo.; * Blair, Mich.; Boyden, N.C.; Callis, Ala.; Clarke, Ohio; Clarke, Kans.; Clift, Ga.; Corley, S.C.; Cullom, Ill.; Delano, Ohio; Dockery, N.C.; Dodge, Iowa; Driggs, Mich.; * Elliott, Ark.; Ferry, Mich.; Gove, Ga.; Haughey, Ala.; Heaton, N.C.; Jones, N.C.; Judd, Ill.; Kellogg, Ala.; Kitchen, W.Va.; Lash, N.C.; Logan, Ill.; * Maynard, Tenn.; McKee, Ky.; Mullins, Tenn.; Newcomb, Mo.; Newsham, La.; Norris, Ala.; Paine, Wis.; Pierce, Ala.; Pile, Mo.; Plants, Ohio; Charles Prince, Ga.; Raum, Ill.; Roots, Ark.; Sawyer, Wis.; Schenck, Ohio; Shellabarger, Ohio; Stover, Mo.; Sypher, La.; Van Horn, Mo.; Welker, Ohio; Whittemore, S.C.; Windom, Minn.; *Loan, Mo.; Nunn, Tenn.; Polsley, W.Va.; Williams, Ind.* (Republicans)
Fox, N.Y. (Democrat)

GROUP 2 (EXPANSIONISTS): *Stevens, N.H.;* Baker, Ill.; Beatty, Ohio; Bromwell, Ill.; Buckland, Ohio; Butler, Mass.; * Butler, Tenn.; Cobb, Wis.; Coburn, Ind.; Cook, Ill.; Deweese, N.C.; Donnelly, Minn.; Eggleston, Ohio; Farnsworth, Ill.; French, N.C.; Goss, S.C.; Gravely, Mo.; Hawkins, Tenn.; Hopkins, Wis.; Hunter, N.Y.; Ingersoll, Ill.; Lawrence, Ohio; Loughbridge, Iowa; Orth, Ind.; Shanks, Ind.; Stokes, Tenn.; Taffe, Nebr.; Washburn, Ind.; Wilson, Ohio (Republicans)

* Archer, Md.; Beck, Ky.; Burr, Ill.; Cary, Ohio; Eldridge, Wis.; Golladay, Tenn.; * Grover, Ky.; * Haight, N.J.; Holman, Ind.; * Jones, Ky.; * Kerr, Ind.; Knott, Ky.; * McCormick, Mo.; Marshall, Ill.; Mungen, Ohio; Niblack, Ind.; * Nicholson, Del.; Ross, Ill.; * Stone, Md.; Tift, Ga.; Trimble, Ky.; Van Trump, Ohio; Woodward, Pa.; Young, Ga. (Democrats and Independent Republican)

NONSCALAR: Cake, Pa.; Edwards, Ga.; Ela, N.H.; Harding, Ill.; Pike, Me.; F. Thomas, Md. (Republicans)
Boyer, Pa.; Getz, Pa.; Humphrey, N.Y.; Johnson, Calif.; Phelps, Md.; Pruyn, N.Y.; Randall, Pa.; Sitgreaves, N.J.; Wood, N.Y. (Democrats)

NOT VOTING: Arnell, Tenn.; Bailey, N. Y.; Blackburn, La.; Blaine, Me.; Boles, Ark.; Bowen, S.C.; Hamilton, Ohio; Hubbard, Iowa; Lincoln, N.Y.; McClurg, Mo.; Stevens, Pa.; Trimble, Tenn.; Washburne, Ill.; Wilson, Pa. (Republicans)
Adams, Ky; Glossbrenner, Pa.; McCullough, Md.; Mann, La.; Morgan, Ohio; Morrissey, N.Y.; Van Auken, N.Y. (Democrats)

■ 41 Congress

GROUP 0 (ANTI–EXPANSIONISTS): Ambler, Ohio; Bailey, N.Y.; Banks, Mass.; * Beaman, Mich.; Benton, N.H.; Blair, Mich.; Brooks, N.Y.; Buffiington, Mass.; Burchard, Ill.; Churchill, N.Y.; * Davis, N.Y.; Dawes Mass.; * Dixon, R.I.; Donley, Pa.; * Duval, W. Va.; Ela, N.H.; Ferriss, N.Y.; Fisher, N.Y.; Garfield, Ohio; Gilfillam, Pa.; * Hale, Me.; Hoar, Mass.; Hooper, Mass.; * Hotchkiss, N.Y.; Kelley, Pa.; Kellogg, Ala.; *Kelsey, N.Y.; Ketcham, N.Y.; *Knapp, N.Y.; Laflin, N.Y.; McGrew, W.Va.; McKee, Ky.; Mercur, Pa.; Moore, N.J.; Morrell, Pa.; * Morrill, Vt.; Myers, Pa.; O'Neill, Pa.; * Peters, Me.; Platt, Va.; Poland, Vt.; Sargent, Calif.; * Scofield, Pa.; Sheldon, N.Y.; * Smith, Vt.; Starkweather, Ohio; Stevens, N.H.; Strong, Conn.; Tanner, N.Y.; Townsend, Pa.; Ward, N.Y.; Washburn, Ind.; * Washburn, Mass.; Wheeler, N.Y.; Whittemore, S.C.; Willard, Vt.; *James Winans, Ohio; *Buck, Ala.; Strickland, Mich.* (Republicans)
Axtell, Calif.; Barnum, Conn.; * Cox, Ohio; * Getz, Pa.; * Haight, N.J.; Haldeman, Pa.; * Potter, N.Y.; * Randall, Pa.; * Reading, Pa.; * Woodward, Pa.; *Slocum, N.Y.; Stiles, Pa.* (Democrats)

GROUP 1 (MODERATE EXPANSIONISTS): *Benjamin, Mo.; Cowles, N.Y.; * Finkelnberg, Mo.; * Logan, Ill.; Stokes, Tenn.;* Armstrong, Pa.; * Asper, Mo.; * Ayer, Va.; Barry, Miss.; Bingham, Ohio; Blaine, Me.; * Burdett, Mo.; * Conger, Mich.; * Covode, Pa.; Degener, Tex.; * Dickey, Pa.; Farnsworth, Ill.; Ferry, Mich.; * Harris, Miss.; Hawley, Ill.; * Jones, N.C.; * Judd, Ill.; Julian, Ind.; * Lash, N.C.; McCarthy, N.Y.; John B. Packer, Pa.; Frank W. Palmer, Iowa; Peck, Ohio; * Perce Miss.; * Pomeroy, Iowa; Charles H. Porter, Va.; * Schenk, Ohio; * William L. Stoughton, Mich.; Van Wyck, N.Y.; * Wallace, S.C.; Welker, Ohio; Wilkinson, Minn.; Williams, Pa.; *Boles, Ark.; Clarke, Kans.; Hamilton, Fla.;* * McCrary, Iowa; *Moore, Ill.;* * Paine, Wis.; *Prosser, Tenn.;* * Shanks, Ind.* (Republicans)
Heaton, N.C.; Schumaker, N.Y.; Sheldon, La.; Swann, Md. (Democrats)

GROUP 2 (EXTREME EXPANSIONISTS): *Coburn, Ind.;* Allison, Iowa; Beatty, Ohio; Bennett, N.Y.; Butler, Mass.; * Butler, Tenn.; Cobb, Wis.; Cook, Ill.; Cullom, Ill.; Deweese, N.C.; * Dockery, N.C.; Dyer, Mo.; Hawkins, Tenn.; Hay, Ill.; * Hays, Ala.; * Heflin, Ala.; * Hoge, S.C.; Ingersoll, Ill.; Lawrence, Ohio; Loughbridge, Iowa; Maynard, Tenn.; Orth, Ind.; * Packard, Ind.; * Ridgway, Va.; * Roots, Ark.; * Smyth, Iowa; Taffe, Nebr.; Tyner, Ind.; Van Horn, Mo.; Wilson, Ohio; Witcher, W.Va. (Republicans)
Adams, Ky.; Archer, Md.; Beck, Ky.; Burr, Ill.; * Conner, Tex.; Crebs, Ill.; Dickinson, Ohio; Dox, Ala.; Eldridge, Wis.; Gibson, Va.; Griswold, Ky.; Hamill, Md.; * Holman, Ind.; Johnson, Calif.; Jones, Ky.; Kerr, Ind.; Knott, Ky.; Lewis, Ky.; McCormick, Mo.; McNeeley, Ill.; Marshall, Ill.; Mayham, N.Y.; * Milnes, Va.; Morgan,

Ohio; Niblack, Ind.; Rice, Ky.; Rogers, Ark.; * Sherrod, Ala.; * Shober, N.C.; Smith, Ore.; Stone, Md.; Strader, Nebr.; Sweeney, Ky.; Trimble, Ky.; Van Auken, Pa.; Van Trump, Ohio; Wells, Mo.; Wilson, Minn.; Winchester, Ky.; Wood, N.Y. (Democrats)

NONSCALAR: Ames, Mass.; Arnell, Tenn.; Boyd, Mo.; Buckley, Ala.; Cessna, Pa.; Fitch, Nev.; Jenckes, R.I.; McKenzie, Va.; Moore, Ohio; Morphis, Miss.; Negley, Pa.; Newsham, La.; Phelps, Pa.; Sawyer, Wis.; Smith, Ohio; Tillmann, Tenn.; Twitchell, Mass.; Upson, Mich. (Republicans)
    Biggs, Del.; Bird, N.J.; Brooks, N.Y.; Calkin, N.Y.; Mungen, Ohio (Democrats)

NOT VOTING: Atwood, Wis.; Bowen, S.C.; Cake, Pa.; Clark, Tex.; Cobb, N.C.; Hill, Ohio; Hopkins, Wis.; Lynch, Me.; Sanford, N.Y.; Smith, Tenn.; Taylor, Pa.; Whitmore, Tex. (Republicans)
    Cleveland, N.J.; Corker, Ga.; Fox, N.Y.; Golladay, Tenn.; Greene, N.Y.; Hambleton, Md.; Hoag, Ohio; Moffet, Pa.; Morrissey, N.Y.; Reeves, N.Y.; Voorhees, Ind. (Democrats)

APPENDIX I

SCALE ANALYSIS

IN ANALYZING the factional and ideological alignments of Congress during Reconstruction, I have utilized the method of scale analysis Louis Guttman developed as a tool to help psychologists measure attitudes. The method assumes that if a common attitude dictates a series of responses by several respondents, then a pattern will emerge in which respondents will range themselves in a continuum according to the intensity with which they hold those attitudes. In the case of measuring attitudes toward Reconstruction (that is, radicalism), the individual responses consist of the votes on questions involving Reconstruction. The method assumes there will be propositions (items) so mild, so conservative, that only the most conservative respondents would vote against the radical position upon them. As items become more radical, more and more respondents will vote against the radical position, until only the respondents with the most radical attitude towards Reconstruction continue to vote for them. In that case the following pattern will emerge:

	Items (Propositions)				
Respondents	1	2	3	4	5
A	O	O	O	O	O
B	X	O	O	O	O
C	X	X	O	O	O
D	X	X	X	O	O
E	X	X	X	X	O
F	X	X	X	X	X

X = radical vote; O = antiradical vote

A's responses indicate his is the most conservative or antiradical attitude, while F's is the most radical. The Guttman method further assumes that if a respondent votes against the radical position when it is mild (as in item 1 above), then he should not vote in favor of the radical position when it is more radical. If he does, the response has *deviated* from the pattern. That is, if Respondent A had voted as follows:

1	2	3	4	5
O	O	O	X	O

then the vote on item 4 breaks the pattern. Either it is deviant or items 1 through 3 are deviant. Given the clarity of the pattern, we may presume that the vote on item 4 is indeed a deviant vote. If enough respondents break the pattern on a given response, then we must assume that the item itself does not test the same attitude as the others, and it is eliminated from the group. In this way we devise a *unidimensional universe* of responses. Most analysts desire strict unidimensionality and therefore will tolerate few deviant responses on an item before it is eliminated.

Where there have been responses to a large number of propositions, or items, the analyst often will fashion "artificial items." The artificial item consists of propositions on which responses are so similar that they are grouped together and counted as one item. In my analysis, where as many as one hundred items may make up the universe, I have nearly always combined large numbers of items into artificial items, which I have called *groups*. Congressmen's attitudes toward Reconstruction, railroads, blacks, and financial matters have been measured in reference to these groups. For example, when measuring radicalism, those respondents who voted against the radical position on the majority of items making up the first group and all succeeding groups have been classified "Group 0." Those voting for the radical position on the majority of items in the first group but not on the second or succeeding groups have been denominated "Group 1," and so on. A respondent who has voted against the radical position on the majority of items in the first group but in favor of the radical position on those items in the second has deviated, and generally is designated as "nonscalar."

The actual steps involved in the process were as follows:

1. A list was made of all votes which the analyst believed to have involved the particular attitude in which he was interested. The responses of individual congressmen were recorded.

2. The votes were put in *marginal frequency order*. That is, the vote on which the largest number of respondents agreed to the radical position was put first, the vote on which the next largest number supported the radical position was put second, and so on.

3. The responses were checked for deviations through *Yule's Q*. *Yule's Q* is a formula to test the scalability of pairs of roll calls. The results are expressed in a range of -1.0 to 1.0, signifying negative or positive scalability. The higher the numerical value, whether positive or negative, the greater the degree of scalability. My Qmin (the minimum numerical expression of scalability acceptable to the analyst) was set at .6. All items with a scalability below the Qmin were eliminated and checked for subscales. In some cases the low Q was caused by the conscious decision of some respondents to vote against their own principles in an effort to defeat legislation of which they disapproved. In these cases, those votes were adjusted and checked for scalability once again.

4. Items still included in the universe after checking for deviation were combined into artificial items, or "groups."

5. Individual respondents were classified according to the attitudes they displayed through their responses to the items.

A few *caveats* should be added here. First, although one of the primary goals in Guttman analysis is unidimensionality, I have consciously liberalized my universes, particularly those involving Reconstruction, as much as possible by allowing a lower Qmin (.6) than is customary. I did not want separate scales on each piece of Reconstruction legislation, which I certainly would have gotten had I been stricter. (See, for instance, Edward L. Gambill, "Who Were the Senate Radicals?" *Civil War History*, XI (June 1965), 237–43; Gambill found nine separate scales for only one session of Congress.) The relaxed requirements for scalability lead to a lower *reproducibility* in a few cases than is customarily allowed (reproducibility is an expression of the degree of perfection in the scale; a perfect scale has no deviating responses). Therefore, the reader must recognize that the charts giving the factional alignments in Congress define not static but fluid groups, gaining and losing members from vote to vote. Second, I have not taken Charles D. Farris's advice to eliminate nearly unanimous and partisan roll calls (partisan roll calls are those on which a certain percentage of one party votes in opposition to a similar percentage of the other; the analyst sets the significant percentage, usually 90, 60, or 50 per cent). Farris's warning that nearly unanimous roll calls inflate the "reproducibility" of the scale, while true, does not pertain here, where reproducibility is deemphasized. As to Farris's stricture on partisan roll calls, I simply do not agree. Finally, it should be pointed out that the scales on Reconstruction are not as "dichotomized" as one would expect. Instead of sharply defined, hostile groups, the Reconstruction scales marked a gradual shading among Republicans from conservatism to radicalism. But this is in part a result of my method. Had only "significant" roll calls been analyzed (that is roll calls marked by nearly even division), as in the program most analysts follow, an artificial dichotomy would have appeared, fostered by the nature of the input. The same would have been true if "partisan" roll calls had been excluded.

For a more detailed, but elementary, explanation of roll call analysis, including the formula for computing Yule's Q, see Lee F. Anderson, Meredith W. Watts, Jr., and Allen R. Wilcox, *Legislative Roll-Call Analysis* (Evanston, Ill.: Northwestern University Press, 1966), 89–121. (I am giving complete cites to works that are not included in the bibliography.) Major contributions to the development of scale analysis are George M. Belknap, "A Method for Analyzing Legislative Behavior," *Midwest Journal of Political Science*, II (November 1958), 377–402; Charles D. Farris, "A Method for Determining Ideological Groupings in the Congress," *Journal of Politics*, XX (May 1958), 308–38; Bert F. Green, "Attitude Measurement," in Gardner Lindzey (ed.), *Handbook of Social Psychology* (2 vols., Cambridge, Mass.: Addison-Wesley Publishing Co., 1954); Louis Guttman, "A Basis for Scaling Qualitative Data," *American Sociological Review*, IX (April 1944), 139–50; Duncan MacRae, Jr., *Dimensions of Congressional Voting: A Statistical Study of the House of Representatives in the Eighty-first Congress* (Berkeley, Calif.: University of California Press, 1958); Samuel A. Stouffer, *et al., Measurement and Prediction* (Princeton, N.J.; Princeton University Press, 1950). The last-cited work is volume IV of the monumental *Studies in Social Psychology in World War II,* sponsored by the Social Science Research Council.

APPENDIX II

THE MONEY QUESTION IN THE HOUSE
OF REPRESENTATIVES, 39–41 CONGRESSES

REPRESENTATIVES in Group 0 of Appendix A voted against the inflationist position on roll calls in Group 1 of this Appendix and in all succeeding groups. Representatives in Group 1 of Appendix A voted for the inflationist position on roll calls in Group 1 of this Appendix but against the inflationist position on roll calls in all succeeding groups. The representatives in Group 2 voted for the inflationist position on roll calls in Group 2 of this Appendix but not for the inflationist position in succeeding groups, and so on.

▪ 39 Congress

Main Scale

GROUP 1: *Cong. Globe*, 39 Cong., 2 Sess., 1426 (Feb. 21, 1867; anticontractionist vote = yea; final vote = 95–65–30), 1666–67 (Feb. 28, 1867; nay; 56–83–51), 992 (Feb. 4, 1867; yea; 87–66–41) 992 (Feb. 4, 1867; nay; 71–82–37), 1 Sess., 1468 (March 16, 1866; nay; 64–70–49), in order of marginal frequency.

GROUP 2: *Cong. Globe*, 39 Cong., 2 Sess., 1424 (Feb. 21, 1867; yea; 74–84–32), 1 Sess., 1496 (March 19, 1866; yea; 70–78–35), 1500 (March 19, 1866; nay; 81–67–35), 1467 (March 16, 1866; yea; 61–75–47), 2 Sess., 151 (Dec. 17, 1866; nay; 88–58–45), 1 Sess., 1614 (March 23, 1866; nay; 83–53–47).

GROUP 3: *Cong. Globe,* 39 Cong., 1 Sess., 1467 (March 16, 1866; yea; 37–98–48).

GROUP 4: *Cong. Globe,* 39 Cong., 1 Sess., 75 (Dec. 18, 1865; nay; 144–6–32).

Subscale

Cong. Globe, 39 Cong., 1 Sess., 4154 (July 25, 1866; yea; 28–87–71), 2 Sess., 49 (Dec. 10, 1866; nay; 94–60–47).

▪ 40 Congress

Main Scale

GROUP 1: *Cong. Globe,* 40 Cong., 3 Sess., 1325 (Feb. 17, 1869; nay; 65–107–50), 1816 (March 2, 1869; nay; 70–108–44), 1333 (Feb. 18, 1869; yea; 106–77–39), 1331 (Feb. 18, 1869; yea; 97–76–49), 1325 (Feb. 17, 1869); yea; 93–86–43), 2 Sess., 1761 (March 9, 1868; nay; 56–65–68), 3 Sess., 1327 (Feb. 17, 1869; nay; 92–78–52).

GROUP 2: *Cong. Globe,* 40 Cong., 3 Sess., 1883 (March 3, 1869; nay; 118–57–48), 1538 (Feb. 24, 1869; nay; 120–60–42), 1471 (March 3, 1869; yea; 53–119–51), 1538 (Feb. 24, 1869; yea; 54–133–35).

Subscale

GROUP 1: *Cong. Globe,* 40 Cong., 2 Sess., 70 (Dec. 7, 1867; yea; 127–32–28), 4310 (July 21, 1868; yea; 86–49–80).

GROUP 2: *Cong. Globe,* 40 Cong., 3 Sess., 1538 (Feb. 24, 1869; yea; 72–100–50).

▪ 41 Congress

Main Scale

Roll calls relating to currency expansion.

GROUP 1: *Cong. Globe,* 41 Cong., 2 Sess., 1460 (Feb. 21, 1870; yea; 108–72–38), 76 (Dec. 11, 1870; nay; 64–89–58), 1263 (Feb. 14, 1870; nay; 73–93–52).

GROUP 2: *Cong. Globe,* 41 Cong., 2 Sess., 4478 (June 15, 1870; yea; 77–95–58), 76 (Dec. 11, 1870; nay; 99–57–55), 4471 (June 15, 1870; yea; 51–103–76).

Subscale

Roll calls relating to payment of government bonds in gold and allowing private contracts to require performance in gold.

GROUP 1: *Cong. Globe,* 41 Cong., 2 Sess., 4970 (June 29, 1870; nay; 53–127–49), 1 Sess., 60 (March 12, 1869; yea; 86–57–51).

GROUP 2: *Cong. Globe,* 41 Cong., 1 Sess., 61 (March 12, 1869; nay; 98–47–53), 2 Sess., 5070–71 (July 1, 1870; nay; 128–43–58), 5059 (July 1, 1870; yea; 41–127–61).

APPENDIX III
THE MONEY QUESTION IN THE SENATE
40–41 CONGRESSES

DEMOCRATIC VOTE not included where Democrats vote inconsistently for partisan reasons.

First Scale

40 Congress; all but one roll call relating to contraction of the currency. Those voting to expand the currency on roll calls in Group 3 were the most committed inflationists. Those voting against expanding the currency on roll calls in Group 1 were the most committed contractionists.

GROUP 1: *Cong. Globe,* 40 Cong., 2 Sess., 501 (Jan. 14, 1868; anticontraction vote = nay; final vote = 1–40–12), 537 (Jan. 15, 1868; yea; 33–4–16), 503 (Jan. 14, 1868; nay; 6–37–10), in order of marginal frequency.

GROUP 2: *Cong. Globe,* 40 Cong., 2 Sess., 438–39 (Jan. 10, 1868; nay; 17–30–6), 537 (Jan. 15, 1868; nay; 15–23–15).

GROUP 3: *Cong. Globe,* 40 Cong., 3 Sess., 1126 (Feb. 2, 1869; yea; 8–39–19), 1661 (Feb. 27, 1869; yea; 7–36–23), 2 Sess., 3998 (July 13, 1868; yea; 6–29–22).

Second Scale

Primarily 41 Congress; relating to payment of national bonds in gold and allowing private contracts specifically requiring performance in gold. Those voting against requiring a gold standard on roll calls in Group 3 were the most opposed to resumption of mandatory use of gold in contracts and in payment of government bonds. Those voting in favor of requiring gold payments on roll calls in Group 1 favored quickest resumption.

GROUP 1: *Cong. Globe,* 41 Cong., 2 Sess., 943 (Feb. 1, 1870; yea; 39–21–8).

GROUP 2: *Cong. Globe,* 41 Cong., 2 Sess., 970 (Feb. 2, 1870; yea; 29–29–10), 40 Cong., 3 Sess., 1834 (March 3, 1869; nay; 31–24–11), 1678 (Feb. 27, 1869; nay; 30–16–20), 41 Cong., 1 Sess., 46 (March 11, 1869; nay; 36–18–11).

GROUP 3: *Cong. Globe,* 41 Cong., 1 Sess., 56 (March 11, 1869; yea; 14–32–19), 53 (March 11, 1869; yea; 12–31–22), 70 (March 12, 1869; nay; 42–13–10), 2 Sess., 968 (Feb. 2, 1870; nay; 44–13–11).

APPENDIX IV
THE TARIFF IN THE HOUSE OF REPRESENTATIVES
39 CONGRESS, SECOND SESSION

GROUP 1: *Cong. Globe,* 39 Cong., 2 Sess., 1590 (Feb. 26, 1867; protariff vote= yea; final vote = 85–49–46); 1658 (Feb. 28, 1867; yea; 106–64–20), in order of marginal frequency.

GROUP 2: *Cong. Globe,* 39 Cong., 2 Sess., 1659 (Feb. 28, 1867; yea; 95–71–24).

APPENDIX V
THE TARIFF IN THE SENATE, 39 CONGRESS

THE TARIFF did not lend itself to scale analysis, and votes on it were not arranged in marginal frequency order.

Cong. Globe, 39 Cong., 1 Sess., 3758 (July 12, 1866; Pro-high-tariff vote = nay; final vote = 23–17–9), 4068 (July 24, 1866; nay; 26–11–11), 4290 (July 28, 1866; nay; 22–11–17), 2 Sess., 678 (Jan. 23, 1867; yea; 13–19–20), 682 (Jan. 23, 1867; nay; 11–18–23), 684 (Jan. 23, 1867; nay; 9–10–33), 700 (Jan. 24, 1867; nay; 23–13–17), 703 (Jan. 24, 1867; nay; 5–32–15), 736 (Jan. 25, 1867; yea; 26–14–12), 737 (Jan. 25, 1867; yea; 11–22–19), 741 (Jan. 25, 1867; yea; 20–17–15), 745 (Jan. 25, 1867; yea; 15–17–20), 749 (Jan. 25, 1867; yea; 8–17–27), 765 (Jan. 26, 1867; yea; 10–17–25), 770 (Jan. 26, 1867; yea; 13–22–17), 798 (Jan. 28, 1867; yea; 19–23–10), 802 (Jan. 28, 1867; yea; 16–20–16), 802 (Jan. 28, 1867; yea; 16–19–17), 821 (Jan. 29, 1867; yea; 16–21–15), 822 (Jan. 29, 1867; yea; 17–15–20), 822 (Jan. 29, 1867; yea; 12–19–21), 828 (Jan. 29, 1867; nay, 15–25–12), 829 (Jan. 29, 1867; nay; 23–13–16), 857 (Jan. 30, 1867; yea; 21–14–17), 860 (Jan. 30, 1867; yea; 18–14–20), 862 (Jan. 30, 1867; yea; 18–15–19), 911 (Jan. 31, 1867; yea; 19–15–18), 915 (Jan. 31, 1867; nay; 20–11–21), 919 (Jan. 31, 1867; yea; 1–28–23), 920 (Jan. 31, 1867; nay; 17–17–18), 921 (Jan. 31, 1867; nay; 15–24–13), 922 (Jan. 31, 1867; nay; 12–26–14), 924 (Jan. 31, 1867; nay; 14–20–18), 927 (Jan. 31, 1867; nay; 11–26–15), 927 (Jan. 31, 1867; nay; 8–23–21), 928 (Jan. 31, 1867; nay; 20–17–15), 930 (Jan. 31, 1867; yea; 19–15–18), 931 (Jan. 31, 1867; yea; 27–10–15), 1958 (March 2, 1867; yea; 31–12–9).

APPENDIX VI
LAND GRANTS TO RAILROADS IN
THE HOUSE OF REPRESENTATIVES
40 CONGRESS

Main Scale

Those voting against aid on the roll calls in Group 1 *opposed* aid throughout the 40th Congress; those voting in favor of aid on the roll calls in Group 3 *supported* aid throughout the Congress. Those who supported aid on roll calls in Groups 1 or 2 but not in Group 3 began opposing aid at some time during this Congress.

GROUP 1: *Cong. Globe,* 40 Cong., 2 Sess., 3588 (June 29, 1868; pro-land-grant vote = yea; final vote = 96–33–65); 1632 (March 3, 1868; yea; 78–44–67, in order of marginal frequency.

GROUP 2: *Cong. Globe,* 40 Cong., 3 Sess., 587 (Jan. 25, 1869; nay; 86–92–44); 1 Sess., 797 (Nov. 26, 1867; nay; 70–66–45).

GROUP 3: *Cong. Globe,* 40 Cong., 3 Sess., 424 (Jan. 18, 1869; nay; 90–67–65).

Subscale (Midwestern Railroads)

Cong. Globe, 40 Cong., 2 Sess., 571 (Jan. 16, 1868; yea; 106–27–55), 571 (Jan. 16, 1868; nay; 27–92–69), 106 (Dec. 10, 1867; nay; 35–111–41), 570 (Jan. 16, 1868; nay; 33–104–51), 107 (Dec. 10, 1867; yea; 108–39–40).

APPENDIX VII
RADICALISM IN THE SENATE
38–40 CONGRESSES

■ 38 Congress, first session

GROUP 1: *Cong. Globe,* 38 Cong., 1 Sess., 1425 (April 5, 1864; radical vote = nay; final vote = 2–34), 3461 (July 1, 1864; yea; 26–3–20), 1424 (April 5, 1864; nay; 5–32), 1490 (April 8, 1864; yea; 38–6), 1809 (April 22, 1864; nay; 5–31), 3303 (June 27, 1864; nay; 5–29–15), 522 (Feb. 8, 1864; nay; 8–31), 1370 (March 31, 1864; nay; 6–28), 3378 (June 29, 1864; nay; 8–25–16), 2963 (June 15, 1864; nay; 6–26–17), 2970 (June 15, 1864; nay; 8–20–12), in order of marginal frequency.

GROUP 2: *Cong. Globe,* 38 Cong., 1 Sess., 3264 (June 25, 1864; yea; 29–10–10), 3176 (June 22, 1864; nay; 8–28–13), 331 (Jan. 25, 1864; yea; 28–11), 1709 (April 19, 1864; yea; 26–10), 3350 (June 28, 1864; yea; 21–9–19), 2931 (June 14, 1864; yea; 23–11–15), 3177 (June 22, 1864; yea; 25–11–31), 3293 (June 27, 1864; yea; 20–8–21), 3177 (June 22, 1864; yea; 26–12–11), 2970 (June 15, 1864; nay; 13–23–13); 54 (Dec. 18, 1863; nay; 15–26).

GROUP 3: *Cong. Globe,* 38 Cong., 1 Sess., 3327 (June 28, 1864; yea; 23–14–11), 3264 (June 25, 1864; yea; 23–14–12), 1207 (March 21, 1864; nay; 14–22), 3491 (July 2, 1864; yea; 18–14–17), 2963 (June 15, 1864; nay; 14–21–14), 102 (Jan. 6, 1864; nay; 16–21), 3261 (June 25, 1864; yea; 22–16–11), 3129 (June 21, 1864; yea; 25–17–5), 3350 (June 28, 1865; nay; 13–16–20).

GROUP 4: *Cong. Globe,* 38 Cong., 1 Sess., 2545 (May 28, 1864; yea; 18–20–11), 96 (Jan. 5, 1864; nay; 20–15), 1714 (April 19, 1864; nay; 24–17), 3460 (July 1, 1864; nay; 17–16–16), 3256 (June 25, 1864; yea; 13–20–16).

GROUP 5: *Cong. Globe,* 38 Cong., 1 Sess., 3407 (June 29, 1864; yea; 11–17–21).

GROUP 6: *Cong. Globe,* 38 Cong., 1 Sess., 2545 (May 28, 1864; yea; 8–27–14).

■ 38 Congress, second session

GROUP 1: *Cong. Globe,* 38 Cong., 2 Sess., 1108 (Feb. 25, 1865; nay; 8–19–23), 1107 (Feb. 25, 1865; nay; 12–19–19), 849 (Feb. 17, 1865; yea; 29–13–8), 1107 (Feb. 25, 1865; yea; 12–18–20), 1107 (Feb. 25, 1865; yea; 11–18–21), 595 (Feb. 4, 1865; yea; 29–10–12), 583 (Feb. 3, 1865; nay; 13–21–8), 595 (Feb. 4, 1865; nay; 7–30–14), 582 (Feb. 3, 1865; nay; 12–31–8), 582 (Feb. 3, 1865; nay; 16–22–14), 561 (Feb. 2, 1865; nay; 11–26–14).

The subgroups of Group 0 consisted of Democrats who voted with the radicals on some or all of the roll calls in Group 6.

GROUP 2: *Cong. Globe,* 38 Cong., 2 Sess., 849 (Feb. 17, 1865; yea; 29–13–8), 595 (Feb. 4, 1865; nay; 7–30–14), 595 (Feb. 4, 1865; yea; 29–10–12).

GROUP 3: *Cong. Globe,* 38 Cong., 2 Sess., 583 (Feb. 3, 1865; nay; 12–31–8), 561 (Feb. 2, 1865; nay; 11–26–14), 582 (Feb. 3, 1865; nay; 12–30–9).

GROUP 4: *Cong. Globe,* 38 Cong., 2 Sess., 582 (Feb. 3, 1865; nay; 16–22–14).

GROUP 5: *Cong. Globe,* 38 Cong., 2 Sess., 632 (Feb. 7, 1865; nay; 29–14–8).

GROUP 6: *Cong. Globe,* 38 Cong., 2 Sess., 1065 (Feb. 24, 1865; yea; 10–25–15), 1107 (Feb. 25, 1865; yea; 12–19–19), 1011 (Feb. 23, 1865; yea; 8–29), 1107 (Feb. 25, 1865; yea; 12–18–20), 1107 (Feb. 25, 1865; yea; 12–17–21), 1107 (Feb. 25, 1865; yea; 11–18–21), 1108 (Feb. 25, 1865; yea; 8–19–23).

■ 39 Congress, first session

Democratic Scale

GROUP 1: *Cong. Globe,* 39 Cong., 1 Sess., 397 (Jan. 22, 1866; nay; 10–36–4), 607 (Feb. 2, 1866; nay; 7–39–4), 1205 (March 6, 1866; yea; 32–5–13), 374 (Jan. 22, 1866; yea; 36–7–6).

GROUP 2: *Cong. Globe,* 39 Cong., 1 Sess., 400 (Jan. 24, 1866; nay; 8–37–5), 2066 (April 20, 1866; yea; 30–4–15), 2899 (May 30, 1866; nay; 8–34–7), 747 (Feb. 8, 1866; yea; 29–7–14), 402 (Jan. 24, 1866; nay; 8–32–10), 399 (Jan. 24, 1866; nay; 8–34–8), 399 (Jan. 24, 1866; nay; 9–36–5), 395 (Jan. 24, 1866; nay; 9–32–8), 421 (Jan. 25, 1866; yea; 37–10–3), 397 (Jan. 24, 1866; nay; 10–36–4), 748 (Feb. 8, 1866; nay; 8–25–17), 747 (Feb. 8, 1866; nay; 11–28–11), *Senate Executive Journal,* XIV, 677 (March 16, 1866; nay; 11–20–18).

GROUP 3: *Cong. Globe,* 39 Cong., 1 Sess., 2986 (June 6, 1866; nay; 7–31–11), 2037 (April 19, 1866; yea; 19–15–15), 2180 (April 25, 1866; yea; 19–13–16), 1288 (March 9, 1866; nay; 12–31–7), 30 (Dec. 12, 1865; yea; 33–11–5), 29 (Dec. 12, 1865; nay; 12–31–6).

Republican Scale

GROUP 3: *Cong. Globe,* 39 Cong., 1 Sess., 2066 (April 20, 1866; yea; 30–4–15), 30 (Dec. 12, 1865; yea; 33–11–5), 1730 (April 3, 1866; yea; 26–9–14), 347 (Jan. 22, 1866; nay; 11–33–5), 348 (Jan. 22, 1866; nay; 8–31–10), 374 (Jan. 22, 1866; yea; 36–7–6), 395 (Jan. 24, 1866; nay; 9–32–8), 397 (Jan. 24, 1866; nay; 10–36–4), 399 (Jan. 24, 1866; nay; 8–34–8), 399 (Jan. 24, 1866; nay; 9–36–5), 400 (Jan. 24, 1866; nay; 8–37–5), 402 (Jan. 24, 1866; nay; 8–32–10), 421 (Jan. 25, 1866; yea; 37–10–3), 395 (Jan. 22, 1866; nay; 10–32–8), 3411 (June 26, 1866; nay; 6–26–17), 747 (Feb. 8, 1866; yea; 29–7–14), 397 (Jan. 22, 1866; nay; 10–36–4), 2986 (June 6, 1866; nay; 7–31–11), 607 (Feb. 2, 1866; nay; 7–39–4), 1284 (March 9, 1866; yea; 10–37–3), 3409 (June 26, 1866; nay; 6–27–16), 29 (Dec. 12, 1865; nay; 12–31–6), 3040 (June 8, 1866; nay; 11–33–5), 3842 (July 16, 1866; yea; 33–12–4), 3042 (June 8, 1866; yea; 33–11–5), 606–607 (Feb. 2, 1866; yea; 33–12–4), 606 (Feb. 2, 1866; nay; 12–34–5), 2921 (May 31, 1866; yea; 31–11–7), 2900 (May 30, 1866; nay; 11–31–7), 2899 (May 30, 1866; nay; 8–34–7), 1288 (March 9, 1866; nay; 12–31–7), 575 (Feb. 1, 1866; yea; 31–10–9), *Sen. Exec. Jour.,* XIV, 883 (June 30, 1866; nay; 9–21–18), 832 (May 24, 1866; nay; 9–17–23), *Cong. Globe,* 39 Cong., 1 Sess., 3839 (July 16, 1866; nay; 13–31–5), 1809 (April 9, 1866; yea; 33–15–1), 2942 (June 4, 1866; nay; 9–26–14).

GROUP 4: *Cong. Globe,* 39 Cong., 1 Sess., 1146 (March 2, 1866; nay; 17–29–4), 943 (Feb. 20, 1866; yea; 30–18–2), 1147 (March 2, 1866; yea; 29–18–3), 1027 (Feb. 26, 1866; nay; 17–29–4), 1677 (March 27, 1866; nay; 27–16–6), 918 (Feb. 19, 1866; nay; 17–29–4), 918 (Feb. 19, 1866; nay; 17–28–5), *Sen. Exec. Jour.,* XIV, 777 (May 2, 1866; nay; 8–21–19), *Cong. Globe,* 39 Cong., 1 Sess., 984 (Feb. 23, 1866; yea; 26–19–5), 2339 (May 2, 1866; yea; 19–11–19), 918 (Feb. 19, 1866; nay; 19–25–6), *Sen. Exec. Jour.,* XIV, 677 (March 16, 1866; nay; 11–20–18).

GROUP 5: *Cong. Globe,* 39 Cong., 1 Sess., 1679 (March 27, 1866; yea; 22–21–6), 1677 (March 27, 1866; yea; 22–21–6), 3622 (July 6, 1866; yea; 17–13–19), 1601–1602 (March 23, 1866; yea; 19–21–10).

GROUP 6: *Cong. Globe,* 39 Cong., 1 Sess., 2429 (May 7, 1866; nay; 21–18–10), 2559 (May 11, 1866; yea; 16–23–10), 3134 (June 13, 1866; nay; 23–14–12), 4245 (July 27, 1866; nay; 21–11–18).

GROUP 7: *Cong. Globe,* 39 Cong., 1 Sess., 1284 (March 9, 1866; yea; 8–39–3), 920 (July 13, 1866; nay; 31–8–9), 1287 (March 9, 1866; yea; 7–38–5).

GROUP 8: *Cong. Globe,* 39 Cong., 1 Sess., 4000 (July 21, 1866; yea; 4–34–10), 4219 (July 27, 1866; nay; 35–2–13), 4001 (July 21, 1866; nay 28–4–16).

■ 39 Congress, second session

NOTE: Democrats sustained the radical position on several of the following roll calls in efforts to prevent passage of Republican legislation. For that reason, Democrats and Johnson Conservatives in Group 0 were scaled separately, based on the roll calls listed in Group 2 with their votes adjusted. The Republican scale begins with the roll calls of Group 2.

GROUP 2: *Cong. Globe,* 39 Cong., 2 Sess.; 277 (Jan. 4, 1867; yea; 21–7–18), 381 (Jan. 10, 1867; yea; 26–7–19), 1645 (Feb. 20, 1867; nay; 8–34–10), 1795 (Feb. 23, 1867; yea; 25–6–21), 404 (Jan. 11, 1867; nay; 6–23–23), 1469 (Feb. 16, 1867; yea; 29–10–13), 1636 (Feb. 20, 1867; yea; 23–12–17), 1461 (Feb. 16, 1867; nay; 8–28–16), 1948 (March 1, 1867; nay; 25–15–12), 550 (Jan. 18, 1867; yea; 29–9–14), 1963 (March 2, 1867; nay; 9–29–14), 1467 (Feb. 16, 1867; yea; 32–3–17), 1467 (Feb. 16, 1867; yea; 9–30–15), 1966 (March 2, 1867; yea; 35–11–6), 948 (Feb. 1, 1867; yea; 31–6–15), 1976 (March 2, 1867; yea; 8–33–11), 1964 (March 2, 1867; yea; 36–8–8), 1855 (Feb. 26, 1867; nay; 8–28–6), 603 (Jan. 21, 1867; yea; 25–9–18), 382 (Jan. 10, 1867; yea; 24–7–21), 109 (Dec. 13, 1866; yea; 32–13–7), 313 (Jan. 7, 1867; yea; 29–10–13), 1518 (Feb. 18, 1867; yea; 22–10–20).

GROUP 3: *Cong. Globe,* 39 Cong., 2 Sess., 1849 (Feb. 26, 1867; yea; 23–11–18).

GROUP 4: *Cong. Globe,* 39 Cong., 2 Sess., 354 (Jan. 9, 1867; yea; 16–17–19).

GROUP 5: *Cong. Globe,* 39 Cong., 2 Sess., 1509 (Feb. 18, 1867; yea; 15–20–17), 1047 (Feb. 6, 1867; yea; 17–28–7), 1948 (March 1, 1867; nay; 25–15–12), 548 (Jan. 18, 1867; yea; 13–27–12).

GROUP 6: *Cong. Globe,* 39 Cong., 2 Sess., 1911 (Feb. 28, 1867; nay; 27–12–13), 1903 (Feb. 28, 1867; nay; 33–13–6), 1509 (Feb. 18, 1867; yea; 15–20–17), 1009 (Feb. 5, 1867; yea; 10–30–12), *Sen. Exec. Jour.,* XV, 338 (March 2, 1867; nay; 32–10–11), *Cong. Globe,* 39 Cong., 2 Sess., 1902 (Feb. 28, 1867; nay; 37–10–5), 1397 (Feb. 15, 1867; yea; 10–37–5), *Sen. Exec. Jour.,* XV, 338 (March 2, 1867; nay; 33–6–14).

GROUP 7: *Cong. Globe,* 39 Cong., 2 Sess., 403 (Jan. 11, 1867; yea; 1–30–21).

■ 40 Congress, first session

Democratic Scale

GROUP 1: *Cong. Globe,* 40 Cong., 1 Sess., 181 (March 18, 1867; yea; 39–5–9), 408 (March 28, 1867; nay; 25–14–14), 171 (March 16, 1867; yea; 38–2–13), 628 (July 13, 1867; yea; 31–6–16), 438 (March 29, 1867; nay; 7–32–14), 644 (July 15, 1867; yea; 29–3–21), 303 (March 23, 1867; yea; 40–7–6).

GROUP 2: *Cong. Globe,* 40 Cong., 1 Sess., 628 (July 13, 1867; yea; 31–6–16), 303 (March 23, 1867; yea; 40–7–6), *Sen. Exec. Jour.,* XV, 572 (March 28, 1867; nay; 5–35–13), *Cong. Globe,* 40 Cong., 1 Sess., 586 (July 11, 1867; yea; 32–6–15), 181 (March 18, 1867; yea; 39–5–9), 171 (March 16, 1867; yea; 38–2–13), 732 (July 19, 1867; yea; 30–6–17), 644 (July 15, 1867; yea; 29–3–21), 732 (July 19, 1867; yea; 32–4–17), 665 (July 16, 1867; nay; 7–28–18), *Sen. Exec. Jour.,* XV, 681 (April 10, 1867; nay; 8–27–18), *Cong. Globe,* 40 Cong., 1 Sess., 677 (July 17, 1867; yea; 25–5–23).

Republican Scale

GROUP 3: *Cong. Globe,* 40 Cong., 1 Sess., 586 (July 11, 1867; yea; 21–8–24).

GROUP 4: *Cong. Globe,* 40 Cong., 1 Sess., 582 (July 11, 1867; yea; 18–18–17), 584 (July 11, 1867; yea; 20–11–22).

GROUP 5: *Cong. Globe,* 40 Cong., 1 Sess., 170 (March 16, 1867; yea; 20–20–13), 360 (March 26, 1867; nay; 21–17–15), 615 (July 12, 1867; yea; 12–22–19), 754 (July 20, 1867; nay; 17–14–22), 303 (March 23, 1867; yea; 19–28–6), 303 (March 23, 1867; yea; 17–25–11), 734–35 (July 19, 1867; nay; 23–14–16), 755 (July 20, 1867; yea; 13–19–21).

GROUP 6: *Cong. Globe,* 40 Cong., 1 Sess., 308 (March 23, 1867; nay; 29–16–8), 360 (March 26, 1867; yea; 15–26–12), 533 (July 9, 1867; yea; 11–21–21), 360 (March 26, 1867; yea; 14–27–12), 303–304 (March 23, 1867; yea; 14–31–8), 441 (March 29, 1867; yea; 13–28–12), 581 (July 11, 1867; yea; 11–22–20), 408 (March 28, 1867; yea; 14–27–12), 441 (March 29, 1867; nay; 28–12–13).

GROUP 7: *Cong. Globe,* 40 Cong., 1 Sess., 408 (March 28, 1867; nay; 25–14–14), 56 (March 11, 1867; nay; 36–10–7).

■ 40 Congress, second session

GROUP 1: *Cong. Globe,* 40 Cong., 2 Sess., 3060 (June 11, 1868; yea; 23–5–26), 3363 (June 22, 1868; yea; 30–7–17), 3058 (June 11, 1868; nay; 5–28–21), 2749 (June 1, 1868; yea; 34–8–12), 3029 (June 10, 1868; yea; 31–5–18), 1417 (Feb. 25, 1868; yea; 28–6–19), 4236 (July 20, 1868; yea; 45–8–7), 4451 (July 25, 1868; yea; 42–5–17), 4251 (July 20, 1868; nay; 3–29–30), 2769 (June 2, 1868; yea; 29–8–17), 4466 (July 25, 1868; yea; 35–8–13), 3607 (June 30, 1868; yea; 34–6–16), 3956 (July 11, 1868; yea; 34–3–20), 3926 (July 10, 1868; yea; 29–5–23), 3955 (July 11, 1868; nay; 3–26–28), 2736 (June 1, 1868; yea; 37–11–6), 778 (Jan. 27, 1868; yea; 26–5–22), 2735 (June 1, 1868; nay; 11–30–13).

GROUP 2: *Cong. Globe,* 40 Cong., 2 Sess., 3607 (June 30, 1868; nay; 13–31–12), 2749 (June 1, 1868; nay; 15–26–13), 2749 (June 1, 1868; nay; 18–22–14).

GROUP 3: *Cong. Globe,* 40 Cong., 2 Sess., 2701 (May 30, 1868; nay; 30–16–8).

GROUP 4: *Cong. Globe,* 40 Cong., 2 Sess., 3385 (June 23, 1868; nay; 29–8–17), 1496 (Feb. 28, 1868; nay; 23–13–16).

GROUP 5: *Cong. Globe,* 40 Cong., 2 Sess., 1028 (Feb. 7, 1868; yea; 8–30–15), 38 (Dec. 5, 1867; yea; 9–36–8).

■ 40 Congress, third session

First Scale—Electoral Vote Count

GROUP 1: *Cong. Globe,* 40 Cong., 3 Sess., 978 (Feb. 8, 1869; yea; 34–11–21).

GROUP 2: *Cong. Globe,* 40 Cong., 3 Sess., 1029 (Feb. 9, 1869; nay; 9–35–22), 1044 (Feb. 9, 1869; yea; 39–16–11).

GROUP 3: *Cong. Globe,* 40 Cong., 3 Sess., 1054 (Feb. 10, 1869; nay; 32–27–7), 1055 (Feb. 10, 1869; yea; 25–34–7), 1050 (Feb. 10, 1869; yea; 24–35–7).

GROUP 4: *Cong. Globe,* 40 Cong., 3 Sess., 1050 (Feb. 10, 1869; nay; 51–7–8), 1840 (March 3, 1869; nay; 34–3–29).

Second Scale—Passage of the Fifteenth Amendment

GROUP 1: *Cong. Globe,* 40 Cong., 3 Sess., 1315 (Feb. 17, 1869; nay; 10–39–17), 1040 (Feb. 9, 1869; nay; 11–45–10), 1304 (Feb. 17, 1869; nay; 6–29–31), 28 (Dec. 8, 1868; yea; 46–6–14), 1314 (Feb. 17, 1869; nay; 12–40–14), 1641 (Feb. 26, 1869; yea; 39–13–14), 121 (Dec. 17, 1868; yea; 44–3–19), 542 (Jan. 23, 1869; yea; 33–9–

24), 1306 (Feb. 17, 1869; nay; 5–30–31), 1040 (Feb. 9, 1869; nay; 13–43–10), 1305 (Feb. 17, 1869; nay; 13–30–23).

GROUP 2: *Cong. Globe,* 40 Cong., 3 Sess., 1301 (Feb. 17, 1869; nay; 14–28–24), 1043 (Feb. 9, 1869; nay; 17–38–11), 1302 (Feb. 17, 1869; nay; 8–24–34), 908 (Feb. 5, 1869; nay; 10–20–36), 1301 (Feb. 17, 1869; nay; 18–31–17), 1300 (Feb. 17, 1869; nay; 21–35–10), 1303 (Feb. 17, 1869; nay; 14–23–29), 1303 (Feb. 17, 1869; nay; 12–25–29), 1029 (Feb. 9, 1869; nay; 21–32–13), 1305 (Feb. 17, 1869; nay; 18–22–26).

Third Scale—Expanding Fifteenth Amendment Coverage

GROUP 1: *Cong. Globe,* 40 Cong., 3 Sess., 1040 (Feb. 9, 1869; yea; 31–27–8).

GROUP 2: *Cong. Globe,* 40 Cong., 3 Sess., 1300 (Feb. 17, 1869; yea; 24–32–10).

GROUP 3: *Cong. Globe,* 40 Cong., 3 Sess., 1295 (Feb. 17, 1869; nay; 33–24–9), 1481 (Feb. 23, 1869; nay; 32–17–17), 908 (Feb. 5, 1869; yea; 9–13–44).

GROUP 4: *Cong. Globe,* 40 Cong., 3 Sess., 1481 (Feb. 23, 1869; nay; 14–36–17).

APPENDIX VIII

RADICALISM IN THE HOUSE OF REPRESENTATIVES
38–40 CONGRESSES

■38 Congress, first session

GROUP 1: *Cong. Globe,* 38 Cong., 1 Sess., 3436 (July 1, 1864; radical vote = nay; final vote = 11–89), 261 (Jan. 18, 1864; yea; 112–16), 1519 (April 9, 1864; yea; 93–18), 261 (Jan. 18, 1864; nay; 27–101), 878 (Feb. 29, 1864; nay; 22–96), in order of marginal frequency.

GROUP 2: *Cong. Globe,* 38 Cong., 1 Sess., 1519 (April 9, 1864; nay; 23–80), 127 (Jan. 7, 1864; yea; 88–24), 768 (Feb. 23, 1864; yea; 71–23), 2579 (May 30, 1864; yea; 79–42), 14 (Dec. 10, 1863; yea; 106–46), 399 (Jan. 28, 1864; yea; 100–44), 2771 (June 6, 1864; nay; 35–67), 846 (Feb. 26, 1864; yea; 82–44), 399 (Jan. 28, 1864; nay; 47–94), 1325 (March 28, 1864; nay; 38–69), 2427 (May 23, 1864; nay; 54–79), 46 (Dec. 17, 1863; nay; 60–100).

GROUP 3: *Cong. Globe,* 38 Cong., 1 Sess., 334 (Jan. 25, 1864; yea; 92–54), 2772 (June 6, 1864; yea; 72–37), 629 (Feb. 12, 1864; nay; 48–87), 2774 (June 6, 1864; nay; 44–66), 2289 (May 16, 1864; yea; 76–53), 21 (Dec. 14, 1863; yea; 98–59), 3179 (June 22, 1864; nay; 50–78), 259 (Jan. 18, 1864; yea; 91–56), 879 (Feb. 29, 1864; nay; 47–76), 2030 (May 2, 1864; yea; 70–50), 631 (Feb. 12, 1864; yea; 94–60), 2995 (June 15, 1864; yea; 93–65), 184 (Jan. 13, 1864; yea; 78–54), 71 (Dec. 21, 1863; yea; 79–55), 3402 (June 29, 1864; yea; 67–47), 8 (Dec. 7, 1863; nay; 74–101), 258 (Jan. 18, 1864; yea; 79–56), 3402 (June 29, 1864; nay; 47–66), 8 (Dec. 7, 1863; yea; 101–71), 659 (Feb. 15, 1864; nay; 58–79), 45 (Dec. 17, 1863; yea; 90–66), 1518 (April 9, 1864; yea; 81–58), 22 (Dec. 14, 1863; yea; 88–66), 2612 (May 31, 1864; nay; 55–76), 3278 (June 25, 1864; nay; 57–78), 2920 (June 14, 1864; yea; 82–57), 45 (Dec. 17, 1863; nay; 67–90), 1635 (April 14, 1864; yea; 78–63), 660 (Feb. 15, 1864; yea; 78–62), 14 (Dec. 10, 1863; yea; 94–73), 2253 (May 12, 1864; yea; 75–64), 3525 (July 2, 1864; yea; 65–53), 1532 (April 11, 1864; yea; 81–64), 629 (Feb. 12, 1864; yea; 83–67), 2578 (May 30, 1864; yea; 81–66), 2108 (May 4,

1864; yea; 73–59), 1634 (April 14, 1864; yea; 80–69), 1634 (April 14, 1864; nay; 70–79).

GROUP 4: *Cong. Globe,* 38 Cong., 1 Sess., 501 (Feb. 4, 1864; nay; 71–83), 895 (March 1, 1864; nay; 62–68), 508 (Feb. 5, 1864; nay; 72–80), 519 (Feb. 5, 1864; yea; 83–74), 3058 (June 17, 1864; yea; 70–61), 34 (Dec. 15, 1863; yea; 91–80), 1626 (April 14, 1864; yea; 75–71), 3357 (June 28, 1864; yea; 82–77), 895 (March 1, 1864; yea; 69–67), 507 (Feb. 4, 1864; yea; 81–79), 3145 (June 21, 1864; nay; 75–76), 1652 (April 15, 1864; nay; 66–66), 1634–35 (April 14, 1864; nay; 71–69), 760 (Feb. 19, 1864; nay; 76–69), 519 (Feb. 5, 1864; nay; 75–73), 759 (Feb. 19, 1864; yea; 67–74), 1652 (April 15, 1864; nay; 75–67), 760 (Feb. 19, 1864; nay; 76–64).

GROUP 5: *Cong. Globe,* 38 Cong., 1 Sess., 2107 (May 4, 1864; yea; 57–76), 1652 (April 15, 1864; yea; 54–85).

GROUP 6: *Cong. Globe,* 38 Cong., 1 Sess., 1289 (March 25, 1864; nay; 53–39), 38 (Dec. 16, 1863; yea; 52–114).

GROUP 7: *Cong. Globe,* 38 Cong., 1 Sess., 2386 (May 20, 1864; nay; 102–26), 2578 (May 30, 1864; yea; 27–114).

■ 38 Congress, second session

GROUP 1: *Cong. Globe,* 38 Congress, 2 Sess., 416 (Jan. 25, 1865; yea; 131–2–49).

GROUP 2: *Cong. Globe,* 38 Cong., 2 Sess., 531 (Jan. 31, 1865; yea; 112–57–13), 531 (Jan. 31, 1865; yea; 119–56–8), 530 (Jan. 31, 1865; nay; 57–111–14), 4 (Dec. 6, 1864; yea; 82–37–63).

GROUP 3: *Cong. Globe,* 38 Cong., 2 Sess., 1160 (Feb. 27, 1865; nay; 27–95–60), 1160–61 (Feb. 27, 1865; yea; 83–46–53), 1264 (March 1, 1865; nay; 49–80–53).

GROUP 4: *Cong. Globe,* 38 Cong., 2 Sess., 1025 (Feb. 23, 1865; yea; 67–54–61), 1025 (Feb. 23, 1865; nay; 52–61–69), 1026 (Feb. 23, 1865; yea; 72–71–39), 1025–26 (Feb. 23, 1865; nay; 68–68–46).

GROUP 5: *Cong. Globe,* 38 Cong., 2 Sess., 970 (Feb. 21, 1865; nay; 91–64–27), 971 (Feb. 21, 1865; nay; 92–57–33).

GROUP 6: *Cong. Globe,* 38 Cong., 2 Sess., 301 (Jan. 17, 1865; nay; 103–34–45).

■ 39 Congress, first session

* *Democratic votes changed from nays to yeas.*

GROUP 1: *Cong. Globe,* 39 Cong., 1 Sess., 946 (Feb. 20, 1866; nay; 18–115–50).

GROUP 2: *Cong. Globe,* 39 Cong., 1 Sess., 921 (Feb. 19, 1866; yea; 117–23–42), 3089 (June 11, 1866; yea; 97–20–66), 698 (Feb. 6, 1866; yea; 112–24–46), 921 (Feb. 19, 1866; yea; 120–26–36), 2572 (May 14, 1866; nay; 19–84–30), 2430 (May 7, 1866; yea; 100–24–59), 2572 (May 14, 1866; yea; 87–22–49), 71 (Dec. 18, 1865; nay; 32–125–23), 688 (Feb. 6, 1866; nay; 34–131–17), 2372 (May 3, 1866; nay; 29–109–45), 6 (Dec. 4, 1865; yea; 133–36–13), 3149 (June 13, 1866; yea; 120–32–32), 1032 (Feb. 26, 1866; yea; 102–27–54), 6 (Dec. 4, 1865; nay; 37–133–12), 4056 (July 23, 1866; yea; 93–26–62), 1368 (March 13, 1866; yea; 107–32–44), 159 (Jan. 9, 1866; yea; 107–32–43).

GROUP 3: *Cong. Globe,* 39 Cong., 1 Sess., 2725 (May 21, 1866; yea; 92–30–61), 33 (Dec. 12, 1865; yea; 126–42–14), 920 (Feb. 19, 1866; yea; 104–33–45), 2878 (May 29, 1866; yea; 96–32–55), 2725 (May 21, 1866; yea; 86–30–67), 69–70 (Dec. 18, 1865; nay; 35–106–41), 1367 (March 13, 1866; yea; 111–38–34), 2429 (May 7, 1866; nay; 29–76–78), 966 (Feb. 21, 1866; yea; 108–38–37), 920 (Feb. 19, 1866; yea; 102–36–44), 4273 (July 27, 1866; yea; 88–31–67), 1861 (April 9, 1866; yea;

122–41–21), 4264 (July 27, 1866; yea; 78–28–70), 950 (Feb. 20, 1866; yea; 109–40–34), 1095 (Feb. 28, 1866; nay; 41–110–32), 310 (Jan. 18, 1866; nay; 47–123–12), 1190 (March 5, 1866; nay; 38–100–45), 61 (Dec. 14, 1865; nay; 42–109–31), 137 (Jan. 8, 1866; yea; 94–37–51), 538 (Jan. 31, 1866; yea; 120–46–16), 2878 (May 29, 1866; nay; 35–86–62), 4264 (July 27, 1866; yea; 81–33–72), 2575 (May 14, 1866; yea; 72–30–81), 311 (Jan. 18, 1866; yea; 116–54–12), 2724 (May 21, 1866; yea; 73–25–85), 62 (Dec. 14, 1865; yea; 107–56–19), 2808 (May 24, 1866; yea; 79–46–58), 2809 (May 24, 1866; nay; 51–81–51).

GROUP 4: *Cong. Globe,* 39 Cong., 1 Sess., 507–508 (Jan. 30, 1866; nay; 64–94–24), 33 (Dec. 12, 1865; yea; 90–63–29), 310 (Jan. 18, 1866; nay; 34–135–15) *, 3985 (July 20, 1866; nay; 53–68–61), 1423 (March 15, 1866; nay; 55–70–58), 4017 (July 21, 1866; yea; 59–52–70), 813 (Feb. 13, 1866; yea; 78–69–33).

GROUP 5: *Cong. Globe,* 39 Cong., 1 Sess., 1296 (March 9, 1866; nay; 82–70–31), 311 (Jan. 18, 1866; nay; 53–117–12) *, 1495 (March 19, 1866; nay; 80–63–40), 3949–50 (July 19, 1866; yea; 43–63–76), 3949 (July 19, 1866; yea; 46–68–68), 3949 (July 19, 1866; yea; 49–71–62).

GROUP 6: *Cong. Globe,* 39 Cong., 1 Sess., 3949 (July 19, 1866; nay; 71–34–77), 2373 (May 3, 1866; yea; 37–95–51), 3948 (July 19, 1866; yea; 31–92–59), 4275 (July 27, 1866; nay; 62–52–72) *, 4276 (July 27, 1866; nay; 62–52–72) *.

▪ 39 Congress, second session

Democratic votes changed from nays to yeas.

GROUP 1: *Cong. Globe,* 39 Cong., 2 Sess., 1535 (Feb. 23, 1867; yea; 96–27–67), 1739 (March 2, 1867; yea; 133–37–21), 646 (Jan. 22, 1867; yea; 109–37–45), 30 (Dec. 6, 1866; nay; 30–124–36), 11 (Dec. 4, 1866; nay; 32–119–40), 324 (Jan. 7, 1867; yea; 111–26–54), 1661 (Feb. 28, 1867; yea; 97–30–63), 4 (Dec. 3, 1866; yea; 116–28–45), 619 (Jan. 21, 1867; yea; 109–37–45), 447 (Jan. 14, 1867; yea; 107–36–48), 322–23 (Jan. 7, 1867; yea; 107–26–58), 1340 (Feb. 19, 1867; yea; 111–41–38), 616 (Jan. 21, 1867; yea; 94–33–74), 1400 (Feb. 20, 1867; yea; 126–46–18), 319 (Jan. 7, 1867; yea; 107–30–54), 1733 (March 2, 1867; yea; 135–48–9), 970 (Feb. 2, 1867; yea; 111–38–41), 685 (Jan. 23, 1867; yea; 108–42–41), 994 (Feb. 4, 1867; yea; 96–36–48), 1175 (Feb. 12, 1867; yea; 113–47–30), 11 (Dec. 4, 1866; yea; 107–37–47), 321 (Jan. 7, 1867; yea; 107–39–45), 320 (Jan. 7, 1867; nay; 40–104–47), 320 (Jan. 7, 1867; nay; 39–105–47), 1215 (Feb. 13, 1867; yea; 109–55–26).

GROUP 2: *Cong. Globe,* 39 Cong., 2 Sess., 1133 (Feb. 11, 1867; yea; 84–59–47), 1399–400 (Feb. 15, 1867; yea; 99–70–21), 970 (Feb. 2, 1867; yea; 82–63–55), 969–70 (Feb. 2, 1867; yea; 75–66–49).

GROUP 3: *Cong. Globe,* 39 Cong., 2 Sess., 1281 (Feb. 16, 1867; nay; 64–69–57), 1215 (Feb. 13, 1867; nay; 69–94–27 *, 817 (Jan. 28, 1867; nay; 88–65–38).

GROUP 4: *Cong. Globe,* 39 Cong., 2 Sess., 1213 (Feb. 13, 1867; nay; 85–78–27) *.

▪ 40 Congress, first session

Group 1: *Cong. Globe,* 40 Cong., 1 Sess., 289 (March 22, 1867; yea; 102–28–34), 504 (July 5, 1867; yea; 111–17–39), 637 (July 13, 1867; yea; 108–20–42), 314 (March 23, 1867; yea; 114–25–25), 638 (July 13, 1867; yea; 112–22–36), 747 (July 19, 1867; yea; 96–24–50), 215 (March 19, 1867; nay; 26–101–36), 747 (July 19, 1867; yea; 108–25–33), 747 (July 19, 1867; yea; 100–22–48), 620 (July 12, 1867; yea; 113–32–25), 17 (March 7, 1867; yea; 111–31–18), 201 (March 19, 1867; yea; 103–24–36), 695 (July 17, 1867; yea; 100–18–52), 642 (July 15, 1867; yea; 84–20–66), 67 (March 11, 1867; yea; 117–27–16), 66 (March 11, 1867; nay; 27–115–18), 546 (July 9, 1867; yea; 119–31–18), 17 (March 7, 1867; yea; 114–33–13), 26 (March 8, 1867; yea; 111–28–21), 500 (July 5, 1867; yea; 110–18–39), 560 (July

10, 1867; yea; 100–29–39), 22 (March 7, 1867; nay; 32–119–9), 190 (March 18, 1867; yea; 98–29–36).

GROUP 2: *Cong. Globe,* 40 Cong., 1 Sess., 559 (July 10, 1867; yea; 79–37–52), 452 (March 29, 1867; nay; 38–63–63), 391 (March 27, 1867; yea; 75–51–38).

GROUP 3: *Cong. Globe,* 40 Cong., 1 Sess., 450 (March 29, 1867; nay; 52–56–56), 320 (March 23, 1867; yea; 64–62–38), 454 (March 29, 1867; nay; 53–45–66).

■ 40 Congress, second session

GROUP 1: *Cong. Globe,* 40 Cong., 2 Sess., 4296 (July 21, 1868; yea; 127–35–53), 2217 (March 28, 1868; yea; 102–30–57), 489 (Jan. 13, 1868; yea; 116–39–33), 478 (Jan. 13, 1868; yea; 113–38–37), 1997 (March 19, 1868; nay; 35–101–53), 210 (Dec. 16, 1867; yea; 112–32–43), 333 (Jan. 6, 1868; nay; 28–80–79), 332 (Jan. 6, 1868; yea; 86–28–73), 209–10 (Dec. 16, 1867; nay; 32–113–42), 332 (Jan. 6, 1868; nay; 28–86–72), 4294 (July 21, 1868; yea; 125–33–52), 1400 (Feb. 24, 1868; yea; 126–47–17), 543 (Jan. 15, 1868; yea; 114–30–35), 488 (Jan. 13, 1868; nay; 39–113–36), 489 (Jan. 13, 1868; yea; 111–38–39), 2505 (May 16, 1868; yea; 88–14–87), 2528 (May 18, 1868; nay; 27–69–93).

GROUP 2: *Cong. Globe,* 40 Cong., 2 Sess., 4473 (July 25, 1868; yea; 103–31–86).

GROUP 3: *Cong. Globe,* 40 Cong., 2 Sess., 2463–64 (May 14, 1868; nay; 60–74–55).

GROUP 4: *Cong. Globe,* 40 Cong., 2 Sess., 68 (Dec. 6, 1867; yea; 57–108–22), 663 (Jan. 21, 1868; yea; 53–112–23).

GROUP 5: *Cong. Globe,* 40 Cong., 2 Sess., 489 (Jan. 13, 1868; yea; 25–124–39).

■ 40 Congress, third session

GROUP 1: *Cong. Globe,* 40 Cong., 3 Sess., 1428 (Feb. 20, 1869; yea; 140–37–46), 1563–64 (Feb. 25, 1869; yea; 144–44–35), 745 (Jan. 30, 1869; yea; 150–42–31), 674 (Jan. 28, 1869; yea; 128–34–60), 35 (Dec. 9, 1868; yea; 128–38–55), 744 (Jan. 30, 1869; yea; 144–45–33).

GROUP 2: *Cong. Globe,* 40 Cong., 3 Sess., 1062 (Feb. 10, 1869; nay; 117–57–48).

GROUP 3: *Cong. Globe,* 40 Cong., 3 Sess., 1057 (Feb. 10, 1869; nay; 137–63–22), 1148 (Feb. 12, 1869; nay; 130–55–38).

APPENDIX IX
IMPEACHMENT IN THE SENATE
40 CONGRESS, SECOND SESSION

Main Scale

GROUP 1: *Trial of Andrew Johnson,* I, 487 (April 11, 1868; pro-conviction vote = nay; final vote = 2–49–3), 1503 (March 2, 1868; nay; 8–22–23), 325 (April 3, 1868; yea; 35–11–8), *Cong. Globe,* 40 Cong., 2 Sess., 1531 (Feb. 29, 1868; nay; 13–27–13), *Trial,* II, 476 (May 7, 1868; nay; 13–37–4), 497 (May 26, 1868; yea; 34–16–4), in order of marginal frequency.

GROUP 2: *Trial of Andrew Johnson,* II, 495 (May 26, 1868; nay; 15–39–0), 494 (May 26, 1868; yea; 35–18–1), I, 507 (April 13, 1868; nay; 15–35–4), II, 487 (May 16, 1868; yea; 35–19–0), 496 (May 26, 1868; yea; 35–19–0), 497 (May 26, 1868; yea; 35–19–0), 435 (May 16, 1868; yea; 34–19–1), I, 633 (April 17, 1868; yea; 29–14–11), *Cong. Globe,* 40 Cong., 2 Sess., 1533 (Feb. 29, 1868; nay; 12–23–18), *Trial,* II, 488 (May 16, 1868; nay; 20–34–0), I, 336 (April 3, 1868; nay; 16–29–9), 693 (April 18, 1868; nay; 19–30–5), II, 489 (May 16, 1868; yea; 32–21–1), 508 (April 13, 1868; nay; 18–32–4), 701 (April 18, 1868; nay; 18–26–10), 474 (May 6, 1868; yea; 28–20–6), I, 693 (April 18, 1868; nay; 20–29–5), 276 (April 2, 1868; yea; 27–17–10), 716 (April 18, 1868; nay; 20–26–8), 35 (March 13, 1868; yea; 28–20–6), 247 (April 2, 1868; nay; 20–29–5), 85 (March 24, 1868; yea; 28–24–2), 214 (April 2, 1868; yea; 28–22–4), II, 494 (May 26, 1868; nay; 24–30–0), I, 697 (April 18, 1868; nay; 22–26–6), 481 (April 11, 1868; nay; 23–28–3), II, 488 (May 16, 1868; nay; 24–30–0), 491 (May 26, 1868; yea; 29–25–0), *Cong. Globe,* 40 Cong., 2 Sess., 1578 (March 2, 1868; nay; 20–24–9).

GROUP 3: *Trial of Andrew Johnson,* II, 491 (May 26, 1868; nay; 26–28–0), 495 (May 26, 1868; yea; 27–27–0), I, 485 (April 11, 1868; nay; 23–29–2), 25 (March 13, 1868; yea; 25–26–3), 521 (April 13, 1868; nay; 25–26–3), 536 (April 15, 1868; yea; 24–26–4), 609 (April 16, 1868; nay; 27–23–4), 612 (April 16, 1868; nay; 27–23–4), 185 (March 31, 1868; yea; 22–26–6), 518 (April 13, 1868; nay; 26–22–6), 35 (March 13, 1868; nay; 27–23–4), 85 (March 24, 1868; nay; 29–23–2), 187 (April 1, 1868; yea; 21–27–6), 605 (April 16, 1868; nay; 29–21–4), II, 141 (April 24, 1868; nay; 21–13–20).

GROUP 4: *Cong. Globe,* 40 Cong., 2 Sess., 2598 (May 27, 1868; nay; 23–14–17), *Trial of Andrew Johnson,* I, 185 (March 31, 1868; nay; 32–18–4), II, 485 (May 16, 1868; nay; 34–19–1), I, 515 (April 13, 1868; nay; 34–17–3), II, 477 (May 7, 1868; yea; 16–36–2), I, 568 (April 15, 1868; nay; 36–15–3), II, 477 (May 7, 1868; yea; 15–38–1).

GROUP 5: *Trial of Andrew Johnson,* I, 489 (April 11, 1868; yea; 12–38–4), II, 307 (April 30, 1868; nay; 35–10–9), I, 426 (April 10, 1868; nay; 42–10–2), II, 476 (May 7, 1868; yea; 6–42–6).

Subscale

GROUP 1: *Trial of Andrew Johnson,* I, 489 (April 11, 1868; nay; 25–27–2), 489 (April 11, 1868; nay; 25–27–2), 268 (April 2, 1868; yea; 22–27–5), *Cong. Globe,* 40 Cong., 2 Sess., 1698 (March 6, 1868; nay; 24–20–9), *Trial,* I, 186 (March 31, 1868; yea; 20–30–4), 186 (March 31, 1868; nay; 31–19–4), II, 478 (May 7, 1868; nay; 22–15–17), *Cong. Globe,* 40 Cong., 2 Sess., 1531 (Feb. 29, 1868; nay; 25–15–13).

GROUP 2: *Trial of Andrew Johnson,* I, 633 (April 17, 1868; yea; 13–30–11).

GROUP 3: *Trial of Andrew Johnson,* I, 371 (April 4, 1868; nay; 37–10–7).

Notes

1. RADICAL RADICALS AND CONSERVATIVE RADICALS

1. Bernard Weisberger, "The Dark and Bloody Ground of Reconstruction Historiography," *Journal of Southern History,* XXV (Nov. 1957), 427–47. The best and most recent historiographies of Reconstruction are Larry G. Kincaid, "Victims of Circumstance: An Interpretation of Changing Attitudes Toward Republican Policy Makers and Reconstruction," *Journal of American History,* LVII (June 1970), 48–66 and Harold M. Hyman's introduction to his edited work, *The Radical Republicans and Reconstruction, 1861–1870* (N.Y., 1967), xvii–lxviii.

2. William A. Dunning, *Essays on the Civil War and Reconstruction, and Related Topics* (N.Y., 1898) and *Reconstruction, Political and Economic, 1865–1877* (N.Y. and London, 1907); John W. Burgess, *Reconstruction and the Constitution, 1866–1876* (N.Y., 1902). Also influential was James Ford Rhodes's *History of the United States From the Compromise of 1850 to the Final Restoration of Home Rule at the South in 1877* (7 vols., N.Y., 1893–1906). Rhodes was a nationalist sympathetic to the opinions of the North in his account of the developments leading to the Civil War, but he condemned Radical Reconstruction in light of what passed in his time for scientific evidence of Negro racial inferiority. Especially important in popularizing the pro-southern interpretation were Claude Bowers, *The Tragic Era: The Revolution After Lincoln* (Cambridge, Mass., 1929) and James G. Randall's synthetic *The Civil War and Reconstruction* (Boston, 1939). In the 1930s "revisionists" emphasized the role of economics in Reconstruction policy-making but shared the anti-Radical Republican, pro-southern bias of their predecessors. See Howard K. Beale's *The Critical Year: A Study of Andrew Johnson and Reconstruction* (N.Y., 1930).

Bowers's *Tragic Era* was sympathetic to Johnson, but more laudatory yet were Robert W. Winston, *Andrew Johnson: Plebeian and Patriot* (N.Y., 1928); Lloyd Paul Stryker, *Andrew Johnson: Profile in Courage* (N.Y., 1929); and George Fort Milton, *The Age of Hate: Andrew Johnson and the Radicals* (N.Y., 1930). Pro-Johnson sentiment lingered into the 1960s with Milton Lomask's *Andrew Johnson: President on Trial* (N.Y., 1960) and Lately Thomas's *The· First President Johnson* (N.Y., 1968).

3. The monographic works which have brought about this revolution include William R. Brock, *An American Crisis: Congress and Reconstruction, 1865–1867* (N.Y. 1963); LaWanda and John H. Cox, *Politics, Principle, and Prejudice, 1865–1866: Dilemma of Reconstruction America* (N.Y., 1963); John Hope Franklin, *Reconstruction: After the Civil War* (Chicago, 1961); Eric L. McKitrick, *Andrew Johnson and Reconstruction* (Chicago, 1960); James M. McPherson, *The Struggle for Equality: The Abolitionists and the Negro in the Civil War and Reconstruction* (Princeton, 1964); Kenneth M. Stampp, *The Era of Reconstruction, 1865–1877* (N.Y., 1965; Hans L. Trefousse, *The Radical Republicans: Lincoln's Vanguard for Racial Justice* (N.Y., 1969).

4. McKitrick, *Johnson and Reconstruction, passim;* Brock, *An American Crisis,* 153–211; David Donald, *The Politics of Reconstruction, 1863–1867* (Baton Rouge, 1968), 53–82; Charles Fairman, *History of the Supreme Court of the United States: Volume VI, Reconstruction and Reunion, 1864–88: Part One* (N.Y., 1971), 253–365.

5. The best discussions of radicalism during the war are T. Harry Williams's *Lincoln and the Radicals* (Madison, 1941) and Trefousse's *The Radical Republicans,* 137–265. Williams's intense anti-radicalism should be taken into account by his readers, however.

6. *Congressional Globe*, 40 Cong., 1 Sess., 100–101 (March 14, 1867; Drake), 638 (July 13, 1867; Stevens). Fessenden referred to "Radical-Radicals" in a letter to Elizabeth Fessenden Warriner, Dec. 15, 1867, William Pitt Fessenden Mss., Bowdoin College Library, Brunswick, Me. See also James W. Nye's castigation of Henry Wilson on one of Wilson's frequent alliances with the less extreme elements of his party, *Cong. Globe*, 40 Cong., 1 Sess., 114 (March 15, 1867), and Henry S. Lane's disgust with "a few extreme Radicals" in the House, *ibid.*, 39 Cong., 2 Sess., 1557 (Feb. 19, 1867).

7. The Rice index of cohesion is a measure of party or group solidarity. Maximum cohesion is represented by 100, minimum by 0.00. The index is found for any roll call by subtracting the percentage of voting members of a group voting in the minority from the percentage voting in the majority and multiplying by one hundred. In the case noted here, the average Reconstruction-connected vote found Republicans divided 84 percent in the majority and 16 percent in the minority. See Lee F. Anderson *et al.*, *Legislative Roll-Call Analysis* (Evanston, Ill., 1966), 32–35.

8. Trumbull to Mrs. Julia Jayne Trumbull, May 8, 1866, copied by Mrs. Mary Ingraham Trumbull, Lyman Trumbull Mss., Illinois State Historical Library. Timothy Otis Howe blamed Fessenden, the leading nonradical in the Senate, personally for the failure of the tenure of office amendment. Howe to Horace Rublee, April 13, 1867. Timothy Otis Howe Mss., Wisconsin State Historical Library. Conness's comments are in the *Cong. Globe*, 40 Cong., 2 Sess., 2901 (June 6, 1868).

9. Howe to Grace T. Howe, Feb. 21, 1866. Howe Mss.

10. *Cong. Globe*, 40 Cong., 2 Sess., 2901 (June 6, 1868).

11. There is no definitive work on the institutional structure of Congress in the 1860s, but anyone working extensively with congressional records will recognize patterns similar to those described in Woodrow Wilson's *Congressional Government: A Study in American Politics* (Boston and N.Y., 1913), first published in 1885. I am indebted to Mrs. Nancy Bowen for allowing me to benefit from her study of the influence of selected Senate committees in the 1860s, "The Top of an Iceberg: Quantitative Analysis Applied to the Finance and Judiciary Committees of the 39th Congress" (unpublished seminar paper, Rice University, 1969).

12. See pp. 185–86, 235, *infra.* I have counted twenty such meetings held from December 1865 until July 1867, when party harmony deteriorated so badly that Republicans feared a caucus would formalize a division rather than promote unity. Reported by newspapers the following day or the next, these caucuses met Dec. 2, 11, 1865; Jan. 10, 16, 1866; Feb. 23, 1866; May 25, 28, 29, 1866; July 11, 14, 1866; Dec. 1, 5, 1866; Jan. 5, 1867; Jan. or Feb. 1867 (discussed in *Cong. Globe*, 40 Cong., 1 Sess., 489–95 [July 5, 1867]); Feb. 16, 1867; Mar. 6, 7, 11, 1867; July 5, 16, 1867.

13. There have been several attempts to use techniques of roll call analysis to investigate Republican radicalism. Glenn M. Linden's "Congressmen, 'Radicalism,' and Economic Issues, 1861–1873" (unpublished Ph.D. dissertation, University of Washington, 1963) was among the first, but used rather crude methodology. Much of the information from his studies appears in two articles: Linden, " 'Radicals' and Economic Policies: The House of Representatives, 1861–1873," *Civil War History*, XIII (March 1967), 51–65, and " 'Radicals' and Economic Policies: The Senate, 1861–1873," *Journal of Southern History*, XXXII (May 1966), 189–99. More sophisticated is Edward L. Gambill, "Who Were the Senate Radicals?" *Civil War History*, XI (June 1965), 237–44. David Donald studied roll calls from 1863 to 1867 closely, although he did not use any established statistical technique, in his *Politics of Reconstruction*. The most sophisticated techniques of analysis appear in Larry George Kincaid, "The Legislative Origins of the Military Reconstruction Act, 1865–1867" (unpublished Ph.D. dissertation, Johns Hopkins University, 1968) and John L. McCarthy, "Reconstruction Legislation and Voting Alignments in the House of Representatives, 1863–1869" (unpublished Ph.D. dissertation, Yale University, 1970).

14. For an explanation of the process of scale analysis, see Appendix I, pp. 381–83.

15. The results of these analyses are presented in appropriate places throughout this study.

16. In the second session of the Thirty-ninth Congress, only Stevens and Boutwell sustained the radical position completely. Morrill and Wilson voted with radicals and radical centrists during the last-minute compromises on the Reconstruction bill. Blaine, Garfield, Schenck, Banks, Bingham, Farnsworth, Hooper, and Allison all opposed them. See List 13, pp. 358–60.

17. *Cong. Globe*, 40 Cong., 1 Sess., 638 (July 13, 1868).

18. The number of man/sessions of support for radicalism is simply the total number of congressional sessions in which each member of a committee ranked either as a radical or radical centrists; the number of man/sessions of opposition to radicalism is the total number of sessions in which each committee member voted with centrists, conservative centrists, or conservatives.

19. Alexander K. McClure, *Colonel Alexander K. McClure's Recollections of Half a Century* (Salem, Mass., 1902), 415.

20. Ben Perley Poore, *Perley's Reminiscences of Sixty Years in the National Metropolis* (2 vols., Philadelphia, Chicago, and Kansas City, 1886), II, 101.

21. James G. Blaine, *Twenty Years of Congress: From Lincoln to Garfield with a Review of the Events Which Led to the Political Revolution of 1860* (2 vols., Norwich, Conn., 1884–86), I, 325.
22. Boston *Daily Advertiser*, Aug. 13, 1868, p. 2; Alexander K. McClure, *Abraham Lincoln and Men of War-Times: Some Personal Recollections of War and Politics during the Lincoln Administration* (3rd edn., Philadelphia, 1892), 264; N.Y. *Independent*, Aug. 20, 1868, p. 4.
23. *N.Y. Tribune*, April 6, 1866, p. 4.
24. Poore, *Reminiscences*, II, 210; Blaine, *Twenty Years of Congress*, II, 289.
25. George A. Townshend, Washington correspondent of the Philadelphia *Telegraph*, in the Centreville *Indiana True Republican*, March 19, 1868, p. 149.
26. Sumner to Francis Lieber, Feb. 18, 1865. Charles Sumner Mss., Houghton Library, Harvard University, Cambridge, Mass.
27. George F. Hoar, *Autobiography of Seventy Years* (2 vols., N.Y., 1908), I, 214.
28. Blaine, *Twenty Years of Congress*, I, 318.
29. Henry Cabot Lodge, *Early Memories* (N.Y. 1913), 289.
30. *Ibid.*, 290.
31. Carl Schurz, *Charles Sumner: An Essay by Carl Schurz*, ed. by Arthur Reed Hogue (Urbana, Ill., 1951), 113.
32. Sumner to Edward L. Pierce, March 11, 1867. Sumner Mss.
33. Moorfield Storey, *Charles Sumner: An American Statesman* (Boston and N.Y., 1900), 86–87.
34. Blaine, *Twenty Years of Congress*, II, 200.
35. *Cong. Globe*, 39 Cong., 1 Sess., 704–705 (Feb. 7, 1866).
36. Howe to Grace T. Howe, July 4, 1866. Howe Mss.
37. Boston *Traveller*, May 9, 1868, p. 1; Fessenden to Francis Fessenden, Dec. 20, 1868. There is scarcely a letter in the Fessenden collection at Bowdoin College that does not make some disparaging remark about the Massachusetts senator.
38. *Cong. Globe*, 39 Cong., 1 Sess., 27 (Dec. 12, 1865).
39. Boston *Commonwealth*, Sept. 9, 1865, p. 2, quoting a correspondent of the Gold Hill (California) *News*.
40. *Cong. Globe*, 41 Cong., 2 Sess., 422 (Jan. 13, 1870).
41. Hoar, *Autobiography*, I, 388.
42. Poore, *Reminiscences*, II, 205–206.
43. Rhodes, *History of the United States from the Compromise of 1850*, VI, 39.
44. See *ibid.*, 39–45; Burgess, *Reconstruction and the Constitution*, 133; Dunning, *Reconstruction*, 213–14.
45. The "radical as vindictive" theme has continued, much abated, to the present. For instance, Lomask, *Andrew Johnson: President on Trial;* T. Harry Williams, "Lincoln and the Radicals: An Essay in Civil War History and Historiography," in Grady McWhiney (ed.), *Grant, Lee, Lincoln and the Radicals: Essays on Civil War Leadership* (Evanston, Ill., 1964), 92–115; Avery Craven, *Re-*

construction: The Ending of the Civil War (N.Y., 1969).
46. Beale, *The Critical Year*. In his excellent historiographical essay, "Victims of Circumstance," Kincaid points out that the economic interpretation of men's motivation was so fundamental to historians when Beale wrote that it was not necessary for him to prove that motivation. Its existence was axiomatic. Beale rather attempted to explain why the northern masses, whose economic interests should have led them to support Johnson, supported the northeastern, business-dominated Congress instead. Kincaid, "Victims of Circumstance," 56–58.
47. Robert P. Sharkey, *Money, Class, and Party: An Economic Study of Civil War and Reconstruction* (Baltimore, 1959).
48. McKitrick studied and rejected the notion that radicalism could be defined in terms of support for black suffrage or opposition to restoring southern states to normal relations in the Union in 1866. Finally he suggested that radicals were bound together by a suspicion of President Johnson in the summer and fall of 1865, but only after he had already conceded that most men known to contemporaries as radicals viewed Johnson with benevolence. McKitrick, *Johnson and Reconstruction*, 53–67. Donald, the Coxes, and Brock have also emphasized the difficulty of differentiating a radical program or ideology from that of the Republican moderates. Donald, "Devils Facing Zionward," in McWhiney (ed.), *Grant, Lee, Lincoln and the Radicals*, 72–88; LaWanda and John Cox, *Politics, Principle, and Prejudice*, 208–10; Brock, *An American Crisis*, 73–74. Harold Hyman, tracing the factors which influenced historians to condemn Republican postwar Reconstruction policy, drew a distinction between older, more idealistic Republican leaders and the rising, practical, young politicians of the 1860s. Hyman (ed.), *The Radical Republicans*, lxvii–lxviii. Among the recent studies which try to determine what radicals did and did not have in common are Stanley Coben, "Northeastern Business and Radical Reconstruction: A Re-examination," *Mississippi Valley Historical Review*, XLVI (June 1959), 67–90; Peter Kolchin, "The Business Press and Reconstruction," *Journal of Southern History* XXXIII (May 1967), 183–96; Gambill, "Who Were the Senate Radicals?"; Linden's dissertation, "Congressmen, 'Radicalism,' and Economic Issues, 1861–1873," his articles, "'Radicals' and Economic Policies: The Senate, 1861–1873," "'Radicals' and Economic Policies: The House of Representatives," and "'Radical' Political and Economic Policies: The Senate, 1873–1877"; Donald's *Politics of Reconstruction* and his "Devils Facing Zionwards," in McWhiney (ed.), *Grant, Lee, Lincoln and the Radicals*, 72–91; and T. Harry Williams, "Lincoln and the Radicals," *ibid.*, 92–117.
49. Linden's crude technique of analysis led

him to categorize too many Republicans as radical, but this is easily remedied by separating congressmen in his list who qualify as radicals after more sophisticated analysis from those who do not. This does not affect the validity of Linden's conclusion. Linden incorporated into his study myriad issues, among them the Homestead bill, tariff regulation, various loan bills, currency measures, tax legislation, and funding bills. The fact that radicals manifested no common voting patterns on all these measures demonstrates the error in Beale's depiction of a monolithic procapitalist and pro-industrialist Radical party, but it does not answer suggestions that radicals may have shared common attitudes toward specific issues —money questions or the tariff, for example.

50. Among the issues I studied were fiscal conservatism (that is, tightfistedness with public money), government subsidies for economic development, national bankruptcy legislation, legislation generally involving expansion of national government activities, legislation to aid agriculture, antimonopoly legislation, and currency regulation. Only the last named seemed to bear a definite relationship with radicalism. I discuss that relationship *infra.*

51. The Rice index of likeness is found by subtracting the percentage of one party's membership voting for a measure from the percentage of the other party's membership voting for it, always subtracting the smaller number from the larger. The difference is subtracted from 100 and then multiplied by 100. Thus a roll call on which the parties split 75–25 percent and 25–75 percent respectively will have an index of likeness equal to a roll call on which they split 90–10 percent and 40–60 percent respectively (that is, 50.00). An index equaling less than 50.00 marks a rather large disagreement.

52. *Cong. Globe,* 38 Cong., 1 Sess., 1361 (March 31, 1864).
53. *Ibid.,* 1652 (April 15, 1864).
54. The Republican candidate for governor of Connecticut in April 1865 won 42,374 votes; in March 1866 the gubernatorial candidate won 43,974 votes. In October 1865 a proposition to amend the Connecticut constitution to allow blacks to vote won 27,217 votes— roughly two-thirds of that cast for the Republican candidates in the regular elections. In Minnesota the Republican candidate for governor garnered 17,355 votes; a black suffrage amendment to the state constitution received 12,318. In Wisconsin, the Republican gubernatorial candidate received 58,322 votes, while a black suffrage amendment received 46,588. All statistics come from the *American Annual Cyclopedia and Registry of Important Events for 1865 and 1866* (N.Y., 1866 and 1867, respectively).
55. D.W. Vaughan, "Conservatism," *The Radical,* II (April 1867), 474, 476.
56. Boston *Evening Journal,* Nov. 9, 1867,

p. 4; Joseph A. Wheelock to Ignatius Donnelly, Oct. 9, 1865. Ignatius Donnelly Mss., Minnesota State Historical Society. Wheelock was coeditor of the St. Paul *Press,* the organ of the state party.

57. Quoted on page 105 of volume two of *The Campaign of 1867,* one of Edward M. McPherson's scrapbooks in the McPherson Mss. in the Library of Congress.
58. γ (gamma) is a measure of correlation for ranked ordinal variables developed by Leo A. Goodman and William H. Kruskal. I have used the computation method described in Theodore K. Anderson and Morris Zelditch, Jr., *A Basic Course in Statistics with Sociological Applications* (2nd edn., N.Y. and other cities, 1968), 152–55. +1.000 would be a perfect positive correlation.
59. Sharkey, *Money, Class, and Party,* 282.
60. It is extremely difficult to prove a negative statement like this. But in all my reading in the *Congressional Globe* from the Thirty-eighth to the Forty-first Congresses, I have never seen the issues connected by a radical and only once by a conservative. Moreover, Sharkey also seems to have been unable to find such references. He offers none in his work. But he does find numerous indications that conservatives connected the two issues, that conservatism and contractionism were somehow related. This offers the real key to the problem, I believe.
61. The seven opponents of the tariff were B. Gratz Brown, Joseph S. Fowler, James W. Grimes, John B. Henderson, Samuel J. Kirkwood, Henry S. Lane, and Lyman Trumbull.
62. See pp. 262–65, *infra.*
63. For roll calls relating to land grants, see Appendix VI, p. 386.
64. Proponents and opponents of currency expansion from the Thirty-ninth through the Fortieth Congresses are listed in Appendix A, pp. 378–81.
65. Donald, *Politics of Reconstructions,* 26–52.
66. There is also the problem of the simple vagary of statistics. When I first compiled a list of consistent radicals and nonradicals for my doctoral dissertation, the voting patterns of their constituents seemed to verify Donald's conclusion. But in that analysis I deliberately excluded roll calls involving the rights of black Americans unless directly relating to the South. The minor changes that resulted in the list of consistent factionists when I included those roll calls completely disrupted the correlation between radicalism and political security that I thought I had confirmed. See Michael Les Benedict, "The Right Way: Congressional Republicans and Reconstruction, 1863–1869" (unpublished Ph.D. dissertation, Rice University, 1971), 50–51.
67. Reported in the Boston *Commonwealth,* Jan. 27, 1866, p. 2.
68. Garfield to James M. Comly, Dec. 12, 1865. James M. Comly Mss., Ohio State Historical Society.

69. Julian, *Political Recollections,* 331; Blaine *et al.,* "Ought the Negro to Be Disfranchised?" 270–71.
70. Spalding in the *Cong. Globe,* 39 Cong., 2 Sess., 290 (Jan. 5, 1867); Grinnell, *ibid.,* 287 (Jan. 4, 1867). See also Hamilton Ward, *ibid.,* 116 (Dec. 13, 1866).
71. Sidney H. Morse, "Concerning the Nation's Soul," *The Radical,* I (April 1866), 287.
72. Fessenden, *ibid.,* 1 Sess., 705 (Feb. 7, 1866), 1275 (March 9, 1866); Sumner, *ibid.,* 673 (Feb. 6, 1866).

2. The Politics of Radicalism

1. Greeley to Alonzo B. Cornell, Oct. 16, 1871. Horace Greeley Mss., Manuscripts Div., L. C.
2. Greeley to Justin S. Morrill, March 12, 1872, quoted in William Belmont Parker, *The Life and Public Services of Justin Smith Morrill* (Boston and N.Y., 1924), 239–40.
3. The long story of factional strife in New York before 1869 is well documented by historians. The profession has done less well in elucidating the origins of the liberal movement in that state. Glyndon G. Van Deusen's three studies of the old liberal Whig triumvirate, taken together, offer an excellent panorama of New York politics. They are: *Horace Greeley, Nineteenth Century Crusader* (N.Y., 1964; originally published 1953); *William Henry Seward* (N.Y., 1967); *Thurlow Weed: Wizard of the Lobby* (Boston, 1947), Sidney David Brummer, *Political History of New York State During the Period of the Civil War* (N.Y., 1911) and Homer Adolph Stebbins, *A Political History of the State of New York, 1865–1869* (N.Y., 1913) are detailed accounts of politics in the state. Greeley has been the subject of numerous biographies. Most useful are Jeter Allen Isely, *Horace Greeley and the Republican Party, 1853–1861: A Study of the New York Tribune* (Princeton, N.J., 1947) and Don C. Seitz, *Horace Greeley: Founder of the New York Tribune* (Indianapolis, 1926). LaWanda and John H. Cox discuss Seward and Weed's machinations during the first year of Andrew Johnson's presidential term in their *Politics, Principle, and Prejudice, 1865–1866: Dilemma of Reconstruction America* (N.Y., 1963), 1–49, 68–87, 107–28. The development of the liberal Republican movement in New York wants doing. Sources I have used in my sketch of that development include the Horace Greeley, Whitelaw Reid, Hamilton Fish, and Roscoe Conkling Mss. at the Library of Congress; the Charles Eliot Norton Mss. at the Houghton Library at Harvard University, Cambridge, Massachusetts (particularly George William Curtis to Norton, Sept. 17, 1870); the *N.Y. Times* and *N.Y. Tribune*; Donald Barr Chidsey, *The Gentleman from New York: A Life of Roscoe Conkling* (New Haven, Conn., 1935); Alfred R. Conkling, *The Life and Letters of Roscoe Conkling: Orator, Statesman, Advocate* (N.Y., 1889); Chauncey M. Depew, *My Memories of Eighty Years* (N.Y., 1924); Thomas Collier Platt, *The Autobiography of Thomas Collier Platt,* comp. and ed. by Louis J. Lang (N.Y.,

1910); Beman Brockway, *Autobiography of Beman Brockway* (N.Y., 1891). Harry J. Carman and Reinhard H. Luthin's *Lincoln and the Patronage* (N.Y., 1943) is indispensable to an understanding of the factional problems among Republicans during the war.
4. [Joseph] Allan Nevins, *The Evening Post: A Century of Journalism* (N.Y., 1968), 284–330. The Coxes discuss the Democrats' relations to the new President in *Politics, Principle, and Prejudice,* 50–87. Stebbins discusses New York politics in pp. 44–80 of his *Political History of the State of New York.* The *N.Y. Times* and *N.Y. Tribune,* detailing accounts of the myriad political meetings of 1865 and early 1866, are the best sources for what politicians supported what policies at any given time during this hectic era.
5. Historians have not yet offered detailed accounts of factional divisions within the state Republican parties. The outlines of these rivalries can be discovered by looking at various sources not directly dealing with them. Maine: Gaillard Hunt, *Israel, Elihu and Cadwallader Washburn: A Chapter in American Biography* (N.Y., 1925), 54–55, 67, 69–75, 100, 106, 112; Charles Eugene Hamlin, *The Life and Times of Hannibal Hamlin* (Cambridge, Mass., 1899); H. Draper Hunt, *Hannibal Hamlin of Maine: Lincoln's First Vice President* (Syracuse, N.Y., 1969); Charles A. Jellison, *Fessenden of Maine: Civil War Senator* (Syracuse, 1962); David Saville Muzzey, *James G. Blaine: A Political Idol of Other Days* (N.Y., 1934); Charles Edward Russell, *Blaine of Maine: His Life and Times* (N.Y., 1931); Fessenden to Hugh McCulloch, April 24, 1865. Hugh McCulloch Mss., L.C.; C. Peters to Fessenden, Aug. 21, 1867. William Pitt Fessenden Mss., L.C.; Massachusetts: Fred Harvey Harrington, *Fighting Politician: Major General N.P. Banks* (Philadelphia, 1948); Samuel Shapiro, *Richard Henry Dana, Jr., 1815–1882* (East Lansing, Mich., 1961); Edward L. Pierce, *Memoirs and Letters of Charles Sumner* (4 vols., Boston, 1893); Henry Greenleaf Pearson, *The Life of John A. Andrew: Governor of Massachusetts, 1861–1865* (2 vols., Boston & N.Y., 1904); David Donald, *Charles Sumner and the Coming of the Civil War* (N.Y., 1960); Donald, *Charles Sumner and the Rights of Man* (N.Y., 1970); Edith Ellen Ware, *Political Opinion in Massachusetts during the Civil War and Reconstruction* (N.Y., 1916); the Andrew and Edward Atkinson Mss. in the Massachu-

setts Historical Society, Boston, Mass.; and the Sumner Mss. at the Houghton Library of Harvard University; Pennsylvania: Erwin Stanley Bradley, *The Triumph of Militant Republicanism: A Study of Pennsylvania and Presidential Politics, 1860–1872* (Philadelphia, 1964); Bradley, *Simon Cameron: A Political Biography* (Philadelphia, 1966); Alexander K. McClure, *Abraham Lincoln and Men of War-Times: Some Personal Recollections of War and Politics During the Lincoln Administration* (3rd edn., Philadelphia, 1892); William H. Egle, *Andrew Gregg Curtin: His Life and Services* (Philadelphia, 1895); Reinhard H. Luthin, "Pennsylvania and Lincoln's Rise to the Presidency," *Pennsylvania Magazine of History and Biography*, LXVIII (Jan. 1943), 61–82; Rebecca Gifford Albright, "The Civil War Career of Andrew Gregg Curtin, Governor of Pennsylvania," *Western Pennsylvania Historical Magazine*, XLVII (Oct. 1964), 323–41, XLVIII (Jan. 1965), 19–42, (Apr. 1965), 151–74; the Stevens and Cameron Mss. in the Library of Congress; Indiana: Emma Lou Thornbrough, *Indiana in the Civil War Era, 1850–1880* (Indianapolis, 1965), 38–123, 180–273; Kenneth M. Stampp, *Indiana Politics During the Civil War* (Indianapolis, 1949); William Dudley Foulke, *Life of Oliver P. Morton, Including His Important Speeches* (2 vols., Indianapolis and Kansas City, 1899); George W. Julian, *Political Recollections, 1840–1872* (Chicago, 1884); Patrick W. Riddleberger, *George Washington Julian, Radical Republican: A Study in Nineteenth Century Politics and Reform* (Indianapolis, 1966); the Indianapolis *Daily Journal* (Morton's organ) and the Centreville *Indiana True Republican*, later the Richmond (Indianapolis) *Radical* (Julian's organ); the George W. Julian Mss. in the Indiana Division of the Indiana State Library; Wisconsin: James L. Sellers, "James R. Doolittle," *Wisconsin Magazine of History*, XVII (Dec. 1933), 168–78, (March 1934), 277–306, (June 1934), 393–401, XVIII (Sept. 1934), 20–41, (Dec. 1934), 178–87; Richard W. Hantke, "Elisha Keyes and the Radical Republicans," *ibid.*, XXXV (Spring 1952), 203–208; Helen J. and Harry Williams, "Wisconsin Republicans and Reconstruction," *ibid.*, XXIII (Sept. 1939), 17–39; William H. Russell, "Timothy O. Howe, Stalwart Republican," *ibid.*, XXXV (Winter 1951), 90–99; Leslie H. Fishel, Jr., "Wisconsin and Negro Suffrage," *ibid.*, XLVI (Spring 1963), 192; Minnesota: John C. Haugland, "Alexander Ramsey and the Republican Party, 1855–1875: A Study of Personal Politics" (unpublished Ph.D. dissertation, University of Minnesota, 1961); Martin Ridge, *Ignatius Donnelly: Portrait of a Politician* (Chicago, 1962); Rhoda R. Gilman, "Ramsey, Donnelly, and the Congressional Campaign of 1868," *Minnesota History*, XXXVI (Dec. 1959), 300–308; John D. Hicks, "The Political Career of Ignatius

Donnelly," *Mississippi Valley Historical Review*, VIII (June–Sept. 1921), 80–96; Iowa: Johnson Brigham, *James Harlan* (Iowa City, Iowa, 1913); Leland L. Sage, "William Boyd Allison and Iowa Senatorial Politics, 1865–1870," *Iowa Journal of History and Politics*, LII (Apr. 1954), 97–128; Sage, *William Boyd Allison: A Study in Practical Politics* (Iowa City, 1956); William Salter, *The Life of James W. Grimes: Governor of Iowa, 1854–1858; Senator of the United States, 1859–1869* (N.Y., 1876); Stanley P. Hirshson, *Grenville M. Dodge: Soldier, Politician, Railroad Pioneer* (Bloomington, Ind., 1967).

6. Brother J. Robert Lane's *A Political History of Connecticut During the Civil War* (Washington, 1941) gives a thorough account of wartime factional disputes. There is no account of intraparty struggles in Connecticut during the Reconstruction era. In developing the outline presented here I have used Lane; the *N.Y. Times's* account of the 1866 battle for Foster's Senate seat, May 16, 1866, p. 5; the Foster scrapbook in the Lafayette S. Foster Mss. in the Massachusetts Historical Society, Boston, Mass.; Gideon Welles, *Diary of Gideon Welles—Secretary of the Navy Under Lincoln and Johnson* (3 vols., Boston and N.Y., 1911), II, 502 (May 5, 1866), 507–508 (May 14, 1866); William M. Grosvenor to Charles Sumner, Sept. 5, 1865. Sumner Mss., Houghton Library; E.W. Palmer to Lyman Trumbull, May 3, 1866. Trumbull Mss. L.C.; J.R. Doolittle to Mrs. Mary Doolittle, May 20, 1866. James Rood Doolittle Mss., Wisconsin State Historical Society Library. Due to the scarcity of secondary literature on the factional disputes in this and other states during Reconstruction, I have had to make inferences and deductions from evidence I have found in light of the information that is available for the earlier period during the war.

7. James G. Blaine, *Twenty Years of Congress: From Lincoln to Garfield with a Review of the Events Which Led to the Political Revolution of 1860* (2 vols., Norwich, Conn., 1884–86), II, 185.

8. *Ibid.*, II, 186, 188; William Frank Zornow, *Kansas: A History of the Jayhawk State* (Norman, Okla., 1957), 119–22; Wendell Holmes Stephenson, *The Political Career of General James H. Lane* (Topeka, 1930); Samuel J. Crawford, *Kansas in the Sixties* (Chicago, 1911), 234–35; Mark A. Plummer, *Frontier Governor: Samuel J. Crawford of Kansas* (Lawrence, 1971); Zornow, "The Kansas Senators and the Re-election of Lincoln," *Kansas Historical Quarterly*, XIX (May 1951), 133–44; Plummer, "Governor Crawford's Appointment of Edmund G. Ross to the United States Senate," *ibid.*, XXVIII (Summer 1962), 145–53; *N.Y. Times*, Jan. 29, 1865, p. 3.

9. The politics of Ohio during the Civil War and Reconstruction are detailed in Eugene H. Roseboom, *The Civil War*

Era, 1850–1873 (N.Y., 1911); Donnal
V. Smith, *Chase and Civil War Politics*
(Columbus, 1931); Felice A. Bonadio,
*North of Reconstruction: Ohio Politics,
1865–1870* (N.Y., 1970). I have also
used the Sherman and Chase Mss. in
the Library of Congress; the Schenck
Mss. in the Rutherford B. Hayes Library in Fremont, Ohio; the William
Henry Smith Mss. in the Ohio Historical
Society Library, Columbus, Ohio; James
R. Therry, "The Life of General Robert
Cummings Schenck" (unpublished Ph.D.
dissertation, Georgetown University,
1968); and Hans L. Trefousse, *Benjamin Franklin Wade: Radical Republican from Ohio* (N.Y., 1963).

10. Campbell to Sherman, Jan. 18, 1866,
John Sherman Mss., Manuscripts Div.,
L.C.

11. Bonadio, *North of Reconstruction, passim.*

12. Foulke, *Morton,* I, 152–53; Centreville
Indiana True Republican, Nov. 30, 1865,
p. 86; Riddleberger, *Julian,* 139–40, 195–
97, 217–18.

13. *Senate Executive Journal,* XV, 136, 156.

14. Clark to John Sherman, Feb. 25, 1866.
John Sherman Mss.

15. Sloan's testimony on impeachment,
House Report No. 7, 40 Cong., 1 Sess.,
appendix, 268–71.

16. E.C. Ingersoll to John H. Bryant, Dec.
18, 1865; Bryant to Trumbull, Dec. 19,
22, 30, 1865, Jan. 8, 1866; E. Emery to
Trumbull, Jan. 5, 1866; Clark E. Carr
to Trumbull, Jan. 8, 1866; Bryant to
Trumbull, May 16, 1866; Emery to
Trumbull, May 22, 1866; John Olney
to Trumbull, Nov. 16, 1865, Apr. 19,
1866; J.C. Sloo *et al.* to Trumbull, May
3, 1866; Peter Page to Trumbull, May
18, 1866; E. Ketchill to Trumbull,
Oct. 21, 1865; E.W. Weldoen, Oct. 23,
1865; J.G.D. Pettijohn to Trumbull,
Nov. 20, 1865; T.J. Johnson to Trumbull, Dec. 3, 1865; D. Clarke to Trumbull, Dec. 6, 1865; Pettijohn to
Trumbull, Dec. 6, 1865; E.S. Condit to
Trumbull, Dec. 9, 1865; Pettijohn to
Trumbull, Jan. 15, 1866; J.L. Hallam
to Trumbull, May 14, 1866; C.D. Hay
to Trumbull, May 16, 1866. Trumbull
Mss., Manuscripts Div., L.C.

3. THE WADE-DAVIS BILL

1. For the most complete discussion of efforts to formulate Reconstruction policy,
see Herman Belz, *Reconstructing the
Union: Theory and Policy During the
Civil War* (Ithaca, N.Y., 1968).

2. James D. Richardson (ed.), *Messages
and Papers of the Presidents, 1789–1897*
(10 vols., Washington, 1896–99), VI,
213–15. Lincoln's attitude toward restoration policy before 1864 is discussed in Charles H. McCarthy, *Lincoln's Plan of Reconstruction* (N.Y.,
1966), 10–23, 38–53, 79–85; William B.
Hesseltine, *Lincoln's Plan of Reconstruction* (Tuscaloosa, Ala., 1960), 48–70;
Belz, *Reconstructing the Union,* 126–
55.

3. John G. Nicolay and John Hay, *Abra-
ham Lincoln: A History* (10 vols., N.Y.,
1890), IX, 109–12; William Frank
Zornow, *Lincoln and the Party Divided*
(Norman, Okla., 1954) 17–18; Belz,
Reconstructing the Union, 166–67.

4. T. Harry Williams, *Lincoln and the
Radicals* (Madison, 1941), 318.

5. *Ibid.,* 317–19; Hesseltine, *Lincoln's
Plan of Reconstruction,* 110–14; Mc-
Carthy, *Lincoln's Plan of Reconstruction,* 275; James G. Randall and David
Donald, *The Civil War and Reconstruction* (2nd edn., Boston, 1961), 551–
53; Zornow, *Lincoln & the Party Divided.* 16–19, 108–109; Belz, *Reconstructing the Union,* 198–200, 232–33.
Belz gives a detailed account of the
bill's passage on pp. 198–223.

6. Thomas J. Durant to Chase, Feb. 21,
1864; March 5, 1864. Salmon P. Chase
Mss., Manuscripts Div., L.C.; Durant
to Lincoln, Feb. 26, 28, 1864. Robert
Todd Lincoln collection of the papers
of Abraham Lincoln (hereafter Lincoln
Mss.), Manuscripts Div., L.C.; Durant
to George S. Boutwell, Feb. 25, 1864;

Durant to Thaddeus Stevens, Feb. 29,
1864; Durant to Henry L. Dawes, March
31, 1864; Durant to Davis, March 31,
1864. Thomas J. Durant Mss., New
York Historical Society; New York,
N.Y.; Benjamin F. Flanders to Lincoln,
Jan. 16, 1864. Lincoln Mss.

7. Thomas W. Conway to Banks, August
29, 31, 1864, Nathaniel Banks Mss.,
Manuscripts Div., L.C.; George S.
Denison to Chase, Feb. 5, 19, March
5, 1864, in Salmon Portland Chase,
*Diary and Correspondence of Salmon
P. Chase,* ed. by Edward G. Bourne
et al., vol. two of the *Annual Report of
the American Historical Association for
the Year 1902* (2 vols., Washington,
1903), 430–35.

8. Criticisms: Davis in *Cong. Globe,* 38
Cong., 1 Sess., 682 (Feb. 16, 1864);
Ashley, *Ibid.,* 1358–59 (March 30,
1864); Smithers, *ibid.,* 1742–43 (April
19, 1864); Kelley, *ibid.,* 2080 (March 3,
1864). Support: Beaman, *ibid.,* 1245–46
(Feb. 16, 1864); Ashley, *ibid.,* 1357
(March 30, 1864); Broomall, *ibid.,* 1769
(Apr. 20, 1864); Donnelly, *ibid.,* 2035
(May 2, 1864); Gooch, *ibid.,* 2071 (May
3, 1864); Boutwell, *ibid.,* 2102 (May 4,
1864).

9. *Ibid.,* 2108 (May 4, 1864), 3491 (July 2,
1864).

10. *Cong. Globe,* 38 Cong., 1 Sess., 1829
(April 23, 1864), 2079–80 (May 3);
Hutchins to Chase, Feb. 12, 24, 1864.
Chase Mss.; George S. Denison to
Chase, Feb. 19, March 5, 1864 in
Bourne *et al.* (eds.), *Diary and Corre-
spondence of Salmon P. Chase,* 430–32
and 432–35, respectively; Frank E.
Howe to Chase, Feb. 6, 1864; Chase to
Howe (copy), Feb. 20, 1864; Benjamin
Rush Plumly to Chase, March 4, 1864.
Chase Mss., L.C.

11. William Whiting, "Military Government," in *War Powers Under the Constitution of the United States* (43rd edn., Boston and N.Y., 1871), 310–12, 314; Ashley to Stanton, Dec. 24, 1863. Letters rec'd. by the Secretary of War, Irregular Series, 1861–66. Record Group 107, National Archives.

12. *Cong. Globe,* 38 Cong., 1 Sess., 1357 (March 30, 1865). Whiting completed his treatise sometime before March 24, 1864. Whiting, *War Powers Under the Constitution,* 259.

13. *Cong. Globe,* 38 Cong., 1 Sess., 1769 (April 20, 1864). See also Sumner's observation to the same effect, *ibid.,* 2898 (June 13, 1864); Representative Daniel Gooch, *ibid.,* 2071 (May 3, 1864); Fernando C. Beaman, *ibid.,* 1246 (Mar. 22, 1864); George S. Boutwell, *ibid.,* 2102 (May 4, 1864).

14. Francis Lieber, *On Civil Liberty and Self-Government* (2nd edn., Philadelphia, 1859), 154. The work first appeared in 1853. See also James Madison, *Federalist No. 48;* William Alexander Duer, *A Course of Lectures on the Constitutional Jurisprudence of the United States, Delivered Annually in Columbia College, New York* (N.Y., 1843), 45; James Wilson, *Of Government,* in *The Works of James Wilson,* ed. by Robert Green McCloskey (2 vols., Cambridge, Mass., 1967), I, 290–99; St. John Tucker (ed.), *Blackstone's Commentaries: with Notes of Reference, to the Constitution and Laws, of the Federal Government of the United States; and of the Common Wealth of Virginia* (5 vols., Philadelphia, 1803), I, appendix, 33–35; Joseph Story, *Commentaries on the Constitution of the United States* (2 vols., Boston, 1851), I, 363–68; James Kent, *Commentaries on American Law* (3 vols., N.Y., 1836), I, 220.

15. The best overall study of the exercise of presidential powers during the Civil War is in James G. Randall, *Constitutional Problems Under Lincoln* (Urbana, 1964). See also Edward S. Corwin, *The President: Office and Powers 1787–1957, History and Analysis of Practice and Opinion* (4th rev. edn., N.Y., 1957), 228–34.

16. *Cong. Globe,* 38 Cong., 1 Sess., 682 (Feb. 16, 1864), 2012 (April 30, 1864).

17. *Luther v. Borden,* 7 Howard 1 (1849). The Supreme Court would follow this precedent in 1866, when it simply added West Virginia to the circuit, thus virtually deciding the state's legitimacy before any case was even brought before it.

18. *Cong. Globe,* 38 Cong., 1 Sess., 1357 (Mar. 30, 1864).

19. *Ibid.,* 681, 682 (Feb. 16, 1864).

20. *Ibid.,* 2038 (May 2, 1864).

21. *Ibid.,* 33–34 (Dec. 15, 1863).

22. *Ibid.,* 681 (Feb. 16, 1864). Ohio Representative Robert C. Schenck responded to Davis's objections by moving that the House instruct the Elections committee to investigate and report on Arkansas's status "by bill or otherwise" before deciding whether its representatives should be seated. Dawes objected to treating his committee "differently from what you would any other committee," and with the issue clouded by the question of committee rights, Schenck's motion was defeated by a coalition of thirty-six Republicans—including six clearly identifiable as radicals—and all the Democrats voting.

Davis had every reason to worry that Dawes would indeed limit his investigation simply to whether the claimants' credentials were in proper form. During the previous Congress, his committee had reported in favor of seating representatives from Tennessee, Virginia, and Louisiana after just such a cursory examination. *Ibid.,* 680–87 (Feb. 16, 1864).

23. *Ibid.,* 2392 (May 21, 1864), 2458–59 (May 25, 1864), 2586 (May 31, 1864), 2895–907 (June 13, 1964).

24. *Ibid.,* appendix, 85 (March 22, 1864); *ibid,.* 1245 (March 22).

25. *Ibid.,* appendix, 85 (March 22, 1864).

26. *Ibid.* (March 22, 1864). Davis may have been oversanguine regarding the limitations the court acknowledged on its power to challenge state constitutions. In 1866 the court would void a provision of a state constitution as conflicting with the national Constitution's ban on *ex post facto* laws. If that decision were carried to its logical conclusion, then an abolition provision in a state constitution might be held to violate the national Constitution (which the court had decided protected citizens' rights to slave property in *Dred Scott)* in the same way, especially if it took national action to recognize the state government. *Cummings* v. *Missouri,* 71 U.S. 277 (1866).

27. For a discussion of Ashley's bill, see Belz, *Reconstructing the Union,* 176–82. Belz suggests that Ashley's bill was really more conservative than the Wade-Davis bill, despite Ashley's inclusion of black suffrage in its provisions, because given the situation the later measure was "charged with a radical purpose"—the overthrow of the Louisiana and Arkansas regimes. Belz correctly indicates that Ashley did not consider his bill to conflict with Lincoln's policy. We differ in my conclusion that the Wade-Davis bill's primary purpose was no different than Ashley's: to regularize and legalize Lincoln's program. Thus, in my view, Ashley's bill, incorporating black suffrage where the Lincoln plan and the Reconstruction bill did not, is the more radical measure.

28. *Cong. Globe,* 38 Cong., 1 Sess., 1345–46 (March 30, 1864), 1361–64 (March 31, 1864). One Republican who voted against the amendment abstained on the vote passing the bill; five others voted for it.

29. The vote provides a clue to the position of the special committee which reported the Reconstruction bill. Only Ashley voted to concur in the Negro suffrage amendment. Davis, Nathaniel B. Smith-

ers (both Republicans), James C. Allen, and William S. Holman (Democrats) opposed it. Republicans Reuben E. Fenton and Henry T. Blow did not vote, nor did Democrat James E. English, although there was no doubt as to his position. *Ibid.,* 1652 (April 15, 1864).

30. *Ibid.*
31. *Ibid.,* 1706 (April 19, 1864).
32. *Ibid.,* 1639–40 (April 15, 1864), 1697–98, 1694 (April 18), 1704–706 (April 19), 1744–46 (April 20), 1842–46 (April 25), 2347–51 (May 19), 2385–86 (May 20).
33. *Ibid.,* 2349 (May 19, 1864).
34. *Ibid.,* 2104 (May 4, 1864).
35. *Ibid.,* 2107 (May 4, 1864).
36. *Ibid.,* 3448 (July 1, 1864).
37. *Ibid.,* 3862 (June 29, 1864).
38. The text of Brown's amendment may be found *ibid.,* 3449.
39. *Ibid.,* 3449–50, 3460–61 (July 1, 1864), 3491 (July 2, 1864). Belz suggests that the five Senators who had supported the amendment July 1 but were absent the next day had been subject to backstage pressures. But close analysis of the *Globe* indicates that they were absent for the whole evening of July 2, during which the Reconstruction bill was only a small part of the business. However, five other Republicans do seem to have abstained from this particular roll call. Belz, *Reconstructing the Union,* 222–23.
40. Provisions forbidding high-ranking rebels from holding office and repudiating debts incurred during the rebellion also were required in the constitutions.
41. *Cong. Globe,* 38 Cong., 1 Sess., 1354, 1356 (March 30, 1864).
42. Carl Schurz, *The Reminiscences of Carl Schurz* (3 vols., N.Y., 1908–1909), III, 222. See also Harold M. Hyman's discussion of the dangers of reviving one's allegiance to the Union during the war in his "Deceit in Dixie," *Civil War History,* III (March 1957), 68–69.
43. Richardson (ed.), *Messages and Papers*

of the Presidents, VI, 189. Schurz offered a similar analysis in his *Reminiscences,* III, 221–22.

44. Richardson (ed.), *Messages and Papers of the Presidents,* VI, 189, 214–15.
45. *Cong. Globe,* 38 Cong., 1 Sess., 1245 (March 22, 1864).
46. John Hay, *Lincoln and the Civil War in the Diaries and Letters of John Hay,* ed. by *Tyler Dennett* (N.Y., 1939), 204; Nicolay and Hay, *Lincoln,* IX, 120. The Constitution provides that any bill not signed by the president within ten days of his receipt becomes law unless Congress first adjourns. If the president withholds his signature in such a situation, and Congress adjourns, he is said to have executed a "pocket veto."
47. Denison to Chase, Aug. 12, 1863, Feb. 19, Mar. 5, 1864, in Bourne *et al.* (eds.), *Diary and Correspondence of Salmon P. Chase,* 399–402, 430–32, and 432–35, respectively; Chase to Frank E. Howe, Feb. 20, 1864; J.L. Whitaker to Chase, May 20, 1864. Chase Mss., L.C.; Stephen Hoyt to Banks, Apr. 25, 1864; J.R. Hamilton to Henry J. Raymond (copy), May 27, 1864; B.R. Plumly to Banks, June 24, Aug. 9, 1864. Banks Mss., L.C.
48. Noah Brooks, *Washington in Lincoln's Time,* ed. by Herbert Mitgang (N.Y. and Toronto, 1958), 154–55; Nicolay and Hay, *Lincoln,* IX, 121.
49. The text of the Wade-Davis manifesto may be found in *Appleton's Annual Cyclopaedia, 1864,* 307–10n. Stevens believed the President's proclamation "infamous." Stevens to Edward M. McPherson, July 10, 1864. Stevens Mss., L.C.; Albert Gallatin Riddle, *Recollections of War Times: Reminiscences of Men and Events in Washington, 1860–1865* (Cleveland, 1887), 304–305; Belz, *Reconstructing the Union,* 228–31; Hans L. Trefousse, *Benjamin Franklin Wade: Radical Republican from Ohio* (N.Y., 1963), 227–29; Trefousse, *The Radical Republicans: Lincoln's Vanguard for Racial Justice* (N.Y., 1968), 293–94.

4. THE RADICALS ON THE DEFENSIVE

1. Radical-conservative lines in the Senate were so altered during the second session of the Thirty-eighth Congress that the votes taken during its course displayed configurations similar to only two votes taken during the first. That this shift is due primarily to the change in issue is indicated by the fact that those two votes dealt with Reconstruction: the recognition of Arkansas.
2. *Cong. Globe,* 38 Cong., 2 Sess., 969 (Feb. 21, 1865).
3. For accounts of the election of 1864 generally, see Hans L. Trefousse, *The Radical Republicans: Lincoln's Vanguard for Radical Justice* (N.Y., 1968), 289–98; William Frank Zornow, *Lincoln & the Party Divided* (Norman, Okla., 1959), *passim;* and more specialized studies, such as Donnal V. Smith,

Chase and Civil War Politics Volume II of the Ohio Historical Collections (Columbus, 1931); Winfred A. Harbison, "Indiana Republicans and the Re-election of President Lincoln," *Indiana Magazine of History,* XXXIV (March 1938), 42–64; Zornow, "The Kansas Senators and the Re-election of Lincoln," *Kansas Historical Quarterly,* XIX (May, 1951), 133–44.

The president's patronage power was by no means absolute. Custom dictated that the president honor the advice of local politicians in making appointments. Each congressman could name the postmaster of his home town. Where a state or local party was united, the president appointed officers not suggested by party workers only at his peril. But where there were factional disputes, his options multiplied. He could favor one side or the other or he could try to deal even-handedly so as to give neither an advantage. Presidential favor could be critical in local disputes, therefore, and here his power was great. For the only major study of Lincoln's use of the patronage, see Harry J. Carman and Reinhard H. Luthin, *Lincoln and the Patronage* (N.Y., 1943).

4. Weed, after taking a leading role in forcing Lincoln's renomination on New York Republicans, threatened to sit out the campaign unless Lincoln appointed men acceptable to him to powerful patronage positions in New York, according to the recollections of his old enemy, radical Reuben Fenton, the Republican candidate for governor at the time. At the urging of Fenton and other radicals, who probably foresaw their own defeats as well as Lincoln's if Weed made his threat good, Lincoln acquiesced. Allen Thorndike Rice (ed.), *Reminiscences of Abraham Lincoln by Distinguished Men of His Time* (N.Y., 1888), 68–70; Glydon G. Van Deusen, *Thurlow Weed: Wizard of the Lobby* (Boston, 1947), 308–12; Ralph Lee Fahrney, *Horace Greeley and the Tribune in the Civil War* (Cedar Rapids, Iowa, 1936), 175–91, 194–210.

5. Phillips to Moncure D. Conway, Jan. 18 [?], 1865. McKim-Garrison Mss. in the Maloney Collection (hereafter McKim-Garrison Mss.), New York City Public Library. See also George W. Julian's complaints to the same effect in "George W. Julian's Journal," *Indiana Magazine of History,* XI (Dec. 1915), 228.

6. Lincoln to Banks, Dec. 24, 1863, in Lincoln, *The Collected Works of Abraham Lincoln,* ed. by Roy P. Basler (9 vols., New Brunswick, 1953), VII, 89–90; Willie Malvin Caskey, *Secession and Restoration of Louisiana,* Louisiana State University Studies, Number 36 (Baton Rouge, 1938), 92–94.

7. Fred Harvey Harrington, *Fighting Politician: Major General N.P. Banks* (Philadelphia, 1948), 14–51.

8. Caskey, *Secession and Restoration of Louisiana,* 86–88; Gerald M. Capers, *Occupied City: New Orleans Under the Federals, 1862–1865* (Lexington, Ky., 1965), 106–107, 222–26.

9. Harrington, *Fighting Politician,* 101.

10. Caskey, *Secession and Restoration of Louisiana,* 92–140; Harrington, *Fighting Politician,* 100–102, 144–50; Capers, *Occupied City,* 133–41; Charles H. McCarthy, *Lincoln's Plan of Reconstruction* (N.Y., 1966), 61–76. Inside views of the radical-conservative (or perhaps more accurately Flanders-Hahn) split were steadily sent to Chase and are a valuable source of information. See the George S. Denison-Chase letters in Edward G. Bourne *et al.* (eds.), *Diary and Correspondence of Salmon P. Chase* (Washington, 1903), 297–458.

11. J.V.C. Smith to Banks, July 13, 1864; Conway to Banks, Aug. 29, 31, 1864. Banks Mss., L.C.; Plumly to Garrison,

Oct. 20, 1864, quoted in the Boston *Liberator,* Nov. 11, 1864, p. 182; Banks, *Address of Major General Nathaniel P. Banks, on the Condition of the Negro Population as Connected with the Reorganization of Government in the Rebel States,* quoted *ibid.,* Dec. 30, 1864, p. 209; *ibid.,* Jan. 13, 1865, p. 6.

12. Wendell Phillips, *The Immediate Issue: A Speech . . . at the Annual Meeting of the Massachusetts Anti-Slavery Society at Boston,* in George Luther Stearns (comp.), *The Equality of All Men Before the Law Claimed and Defended* (Boston, 1865), 34.

13. *Cong. Globe,* 38 Cong., 1 Sess., 1895 (March 1, 1864), 3350 (June 28, 1864). In the first session four Republican representatives who abstained or voted against the Freedmen's Bureau bill on passage had supported it on preliminary votes. In the second session twenty-three representatives who either abstained or opposed the bill on the final vote joined in defeating Democratic efforts to table it. Only two Republicans aided the tabling effort. *Ibid.,* 2 Sess., 566 (Feb. 2, 1865), 694 (Feb. 9), 1402 (March 3).

14. See Thomas D. Eliot's justification of the bill, *ibid.,* 38 Cong., 1 Sess., 573 (Feb. 10, 1864); William D. Kelley's, *ibid.,* 774 (Feb. 23).

15. All knew that Davis bitterly opposed the Lincoln-Banks-Hahn Louisiana government. Four of the five Republicans on his committee were known as pronounced radicals. James F. Wilson, the respected chairman of the Judiciary committee, himself had been the strongest radical on his committee during the first session. Three other members, though radical, had not been as consistent in their votes as members of the Reconstruction committee.

16. *Ibid.,* 2 Sess., 26 (Dec. 13, 1864). A somewhat modified version of the Eliot resolution is quoted *ibid.,* 281 (Jan. 16, 1865). Herman Belz discusses the resolution in *Reconstructing the Union: Theory and Policy during the Civil War* (Ithaca, 1969), 250–51.

17. *House Report No. 13,* 38 Cong., 2 Sess. (Feb. 11, 1865). Banks's testimony is given on pp. 15–25; *Suggestions Presented to the Judiciary Committee of the Senate of the U.S. by Major General N.P. Banks Relating to the State of Louisiana,* Senate *Miscellaneous Document No. 9,* 38 Cong., 2 Sess. (Jan. 11, 1865).

18. Hahn to Hurlbut, Dec. 5, 1864. Mss., Manuscripts Div., L.C.

19. V.J.C. Smith to Banks, Oct. 15, 1864; B.R. Plumly to Banks, Oct. 20, 1864; Hahn to Banks, Oct. 25, 1864; Stephen Hoyt to Banks, Dec. 3, 1864. Banks Mss., L.C.

20. Stanton to Banks, Dec. 6, 1864. Banks Mss., L.C.; Banks to Stanton, Dec. 7, 1864. Lincoln Mss.; Banks to Lincoln, Dec. 2, 1864. Banks Mss., L.C. Lincoln did attempt to control the military hostility to the restored Louisiana state government, however. Lincoln to Hurlbut, Nov. 14, 1864, and Lincoln to

Canby, Dec. 12, 1864, in Lincoln, *Works,* VIII, 106–107, 163–64.

21. Chase mentioned this conversation to Lincoln and George S. Denison. Chase to Lincoln, April 12, 1865, in Lincoln, *Works,* VIII, 399–401n; Denison to Chase, Jan. 15, 1865, quoted in Bourne *et al.* (eds.), *Diary and Correspondence of Salmon P. Chase,* 455–56. Denison informed Chase that he doubted that Louisianans would agree to extend the vote to blacks, however. Eliot announced in the House, while advocating recognition of Louisiana, that he was satisfied "from information derived from the highest sources" that the Louisiana legislature would quickly enfranchise qualified blacks. *Cong. Globe,* 38 Cong., 2 Sess., 300 (Jan. 17, 1865).

22. Harrington, *Fighting Politician,* 42, 50–51. Hooper had been defending Banks's activities at least since October. Samuel Hooper to Banks, Oct. 7, 1864. Banks Mss., L.C.

23. See Field's testimony in *House Report No. 13,* 38 Cong., 2 Sess., 26–35.

24. A.P. Field *et al.* to Banks, Dec. 12, 1864. Banks Mss., L.C.

25. *N.Y. Tribune,* Dec. 17, 1864, p. 4.

26. Sumner to Bright, Jan. 1, 1865, quoted in Edward L. Pierce, *Memoir and Letters of Charles Sumner,* (4 vols., Boston, 1893), IV, 221.

27. Lincoln to Trumbull, Jan. 9, 1865, in Lincoln, *Works,* VIII, 206–207.

28. Lincoln, *Works,* VIII, 399–405.

29. Memorial of Citizens of Louisiana, *Sen. Misc. Doc. No. 6,* 38 Cong., 2 Sess. (Dec. 7, 1867). The memorial was presented to the House also. *House Misc. Doc. No. 6,* 38 Cong., 2 Sess. (Dec. 13, 1864).

30. Phillips to Moncure Daniel Conway, Jan. 18 [?], 1865. McKim-Garrison Mss.; Phillips, *The Immediate Issue,* in Stearns (comp.), *Equality Before the Law,* 29–35; Frederick Douglass, *What the Black Man Wants: Speech of Frederick Douglass at the Annual Meeting of the Massachusetts Anti-Slavery Society at Boston, ibid.,* 36–39; Grosvenor, "The Law of Conquest the True Basis of Reconstruction," *New Englander,* XXIX (Jan., 1865), 111–31; McKim to Garrison, Jan. 17, 1865, quoted in the Boston *Liberator,* Jan. 27, 1865, p. 15; Boston *Commonwealth,* Feb. 4, 1865, pp. 1, 2.

31. *Cong. Globe,* 38 Cong., 2 Sess., 53 (Dec. 15, 1864). Belz describes the bill's provisions in *Reconstructing the Union,* 251–52.

32. John Hay, *Lincoln and the Civil War in the Diaries and Letters of John Hay,* ed. by Tyler Dennet (N.Y., 1939), 244–46 (Dec. 18, 1864).

33. Davis to S.F. du Pont, Dec. 20, 1864. du Pont Mss., Eleutherian Mills Historical Library; *N.Y. Times,* Dec. 19, 1864, p. 1.

34. *Cong. Globe,* 38 Cong., 2 Sess., 290 (Jan. 16, 1865). Kelley proposed amendments to enfranchise all black men in the South. *Ibid.,* 281 (Jan. 16, 1865), 968 (Feb. 21, 1865). Both Stevens and

Julian opposed Ashley's proposition on test votes until he eliminated the provision recognizing Lincoln's reorganized governments. *Ibid.,* 310 (Jan. 17, 1865), 970, 971 (Feb. 21, 1865), 1002 (Feb. 22, 1865). Julian acidly attacked the Lincoln administration's conservatism in a prepared speech February 7, 1865. *Ibid.,* appendix, 65–68. See also Phillips, *The Immediate Issue,* in Stearns (comp.), *Equality Before the Law,* 30, and the Boston *Commonwealth,* Jan. 21, 1865, p. 2; Feb. 4, 1865, p. 2; Feb. 25, 1865, p. 2.

35. Both amendments are in *Cong. Globe,* 38 Cong., 2 Sess., 280–81 (Jan. 16, 1865).

36. *Ibid.,* 301 (Jan. 17, 1865), 628 (Feb. 6, 1865), 643–44 (Feb. 7, 1865); Belz, *Reconstructing the Union,* 263.

37. *Ibid.,* 934–37 (Feb. 20, 1865).

38. *Ibid.,* 968 (Feb. 21, 1865).

39. *Ibid.,* 970–71 (Feb. 21, 1865.

40. *Ibid.,* 970 (Feb. 21, 1865). Radicals made one last futile effort in the House to pass a Reconstruction law. On February 22 Wilson reported a bill similar to his delaying amendment from his Judiciary committee. Ashley succeeded in defeating his effort to prevent amendment by calling the previous question and once more proposed his Reconstruction bill, as a substitute, for the Wilson measure. But the whole subject was again—and finally—laid upon the table. *Ibid.,* 997–1003 (Feb. 22, 1865).

41. *House Report No. 13,* 38 Cong., 2 Sess. (Feb. 11, 1865); Minutes of the House Committee on Elections, 1856–67. R. G. 233, N. A., Washington, D.C.

42. The majority consisted of Republicans Portus Baxter, Glenni W. Scofield, Green Clay Smith, and Dawes, and Democrats James S. Brown and John Ganson. The Republican dissenters were Nathaniel B. Smithers and Charles Upson.

43. *Cong. Globe,* 38 Cong., 2 Sess., 870 (Feb. 17, 1865).

44. *Ibid.,* 505 (Jan. 30, 1865).

45. *Ibid.,* 533, 535 (Feb. 1, 1865).

46. *Ibid.,* 582 (Feb. 3, 1865). The entire debate may be found *ibid.,* 532–33, 534–37 (Feb. 1, 1865), 548–63 (Feb. 2, 1865), 574–86 (Feb. 3, 1865), 590–95 (Feb. 4, 1865).

47. *Ibid.,* 711 (Feb. 9, 1865).

48. *Ibid.,* 1011 (Feb. 23, 1865).

49. *Ibid.,* 1107 (Feb. 25, 1865).

50. *Ibid.,* 1108 (Feb. 25, 1865).

51. *Ibid.*

52. "We killed the Louisiana Bill . . . so dead, that it will not pass this session," Zachariah Chandler wrote his wife after the Senate adjourned. Chandler to Mrs. Letitia Chandler, Feb. 27, 1865, quoted in Sister Mary Karl George, "Zachariah Chandler: Radical Revisited" (unpublished Ph.D. dissertation, St. Louis University, 1965), 170; Sumner to George Bancroft, Feb. 28, 1865. George Bancroft Mss., Massachusetts Historical Society.

53. *Cong. Globe,* 38 Cong., 2 Sess., 1129 (Feb. 27, 1865). The entire debate may

be found *ibid.*, 1011–12 (Feb. 23, 1865), 1061–70 (Feb. 27, 1865), 1091–99, 1101–11 (Feb. 25, 1865), 1126–29 (Feb. 27, 1865).

54. Sumner to George Bancroft, Feb. 28, 1865. George Bancroft Mss.; Wendell Phillips to Sumner, Mar. 1, 1865; Parker Pillsbury to Sumner, June 2, 1865. Sumner Mss.

55. Phillips to Sumner, Mar. 1, 1865. Sumner Mss.; letter fragment from Phillips to Conway, sent in spring, 1865. McKim-Garrison Mss.

56. Gideon Welles, *Diary of Gideon Welles —Secretary of the Navy Under Lincoln and Johnson* (3 vols., Boston, 1911), II, 237 (Feb. 6, 1865).

57. It was not at all legally certain that a presidential pardon would exempt the pardoned individual's property from confiscation. What Lincoln evidently intended was to order United States officials in Virginia to cease enforcing the Confiscation acts. Lincoln may have been showing himself willing to disregard a congressional law once again, as he had considered the possibility of disregarding the proposed Reconstruction bill in December 1864 (see pp. 90–91, *supra*).

58. Lincoln expressed these hopes to Welles. Welles, *Diary*, II, 279–80 (Apr. 13, 1865).

59. Lincoln to Major General Godfrey Weitzel, April 12, 1865, in Lincoln, *Works*, VIII, 406–407.

60. Nicolay and Hay, *Lincoln*, IX, 456–63; Lincoln, *Works*, VIII, 399–405.

61. Sumner to Lieber, April 11, 1865, in Pierce, *Sumner*, IV, 236; Adolphe de Chambrun, *Impressions of Lincoln and the Civil War: A Foreigner's Account*, trans. by Aldebert de Chambrun (N.Y., 1952), 94.

62. For Lincoln's efforts to employ the Virginia rebel legislature to secure peace, and Republican reaction, see U.S. House of Representatives, Committee on the Judiciary, *Report on the Impeachment of the President, House Report No. 7*, 40 Cong., 1 Sess. (Nov. 25, 1865), appendix, 400; Welles, *Diary*, II 279–80 (Apr. 14, 1865); Benjamin P. Thomas and Harold M. Hyman, *Stanton: The Life and Times of Lincoln's Secretary of War* (N.Y., 1962), 353–56; Lincoln, *Works*, VIII, 386–89, 405–407.

63. Thomas and Hyman, *Stanton*, 357–58.

64. Chase to Lincoln, April 11, 12, 1865, in Lincoln, *Works*, VIII, 399–401n.; Springfield *Illinois State Journal*, April 17, 1865, p. 1.

65. Wendell Phillips, *Abraham Lincoln*, in his *Speeches, Lectures, and Letters* (2nd series, Boston, 1894), 446, 448; Alley to Sumner, May 6, 1865. Sumner Mss.

5. The Radicals on the Offensive

1. George W. Julian, "George W. Julian's Journal—Assassination of Lincoln," *Indiana Magazine of History*, XI (Dec. 1915), 335. (April 16, 1865).

2. The Coxes have devoted more energy to exploring the byzantine politics of 1865 than any other historians, but they approached the subject from the vantage point of Johnson and his allies, tracing their hopes and expectations rather than those of the conservative and center Republicans who did not follow Johnson out of the party. Nonetheless they recognized the conservative Seward's and Weed's intention to build a broad Union organization that would isolate both radicals and Peace Democrats. LaWanda and John H. Cox, *Politics, Principle, and Prejudice: Dilemma of Reconstruction, America* (N.Y., 1963), *passim*; Eric L. McKitrick, *Andrew Johnson and Reconstruction* (Chicago and London, 1960), 42–92; W.R. Brock, *An American Crisis: Congress and Reconstruction, 1865–1867* (N.Y., 1963), 15–48.

3. Julian, "Journal," 335, 336 (April 16, 1865).

4. John Savage, *The Life and Public Services of Andrew Johnson, Seventeenth President of the United States* (N.Y., 1866), 338, 348.

5. Sumner to John Bright, April 18, 1865, quoted in Edward L. Pierce, *Memoir and Letters of Charles Sumner* (4 vols., Boston, 1893), IV, 239–40; James G. Blaine, *Twenty Years of Congress: From Lincoln to Garfield with a Review of the Events Which Led to the Political Revolution of 1860* (2 vols., Norwich, Conn., 1884–86), II, 7–15.

6. Chambrun to Martha Corcelle de Chambrun, April 21, 1865, quoted in Chambrun, *Impressions of Lincoln and the Civil War: A Foreigner's Account* (N.Y., 1952), 109–16.

7. Benjamin P. Thomas and Harold M. Hyman, *Stanton: The Life and Times of Lincoln's Secretary of War* (N.Y., 1962), 405–18; Raoul S. Naroll, "Lincoln and the Sherman Peace Fiasco—Another Fable?" *Journal of Southern History*, XX (Nov. 1954), 459–83.

8. Gideon Welles, *Diary of Gideon Welles —Secretary of the Navy Under Lincoln and Johnson* (3 vols., Boston and N.Y., 1911), II, 294 (April 21, 1865), 301 (May ?, 1865), 301–304 (May 9, 1865).

9. Stearns to Sumner, April 30, 1865. Sumner Mss.; Sumner to Bright, May 1, 1865, quoted in Pierce, *Sumner*, IV, 241–42.

10. The pamphlet was George L. Stearns (comp.), *Equality of All Men before the Law Claimed and Defended* (Boston, 1865).

11. The *Independent* reprinted an editorial in favor of suffrage extension from the *Methodist Quarterly Review*, on Feb. 9, 1865, p. 6. The N.Y. *National Anti-Slavery Standard* reprinted one of Henry Ward Beecher's sermons on the same subject March 4, 1865, p. 1; Boston *Liberator*, Jan. 13, 1865, p. 6; Boston

Commonwealth, Mar. 11, 1865, p. 2; May 20, 1865, p. 2; June 3, 1865, p. 1.

12. Atkinson to [Sumner?], Feb. 17, 1865. Edward Atkinson Mss., Massachusetts Historical Society; Frank Preston Stearns, *The Life and Public Services of George Luther Stearns* (Philadelphia and London, 1907), 332–38; Chase to William D. Kelley, Jan. 22, 1865, quoted in Robert Bruce Warden, *An Account of the Private Life and Public Services of Salmon P. Chase* (Cincinnati, 1968), 633; Chase to Francis Lieber, Feb. 14, 18, 1865. Francis Lieber Mss., Huntington Library; Chase to Rev. J.M. Reid, Jan. 23, 1865, quoted in James W. Schuckers, *The Life and Public Services of Salmon Portland Chase* (N.Y., 1874), 514.

13. Stearns to Sumner, May 8, 1865. Sumner Mss; Sumner, *Promises of the Declaration of Independence, and Abraham Lincoln: Eulogy on Abraham Lincoln, before the Municipal Authorities of the City of Boston, June 1, 1865,* in *The Works of Charles Sumner* (15 vols., Boston, 1870–1883), IX, 367–428; Wendell Phillips, "Abraham Lincoln," in *Speeches, Lectures and Letters* (2nd series, Boston, 1894), 446–53; George B. Loring, *The Present Crisis: A Speech Delivered by Dr. Geo. B. Loring at Lyceum Hall, Salem, Wednesday Evening, April 26, 1865, on the Assassination of President Lincoln. Dr. Loring's Letter to the Salem Gazette, on Reconstruction* (South Danvers, Mass., 1865); John Greenleaf Whittier, *The Lesson and Our Duty,* in Whittier, *The Prose Works of John Greenleaf Whittier* (3 vols., N.Y., 1894), III, 148–54; Gilbert Haven, *A Memorial Discourse on the Character & Career of Abraham Lincoln,* in Gilbert Haven, *National Sermons: Speeches and Letters on Slavery and Its War* (Boston, 1869), 551–80.

14. Phillips to Sumner, May 5, 1865; Edward L. Pierce to Sumner, March 12, 1865; George Bailey Loring to Sumner, April 23, May 1, 1865. Sumner Mss.

15. Chambrun to Martha de Corcelle de Chambrun, June 4, 5, 1865, quoted in Chambrun, *Impressions of Lincoln and the Civil War,* 155–58.

16. Chase to Johnson, April 18, 1865. Andrew Johnson Mss., Manuscripts Div., L.C.; Sumner to F.W. Bird, Apr. 25, 1865; Sumner to Bright, May 1, 1865, quoted in Pierce, *Sumner,* IV, 241, 241–42; Sumner, *The One Man Power vs. Congress,* delivered Oct. 2, 1866, at the Boston Music Hall, quoted in the Boston *Daily Advertiser,* Oct. 3, 1866, p. 1.

17. William Dudley Foulke, *Life of Oliver P. Morton, Including His Important Speeches* (2 vols., Indianapolis and Kansas City, 1899), I, 440–41; Edward McPherson (ed.), *The Political History of the United States of America, During the Period of Reconstruction . . .* (3rd edn., Washington, 1880) 45–47; Julian, "Journal," 337 (May 24, 1867); Julian, *Political Recollections, 1840–1872* (Chicago, 1884), 260–62.

18. Sumner to Bright, May 1, 1865; Sumner

to Lieber, May 2, 1865, quoted in Pierce, *Sumner,* IV, 241–42 and 243, respectively; Sumner to Stearns, May 4, 1865, quoted in Stearns, *Stearns,* 344.

19. Chase to Johnson, May 4, 7, 12, 17, 21, 23, 1865. Johnson Mss.

20. Sumner to Lieber, May 2, 1865, quoted in Pierce, *Sumner,* IV, 243; Sumner to Stearns, May ?, 1865, quoted in Stearns, *Stearns,* 344; R.B. Hayes to Sophie B. Hayes, May 7, 1865. Rutherford B. Hayes Mss., Rutherford B. Hayes Library; Stearns to Sumner, May 8, 1865. Sumner Mss.

21. Welles, *Diary,* II, 281–82 (April 14, 1865), 301 (May ?, 1865); McPherson (ed.), *Political History of . . . Reconstruction* 8–9.

22. Stevens to Sumner, May 10, 1865. Sumner Mss.

23. Thomas and Hyman, *Stanton,* 403–404.

24. Welles, *Diary,* II, 301–303; Thomas and Hyman, *Stanton,* 444–46.

25. Julian, *Political Recollections,* 263; Patrick W. Riddleberger, *George Washington Julian, Radical Republican: A Study in Nineteenth Century Politics and Reform,* volume XLV of the Indiana Historical Collections (Indianapolis, 1966), 211.

26. Stevens to Johnson, May 15, 1865. Johnson Mss.

27. James D. Richardson (ed.), *A Compilation of the Messages and Papers of the Presidents of the United States* (10 vols., Washington, 1896–99) VI, 312–14; Sumner to Bright, June 5, 1865, quoted in Pierce, *Sumner,* IV, 253.

28. John H. and LaWanda Cox, *Politics, Principle and Prejudice,* 150–71; Hans L. Trefousse, "Ben Wade and the Negro," *Ohio Historical Quarterly,* LXVIII (April, 1959), 161–76.

29. Johnson to Sharkey, Aug. 15, 1865, quoted in McPherson (ed.), *Political History of . . . Reconstruction,* 19–20; Henderson's speech, reported in the Indianapolis *Daily Journal,* Oct. 25, 1865, p. 2; Henderson's explanation, in *Cong. Globe,* 39 Cong., 1 Sess., 1438 (March 16, 1866).

30. McPherson (ed.), *Political History of . . . Reconstruction,* 48–49. Stearns published the interview in the Boston *Daily Advertiser,* Oct. 23, 1865, p. 2.

31. Richardson (ed.), *Messages and Papers of the Presidents,* VI, 313.

32. *N.Y. Independent,* June 22, 1865, p. 3; Sumner to Lieber, May 7, 1865. Sumner Mss. Also Henry Winter Davis, Letter to a Friend, May 27, 1865, in Davis, *Speeches and Addresses Delivered in the Congress of the United States, and on Several Public Occasions* (N.Y., 1867), 556–63, at 562; Isaac F. Redfield to Solomon Foot, Sept. 9, 1865, quoted in Joel Parker, *Revolution and Reconstruction. Two Lectures Delivered in the Law School of Harvard College in Jan., 1865, and Jan., 1866* (N.Y., 1866), 78–79.

33. Sumner to Wade, June 9, 1865. Sumner Mss.

34. *Ibid.;* Stevens to Sumner, May 10, 30, Oct. 7, 1865. Sumner Mss.

35. Phillips to Moncure D. Conway, Sept. 12, 1865. McKim-Garrison Mss., N.Y. Pub. Library; Davis to Sumner, June 20, 1865; Wade to Sumner, July 29, 1865. Sumner Mss.; Welles, *Diary,* II, 325 (June 30, 1865); Senator William Sprague to Chase, Sept. 6, 1865. Chase Mss., L.C.
36. N.Y. *Independent,* June 8, 1865, p. 8.
37. Boutwell to Sumner, June 12, 1865. Sumner Mss.; Carl Schurz, *Reminiscences of Carl Schurz* (3 vols., N.Y., 1908–1909), III, 157–86; Claude Moore Fuess, *Carl Schurz: Reformer (1829–1906),* (N.Y., 1932), 130–33; Schurz to Johnson, Aug. 18, 21, 29, Sept. 4, 6, 15, 23 (2 letters). Johnson Mss.
38. Sumner to Chase, June 25, 1865. Chase Mss., L.C.; Harlan to Sumner, June 15, 19, Aug. 21, 1865. Sumner Mss.; Sumner to McCulloch, July 12, 1865; McCulloch to Sumner, Aug. 15, 1865. Hugh McCulloch Mss., L.C.
39. George S. Boutwell, *Reminiscences of Sixty Years in Public Affairs* (N.Y., 1902), 103–104; Boutwell to McCulloch, July 1, 1865; McCulloch to Forbes, June 27, July 3, July 10, 1865; R.D. Mussey to McCulloch, July 11, 1865; McCulloch to Atkinson, June 30, 1865; Medill to McCulloch, June 16, 1865; Reid to McCulloch, July 9, 1865; McCulloch to Sumner, Aug. 15, 1865. McCulloch Mss., L.C.
40. George S. Boutwell, *Reconstruction: Its True Basis, Speech at Weymouth, Mass., July 4, 1865,* in Boutwell, *Speeches and Papers Relating to the Rebellion and the Overthrow of Slavery* (2 vols., Boston, 1867), II, 372–407, at 378–79; Henry Wilson in Washington and John B. Alley at Salem, Mass., July 4, 1865, quoted in the Boston *Liberator,* July 21, 1865, p. 113; N.Y. *Independent,* July 13, 1865, p. 8; Springfield *Illinois State Journal,* July 19, 1865, p. 2, quoting the *Chicago Tribune* and *Albany Evening Journal;* Buffalo *Morning Express,* July 31, 1865, p. 1.
41. Michael Les Benedict, *The Impeachment and Trial of Andrew Johnson* (N.Y., 1973), 37–44.
42. Hooper to Banks, Aug. 27, 1865. Banks Mss., Illinois State Historical Library. Chase to Sprague, Sept. 6, 1865; Sprague to Chase, Sept. 6, 1865. Chase Mss., L.C.; Boutwell to McCulloch, Sept. 29, 1865. McCulloch Mss., L.C.
43. Davis, *Letter to a Friend,* May 27, 1865, in Henry Winter Davis, *Speeches and Addresses Delivered in the Congress of the United States, and on Several Public Occasions* (N.Y., 1867), 556–63; Henry Whitney Bellows, *Historical Sketch of the Union League Club of New York: Its Origin, Organization, and Work, 1863–1879* (N.Y., 1879), 87; N.Y. *Tribune,* May 29, 1865, p. 4; May 30, p. 4; May 31, p. 4; June 1, p. 4; June 6, p. 4; June 13, p. 4; June 14, p. 4; June 15, p. 4; June 23, p. 4; New York *Nation,* July 6, 1865, p. 4; July 20, p. 68; July 27, pp. 101–102; Boston *Evening Journal,* June 21, 1865, p. 4; Sept. 16, p. 4; Boston *Daily Advertiser,* June 6, 1865, p. 2; Harris L. Dante, "Reconstruction Politics in Illinois" (unpublished Ph.D. dissertation, University of Chicago, 1950), 108–109.
44. N.Y. *Times,* June 22, 1865, p. 5; June 25, p. 6. A copy of Andrew's letter may be found in the John Albion Andrew Mss., dated June 19, 1865, at the Massachusetts Historical Society. It is quoted in the N.Y. *Times,* June 25, p. 6. The committee consisted of Dana, Parsons, Charles G. Loring, John Greenleaf Whittier, Jacob M. Manning, Samuel Gridley Howe, George Luther Stearns, John Murray Forbes, and William Endicott, Jr.
45. Forbes to N.M. Beckwith, June 25, 1865, quoted in Forbes, *Letters and Recollections of John Murray Forbes,* ed. by Sarah F. Hughes (2 vols., Boston, 1899), 143–45; Boston *Liberator,* Aug. 25, 1865, p. 134; Boston *Daily Advertiser,* Sept. 26, 1865, p. 2. Among the signers were Loring, Emory Washburn, Peleg W. Chandler, John B. Alley, Nathaniel Thayer, and Jared Sparks.
46. N.Y. *Tribune,* June 14, 1865, p. 1.
47. James Abram Garfield, *Suffrage and Safety: Oration delivered at Ravenna, Ohio, July 4, 1865,* in Garfield, *The Works of James Abram Garfield,* ed. by Burke A. Hinsdale (2 vols., Boston, 1882), I, 85–94; Davis, *Lessons of the War: Speech in Chicago on July 4,* in Davis, *Speeches and Addresses,* 564–84; Edwin Channing Larned, *The Great Conflict, What Has Been Gained, and What Remains to be Accomplished* (Chicago, 1865); Richard Yates, *Speech of the Hon. Richard Yates delivered at Elgin, Ill. on the 4th of July, A.D., 1865* (Jacksonville, Ill., 1865); George S. Boutwell, *Reconstruction: Its True Basis,* in Boutwell, *Speeches,* 372–407; Boston *Liberator,* July 14, 1865, p. 112; July 21, p. 113; Nathaniel P. Banks, *An Address Delivered at the Custom-house, New Orleans, on the Fourth of July, 1865* (New Orleans, [1865]).
48. Dixon to Sumner, June 6, 1865; Morgan to Sumner, July 21, 1865; Sumner to Wade, Aug. 3, 1865. Sumner Mss.; G. Galin Berrier, "The Negro Suffrage Issue in Iowa—1865–1868," *Annals of Iowa,* XXXIX (Spring, 1968), 245; N.Y. *Tribune,* Sept. 8, 1865, p. 1; Sept. 9, 1865, p. 1; Springfield *Illinois State Journal,* Sept. 19, 1865, p. 2; N.Y. *Times,* June 30, 1865, p. 1; Boston *Daily Advertiser,* Aug. 11, 1865, p. 1; N.Y. *Tribune,* Sept. 15, 1865, p. 1; Medill to McCulloch, June 16, 1865; Boutwell to McCulloch, July 1, 1865. McCulloch Mss., L.C.; N.Y. *Times,* June 21, 1865, p. 4; June 28 ,1865, p. 4.
49. Morgan to Sumner, July 21, 1865; Howard to Sumner, July 26, 1865; Morrill to Sumner [July or August?], 1865; Sumner to Wade, Aug. 3, 1865; Conness to Sumner, Aug. 22, 1865; Brown to Sumner, Sept. 12, 1865. Sumner Mss.; Sprague to Chase, Sept. 6, 1865. Chase Mss., L.C.; Grimes to E. H. Stiles, Sept. 14, 1865, quoted in William Salter, *The Life of James W. Grimes, Gov-*

ernor of Iowa, 1854–1858; Senator of the United States, 1859–1869 (N.Y., 1876), 280–82; James W. Grimes to Charles H. Ray, Oct. 28, 1865, quoted in Logsdon, "White," 148n; Welles, *Diary,* II, 322–23 (June 24, 1865).

50. McCulloch to Susan McCulloch, June 25, 1865. McCulloch Mss., Lilly Library, Indiana University, Bloomington, Indiana; Welles, *Diary,* III, 363 (Aug. 19, 1865). The Maine convention, as noted, endorsed black suffrage. Welles concluded that hostile elements controlled Pennsylvania's convention because although it endorsed President Johnson, it averred that Congress had ultimate control over Reconstruction, a position neither Lincoln, Johnson, nor any other member of the Cabinet yet contravened.

51. Johnson to Governor William Sharkey, Aug. 15, 1865, quoted in McPherson (ed.), *Political History of . . . Reconstruction,* 19–20.

52. Washington *Daily Morning Chronicle,* July 10, 1865, p. 2; July 11, p. 2; Forney to Sumner, May 20, 1865; Morgan to Sumner, July 21, 1865; Dana to Sumner, Sept. 1, 1865. Sumner Mss.; Francis Lieber to Morgan, Oct. 6, 1865. Edwin D. Morgan Mss., New York State Library.

53. Phillips to Moncure D. Conway, Sept. 12, 1865. McKim–Garrison Mss.

54. Springfield *Illinois State Journal,* Aug. 16, 1865, p. 2. The *Journal* was the most important Republican paper in southern Illinois. Phillips was United States marshal for the southern Illinois district. Other newspapers that took similar views, at least arguing against premature attacks against the president, were Forney's Philadelphia *Press* and Washington *Daily Morning Chronicle,* the San Francisco *Alta California,* the Philadelphia *North American,* edited by Mayor Morton McMichael, Dana's Chicago *Republican,* the Toledo *Blade,* Cincinnati *Commercial,* Boston *Liberator,* the *New York Times,* New York *Evening Post,* the Indianapolis *Daily Journal,* Governor Morton's organ, and the Madison *Wisconsin State Journal,* edited by state party chairman Horace Rublee.

55. Indianapolis *Daily Journal,* Oct. 24, 1865, p. 2; Nov. 1, 1865, p. 2; Nov. 3, 1865, p. 2; Foulke, *Morton,* I, 448–51; Riddleberger, *Julian,* 212–18; Emma Lou Thornbrough, *Indiana in the Civil War Era, 1850–1880* (Indianapolis, 1965), 228–31.

56. *N.Y. Times,* Mar. 2, 1865, p. 4; May 6, 1865, p. 4; May 7, 1865, p. 4; July 13, 1865, p. 4; Aug. 26, 1865, pp. 4–5; LaWanda and John H. Cox, *Politics, Principle, and Prejudice,* 31–87. The Coxes view the Seward-Weed offensive as an effort to build a national conservative party as well as to gain control of New York.

57. Homer Adolph Stebbins, *A Political History of the State of New York, 1865–1869,* vol. LV of Studies in History, Economics and Public Law ed. by the Faculty of Political Science of Columbia University (N.Y., 1913), 57–63;

N.Y. Times, Sept. 16, 1865, p. 8; Sept. 20, 1865, p. 1; Sept. 21, 1865, p. 1; *N.Y. Tribune,* Sept. 21, 1865, p. 1; Boston, *Daily Advertiser,* Sept. 26, 1865, p. 1; "Though the Convention was Radical in sentiment, the Conservatives had their way in it, because it was deemed best to attach President Johnson more firmly to the Union party, and not drive him over to the Democracy," Greeley recalled. *N.Y. Tribune,* Mar. 5, 1866, p. 4. Greeley's language implied that he had shared this spirit, but his statements at the time clearly demonstrate that he did not. Instead, he complained of the lack of radical leadership. Putting the two statements together, the implication is that because radicals had no individual leader, a number of them were persuaded to support the conservative program for fear of alienating the President with a radical one.

58. See, for instance, Greeley's speech at a Union meeting held in Cooper Union, October 20, attended by members of both factions of the party. *N.Y. Times,* Oct. 21, 1865, pp. 1, 8; *N.Y. Tribune,* Oct. 20, 1865, p. 4. Other radicals feared a New York victory would entrench conservatives in the great state's party, and hoped for a Republican defeat to demonstrate the unviability of the conservative position. Stevens to Sumner, Oct. 25, 1865. Sumner Mss. Simeon Draper, the former collector of the port of New York and ally of the radical faction, refused to contribute to the Republican cause, and, Weed suspected, did not vote the Republican ticket after his removal in August. Weed to Seward, Nov. 14, 1866. William Henry Seward Mss., Rush Rhees Library, University of Rochester, Rochester, N.Y.

59. Doolittle to Johnson, Sept. 9, 1865, Johnson Mss.; Madison *Wisconsin State Journal,* Sept. 5, 6, 7, 8, 1865; *N.Y. Tribune,* Oct. 3, 1865, p. 4; Leslie H. Fishel, Jr., "Wisconsin and Negro Suffrage," *Wisconsin Magazine of History,* XLVI (Spring 1963), 192–93; Helen J. and Harry Williams, "Wisconsin Republicans and Reconstruction," *ibid.,* XXIII (Sept. 1939), 20–25; Richard W. Hantke, "Elisha W. Keyes and the Radical Republicans," *ibid.,* XXXV (Spring 1952), 203–208.

60. William Henry Smith, *A Political History of Slavery* (2 vols., N.Y. & London, 1903), 239; Baber to Seward, Nov. 4, 1865. Seward Mss.; Lewis D. Campbell to Johnson, Aug. 21, 1865. Johnson Mss.

61. The letter and Cox's answer are quoted in the N.Y. *Independent,* Aug. 17, 1865, p. 4.

62. Bannister to Chase, Sept. 19, 1865. Chase Mss.; Baber to Johnson, July 4, 1865. Johnson Mss.

63. Cox to Garfield, July 21, Dec. 13, 1865. James A. Garfield Mss., Manuscripts Div., L.C.

64. *N.Y. Times,* Aug. 21, 1865, p. 3.

65. N.Y. *Independent,* Sept. 14, 1865, p. 1; Flamen Ball to Chase, Aug. 22, 1865. Chase Mss. L.C.; George H. Porter,

Ohio Politics During the Civil War Period, vol. CV of the Studies in History, Economics and Public Law ed. by the Faculty of Political Science of Columbia University (N.Y., 1911), 206–19.

66. Welles, *Diary,* II, 349 (Aug. 2, 1865); Philadelphia *North American,* Aug. 18, 1865, p. 2; Aug. 19, 1865, p. 2. At Stevens's urging the convention took a strong stand on the issue of black civil rights, saying no southern state should be readmitted until the security of the freedmen was guaranteed. By this time radicals had given up hope of winning endorsements of black suffrage, and Stevens was pleased with his relatively small victory. Stevens to Sumner, Oct. 25, 1865. Sumner Mss.

67. *N.Y. Times,* Jan. 29, 1865, p. 3; Mark A. Plummer, "Governor Crawford's Appointment of Edmund G. Ross to the United States Senate," *Kansas Historical Quarterly,* XXVIII (Summer 1962), 145–47; William Frank Zornow, *Kansas: A History of the Jayhawk State* (Norman, Okla., 1957), 123–24.

68. S.F. *Daily Alta California,* July 17, 1865, p. 1; Aug. 17, p. 1; Aug. 18, p. 1; Aug. 22, p. 2; Berrier, "Negro Suffrage Issue in Iowa," 241–45; Arthur Charles Cole, The *Era of the Civil War, 1848–1870,* vol. III of *The Centennial History of Illinois* (Springfield, 1919), 392–95.

69. *N.Y. Times,* June 25, 1865, p. 6. Andrew was leaving office. His friends clearly intended to make him president, but most avenues of advancement were closed to him. In January and February the governor's friends had dickered for a seat in the cabinet for him. These hopes did not vanish. Andrew also began to stake out a position independent of Sumner, whose Senate seat was the next available. He retained his cordial relationship with the Blairs, who believed him secretly the president's supporter even after open warfare broke out between Johnson and the party. Montgomery Blair to Andrew, March 13, 1866; Andrew to Francis Preston Blair, Sr., March 18, 1866; Andrew to Montgomery Blair, March 26, 1866; F.P. Blair, Sr. to Andrew, April 26, 1866; William L. Burt to Andrew, May 21, 24, 1866; William S. King to Andrew, June 21, 1866; M. Blair to Andrew, July 1, 1866. Andrew Mss.; William S. Robinson to Sumner, March 7, 1866. Sumner Mss.; William E. Smith, *The Francis Preston Blair Family in Politics* (2 vols.), N.Y., 1933), II, 332.

70. Henry Greenleaf Pearson, *The Life of John A. Andrew: Governor of Massachusetts, 1861–1865* (2 vols., Boston and New York, 1904), II, 251; Andrew to Sumner, Nov. 21, 1865. Sumner Mss.; Sumner to Andrew [Dec. 1865?]. Andrew Mss. The second letter is filed under November 1865 in the Andrew Mss., at the Massachusetts Historical Society. The letters are reprinted, with changes in punctuation, in Pearson, *Andrew,* II, 273–76.

71. *N.Y. Times,* Oct. 21, 1865, p. 4.

72. *N.Y. Independent,* Sept. 28, 1865, p. 4; Oct. 5, 1865, p. 4; *N.Y. Tribune,* Sept. 12, 1865, p. 4; Sept. 14, 1865, p. 4; Oct. 3, 1865, p. 4.

73. *Appleton's Annual Cyclopaedia,* V (1865), 301–302, 304, 823; *Tribune Almanac and Political Register for 1867* (N.Y., 1867), 64 (hereafter *Tribune Almanac, 1867*).

74. *N.Y. Independent,* Oct. 5, 1865, p. 4; Sumner to McCulloch, Aug. 28, 1865. McCulloch Mss., L.C.

75. Defrees to Doolittle, Oct. 20, 1865, quoted in James Rood Doolittle, "Doolittle Correspondence," *Publications of the Southern History Association,* XI (March 1907), 104–105; H. Doolittle to Weed, Sept. 6, 1865. Thurlow Weed Mss., Rush Rhees Library, University of Rochester, Rochester, N.Y.

76. Welles, *Diary,* II, 379 (Oct. 1865).

77. Lieber to Sumner, Oct. 5, 1865, quoted in Frank Freidel, *Francis Lieber, Nineteenth-Century Liberal* (Baton Rouge, 1947), 378; Garfield to Chase, Oct. 4, 1865. Chase Mss., L.C.

6. THE CENTER REPUBLICANS CHANGE THEIR MINDS

1. Hahn to Banks, Oct. 28, 1864; Stephen Hoyt to Banks, Dec. 3, 1864. Nathaniel Banks Mss., Manuscripts Div., L.C.; Hahn to Hurlbut, Dec. 5, 1864. Lincoln Mss.; Gerald M. Capers, *Occupied City: New Orleans Under the Federals, 1862–1865* (Lexington, Ky., 1965), 117–19, 142; Fred Harvey Harrington, *Fighting Politician: Major General N.P. Banks* (Philadelphia, 1948), 166.

2. Harrington, *Fighting Politician,* 166.

3. N.C. Brooks to Johnson, May 5, 1865; Banks to Preston King, May 6, 1865; A.P. Dostie to Johnson, May 16, 1865; George Ashmun to Johnson, May 7, 1865; Hahn to Seward, May 19, 1865; Wells to Johnson, May 22, 1865. Andrew Johnson Mss., Manuscripts Div., L.C.; Wells to Johnson, May 26, 1865. Hugh McCulloch Mss., Manuscripts Div., L.C.; Harrington, *Fighting Politician,* 168–69; Capers, *Occupied City,* 143–44; Willie Marvin Caskey, *Secession and Restoration in Louisiana,* Louisiana State University Studies Number 36 (Baton Rouge, 1938), 164–70; Emily Hazen Reed, *Life of A.P. Dostie; or, The Conflict in New Orleans* (N.Y., 1868), 189–200.

4. Caskey, *Secession and Restoration of Louisiana,* 172–78.

5. *Ibid.,* 179–80; Harrington, *Fighting Politician,* 168–69; Capers, *Occupied City,* 143–44; Reed, *Dostie,* 175–81.

6. Harrington, *Fighting Politician,* 168.

7. Covode report to Stanton, undated copy in the John Covode Mss., Manuscripts Div., L.C. Also Covode to Wade, July 11, 1865. Benjamin F. Wade Mss., Manuscripts Div., L.C.

8. Schurz to Johnson, Sept. 4, 1865, and enclosures. Johnson Mss.
9. Wells to Johnson, Sept. 23, Oct. 6, 1865. Johnson Mss.
10. Taliaferro to Mrs. Susan B. (Taliaferro) Alexander, July 15, 1865. Taliaferro Mss., Louisiana State University Archives, Baton Rouge, Louisiana; Schurz to Johnson, Sept. 23, 1865. Johnson Mss.
11. Field to Banks, Nov. 20, 1865. Banks Mss., L.C.
12. Field to Stevens, Dec. 4, 1865. Thaddeus Stevens Mss., Manuscripts Div., L.C. In a long, unsigned letter another Louisiana conservative expressed himself similarly to Elihu B. Washburne, suggesting that James G. Taliaferro replace Wells as provisional governor. The letter gives a detailed account of Wells's betrayal of the Conservative Unionists. ? to E.B. Washburne [Nov.–Dec. 1865]. Elihu B. Washburne Mss., Manuscripts Div., L.C.
13. Boston *Evening Journal*, Oct. 10, 1865, p. 4; *N.Y. Tribune*, Nov. 18, 1865, p. 4.
14. Cutler to Trumbull, Dec. 6, 1865. See also Cutler to Trumbull, Aug. 29, 1865. Lyman Trumbull Mss., Manuscripts Div., L.C.
15. Fessenden to Grimes, July 14, 1865; Lot M. Morrill to Fessenden, July 19, 1865. William Pitt Fessenden Mss., Bowdoin College Library, Brunswick, Me.; Andrew to Sumner, Nov. 21, 1865. Charles Sumner Mss., Houghton Library, Harvard University, Cambridge, Mass.; S.F. Wetmore to Andrew, Nov. 14, 20, 1865. John Albion Andrew Mss. Massachusetts Historical Society; James A. Garfield to J.D. Cox, July 26, 1865. Jacob D. Cox Mss., Oberlin College Library, Oberlin, Ohio.
16. Raymond to George Jones, Aug. 6, 1865. George C. Jones Mss., New York Public Library.
17. *N.Y. Times*, Aug. 18, 1865, p. 4.
18. Lieber to Martin Russell Thayer, Feb. 3, 1864. Francis Lieber Mss., Huntington Library. The letter is quoted in Thomas Sargeant Perry, *Life and Letters of Francis Lieber* (Boston, 1882), 339–41; James Albert Woodburn, *Life of Thaddeus Stevens* (Indianapolis, 1913), 207–38. See also R.F.F., "Right to Confiscate and Emancipate," *Monthly Law Reporter*, XXIV (Sept. 1862), 646; J.H.A., "Legal Miscellany: Martial Law," *American Law Register*, IX (June 1861), 498–511; D. [Theodore W. Dwight?], "Writ of Habeas Corpus," *American Law Register*, IX (Oct. 1861), 705–17; Sidney George Fisher, *The Trial of the Constitution* (Philadelphia, 1862), 63–64, 199; Grosvenor P. Lowrey, *The Commander in Chief: A Defence Upon Legal Grounds of the Proclamation of Emancipation, and an Answer to Ex-Judge Curtis' Pamphlet Entitled "Executive Power"* (N.Y., 1862); Oliver Wendell Holmes, *Oration Delivered Before the City Authorities of Boston on the Eighty-Seventh Anniversary of the National Independence of America* (Philadelphia, 1863), 26–27; Matthew Hale Carpenter,

Letter on Martial Law (N.Y., 1865), 3–4.
19. Daniel Agnew, *Our National Constitution: Its Adaption to a State of War or Insurrection* (2nd edn., Philadelphia, 1863), 11; Joel Parker, *Habeas Corpus and Martial Law: A Review of the Opinion of Chief Justice Taney, in the Case of John Merryman* (Philadelphia, 1862); "Rightful Power of Congress to Confiscate and Emancipate," *Monthly Law Reporter*, XXIV (Sept. 1862), 469–93; Jehu Baker, *The Rebellion: Speech Delivered in Hall of Representatives, Springfield, Ill., Feb. 4, 1863* (Belleville, Ill., 1863); Oliver P. Morton's speech in New York, April 11, 1863 in Loyal National League, *The Sumter Anniversary, 1863: Opinions of Loyalists Concerning the Great Questions of the Times* (N.Y., 1863), 40–50, especially 47–48; Lyman Trumbull's defense of the constitutionality of confiscation in *Cong. Globe*, 38 Cong., 1 Sess., 3306 (June 27, 1864), and also *Argument of Hon. Lyman Trumbull in the Supreme Court of the United States, Mar. 4, 1868, in the Matter of Ex Parte WILLIAM H. McCARDLE, Appellant* (Washington, 1868), 24.
20. For fuller discussion of this aspect of wartime Reconstruction legislation, see Herman Belz, "Henry Winter Davis and the Origins of Congressional Reconstruction," *Maryland Historical Magazine*, LXVII (Summer 1972), 129–43.
21. Wendell Phillips, Speech to the Massachusetts Anti-Slavery Society, Jan. 26, 1865, in George Luther Stearns (comp.), *The Equality of All Men, Before the Law Claimed and Defended* (Boston, 1865), 31.
22. Boston *Evening Journal*, June 27, 1865, p. 4.
23. See also Thaddeus Stevens, *Reconstruction: Speech of the Hon. Thaddeus Stevens, Delivered in the City of Lancaster, September 7th, 1865* (Lancaster, Pa., 1865), 3, 7; Oliver P. Morton in *Cong. Globe*, 40 Cong., 2 Sess., 2603 (May 27, 1868); William Whiting, *The Return of the Rebellious States to the Union: A Letter from Hon. Wm. Whiting to the Union League of Philadelphia* (Philadelphia, 1864), 3–4; Carl Schurz, "The Logical Results of the War," in Carl Schurz, *Speeches, Correspondence, and Political Papers of Carl Schurz*, ed. by Frederic Bancroft (6 vols., N.Y., 1913), I, 378–79; Alpheus Crosby, *The Present Position of the Seceded States and the Rights and Duties of the General Government in Respect to Them: An Address to the Phi Beta Kappa Society of Dartmouth College, July 19, 1865* (Boston, 1865), 12; T.W. Higginson, "Fair Play the Best Policy," *Atlantic Monthly*, XV (May 1865), 628; and Count A. de Gasparin, *Reconstruction, A Letter to President Johnson* (N.Y., 1865), 13.
24. [James Russell Lowell], "Reconstruction," *North American Review*, C (April 1865), 553; E.P. Whipple, "Reconstruction and Negro Suffrage," *Atlantic*

Monthly, XVI (Aug. 1865), 247; Edwin L. Godkin, "Universal Suffrage and Universal Amnesty," N.Y. *Nation,* Nov. 29, 1866, p. 430. See also Senator William Sprague's comments in *Cong. Globe,* 38 Cong., 2 Sess., 960 (Feb. 21, 1865); Joseph Medill to Hugh Mc-Culloch, June 10, 1865. McCulloch Papers, Library of Congress; Henry Winter Davis, *Lessons of the War* (speech in Chicago, July 4, 1865), in Davis, *Speeches and Addresses Delivered in the Congress of the United States, and on Several Public Occasions* (N.Y., 1867), 579–81; "Letters to the Editor: Winter Davis on Reconstruction," N.Y. *Nation,* Nov. 30, 1865, p. 681; Letter from John Stuart Mill to the Cincinnati *Commercial,* quoted in *Littel's Living Age,* LXXXVII (Oct. 7, 1865), 47–48; Gasparin, *Reconstruction,* 37–38; Col. J.L. Haynes to Nathaniel P. Banks, Jan. 11, 1866. Banks Mss., Illinois Historical Library; John Covode to Edwin M. Stanton, summer, 1865, undated draft of letter in the Covode papers, L.C.

25. Among the proponents of territorialization were Stevens, Julian, Butler, Ashley, and Kelley. Boutwell advocated this policy for some of the rebel states. See Stevens's *Reconstruction,* 3–4, and his exposition in Congress in *Cong. Globe,* 39 Cong., 1 Sess., 74 (Dec. 18, 1865); Julian, *Dangers and Duties of the Hour—Reconstruction and Suffrage* in Julian, *Speeches on Political Questions* (N.Y. and Cambridge, Mass., 1872), 287–88; Benjamin F. Butler, *Butler's Book: Autobiography and Personal Reminiscences of Major-General Benjamin F. Butler* (Boston, 1892), 960–61; Boutwell, *Reconstruction: Its True Basis,* in George S. Boutwell, *Speeches and Papers Relating to the Rebellion and the Overthrow of Slavery* (2 vols., Boston, 1867), II, 389–90.

26. Woodbury Davis, "Political Problems and Conditions of Peace," *Atlantic Monthly,* XII (Aug. 1863), 254.

27. The text may be found in the *N.Y. Times,* June 24, 1865, p. 8. I have omitted italics in the quoted material.

28. Huntington to McCulloch, Oct. 19, 1865. McCulloch Mss., L.C.; *N.Y. Times,* Jan. 14, 1866, p. 3; letter from Colfax to the Union party convention of Indiana's ninth congressional district, quoted in O.J. Hollister, *The Life of Schuyler Colfax* (N.Y. and London, 1886), 286; Francis Fessenden, *Life and Public Services of William Pitt Fessenden* (2 vols., Boston and N.Y., 1907), II, 36–37; George S. Boutwell, *Reconstruction: Its True Basis,* in *Speeches and Papers,* II, 386–88; Chase to Francis Lieber, Feb. 14, 1865; Lieber Mss., Huntington Library; William Lawrence in *Cong. Globe,* 39 Cong., 2 Sess., 1083; Schurz, "Logical Results of the War," in Carl Schurz, *Speeches,* I, 405–406. See also Howard K. Beale (ed.), *Diary of Edward Bates, 1859–1866* (Washington, 1933), 543. Fessenden, Boutwell, and Lawrence all were named

to the Joint Committee on Reconstruction, which formulated Congress's Reconstruction policy.,

29. A word should be inserted here about the use Republicans made of the clause of the Constitution obligating the national government to guarantee each state a republican form of government. Some historians have suggested Republicans used this as their constitutional basis for Reconstruction. In general, however, Republicans were reluctant to use the guarantee clause as a source of power in Reconstruction, because it implied a permanent authority in Congress to regulate suffrage in states—all states, whether they had been in rebellion or not. See, for instance, Senator Richard Yates's exposition of the guarantee power in *Cong. Globe,* 40 Cong., 2 Sess., 2746 (June 1, 1868) and Sumner's, *ibid.,* 3 Sess., 903 (Feb. 5, 1869). When in 1869 Sumner and Senator Henry Wilson proposed to enfranchise all black Americans by act of Congress under the guarantee clause rather than by constitutional amendment, they received the support of only eight Republicans. *Cong. Globe,* 40 Cong., 3 Sess., 5 (Dec. 7, 1868), 38, 43 (Dec. 10, 1868), 378 (Jan. 15, 1869), 1041 (Feb. 9, 1869). Republicans preferred to use the guarantee clause as a vague guide in setting the conditions that southern states had to meet under the "grasp of war" approach. For instance, the report of the Reconstruction committee in 1866 said, "The first step towards that end [of placing the state in a condition to resume its political relations to the Union] would necessarily be the establishment of a republican form of government by the people." U.S. Congress, *Report of the Joint Committee on Reconstruction at the First Session Thirty-Ninth Congress* (Washington, 1866), xiv. For a study that presents a different opinion, see Charles O. Lerche, "Congressional Interpretations of the Guarantee of a Republican Form of Government During Reconstruction," *Journal of Southern History,* XV (May 1949), 192–211.

30. Dana to Adams, June 1865, quoted in Charles Francis Adams, Jr., *Richard Henry Dana: A Biography* (Boston and N.Y., 1891), 330–31.

31. Boston *Daily Advertiser,* June 6, 1865, p. 2.

32. The best discussion of the relations between the president and the Democrats is in LaWanda and John H. Cox, *Politics, Principle, and Prejudice, 1865–1866: Dilemma of Reconstruction America* (N.Y., 1963), 50–106, *passim.*

33. N.Y. *Herald,* Oct. 31, 1865, p. 4; N.Y. *Evening Post,* Nov. 22, 1865, p. 3; Chicago *Times,* quoted in the Springfield *Illinois State Journal,* Aug. 30, 1865, p. 2.

34. Johnson to Governor W.L. Sharkey, Aug. 15, 1865; Johnson to Gov. W.W. Holden, Oct. 18, 1865; Seward to Gov. James Johnson, Oct. 28, 1865; Johnson to Gov. B.F. Perry, Oct. 28, 31, Nov.

6, 20, 1865, quoted in Edward Mc-Pherson (ed.), *The Political History of the United States of America During the Period of Reconstruction* . . . (3rd edn., Washington, 1880), 19–20, 19, 20–21, 22–23, respectively; Seward to Holden, Nov. 21, 1865; Seward to Perry, Nov. 9, 10, 20, 1865; Seward to Gov. William Marvin, Nov. 20, 1865, quoted in *Senate Executive Document No. 26*, 39 Cong., 1 Sess., 47, 198, 198–99, 200, 215, respectively.
35. *N.Y. Times*, Nov. 6, 1865, p. 4.
36. Indianapolis *Daily Journal*, Oct. 25, 1865, p. 2; Boston *Daily Advertiser*, Oct. 23, 1865, p. 2; Philadelphia *North American*, Aug. 26, 1865, p. 2; Henry Wilson to Sumner, Sept. 9, 1865. Sumner Mss.; Horace White to Fessenden, Oct. 9, 1865. White Mss., Illinois State Historical Library (copy of original in Fessenden Mss., Beloit College, Beloit, Wis.); George T. Brown to Trumbull, Sept. 8, 1865. Trumbull Mss., L.C.
37. McCulloch to Sumner, Aug. 22, 1865. Sumner Mss.
38. LaWanda and John Cox suggest that Seward wished to win the support of the Democratic masses and combine them in a party with conservative and moderate Republicans, leaving both the Democratic leaders and the radicals in opposition. See their *Politics, Principle, and Prejudice*, 31–49.
39. See also the *N.Y. Times*, June 15, 1865, p. 4.
40. Seward to Sharkey, July 24, 1865, quoted in *Senate Executive Document No. 26*, 39 Cong., 1 Sess., 60.
41. Seward to Marvin, Sept. 12, 1865, quoted in McPherson (ed.), *Political History of . . . Reconstruction*, 25. Seward later admitted that the messages had been prepared in haste and that Johnson had not thoroughly considered them. "The language used was stronger than he [Johnson] considered it to be," the Secretary conceded. See Seward's testimony on impeachment, *House Report No. 7*, 40 Cong., 1 Sess., appendix, 382.
42. Gideon Welles, *Diary of Gideon Welles—Secretary of the Navy Under Lincoln and Johnson* (3 vols., Boston and N.Y., 1911) II, 378–79 (Oct. 1865).
43. *N.Y. Times*, Nov. 15, 1865, p. 4; Sept. 21, 1865, p. 4.
44. *N.Y. Nation*, Nov. 16, 1865, p. 614.
45. Springfield (Massachusetts) *Republican*, Nov. 14, 1865, p. 2; Springfield *Illinois State Journal*, Sept. 26, 1865, p. 2; Oct. 6, 1865, p. 2; Nov. 8, 1865, p. 2; Boston *Evening Journal*, Oct. 24, 1865, p. 4; Philadelphia *North American*, Nov. 15, 1865, p. 2; Buffalo (N.Y.) *Morning Express*, Nov. 27, 1865, p. 1.
46. Howard to Sumner, Nov. 12, 1865. See also James M. Scovel to Sumner, Nov. 13, 1865. Sumner Mss.; E.D. Morgan to Lieber, Oct. 6, 1865. Edmund Morgan Mss., New York State Library: "I believe we shall all agree upon some plan by which we shall as friends of the Administration continue to act harmoniously— Of course I hope this, but I also *believe it*."

47. Johnson to Humphreys, Nov. 17, 1865, quoted in the Springfield *Illinois State Journal*, Nov. 27, 1865, p. 2. Italics mine. Historians have not recognized the importance of Johnson's apparent shift, nor Seward's central role.
48. Quoted in the *N.Y. Times*, Nov. 20, 1865, p. 1.
49. Indianapolis *Daily Journal*, Nov. 24, 1865, p. 2; Buffalo *Morning Express*, Nov. 21, 1865, p. 1; Springfield *Illinois State Journal*, Nov. 28, 1865, p. 2; Washington *Daily Morning Chronicle*, Nov. 27, 1865, p. 2.
50. Blaine to Colfax, Nov. 22, 1865. James G. Blaine Mss., Manuscripts Div., L.C.; Colfax to ?, Dec. 6, 1865. Schuyler Colfax Mss., Indiana State Library, Indiana Division; Garfield to Jacob D. Cox, Nov. 28, 1865. Cox Mss.
51. Johnson to Perry, Nov. 27, 1865, quoted in McPherson (ed.), *Political History of . . . Reconstruction*, 24.
52. This wording, however, was far less explicit and firm than the earlier demand Johnson made of Humphreys.
53. Johnson to Holden, Nov. 27, 1865, quoted in William W. Holden, *Memoirs of W.W. Holden* (Durham, N.C., 1911), 69.
54. Alice M. Hooper to Sumner, Nov. 22, 1865; Sumner to Lieber, Dec. 3, 1865. Sumner Mss.; Bancroft to Johnson, Dec. 1, 1865. Johnson Mss.
55. Lane to A.H. Blair, Dec. 2, 1865. Henry S. Lane Mss., William Henry Smith Library of the Indiana Historical Society; *N.Y. Times*, Nov. 21, 1865, p. 4; Fessenden to Elizabeth Fessenden Warriner, Dec. 3, 1865. Fessenden Mss., Bowdoin College Library.
56. Before receiving the message, the House passed a joint resolution to appoint a joint committee on Reconstruction (see Chapter Eight).
57. Seward's draft of the annual message is in the Johnson Mss.
58. James D. Richardson (ed.), *A Compilation of the Messages and Papers of the Presidents of the United States* (10 vols., Washington, 1896–99), VI, 353–71.
59. In a thorough analysis, the Coxes demonstrate the ambiguity of the message in their *Politics, Principle and Prejudice*, 129–34.
60. Boston *Evening Journal*, Dec. 6, 1865, p. 1; N.Y. *Nation*, Dec. 14, 1865, pp. 739, 742; *Chicago Tribune*, Dec. 13, 1865, p. 2; Dec. 14, p. 2; Madison *Wisconsin State Journal*, Dec. 11, 1865, p. 1; Indianapolis *Daily Journal*, Dec. 6, 1865, p. 2; *N.Y. Tribune*, Dec. 9, 1865, p. 4; Boston *Daily Advertiser*, Dec. 13, 1865, p. 2; Springfield *Illinois State Journal*, Dec. 12, 1865, p. 2; Philadelphia *North American*, Dec. 10, 1865, p. 2; Buffalo *Morning Express*, Dec. 6, 1865, p. 1; Dec. 7, 1865, p. 4; Washington *Daily Morning Chronicle*, Dec. 8, 1865, p. 1; Dec. 21, 1865, p. 2; "The President's Message," *North American Review*, CII (June 1866), 250–60; John M. Harrison, *The Man Who Made Nasby, David Ross Locke* (Chapel Hill,

1969), 131; W.W. Holden to Johnson, Dec. 6, 1865. Johnson Mss.; Isaac Baldwin to E.B. Washburne, Dec. 8, 1865. E.B. Washburne Mss.; Carl Schurz to Mrs. Margaretha Meyer Schurz, Dec. 5, 1865, quoted in Schurz, *Intimate Letters of Carl Schurz, 1841–1869,* ed. by Joseph Shafer, Publications of the State Historical Society of Wisconsin, XXX (Madison, 1928), 354; Garfield to Burke A. Hinsdale, Dec. 11, 1865, quoted in Mary L. Hinsdale (ed.), *Garfield-Hinsdale Letters: Correspon-*

dence Between James Abram Garfield and Burke Aaron Hinsdale (Ann Arbor, 1949), 76–77; C.A. Trimble to John Sherman, Dec. 11, 1865. Sherman Mss., L.C.

61. Bancroft to Johnson, Dec. 6, 1865; Morton to Johnson, Dec. 7, 1865. Johnson Mss.

62. Stevens to Theodore Tilton, Dec. 7, 1865. Single Stevens letter in the Illinois State Historical Library, Springfield, Illinois.

7. CONSERVATIVE RECONSTRUCTION—PART ONE

1. *Cong. Globe,* 39 Cong., 1 Sess., 990 (Feb. 23, 1866).
2. *Ibid.*
3. *Ibid.,* 293 (Jan. 18, 1866).
4. *The* (Boston) *Right Way,* Dec. 2, 1865, p. 2.
5. George W. Julian, *Political Recollections, 1840–1872* (Chicago, 1884), 305–306.
6. Although Congress finally abandoned confiscation as an element of Reconstruction, as of fall 1865 black men had good reason to believe Republicans intended to inaugurate land redistribution in the South. The expectation of "forty acres and a mule" at which historians have scoffed was a real one, and one with foundation in fact. See especially LaWanda Cox, "The Promise of Land to the Freedmen," *Mississippi Valley Historical Review,* XLV (Dec. 1958), 413–40. Wendell Phillips, Thaddeus Stevens, Benjamin F. Butler, and the American Anti-Slavery Society continued to advocate such a program through 1867, and southern blacks hoped to receive land as part of the congressional program in the spring of 1867. See pp. 258–59, *infra.*

   National supervision over the education of freedmen loomed large in the drive for a national bureau of education from 1864–1867. Although educators envisioned the bureau as noncoercive, its special goal was to be the extension of the free school system into the South. Moreover, some of its proponents suggested financial inducements to the states to meet certain educational standards. Many educators advocated a national system of education for freed blacks operated separately from the proposed bureau. E.E. White, "National Bureau of Education," *American Journal of Education,* XVI (March 1866), 177–86; Andrew Jackson Rickoff, "A National Bureau of Education," *ibid.* (June 1866), 299–310; J.P. Wickersham, "Education as an Element of Reconstruction," *ibid.,* 283–97. The 1865 convention of the National Teachers Association passed resolutions endorsing national encouragement of educational reform and a national bureau of education. The National Association of School Superintendents, meeting in Washington in February 1866, followed suit. *Ibid.,* XV (Dec. 1865), 805–806, 809–

10; Boston *Right Way,* Dec. 10, 1865, p. 2.
7. Radicals, conservatives, and centrists recorded their positions on Reconstruction in numerous speeches in and out of Congress. The foregoing discussion is based on analysis of their opinions.

   Conservatives and centrists—John A. Andrew (governor of Massachusetts): Andrew, *Valedictory Address to the Two Branches of the Legislature of Massachusetts, Jan. 4, 1866* (Boston, 1866); Delos R. Ashley (Nevada representative): *Cong. Globe,* 39 Cong., 1 Sess., 1314–16 (March 10, 1866); John A. Bingham (Ohio representative): *ibid.,* 156–59 (Jan. 9, 1866), 428–31 (Jan. 25, 1866); Reader W. Clarke (Ohio representative): *ibid.,* 1006–10 (Feb. 24, 1866); Schuyler Colfax (Speaker of the House of Representatives): speech of Nov. 18, 1865, quoted in the *N.Y. Times,* Nov. 20, 1865, p. 1; Henry C. Deming (Connecticut representative): *Cong. Globe,* 39 Cong., 1 Sess., 331 (Jan. 19, 1866); Lucius Fairchild (governor of Wisconsin): message to the state legislature, quoted in *N.Y. Times,* Jan. 4, 1866, p. 1; James R. Hubbell (Ohio representative): *Cong. Globe,* 39 Cong., 1 Sess., 659–62 (Feb. 5, 1866); James H. Lane (Kansas senator): report of pro-Johnson rally in Leavenworth, Kans., *N.Y. Times,* Jan. 21, 1866, p. 3; Henry J. Raymond (N.Y. representative; ed. *N.Y. Times*): *Cong. Globe,* 39 Cong., 1 Sess., 120–25 (Dec. 21, 1865), 483–92 (Jan. 29, 1866); Rufus P. Spalding (Ohio representative): *ibid.,* 133 (Jan. 5, 1866).

   Radicals—James M. Ashley (Ohio representative): Speech at San Francisco, California, September 17, 1865, in Ashley, *Duplicate Copy of the Souvenir from the Afro-American League of Tennessee to Hon. James M. Ashley of Ohio* (Philadelphia, 1894), 370–84; George S. Boutwell (Massachusetts representative): Boutwell, *Reconstruction: Its True Basis,* in *Speeches and Papers Relating to the Rebellion and the Overthrow of Slavery* (2 vols., Boston, 1867), II, 372–407; Burton C. Cook (Illinois representative): *Cong. Globe,* 39 Cong., 1 Sess., 903–904 (Feb. 17, 1866); Timothy Otis Howe (Wisconsin senator): *ibid.,* 162–70 (Jan. 10, 1866), 293–96 (Jan. 18, 1866), 438–45 (Jan.

26, 1866); George W. Julian (Indiana representative): Julian, *Dangers and Duties of the Hour—Reconstruction and Suffrage: In the Hall of the House of Representatives, Indianapolis, November 17, 1865,* in Julian, *Speeches on Political Questions* (N.Y., 1872), 262–90; *John R. Kelso* (Missouri representative): *Cong. Globe,* 39 Cong., 1 Sess., 730–33 (Feb. 7, 1866); Halbert E. Paine (Wisconsin representative): *ibid.,* 562–66 (Jan. 31, 1866); Samuel C. Pomeroy (Kansas senator): *ibid.,* 1180–84 (March 5, 1866); Thaddeus Stevens (Pennsylvania representative): Stevens, *Reconstruction: Speech of the Hon. Thaddeus Stevens, Delivered in the City of Lancaster, Sept. 7, 1865* (Lancaster, 1865), *passim; Cong. Globe,* 39 Cong., 1 Sess., 72–75 (Dec. 18, 1865), 1307–10 (March 10, 1866); Charles Sumner (Massachusetts senator): Sumner, *The National Security and the National Faith: Guaranties for the National Freedman and the National Creditor— Speech at the Republican State Convention, in Worcester, Massachusetts, September 14, 1865,* in Sumner, *The Works of Charles Sumner* (15 vols., Boston, 1870–1883), IX, 437–77; resolutions in Senate, *Cong. Globe,* 39 Cong., 1 Sess., 2 (Dec. 4, 1865); Hamilton Ward (N.Y. representative): *ibid.,* 783 (Feb. 10, 1866); Thomas Williams (Pennsylvania representative): *ibid.,* 784–98 (Feb. 10, 1866). Also Julian, *Political Recollections,* 305–308; Benjamin F. Butler, *Butler's Book: Autobiography and Personal Reminiscences of Major-General Benjamin F. Butler* (Boston, 1892), 960–61. For insight into radicals' efforts to promote black landholding, see Paul Wallace Gates, "Federal Land Policy in the South, 1866–1868," *Journal of Southern History,* VI (Aug. 1940), 304–308.

8. Generally historians have not realized how sure moderate Republicans must have been of the president's cooperation, especially after they read his annual message. This is due in large part to their failure to recognize that the non-radicals were proceeding on the same constitutional theory as they believed the president espoused. Failing to see how close the conservatives and centrists believed they were to Johnson, they naturally failed to see how far they believed they were from the radicals.

9. See, for instance, Doolittle to Johnson, Sept. 9, 1865; Dixon to Johnson, Sept. 26, Oct. 8, 1865. Andrew Johnson Mss., Manuscripts Div., L.C.; Gideon Welles, *Diary of Gideon Welles—Secretary of the Navy Under Lincoln and Johnson* (3 vols., Boston and N.Y., 1911), II, 330 (July 10, 1865), 369 (Aug. 30, 1865).

10. Robert P.L. Baber to Doolittle, Feb. 28, 1866. James Rood Doolittle Mss., Manuscripts Div., L.C.

11. For an example of this confusion, see the entries in Welles's *Diary* from July

to December 1865, and try to determine to whom he refers by the term "radical."

12. Morton, of course, was engaged in his bitter duel with Julian (see pp. 64–65, 113, *supra*). Doolittle was battling a radical faction in the Wisconsin state party, led by the formerly conservative Timothy Otis Howe. See pp. 65, 113, *supra.*

13. A.K. McClure, *Colonel Alexander K. McClure's Recollections of Half a Century* (Salem, Mass., 1902), 301–302.

14. Johnson to Benjamin F. Perry, Nov. 27, 1865, quoted in Edward McPherson (ed.), *The Political History of the United States of America, During the Period of Reconstruction . . .* (3rd edn., Washington, 1880), p. 24.

15. Welles, *Diary,* II, 387 (Dec. 3, 1865).

16. *N.Y. Tribune,* Dec. 4, 1865, p. 1; *Boston Evening Journal,* Dec. 4, 1865, p. 2; Rutherford B. Hayes, *Diary and Letters of Rutherford B. Hayes, Nineteenth President of the United States,* ed. by Charles Richard Williams (5 vols., Columbus, Ohio, 1922–26), III, 7–8 (Dec. 1, 1865); *Cong. Globe,* 39 Cong., 1 Sess., 6–7 (Dec. 4, 1867); Marvin Schlegel, "The Dawes Plan: The Origin of the Joint Committee on Reconstruction," *Virginia Social Science Journal,* VI (Nov. 1971), 134–42. Schlegel is the first scholar to have suggested that Dawes and not Stevens himself originated the plan for a joint committee on Reconstruction. The plan bears a definite resemblance to Dawes's proposition of the first session of the Thirty-eighth Congress to appoint a presidential commission to report to Congress on conditions in the southern states where civil government was being restored under President Lincoln's authority. See *Cong. Globe,* 38 Cong., 1 Sess., 3178 (June 22, 1864).

17. Cincinnati *Commercial,* Dec. 12, 1865, p. 1; Welles, *Diary,* II, 405 (Dec. 28, 1865); Morgan to [John] Jay, Dec. 25, 1865. Edwin D. Morgan Mss., New York State Library; *Cong. Globe,* 39 Cong., 1 Sess., 24–30 (Dec. 12, 1865), 46–47 (Dec. 13, 1865); Springfield *Illinois State Journal,* Dec. 22, 1865, p. 2.

18. *Cong. Globe,* 39 Cong., 1 Sess., 31–34 (Dec. 12, 1865).

19. Washington *Daily Morning Chronicle,* Dec. 9, 1865, p. 1; Boston *Evening Journal,* Dec. 8, 1865, p. 2; N.Y. *Independent,* Dec. 14, 1865, p. 1.

20. Sumner to Lieber, Dec. 16, 1865, Charles Sumner Mss., Houghton Library, Harvard University, Cambridge, Mass.

21. *Cong. Globe,* 39 Cong., 1 Sess., 72–75 (Dec. 18, 1865); quoted material at p. 74.

22. *Ibid.,* 120–25 (Dec. 21, 1865).

23. Washington *Daily Morning Chronicle,* Dec. 20, 1865, p. 2; N.Y. *Independent,* Dec. 28, 1865, p. 1; N.Y. *Nation,* Dec. 28, 1865, p. 803.

24. *Cong. Globe,* 39 Cong., 1 Sess., 39–43 (Dec. 13, 1865), 79–80 (Dec. 19), 90–95 (Dec. 20), 111–12 (Dec. 21).
25. Alice Hooper to Sumner, Dec. 16, 1865. Sumner Mss.
26. Phillips to Sumner, Dec. 25, 1865. Sumner Mss.
27. Phillips to Lyman Trumbull, Dec. 26, 1865. Lyman Trumbull Mss., Manuscripts Div., L.C.; N.Y. *Nation,* Dec. 28, 1865, pp. 806–807.
28. Weed to E.D. Morgan, Dec. 20, 1865. Morgan Mss.; Andrew, *Valedictory Address, passim;* George B. Loring to Sumner, Jan. 7, 1866. Sumner Mss. The addresses of Governors Cony of Maine and Fairchild of Wisconsin were reported by the *N.Y. Times* as examples of endorsements of the president. *N.Y. Times,* Jan. 4, 1866, p. 1; Jan. 5, 1866, pp. 4, 5. Also Hayes, *Diary,* III, 11 (Dec. 12, 1865); Carl Schurz to Mrs. Margaretha Meyer Schurz, Dec. 17, 1865, quoted in Schurz, *Intimate Letters,* 354–55; Horace Greeley to Colfax, Dec. 11, 1865. Schuyler Colfax Mss., N.Y. Public Library; Garfield to Eliza Ballow Garfield, Dec. 17, 1865, quoted in Theodore Clark Smith, *The Life and Letters of James Abram Garfield* (2 vols., New Haven, 1925), I, 392; Trumbull to D.L. Phillips, Dec. 21, 1865, quoted in Arthur Charles Cole, *The Era of the Civil War, 1848–1870,* vol. III of *The Centennial History of Illinois* (Springfield, 1919), 395n; Trumbull to William Jayne, Dec. 24, 1865, quoted in Mark Krug, *Lyman Trumbull: Conservative Radical* (N.Y., 1965), 232; Allen C. Fuller to Trumbull, Dec. 27, 1865; F.A. Eastman to Trumbull, Jan. 4, 1866. Trumbull Mss., L.C.; D.L. Phillips to Richard Yates, Dec. 26, 1865. Richard Yates Mss., Illinois State Historical Library; J.A. Wheelock to Ignatius Donnelly, Dec. 27, 1865. Ignatius Donnelly Mss., Minnesota State Library; John Binny to John A. Andrew, Dec. 27, 1865. John Albion Andrew Mss., Massachusetts Historical Society; Washington *Daily Morning Chronicle,* Dec. 22, 1865, p. 2; *Chicago Tribune,* Dec. 18, 1865, p. 1; Boston *Daily Advertiser,* Dec. 23, 1865, p. 2; Buffalo *Morning Express,* Dec. 22, 1865, p. 4; Springfield *Illinois State Journal,* Dec. 27, 1865, p. 2; Jan. 1, 1866, p. 2.
29. *Cong. Globe,* 39 Cong., 1 Sess., 27 (Dec. 12, 1865).
30. For Harris's statement to Welles, see Welles, *Diary,* II, 401 (Dec. 21, 1865).
31. Fessenden to Samuel Fessenden, Dec. 31, 1865. William Pitt Fessenden Mss., Bowdoin College Library, Brunswick, Me.
32. See Charts 9 and 10. Earlier historians of Reconstruction, men like Bowers, Randall, and Beale, did not recognize the essential differences among Republicans. More recent historians—McKitrick, Brock, and the Coxes, for example —realize that Republicans settled on a moderate policy during the first session of the Thirty-ninth Congress, but only

Brock has remarked on the radicals' attempt to seize the initiative early in its early months. W.R. Brock, *An American Crisis: Congress and Reconstruction, 1865–1867* (N.Y., 1903), 97–104. McKitrick recognized the importance of Sumner's failure to win a place on the Reconstruction committee. Eric L. McKitrick, *Andrew Johnson and Reconstruction* (Chicago and London, 1960), 276–77.
33. Welles, *Diary,* II, 412–13 (Jan. 8, 1866).
34. *Ibid.,* 387 (Dec. 3, 1865), 393–95 (Dec. 8), 396 (Dec. 13), 398–99 (Dec. 18), 399 (Dec. 19), 407 (Dec. 30), 414–17 (Jan. 13, 1866), 421 (Jan. 30). Also Edward Bates to Johnson, Feb. 10, 1866, quoted in Bates *Diary of Edward Bates,* ed. by Howard K. Beale (Washington, 1933), 547–51 (Feb. 10, 1866).
35. See pp. 128–29, above.
36. Seward to Holden, Dec. 4, 1865, in *Senate Executive Document No. 26,* 39 Cong., 1 Sess., 47.
37. *N.Y. Times,* Dec. 5, 1865, p. 4.
38. *Ibid.,* Dec. 25, 1865, p. 4.
39. *Chicago Tribune,* Jan. 11, 1866, p. 2; Boston *Evening Journal,* Dec. 20, 1865, p. 2; Dec. 23, 1865, p. 4; Jan. 15, 1866, p. 4.
40. Benjamin B. Kendrick (ed.), *The Journal of the Joint Committee of Fifteen on Reconstruction: 39th Congress, 1865–1867* (N.Y. and London, 1914), 40–41 (Jan. 9, 1866); Washburne to Mrs. Adele Washburne, Jan. 7, 1866, quoted in Russell K. Nelson, "The Early Life and Congressional Career of Elihu B. Washburne" (unpublished Ph.D. dissertation, University of North Dakota, 1953), 482; Daniel Clark to George G. Fogg, Jan. 20, 1866. Clark Mss., New Hampshire Historical Society, Concord, N.H.; Fessenden to Samuel Fessenden, Dec. 31, 1865. Fessenden Mss., Bowdoin College Library; Forney to Sumner, Dec. 26, 1865. Sumner Mss.; Forney to Andrew Johnson, Jan. 2, 1866. Johnson Mss.; Henry S. Lane to Richard Thompson, Dec. 29, 1965. Richard Thompson Mss., Indiana State Historical Library, Indiana Division; Willard H. Smith, *Schuyler Colfax: The Changing Fortunes of a Political Idol,* vol. XXXIII of the Indiana Historical Collections (Indianapolis, 1952), 230–31; E.D. Morgan to J. Morgan, Jan. 3, 1866, quoted in James A. Rawley, *Edwin D. Morgan, 1811–1883: Merchant in Politics,* vol. DLXXXII of the Studies in History, Economics and Public Law ed. by the Faculty of Political Science of Columbia University (N.Y., 1956), 216; Washington *Daily Morning Chronicle,* Dec. 22, 1865, p. 2; Fessenden in *Cong. Globe,* 39 Cong., 1 Sess., 366–67 (Jan. 23, 1866); Springfield *Illinois State Journal,* Jan. 26, 1866, p. 2; Boston *Evening Journal,* Jan. 25, 1866, p. 4; Philadelphia *North American,* Jan. 16, 1866, p. 2; Toledo *Blade,* Jan. 9, 1866, p. 2; Jan. 18, p. 2.
41. N.Y. *Independent,* Dec. 25, 1865, p. 1; Jan. 4, 1866, p. 1; Hayes, *Diary,* III,

12–13 (Jan. 10, 1866); *N.Y. Times,* Jan. 11, 1866, p. 1; Jan. 13, 1866, p. 4, 5; Jan. 17, 1866, p. 1; Boston *Evening Journal,* Jan. 11, 1866, p. 4; Jan. 13, 1866, p. 4; Jan. 16, 1866, p. 4; Jan. 17, 1866, p. 4; Jan. 18, 1866, p. 4; Boston *Daily Advertiser,* Jan. 15, 1866, p. 2; *Cong. Globe,* 39 Cong., 1 Sess., 310–11 (Jan. 18, 1866).

42. Poore ("Perley") in the *Boston Evening Journal,* Jan. 21, 1866, p. 4.

43. Fessenden to Elizabeth Fessenden Warriner, Jan. 14, 1866. Fessenden Mss., Bowdoin College Library.

44. Forney ("Occasional") in the Washington *Daily Morning Chronicle,* Feb. 21, 1866, p. 1.

45. *Cong. Globe,* 39 Cong., 1 Sess. (Feb. 8, 1866).

46. Springfield *Illinois State Journal,* Jan. 27, 1866, p. 2; Welles, *Diary,* II, 435 (Feb. 19, 1866); Krug, *Trumbull,* 231–43.

47. Trumbull speaking at a reception for him in Chicago in the summer of 1866. Trumbull scrapbook. Trumbull Mss., Illinois State Historical Library; Welles, *Diary,* II, 489 (April 19, 1866); Trumbull in *Cong. Globe,* 39 Cong., 1 Sess., 1760 (Feb. 4, 1866); Oliver Otis Howard, *Autobiography of Oliver Otis Howard, Major General United States Army* (2 vols., N.Y., 1907), II, 208.

48. The bill is described in *Cong. Globe,* 39 Cong., 1 Sess., 211–12 (Jan. 12, 1866).

49. *Ibid.,* 364–66 (Jan. 23, 1866).

50. The original version of the bill may be found *ibid.,* 211–12 (Jan. 12, 1866).

51. *Ibid.,* 474 (Jan. 29, 1866). This was later modified to read "All persons born in the United States and not subject to any foreign Power, excluding Indians not subject to tribal authority, are hereby declared to be citizens of the United States . . . ."

52. On constitutional questions not involving Reconstruction, Trumbull, Fessenden, Daniel Clark, Dixon, Doolittle, Foster, Grimes, Henderson, Cowan, Lot M. Morrill, Daniel Norton, Peter G. Van Winkle, Waitman T. Willey, Sprague, and Samuel J. Kirkwood would join the Democrats in voting against proposals to increase the functions of the national government. See the votes on proposals for a nationwide quarantine to protect against cholera, *Cong. Globe,* 39 Cong., 1 Sess., 2586, 2589 (May 15, 1866); to facilitate interstate commerce and communications, *ibid.,* 2870, 2876 (May 29, 1866); to repair levees on the Mississippi River, *ibid.,* 4083 (July 24, 1866).

53. *Ibid.,* 476 (Jan. 29, 1866). This interpretation is in flat disagreement with that expounded by the Supreme Court in *Jones* v. *Alfred H. Mayer Co.,* 392 U.S. 409 (1968), and Robert L. Kohl in "The Civil Rights Act of 1866, Its Hour Come Round at Last: *Jones* v. *Alfred H. Mayer Co,*" *Virginia Law Review,* LV (March 1969), 272–300. Both the opinion and the article are long on inference but short on evidence. The Su-

preme Court in the Jones case cites the provisions of the Freedmen's Bureau bill as evidence for interpreting the meaning of the Civil Rights bill. But, as the court recognizes, Trumbull left the key word "prejudice" out of the Civil Rights bill when defining the conditions in which discrimination in civil rights was illegal. To one familiar with Trumbull's extreme conservatism in constitutional matters, the reason is clear: the Freedmen's Bureau bill, a war measure, was justified under Congress's war powers, which were in Trumbull's opinion limited only by the law of nations. Therefore a provision against denial of rights based on personal prejudice was constitutionally justifiable. The Civil Rights bill he justified under peacetime provisions of the Constitution. That legislation would be permanent, and Trumbull intended no permanent extension of federal power of this magnitude. The statement just quoted in the text is a clear implication of this.

Kohl, in defending the court's decision, argues that the Civil Rights bill was framed in response to extralegal as well as legal discrimination against black men in the South. He gives no hard evidence to this effect, relying instead on the fact that testimony before the Joint Committee on Reconstruction indicated that such discrimination existed. Kohl assumes that the prohibition on discrimination in civil rights due to "custom" in the Civil Rights bill must have been intended to combat this type of discrimination. But Trumbull framed the section involved before the Reconstruction committee had received any testimony, and the bill was reported not from the Reconstruction committee, but from the Judiciary committee. This does not mean that Trumbull could not have had such discrimination in mind; he had access to Freedmen's Bureau correspondence which offered testimony similar to that the Reconstruction committee heard. It only means that it is not certain that he had it in mind. Given this uncertainty, it would be helpful to have just one indication that Trumbull did indeed intend to combat extralegal prejudice. But instead, his statements, such as the one I have given in the text, imply a contrary view. Moreover, Trumbull later opposed legislation operating directly on extralegal criminal conspiracies to violate citizens' rights. See his arguments on the Ku Klux Klan Act of 1871 in the *Cong. Globe,* 42 Cong., 1 Sess., 578–79 (April 11, 1871). Of course this may indicate no more than that Trumbull had changed his mind along witih his politics (by 1871 he was in open revolt against the Republican party). See also Charles Fairman's discussion in *History of the Supreme Court of the United States: Volume VI, Reconstruction and Reunion, 1864–88: Part One* (N.Y., 1971), 1207–59.

54. Doolittle's bill authorized the president to maintain the bureau in the slave states

until all discriminatory laws "have been repealed or modified so as to secure the equal protection of all persons in all the civil rights of person and property known to or secured by the common law, without distinction of class, race, or color . . . ." He specifically included all the rights Trumbull had listed. Senate bill number 50, Senate bill file, 39 Cong. R.G. 46, N.A.

55. D.C. Phillips to Trumbull, Jan. 7, 1866. Trumbull Mss., L.C.; *N.Y. Times,* Jan. 15, 1866, p. 4; Philadelphia *North American,* Feb. 5, 1866, p. 2; Buffalo *Morning Express,* Feb. 8, 1866, p. 4; Forney ("Occasional") in Washington *Daily Morning Chronicle,* Jan. 10, 1866, p. 1; Poore ("Perley") in Boston *Evening Journal,* Jan. 17, 1866, p. 2; Jan. 18, p. 2; "Dixon" in Boston *Daily Advertiser,* Feb. 20, 1866, p. 1; Carl Schurz, *Reminiscences of Carl Schurz* (3 vols., N.Y., 1908), III, 255.

56. Washington *Daily Morning Chronicle,* Feb. 20, 1866, p. 1. Newspaper correspondence from "Herman" in the Trumbull scrapbook at the Illinois State Historical Library makes similar observations. Trumbull Mss., Illinois State Historical Library.

57. *Cong. Globe,* 39 Cong., 1 Sess., 421 (Jan. 25, 1866).

58. *Ibid.,* 585–90 (Feb. 1, 1866).

59. *Ibid.,* 298–99 (Jan. 18, 1866), 323 (Jan. 19, 1866), 655, 658 (Feb. 5, 1866), 688 (Feb. 6, 1866).

60. *Ibid.,* 606–607 (Feb. 2, 1866). Doolittle was absent when the Civil Rights bill passed, but he had voted with the Republican majority on preliminary roll calls and declared he would have voted for the bill if present. *Ibid.,* 1804–805 (April 6, 1866), 575 (Feb. 1, 1866), 606 (Feb. 2, 1866).

61. *Ibid.,* 351 (Jan. 22, 1866).

62. The votes are *ibid.,* 538 (Jan. 31, 1866). The entire debate may be found *ibid.,* 351–59 (Jan. 22, 1866), 376–89 (Jan. 23), 403–12 (Jan. 24), 422–35 (Jan. 25), 447–60 (Jan. 26), 483–94 (Jan. 29), 508–509 (Jan. 30), 535–38 (Jan. 31); McPherson (ed.), *Political History of . . . Reconstruction,* 51–52; Boston *Evening Journal,* Jan. 30, 1866, p. 4; *Chicago Tribune,* Jan. 30, 1866, p. 1; Boston *Daily Advertiser,* Feb. 1, 1866, p. 1.

63. Moncure Conway, "Sursum Corda!" *The Radical,* I (April 1866), 291.

64. Fessenden to Elizabeth Fessenden Warriner, Feb. 3, 1866, Fessenden Mss., Bowdoin College Library.

65. Smith to Sumner, Mar. 23, 1866; Schurz to Sumner, Feb. 8, 1866; Theodore Tilton to Sumner, Feb. 3, 1866; Israel Washburn to Sumner, Feb. 8, Mar. 8, 1866; Edward L. Pierce to Sumner, Feb. 8, 1866; Garrison to Sumner, Feb. 11, 1866; Elizabeth Cady Stanton to Sumner, Feb. 15, 1866; Loring to Sumner, Feb. 16, 1866; Thomas Wentworth Higginson to Sumner, Feb. 18, 1866; Susan B. Anthony to Sumner, March 8, 1866; Edward Channing Larned to Sumner, March 10, 1866; Pillsbury to Sumner,

March 12, 1866; William E. Whiting to Sumner, March 12, 1866; Elizur Wright to Sumner, March 14, 1866; Wendell Phillips to Sumner, March 17, 1866. Sumner Mss.; *Senate Miscellaneous Document No. 56,* 39 Cong., 1 Sess.; N.Y. *Independent,* Feb. 8, 1866, p. 4; Gerritt Smith to Sumner, ?, quoted in the the *Cong. Globe,* 39 Cong., 1 Sess., 1281 (March 9, 1866).

66. *Ibid.,* 592 (Feb. 1, 1866).

67. *Ibid.,* 685 (Feb. 6, 1866).

68. *Ibid.,* 673 (Feb. 6, 1866).

69. *Ibid.,* 1224–25 (March 7, 1866).

70. *Ibid.,* 704–705 (Feb. 7, 1866).

71. *Ibid.,* 1239 (March 9, 1866).

72. *Ibid.,* 1281 (March 9, 1866); Sumner and Fessenden's speeches are *ibid.,* 673–87 (Feb. 5, 6, 1866), 702–708 (Feb. 7, 1866), 1224–33 (March 7, 1866), 1275–82 (March 9, 1866).

73. Springfield *Illinois State Journal,* Feb. 6, 1866, p. 1; *Chicago Tribune,* Feb. 3, 1866, p. 2; Feb. 4, 1866, p. 4; Washington *Daily Morning Chronicle,* Feb. 9, 1866, p. 2; *N.Y. Tribune,* Feb. 10, 1866, p. 1; newspaper correspondence from "Herman" in the Trumbull scrapbook. Trumbull Mss., Illinois State Historical Library; Schurz, *Reminiscences,* III, 255.

74. David W. Bartlett ("D.W.B.") in the N.Y. *Independent,* Feb. 15, 1866, p. 1; McPherson (ed.), *Political History of . . . Reconstruction,* 52–56.

75. Poore in the Boston *Evening Journal,* Feb. 12, 1866, p. 4; Bartlett in the N.Y. *Independent,* Feb. 15, 1866, p. 1; Garfield to Burke Hinsdale, Feb. 13, 1866, quoted in Hinsdale (ed.), *Garfield-Hinsdale Letters,* 77–79.

76. Fessenden to Elizabeth Fessenden Warriner, Feb. 17, 1866. Fessenden Mss., Bowdoin College Library; Fessenden to George Harrington, Feb. 3, 1866, quoted in Charles A. Jellison, *Fessenden of Maine, Civil War Senator* (Syracuse, 1962); Dawes to Mr. Electa Dawes, Feb. 1, 1866. Henry L. Dawes Mss., Manuscripts Div., L.C.

77. Welles, *Diary,* II, 425–26 (Feb. 2, 1866), 432 (Feb. 13, 1866).

78. Seward's draft is in the Johnson Mss.; LaWanda and John H. Cox, "Andrew Johnson and His Ghost Writers," *Mississippi Valley Historical Review,* XLVIII (Dec. 1961), 465–66, 467, 472–73; Glyndon G. Van Deusen, *William Henry Seward* (N.Y., 1967), 442–44. Seward expressed similar opinions in a speech at a pro-Johnson rally February 22, 1866. Seward, Speech at Cooper Union, Feb. 22, 1866, in Seward, *The Works of William H. Seward,* ed. by George E. Baker (5 vols., Boston, 1884), 538–39.

79. *Cong. Globe,* 39 Cong., 1 Sess., 915–17 (Feb. 19, 1866).

80. Boston *Daily Advertiser,* Feb. 20, 1866, p. 1; Feb. 21, 1866, p. 2.

81. Philadelphia *North American,* Feb. 21, 1866, p. 2; Buffalo *Morning Express,* Feb. 21, 1866, p. 1; Boston *Evening Journal,* Feb. 20, 1866, p. 2; Springfield

Illinois State Journal, Feb. 24, 1866, p. 2.

82. Trumbull's rebuttal is in the *Cong. Globe,* 39 Cong., 1 Sess., 936–43 (Feb. 20, 1866).

83. *Ibid.,* 991 (Feb. 23, 1866). Fessenden disscussed the veto *ibid.,* 984–91 (Feb. 23, 1866).

84. Kendrick (ed.), *Journal of the Joint Committee,* 71–72 (Feb. 20, 1866).

85. *Cong. Globe,* 39 Cong., 1 Sess., 950 (Feb. 20, 1866), 966 (Feb. 21, 1866).

86. *Ibid.,* 1143–47 (March 2, 1866). Fessenden's discussion of the effect of the concurrent resolution was correct. A *concurrent* resolution is passed by the separate action of each house. It is not an act of Congress, and may be repealed by either house without the consent of the other.

87. Howe to Horace Rublee, Feb. 28, 1866. Timothy Otis Howe Mss., State Historical Society of Wisconsin.

88. *Cong. Globe,* 39 Cong., 1 Sess., 943 (Feb. 20, 1866). On February 23 James H. Lane joined the dissenters after the Senate refused to take up his resolution to seat Arkansas's senators-elect. *Ibid.,* 1026–27 (Feb. 26, 1866).

89. *Ibid.,* 920–21 (Feb. 19, 1866).

90. Indianapolis *Daily Journal,* Feb. 23, 1866, p. 2; J.S. Scobey to Henry S. Lane, Mar. 4, 1866. Henry S. Lane Mss, Lilly Library, Indiana University, Bloomington, Indiana; Mathilda Gresham, *Life of Walter Quentin Gresham, 1832–1895* (2 vols., Chicago, 1919), 331–32.

91. Prosper Wetmore to McCulloch, Feb. 26, 1866. McCulloch Mss., L.C.; John and LaWanda Cox, *Politics, Principle, and Prejudice,* 185, 186–89; Van Deusen, *Seward,* 443–44.

92. William S. Robinson to Sumner, March 7, 1866; Samuel A. Stone to Sumner, March 16, 1866; George L. Sawin to Sumner, March 21, 1866. Sumner Mss.; Montgomery Blair to Andrew, March 13, 1866; Andrew to Francis Preston Blair, Sr., March 18, 1866. Andrew Mss.

93. *Cong. Globe,* 39 Cong., 1 Sess., appendix, 132 (Feb. 26, 1866). Sherman's entire speech is *ibid.,* 124–33 (Feb. 26, 1866); Boston *Evening Journal,* Feb. 27, 1866, p. 4; *N.Y. Times,* Feb. 27, 1866, p. 1.

94. Cox to George B. Wright, Feb. 26, 1866, quoted in *N.Y. Times,* Feb. 27, 1866, p. 1; Welles, *Diary,* II, 440 (Feb. 26, 1866).

95. Boston *Evening Journal,* Feb. 28, 1866, p. 2; Welles, *Diary, II,* 441 (March 3, 1866), 446–47 (March 8, 1866), 447–50 (March 9, 1866); Hayes to Sardis Birchard, March 4, 1866, quoted in Hayes, *Diary,* III, 19–20.

96. Bingham and Grider were the other two members.

97. Kendrick (ed.), *Journal of the Joint Committee,* 63–64 (Feb. 15, 1866), 64–69 (Feb. 17, 1866), 69–71, 73–78 (Feb. 20, 1866), 78–81 (March 5, 1866); *House Report No. 29,* 39 Cong., 1 Sess. (March 6, 1866); *Chicago Tribune,* March 11, 1866, p. 2; Boston *Evening Journal,* March 3, 1866, p. 4; March 5, 1866, p. 4; March 6, 1866, p. 4; Boston *Daily Advertiser,* March 6, 1866, p. 1; *N.Y. Independent,* March 15, 1866, p. 4; Boston *Right Way,* March 17, 1866, p. 1; Boston *Commonwealth,* Feb. 17, 1866, p. 2.

98. *Cong. Globe,* 39 Cong., 1 Sess., 1095 (Feb. 28, 1866).

99. *Ibid.,* 1296 (March 9, 1866).

100. *Ibid.,* 1284, 1287, 1288 (March 9, 1866).

101. *Ibid.,* 1289 (March 9, 1866); Stevens to Sumner, March ?, 1866; Chase to Sumner, March 9, 1866. Sumner Mss.

102. Stevens in *Cong. Globe,* 39 Cong., 1 Sess., 2459 (May 8, 1866); Fessenden to Elizabeth Fessenden Warriner, March 10, 1866. Fessenden Mss., Bowdoin College Library; Dawes to Mrs. Electa Dawes, March 16, 1866. Dawes Mss.; Toledo *Blade,* March 10, 1866, p. 2; *N.Y. Tribune,* March 10, 1866, p. 2.

103. *Chicago Tribune,* March 14, 1866, p. 1; E.B. Washburne to Mrs. Adele Washburne, March 11, 1866, quoted in Russell K. Nelson, "Washburn," 485.

8. Conservative Reconstruction—Part Two

1. Wentworth to John Haines, March 7, 1866. Wentworth Mss., Chicago Historical Society, Chicago, Illinois.

2. *Cong. Globe,* 39 Cong., 1 Sess., 1367 (March 13, 1866). The three Johnson supporters were Columbus Delano, Andrew J. Kuykendall, and Kellian V. Whaley. Raymond and three other administration supporters, Robert S. Hale, Thomas E. Noell, and Thomas N. Stilwell, did not vote. The vote in the Senate may be found *ibid.,* 1413 (March 15, 1866).

3. McCulloch to Wilson, March 12, 1866. Henry Wilson Mss., Manuscripts Div., L.C.; Gideon Welles, *Diary of Gideon Welles—Secretary of the Navy Under Lincoln and Johnson* (3 vols., Boston and N.Y., 1911), II, 446–47 (March 8, 1866).

4. *N.Y. Times,* Mar. 14, 1866, p. 1.

5. Sherman, speech at Bridgeport, Conn., quoted in the *N.Y. Times,* March 19, 1866, pp. 1, 8; *N.Y. Tribune,* March 17, 1866, p. 1; *Chicago Tribune,* March 27, 1866, p. 2.

6. *Chicago Tribune,* March 27, 1866, p. 2; *N.Y. Tribune,* March 21, 1866, p. 1; March 22, p. 1; March 23, p. 1; *N.Y. Times,* March 24, p. 1; Boston *Daily Advertiser,* March 25, 1866, p. 1.

7. E.B. Sadler to Sherman, March 23, 1866. John Sherman Mss., Manuscripts Div., L.C. Sadler was one of the leading Republicans in the Ohio state senate. He had been in close contact with Sherman in the previous months, during Sherman's campaign for reelection to the Senate. D.L. Phillips wrote Trumbull in the same vein. Phillips to Trumbull, March 22, 1866. Lyman Trumbull Mss., Manuscripts Div., L.C.

8. Cox to Johnson, March 22, 1866. Andrew Johnson Mss., Manuscripts Div., L.C.; William Dudley Foulke, *Life of Oliver P. Morton, Including his Important Speeches* (2 vols., Indianapolis and Kansas City, 1899), I, 467; Welles, *Diary,* II, 463–64 (March 26, 1866); LaWanda and John Cox, *Politics, Principle, and Prejudice, 1865–1866: Dilemma of Reconstruction America* (Glencoe, 1963), 196–97.

9. Welles, *Diary,* II, 463 (March 26, 1866).

10. Seward's draft is in the Johnson papers at the Library of Congress; Seward to Johnson, Mar. 27, 1866. Johnson Mss., L.C. See LaWanda and John Cox, "Andrew Johnson and His Ghost Writers: An Analysis of the Freedmen's Bureau and Civil Rights Veto Messages," *Mississippi Valley Historical Review* XLVIII (Dec. 1961), 474–75.

11. The veto message is quoted in James D. Richardson (ed.), *Messages and Papers of the Presidents of the Uniited States, 1789–1897* (10 vols., Washington, 1896–99), VI, 405–16.

12. Morgan to Thurlow Weed, April 8, 1866. Weed Mss., Rush Rhees Library, University of Rochester, Rochester, N.Y.; Raymond to Seward, n.d. [April 1866]. William Henry Seward Mss., Rush Rhees Library, University of Rochester, Rochester, N.Y.

13. Willard Warner to Sherman, Mar. 28, 1866. John Sherman Mss.; N.Y. *Independent,* March 31, 1866, p. 1. Warner was an important Ohio state legislator. He later served the Freedmen's Bureau in Alabama and was elected to the United States Senate from that state in 1868.

14. Cox to Johnson, March 22, 1866. Johnson Mss.; Stewart in *Cong. Globe,* 39 Cong., 1 Sess., 1785 (April 5, 1866).

15. *Ibid.,* 1809 (April 6, 1866).

16. Howe to Grace T. Howe, Apr. 7, 1866. Timothy Otis Howe Mss., Wisconsin State Historical Library; N.Y. *Independent,* April 12, 1866, p. 4.

17. *Ibid.,* 1861 (April 9, 1866).

18. Colfax to Mary Clemmer Ames, April 10, 1866. Ames Mss., Rutherford B. Hayes Library.

19. Philadelphia *North American,* April 2, 1866, p. 2.

20. Charles Sumner, *The Works of Charles Sumner* (15 vols., Boston, 1870–83), X, 274–75.

21. Wendell Phillips to Sumner, March 24, 1866. Charles Sumner Mss., Houghton Library, Harvard University.

22. *Chicago Tribune,* March 28, 1866, p. 2.

23. Dawes to Mrs. Electa Dawes, Mar. 31, 1866. Dawes Mss.; Foster to Anna ? (Foster's sister), April 17, 1866. Lafayette S. Foster Mss., Massachusetts Historical Society.

24. Bateman to Sherman, Feb. 21, March 30, 1866. John Sherman Mss. Bateman's first letter was endorsed by E.B. Sadler and William Henry Smith. Smith was Ohio secretary of state; Bateman and Sadler Ohio state senators.

25. Colfax to Judge David Turner, May ?, 1866, quoted in O.J. Hollister, *The Life*

of Schuyler Colfax (N.Y. and London, 1866), 284–85; Robert Dale Owen, "Political Results from the Varioloid," *Atlantic Monthly,* XXXV (June 1875), 666; *N.Y. Times,* April 27, 1866, p. 1; Welles, *Diary,* II, 490 (April 19, 1866); George S. Boutwell, *Reminiscences of Sixty Years in Public Affairs* (2 vols., N.Y., 1902), II, 41–42.

26. Bryant quoted in Allan Nevins, *The Evening Post: A Century of Journalism* (N.Y., 1968), 329–30; Rutherford B. Hayes to Mrs. Sophie B. Hayes, April 12, 1866. Hayes Mss., Rutherford B. Hayes Library; Grimes to Mrs. Grimes, Apr. 16, 1866, quoted in William Salter, *The Life of James W. Grimes, Governor of Iowa, 1854–1858; Senator of the United States, 1859–1869* (N.Y., 1876), 291.

27. *Cong. Globe,* 39 Cong., 1 Sess., 2180 (April 25, 1866), 2373–74 (May 3, 1866).

28. Benjamin B. Kendrick (ed.), *Journal of the Joint Committee of Fifteen on Reconstruction: 39 Congress, 1865–1867* (N.Y., 1914), 100–106 (April 28, 1866).

29. *Cong. Globe,* 39 Cong., 1 Sess., 2286 (Apr. 30, 1866).

30. U.S. Congress, *Report of the Joint Committee on Reconstruction,* xix–xx (quoted material at xx).

31. Quoted in Charles Fairman, "Does the Fourteenth Amendment Incorporate the Bill of Rights?: The Original Understanding," *Stanford Law Review,* II (Dec. 1949), 96. The scope of the Fourteenth Amendment has been a center of whirling controversy since its proposal, but nearly all scholars agree that it placed an obligation *upon states* either merely to refrain from discrimination in laws and procedures involving civil rights or to offer full protection for those rights. That is, the quarrel among lawyers and historians has been over whether the Fourteenth Amendment grants Congress power to intervene in cases of state *inaction* or merely in cases of overt discrimination. No matter which interpretation is correct (and I lean toward the first), it is clear that the framers of the Fourteenth Amendment considered protection of rights to be primarily a state responsibility, and gave Congress the power to intervene only where the state failed to meet its obligation. For a clear indication of how state-centered Republicans believed the constitutional amendment to be as they passed and ratified it, see the compendia of Republican arguments offered *ibid.,* especially at 41–134. The evidence is all the more persuasive because Fairman was dealing with another point entirely.

32. Boutwell, *Reminiscences,* II, 42.

33. Kendrick (ed.), *Journal of the Joint Committee,* 82–120 (April 21, 23, 25, 28, 1866). Three monographs have dealt specifically with the activities of the Reconstruction committee and the framing of the Fourteenth Amendment. They are Horace Edgar Flack, *The Adoption of the Fourteenth Amendment* (Baltimore, 1908); the second part of Ken-

drick's *Journal of the Joint Committee;* and Joseph B. James, *The Framing of the Fourteenth Amendment* (Urbana, Ill., 1956). James's work is the most recent and takes advantage of more sources than were available to the earlier historians.

34. *Cong. Globe,* 39 Cong., 1 Sess., 2459 (May 8, 1866).
35. Phillips to Sumner, April 30, 1866. Sumner Mss.; Washington *Daily Morning Chronicle,* May 31, 1866, p. 1.
36. *Chicago Tribune,* May 1, 1866, p. 2; Medill to Trumbull, May 2, 1866. Trumbull Mss., L.C. Boston *Daily Advertiser,* May 12, 1866, p. 1; N.Y. *Herald,* May 12, 1866, p. 1; N.Y. *Tribune,* April 30, 1866, p. 4; N.Y. *Independent,* May 3, 1866, p. 4; Julius Bing to Sumner, May 3, 1866. Sumner Mss.; Thomas Richmond to Trumbull, May 12, 1866; Daniel Richards to Trumbull, May 7, 1866. Trumbull Mss., L.C.; Richards to E.B. Washburne, May 7, 1866. Washburne Mss.; Virginia Unionist Convention, reported in the Buffalo *Morning Express,* May 23, 1866, p. 4; N.Y. *National Anti-Slavery Standard,* May 5, 1866, p. 2; May 26, 1866, p. 2; Boston *Right Way,* May 5, 1866, p. 2.
37. N.Y. *Independent,* June 7, 1866, p. 1; Colfax to Samuel Sinclair, quoted in Hollister, *Colfax,* 284. Hollister did not give the exact date.
38. *Cong. Globe,* 39 Cong., 1 Sess., 2462–63 (May 8, 1866).
39. *Ibid.,* 2543–45 (May 10, 1866).

40. *Ibid.,* 2545 (May 10, 1866).
41. Hayes to Bateman, May 15, 1866. Transcript in the Hayes Mss., original owned by the Western Reserve Historical Society.
42. *Cong. Globe,* 39 Cong., 1 Sess., 2767–68 (May 23, 1866); Trumbull to Mrs. Julia Swayne Trumbull, May 13, 1866. Trumbull Mss., Illinois State Historical Library; Salter, *Grimes,* 297.
43. *Cong. Globe,* 39 Cong., 1 Sess., 2766 (May 23, 1866).
44. Seward's and Stanton's addresses are quoted in the Boston *Daily Advertiser,* May 23, 1866, p. 1. Most newspapers carried them in full.
45. *N.Y. Times,* May 30, 1866, p. 8; May 31, 1866, p. 4; June 4, 1866, p. 4; Forney ("Occasional") in the Washington *Daily Morning Chronicle,* May 31, 1866, p. 1; June 2, 1866, p. 1.
46. Washington *National Intelligencer,* May 29, 1866, p. 2.
47. Trumbull to Julia Jayne Trumbull, May 27, 1866. Trumbull Mss., Illinois State Historical Library; *N.Y. Times,* May 26, 1866, p. 1; May 29, 1866, p. 1; May 30, 1866, p. 8; Boston *Daily Advertiser,* May 30, 1866, p. 1; James, *Framing of the Fourteenth Amendment,* 140–41.
48. *Cong. Globe,* 39 Cong., 1 Sess., 3042 (June 8, 1866).
49. *Ibid.,* 3149 (June 13, 1866).
50. N.Y. *Independent,* June 21, 1866, p. 4.
51. *Cong. Globe,* 39 Cong., 1 Sess., 3148 (June 13, 1866); N.Y. *Independent,* June 21, 1866, p. 4.

9. THE ELECTIONS OF 1866

1. Trumbull to Mrs. Julia Jayne Trumbull, May 15, 1866, Lyman Trumbull Mss., Illinois State Historical Library. See also J. Sherman to W.T. Sherman, July 8, 1866, quoted in Rachel Sherman Thorndike (ed.), *The Sherman Letters: Correspondence Between General and Senator Sherman from 1837 to 1891* (N.Y., 1894), 276.
2. Cox to Garfield, June 22, 1866. James A. Garfield Mss., Manuscripts Div., L.C.
3. Field to Chase, June 30, 1866. Salmon P. Chase Mss., Manuscripts Div., L.C.; Chase to James W. Schuckers, May 15, 1866. Chase Mss. (second series), L.C.; Toledo *Blade,* June 13, 1866, p. 2. See also Warner M. Bateman to John Sherman, July 9, 1866. John Sherman Mss. Manuscripts Div., L.C.; Fessenden to Elizabeth Fessenden Warriner, June 2, 1866. Fessenden Mss., Bowdoin College Library, Brunswick, Me.; James Speed to Francis Lieber, May 26, 1866. Francis Lieber Mss., Huntington Library, San Marino, Calif.; Trumbull to Mrs. Julia Jayne Trumbull, May 29, 1866. Trumbull Mss., Illinois State Historical Library; Timothy Otis Howe to Grace T. Howe, June 2, 1866. Howe Mss., Wisconsin State Historical Society Library.
4. Gideon Welles, *Diary of Gideon Welles —Secretary of the Navy Under Lincoln and Johnson* (3 vols., Boston and N.Y.,

1911), II, 521–22 (June 4, 1866); Trumbull to Mrs. Julia Jayne Trumbull, May 29, 1866. Trumbull Mss., Illinois State Historical Library.
5. Raymond in the *N.Y. Times,* June 12, 1866; Hayes to Birchard A. Hayes, June 8, 1866. Rutherford B. Hayes Mss., Rutherford B. Hayes Library; Toledo *Blade,* June 15, 1866, p. 2; Warner M. Bateman to John Sherman, July 9, 1866. John Sherman Mss.
6. Cox to Johnson, June 21, 1866; Sloane to Johnson, May 5, 1866. Andrew Johnson Mss., Manuscripts Div., L.C.; Aaron F. Perry to Cox, June 22, 1866. Jacob D. Cox Mss., Oberlin College Library, Oberlin, Ohio; Toledo *Blade,* June 22, 1866, p. 2.
7. *Cong. Globe,* 39 Cong., 1 Sess. (June 13, 1866).
8. *N.Y. Times,* June 4, 1866, p. 4; June 6, 1866, p. 4; June 9, 1866, p. 4. Seward's speech is quoted *ibid.,* May 23, 1866, pp. 4–5.
9. Welles, *Diary,* II, 527 (June 11, 1866).
10. Bingham proposed an amendment to this effect on May 1, 1866, and the Senate Republican caucus agreed to a similar one on May 29. *Cong. Globe,* 39 Cong., 1 Sess. (May 1, 1866); House Resolution No. 543 in the House Bill file, 39 Cong. R.G. 233, N.A.
11. Boutwell to Sumner, June 17, 1866. Charles Sumner Mss., Houghton Li-

brary, Harvard University, Cambridge, Mass.

12. *Cong. Globe,* 39 Cong., 1 Sess., 2313 (May 1, 1866), 2597 (May 15, 1866), 2880 (May 29, 1866).

13. Stevens introduced his bill on May 28, but he did not have it read into the record until the closing days of the session. *Ibid.,* 2858 (May 28, 1866), 4157 (July 25, 1866).

14. *Ibid.,* 2598–99 (May 15, 1866).

15. "R." in the *N.Y. Times,* June 12, 1866, p. 4; *ibid.,* June 4, 1866, p. 4; June 6, 1866, p. 4.

16. Raymond to Weed, June 12, 1866. Thurlow Weed Mss., Rush Rhees Library, University of Rochester, Rochester, N.Y.

17. *Cong. Globe,* 39 Cong., 1 Sess., 3241–50 (June 18, 1866); *N.Y. Times,* June 22, 1866, p. 4.

18. N.Y. *World,* June 15, 1866, p. 4; May 24, 1866, p. 4; May 28, 1866, p. 4; May 30, 1866, p. 4; June 5, 1866, p. 4; June 7, 1866, p. 4; Washington *National Intelligencer,* June 13, 1866, p. 2; June 7, 1866, p. 2; June 11, 1866, p. 2; June 12, 1866, p. 2; June 19, 1866, p. 2.

19. N.Y. *World,* June 16, 1866, p. 4; Welles, *Diary* II, 523 (June 6, 1866); Doolittle to Mrs. Mary Doolittle, June 20, 1866. James Rood Doolittle Mss., Wisconsin State Historical Library; W.B. Phillips to Johnson, May 20, 1866; Randall to Johnson, June 5, 1866. Johnson Mss. The Democrats who met Johnson were appointed by the Democratic congressional caucus. The *World* reported that the visit was "pleasant," but Randall's letter hardly verifies that description. N.Y. *World,* June 5, 1866, p. 1.

20. Welles, *Diary,* II, 528 (June 15, 1866). Doolittle had already met several days earlier with Johnson, Senator Cowan, Green Clay Smith, former Governor Alexander W. Randall of Wisconsin, former Senator Orville H. Browning of Illinois, and other members of the newly formed National Union Club, who agreed that a national convention would be an appropriate way to sustain the president. Orville Hickman Browning, *Diary of Orville Hickman Browning,* ed. by James G. Randall (2 vols., Springfield, Ill., 1938), II, 79 (June 11, 1866).

21. Raymond, "Extracts from the Journal of Henry J. Raymond," *Scribner's Monthly,* XX (June 1880), 276.

22. Welles, *Diary,* II, 529–30 (June 18, 1866).

23. *Ibid.,* 540 (June 25, 1866). The maneuvering which led to the call for the convention is chronicled *ibid.,* 528–29 (June 15, 1866), 529–31 (June 18, 1866), 533 (June 20, 1866), 533–35 (June 21, 1866), 535–40 (June 23, 1866), 540–41 (June 25, 1866); Browning, *Diary,* II, 79 (June 11, 1866), 81 (June 23, 1866). The call itself was published in most newspapers on June 26, 1866 and may be found in Edward McPherson (ed.), *The Political History of the United States of America, During the Period of Reconstruction* . . . (3rd edn., Washington, 1880), 118–19.

24. The message may be found *ibid.,* 83–84.

25. N.Y. *World,* June 23, 1866, p. 4.

26. The address of the congressional Democrats was issued July 4, 1866, and may be found in McPherson (ed.), *Political History of . . . Reconstruction,* 119–20. The supplementary call appeared July 10, signed by Blair, Alexander W. Randall, Postmaster General and president of the National Union Club, and Lewis D. Campbell. It may be found in the N.Y. *World,* August 15, 1867, pp. 1, 8.

27. Raymond to Weed, July 12, 1866, quoted in Thurlow Weed Barnes, *Memoir of Thurlow Weed* (Boston, 1884), 452.

28. Raymond, "Journal," 276–78.

29. *N.Y. Times,* July 2, 1866, p. 4; July 6, 1866, p. 4; July 11, 1866, p. 4; July 23, 1866, p. 4; July 25, 1866, p. 4; July 26, 1866, p. 4; July 27, 1866, p. 4; Aug. 9, 1866, p. 4; N.Y. *World,* June 27, 1866, p. 4; June 28, 1866, p. 4; June 29, 1866, p. 4; July 12, 1866, p. 4; July 24, 1866, p. 4.

30. N.Y. *World,* July 24, 1866, p. 4. For examples of the *Herald's* warnings, see the issues of July 16, 1866, p. 4; July 24, 1866, p. 4.

31. Richard W. Thompson, quoted in the Toledo *Blade,* June 11, 1866, p. 2.

32. Traditionally, historians interpreted Stanton's position as hypocritical, but his most recent biographers have argued cogently that in fact he made a significant sacrifice to stay where he, leading military men, and Republicans felt duty required him to remain. Benjamin P. Thomas and Harold M. Hyman, *Stanton: The Life and Times of Lincoln's Secretary* (N.Y., 1962), 471–94.

33. N.Y. *Evening Post,* July 19, 1866, p. 2. For earlier *Post* opinions of the convention and the Republican party, see July 10, 1866, p. 2; July 12, 1866, p. 2; July 16, 1866, p. 2; July 17, 1866, p. 2.

34. Raymond, "Journal," 279–80; Eric L. McKitrick, *Andrew Johnson and Reconstruction* (Chicago and London, 1960), 410–12. The resolutions are given in McPherson (ed.), *Political History of . . . Reconstruction,* 240–41.

35. Weed had hoped to convince the Democrats to restrain themselves through his influence with Richmond, the Albany Regency's chief, but Richmond died shortly before the state convention, leaving the party with no man powerful enough to harmonize the factions. Glyndon G. Van Deusen, *Thurlow Weed: Wizard of the Lobby* (Boston, 1947), 321–22; Howard K. Beale, *The Critical Year: A Study of Andrew Johnson and Reconstruction* (N.Y., 1930), 394–96; N.Y. *Herald,* Aug. 26, 1866, p. 5; Aug. 31, 1866, p. 5; Sept. 2, 1866, p. 8; Weed in the *N.Y. Times,* Oct. 9, 1866, pp. 4–5; Sept. 11, 1866, p. 3; Sept. 12, 1866, p. 3; Sept. 13, 1866, p. 7; N.Y. *World,* Sept. 11, 1866, p. 1; Sept. 12, 1866, p. 4; Sept. 13, 1866, p. 1.

36. N.Y. *Herald,* October 8, 1866, p. 4; W.B. Phillips to Johnson, Sept. 3, 1866. Johnson Mss.

37. *N.Y. Times,* Sept. 20, 1866, p. 4; Sept.

25, 1866, p. 4; Oct. 3, 1866, p. 4. John Cochrane, John A. Dix, and Henry Ward Beecher, all leading Johnson-supporting conservative Unionists, generally abandoned their efforts. Cochrane to Johnson, Oct. ?, 1866; Dix to Johnson, Nov. 8, 1866; Samuel N. Smith to Johnson, Nov. 10, 1866. Johnson Mss.; Beecher, Address at the Brooklyn Academy of Music, Oct. 15, 1866, quoted in the *N.Y. Times,* Oct. 16, 1866, pp. 1, 8. Even the extremely conservative Orville H. Browning and Welles blamed the Democrats for the defeats. Browning to Doolittle, Oct. 13, 1866. Doolittle Mss., Wisconsin State Historical Library; Welles, *Diary,* II, 617 (Oct. 11, 1866). See also Dix to Doolittle, Jan. 8, 1867. Doolittle Mss., Wisconsin State Historical Library.

38. *Cong. Globe,* 39 Cong., 1 Sess., 3948–49 (July 19, 1866).

39. *Ibid.,* 3977 (July 20, 1866).

40. *Ibid.,* 3980–81 (July 20, 1866). The vote was 125 to 12, but one more radical paired against the resolution; fifteen more Republicans were declared to be in favor. The radical dissenters were John B. Alley, John F. Benjamin, Boutwell, Eliot, William Higby, Thomas A. Jenckes, Julian, Kelley, Benjamin F. Loan, Joseph W. McClurg, Halburt E. Paine, Thomas Williams, and John M. Broomall (who was paired).

41. *Ibid.,* 4000 (July 21, 1866).

42. *Ibid.,* 4007 (July 21, 1866).

43. *N.Y. Herald,* July 23, 1866, p. 4; *N.Y. National Anti-Slavery Standard,* July 26, 1866, p. 2; *N.Y. Independent,* Aug. 2, 1866, p. 4. See also the Boston *Commonwealth,* July 28, 1866, [no page number].

44. Albany *Evening Journal,* quoted in the *N.Y. Tribune,* July 27, 1866, p. 5; Cleveland *Herald,* Sept. 27, 1866, p. 2; Representative Robert S. Hale, answering an invitation to endorse the Philadelphia National Union Convention, quoted in the *N.Y. Tribune,* Aug. 20, 1866, p. 4; "The Seward-Johnson Reaction," *North American Review,* CIII (Oct. 1866), 534–35.

45. Lane, Speech at Indianapolis, Aug. 18, 1866, quoted in the Cincinnati *Commercial* (ed.), *Speeches of the Campaign of 1866, in the States of Ohio, Indiana and Kentucky* (Cincinnati, 1866), 13.

46. Sherman, Speech at Mozart Hall, Sept. 28, 1866, *ibid.,* 39. See also William Dennison, Speech at Columbus, no date given, quoted in the Cleveland *Herald,* Aug. 13, 1866, p. 2.

47. James G. Blaine, "The Fourteenth Amendment as a Basis of Reconstruction," delivered at Skowhegan, Maine, Aug. 29, 1866, in *Political Discussions, Legislative, Diplomatic, and Peculiar, 1856–1886* (Norwich, Conn., 1887), 65. Especially effective in emphasizing the conservatism of the Republican program were the speeches of Republicans who had originally supported the president. See for instance Jacob D. Cox, Speech at the Brooklyn Academy of Music, Oct. 17, 1866, quoted in the *N.Y. Herald,* Oct. 18, 1866, p. 10; Cox, Speech at Columbus, Ohio, Aug. 21, 1866, quoted in the Cincinnati *Commercial* (ed.), *Campaign of 1866,* p. 17; William Dennison, Speech at Columbus, no date given, quoted in the Cleveland *Herald,* Aug. 13, 1866, p. 2. See also Rutherford B. Hayes, "The Question of the Day," delivered at Cincinnati, Sept. 7, 1866, quoted in the Cincinnati *Daily Gazette,* Sept. 8, 1866, p. 1; Benjamin F. Wade, Speech at Ottawa, Ohio, Sept. 11, 1866, in Cincinnati *Commercial* (ed.), *Campaign of 1866,* 31; General M.F. Force, Speech at Chillicothe, Ohio, Sept. 22, 1866, *ibid.,* 34; Sherman, Speech at Mozart Hall, Sept. 28, 1866, *ibid.,* 39; James A. Garfield, "National Politics," delivered at Warren, Ohio, Sept. 1, 1866, in Garfield, *Works of James Abram Garfield,* ed. by Burke A. Hinsdale (2 vols., Boston, 1883), I, 216–42. Less blatant in their appeal to conservative Republicans, but still clearly avoiding implications of radicalism, were Oliver P. Morton, Speech at New Albany, Indiana, no date given, in Cincinnati *Commercial* (ed.), *Campaign of 1866,* p. 2; Robert C. Schenck, Speech at Dayton, Ohio, Aug. 18, 1866, *ibid.,* 12–13; Schuyler Colfax, Speech at Indianapolis, Aug. 7, 1866, *ibid.,* 14; Columbus Delano, Speech at Coshocton, Ohio, Aug. 28, 1866, *ibid.,* 23.

48. Carl Schurz, "The Logical Results of the War," delivered in Philadelphia, Sept. 8, 1866, in Schurz, *Speeches, Correspondence, and Political Papers of Carl Schurz* (3 vols., N.Y., 1913), I, 403. See, for example, Benjamin F. Butler's speech at the Republican Soldiers' and Sailors' Convention, Sept. 25, 1866, quoted in the *N.Y. Times,* Sept. 27, 1866, p. 5; the speeches of former vice president Hannibal Hamlin and Senator Henry Wilson at a Republican rally at the Cooper Institute in New York City, Oct. 15, 1866, quoted in the N.Y. *Herald,* Oct. 16, 1866, p. 3: Hannibal Hamlin, Speech in Philadelphia, Oct. 3, 1866, quoted in the *N.Y. Tribune,* Oct. 4, 1866, p. 1; Henry Wilson, Speech in New York City, Oct. 15, 1866, quoted *ibid.,* Oct. 16, 1866, p. 8.

49. Morton, Speech at New Albany, Indiana, in Cincinnati *Commercial* (ed.), *Campaign of 1866,* II, 2 Lane, Speech at Indianapolis, Aug. 18, 1866, *ibid.,* 13–14; Delano, Speech at Coshocton, Ohio, Aug. 28, 1866, *ibid.,* 23; Beale, *The Critical Year,* 195; Resolutions of the Unconditional Union Convention of Maryland, June 6, 1866, quoted in McPherson (ed.), *Political History of . . . Reconstruction,* 124.

50. Address of the National Union Executive Committee, quoted in the *N.Y. Times,* Aug. 30, 1866, p. 4; *N.Y. Nation,* Oct. 4, 1866, p. 270; *N.Y. Evening Post,* Sept. 24, 1866, p. 2; John Sherman, quoted in the Boston *Daily Adver-*

tiser, Oct. 5, 1866, p. 2; James A. Garfield, "National Politics," in Garfield, *Works,* I, 140.

51. N.Y. *Herald,* Sept. 13, 1866, p. 6; Sept. 15, 1866, p. 4; Sept. 19, 1866, p. 6; Sept. 20, 1866, p. 6; Sept. 24, 1866, p. 1; Sept. 28, 1866, p. 1; N.Y. *Evening Post,* Sept. 24, 1866, p. 2; Sept. 26, 1866, p. 2; *N.Y. Times,* Sept. 24, 1866, p. 4. Weed's visit is reported in the *Chicago Tribune,* Sept. 19, 1866, p. 1.

52. Tilton in the N.Y. *Independent,* Sept. 27, 1866, p. 4; Oct. 18, 1866, p. 4. See also the Boston *Right Way,* Sept. 29, 1866, p. 1; Oct. 6, 1866, p. 1.

53. Phillips, quoted in the Boston *Commonwealth,* Nov. 10, 1866, p. 2.

54. *Reporter,* II (Sept. 24, 1866), 14.

55. *Ibid.,* (Oct. 22, 1866), 8–9.

56. *Ibid.,* 11.

57. The most complete report of the convention appeared in the *Reporter,* II (Sept. 17, 24, Oct. 1, 8, 22, 29, Nov. 5, 1866), *passim.* The tension and bitterness of the contest is clear from newspaper reports. Boston *Evening Journal,* Sept. 5, 1866, p. 4; Sept. 6, 1866, p. 4; Sept. 7, 1866, p. 4; Boston *Daily Advertiser,* Sept. 4, 1866, p. 1; Washington *National Intelligencer,* Sept. 4, 1866, p. 2; Sept. 5, 1866, p. 2; Sept. 6, 1866, p. 2; Sept. 7, 1866, p. 2; Sept. 8, 1866, p. 2; *N.Y. Times,* Sept. 4, 1866, p. 1; N.Y. *Herald,* Sept. 5, 1866, p. 3; Sept. 6, 1866, p. 3; Sept. 7, 1866, p. 7; Sept. 8, 1866, p. 1; Sept. 10, 1866, p. 4; Tilton in the N.Y. *Independent,* Sept. 13, 1866, p. 4; N.Y. *Evening Post,* Sept. 8, 1866, p. 3.

58. N.Y. *Herald,* Sept. 14, 1866, p. 8.

59. James G. Blaine, *Twenty Years of Congress: From Lincoln to Garfield with a Review of the Events Which Led to the Political Revolution of 1860* (2 vols., Norwich, Conn., 1884–86), II, 230–33; N.Y. *Herald,* Sept. 26, 1866, p. 10; Sept. 27, 1866, p. 5; *N.Y. Times,* Sept. 26, 1866, p. 1; Sept. 27, 1866, p. 5.

60. Blaine, *Twenty Years,* II, 228.

61. Boston *Right Way,* Oct. 13, 1866, p. 1; *N.Y. Times,* Sept. 29, 1866, p. 4; Oct. 11, 1866, p. 4; Washington *National Intelligencer,* Nov. 10, 1866, p. 2.

62. Quoted in McPherson (ed.), *Political History of . . . Reconstruction,* 241.

63. Johnson made the statement in his response to a delegation which presented him with the proceedings of the National Union convention, August 18, 1866. It was reported in newspapers throughout the country and is quoted *ibid.,* 127.

64. McKitrick, *Johnson and Reconstruction,* 428–38.

65. New Jersey Democratic Representative Andrew J. Rogers, at a rally in Washington, D.C., quoted in the Washington *National Intelligencer,* Aug. 28, 1866, p. 3.

66. *Cong. Globe,* 39 Cong., 1 Sess., appendix, 304 (March 2, 1866).

67. N.Y. *World,* April 9, 1866, p. 4; Ewing in a public letter to Orville H. Browning, quoted in the Washington *National Intelligencer,* Aug. 9, 1866, p. 2; resolutions of a Johnson rally in Washington, D.C., quoted *ibid.,* Aug. 27, 1866, p. 2. See also the speech of Representative Andrew J. Rogers (D–N.J.) at the D.C. rally, quoted *ibid.,* Aug. 28, 1866, p. 3, and the *Intelligencer's* own forebodings, *ibid.,* July 20, 1866, p. 2. Raymond too warned of inevitable violence before he left the Johnson camp. See his address at the National Union convention, quoted in the N.Y. *World,* Aug. 17, 1866, p. 8.

68. Blair affirmed his position in speeches regularly. See the N.Y. *World,* July 19, 1866, p. 1; Boston *Daily Advertiser,* Aug. 28, 1866, p. 2; N.Y. *Evening Post,* Sept. 4, 1866, p. 2. For the *N.Y. Times's* position, see its issue of Sept. 12, 1866, p. 4. See also the speech of former Mayor Richard Vaux of Philadelphia at a Johnson rally in Reading, Pennsylvania, July 13, 1866 and the rally's subsequent resolution calling on the president "in the name of an outraged and violated Constitution, and an imperilled Union to make the Congress what the Constitution requires it to be—the representative body of the whole people." Washington *National Intelligencer,* July 20, 1866, p. 3. Garfield worried that the president intended to follow this program as early as February 1866. Justin Morrill, another leader of the House, expressed the same fear by May. Garfield to James M. Comly, Feb. 21, 1866. James R. Comly Mss., Ohio Historical Society; Morrill to ――― Jewett, May 4, 1866, quoted in William Belmont Parker, *The Life and Public Services of Justin Smith Morrill* (Boston and N.Y., 1924), 229–30. See also William Lloyd Garrison to James Miller McKim, March 3, 1866. McKim-Garrison Mss. in the Maloney Collection, New York Public Library.

69. Dawes to Mrs. Electa Dawes, July 12, 14, 1866. Henry L. Dawes Mss., Manuscripts Div., L.C. See also William P. Fessenden to Daniel Fessenden, July 8, 1866, quoted in Francis Fessenden, *Life and Public Services of William Pitt Fessenden* (2 vols., Boston and N.Y., 1907), II, 117–18.

70. Dawes to Mrs. Electa Dawes, July 15, 1866. Dawes Mss.

71. *N.Y. Times,* July 16, 1866, pp. 4–5; July 18, 1866, p. 4; John A. Krout (ed.), "Henry J. Raymond on the Republican Caucuses of July, 1866," *American Historical Review,* XXXIII (July 1928), 835–42; *Cong. Globe,* 39 Cong., 1 Sess., 3912–13 (July 18, 1866), 3933–34 (July 19, 1866), 3981–85 (July 20, 1866), 4009, 4017 (July 21, 1866), 4113–15, 4155–56 (July 25, 1866).

72. E.D. Townsend ("by order of the President") to Gen. Absalom Baird, Aug. 1, 1866; Townsend to Voorhies and Herron, Aug. 1, 1866; Voorhies and Herron to Townsend, Aug. 2, 1866. Johnson Mss. Johnson retreated from his orders when Sheridan firmly expressed his conviction that martial law

must be maintained. Report of the Select Committee on the New Orleans Riot, *House Report No. 16,* 39 Cong., 2 Sess.; Willie Malvin Caskey, *Secession and Restoration of Louisiana* (Baton Rouge, 1938), 211–24; Beale, *The Critical Year,* 344–53. The best account of the riot is in Fawn Brodie, *Thaddeus Stevens: Scourge of the South* (N.Y., 1959), 273–82. Pro-southern historians like Caskey have tried to minimize the importance and savagery of the New Orleans bloodshed, accepting only southern white anti-loyalist testimony. The actual facts are readily apparent to an unprejudiced reader of the testimony offered by both loyalists and anti-loyalists to the select committee. That testimony is included in the committee's report.

73. N.Y. *Evening Post,* Aug. 2, 1866, p. 2; Aug. 6, 1866, p. 2; Charles Nordhoff to Parke Godwin, Aug. 3, 1866. William Cullen Bryant and Parke Godwin Mss., New York Public Library.

74. The *N.Y. Times,* before it abandoned Johnson, called on Congress to solve the problem by admitting southern representatives, Sept. 12, 1866, p. 4. The quotation is from the N.Y. *Nation,* Sept. 20, 1866, p. 230.

75. E.B. Washburne to Thomas J. Turner, Sept. 17, 1866, a public letter quoted in the *Chicago Tribune,* Sept. 19, 1866, p. 1. Ohio Republicans picked up Washburne's question in their canvasses. N.Y. *Evening Post,* Oct. 4, 1866, p. 2.

76. N.Y. *Nation,* Sept. 20, 1866, p. 231. For Republican allusions to the probability of a presidential *coup,* see James A. Garfield's speech at Toledo, Ohio, Aug. 22, 1866, in Cincinnati *Commercial* (ed.), *Campaign of 1866,* 18; Garfield, "National Politics," Speech delivered Warren, Ohio, Sept. 1, 1866, in Garfield, *Works,* I, 237; Wade, Speech at Ottawa, Ohio, Sept. 11, 1866, in Cincinnati *Commercial* (ed.), *Campaign of 1866,* 31; Henry Wilson, Speech at Anderson, Ind., Sept. 22, 1866, *ibid.,* 34; Oliver P. Morton, Speech at Anderson, Ind., Sept. 22, 1866, *ibid.,* 35; George S. Boutwell, "The Usurpation," *Atlantic Monthly,* XVIII (Oct. 1866), 506–13; *Chicago Tribune,* July 17, 1866, p. 2; Sept. 1,

1866, p. 2; Sept. 14, 1866, p. 2; Sept. 15, 1866, p. 2; Oct. 10, 1866, p. 2; N.Y. *Independent,* Aug. 9, 1866, p. 4; N.Y. *Tribune,* Sept. 15, 1866, p. 4; Sept. 18, 1866, p. 4; Sept. 20, 1866, p. 4; N.Y. *Evening Post,* Oct. 4, 1866, p. 2; Boston *Right Way,* Aug. 18, 1866, p. 1; Sept. 22, 1866, p. 1; Boston *Daily Advertiser,* Aug. 20, 1866, p. 1; Aug. 21, 1866, p. 2; Oct. 11, 1866, p. 2; Toledo *Blade,* Sept. 5, 1866, p. 2. These fears did not affect only politicians. Stanton decided to remain at the War Department at least in part because, as outgoing Postmaster General Dennison confided to Cox, "He is *alarmed* at the prospects." Dennison added, "It is not at all clear but that he had better remain in the Cabinet as long as possible." Dennison to Cox, July 16, 1866. Cox Mss. Grant later testified before the House committee investigating impeachment that he often heard Johnson say "that if the Conservatives of the North carried the elections by members enough to give them, with the Southern members, a majority, why would they not be the Congress of the United States?" Privately, Grant warned Sheridan that he feared "that we are fast approaching the time when he [Johnson] will want to declare the body itself [Congress] illegal, unconstitutional, and revolutionary. Commanders in Southern States will have to take a great care to see, if a crisis does come, that no armed headway can be made against the Union." Testimony on impeachment, *House Report No. 7,* 40 Cong., 1 Sess., appendix, 833–34; Grant to Sheridan, Oct. 12, 1866, in Adam Badeau, *Grant in Peace: From Appomatox to Mount McGregor —A Personal Memoir* (Hartford, 1887), 51.

77. N.Y. *World,* Oct. 12, 1866, p. 4.

78. Browning's letter is quoted in the Washington *National Intelligencer,* Oct. 24, 1866, p. 2.

79. N.Y. *Evening Post,* Oct. 12, 1866, p. 2; Boston *Daily Advertiser,* Oct. 16, 1866, p. 2; N.Y. *Independent,* Oct. 25, 1866, p. 4.

80. Cox to Monroe Cox, Nov. 21, 1866. Cox Mss.

10. "RADICAL" RECONSTRUCTION—PART ONE

1. Boutwell, "Policy and Justice in Public Affairs," delivered before the Mercantile Library Association, Boston, Nov. 7, 1866, in George S. Boutwell, *Speeches and Papers Relating to the Rebellion and the Overthrow of Slavery* (2 vols., Boston, 1867), II, 509–37; Boutwell, "Reconstruction, And Its Relations to the Business of the Country," delivered before the Old Bay State Association, Boston, Dec. 27, 1866, *ibid.,* II, 547. Stevens, Speech at Bedford, Pennsylvania, Sept. 4, 1866, quoted in the *N.Y. Times,* Sept. 11, 1866, p. 8; Stevens, Speech at Lancaster, Pennsylvania, Sept. 27, 1866, quoted *ibid.,* Oct. 3, 1866, p. 5; Sumner, "The One Man Power vs.

Congress," delivered at the Boston Music Hall, Oct. 2, 1866, in Sumner, *The Works of Charles Sumner* (15 vols., Boston, 1870–83), XI, 1–39.

2. Butler, Address to the Massachusetts Republican state convention, Sept. 13, 1866, quoted in the Boston *Daily Advertiser,* Sept. 14, 1866, p. 1.

3. Broomall to Stevens, Oct. 27, 1866. Thaddeus Stevens Mss., Manuscripts Div., L.C.

4. *Cong. Globe,* 39 Cong., 2 Sess., 124–25, 128 (Dec. 14, 1865); Sherman to Bateman, Dec. 3, 1866. Warner Bateman Mss., Western Reserve Historical Society, Cleveland, Ohio; Chandler recalled his position in a speech at Ashtabula, Ohio,

Oct. 1, 1867, a copy of which may be found in the McPherson scrapbook: Campaign of 1867, II, 135. Edward McPherson Mss., Manuscripts Div., L.C.; James G. Blaine, *Twenty Years of Congress: From Lincoln to Garfield with a Review of the Events Which Led to the Political Revolution of 1860* (2 vols., Norwich, Conn., 1884–86), II, 245.

5. N.Y. *Herald,* Sept. 29, 1866, p. 6 and Oct. 11, 1866, p. 6 (I have combined quotations from separate editorials). See also *ibid.,* Oct. 14, 1866, p. 4; Oct. 23, 1866, p. 4; Oct. 29, 1866, p. 4.

6. *Ibid.,* Oct. 7, 1866, p. 4; Oct. 10, 1866, p. 6; Nov. 8, 1866, p. 4; Nov. 14, 1866, p. 4; N.Y. *Evening Post,* Oct. 17, 1866, p. 2; Oct. 19, 1866, p. 2; *N.Y. Times,* Oct. 8, 1866, p. 4; Oct. 9, 1866, p. 4; Oct. 20, 1866, p. 4; Oct. 30, 1866, p. 4; Oct. 31, 1866, p. 4; Nov. 23, 1866, p. 4; Boston *Daily Advertiser,* Dec. 1, 1866, p. 1; Adam Badeau, *Grant in Peace: From Appamatox to Mount McGregor—A Personal Memoir* (Hartford, 1887), 42–45.

7. Chase to Greeley, Nov. 21, 1866. Horace Greeley Mss., Manuscripts Div., L.C.; Boston *Daily Advertiser,* Nov. 12, 1866, p. 2; Nov. 19, 1866, p. 1; Nov. 20, 1866, p. 1; Nov. 24, 1866, p. 1; N.Y. *Herald,* Nov. 15, 1866, p. 4; Nov. 17, 1866, p. 4; Nov. 18, 1866, p. 4; Nov. 19, 1866, p. 5; Nov. 20, 1866, p. 5; Nov. 21, 1866, p. 6; Nov. 23, 1866, p. 4; Nov. 30, 1866, p. 6; N.Y. *National Anti-Slavery Standard,* Nov. 24, 1866, pp. 2, 3; *N.Y. Tribune,* Nov. 19, 1866, p. 4; Nov. 23, 1866, p. 4; Nov. 27, 1866, p. 4; Dec. 3, 1866, p. 4; Gideon Welles, *Diary of Gideon Welles—Secretary of the Navy Under Lincoln and Johnson* (3 vols., Boston and N.Y., 1911), II, 619 (Nov. 17, 1866); Howard K. Beale, *The Critical Year: A Study of Andrew Johnson and Reconstruction* (N.Y., 1930), 399–403. At the same time Chase was trying to promote a movement in the South to ratify the Fourteenth Amendment. Michael Perman, *Reunion Without Compromise: The South and Reconstruction, 1865–1868* (Cambridge, Eng., 1973), 255–59.

8. Doolittle to Browning, Nov. 8, 1866. Orville H. Browning Mss., transcripts in the Illinois Historical Survey, University of Illinois, Urbana, Ill.

9. Wager Swayne to Chase, Nov. 27, Dec. 10, 1866. Salmon P. Chase Mss., Manuscripts Div., L.C.; Alexander Sharp to E.B. Washburne, Dec. 19, 1866, Jan. 10, 1867. Elihu B. Washburne Mss., Massachusetts Historical Society; McPherson scrapbook: Fourteenth Amendment, 60. McPherson Mss.; *House Report No. 7,* 40 Cong., 1 Sess., appendix, 297–301, 304–305; Eric L. McKitrick, *Andrew Johnson and Reconstruction* (Chicago and London, 1960), 467–72. For the southern view of the rejection of the Fourteenth Amendment, see Michael Perman, "The South and Congress's Reconstruction Policy, 1866–67," *American Studies,* IV (Feb. 1971), 183–

94; Perman, *Reunion Without Compromise,* 229–65.

10. McKitrick, *Johnson and Reconstruction,* 473–85; David Donald, *The Politics of Reconstruction, 1863–1867* (Baton Rouge, 1965), 53–82; W.R. Brock, *An American Crisis: Congress and Reconstruction, 1865–1867* (N.Y., 1963), 473–85. Four studies appearing in the past five years—besides my own dissertation, "The Right Way: Congressional Republicans and Reconstruction, 1863–1869" (unpublished Ph.D. dissertation, Rice University, 1971)—have suggested what I argue in the following pages, that the Reconstruction acts embodied the views of nonradical rather than radical Republicans. They are Charles Fairman, *History of the Supreme Court of the United States: Volume VI, Reconstruction and Reunion, 1864–88: Part One* (N.Y., 1971), 253–309; Larry George Kincaid, "The Legislative Origins of the Military Reconstruction Act, 1865–1867" (unpublished Ph.D. dissertation, Johns Hopkins University, 1968); Martin E. Mantell, *Johnson, Grant, & the Politics of Reconstruction* (N.Y. and London, 1973), 22–26; and Allen W. Trelease, *Reconstruction: The Great Experiment* (N.Y., 1972), 72–77.

11. George W. Julian, *Political Recollections 1840–1872* (Chicago, 1884), 305–308; Julian in the *Cong. Globe,* 39 Cong., 2 Sess., appendix, 77–80 (Jan. 28, 1867); Josiah B. Grinnell, *Men and Events of Forty Years: Autobiographical Reminiscences of an Active Career* (Boston, 1891), 158; Detroit *Post and Tribune, Zachariah Chandler: An Outline Sketch of his Life and Public Services* (Detroit, 1880), 288, 292–93; Sumner to John Bright, May 27, 1867, in Edward L. Pierce, *Memoir and Letters of Charles Sumner* (4 vols., Boston, 1893), IV, 319–20; Stevens in the N.Y. *Herald,* July 8, 1867, p. 6; Timothy Otis Howe to Horace Rublee, Jan. 15, 1868. Timothy Otis Howe Mss., Wisconsin State Historical Society Library; Wendell Phillips in James G. Blaine *et al.,* "Ought the Negro to Be Disfranchised? Ought He to Have Been Enfranchised?" *North American Review,* CXXVIII (March 1879), 257–62. Julian was the only congressman to refuse to concede defeat for territorialization in 1867. He was one of the few congressmen to propose legislation to erect territorial governments in the South, and even his bill implied rather quick restoration, specifically outlining steps to that end. House Resolution 894, House of Representatives bill file, 39 Cong., R.G. 233, N.A.; see his correspondence to his brother's newspaper, the Centreville *Indiana True Republican,* Jan. 24, 1867, p. 114; *Cong. Globe,* 39 Cong., 2 Sess., appendix, 77–80 (Jan. 28, 1867).

12. *Cong. Globe,* 39 Cong., 2 Sess., 117 (Dec. 13, 1866). See also similar comments by Rep. Frederick A. Pike, *ibid.,* 255 (Jan. 3, 1867); Broomall, *ibid.,* 351 (Jan. 8, 1867); Glenni W. Scofield, *ibid.,* 598 (Jan. 19, 1867); Julian, *ibid.,*

appendix, 78 (Jan. 28, 1867); Farnsworth, *ibid.,* 99 (Feb. 7, 1867).

13. J.C. Emerson to Daniel Richards, Jan. 11, 1867. Fessenden Mss., L.C.

14. Jonathan F. Turner to Richards, Jan. 12, 1867. See also O.B. Hart to Richards, Jan. 8, 1867; Norman Brownson to Richards, Jan. 12, 1867. Richards forwarded these letters to Fessenden in a letter Jan. 15. They are in the Fessenden Mss., L.C. Also Alexander H. Jones to Schuyler Colfax, Dec. 3, 1866, in the papers of the Joint Committee on Reconstruction, 39 Cong., R.G. 128, N.A.; Memorial of Citizens of Louisiana, quoted in *Cong. Globe,* 39 Cong., 2 Sess., 537 (Jan. 17, 1867); Memorial of Citizens of Arkansas, quoted in the Boston *Right Way* (Jan. 12, 1867), p. 4; Boston *Daily Advertiser,* January 16, 1867, p. 2; *N.Y. Times,* Dec. 10, 1866, p. 4; Dec. 13, 1866, p. 1; Dec. 14, 1866, p. 1. Richards and Hart were leading Florida Unionist politicians. Jones was a representative-elect from North Carolina. He would represent the reconstructed state in Congress upon its restoration. The Louisiana petition was organized by Durant.

15. Boutwell in a speech at Tremont Temple, Boston, in the week of Jan. 5–12, quoted in the N.Y. *National Anti-Slavery Standard,* Jan. 12, 1867, p. 1. Radicals proposed several bills embodying their ideas. Of those which Congress considered, only Stevens's and the bill to restore civil government in Louisiana embodied the radical position. These are at *Cong. Globe,* 39 Cong., 2 Sess., 250 (Jan. 3, 1867) and 1128–29 (Feb. 11, 1867), respectively. Note the modification of Stevens's bill under radical pressure. See Ashley's amendment to H.R. 543, *ibid.,* 253–54 (Jan. 3, 1867); Hezekiah S. Bundy's Texas territorial government bill (H.R. 223); Julian's bill to establish territorial governments in the rebellious states (H.R. 894), and Henry D. Washburn's bill to reestablish civil governments in the rebellious states (H.R. 985), all in the House of Representatives bill file, 39 Cong., R.G. 233, N.A.; Hamilton Ward's bill to guarantee republican forms of government in the rebellious states (H.R. 856), resubmitted as H.R. 5 in the Fortieth Congress, in the House bill file, 40 Cong. R.G. 233, N.A. and in the Thaddeus Stevens Mss., Manuscripts Div., L.C. For radicals' views as expressed in Congress, see *ibid.,* 349–52 (Jan. 8, 1867; Broomall); *ibid,* 264–66 (Jan. 3, 1867, Holmes); *ibid.,* appendix, 77–80 (Jan. 28; Julian); *ibid.,* 86 (Dec. 12, 1866; resolution by George F. Miller); *ibid.,* 282–86 (Jan. 4, 1867; Newell); *ibid.,* 499 (Jan. 16; Paine); *ibid.,* 254–56 (Jan. 3, 1867; Pike); *ibid.,* 211–14 (Dec. 20, 1866; Senator Edmund G. Ross); *ibid.,* 596–98 (Jan. 19, 1867; Scofield); *ibid.,* 15 (Dec. 5, 1866; resolutions by Sumner); *ibid.,* 115–18 (Dec. 13, 1866; Ward). Outside Congress: Wendell Phillips's speech to the Pennsylvania Anti-Slavery Society, Nov. 22,

1866, quoted in the N.Y. *National Anti-Slavery Standard,* Dec. 1, 1866, p. 2.
For impeachment: Stevens to Schenck, Aug. 31, 1866. Norcross Collection Massachusetts Historical Society; Schenck to Stevens, Sept. 23, 1866. Stevens Mss.; Wendell Phillips in a speech at Cooper Institute, Oct. 25, 1866, quoted in the N.Y. *National Anti-Slavery Standard,* Nov. 3, 1866, pp. 1–2; Boutwell in a speech at the Mercantile Library, Boston, in Nov., 1866, quoted in the Boston *Commonwealth,* Nov. 17, 1866, p. 1; William Lloyd Garrison in the N.Y. *Independent,* Jan. 17, 1867, p. 1; Julian in the Centreville *Indiana True Republican,* Jan. 18, 1867, p. 106; Sidney H. Morse, "Impeachment," *Radical,* II (Feb. 1867), 373–75. Radical newspapers endorsed impeachment. See, for instance, the Boston *Right Way,* Jan. 12, 1867, p. 2; Jan. 19, 1867, p. 2; Boston *Commonwealth,* Jan. 12, 1867, p. 2; Jan. 19, 1867, p. 2; *Wilkes' Spirit of the Times,* quoted in the N.Y. *National Anti-Slavery Standard,* Jan. 26, 1867, p. 1. The *Right Way* reprinted opinions favorable to impeachment appearing in other newspapers, Feb. 9, 1867, p. 3; Feb. 16, 1867, p. 3. The N.Y. *Independent* and *Anti-Slavery Standard* indicated their support for the action by printing the opinions of Garrison and Phillips.

16. Sherman to Cox, Jan. 7, 1867. Jacob D. Cox Mss., Oberlin College Library, Oberlin, Ohio; Fessenden to F.H. Morse, ?, 1868, quoted in Francis Fessenden, *Life and Public Services of William Pitt Fessenden* (2 vols., Boston and N.Y., 1907), II, 306–308. See also Cox to Monroe Cox, Nov. 21, 1866. Cox Mss.

17. *Cong. Globe,* 39 Cong., 2 Sess., 250 (Jan. 3, 1867).

18. *Ibid.,* 499 (Jan. 16, 1867), appendix 75, 536 (Jan. 17, 1867). Kincaid submits Stevens's bill had firmer radical backing than it probably did, arguing that even the radicals who had presented bills of their own waited for his lead. Actually they had no choice. Under the rules, their bills went directly to the joint committee without debate. Only the committee could report them, and it had not met. Kincaid, "The Military Reconstruction Act," 122n.

19. *Ibid.,* 253–54 (Jan. 3, 1867).

20. *Ibid.,* 505 (Jan. 16, 1867).

21. *Ibid.,* 500–501 (Jan. 16, 1867).

22. *Ibid.,* 504. Bingham's entire speech is in *ibid.,* 500–505 (Jan. 16, 1867).

23. *Ibid.,* 625 (Jan. 21, 1867).

24. *Ibid.,* 715, 721 (Jan. 24, 1867).

25. *Ibid.,* 781, 782 (Jan. 26, 1867).

26. *Ibid.,* 816 (Jan. 28, 1867).

27. *Ibid.,* 817 (Jan. 28, 1867).

28. Sherman to Cox, Jan. 7, 1867. Cox Mss.; *N.Y. Times,* Jan. 28, 1867, p. 4.

29. Orville H. Browning, *The Diary of Orville Hickman Browning,* ed. by James G. Randall and Theodore C. Pease (2 vols., Springfield, Ill., 1933), II, 115 (Dec. 4, 1866).

30. E.R. Hill to Banks, Dec. 8, 1866; W.A.

Harrington to Banks, Dec. 13, 1866; David K. Hitchcock to Banks, Feb. 13, 22, 1867; Ebenezer Nelson to Banks, Feb. 24, 1867; D.N. Haskell to Banks, Feb. 24, 1867; A.C. Mayhew to Banks, Feb. 25, 1867; Thomas Russell to Banks, Mar. 25, 1867. Nathaniel Banks Mss., Illinois State Historical Library.

31. *N.Y. Times,* Dec. 6, 1866, p. 1.
32. Browning, *Diary,* II, 127 (Jan. 29, 1867); Moore, notes, Jan. 30, 31, 1867. Johnson Mss.; Welles, *Diary,* III, 31–33 (Jan. 31, 1867), 37–38 (Feb. 5, 1867); *N.Y. Times,* Feb. 5, 1867, p. 5; Michael Perman, "The South and Congress's Reconstruction Policy, 1866–67," *American Studies,* IV (Feb. 1971), 195–99. Kincaid offers an excellent discussion of the Orr plan's motives and effect. Kincaid, "The Military Reconstruction Act," 162–71.
33. Boston *Daily Advertiser,* Feb. 6, 1867, p. 1. Even the conservative *N.Y. Times* rejected it. Feb. 7, 1867, p. 4.
34. See, for instance, W.M. Dickson to R.B. Hayes, Feb. 25, 1867. On January 30 Hayes had assured his uncle that Reconstruction legislation was dead for the session. Hayes to Sardis Birchard, Jan. 30, 1867. Rutherford B. Hayes Mss., Rutherford B. Hayes Library.
35. Carl Schurz, *Reminiscences of Carl Schurz* (3 vols., N.Y., 1908–1909), III, 246; James G. Blaine in Blaine *et al.,* "Ought the Negro to Be Disfranchised?"

230–31; Garfield, *ibid.,* 246; for conservative views, see Fessenden to Morse, ?, 1868, quoted in Fessenden, *Fessenden,* II, 306–307; Fessenden to Samuel Fessenden, Jan. 19, 1867. Fessenden Mss., Bowdoin College Library; Fessenden to Richard Henry Dana, Feb. 9, 1867. Richard Henry Dana Mss., Massachusetts Historical Society; outline of speech prepared for delivery in Congress in 1868 in the Fessenden Mss., Manuscripts Div., L.C.; Jacob D. Cox to John Sherman, Feb. 15, 1867. John Sherman Mss., Manuscripts Div., L.C.; Bingham in *Cong. Globe,* 39 Cong., 2 Sess., 500–505 (Jan. 16, 1867); Rep. William E. Dodge, *ibid.,* 627 (Jan. 21, 1867); Rep. John A. Griswold, *ibid.,* 1101 (Feb. 8, 1867); Rep. Rufus P. Spalding, *ibid.,* 290 (Jan. 5, 1867); Sen. William M. Stewart, *ibid.,* 1367–69 (Feb. 15, 1867).

36. Edwin L. Godkin, "Universal Suffrage and Universal Amnesty," in the N.Y. *Nation,* Nov. 29, 1866, p. 430. See also Carl Schurz, "The True Problem," *Atlantic Monthly,* XIX (March 1867), 377; Schurz, *Reminiscences,* III, 246; Sen. Stewart in *Cong. Globe,* 39 Cong., 2 Sess., 1361 (Feb. 15, 1867); Sen. Edwin D. Morgan, Speech at Cooper Institute, Oct. 15, 1867, quoted in the *N.Y. Tribune,* Oct. 16, 1867, p. 2; Sen. Morton in the *Cong. Globe,* 40 Cong., 2 Sess., 725 (Jan. 24, 1868).

11. "RADICAL" RECONSTRUCTION—PART TWO

1. The original Reconstruction bill provided restoration for states meeting its requirements only after the Fourteenth Amendment had become part of the Constitution. But Bingham, like Stevens, believed that three-fourths of only the *loyal* states were required to ratify it. Therefore in his opinion it had already been adopted.
2. Benjamin B. Kendrick (ed.), *Journal of the Joint Committee of Fifteen on Reconstruction, 39 Congress, 1865–1867* (N.Y., 1914), 122–24 (Feb. 2, 1867).
3. Kendrick quotes the bill *ibid.,* 380–82. This version, which he reprinted from newspaper reports, varies slightly from the version in the Senate bill file, 39 Cong., R.G. 46, N.A. (Senate Bill No. 564). For some reason, Donald, McKitrick, and Brock attribute the inception of this bill to Julian. In fact, Julian vigorously opposed it, arguing not for military government but territorial government, with civil officials elected by the southerners themselves. See *Cong. Globe,* 39 Cong., 2 Sess., appendix, 77–80 (this is the speech historians usually cite to support their suggestion); Julian in the Centreville *Indiana True Republican,* Jan. 24, 1867, p. 114; Feb. 28, 1867, p. 133.
4. Kendrick (ed.), *Journal of the Joint Committee,* 124–29 (Feb. 6, 1867).
5. *Cong. Globe,* 39 Cong., 2 Sess., 1366 (Feb. 15, 1867).

6. Brandegee, *ibid.,* 1076 (Feb. 7, 1867); Bingham, *ibid.,* 1082 (Feb. 7, 1867). See also Thayer, *ibid.,* 1097; Abner C. Harding, *ibid.,* 1098–99; Shellabarger, *ibid.,* 1102; Garfield, *ibid.,* 1104; John A Kasson, *ibid.,* 1105 (all Feb. 8, 1867).
7. See Banks's comments for an example of the impact of this upon him. *Ibid.,* appendix, 174–75 (Feb. 9, 1867).
8. *Ibid.,* 1076 (Feb. 7, 1867). See also Wendell Phillips's similar exposition in the N.Y. *National Anti-Slavery Standard,* Feb. 16, 1867, p. 2. One should not imagine that the Williams bill conformed exactly to what Stevens had hoped for in 1865, when the question was still fresh. His ideal would have been to provide territorial governments for the southerners. In fact, he specifically objected to placing them under military governments. See his speech in *Cong. Globe,* 39 Cong., 1 Sess., 72–75 (Dec. 18, 1865). Nonetheless, with Republican opinion as strongly in favor of quick restoration as it was, the Military Government bill must have seemed a godsend at first.

McKitrick either missed the clear implication in Stevens's speech that he considered the new bill to be more than merely a temporary measure, or he rejected that interpretation. He suggests that Stevens merely believed that he could pass a measure more to his liking in the Fortieth Congress and wanted only to prevent the Thirty-ninth from passing a more conservative measure. But this does not explain why so many Republicans themselves immediately assummed the Military Government bill would be a long-term measure and why they worked so feverishly to obviate that possibility. McKitrick himself discusses these efforts. Eric L. McKitrick, *Andrew Johnson and Reconstruction* (Chicago and London, 1960), 478–79. See John A. Griswold's comments in *Cong. Globe,* 39 Cong., 2 Sess., 1101 (Feb. 8, 1867), and Banks's, *ibid.,* appendix, 174–75 (Feb. 9, 1867).

9. *Ibid.,* 1037 (Feb. 6, 1867), 1076 (Feb. 7, 1867).

10. Underwood to Banks, Feb. 11, 1867. Nathaniel Banks Mss., Illinois State Historical Library; Durant to Benjamin F. Flanders, Feb. 10, 1867. Flanders Mss., Louisiana State University archives, Baton Rouge. The correspondent of the radical Boston *Commonwealth* reported that southern loyalists in Washington unanimously opposed Stevens's proposal. Boston *Commonwealth,* Feb. 16, 1867, p. 2.

11. Centreville *Indiana True Republican,* Feb. 14, 1867, p. 126.

12. *Cong. Globe,* 39 Cong., 2 Sess., 1081 (Feb. 7, 1867).

13. *Ibid.,* 1083 (Feb. 7, 1867). The entire speech is *ibid.,* 1080–83 (Feb. 7, 1867).

14. *Ibid.,* 1104–105 (Feb. 8, 1867).

15. *Ibid.*

16. *Ibid.,* 1105 (Feb. 8, 1867).

17. Boston *Daily Advertiser,* Feb. 9, 1867, p. 1.

18. *Cong. Globe,* 39 Cong., 2 Sess., 1176–77 (Feb. 12, 1867).

19. *Ibid.,* 1182 (Feb. 12, 1867); 1106 (Feb. 9, 1867).

20. Kasson's amendment may be found *ibid.,* 1104–105 (Feb. 8, 1867); Lawrence's *ibid.,* 1083–84 (Feb. 7, 1867). Banks prepared an amendment but did not offer it. He did frame a version applying to Louisiana. It is in his papers in the Library of Congress and was published in several newspapers on February 11.

21. The bill may be found *ibid.,* 1128–29 (Feb. 11, 1867). Eliot and Shellabarger carefully asked leading Louisiana Republicans for their recommendations regarding Louisiana government. Nearly all urged territorialization. See Durant's opinion in Testimony on the New Orleans Riot, *House Report No. 16,* 39 Cong., 2 Sess., appendix, 11; Rufus Waples's suggestions, *ibid.,* 27; Judge Rufus K. Howells's advice, *ibid.,* 51.

22. In 1865 and 1866, when the military held paramount authority in the South while southerners reorganized their governments under Johnson's direction, the commanders had carefully avoided interference with the civil authorities. The most significant exception was a conflict between General Henry W. Slocum and Mississippi Provisional Governor William L. Sharkey over Sharkey's right to reorganize the state militia. Army officers also had circumscribed the liberties of the newly freed blacks, like white southerners believing them unprepared to cope with freedom—a perhaps not unreasonable conclusion, but one which did little to assure radicals of the army's good intentions. Finally, radicals had distrusted the regular army officer corps throughout the Civil War, believing them secretly proslavery and disinclined to bring all their resources to bear in conquering the South. The only study of the army's role in Reconstruction on the local level in the South is James E. Sefton's *The United States Army and Reconstruction, 1865–1877* (Baton Rouge, 1967). Thoroughly researched, Sefton's book suffers from a lack of interpretation, especially of the army's impact on southern social and political institutions. Did it encourage or discourage social change? Within the framework of Republican politics, did the military authorities favor radicals or conservatives or neither? For the period of presidential Reconstruction, Sefton clearly implies that the military tried to limit its role, gave Johnson's civil authorities maximum freedom, shared with white southerners a concern for social and economic stability which worked against what radicals believed to be the black men's interests, and tried to conduct itself in such a way as to minimize the hostility of white southerners (with all that implies as to the situation of black southerners). See his pp. 25–59.

For the period of congressional Reconstruction, Sefton's conclusions are less apparent. It is clear that the Army considered it a duty to enforce the Reconstruction acts and to encourage southern compliance with them and the formation of new state constitutions. But Sefton pays more attention to details than the broad questions outlined above. It seems important to note that although nearly every important state official in the Johnson governments held office in violation of the disqualification clause of the constitutional amendment, and although the Reconstruction act specifically declared that offices thus held must be vacated, very few officials were ever removed, including only three governors, one of whom—J. Madison Wells of Louisiana—was not disqualified by the act and had allied himself with the extreme radicals of his state. See *ibid.,* 138–41, 162, 195–96; Michael Perman, *Reunion Without Compromise; The South and Reconstruction, 1865–1868* (Cambridge, Eng., 1973), 132–43. Some indications that the military commanders generally did not play the radical role historians traditionally assigned to them are in James M. Schofield, *Forty-Six Years in the Army* (N.Y., 1897), 394–405; James L. McDonough, "John Schofield as Military Dictator of Reconstruction in Virginia," *Civil War History,* XV (Sept. 1969), 237–56; McDonough, *Schofield: Union General in Civil War and Reconstruction* (Tallahassee, Fla., 1972), 160–88; William Watson Davis, *The Civil War and Reconstruction in Florida* (N.Y., 1913), 470–76, 483–516, 522–27; Jerrell H. Shofner, "Political Reconstruction in Florida," *Florida Historical Quarterly,* XLV

(Oct. 1966), 145–52; Merlin G. Cox, "Military Reconstruction in Florida," *ibid.*, XLVI (Jan. 1968), 228–33; J.G. deRoulhac Hamilton, *Reconstruction in North Carolina* (Gloucester, Mass., 1964), 233; W.A. Swanberg, *Sickles the Incredible* (N.Y., 1956), 287–93; Max L. Heyman, Jr., "'The Great Reconstructor': General E.R.S. Canby and the Second Military District," *North Carolina Historical Review*, XXXII (Jan. 1955), 52–80; James Roy Morrill III, "North Carolina and the Administration of Brevet Major General Sickles," *ibid.*, XLII (Summer 1965), 291–305; Thomas S. Staples, *Reconstruction in Arkansas, 1862–1874* (N.Y., 1923), 127–40; James T. Currie, "The Beginnings of Congressional Reconstruction in Mississippi," *Journal of Mississippi History* (Aug. 1973), 267–86; Robert W. Shook, "The Federal Military in Texas, 1865–1870," *Texas Military History*, VI (Spring 1967), 32–38. William S. McFeely suggests that growing regular army influence in the Freedmen's Bureau subverted its mission. McFeely, *Yankee Stepfather: General O.O. Howard and the Freedmen* (New Haven and London, 1968), 291–96.

23. *Cong. Globe*, 39 Cong., 2 Sess., 1182 (Feb. 12, 1867), 1210, 1212 (Feb. 13, 1867).

24. *Ibid.*, 1083 (Feb. 7, 1867), 1211 (Feb. 13, 1867).

25. *Ibid.*, 1375 (Feb. 15, 1867).

26. *Ibid.*, 1210, 1211 (Feb. 13, 1867).

27. *Ibid.*, 1211 (Feb. 13, 1867).

28. *Ibid.*, 1130–31 (Feb. 11, 1867).

29. *Ibid.*, 1130–33 (Feb. 11, 1867).

30. *Ibid.*, 1133 (Feb. 11, 1867); 1175 (Feb. 12, 1867).

31. Boston *Daily Advertiser*, Feb. 14, 1867, p. 1; Centreville *Indiana True Republican*, Feb. 21, 1867, p. 129; Resolutions of the Feb. 11, 1867, meeting of the Southern Republican Association, quoted in *Cong. Globe*, 39 Cong., 2 Sess., 1171 (Feb. 12, 1867); Petition of Arkansas Citizens, *ibid.*, 1223 (Feb. 13, 1867).

32. Laflin to Greeley, Feb. 17, 1867 (misdated February 1). Horace Greeley Mss., Manuscripts Div., L.C.; *N.Y. Tribune*, Feb. 15, 1867, p. 1; Feb. 17, 1867, p. 1; Feb. 18, 1867, p. 1; Moore, notes, Feb. 14, 1867. Johnson Mss.; Unpublished testimony before the Select Committee . . . on a Corrupt Bargain with the President, in the papers of that committee, 39 Cong., R.G. 233, N.A. Warden and Este were uncertain as to the date of the first meeting at the Metropolitan Hotel in their testimony, placing it on either February 12 or 13. The 12th appears more likely because they mentioned that the House passed the Military Government bill *between* the meetings. That bill passed February 13.

33. *Cong. Globe*, 39 Cong., 2 Sess., 1213–15 (Feb. 13, 1867).

34. Senator Henderson mentioned that southern lobbyists had informed him that they favored the Louisiana bill and opposed the other. We may surmise they approached other senators too, especially since the Southern Republican Associa-

tion sent a formal memorial to the Senate embodying these views. Henderson, *ibid.*, 1371 (Feb. 15, 1867); the memorial at *ibid.*, 1553 (Feb. 19, 1867). Virginia radicals sent a petition at this time asking that Virginia be given a territorial government, with Judge Underwood as its governor. *Ibid.* This petition joined one from Arkansas specifically asking the extension of the Louisiana bill's provisions to that state. *Ibid.*, 1223 (Feb. 13, 1867); Boston *Daily Advertiser*, Feb. 14, 1867, p. 1; Wade in *Cong. Globe*, 39 Cong., 2 Sess., 1303 (Feb. 13, 1867); Wilson, *ibid.*, 1511 (Feb. 18, 1867); Conness, *ibid.*, 1555 (Feb. 19, 1867). Sumner's position is easily determined by his course. See *ibid.*, 1302–03 (Feb. 13, 1867).

35. *Ibid.*, 1303 (Feb. 14, 1867). Wade said essentially the same thing. *Ibid.*

36. *Ibid.*, 1304 (Feb. 14, 1867).

37. *Ibid.*, 1302–304 (Feb. 14, 1867).

38. *Ibid.*, 1560 (Feb. 19, 1867).

39. *Ibid.*, 1304 (Feb. 14, 1867), 1360 (Feb. 15, 1867). Reverdy Johnson proposed Williams's amendment when the Oregon senator decided not to propose it. It may be found *ibid.*, 1361 (Feb. 15, 1867).

40. *Ibid.*, 1304 (Feb. 14, 1867).

41. The issues involved in the Blaine amendment were not voted upon in the Senate until a Republican caucus had smoothed differences. The issues which determined radicalism and conservatism in List 12, therefore, related primarily to circumscription of the president's powers, a fundamentally different issue from Reconstruction. On that issue, Stewart, Kirkwood, Lane, and Cragin voted with the radicals. I use the terms *conservative* and *centrist* here with reference to their positions on Reconstruction, best delineated by their positions during the first session. See List 10.

42. *Ibid.*, 1365, 1392, 1392–93 (Feb. 15, 1867).

43. The entire debate is in *ibid.*, 1364–98 (Feb. 15, 1967).

44. *Ibid.*, 1563 (Feb. 19, 1867); Boston *Evening Journal*, Feb. 18, 1867, p. 1; *N.Y. Tribune*, Feb. 18, 1867, p. 1; Boston *Daily Advertiser*, Feb. 18, 1867, p. 1; Edward L. Pierce, *Memoir and Letters of Charles Sumner* (4 vols., Boston, 1893), IV, 313–14; Sumner to John Bright, May 27, 1867, in *ibid.*, 319–20; Gideon Welles, *Diary of Gideon Welles —Secretary of the Navy Under Lincoln and Johnson* (3 vols., Boston and N.Y., 1911), III, 47 (Feb. 18, 1867). The amendment as finally agreed upon is in the *Cong. Globe*, 39 Cong., 2 Sess., 1459 (Feb. 16, 1867).

45. *Ibid.*, 1459–69 (Feb. 16, 1867), 1511, 1518 (Feb. 18, 1867).

46. Sherman to Cox, Feb. 20, 1867. Jacob D. Cox Mss., Oberlin College Library, Oberlin, Ohio.

47. *N.Y. Tribune*, Feb. 18, 1867, p. 1; Boston *Evening Journal*, Feb. 17, 1867, p. 4; Testimony in the papers of the Select Committee on a Corrupt Bargain with the President, 39 Cong., R.G. 233, N.A.

48. Springfield (Massachusetts) *Daily Republican,* Feb. 18, 1867, p. 2.
49. *Cong. Globe,* 39 Cong., 2 Sess., 1316, 1318 (Feb. 18, 1867).
50. *Ibid.,* 1320 (Feb. 18, 1867).
51. The entire debate is *ibid.,* 1315–40 (Feb. 18, 19, 1867). See also Poore's report in the Boston *Evening Journal,* Feb. 20, 1867, p. 2; Boston *Daily Advertiser,* Feb. 20, 1867, p. 1; *N.Y. Tribune,* Feb. 20, 1867, p. 1.
52. See Wade's comments, *Cong. Globe,* 39 Cong., 2 Sess., 1558 (Feb. 19, 1867).
53. *Ibid.,* 1559–60 (Feb. 19, 1867).
54. The entire debate is *ibid.,* 1555–70 (Feb. 19, 1867).
55. *Ibid.,* 1356–58 (Feb. 19, 1867).
56. *Ibid.,* 1399–1400 (Feb. 20, 1867); *N.Y. Tribune,* Feb. 21, 1867, p. 1.
57. *Cong. Globe,* 39 Cong., 2 Sess., 1645 (Feb. 20, 1867).
58. Howe to Grace T. Howe, Feb. 26, 1867. Timothy Otis Howe Mss., Wisconsin State Historical Society Library.
59. Julian in the Centreville *Indiana True Republican,* Mar. 7, 1867, p. 137; Howe to Grace T. Howe, Feb. 26, 1867. Howe Mss.; *N.Y. Times,* Feb. 21, 1867, p. 1; Este to Johnson, Feb. ?, 1867 (erroneously filed under March 1867). Andrew Johnson Mss., Manuscripts Div., L.C.; Springfield (Massachusetts) *Daily Republican,* Feb. 28, 1867, p. 2; March 2, 1867, p. 4; Nordhoff to Parke Godwin, Feb. 21, 1867. William Cullen Bryant and Parke Godwin Mss., New York Public Library.
60. *Cong. Globe,* 39 Cong., 2 Sess., 1626 (Feb. 20, 1867).
61. Kincaid points out positive gains that a strong veto might secure, but Johnson still could have delivered that veto if the Fortieth Congress passed a Reconstruction measure. Kincaid, "The Military Reconstruction Act," 281–84.
62. *Cong. Globe,* 39 Cong., 2 Sess., 1976 (March 2, 1867).
63. *Ibid.,* 40 Cong., 1 Sess., 63 (March 11, 1867). Colfax appointed James F. Wilson (chairman), Boutwell, Francis Thomas, Thomas Williams, Frederick Woodbridge, William Lawrence, John C. Churchill (all Republicans) and Samuel S. Marshall and Charles A. Eldridge (Democrats) to the committee. Woodbridge and Thomas inclined towards conservatism; Wilson and Lawrence had cooperated with Bingham and Blaine but had supported compromise efforts at the end of the session; Boutwell and Williams were radicals. See W.R. Brock, *An American Crisis: Congress and Reconstruction, 1865–1867* (N.Y., 1963), 204.
64. *Cong. Globe,* 40 Cong., 1 Sess., 49, 50–56 (March 11, 1867). Petitions came from Republicans in Virginia, North Carolina, and Arkansas. *Ibid.,* 17 (March 7, 1867), 27 (March 8, 1867), 76 (March 13, 1867). Sumner presented his bill March 6. *Ibid.,* 9–10. The New York radical Hamilton Ward presented a new Reconstruction bill in the House, but like Sumner's, it died in committee. *Ibid.,* 57 (March 11, 1867); House bill file, 40 Cong. (H.R. 5). R.G. 233, N.A.
65. Sumner to Pierce, March 11, 1867.

Charles Sumner Mss., Houghton Library, Harvard University, Cambridge, Mass.
66. *Cong. Globe,* 40 Cong., 1 Sess., 66 (March 11, 1867).
67. For the debates and votes on these questions see *ibid.,* 109–18 (March 15, 1867), 147–51 (March 16, 1867), 158–63 (March 16, 1867), 182–85 (March 18, 1867). As modified in conference between representatives of both houses, the bill required that at least 50 percent of the registered voters vote in each election. See *ibid.,* appendix, 39–40 for the final terms of the bill.
68. *Ibid.,* 99–109 (March 14, 1867), 163–65 (March 16, 1867). Drake's discussion of radicalism is on pp. 100–101.
69. *Ibid.,* 165–70 (March 16, 1867).
70. *Ibid.,* 165 (March 16, 1867).
71. Stevens in the N.Y. *Herald,* July 8, 1867, p. 6; Poore in the Boston *Evening Journal,* March 20, 1867, p. 4; Howe to Horace Rublee, Jan. 15, 1868. Howe Mss.; N.Y. *National Anti-Slavery Standard,* March 2, 1867, p. 2; Garrison and Parker Pillsbury, *ibid.,* March 9, 1867, p. 1 and March 23, 1867, p. 3, respectively.
72. Although congressmen might have justified the Reconstruction acts upon Congress's obligation to guarantee republican forms of government to the states, none did so, arguing the grasp of war theory instead. See Brandegee's constitutional defense of the Military Government bill, *Cong. Globe,* 39 Cong., 2 Sess., 1076 (Feb. 7, 1867); Bingham, *ibid.,* 1082 (Feb. 7, 1867); William Lawrence, *ibid.,* 1083 (Feb. 7, 1867); Martin Russell Thayer, *ibid.,* 1097 (Feb. 8, 1867); Abner C. Harding, *ibid.,* 1098–99 (Feb. 8, 1867); Shellabarger, *ibid.,* 1102 (Feb. 8, 1867); Garfield, *ibid.,* 1104 (Feb. 8, 1867); Kasson, *ibid.,* 1105 (Feb. 8, 1867); Garfield again ("All I ask is, that Congress shall place civil governments before these people of the rebel States, and a cordon of bayonets behind them."), *ibid.,* 1184 (Feb. 12, 1867); Stewart, *ibid.,* 1364 (Feb. 15, 1867); Jacob M. Howard, *ibid.,* 1365 (Feb. 15, 1867); Sherman, *ibid.,* 1462 (Feb. 16, 1867); Lyman Trumbull, *Argument of Hon. Lyman Trumbull in the Supreme Court of the United States, Mar. 4, 1868, in the Matter of* Ex Parte WILLIAM H. McCARDLE, *Appellant* (Washington, 1868), 14, 20–26; Edwin Dennison Morgan in a speech at Cooper Institute, quoted in J. Rawley, *Edwin D. Morgan, 1811–1883: Merchant in Politics* (N.Y., 1956), 226.
   Richard Henry Dana, who had popularized the grasp of war doctrine in his Faneuil Hall speech, wrote to Charles Francis Adams, Jr., "I must shock and dismay you by expressing my great satisfaction in the Reconstruction Bill. . . . [I]t is on the principle which I had the honor to be the first to lay down in my Faneuil Hall speech of June, 1865— what my flattering friends call my 'Grasp-of-war Speech.' Not that my speech had any agency in the result, but that the result justifies it." Dana to Adams, April 14, 1867, quoted in Charles Francis

Adams, Jr., *Richard Henry Dana: A Biography* (Boston & N.Y., 1891), 334–35.
73. George W. Julian, *Political Recollections, 1840–1872* (Chicago, 1884), 306; Albion W. Tourgée, *A Fool's Errand* (N.Y., 1880), 120; Josiah Bushnell Grinnell, *Men and Events of Forty Years: Autobiographical Reminiscences of an Active Career from 1850 to 1890* (Boston,

1891), 158. See also Benjamin F. Butler, *Butler's Book: Autobiography and Personal Reminiscences of Major-General Benjamin F. Butler* (Boston, 1892), 960–61; Wendell Phillips in James G. Blaine *et al.*, "Ought the Negro to be Disfranchised? Ought He to have Been Enfranchised?" *North American Review,* CXXVIII (March 1879), 257–62.

12. THE IMPEACHMENT MOVEMENT AND PRESIDENTIAL OBSTRUCTION

1. N.Y. *National Anti-Slavery Standard,* March 2, 1867, p. 2. See also Colonel Charles E. Moss's correspondence to the *Standard,* March 2, 1867, p. 3; William Lloyd Garrison's call for impeachment, *ibid.,* March 9, 1867, p. 1.
2. Boutwell, Speech in Tremont Temple, week of Jan. 5–12, *ibid.,* Jan. 12, 1867, p. 1; Boston *Right Way,* Jan. 12, 1867, p. 2; Jan. 19, 1867, p. 2; Feb. 9, 1867, p. 3; Feb. 16, 1867, p. 3; *Wilkes' Spirit of the Times,* quoted by the N.Y. *National Anti-Slavery Standard,* Jan. 26, 1867, p. 1; Sidney H. Morse, "Impeachment," *Radical,* II (Feb. 1867), 373–75; Boston *Commonwealth,* Jan. 12, 1867, p. 2; Jan. 19, 1867, p. 2; Garrison article in the N.Y. *Independent,* Jan. 17, 1867, p. 1; Julian in the Centreville *Indiana True Republican,* Jan. 18, 1867, p. 106; Ward circulated petitions for impeachment which reached Congress from Michigan, Ohio, Iowa, Alabama, Illinois, Pennsylvania, Wisconsin, and Indiana. See the papers of the House Committee on the Judiciary, 39 Cong., R.G. 233, N.A.; Ward to Butler, Jan. 27, 1867. Benjamin F. Butler Mss. (impeachment correspondence), Manuscripts Div., L.C.
3. N.Y. *Times,* Jan. 6, 1867, p. 1; Jan. 7, 1867, p. 5; Boston *Evening Journal,* Jan. 7, 1867, p. 4; N.Y. *National Anti-Slavery Standard,* Jan. 19, 1867, p. 2; *Cong. Globe,* 39 Cong., 2 Sess., 319–21 (Jan. 7, 1867), 443–46 (Jan. 14, 1867), 807–808 (Jan. 28, 1867), 991 (Feb. 14, 1867).
4. N.Y. *Times,* March 7, 1867, p. 4; Boston *Evening Journal,* March 6, 1867, p. 4; March 7, 1867, p. 4.
5. N.Y. *Times,* March 7, 1867, p. 4; Boston *Evening Journal,* March 7, 1867, p. 4.
6. Grimes to Mrs. Grimes, March 12, 1867, quoted in William Salter, *The Life of James W. Grimes, Governor of Iowa, 1854–1858; Senator of the United States, 1859–1869* (N.Y., 1876), 323; N.Y. *Times,* March 8, 1867, p. 4.
7. John W. Forney to Sumner, July 10, 1867. Charles Sumner Mss., Houghton Library, Harvard University, Cambridge, Mass. (Forney, the secretary of the Senate, was so certain there would be no July session—he received "the assurances of experienced Senators" to this effect—that he left for Europe.); Zachariah Chandler, speaking at Ashtabula, Ohio, in McPherson scrapbook: Campaign of 1867, II, 135–36. Edward McPherson Mss., Manuscripts Div., L.C.; *Cong. Globe,* 40 Cong., 1 Sess., 16

(March 7, 1867), 303–308, 315–20 (March 23, 1867), 321–22, 331, 334 (March 25, 1867), 352–60 (March 26, 1867), 387–91 (March 27, 1867), 401–408, 419–20, 425–27 (March 28, 1867), 438–41, 446–54 (March 29, 1867).
8. "B" in the N.Y. *Times,* Feb. 13, 1867, p. 2.
9. Moore notes, Feb. 16, 1867. Andrew Johnson Mss., Manuscripts Div., L.C.
10. Sherman to W.T. Sherman, July 8, 1866, in Rachel Sherman Thorndike (ed.), *The Sherman Letters: Correspondence Between General and Senator Sherman from 1837 to 1891* (N.Y., 1894), 276; Trumbull to Mrs. Julia Jayne Trumbull, May 29, 1866. Lyman Trumbull Mss., Illinois State Historical Library.
11. Cox to Monroe Cox [?], Nov. 21, 1866. Jacob D. Cox Mss., Oberlin College Library, Oberlin, Ohio.
12. U.S. *Statutes at Large,* XII, 502–503 (the test oath law), 589–92 (the Confiscation act; the disqualification provision is section 3, on. p. 590).
13. *Ibid. In rem* proceedings lie against property rather than persons. That is, if the property were tainted by ownership by someone adhering to the rebellion, the court would find against it and transfer title to the government.
14. The development and passage of the Confiscation bill and supplementary resolution is discussed in Leonard P. Curry, *Blueprint for Modern America: Non-Military Legislation of the First Civil War Congress* (Nashville, 1968), 75–100.
15. U.S. *Statutes at Large,* XIII, 507–509.
16. A large literature has accumulated recently indicating how close Republicans came during the war to inaugurating a real land reform in the South. See LaWanda Cox, "The Promise of Land to the Freedmen," *Mississippi Valley Historical Review,* XLV (Dec. 1958), 413–40; Paul W. Gates, "Federal Land Policy in the South, 1866–1888," *Journal of Southern History,* VI (Aug. 1940), 303–30; John A. Carpenter, *The Sword and the Olive Branch: Oliver Otis Howard* (Pittsburgh, 1964), 106–107. For experimental land reforms and the pressure leading to creation of the Freedmen's Bureau with its land-reform potential, see John G. Sproat, "Blueprint for Radical Reconstruction," *ibid.,* XXIII (Feb. 1957), 25–44; Willie Lee Rose, *Rehearsal for Reconstruction: The Port Royal Experiment* (N.Y., 1964); George R. Bentley, *A History of the Freedmen's Bureau* (Philadelphia, 1955), 16–49;

William S. McFeely, *Yankee Stepfather: General O.O. Howard and the Freedmen* (New Haven and London, 1958), 45–64.
17. The best study of Reconstruction under the Johnsonian provisional governments is Michael Perman, *Reunion Without Compromise: The South and Reconstruction, 1865–1868* (Cambridge, Eng., 1973), especially pp. 57–181.
18. The most intensive study of the problem of loyalty oaths during the Civil War and Reconstruction is Harold M. Hyman's *The Era of the Oath: Northern Loyalty Tests During the Civil War and Reconstruction* (Philadelphia, 1954). Jonathan Truman Dorris studied the pardon and amnesty question exhaustively in *Pardon and Amnesty Under Lincoln and Johnson: The Restoration of the Confederates to Their Rights and Privileges, 1861–1898* (Chapel Hill, N.C., 1953).
19. J. Hubley Ashton (acting attorney general) to Nathaniel Usher (U.S. attorney, Northern Dist., Fla.), July 25, 27, 1865; Ashton to William Marvin (prov. governor, Fla.), July 27, 1865. Attorney-General's Letterbooks, General Correspondence, R.G. 60, N.A.; Usher to Speed, Aug. 17, 1865. Attorney General's Office, Letters Received, R.G. 60, N.A.
20. Speed to Lucius H. Chandler (U.S. atty., Va.), Sept. 5, 1865; Ashton to James Q. Smith (U.S. atty., Ala.), Sept. 22, 1865. Atty.-Gen'l. Letterbooks, Gen'l. Corres., R.G. 60, N.A.
21. William Stewart (clerk) to Perkins Bass (U.S. atty., N. Dist., Ill.), Sept. 1, 1865; Ashton to Usher, Sept. 1, 1865; H.F. Pleasants (clerk) to Chandler, Sept. 2, 1865; Ashton to William A. Grover (U.S. atty., Mo.), Sept. 2, 1865; Ashton to William J. Jones (U.S. atty., Maryland), Sept. 2, 1865; Speed to Benjamin F. Smith (U.S. atty., W. Va.), Sept. 6, 1865; Speed to William N. Glover (?), Sept. 6, 1865; Speed to James Q. Smith (?), Sept. 22, 1865; Speed to Horace H. Harrison (U.S. atty., Middle Dist., Tenn.), Sept. 27, Oct. 20, 1865; Speed to Isaac Murphy (gov. of Ark.), Nov. 28, 29, 1865; Speed to Harrison, Nov. 30, 1865; Speed to ? Jennings, April 11, 1866; Speed to Bennet Pike (U.S. atty., W. Dist., Mo.), April 11, June 15, 1866; Stanbery to Pike, June 23, 1866; Pleasants (acting chief clerk) to John L. Williamson (U.S. atty., Tenn.), Aug. 20, 1866 (halting confiscation proceeding against (Confederate General P.G.T. Beauregard); Ashton to C.C. Carrington (U.S. atty., Washington), Nov. 10, 1866; Stanbery to James Q. Smith, Jan. 16, 1867 (halting proceedings against Cassius C. Clay); Ashton to the district attorney and U.S. marshall, Georgia, March 27, 1867; Stanbery to L.V.B. Martin (U.S. atty., Ala., March 29, 1867; Pleasants to Henry A. Fitch (U.S. atty., Ga.), April 15, 1867; F.U. Still (acting chief clerk) to Francis Bugbee (U.S. atty., N. Dist., Fla.), Nov. 4, 1867); Binckley (asst. atty.-gen.) to Usher, Nov. 29, 1867; Binckley to Bug-

bee, Dec. 6, 1867. Atty-Gen'l. Letterbooks, Gen'l. Corres., R.G. 60, N.A.
22. Speed to Usher, Dec. 9, 1865. See also Speed to Daniel R. Goodle (U.S. atty., Va.), Nov. 27, 1865; Speed to Crawford W. Hall, Jan. 11, 1866. Atty-Gen'l. Letterbooks, Gen'l. Corres., R.G. 60, N.A. Also the testimony of D.H. Starbuck before the Judiciary committee on impeachment, *House Report No. 7, 40 Cong., 1 Sess.,* appendix, 154–55.
23. Speed to Pike, June 15, Aug. 14, 1866. Atty.-Gen'l. Letterbooks, Gen'l. Corres., R.G. 60, N.A.; Stanbery's testimony before the House Judiciary committee on impeachment, *House Report No. 7, 40 Cong., 1 Sess.,* appendix, 420.
24. Howard to Stanton, Sept. 4, 1865. Johnson Mss.; Howard's testimony on impeachment, *House Report No. 7, 40 Cong., 1 Sess.,* appendix, 89.
25. Message from the President Relative to Pardons and Abandoned Property, *House Executive Document No. 99, 39 Cong., 1 Sess.; House Report No. 7, 40 Cong., 1 Sess.,* appendix, 87–92; *House Report No. 30, 40 Cong., 2 Sess.;* McFeely, *Yankee Stepfather,* 111–17; Oliver Otis Howard, *Autobiography of Oliver Otis Howard* (2 vols., N.Y., 1908), II, 234–36; Dorris, *Pardon and Amnesty,* 227–33; Carpenter, *Sword and the Olive Branch,* 106–109; Martin Abbott, "Free Land, Free Labor, and the Freedmen's Bureau," *Agricultural History,* XXX (Oct. 1956), 151–53.
26. Howard, *Autobiography,* II, 280, 283–84; Carpenter, *Sword and the Olive Branch,* 118–20. McFeely deals with Johnson's relations with Howard and the Bureau throughout his *Yankee Stepfather.*
27. James D. Richardson (ed.), *Messages and Papers of the Presidents of the United States* (10 vols., Washington, 1896–99), VI, 429–32; Benjamin P. Thomas and Harold M. Hyman, *Stanton: The Life and Times of Lincoln's Secretary of War* (N.Y., 1962), 477–79; Grant to General George H. Thomas, April 10, 1866. Headquarters of the Army, letters sent, R.G. 108, N.A.; Davis Tillson to O.O. Howard, April 7, 1866; E.D. Townsend to Tillson, April 17, 1866, quoted in Edward McPherson (ed.), *Political History of the United States of America, During the Period of Reconstruction . . .* (3rd edn, Washington, 1880), 17n.
28. General Order No. 26, May 1, 1866, quoted in Richardson (ed.), *Messages and Papers of the Presidents,* VI, 440–42; Gen. Order No. 46, July 13, 1866, quoted in McPherson (ed.), *Political History of . . . Reconstruction,* 198–99.
29. Richardson (ed.), *Messages and Papers of the Presidents,* VI, 434–38; Thomas and Hyman, *Stanton,* 498–99.
30. Republican fears that Johnson contemplated a *coup* in summer, 1866, are discussed *supra,* 203–209. These fears were aroused again as the date approached for the assembly of the Fortieth Congress. N.Y. *Independent,* Jan. 31, 1867, p. 1. The rumors became especially pronounced and more prevalent in the fall of 1867. Carl Schurz, *Remi-*

niscences of *Carl Schurz* (3 vols., N.Y., 1908–1909), III, 252; Speech of John Sherman in Cincinnati, quoted in the McPherson scrapbook: Campaign of 1867, II, 111. McPherson Mss.; Schurz to Mrs. Margarethe Schurz, *Intimate Letters of Carl Schurz, 1841–1869*, ed. by Joseph Shafer (Madison, Wis., 1928), 392–93 and 412–16, respectively; John Binney to Schuyler Colfax, Sept. 9, 1867, enclosed with Binney to John A. Andrew, Sept. 12, 1867. John Albion Andrew Mss., Massachusetts Historical Society; Boston *Daily Advertiser*, Aug. 29, 1867, p. 2; Sept. 2, 1867, p. 2; *N.Y. Times*, Sept. 17, 1867, p. 4; *Chicago Tribune*, Sept. 27, 1867, p. 2; Oct. 1, 1867, p. 1; Oct. 3, 1867, p. 1; Oct. 11, 1867, p. 2; N.Y. *National Anti-Slavery Standard*, Oct. 27, 1866, p. 2; [Anonymous], "The Conspiracy at Washington," *Atlantic Monthly*, XX (Nov. 1867), 633–38.

The only study of the fears of renewed strife during Reconstruction is William A. Russ, Jr., "Was There Danger of a Second Civil War During Reconstruction?" *Mississippi Valley Historical Review*, XXV (June 1938), 39–58. Russ's study is suggestive, but incomplete. He did not seem to believe that Republican apprehensions were honest, even though he offered no evidence to indicate that they were not and a great deal which indicated that they were. A new look at this question would be most useful.

31. The correspondence of Republicans is filled with evidence of the change which came over southerners when they realized the president's intentions. J.W. Sprague to John Sherman, March 29, April 4, 1866. John Sherman Mss. Manuscripts Div., L.C. Jonathan Roberts to Trumbull, April 21, 1866; A.P. Field to Trumbull, May 17, 1866. Trumbull Mss., L.C.; W.G. Brownlow to Chase, June 20, 1866. Salmon P. Chase Mss., Manuscripts Div. L.C. James Speed to H.S. Lane, Aug. 6, 1866. Henry S. Lane Mss, Lilly Library, Indiana University, Bloomington, Indiana; A. Warren Kelsey to Edward Atkinson, Nov. 13, 1865. Edward Atkinson Mss., Massachusetts Historical Society; William Smith to D.H. Bingham, March 31, 1866. Papers of the Joint Committee on Reconstruction, 39 Cong., R.G. 233, N.A.; Eric L. McKitrick, *Andrew Johnson and Reconstruction* (Chicago and London, 1960), 154–58, 186–213.

32. *Cong. Globe*, 39 Cong., 1 Sess., 688 (Feb. 6, 1866).

33. *Ibid.*, 2 Sess., 1903, 1911 (Feb. 28, 1867); Harold Hyman, *The Era of the Oath*, 60–68.

34. Sheridan to Grant, April 19, 1867, Headquarters of the Army (hereafter HQA), letters rec'd, R.G. 108, N.A.

35. Thomas and Hyman, *Stanton*, 534–35.

36. U.S. Department of Justice, *Opinions of the Attorneys General of the United States*, XII, 182–206.

37. Gideon Welles, *Diary of Gideon Welles —Secretary of the Navy Under Lincoln*

and Johnson (3 vols., Boston and N.Y., 1911), III, 110 (June 20, 1867); Sickles to the Adjutant General, June 19, 1867. Edwin M. Stanton Mss., Manuscripts Div., L.C.

38. George C. Gorham, *Life and Public Services of Edwin M. Stanton* (2 vols., Boston and N.Y., 1899), II, 381.

39. Fessenden to Grimes, June 18, 1867, quoted in Charles A. Jellison, *Fessenden of Maine: Civil War Senator* (Syracuse, 1962), 221; *N.Y. Times*, June 12, 1867, p. 4; Schenck to R.B. Hayes (sent to all representatives), June 21, 1867, Rutherford B. Hayes Mss., Rutherford B. Hayes Library; E.D. Morgan to Fessenden, June 22, 1867; Morgan to Conkling, June 22, 1867; Conkling to Morgan, June 24, 1867. Edmund D. Morgan Mss., New York State Library; Boston *Daily Advertiser*, June 21, 1867, p. 2.

40. Boston *Daily Advertiser*, July 4, 1867, p. 1; *Cong. Globe*, 40 Cong., 1 Sess., 480 (July 3, 1867).

41. The nine senators voted with Sumner either to amend the resolution to remove its restriction, or against the resolution itself. They were Chandler, Drake, Fowler, Howe, Ross, Thayer, Tipton, and Wade among the Republicans and Buckalew among the Democrats. Ross, at least, was primarily interested in legislation to protect the frontier against Indian raids. *Ibid.*, 481–99 (July 5, 1867). The votes are at pp. 487 and 498.

42. Dawes to Mrs. Electa Dawes, July 9, 16, 1867. Henry L. Dawes Mss., Manuscripts Div., L.C.; Boston *Evening Journal*, July 5, 1867, p. 4; July 7, 1867, p. 4; July 8, 1867, p. 4.

43. *Cong. Globe*, 40 Cong., 1 Sess., 589 (July 11, 1867).

44. *Ibid.*, 590 (July 11, 1867).

45. *Ibid.*, 732–35 (July 19, 1867).

46. *Ibid.*, 749 (July 20, 1867).

47. The Chandler-Fessenden exchange is *ibid.*, 749–52 (July 20, 1867).

48. *Ibid.*, 757, 761, 764 (House), 753, 753–54, 755 (Senate; July 20, 1867). In the House 47 Republican radicals and centrists opposed the conference report, which was carried by the united effort of 51 conservative and centrist Republicans and 10 Democrats and Johnsonians. In the Senate 15 conservatives and centrists and two Democrats defeated 14 radicals and centrists.

49. Stevens, managing the Supplementary Reconstruction bill in the House, refused to accept Butler's amendment to remove all state officers. Butler then opposed seconding the previous question, which cut off the possibility of amendment, but he lost. *Ibid.*, 541, 542 (July 9, 1867). Stevens probably agreed with Butler himself, but as manager of the bill he represented the Reconstruction committee which reported it, not his own inclinations. In the Senate, Henry Wilson proposed an amendment similar to Butler's, but it too was defeated, 21 to 11. *Ibid.*, 528–33 (July 9, 1867). Sumner's amendment was ruled

out of order by a vote of 22 to 11. *Ibid.,* 581 (July 11, 1867). The Senate generally rejected a series of amendments Sumner offered, although it finally accepted one forbidding discrimination on account of color in appointing registration boards. *Ibid.,* 580–84, 586 (July 11, 1867).

50. *Ibid.,* 625 (July 13, 1867). See also Schenck's and Logan's remarks, *ibid.,* 596 (July 11, 1867) and appendix, 15 (July 12, 1867), and Julian's letter to his brother's newspaper: Centreville *Indiana True Republican,* July 18, 1867, p. 10. The text of the passed measure is in *Cong. Globe,* 40 Cong., 1 Sess., appendix, 39–40.

51. Grant to Johnson, Aug. 1, 1867. Copy in Moore notes, Johnson Mss.; Browning, *Diary,* II, 153–54 (Aug. 2, 1867); Moore, notes, Aug. 19, 1867. Johnson Mss.

52. Grant to Johnson, Aug. 17, 1867, quoted in McPherson (ed.), *Political History of . . . Reconstruction,* 306–307.

53. Peleg Chandler to Sumner, Aug. 15, 1867. Sumner Mss.; Horace White to Zachariah Chandler, Aug. 20, 1867. Chandler Mss., Manuscripts Div., L.C.; Colfax to Garfield, Sept. 11, 1867. James A. Garfield Mss., Manuscripts Div., L.C.; Willard H. Smith, *Schuyler Colfax: The Changing Fortunes of a Political Idol* (Indianapolis, 1952), 261; *N.Y. Times,* Aug. 26, 1867, p. 4 (for Washburne's views); *N.Y. Times,* Aug.

2, 1867, p. 4; *Chicago Tribune,* Aug. 21, 1867, p. 2; Boston *Daily Advertiser,* Sept. 2, 1867, p. 2; Sept. 3, 1867, p. 2; Indianapolis *Daily Journal,* Sept. 14, 1867, p. 4; Schurz to Mrs. Margarethe Meyer Schurz, Aug. 27, 1867, quoted in Schurz, *Intimate Letters,* 391–92; Burke Hinsdale to Garfield, Sept. 30, 1867, quoted in Mary L. Hinsdale (ed.), *Garfield-Hinsdale Letters: Correspondence Between James Abram Garfield and Burke Aaron Hinsdale* (Ann Arbor, 1949), 107–109.

54. Grant to Pope, Sept. 9, 1867. HQA, letters sent, R.G. 108, N.A.; Swanberg, *Sickles the Incredible,* 290–93.

55. Speed to Sumner, Sept. 12, 1867. Sumner Mss.; *N.Y. Times,* Sept. 14, 1867, p. 4. For a full compilation of sources indicating Republicans seriously worried about the possibilty of a *coup d'état,* see note 30, pp. 434–35, *supra.*

56. *N.Y. National Anti-Slavery Standard,* Aug. 17, 1867, p. 2.

57. Georges Eugène Benjamin Clemenceau, *American Reconstruction,* ed. by Fernand Baldensperger, trans. by Margaret Mac Veagh (N.Y. and Toronto, 1926), 102–103 (Sept. 10, 1867).

58. Logan Uriah Reavis to Trumbull, Aug. 30, 1867. Trumbull Mss., L.C. Reavis was a well-known western nationalist, who among other things advocated moving the national capital to St. Louis. This was not then considered so outlandish a proposition as it seems today.

---

13. The Critical Year: The Elections of 1867

1. Howard K. Beale, *The Critical Year: A Study of Andrew Johnson and Reconstruction* (N.Y., 1930), *passim.*
2. In a long letter to Tilton, Sumner urged his measure as a necessity, without which Republicans would eventually lose power in the North. Tilton published the letter in the *Independent* and endorsed Sumner's position. Sumner's proposition received further support from the Border State Convention, meeting in Baltimore early in September. As the only national Republican meeting of 1867, it was given wide publicity. Presided over by Tennessee Representative Horace Maynard, many leading border state Republicans attended, including Representative Robert T. Van Horn, former Senator John A.J. Creswell, and Tennessee leader (soon to be representative) Roderick R. Butler. N.Y. *Independent,* May 2, 1867, p. 4; McPherson scrapbook: Campaign of 1867, I, 68–73. Edward McPherson Mss., Manuscripts Div., L.C.; *N.Y. Times,* Sept. 13, 1867, p. 1. Trumbull argued that Congress had no power to enfranchise northern blacks. *Ibid.,* Sept. 2, 1867, p. 2.
3. Chicago *Evening Journal,* July 1, 1867, p. 3; Durant to ———, May 27, 1867, quoted in the Richmond *Indiana True Republican,* July 4, 1867, p. 1.
4. *N.Y. Tribune,* May 8, 1867, p. 1.

Thomas Wentworth Higginson, the society's president, seconded the demand for land reform at the same meeting. N.Y. *Independent,* May 2, 1867, p. 4; Stevens letter of April 27, 1867 on Reconstruction, published in the N.Y. *National Anti-Slavery Standard,* May 4, 1867, p. 1; *ibid.,* June 22, 1867, p. 2; Centreville *Indiana True Republican,* July 4, 1867, pp. 2, 4; Boston *Commonwealth* March 23, 1867, p. 2; March 30, 1867, p. 2.

5. Gettysburg (Pa.) *Star and Herald,* quoted in the *N.Y. Times,* May 29, 1867, p. 1. The letter was reported across the nation by the Associated Press; *ibid.,* June 7, 1867, p. 5.
6. *Ibid.,* June 14, 1867, p. 4; Boston *Daily Advertiser,* May 16, 1867, p. 2.
7. Boston *Daily Advertiser,* June 13, 1867, p. 2; Cincinnati *Commercial,* June 15, 1867, p. 4.
8. *N.Y. Times,* May. 2, 1867, p. 4.
9. *N.Y. Independent,* May 9, 1867, p. 1; June 6, 1867, p. 1; Cincinnati *Commercial,* July 8, 1867, p. 5; Boston *Daily Advertiser,* July 4, 1867, p. 2; Richard H. Abbot, *Cobbler in Congress: The Life of Henry Wilson, 1812–1875* (Lexington, Ky., 1972), 186–93.
10. Boston *Evening Journal,* May 24, 1867, p. 2; *N.Y. Tribune,* May 20, 1867, p. 4; May 21, 1867. p. 1; May 28, 1867, p. 4; Gen. John Pope to Schenck, May 20,

1867. Springfield (Massachusetts) *Republican,* March 29, 1867, p. 2. Robert C. Schenck Mss. Rutherford B. Hayes Library; John to William T. Sherman, Aug. 9, 1867, quoted in Rachel Sherman Thorndike (ed.), *The Sherman Letters: Correspondence Between General and Senator Sherman from 1837 to 1891* (N.Y., 1894), 292–94, at 293.

11. Boston *Evening Journal,* May 30, 1867, p. 2.

12. Endorsement by Wade on James G. Brisbin to Wade, April 30, 1867. Zachariah Chandler Mss., Manuscripts Div., L.C.; Cincinnati *Commercial,* July 8, 1867, p. 5.

13. *N.Y. Tribune,* May 17, 1867, p. 1.

14. *N.Y. Tribune,* May 31, 1867, p. 4.

15. Glydon G. Van Deusen, *Horace Greeley: Nineteenth Century Crusader* (N.Y., 1964), 352–56; *N.Y. Tribune,* May 24, 1867, p. 4.

16. Boston *Evening Journal,* May 29, 1867, supplement, 4.

17. Boston *Daily Advertiser,* May 25, 1867, p. 2.

18. Stevens in the Gettysburg *Star and Herald,* quoted in the *N.Y. Times,* May 29, 1867, p. 5; Stevens letter of April 27, quoted in the N.Y. *National Anti-Slavery Standard,* May 4, 1867, p. 1; Stevens to Samuel Schock, August 26, 1867, quoted in the Boston *Evening Journal,* Aug. 29, 1867, p. 4; Phillips, Speech Before the American Anti-Slavery Society, quoted in the *N.Y. Tribune,* May 8, 1867, p. 1; N.Y. *National Anti-Slavery Standard,* March 30, 1867, p. 2; April 6, 1867, p. 2; Oct. 26, 1867, p. 2. The influential abolitionist, Parker Pillsbury, called upon the anti-slavery vanguard to leave the party in a letter published by the *Standard,* Nov. 2, 1867, p. 1.

19. Boston *Daily Advertiser,* Sept. 4, 1867, p. 1.

20. "Last year the extreme radicals kept in the background and enabled judicious Republicans to carry the elections," John Binney observed. He pleaded, "Let them do so now." Binney to John A. Andrew, Sept. 23, 1867. John Albion Andrew Mss., Massachusetts Historical Society; *N.Y. Times,* June 14, 1867, p. 4.

21. McPherson scrapbook: Campaign of 1867, II, 135–36. McPherson Mss.

22. Fessenden to Grimes, Sept. 20, 1867. William Pitt Fessenden Mss., Bowdoin College Library, Brunswick, Me.; Grimes to Atkinson, Sept. 15, 1867. Edward Atkinson Mss.; Indianapolis *Daily Journal,* Aug. 2, 1867, p. 4.

23. Hinsdale to Garfield, Jan. 20, 1868, quoted in Mary L. Hinsdale (ed.), *Garfield-Hinsdale Letters: Correspondence Between James Abram Garfield and Burke Aaron Hinsdale* (Ann Arbor, 1949), 127–30; Horace White to Zachariah Chandler, Aug. 20, 1867. Z. Chandler Mss.; Edwin D. Morgan to D.D.T. Marshall, Sept. 22, 1867, quoted in James A. Rawley, *Edwin D. Morgan, 1811–1883: Merchant in Politics* (N.Y., 1956), 225; Carl Schurz to Mrs. Schurz,

Sept. 21, 1867, quoted in Carl Schurz, *Intimate Letters of Carl Schurz, 1841–1869,* ed. by Joseph Schafer (Madison, Wis., 1928), 398–400.

24. *Cong. Globe,* 39 Cong., 1 Sess., 75 (Dec. 18, 1865).

25. *Ibid.,* 1468 (March 16, 1866), 1614 (March 23, 1866), 1854 (April 9, 1866). The second Loan bill passed 83–53. But the division in the whole House was about 84 to 43 in favor of some contraction. Groups 0 and 1 detailed in Appendix A, pp. 381–83, favored limited contraction, while groups 2, 3 and 4 opposed it.

26. *Ibid.,* 2 sess., 1426 (Feb. 21, 1867). This was defeated by the Senate, however. Robert P. Sharkey, *Money, Class, and Party: An Economic Study of Civil War and Reconstruction* (Baltimore, 1959), 86–88.

27. Those who shifted noticeably toward expansionist views: William Boyd Allison (Iowa), Shelby Moore Cullom * (Ill.), Columbus Delano (Ohio), John F. Farnsworth (Ill.), John H. Farquhar (Ind.), Godlove S. Orth (Ind.), William H. Randall * (Ky.), Philetus Sawyer (Wis.), Thomas N. Stilwell (Ind.), Charles Upson (Mich.), Samuel L. Warner (Conn.), Henry D. Washburn (Ind.), and Kellian V. Whaley * (W. Va.), (all Republicans); Michael C. Kerr, Samuel S. Marshall * (Ill.), Burwell C. Ritter (Ky.), Lewis W. Ross * (Ill.), Nathaniel Taylor (Tenn.), Anthony Thornton * (Ill.), Lawrence S. Trimble * (Ky.), (all Democrats); and Thomas E. Noell (Mo.), (a conservative Unionist who ranked with Democrats by the second session). Those who shifted toward contractionism: Roswell Hart (N.Y.), Demas Hubbard (N.Y.), Calvin T. Hulburd (N.Y.), George F. Miller (Pa.), James K. Moorhead (Pa.), Thomas Williams (Pa.), (all Republicans). An asterisk (*) denotes a shift of major proportions. Representatives from Illinois, Indiana, and Ohio seem to have been most inclined to shift toward expansionism. Sharkey, *Money, Class and Party,* 84–88.

28. For more on the career of this interesting and important reformer, see Harold Francis Williamson's *Edward Atkinson: The Biography of an American Liberal, 1827–1905* (Boston, 1934).

29. Atkinson to McCulloch, Oct. 12, 1866. Atkinson Mss.

30. William Gray *et al.* to McCulloch, Apr. 30, 1867; McCulloch to Ignatius Sargent *et al.,* May 11, 1867; Gray to McCulloch, May 20, 1867. McCulloch Mss., Lilly Library, Indiana University; McCulloch to Gray and others, May 22, 1867. Atkinson Mss.; Gray to McCulloch, May 26, 1867; Atkinson to McCulloch, May 27, 1867. McCulloch Mss., Lilly Library, Indiana University. The hard-money men arranged to have the letter published in the Boston *Daily Advertiser,* May 28, 1867, p. 2.

31. Atkinson to Sumner, July 8, 1867. Charles Sumner Mss., Houghton Li-

brary, Harvard University, Cambridge, Mass.

32. The association's leaders included such financial conservatives as Emory Washburn, ex-Governor Andrew, Richard Henry Dana, Alexander H. Rice, John Murray Forbes, Governor William Claflin, and John G. Palfrey. Although men of conservative tendencies preponderated in its membership, radicals like Forbes and George Bailey Loring joined the organization also. The association's circular is quoted in the N.Y. *National Anti-Slavery Standard,* July 20, 1867, p. 3.

33. Atkinson to McCulloch, May 28, Aug. 7, Sept. 3, 1867. McCulloch Mss., L.C. For a more detailed discussion of the genesis of the hard-money lobby, see Irwin Unger, *Greenback Era: A Social and Political History of American Finance, 1865–1879* (Princeton, 1964), 131–43.

34. Welles, *Diary of Gideon Welles—Secretary of the Navy Under Lincoln and Johnson* (3 vols., Boston and N.Y., 1911), III, 150, 152 (Aug. 2, 1867), 152–54 (Aug. 3); Gideon Orville Hickman Browning, *Diary, of Orville Hickman Browning,* ed. by James G. Randall (Springfield, 1938), II, 153–54 (Aug. 2, 1867).

35. J.R. Flanigen to Johnson, Aug. 25, 1867; R. King Cutler to Johnson, July 26, Aug. 20, 1867; William B. Reed to [Montgomery Blair], Aug. 24, 1867, enclosed with Blair to Johnson, Aug. 26, 1867; William Cassidy to Blair, Sept. 1, 1867; R.W. Latham to Johnson, Oct. 5, 1867. Andrew Johnson Mss., Manuscripts Div., L.C., Boston *Daily Advertiser,* Sept. 11, 1867, p. 1; *N.Y. Times,* Aug. 27, 1867, p. 5; *Chicago Tribune,* Aug. 29, 1867, p. 1; *N.Y. Tribune,* Aug. 25, 1867, p. 4; Washington *National Intelligencer,* Aug. 27, 1867, p. 2; *Boston Evening Journal,* Aug. 27, 1867, p. 4; Aug. 28, 1867, p. 2, 4; Aug. 29, 1867, p. 2.

36. McCulloch to Johnson, Aug. 19, 1867. Johnson Mss. William G. Moore, Johnson's private secretary, recorded that the attacks had an effect on the president, who began to suspect McCulloch of harboring presidential aspirations. Moore, notes, Aug. 14, 1867. Johnson Mss.

37. Andrew's supporters were busily putting him in a position to run for the presidency. When Smythe suggested to one of his principal adherents, Frank E. Howe, that Andrew join the Cabinet, Howe immediately demanded that the ex-governor be given a major say in any further cabinet changes. The importance of this for Andrew's presidential aspirations is obvious. But Howe encouraged Andrew to accept the overture in any case. If he could not dominate the cabinet, he suggested, "Would not an issue with the Pres. and a resignation perchance do you good?" Howe to Andrew, Sept. 25, 1867. Andrew Mss. General Sherman mentioned his suggestions to his brother. William

T. to John Sherman, Oct. 7, 1867, quoted in Rachel Thorndike Sherman (ed.), *The Sherman Letters: Correspondence Between General and Senator Sherman from 1837 to 1891* (N.Y., 1894), 297–98.

38. Sherman to Colfax, Oct. 20, 1867. Schuyler Colfax Mss., Rush Rhees Library, University of Indiana.

39. The legislation had the support of the Military Affairs committee, led by a fellow radical, Robert C. Schenck. *Cong. Globe,* 38 Cong., 1 Sess., 427–31 (Feb. 1, 1864), T. Harry Williams, *Lincoln and the Radicals* (Madison, Wis., 1941), 334–37; William Frank Zornow, *Lincoln & the Party Divided* (Norman, Okla., 1954), 87–88, 94.

40. Hans L. Trefousse, *Ben Butler: The South Called Him Beast!* (N.Y., 1957), 173–76, 183, 193, 205; William B. Hesseltine, *Ulysses S. Grant, Politician* (N.Y., 1935), 44–45; Williams, *Lincoln and the Radicals,* 365–69; William D. Mallam, "The Grant-Butler Relationship," *Mississippi Valley Historical Review,* XLI (Sept. 1954), 259–69.

41. William B. Hesseltine, *Ulysses S. Grant, Politician* (N.Y., 1935), 61.

42. Badeau to E.B. Washburne, Oct. 20, 1865. Elihu B. Washburne Mss., Manuscripts Div., L.C.; Rawlins to Mrs. Rawlins, Aug. 30, Sept. 1, 1866, quoted in James Harrison Wilson, *The Life of John A. Rawlins: Lawyer, Assistant Adjutant-General, Chief of Staff, Major General of Volunteers, and Secretary of War* (N.Y., 1916), 334–36; Browning, *Diary,* II, 103–104 (Oct. 25, 1866).

43. Welles, *Diary,* II, 592, 593, 595 (Sept. 17, 1866), 646–47 (Dec. 24, 1866); Browning, *Diary,* II, 103–104 (Oct. 25, 1866); Sylvester Mowry to Doolittle, Dec. 12, 29, 1867, quoted in "Doolittle Correspondence," *Publications of the Southern History Association,* XI (Jan. 1907), 6–9; Hesseltine, *Grant,* 72–76.

44. Welles, *Diary,* III, 184–85 (Aug. 26, 1867); Thomas Ewing, Jr., to Thomas Ewing, Sr., Sept. 4, 1867. Ewing Family Mss., L.C.

45. William T. to John Sherman, Aug. 3, 1867, quoted in Thorndike (ed.), *Sherman Letters,* 292.

46. *N.Y. Tribune,* May 8, 1867, p. 1; N.Y. *National Anti-Slavery Standard,* Aug. 3, 1867, p. 2; Jame G. Blaine, *Twenty Years of Congress: From Lincoln to Garfield with a Review of the Events Which Led to the Political Revolution of 1860* (2 vols., Norwich, Conn., 1884–86), II, 531.

47. Orth to Colfax [spring, 1867]. Godlove S. Orth Mss., Indiana Division, Indiana State Library.

48. William Henry Smith to Steve ?, [June 1867]; Smith to Joseph H. Barrett, Apr. 25, 27, June 6, 29, 1867. Smith Mss., Ohio State Historical Society; Felice Bonadio, *North of Reconstruction: Ohio Politics, 1865–1870* (N.Y., 1970), 100–104, 141–50.

49. Fessenden to Grimes, June 18, 1867. Fessenden Mss. Wade, as president *pro tempore* of the Senate, was next in line

for the presidency if something happened to Johnson; hence Fessenden's reference to him as "V.P."

50. Thurlow Weed Barnes, *Memoir of Thurlow Weed* (Boston, 1884), 457–58; Glydon G. Van Deusen, *Thurlow Weed: Wizard of the Lobby* (Boston, 1947), 327–28; Hesseltine, *Grant*, 91–92; *N.Y. Times*, Oct. 17, 1867, p. 4; Nov. 10, 1867, p. 4; Nov. 27, 1867, p. 4; Chester L. Barrows, *William Maxwell Evarts: Lawyer, Diplomat, Statesman* (Chapel Hill, 1941), 138.

51. Greeley to Z. Chandler, Aug. 25, 1867. Z. Chandler Mss.; Boston *Commonwealth*, Nov. 16, 1867, p. 2; "Van" in the Springfield (Massachusetts) *Republican*, Aug. 2, 1867, p. 2.

52. Curtin to Washburne, Oct. 17, 1867. Washburne Mss.

53. Boston *Daily Advertiser*, Sept. 4, 1867, p. 1.

54. Adam Badeau, *Grant in Peace: From Appomattox to Mount McGregor—A Personal Memoir* (Hartford, 1887), 59–60.

55. Wilson, *Rawlins*, 338–39, 470–502. Orville E. Babcock, also on Grant's staff, regretted Rawlins's move, fearing it premature. Babcock to Washburne, Aug. 13, 1867. Washburne Mss., L.C.

56. Forney to Sumner, July 10, 1867. Sumner Mss.

57. Cincinnati *Commercial*, July 15, 1867, p. 2. Weed discerned this intention among New York Democrats, and Montgomery Blair discussed the possibility with Gideon Welles, who believed that though Grant preferred Democrats to Republicans, he would rather accept a Republican nomination if offered. Barnes, *Memoir of Thurlow Weed*, 457–58; Welles, *Diary*, III, 121 (June 27, 1867).

58. *N.Y. Herald*, July 6, 1867, p. 4.

59. *Ibid.*, July 14, 1867, p. 6; July 24, 1867, p. 4.

60. John to William T. Sherman, Aug. 9, 1867, quoted in Thorndike (ed.), *Sherman Letters*, 292–94, at 293.

61. *N.Y. Independent*, Aug. 29, 1867, p. 4; Phillips in the *N.Y. National Anti-Slavery Standard*, Aug. 24, 1867, p. 2; Clemenceau, *American Reconstruction*, 93.

62. *N.Y. Tribune*, Aug. 15, 1867, p. 4; Aug. 21, 1867, p. 4; Aug. 17, 1867, p. 4; Aug. 20, 1867, p. 4.

63. *Ibid.*, Aug. 15, 1867, p. 4.

64. Fessenden to Grimes, Sept. 20, 1867. Fessenden Mss. Bowdoin College Library.

65. White to Washburne, Aug. 13, 1867. Elihu B. Washburne Mss., L.C.

66. Grant to Johnson, Aug. 17, 1867, quoted in Edward McPherson (ed.), *The Political History of the United States of America, During the Period of Reconstruction . . .* (3rd edn, Washington, 1880), 306–307; James Sheldon to Washburne, Aug. 26, 1867. Washburne Mss., L.C.; Welles, *Diary*, III, 185–88 (Aug. 27, 1867); Browning, *Diary*, II, 159 (Aug. 27, 1867); Boston *Evening Journal*, Aug. 20, 1867, p. 2; *N.Y. Tri-*

bune, Aug. 27, 1867, p. 4; *N.Y. Times*, Aug. 27, 1867, p. 4, 5; *N.Y. Nation*, Oct. 10, 1867, p. 210.

67. Boston *Evening Journal*, Sept. 6, 1867, p. 2.

68. *N.Y. Independent*, Sept. 5, 1867, p. 4.

69. Blaine to Israel Washburn, Sept. 12, 1867 [?], quoted in Gaillard Hunt, *Israel, Elihu and Cadwallader Washburn: A Chapter in American Biography* (N.Y., 1925), 122–23, at 122. The letter seems to have been dated earlier than one would expect, in light of Blaine's confidence that Republicans were not to succeed at the polls. However, it is dated after the Maine elections, in which Republicans did less well than the previous year.

70. *N.Y. Times*, Sept. 2, 1867, p. 2.

71. Smith to Whitelaw Reid, Oct. 3, 1867, Smith Mss., Ohio Historical Society; Rutherford B. Hayes, *Diary and Letters, of Rutherford B. Hayes, Nineteenth President of the United States*, ed. by Charles Richard Williams (5 vols., Columbus, Ohio, 1922–26), III, 48 (Oct. 6, 1867); John to William T. Sherman, Aug. 9, 1867, quoted in Thorndike (ed.), *Sherman Letters*, 292–94. The election statistics are all from the *Tribune Almanac, 1868*.

72. Lieber to ?, Nov. 6, 1867. Francis Lieber Mss., Manuscripts Div., L.C.; Blaine to Israel Washburn, Sept. 12, 1867, quoted in Hunt, *Washburne*, 122–23, at 122; Springfield (Massachusetts) *Republican*, Oct. 10, 1867, p. 2.

73. Banks to Mrs. Banks, Nov. 13, 1867. Nathaniel Banks Mss., Manuscripts Div., L.C.

74. Colfax to John A.J. Creswell, Sept. 28, 1867. Colfax Mss., Rutherford B. Hayes Library.

75. Sherman to Colfax, Oct. 20, 1867. Colfax Mss., Rush Rhees Library; Cincinnati *Commercial*, quoted in the *N.Y. Times*, Nov. 8, 1867, p. 8; Donald O. Dewey (ed.), "The Journal of David McDonald," *Indiana Magazine of History*, LXII (Sept. 1966), 227; Martin Russell Thayer to Edward M. McPherson, Oct. 10, 1867. McPherson Mss.

76. Binney to John A. Andrew, Sept. 13, 1867. Andrew Mss.; Wade to Chandler, Oct. 10, 1867. Z. Chandler Mss.

77. *N.Y. Times*, Oct. 10, 1867, p. 4; Oct. 14, 1867, p. 4; Cincinnati *Commercial*, Oct. 10, 1867, p. 4. Stebbins, in his *Political History of New York*, says that most New York newspapers blamed the defeat on the radicals (page 209).

78. Fessenden to Grimes, Oct. 20, 1867. Fessenden Mss., Bowdoin College Library.

79. *N.Y. Independent*, Oct. 17, 1867, p. 4; Nov. 14, 1867, p. 4; Stevens quoted in the Indianapolis *Daily Journal*, Oct. 22, 1867, p. 4; Springfield (Massachusetts) *Republican*, Oct. 15, 1867, p. 2.

80. Boston *Evening Journal*, Nov. 9, 1867, p. 4.

81. *N.Y. Independent*, Oct. 24, 1867, p. 1; Nov. 7, 1867, p. 1; Nov. 14, 1867, p. 1.

82. Sharkey, *Money Class, and Party*, 92–101; Richard Smith to Colfax, Oct. 14,

1867; Samuel Shellabarger to Colfax, Oct. 17, 1867; H.S. Bundy to Colfax, Oct. 19, 1867. Colfax Mss., Hayes Library; William Henry Smith to R.D. Mussey, Oct. 21, 1867. William Henry Smith Mss., Ohio Historical Society.

83. Atkinson to ?, Aug. 11, 1867; C.F. Adams, Jr. to Atkinson, Dec. 27, 1867; Atkinson to Sumner, Feb. 19, 25, 1868. Atkinson Mss.; Atkinson to Norton, Dec. 17, 26, 28, 1867, Jan. 21, 24, 28, 31, Feb. 15, 26, March 6, 30, April 6, 8, 1868; C.F. Adams, Jr. to Norton, Dec. 10, 1867. Charles Eliot Norton Mss., Houghton Library. Harvard University, Cambridge, Massachusetts; William Endicott, "Reminiscences of Seventy-five Years," *Proceedings of the Massachusetts Historical Society,* XLVI (Nov. 1912), 230–31. Unger's *Greenback Era* is not organized chronologically before 1868, treating the development of differing financial theories and interests before that date separately. Nonetheless, it is indispensable to an understanding of the financial issue at this time.

84. Grimes to Atkinson, Oct. 14, 1867. Atkinson Mss.; N.Y. *Independent,* Oct. 24, 1867, p. 1; N.Y. *Times,* Nov. 19, 1867, p. 4.

85. Grimes to Atkinson, Sept. 15, 1867. Atkinson Mss.

86. See List 8, Chapter I, p. 347.

87. Cooke to John Sherman, Oct. 12, 1867. John Sherman Mss.; Grimes to Atkinson, Oct. 14, 1867. Atkinson Mss. Grimes was referring to Sumner's Red-

path interview, in which he had complained of the conservatives' obstructiveness. See p. 261 *supra.*

88. Clemenceau, *American Reconstruction,* 118 (Oct. 2, 1867); W. Ralph Thayer to Washburne, Oct. 10, 1867. E.B. Washburne Mss., L.C.

89. Boston *Daily Advertiser,* Oct. 8, 1867, p. 2; Toledo *Blade,* Oct. 11, 1867, p. 2.

90. Raymond to McCulloch, Oct. 11, 1867. McCulloch Mss.; N.Y. *Times,* Oct. 17, 1867, p. 4.

91. Cochrane to Washburne, Nov. 9, 1867; Curtin to Washburne, Oct. 17, 1867; John Meredith Read to Washburne, Nov. 7, 1867; E.H. Rollins to Washburne, Oct. 11, 1867, E.B. Washburne Mss., L.C.; Fessenden to Grimes, Oct. 20, 1867. Fessenden Mss., Bowdoin College Library; E.D. Morgan to C.E. Bishop, Nov. 17, 1867. Edmund Morgan Mss., New York State Library.

92. N.Y. *Nation,* Nov. 14, 1867, p. 385; N.Y. *Independent,* Nov. 14, 1867, p. 4. See also Wade's remarks to the Cincinnati *Commercial* correspondent, Joseph McCullagh, N.Y. *Times,* Nov. 8, 1867, p. 8, and the N.Y. *Tribune,* Oct. 15, 1867, p. 4.

93. N.Y. *Times,* Nov. 8, 1867, p. 8.

94. Bingham to Washburne, Nov. 9, 1867. E.B. Washburne Mss., L.C.; Washburne to Samuel Galloway, Nov. 18, 1867. Norcross collection. Massachusetts Historical Society; Fessenden to Grimes, Oct. 20, 1867. Fessenden Mss., Bowdoin College Library.

14. Congress on the President's Hip

1. Cochrane to Washburne, Nov. 16, 18, 22, 25, Dec. 5, 6, 9, 1867, Jan. 1, 1868; Cochrane, Prosper M. Whetmore, and James Wadsworth to Washburne, Nov. 25, 1867. Elihu B. Washburne Mss., Manuscripts Div., L.C.; Gideon Welles, *Diary of Gideon Welles—Secretary of the Navy Under Lincoln and Johnson* (3 vols., Boston and N.Y., 1911), III, 249–50 (Dec. 27, 1867); Thurlow Weed Barnes, *Memoir of Thurlow Weed* (Boston, 1884), 457–58; Glyndon G. Van Deusen, *Thurlow Weed Wizard of the Lobby* (Boston, 1947), 327–28.

2. Centreville *Indiana True Republican,* Dec. 12, 1867, p. 93 (the dispatch was dated Dec. 12); N.Y. *Herald,* Nov. 30, 1867, p. 5; E.J. Sherman to Butler, Dec. 6, 1867. Benjamin F. Butler Mss., Manuscripts Div., L.C.

3. Jacob William Schuckers, *The Life and Public Services of Salmon P. Chase, U.S. Senator and Governor of Ohio* (N.Y., 1874), 548; Lewis D. Campbell to Johnson, Oct. 12, 1867; Amos Layman to Johnson, Oct. 12, 1867. Andrew Johnson Mss., Manuscripts Div., L.C.; N.Y. *Times,* Nov. 8, 1867, p. 8; Daniel Richards to E.B. Washburne, Nov. 11, 13, 19, 1867; F.W. Kellogg to Washburne, Dec. 16, 1867; J.B. Stockton to Washburne, Jan. 14, 1868; James Bris-

tow to Washburne, Jan. 16, 1868. Washburne Mss., L.C.

4. N.Y. *Times,* Nov. 23, 1867, p. 1; Boston *Daily Advertiser,* Nov. 25, 1867, p. 1; Nov. 26, 1867, p. 1; N.Y. *Independent,* Nov. 30, 1867, p. 1.

5. Fogg to Washburne, Nov. 22, 1867. E.B. Washburne Mss., L.C.; Washburne to Fogg, Nov. 25, 1867. George W. Fogg Mss., New Hampshire Historical Society; Fessenden to William H. Fessenden, Nov. 23, 1867. Fessenden Mss., Bowdoin College Library, Brunswick, Me.; William Henry Smith to C.S. Hamilton, Dec. 2, 1867. Smith Mss., Ohio Historical Society; Emory Washburn to Dawes, Dec. 5, 1867. Henry L. Dawes Mss., Manuscripts Div., L.C.; Toledo *Blade,* Nov. 30, 1867, p. 2; Boston *Daily Advertiser,* Nov. 26, 1867, p. 2; Boston *Evening Journal,* Nov. 27, 1867, p. 4.

6. Garfield to Hinsdale, Dec. 5, 1867, quoted in Mary L. Hinsdale (ed.), *Garfield-Hinsdale Letters: Correspondence Between James Abram Garfield and Burke Aaron Hinsdale* (Ann Arbor, 1949), 117–18; Fessenden to Francis Fessenden, Dec. 1, 1867. Fessenden Mss., Bowdoin College Library; N.Y. *National Anti-Slavery Standard,* Dec. 14, 1867, p. 2.

7. Report on the impeachment of the president, *House Report No. 7*, 40 Cong., 1 Sess., 2.
8. *Ibid.*, 31, 39.
9. *Ibid.*, 29.
10. The entire majority report is *ibid.*, 1–59. Although historians of the Johnson impeachment traditionally have rejected the radicals' argument as faulty in law, in fact it was more consonant with precedents and legal authority of the time (as well as with the opinions of more recent analysts) than that of the conservatives. For a fuller discussion of the law of impeachment in the 1860s, see Michael Les Benedict, *The Impeachment and Trial of Andrew Johnson* (N.Y., 1973), 26–36.
11. *House Report No. 7, 40 Cong., 1 Sess.*, 61–62.
12. *Ibid.*, 105. The whole minority report runs from pages 59–105. Attractively worded, the conservative statement of the law and the case has won the endorsement of most historians, but it both rejected precedents and glossed over the true nature of Johnson's offenses, which involved an effort to use the constitutional power of the presidency to nullify the legislative authority of Congress. See Benedict, *Impeachment and Trial of Johnson*, 26–60, in which some of the material from pp. 282–83, *supra*, is put into legal context.
13. James D. Richardson (ed.), *Messages and Papers of the President of the United States* (10 vols., Washington, 1896–99), VI, 558–81.
14. The president in reality was warning Congress against any attempt to suspend him from office pending a trial on impeachment. He gave as an example of an act to which resistance would be justified one "to abolish a coordinate department of the Government." *Ibid.*, 569. On November 30 Johnson asked his Cabinet's advice on his course in case Congress should attempt to suspend his during an impeachment trial. The members agreed he should not submit. The critical voice was that of Grant, who would control the army. He told the President he would support him with military force, even at the risk of civil war. Orville H. Browning, *Diary of Orville Hickman Browning*, ed. by James G. Randall (Springfield, 1938), II, 167–68 (Nov. 30, 1867).
15. *Cong. Globe*, 40 Cong., 2 Sess., appendix, 62 (Dec. 6, 1867).
16. Boston *Evening Journal*, Dec. 4, 1867, p. 2.
17. Boutwell's speech may be found in *Cong. Globe*, 40 Cong., 2 Sess., appendix, 54–62 (Dec. 5, 6, 1867).
18. Wilson's speech may be found *ibid.*, 62–65 (Dec. 6, 1867).
19. Boston *Evening Journal*, Dec. 5, 1867, p. 2; *Daily Advertiser*, Dec. 9, 1867, p. 1; N.Y. *Independent*, Dec. 12, 1867, p. 4.
20. *Cong. Globe*, 40 Cong., 2 Sess., 64–67 (Dec. 6, 1867), 67–69 (Dec. 7, 1867).
21. Julian to Mrs. Grace Giddings Julian,

Dec 8, 1867, George W. Julian Mss., Indiana Div., Indiana State Library.
22. N.Y. *Independent*, Dec. 12, 1867, p. 4.
23. N.Y. *National Anti-Slavery Standard*, Dec. 14, 1867, p. 2. Butler to E.J. Sherman, Dec. 16, 1867. A copy of Butler's letter is endorsed on Sherman to Butler, Dec. 9, 1867. Butler Mss.
24. N.Y. *National Anti-Slavery Standard*, Dec. 14, 1867, p. 2.
25. *N.Y. Times*, Dec. 21, 1867, p. 4.
26. Fessenden to Elizabeth Fessenden Warriner, Dec. 15, 1867; Fessenden to William H. Fessenden, Dec. 7, 1867; Fessenden to Samuel Fessenden, Dec. 7, 1867; Fessenden Mss., Bowdoin College Library; John Binney to Fessenden, Dec. 9, 1867. Fessenden Mss., Manuscripts Div., L.C.
27. Marble to Doolittle, Dec. 29, 1867, quoted in "Doolittle Correspondence," *Publications of the Southern Historical Association*, XI (Jan. 1907), 6–7.
28. Ewing to Hugh Ewing, Jan. 3, 1868. Hugh Boyle Ewing Mss., Ohio Historical Society Library.
29. Hancock to Grant, Jan. 15, Feb. 7, 9, 11, 27, 1868; Hancock to Lorenzo Thomas, Feb. 27, 1868. HQA letters rec'd, R.G. 108, N.A.; Grant to Hancock, Feb. 21, 29, 1868. HQA letters sent, R.G. 108, N.A. Some of this correspondence and more not cited may be found in *House Executive Documents Nos. 172 and 209, 40 Cong., 2 Sess.*
30. S.B. Packard to Grant, March 13, 1868. HQA letters rec'd, R.G. 108, N.A.
31. Schofield to Grant, Dec. 2, 1867. John M. Schofield Mss., Manuscripts Div., L.C.; Schofield, *Forty-Six Years in the Army* (N.Y., 1897), 397.
32. Pope to Grant, Dec. 27, 1867. HQA letters rec'd, R.G. 108, N.A. The provisional government signaled its renewed recalcitrance by refusing to pay the expenses of the constitutional convention, forcing Pope to remove the governor and state treasurer. *House Exec. Doc. No. 30*, 40 Cong., 2 Sess., pp. 12–18, *passim;* Elizabeth Studley Nathans, *Losing the Peace: Georgia Republicans and Reconstruction, 1865–1871* (Boston, 1968), 70–72.
33. Walter L. Fleming, *Civil War and Reconstruction in Alabama* (N.Y., 1949), 492–500.
34. Howard to Edgar Ketchum, Dec. 30, 1867. Oliver Otis Howard Mss., Bowdoin College Library, Brunswick, Me.; Boston *Commonwealth*, Jan. 4, 1867, p. 2.
35. Blodgett to John Sherman, Dec. 30, 1867. John Sherman Mss., Manuscripts Div., L.C. This was a circular letter sent to many congressmen; Underwood to E.B. Washburne, Dec. 9, 1868. Elihu B. Washburne Mss., Manuscripts Div., L.C.
36. B.W. Norris to [the Republican congressional campaign committee], Jan. 4, 1868; Ed. I. Costello to T.L. Tullock, Jan. 17, 1868. Files of the Select Committee on Reconstruction, 40–41 Congresses, R.G. 233 (file 40A–F29.8 and

40A–F29.23, respectively); Petitions of the Mississippi, Georgia, and Arkansas state constitutional conventions. Senate Petition and Memorial file, 40 Cong., R.G. 46, N.A. Charles Buckley to E.B. Washburne, Jan. 9, 1868; George Ely to Washburne, Feb. 9, 1868; W.H. Gibbs to Washburne, Jan. 18, 1868; Underwood to Washburne, Dec. 16, 1867. Washburne Mss., L.C.; A. Sumner Powell to Stevens, Feb. 18, 1868. Thaddeus Stevens Mss., Manuscripts Div., L.C.; *House Misc. Docs. Nos. 43, 54, 57,* 40 Cong., 2 Sess. (Jan. 27, 28, and 31, respectively).

37. *Chicago Tribune,* Dec. 30, 1867, p. 2.
38. White to Washburne, Jan. 16, 1868. Washburne Mss., L.C.
39. Howe to Horace Rublee, Jan. 15, 1868. Timothy Otis Howe Mss., Wisconsin State Historical Society Library; N.Y. *National Anti-Slavery Standard,* Jan. 11, 1868, p. 1. Boston *Commonwealth,* Jan. 4, 1867, p. 2.
40. Boston *Commonwealth,* Jan. 4, 1867, p. 2.
41. *Cong. Globe,* 40 Cong., 2 Sess., 572 (Jan. 16, 1868).
42. *Ibid.,* 264–65 (Dec. 18, 1867).
43. *Ibid.,* 265–67 (Dec. 18, 1867). In the Senate, radicals tried and failed to force the conservative Judiciary committee to frame a bill similar to Ashley's. *Ibid.,* 384 (Jan. 8, 1868), 405–406 (Jan. 9, 1868).
44. *Cong. Globe,* 40 Cong., 2 Sess., 476 (Jan. 13, 1868).
45. This survey may be found in the subject file: Virginia constitutional convention in the Schofield Mss., L.C.
46. Colfax to J.C. Underwood, Jan. 7, 1868; E.B. Washburne to Underwood, Dec. 7, 1867. John C. Underwood Mss., Manuscripts Div., L.C.; Underwood to Washburne, Dec. 9, 1867. Washburne Mss., L.C.; Underwood was president of the Virginia constitutional convention.
47. C[harles] H. Lewis to Henry Wilson, Nov. 19, 1867. Henry Wilson Mss., Manuscripts Div., L.C.; Hamilton James Eckenrode, *The Political History of Virginia During the Reconstruction* (Baltimore, 1904), 64–103; Alrutheus Ambush Taylor, *The Negro in the Reconstruction of Virginia* (N.Y., 1969), 208–42; Charles H. Amber, *Francis H. Pierpont: Union War Governor of Vir-*

ginia and Father of West Virginia (Chapel Hill, 1937), 293–99; John McDonough, "James L. Schofield as Military Dictator of Reconstruction in Virginia," *Civil War History,* XV (Sept. 1969), 237–56, *passim;* Jack P. Maddex, Jr., *The Virginia Conservatives, 1867–1879: A Study in Reconstruction Politics* (Chapel Hill, 1970), 49–50, 58–59, 60.

48. Alan Conway, *The Reconstruction of Georgia* (Minneapolis, 1966), 150–51; Nathans, *Losing the Peace,* 56–68; Henry Clay Warmoth, *War, Politics and Reconstruction: Stormy Days in Louisiana* (N.Y., 1930), 51–59; John Rose Ficklen, *History of Reconstruction in Louisiana (Through 1868)* (Baltimore, 1910), 194–200; William Watson Davis, *The Civil War and Reconstruction in Florida* (N.Y., 1913), 470–77, 500–16; John Allen Meador, "Florida Political Parties, 1865–1877" (unpublished Ph.D. dissertation, University of Florida, 1964), 72–80, 90–101; Sarah Van Voorhis Woolfolk, "The Role of the Scalawag in Alabama Reconstruction" (unpublished Ph.D. dissertation, Louisiana State University, 1965), 46–82. Albion Tourgée printed a composite of the letters he received from northern Republicans urging moderation upon him as a member of the North Carolina constitutional convention, as well as the acid reply he probably wished he had written. Albion W. Tourgée, *A Fool's Errand* (N.Y., 1880), 143–44.
49. *Cong. Globe,* 40 Cong., 2 Sess., 644–46 (Jan. 20, 1868).
50. *Ibid.,* 662–64 (Jan. 21, 1868).
51. Hassaurek to Sherman, Jan. 27, 1868. John Sherman Mss., L.C.; *Chicago Tribune,* Jan. 30, 1868, p. 2; John Binney to Fessenden, Feb. 5, 1868. Fessenden Mss., L.C.; Hinsdale to Garfield, Jan. 20, 1868, quoted in Hinsdale (ed.), *Garfield-Hinsdale Letters,* 127–30; Boston *Commonwealth,* Jan. 11, 1868, p. 2; N.Y. *Nation,* Jan. 16, 1868, p. 41.
52. William T. to Ellen Ewing Sherman, Jan. 23, 1868. W.T. Sherman Mss., University of Notre Dame Archives (quoted in Mark A. DeWolfe Howe (ed.), *Home Letters of General Sherman* [N.Y., 1909], 367–68).
53. *Cong. Globe,* 40 Cong., 2 Sess., 595 (Jan. 17, 1868).
54. *Ibid.*

15. IMPEACHMENT AND TRIAL

1. Moore notes, Feb. 17, 1868. Andrew Johnson Mss., Manuscripts Div., L.C.; Jerome B. Stillson to Samuel J. Tilden, Feb. 12, 1868. S.L.M. Barlow Mss., Huntington Library.
2. I have discussed the confusing origins of the Tenure of Office act more fully in Michael Les Benedict, *The Impeachment and Trial of Andrew Johnson* (N.Y., 1973), 105–108.
3. Benjamin P. Thomas and Harold M. Hyman, *Stanton: The Life and Times of Lincoln's Secretary of War* (N.Y., 1962), 589.

4. For the best accounts of the role of the Supreme Court during Reconstruction, see Stanley I. Kutler, *Judicial Power and Reconstruction Politics* (Chicago and London, 1968) and Charles Fairman, *History of the Supreme Court of the United States: Volume VI, Reconstruction and Reunion, 1864–88: Part One* (N.Y., 1971).
5. The correspondence in which Grant and Johnson debated what actually occurred at his meeting is reprinted in Edward McPherson (ed.), *The Political History of the United States of America, Dur-*

ing the Period of Reconstruction . . ., (3rd edn, Washington, 1880), 283–88. See also the written testimony of Johnson's cabinet in support of the president's contentions, *ibid.*, 289–92.

6. Sherman was so confident of this that it is probable that he discussed his plan with his brother, Senator John Sherman. Before the Senate voted on accepting Stanton's removal, Thomas Ewing, Jr. told Johnson that he had been assured that Cox's nomination would settle the matter. Ewing to Johnson, [Jan. 12 (?), 1868], Johnson Mss., L.C.

7. W.T. Sherman to Ellen Ewing Sherman, Jan. 13, 1868. W.T. Sherman Mss., Notre Dame University Archives. The letter is excerpted in Mark A. DeWolfe Howe (ed.), *Home Letters of General Sherman* (N.Y., 1909), 364–65.

8. Fawn M. Brodie, *Thaddeus Stevens, Scourge of the South* (N.Y., 1959), 333.

9. W.T. Sherman to Johnson, Jan. 31, Feb. 14, 1868, quoted in Rachel Sherman Thorndike (ed.), *The Sherman Letters: Correspondence Between General and Senator Sherman from 1837 to 1891* (N.Y., 1894), 300–304; Gideon Welles, *Diary of Gideon Welles—Secretary of the Navy Under Lincoln and Johnson* (3 vols., Boston and N.Y., 1911), III, 271–72 (Feb. 5, 1868); W.T. Sherman to Ellen Ewing Sherman, Jan. 28, 30, 1868. W.T. Sherman Mss., University of Notre Dame Archives; Sherman to Thomas Ewing, Sr., Feb. 13, 14, 1868, quoted in Howe (ed.), *Home Letters of General Sherman,* 370–74; Johnson to Grant, Feb. 6, 1868; Johnson to Sherman, Feb. 19, 1868. HQA letters rec'd, R.G. 108, N.A.; W. T. Sherman to John Sherman, Feb. 14, 1868; W.T. Sherman to Grant, Feb. 14, 1868; W.T. Sherman to John Sherman (telegram), Feb. 14, 1868, quoted in Thorndike (ed.), *Sherman Letters,* 305–306.

10. N.Y. *Herald,* June 22, 1868, p. 5; *Cong. Globe,* 40 Cong., 2 Sess., 1326–27 (Feb. 21, 1868). On February 10, the House had transferred the impeachment question from the Judiciary to the Reconstruction committee, where Bingham had smothered it. See *ibid.,* 1087–88 (Feb. 10, 1868); Bingham to Mrs. Bingham, Feb. 16, 1868. John A. Bingham Mss., Ohio Historical Society Library.

11. E.L. Stanton to E.M. Stanton, Feb. 21, 1868. Edwin M. Stanton Mss., Manuscripts Div., L.C.; Sumner to Stanton, Feb. 21, 1868, quoted in E.D. Townshend, *Anecdotes of the Civil War* (N.Y., 1884), 133n. In the Stanton papers at the Library of Congress are messages of February 27 from Boutwell, Howard Wilson, Yates, and Thayer.

12. *Senate Executive Journal,* XVI, 170–72 (Feb. 21, 1868).

13. Shelby Moore Cullom, *Fifty Years of Public Service: Personal Recollections of Shelby M. Cullom, Senior Senator from Illinois* (N.Y., 1911), 154.

14. Fessenden to Elizabeth Fessenden Warriner, Feb. 22, 1868. William Pitt Fessenden Mss., Bowdoin College Library, Brunswick, Me.

15. Schenck to Sally Schenck, Feb. 21, 1868. Robert C. Schenck Mss., Rutherford B. Hayes Library; *Cong. Globe,* 40 Cong., 2 Sess., 1386 (Feb. 24, 1868). Republicans of all shades of radicalism and conservatism echoed Blair's remarks. See Michael Les Benedict, "A New Look at the Impeachment of Andrew Johnson," *Political Science Quarterly,* LXXXVIII (Dec. 1973), 366–67.

16. Allan Nevins and Milton Halsey Thomas (eds.), *The Diary of George Templeton Strong* (4 vols., N.Y., 1952), III, 191 (Feb. 23, 1868); Welles, *Diary,* III, 315 (March 17, 1868).

17. *Cong. Globe,* 40 Cong., 2 Sess., 1402 (Feb. 24, 1868).

18. For a more detailed account of these maneuverings, see Benedict, *Impeachment of Johnson,* 115–25.

19. More than one third of the Senate voted against the pro-conviction position on all the roll calls listed in Groups 2 through 5 of the main scale of Appendix IX (pp. 394–95), and on all those in Groups 1 through 3 of the subscale.

20. Boston *Evening Journal,* April 18, 1868, p. 4.

21. Fessenden to Elizabeth Fessenden Warriner, Dec. 15, 1867; Fessenden to Francis Fessenden, Dec. 20, 1868. Fessenden Mss., Bowdoin College Library; Boston *Traveller,* May 9, 1868, p. 1.

22. Grimes was locked in struggle with his colleague, Harlan, who not surprisingly tendered cordial support to the impeachment. Fessenden's great rival in Maine was Hannibal Hamlin, whom Johnson had replaced as Vice President in 1864 and who had worked for impeachment since the summer of 1866.

23. N.Y. *Independent,* May 21, 1868, p. 1.

24. Boston *Daily Advertiser,* June 17, 1867, p. 2.

25. *Chicago Tribune,* April 21, 1868, p. 2; N.Y. *Evening Post,* April 25, 1868, p. 2.

26. Alley to Butler, May 2, 1868. Benjamin F. Butler Mss., Manuscripts Div., L.C.

27. Garfield to Rhodes, May 7, 1868, quoted in Theodore Clarke Smith, *The Life and Letters of James Abram Garfield* (2 vols., New Haven, 1925), I, 425.

28. *Chicago Tribune,* May 6, 1868, p. 2; George F. Edmunds, "Ex-Senator Edmunds on Reconstruction and Impeachment," *Century Magazine,* LXXXV (April 1913), 863–64; Hans L. Trefousse, "Ben Wade and the Failure of the Impeachment of Johnson," *Bulletin of the Historical and Philosophical Society of Ohio,* XVIII (Oct. 1960), 241–52. See also Fessenden's letter in response to an invitation to be guest of honor at a Boston dinner, published in the Boston *Daily Advertiser,* June 30, 1868, p. 2, where he manifested a hostility to office seekers—"men ready to jump into places to be made vacant, as they hoped and believed, for their benefit"—similar to that Garfield ascribed to conservative Republicans who feared Wade's administration.

29. Atkinson to Sumner, March 4, 1868. Charles Sumner Mss., Houghton Li-

brary, Harvard University, Cambridge, Mass.

30. Dana to Mrs. Sara Dana, March, 22, 1868. Richard Henry Dana Mss., Massachusetts Historical Society; Fessenden to William H. Fessenden, May 3, 1868. Fessenden Mss., Bowdoin College Library.

31. Williams in U.S. Congreess, *The Impeachment and Trial of Andrew Johnson, President of the United States, Before the Senate of the United States, on Impeachment by the House of Representatives for High Crimes and Misdemeanors* (3 vols., Washington, 1868), II, 260 (April 28, 1868); Evarts, *ibid.,* 278 (April 28, 1868). For a fuller discussion of the arguments made during the trial, see Benedict, *Impeachment of Johnson,* 143–67.

32. Irving Brant, *Impeachment: Trials and Errors* (N.Y., 1972), 133–54.

33. Colfax to J.R. Young, April 16, 1868. Jonathan Russell Young Mss., Manuscripts Div., L.C.; Benjamin Perley Poore to W.W. Clapp. William Warland Clapp Mss., Houghton Library, Harvard University, Cambridge, Massachusetts; Julian to Mrs. Laura Giddings Julian, May 5, 1868. George W. Julian Mss., Indiana Div., Indiana State Library.

34. Boston *Daily Advertiser,* May 16, 1868, p. 2.

35. James Lee McDonough and William T. Alderson (eds.), "Republican Politics and the Impeachment of Andrew Johnson," *East Tennessee Historical Quarterly,* XXVI (Summer 1967), 177–83; Moore notes, April 23, 24, May 1, 1868. Johnson Mss.; Welles, *Diary,* III, 364–65 (May 20, 1868), 409–10 (July 21, 1868).

36. Orville H. Browning, *Diary of Orville Hickman Browning,* ed. by James G. Randall (Springfield, 1938), II, 195 (May 5, 1868); James D. Richardson (ed.), *A Compilation of the Messages and Papers of the Presidents of the United States* (10 vols., Washington, 1896–99), VI, 632.

37. Samuel Sullivan Cox, *Union—Disunion —Reunion: Three Decades of Federal Legislation, 1855 to 1885* (Providence, 1886), 592–94. By May 14, Henderson assured Republican representatives that Johnson intended to enforce the Reconstruction laws if acquitted. *House Report No. 75,* 40 Cong., 2 Sess., 18.

38. *Chicago Tribune,* May 14, 1868, p. 2.

39. Boston *Evening Journal,* May 8, 1868, p. 4; *Trial of Andrew Johnson,* II, 475–79 (May 7, 1868).

40. Boston *Evening Journal,* May 12, 1868, p. 4; Edmund G. Ross, *History of the Impeachment of Andrew Johnson, President of the United States, by the House of Representatives, and His Trial by the Senate, for High Crimes and Misdemeanors in Office, 1868* (Santa Fe, 1896), 131–33.

41. Cox, *Three Decades of Federal Legislation,* 592–94; Thomas Graham Belden and Marva Robins Belden, *So Fell the Angels* (Boston, 1956), 187–94; *House Report No. 75,* 40 Cong., 2

Sess., 1–5. Butler argued that the "Chase movement" was really a cover for operations to bribe senators into voting against conviction, but his evidence is scanty, although it is clear a bribe was offered to Senator Pomeroy and that he was very tempted to accept it. *Ibid.,* 8–12; Moore notes, March 18, 1868. Johnson Mss.

42. A copy of Schenck's circular, dated May 12, 1868, is in the Schenck Mss.

43. Morrill to Fessenden, May 10, 1868. Fessenden Mss., Bowdoin College Library. The letter is quoted in Francis Fessenden, *Life and Public Services of William Pitt Fessenden* (2 vols., Boston and N.Y., 1907), II, 205–207.

44. *House Report No. 75,* 40 Cong., 2 Sess., 15–16, 30–32; William S. King to E.B. Washburne, May 12, 1868. Elihu B. Washburne Mss., L.C.; [?] to Butler, May 12, 1868. Butler Mss.; Boston *Evening Journal,* May 13, 1868, p. 4; May 16, 1868, p. 4. The Cincinnati *Commercial's* correspondent reported that the changed cabinet would include Groesbeck as secretary of the treasury, Evarts as secretary of state, Jacob D. Cox as secretary of war, and John D. Catron as secretary of the interior. Reported in the *N.Y. Tribune,* May 20, 1868, p. 4.

45. *N.Y. Evening Post,* May 14, 1868, p. 2. The *Post* reprinted editorials critical of the Republican pressure from newspapers around the country. *Ibid.,* May 15, 1868, p. 2; Boston *Daily Advertiser,* May 15, 1868, p. 2.

46. Cincinnati *Commercial,* May 16, 1868, p. 6; May 13, 1868; p. 4; May 21, 1868, p. 4; *Chicago Tribune,* May 11, 1868, p. 2; *N.Y. Nation,* May 14, 1868, pp. 384–85; John Murray Forbes to William Pitt Fessenden, May 23, 1868, quoted in Sarah F. Hughes (ed.), *Letters and Recollections of John Murray Forbes* (2 vols., Boston, 1899), II, 164–65; Henry J. Bowditch to Sumner, May 18, 1868; F.V. Balch to Sumner, May 18, 1868; Edward Atkinson to Sumner, June 1, 1868. Charles Sumner Mss., Houghton Library, Harvard University, Cambridge, Mass.

47. *N.Y. Nation,* May 28, 1868, p. 421; Cincinnati *Commercial,* May 19, 1868, p. 1; May 22, 1868, pp. 1, 4; *Chicago Tribune,* May 20, 1868, p. 1; Horace White to C.E. Norton, May 20, 1868. Norton Mss.

48. *N.Y. Herald,* May 29, 1868, p. 3; *N.Y. Evening Post,* May 28, 1868, p. 4; May 29, 1868, p. 2.

49. Boston *Evening Journal,* May 23, 1868, p. 4; *N.Y. Nation,* May 21, 1868, p. 402; William Frank Zornow, *Kansas: A History of the Jayhawk State* (Norman, Okla., 1957), 120; George A. Boeck, "Senator Grimes and the Iowa Press, 1867–1868," *Mid-America,* XLVIII (July 1966), 159, 161; R.W. Bayles, "Peter G. Van Winkle and Waitman T. Willey in the Impeachment Trial of Andrew Johnson," *West Virginia History,* XIII (Jan. 1952), 86–87; Charles A. Jellison, *Fessenden of Maine: Civil War Senator* (Syracuse, 1962), 250–51; Mark Krug, *Lyman*

Trumbull: Conservative Radical (N.Y., 1965), 269–72. Historians have recognized that the "martyr" legend has been exaggerated since the publication of Ralph J. Roske's "The Seven Martyrs?" *American Historical Review,* LXIV (Jan. 1959), 323–30.

50. Fessenden's letter was reprinted in the Boston *Daily Advertiser,* June 30, 1868, p. 2.

51. Grimes to Henry W. Starr, Mar. 18, 1869, quoted in William Salter, *The Life of James W. Grimes, Governor of Iowa, 1854–1858; Senator of the United States, 1859–1869* (N.Y., 1876), 367.

16. RESTORING THE STATES . . . AND STATE RIGHTS

1. See pp. 241–42, *supra.*
2. *Cong. Globe,* 40 Cong., 2 Sess., 265–67 (Dec. 18, 1867); H.M. Turner to B.F. Butler, Feb. 2, 1868 (and Butler's endorsement). Benjamin F. Butler Mss., Manuscripts Div., L.C.
3. Of 170,631 registered voters, 69,807 had voted for the constitution and 1005 against it. *House Exec. Doc. No. 284,* 40 Cong., 2 Sess.
4. *Cong. Globe,* 40 Cong., 2 Sess., 1417 (Feb. 25, 1868).
5. *N.Y. Tribune,* May 12, 1868, p. 4.
6. In Florida, Louisiana, North Carolina and South Carolina, the new constitutions won the approval of an absolute majority of the registered voters, so that even if every person who had voted against the constitutions in those states had refused to vote, the constitutions would have been ratified under the original Reconstruction laws. In Arkansas only 37.8 percent of the registered voters had approved the constitution; in Georgia, 46.5. *House Exec. Doc. Nos. 278* and *284,* 40 Cong., 2 Sess.; *Senate Exec. Doc. No. 53,* 40 Cong., 2 Sess. None of these documents give the election results in Florida. Trumbull offered them in the Senate, *Cong. Globe,* 40 Cong., 2 Sess., 2858 (June 5, 1868).
7. The Florida Republican party had been rent by a factional struggle between followers of Dean Richards, Liberty Billings, and William U. Sanders, those of Colonel O.B. Hart, and those of Colonel Thomas W. Osborn. In their efforts to win control of the party Richards, Billings, and Saunders appealed to black Republicans by advocating radical measures and fanning distrust of the southern-born Hart. In the constitutional convention held in compliance with the Reconstruction acts, the Richards-Billings faction maintained a narrow majority over a Union Conservative (i.e., Democratic) and conservative Republican minority of which Harrison Reed, a postal agent appointed by the Johnson administration, became the leader. In an effort to check the radicals' activities, the conservative coalition withdrew from the constitutional convention, depriving it of a quorum. The military forces refused to force the bolters back into the convention, and the radicals were forced to frame a constitution without the presence of a quorum of the convention. On February 10, the bolters slipped into the convention hall, and at their behest the military forced two radicals to join them, making a quorum. The army then protected the new convention from the outraged radicals as it elected Osborn president and framed a second, more conservative constitution. After some confusion, the commanding general fashioned a "compromise," by which Richards, Billings, and Saunders were expelled from the convention and the rest of the radicals forced to remain. With the cooperation of the armed forces, the conservative coalition succeeded in winning ratification for their constitution over radical opposition. In the election for state officers the coalition collapsed, however, and conservative Republicans succeeded in electing Reed governor over a Conservative (i.e., Democratic) opponent. William Watson Davis, *The Civil War and Reconstruction in Florida* (N.Y., 1913), 470–76, 483–516, 522–27; Jerrell H. Schofner, "Political Reconstruction in Florida," *Florida Historical Quarterly,* XLV (Oct. 1966), 145–52; Merlin G. Cox, "Military Reconstruction in Florida," *ibid.,* XLVI (Jan. 1868), 228–33.
8. Drake in *Cong. Globe,* 40 Cong., 2 Sess., 2629 (May 28, 1868); Dawes, *ibid.* at 2213–14 (March 28, 1868); Howe, *ibid.* at 2744–45 (June 1, 1868). See also the comments of Representative Benjamin F. Loan, *ibid.,* 1819–20 (March 10, 1868); Thomas Williams, *ibid.,* 2909–10 (March 28, 1868); Senator George F. Edmunds, *ibid.,* 2662–63 (May 29, 1868), 3009 (June 10, 1868); William M. Stewart, *ibid.,* 2862 (June 5, 1868); Richard Yates, *ibid.,* 2868 (June 5, 1868); Representative Benjamin F. Butler, *ibid.,* 3092 (June 12, 1868).
9. *Ibid.,* 1818 (March 11, 1868).
10. Representative Benjamin F. Loan, *ibid.,* 1819–20 (March 11, 1868).
11. *Ibid.,* 2137 (March 26, 1868); C. Tucker to Stevens, March 21, 1868; J.L. Peasington to Stevens, March 22, 1868. Thaddeus Stevens Mss., Manuscripts Div., L.C.
12. *Cong. Globe,* 40 Cong., 2 Sess., 2138 (March 26, 1868).
13. *Ibid.,* 2214 (March 28, 1868).
14. *Ibid.,* 2216 (March 28, 1868).
15. *Ibid.,* 2211 (March 29, 1868).
16. This proposal was embodied in an amendment to the Alabama Restoration bill suggested by Representative Rufus P. Spalding, quoted *ibid.,* 2216 (March 28, 1868). Alabamans had voted for state officers at the same time they voted on the ratification question. Since the Democrats had refused to participate in the election in an effort to prevent ratification, Republican state candi-

dates won overwhelming majorities of the votes cast.

17. *Ibid.,* 2215 (March 28, 1868).
18. *Ibid.,* 2216 (March 28, 1868).
19. The bill was read *ibid.,* 2390 (May 8, 1868).
20. Trumbull, *ibid.,* 2601–2602 (May 27, 1868); Conkling, *ibid.,* 2604 (May 27, 1868); Sherman, *ibid.,* 2607 (May 27, 1868). Even Stewart, who strongly advocated the conditions in the Senate, finally had to concede, "I do not pretend to say that the insertion of this declaration in the bill will alter either the constitution of the State or of the General Government. It is a notice, however, to these parties; it is a compact; it is a declaration of principle, which has generally been respected." *Ibid.,* 2605 (May 27, 1868).
21. Baker, *ibid.,* 2391; Spalding, *ibid.,* 2397; Blaine, *ibid.,* 2391 (all May 8, 1868).
22. *Ibid.,* 2399 (May 8, 1868). Of the Republicans only the conservatives Baker and Spalding and the radical Thomas Williams opposed passage. Bingham did not vote.
23. *Ibid.,* 2412–13 (May 11, 1868), 2445–56 (May 13, 1868), 2461–65 (May 14, 1868).
24. *Ibid.,* 2744–45 (June 1, 1868).
25. *Ibid.,* 2603 (May 27, 1868).
26. *Ibid.,* 2699 (May 30, 1868); Conkling, *ibid.,* 2663–67 (May 29, 1868); Frelinghuysen, *ibid.,* 2692 (May 30, 1868); Fowler, *ibid.,* 2743–44 (June 1, 1868).
27. *Ibid.,* 3024–25 (June 10, 1868).
28. *Ibid.,* 2701 (May 30, 1868). The amendment came up a second time when the bill was reported to the Senate from the committee of the whole, a parliamentary procedure. This time it lost 18–22, with two opponents of fundamental conditions absent. *Ibid.,* 2749–50 (June 1, 1869).
29. *Ibid.,* 2748, 2750 (June 1, 1868).

30. The new version is given *ibid.,* 2901 (June 6, 1868).
31. *Ibid.,* 2867–68 (June 5, 1868).
32. *Ibid.,* 3029 (June 10, 1868). Besides the long wrangle over restoring Alabama to the bill, Republicans discussed several specific provisions of the state constitutions involving water rights and stay laws, and answered Democratic attacks upon the entire Republican Reconstruction policy.
33. The movement to strike Florida from the restoration bill was led by Illinois representative Farnsworth, a personal and political friend of Daniel Richards, the leader of the defeated radical faction of the Florida Republican party. But archradical Benjamin F. Butler defended the triumphant Reed-Hart-Osborn faction, dividing radical forces in the House. *Ibid.,* 3092–96 (June 12, 1868). The House agreed to the Senate's version of the bill *ibid.,* 3096 (June 12, 1868).
34. James G. Blaine, *Twenty Years of Congress: From Lincoln to Garfield with a Review of the Events which Led to the Political Revolution of 1860* (2 vols., Norwich, Conn., 1884–86), II, 388; Schurz, "The Road to Peace—A Solid, Durable Peace," in Carl Schurz, *Speeches, Correspondence, and Political Papers of Carl Schurz,* ed. by Frederic Bancroft (6 vols., N.Y., 1913), I, 419.
35. *Chicago Tribune,* Aug. 20, 1868, p. 2; Tilton in the N.Y. *Independent,* July 16, 1868, p. 4.
36. *Chicago Evening Journal,* Nov. 10, 1868, p. 2. See also the N.Y. *Nation,* Oct. 29, 1868, p. 344; *N.Y. Tribune,* Nov. 4, 1868, p. 2; "The Beginning of the End," *American Freedman,* III (Dec. 1868), 2–3; "The Moral Significance of the Republican Triumph," *Atlantic Monthly,* XXIII (Jan. 1869), 124–28.

17. Epilogue: The Fifteenth Amendment

1. William Gillette, *The Right to Vote: Politics and the Passage of the Fifteenth Amendment* (Baltimore, 1965); La-Wanda and John H. Cox, "Negro Suffrage and Republican Politics: The Problem of Motivation in Reconstruction Historiography," *Journal of Southern History,* XXXIII (Aug. 1967), 303–30; Glenn M. Linden, "A Note on Negro Suffrage and Republican Politics," *ibid.,* XXXVI (Aug. 1970), 411–20.
2. *Cong. Globe,* 40 Cong., 3 Sess., 560 (Jan. 23, 1869).
3. *Ibid.,* 672 (Jan. 29, 1869).
4. *Ibid.,* 708 (Jan. 29, 1869).
5. Stevens to [Charles E. Spencer], June 24, 1868; Butler to ? (draft), April 8, 1868. Benjamin F. Butler Mss., Manuscripts Div., L.C.; A.H. Hood to Stevens, May 23, 1868. Thaddeus Stevens Mss., Manuscripts Div., L.C.; James G. Blaine, *Twenty Years of Congress: From Lincoln to Garfield with a Review of the Events Which Led to the Political Revolution of 1860* (2 vols., Norwich, Conn.,

1884–86), II, 388; Letter from Carl Roeser, published in the Boston *Commonwealth,* June 6, 1868, p. 1; *ibid.,* June 6, 1868, p. 2; Michael Les Benedict, "Grant and the Decline of Republican Radicalism, 1867–1868," unpublished paper delivered at the conference "Ulysses S. Grant in Perspective," De-Kalb, Illinois, April 27, 1972.
6. George W. Julian, *Political Recollections, 1840–1872* (Chicago, 1884), 319–20; Stevens's comments, reported in the N.Y. *Herald,* July 20, 1868, p. 5; *ibid.,* June 24, 1868, p. 5; William C. Howells to W.H. Smith, June 29, 1868. William H. Smith Mss., Ohio Historical Society; Boston *Daily Advertiser,* July 10, 1868, p. 2; Bartlett in the N.Y. *Independent,* July 23, 1868, p. 1.
7. Besides simply pointing to the possible impact of black voters on state elections, Gillette asserted that Republicans in Congress consistently referred to the Amendment's impact on the North during the debates on its passage. Gillette,

The Right to Vote, 46–50. But this is a matter of interpretation. Gillette sees arguments pertaining to the North as the most important elements of the debate; another reader might disagree. In analyzing the discussions I found Republican speakers clearly referred to the Amendment's impact in the North twelve times and in the South nine times. But three of the speakers who specifically referred to the enfranchisement of northern blacks indicated that the primary purpose of that enfranchisement was to quiet southern white complaints that the North was discriminating against the South in giving black men votes there while resisting the measure at home. Boutwell in *Cong. Globe*, 40 Cong., 3 Sess., 561 (Jan. 23, 1869); Simon Corley, *ibid.*, appendix, 95 (Jan. 28, 1869); W. Jasper Blackburn, *ibid.*, appendix, 241–42 (Jan. 30, 1869).

The only solid piece of evidence Gillette gives of the essentially political motivation behind the Fifteenth Amendment is a letter from Thaddeus Stevens to his friend and ally, Edward McPherson, Aug. 16, 1867: "We must establish the doctrine of National jurisdiction over all the States in State matters of the Franchise, or we shall finally be ruined—We must thus bridle Penna. Ohio Ind. et cetera, or the South, *being in*, we shall drift into democracy." Gillette, *The Right to Vote*, 35. But this letter is susceptible of quite a different interpretation than Gillette gives it. It was written long before the Fifteenth Amendment was put upon its passage (Dec. 1868–Feb. 1869), and may have referred to Republican fears that Reconstruction was not secure in the southern states. Stevens may have meant this: to obviate the danger that southern whites, once restored to the Union, might with impunity repudiate black suffrage, the right to regulate suffrage must be lodged in the national government. The northern states would have to accept such national control ("We must bridle Penna. . . .") in order to safeguard against black disfranchisement in the South. With that evidence rendered questionable, little remains to support Gillette's thesis but carefully culled political justifications for an essentially moral act. See *ibid.*, 48–49. Despite disagreements in interpretation of Republicans' motives, however, all historians owe Gillette their thanks for his careful and detailed analysis of the amendment's ratification.

8. Allen W. Trelease, *White Terror: The Ku Klux Klan Conspiracy and Southern Reconstruction* (N.Y. and other cities, 1971), 111–85; John Welch Patton, *Unionism and Reconstruction in Tennessee* (Chapel Hill, 1934), 142–43; Thomas S. Staples, *Reconstruction in Arkansas, 1862–1874* (N.Y., 1923), 260–65; William Watson Davis, *The Civil War and Reconstruction in Florida* (N.Y., 1913), 540–41; John Rose Ficklen, *History of Reconstruction in Louisiana (Through 1868)*, (Baltimore, 1910), 225–31.

9. Alan Conway, *The Reconstruction of Georgia* (Minneapolis, 1967), 162–68, 171–81.

10. *Cong. Globe*, 40 Cong., 3 Sess., 171 (Jan. 5, 1869). A copy of this bill is in the Benjamin F. Butler papers in the Library of Congress. Although its title referred to Georgia, the text applied to several southern states.

11. *Ibid.*, 6–7, 10 (Dec. 7, 1869).

12. *Ibid.*, 2 (Dec. 7, 1869).

13. *Ibid.*

14. *Ibid.*, 43 (Dec. 10, 1868), 568 (Jan. 25, 1868).

15. *Ibid.*, 972, 978 (Feb. 8, 1869).

16. Bullock to Butler, Feb. 7, 1869. Butler Mss.

17. *Cong. Globe*, 40 Cong., 3 Sess., 1150 (Feb. 10, 1869).

18. *Ibid.*, 1045 (Feb. 10, 1869).

19. *Ibid.*, 1057, 1059 (Feb. 10, 869).

20. *Ibid.*, 1062 (Feb. 10, 1869).

21. Richmond *Radical*, Feb. 18, 1869, p. 134.

22. *Cong. Globe*, 40 Cong., 3 Sess., 1062–67 (Feb. 10, 1869).

23. Colfax to Washburne, Feb. 11, 1869. Elihu B. Washburne Mss., Massachusetts Historical Society.

24. The House version is quoted in the *Cong. Globe*, 40 Cong., 3 Sess., 286 (Jan. 11, 1869) and the Senate version *ibid.*, 379 (Jan. 15, 1869). The same battle which has raged among constitutional analysts regarding the scope of the Fourteenth Amendment pertains also to the Fifteenth. See footnote 31, p. 421, *supra*.

25. *N.Y. Tribune*, Dec. 1, 1868, p. 4.

26. *Cong. Globe*, 40 Cong., 3 Sess., 978 (Feb. 8, 1869).

27. *Ibid.*, 862 (Feb. 3, 1869). See also Howard, *ibid.*, 999 (Feb. 8, 1869); Representative William Lawrence, *ibid.*, 1226 (Feb. 25, 1869); Hamilton Ward, *ibid.*, 724 (Jan. 29, 1869); Senator Morton, *ibid.*, 863 (Feb. 3, 1869); Williams, *ibid.*, 900 (Feb. 5, 1869); Abbott, *ibid.*, 981 (Feb. 8, 1869).

28. *Ibid.*, 1041 (Feb. 9, 1869). For arguments that Congress possessed the power to oversee state voting regulations, see the comments of Representative William A. Pile, *ibid.*, 725 (Jan. 29, 1869); M.C. Hamilton, *ibid.*, appendix, 100 (Jan. 29, 1869); Broomall, *ibid.*, appendix, 102 (Jan. 30, 1869); Senator Sumner, *ibid.*, 902–904 (Feb. 5, 1869); Ross, *ibid.*, 982 (Feb. 8, 1869); Yates, *ibid.*, 2 Sess., 2746 (June 1, 1868).

29. Representatives Thomas A. Jenckes, George W. Julian, and James M. Ashley and Senator George H. Williams all proposed amendments providing broader protection. *Ibid.*, 3 Sess., 728 (Jan. 29, 1868), 491 (Jan. 21, 1869); House Resolutions 371 and 381 in the House Resolution file, 40 Congress, R.G. 233, N.A.

30. *Cong. Globe*, 40 Cong., 3 Sess., 639 (Jan. 27, 1869). Schenck announced that this amendment was offered with the support of a large number of Ohio representatives. *Ibid.*, 743 (Jan. 30, 1869).

31. *Ibid.*, appendix, 97 (Jan. 29, 1869).

32. *Ibid.*, 744 (Jan. 30, 1869).

33. *Ibid.*, 1029, 1040 (Feb. 9, 1869).

34. *Ibid.,* 1226 (Feb. 15, 1869).
35. Wilson, *ibid.,* 1291 (Feb. 17, 1869).
36. *Ibid.,* 1295 (Feb. 17, 1869).
37. *Ibid.,* 1299 (Feb. 17, 1869).
38. *Ibid.,* 1300 (Feb. 17, 1869).
39. *Ibid.,* 1318 (Feb. 17, 1869).
40. *Ibid.,* 1428 (Feb. 20, 1869).
41. *Ibid.,* 1481 (Feb. 23, 1869).

42. *Ibid.,* 1563–64 (Feb. 25, 1869).
43. Pomeroy, *ibid.,* 1623 and Edmunds, 1624 (Feb. 26, 1869).
44. *Ibid.,* 1626 (Wilson), 1628–29 (Sawyer; Feb. 26, 1869).
45. *Ibid.,* 1641 (Feb. 26, 1869).
46. *N.Y. Tribune,* Nov. 4, 1868, p. 2.

Bibliography

GOVERNMENT PAPERS AND DOCUMENTS

UNPUBLISHED

United States, Adjutant-General Letters Received (Main series), 1861–1870. Record Group 94, National Archives, Washington, D.C.

United States. Congress. House of Representatives. Bill file, 38–40 Congresses. R.G. 233, N.A.

United States. Congress. House of Representatives. Joint Resolution file, 38–40 Congresses. R.G. 233, N.A.

United States. Congress. House of Representatives. Committee on Elections. Minutes. 38–40 Congresses. R.G. 233, N.A.

United States. Congress. House of Representatives. Committee on the Judiciary. Minutes. 38–40 Congresses. R.G. 233, N.A.

United States. Congress. House of Representatives. Committee on the Judiciary. Papers, memorials, and petitions. 38–39 Congresses. R.G. 233, N.A.

United States. Congress. House of Representatives. Select Committee of the Managers of Impeachment, 40 Congress. Journal. R.G. 233, N.A.

United States. Congress. House of Representatives. Select Committee on Alleged Private Meetings of Members of the House with a View to a Corrupt Bargain with the President, 39 Congress. Papers. R.G. 233, N.A.

United States. Congress. House of Representatives. Select Committee on Emancipation, 38 Congress. Papers. R.G. 233, N.A.

United States. Congress. House of Representatives. Select Committee on Freedmen's Affairs, 39–40 Congresses. Papers. R.G. 233, N.A.

United States. Congress. House of Representatives. Select Committee on the Rebellious States, 38 Congress. Petitions and memorials. R.G. 233, N.A.

United States. Congress. House of Representatives. Select Committee on Reconstruction, 39 Congress. Papers. R.G. 233, N.A. (These evidently are papers referred to the Joint Committee on Reconstruction but filed under this heading.)

United States. Congress. House of Representatives. Select Committee on Reconstruction, 40–41 Congresses. Papers. R.G. 233, N.A.

United States. Congress. Joint Committee on Reconstruction. Papers, 1866–71. R.G. 128, N.A.

United States. Congress. Senate. Bill file, 38–39 Congresses. R.G. 46, N.A.

United States. Congress. Senate. Joint Resolution file, 39 Congress. R.G. 46, N.A.

United States. Congress. Senate. Petition and Memorial file, 40 Congress. R.G. 46, N.A.

United States. Congress. Senate. Committee on the Judiciary. Papers, 38–42 Congresses. R.G. 46, N.A.

United States. Congress. Senate. Committee on the Judiciary. Petitions and memorials, 39 Congress. R.G. 46, N.A.

United States. Department of Justice. Attorney-General's Official Letterbooks. R.G. 60, N.A.

United States. Department of Justice. Executive and Congressional Letterbooks. R.G. 60, N.A.

United States. Department of Justice. Instruction Books. R.G. 60, N.A.

United States. Department of Justice. Letters Received, 1865–73. R.G. 60, N.A.

United States. Department of Justice. Letters Received from United States Attorneys. R.G. 60, N.A.

United States. Department of Justice. Letters Received from United States Marshals. R.G. 60, N.A.

United States. Department of War. Headquarters of the Army. Letters Received. R.G. 108, N.A.

United States. Department of War. Headquarters of the Army. Letters Sent. R.G. 108, N.A.

PUBLISHED

Congressional Globe

House Executive Documents, 38–40 Congresses

House Miscellaneous Documents, 38–40 Congresses

House Reports, 38–40 Congresses

Senate Executive Documents, 38–40 Congresses

Senate Miscellaneous Documents, 38–40 Congresses

Senate Reports, 38–40 Congresses

United States Department of Justice. *Opinions of the Attorneys General of the United States.*

United States. Congress. Joint Committee on Reconstruction. *The Journal of the Joint Committee of Fifteen on Reconstruction, 39 Congress, 1865–1867.* Ed. by Benjamin B. Kendrick. Studies in History, Economics, and Public Law edited by the Faculty of Political Science of Columbia University, Vol. LXII. N.Y.: Columbia University Press, 1914.

United States. Congress. Senate. *Journal of the Executive Proceedings of the Senate of the United States of America.*

United States. Congress. Senate. *Trial of Andrew Johnson, President of the United States, Before the Senate of the United States, on Impeachment by the House of Representatives, for High Crimes and Misdemeanors.* 3 vols. Washington: Government Printing Office, 1868.

United States. President. *A Compilation of the Messages and Papers of the Presidents of the United States.* Ed. by James D. Richardson. 10 vols. Washington: Government Printing Office, 1896–99.

PRIMARY SOURCES

UNPUBLISHED MANUSCRIPT COLLECTIONS

John Albion Andrew Mss. Massachusetts Historical Society.

Edward Atkinson Mss. Massachusetts Historical Society.

Conrad Baker Mss. William Henry Smith Library of the Indiana State Historical Society.

George Bancroft Mss. Massachusetts Historical Society.

Nathaniel Banks Mss. Illinois State Historical Library.

———. Manuscript Division, Library of Congress.

S.L.M. Barlow Mss. Huntington Library.

Warner Bateman Mss. Western Reserve Historical Society.

Henry W. Bellows Mss. Massachusetts Historical Society.

John A. Bingham Mss. Ohio Historical Society.
James G. Blaine Mss. Manuscripts Division, Library of Congress.
Montgomery Blair Mss. Lilly Library, Indiana University.
Henry P. Bromwell Mss. Manuscripts Division, Library of Congress.
Orville H. Browning Mss. Illinois Historical Survey, University of Illinois.
———. Illinois State Historical Library.
Orestes Brownson Mss. Archives, Notre Dame University.
William Cullen Bryant and Parke Godwin collection. New York Public Library.
Benjamin F. Butler Mss. Manuscripts Division, Library of Congress.
Simon Cameron Mss. Manuscripts Division, Library of Congress.
Lewis D. Campbell Mss. Ohio Historical Society.
William Eaton Chandler Mss. New Hampshire Historical Society.
Zachariah Chandler Mss. Manuscripts Division, Library of Congress.
Salmon P. Chase Mss. Cincinnati Historical Society.
———. Manuscripts Division, Library of Congress.
William Warland Clapp Mss. Houghton Library, Harvard University.
———. Manuscripts Division, Library of Congress.
Daniel Clark Mss. New Hampshire Historical Society.
John Henry Clifford Mss. Massachusetts Historical Society.
Schuyler Colfax Mss. Indiana Division, Indiana State Library.
———. Smith Library, Indiana State Historical Society.
———. Rutherford B. Hayes Library (a collection made up of copies of correspon-
    dence from various collections at the Hayes Library).
———. Manuscript Division, Library of Congress.
———. Rush Rhees Library, University of Rochester.
James R. Comly Mss. Ohio Historical Society.
Roscoe Conkling Mss. Manuscripts Division, Library of Congress.
John Covode Mss. Manuscripts Division, Library of Congress.
Jacob D. Cox Mss. Oberlin College Library.
Will Cumback Mss. Lilly Library, Indiana University.
Benjamin Robbins Curtis Mss. Manuscripts Division, Library of Congress.
George William Curtis Mss. Houghton Library, Harvard University.
Richard Henry Dana Mss. Massachusetts Historical Society.
David Davis Mss. Illinois State Historical Library.
Henry L. Dawes Mss. Manuscripts Division, Library of Congress.
Frederick M. Dearborn Mss. Houghton Library, Harvard University.
Ignatius Donnelly Mss. Minnesota Historical Society.
James Rood Doolittle Mss. Manuscripts Division, Library of Congress.
———. Wisconsin State Historical Society Library.
———. New York Public Library.
Frederick Douglass Mss. Headquarters of the National Capitol Parks—East.
Douglass, Morrison, Walker Mss. Cincinnati Historical Society.
S.F.DuPont Mss. Eleutherian Mills Historical Library.
Thomas J. Durant Mss. New York Historical Society.
William Maxwell Evarts Mss. Manuscripts Division, Library of Congress.
Hugh Boyle Ewing Mss. Ohio Historical Society.
Philemon B. Ewing Mss. Ohio Historical Society.
Thomas Ewing, Sr. Mss. Ohio Historical Society.
Ewing Family Mss. Manuscripts Division, Library of Congress.
Jesse W. Fell Mss. Illinois Historical Survey, University of Illinois.
Reuben E. Fenton Mss. New York State Library.
William Pitt Fessenden Mss. Bowdoin College Library.
———. Manuscripts Division, Library of Congress.
Hamilton Fish Mss. Manuscripts Division, Library of Congress.
Flagg Family Mss. Illinois Historical Survey, University of Illinois.
George W. Fogg Mss. New Hampshire Historical Society.
LaFayette S. Foster Mss. Massachusetts Historical Society.
Joseph S. Fowler Mss. Manuscripts Division, Library of Congress.
James A. Garfield Mss. Manuscripts Division, Library of Congress.

———. Ohio Historical Society.

John Hatch George Mss. New Hampshire Historical Society.

Ulysses S. Grant-Elihu B. Washburne Correspondence. Illinois State Historical Library.

Horace Greeley Mss. Manuscripts Division, Library of Congress.

Horace Greeley-Schuyler Colfax Correspondence. New York Public Library.

Murat Halstead Mss. Cincinnati Historical Society.

John Hanna Mss. Lilly Library, Indiana University.

Friedrich Hassaurek Mss. Ohio Historical Society.

John H. Hay Mss. Manuscripts Division, Library of Congress.

Rutherford B. Hayes Mss. Rutherford B. Hayes Library.

Thomas Wentworth Higginson Mss. Houghton Library, Harvard University.

Houghton Library Autograph File. Houghton Library, Harvard University.

Oliver Otis Howard Mss. Bowdoin College Library.

Timothy Otis Howe Mss. Wisconsin State Historical Society Library.

Julia Ward Howe and Samuel Gridley Howe Mss. Houghton Library, Harvard University.

Andrew Johnson Mss. Manuscripts Division, Library of Congress.

George C. Jones Mss. New York Public Library.

George W. Julian Mss. Indiana Division, Indiana State Library.

Elisha Keyes Mss. Wisconsin State Historical Society Library.

Nathan Kimball Mss. Lilly Library, Indiana University.

Henry S. Lane Mss. Smith Library. Indiana State Historical Society.

———. Indiana Division, Indiana State Library.

———. Lilly Library, Indiana University.

Amos A. Lawrence Mss. Massachusetts Historical Society.

Francis Lieber Mss. Huntington Library.

———. Manuscripts Division, Library of Congress.

Robert Todd Lincoln Mss. Manuscripts Division, Library of Congress.

Alexander Long Mss. Cincinna : Historical Society.

Henry Wadsworth Longfellow Mss. Houghton Library, Harvard University.

Hugh McCulloch Mss. Lilly Library, Indiana University.

———. Manuscripts Division, Library of Congress.

James Miller McKim-William Lloyd Garrison Mss. New York Public Library.

Edward McPherson Mss. Manuscripts Division, Library of Congress.

Margaret S. Maloney Collection. New York Public Library.

William G. Moore Mss. Manuscripts Division, Library of Congress.

Edwin D. Morgan Mss. New York State Library.

Oliver P. Morton Mss. Indiana Division, Indiana State Library.

———. Smith Library, Indiana State Historical Society.

Otis Norcross Mss. Massachusetts Historical Society.

Charles Eliot Norton Mss. Houghton Library, Harvard University.

Ohio Historical Society Individual Letters. Division of Archives and Manuscripts, Ohio Historical Society.

William W. Orme Mss. Illinois Historical Survey, University of Illinois.

Godlove S. Orth Mss. Indiana Division, Indiana State Library.

John Gorham Palfrey Mss. Houghton Library, Harvard University.

George W. Patterson Mss. Rush Rhees Library, University of Rochester.

Daniel D. Pratt Mss. Indiana Division, Indiana State Library.

John M. Palmer Mss. Illinois State Historical Library.

Charles A. Ray Mss. Chicago Historical Society Library.

Henry J. Raymond Mss. New York Public Library.

Whitelaw Reid Mss. Manuscripts Division, Library of Congress.

Horace Rublee Mss. Wisconsin State Historical Society Library.

Robert C. Schenck Mss. Rutherford B. Hayes Library.

John M. Schofield Mss. Manuscripts Division, Library of Congress.

James W. Schuckers Mss. Manuscripts Division, Library of Congress.

William Henry Seward Mss. Rush Rhees Library, University of Rochester.

Horatio Seymour Mss. New York State Library.

John Sherman Mss. Manuscripts Division, Library of Congress.
William T. Sherman Mss. Archives, Notre Dame University.
William Henry Smith Mss. Ohio Historical Society.
————. Smith Library, Indiana State Historical Society.
Edwin M. Stanton Mss. Manuscripts Division, Library of Congress.
Thaddeus Stevens Mss. Manuscripts Division, Library of Congress.
John D. Strong Mss. Illinois State Historical Library.
Charles Sumner Mss. Houghton Library, Harvard University.
Charles Sumner-Storer Correspondence. Cincinnati Historical Society.
Richard W. Thompson Mss. Indiana Division, Indiana State Library.
————. Lilly Library, Indiana University.
Samuel J. Tilden Mss. New York Public Library.
Lyman Trumbull Mss. Illinois State Historical Library.
————. Manuscripts Division, Library of Congress.
Jonathan B. Turner Mss. Illinois Historical Survey, University of Illinois.
John C. Underwood Mss. Manuscripts Division, Library of Congress.
Benjamin F. Wade Mss. Manuscripts Division, Library of Congress.
Benjamin F. Wade-Storer Correspondence, Cincinnati Historical Society.
Amasa Walker Mss. Massachusetts Historical Society.
Lew Wallace Mss. Smith Library, Indiana State Historical Society.
Israel Washburn Mss. Manuscripts Division, Library of Congress.
Elihu B. Washburne Mss. Manuscripts Division, Library of Congress.
————. Massachusetts Historical Society.
Thurlow Weed Mss. Rush Rhees Library, University of Rochester.
Gideon Welles Mss. New York Public Library.
John Wentworth Mss. Chicago Historical Society.
Henry Wilson Mss. Manuscripts Division, Library of Congress.
Robert C. Winthrop Mss. Massachusetts Historical Society.
Horatio Woodman Mss. Massachusetts Historical Society.
Charles J. Worden Mss. Indiana Division, Indiana State Library.
Richard Yates Mss. Illinois State Historical Library.
Jonathan R. Young Mss. Manuscripts Division, Library of Congress.

PUBLISHED COLLECTIONS OF WORKS, DIARIES, LETTERS, MEMOIRS, SEMI-AUTOBIOGRAPHICAL FICTION

Adams, Charles Francis *et al. A Cycle of Adams Letters, 1861–1865*. Ed. by Chauncey Worthington Ford. Boston and N.Y.: Houghton Mifflin Company, 1920.
Ashley, James M. *Duplicate Copy of the Souvenir from the Afro-American League of Tennessee to Hon. James M. Ashley of Ohio*. Philadelphia: Publishing House of the A.M.E. Church, 1894.
Bates, Edward. *Diary of Edward Bates, 1859–1866*. Ed. by Howard K. Beale. Volume IV of the *Annual Report of the American Historical Association, 1930*. Washington: Government Printing Office, 1933.
Bigelow, John. *Retrospections of an Active Life*. 4 vols. N.Y.: The Baker and Taylor Co., 1909.
Blaine, James G. *Political Discussions, Legislative, Diplomatic, and Peculiar, 1856–1886*. Norwich, Conn.: Henry Bill Publishing Company, 1887.
————. *Twenty Years of Congress: From Lincoln to Garfield with a Review of the Events Which Led to the Political Revolution of 1860*. 2 vols. Norwich, Conn.: Henry Bill Publishing Company, 1884–86.
Boutwell, George S. *Reminiscences of Sixty Years in Public Affairs*. N. Y.: McClure, Phillips and Co., 1902.
————. *Speeches and Papers Relating to the Rebellion and the Overthrow of Slavery*. 2 vols. Boston: Little, Brown and Company, 1867.

Breen, Matthew P. *Thirty Years of New York Politics.* N.Y.: privately published, 1899.

Bright, John. "Letters to Charles Sumner, 1861–1872." *Massachusetts Historical Society Proceedings,* XLVI (Oct. 1912), 93–164.

Brockway, Beman. *Autobiography of Beman Brockway.* Watertown, N.Y.: Daily Times Printing and Publishing House, 1891.

Brooks, Noah. *Washington in Lincoln's Time.* Ed. by Herbert Mitgang. N.Y. and Toronto: Rinehart and Company, 1958.

Browning, Orville Hickman. *Diary of Orville Hickman Browning.* Ed. by James G. Randall. Collections of the Illinois State Historical Library. 2 vols. Springfield, Ill.: Illinois State Historical Library, 1938.

Butler, Benjamin F. *Butler's Book: Autobiography and Personal Reminiscences of Major-General Benjamin F. Butler.* Boston: A.M. Thayer, 1892.

Carpenter, F.B. *The Inner Life of Abraham Lincoln: Six Months at the White House.* N.Y.: Hurd and Houghton, 1868.

Chambrun, Adolphe de. *Impressions of Lincoln and the Civil War: A Foreigner's Account.* N.Y.: Random House, 1952.

Chase, Salmon P. *Diary and Correspondence of Salmon P. Chase.* Ed. by Edward G. Bourne *et al.* Volume II of the *Annual Report of the American Historical Association of the Year 1902.* Washington: Government Printing Office, 1903.

Chittenden, L.E. *Recollections of President Lincoln and His Administration.* N.Y.: Harper and Bros., 1891.

Cole, Cornelius. *The Memoirs of Cornelius Cole, Ex-Senator of the United States from California.* N.Y.: McLoughlin Brothers, 1908.

Conness, John. *Some of the Men and Measures of the War and Reconstruction Period: Address Before the Mercantile Library Association, Mar. 4, 1882.* Boston: N. Sawyer and Son, 1882.

Conway, Moncure D. *Autobiography, Memoirs, and Experiences.* 2 vols. Boston: Houghton Mifflin Company, 1904.

Cox, Samuel Sullivan. *Union—Disunion—Reunion. Three Decades of Federal Legislation. 1855 to 1885.* Providence, R.I.: J.A. & R.A. Reid, 1886.

Crawford, Samuel. *Kansas in the Sixties.* Chicago: A.C. McClurg, 1911.

Cullom, Shelby Moore. *Fifty Years of Public Service: Personal Recollections of Shelby M. Cullom, Senior Senator from Illinois.* N.Y.: A.C. McClurg, 1911.

Curtis, Benjamin Robbins. *A Memoir of Benjamin Robbins Curtis, LL.D., with Some of his Professional and Miscellaneous Writings.* 2 vols. Boston: Little, Brown and Company, 1879.

Davis, Henry Winter. *Speeches and Addresses Delivered in the Congress of the United States, and on Several Public Occasions.* N.Y.: Harper Brothers, 1867.

Dawes, Henry L. "Recollections of Stanton Under Johnson." *Atlantic Monthly,* LXXXIV (Oct. 1894), 494–504.

Depew, Chauncey M. *My Memories of Eighty Years.* N.Y.: Charles Scribner's Sons, 1924.

Dodge, Grenville. *Personal Recollections of President Abraham Lincoln, General Ulysses S. Grant, William T. Sherman.* Council Bluffs, Iowa: Monarch Printing Company, 1914.

Doolittle, James Rood. "Doolittle Correspondence." *Publications of the Southern History Association,* XI (Jan. 1907), 6–9, (March 1907), 94–105.

Edmunds, George F. "Ex-Senator Edmunds on Reconstruction and Impeachment." *Century Magazine,* LXXXV (April 1913), 863–64.

Forbes, John Murray. *Letters and Recollections of John Murray Forbes.* Ed. by Sarah F. Hughes. 2 vols. Boston: Houghton Mifflin Company, 1899.

Forney, John W. *Anecdotes of Public Men.* 2 vols. N.Y.: Harper and Brothers., 1873, 1881.

Garfield, James Abram. *The Diary of James A. Garfield.* Ed. by Frederick D. Williams and Harry James Brown. 2 vols. East Lansing, Mich.: Michigan State University Press, 1967.

————— and Burke A. Hinsdale. *Garfield-Hinsdale Letters: Correspondence Between James Abram Garfield and Burke Aaron Hinsdale,* ed. by Mary L. Hinsdale. Ann Arbor: University of Michigan Press, 1949.

—————. *The Works of James Abram Garfield,* ed. by Burke Aaron Hinsdale. 2 vols. Boston: James R. Osgood and Company, 1883.

Grant, Ulysses Simpson. *General Grant's Letters to a Friend, 1861–1880.* Ed. by James Grant Wilson. N.Y. and Boston: T.Y. Crowell, 1897.

—————. *Personal Memoirs of U.S. Grant.* 2 vols. N.Y.: Charles L. Webster, 1885–86.

Grinnell, Josiah Bushnell. *Men and Events of Forty Years: Autobiographical Reminiscences of an Active Career from 1850 to 1890.* Boston: D. Lothrop, 1891.

Haven, Gilbert. *National Sermons: Sermons, Speeches and Letters on Slavery and Its War From the Passage of the Fugitive Slave Bill to the Election of President Grant.* Boston: Lee and Shepard, 1869.

Hay, John. *Letters of John Hay and Extracts from his Diary.* 3 vols. Washington: printed, but not published, 1908.

—————. *Lincoln and the Civil War in the Diaries and Letters of John Hay.* Ed. by Tyler Dennet. N.Y.: Dodd, Mead & Co., 1939.

Hayes, Rutherford B. *Diary and Letters of Rutherford B. Hayes, Nineteenth President of the United States.* Ed. by Charles Richard Williams. 5 vols. Columbus, Ohio: Ohio State Archaeological and Historical Society, 1922–26.

Henderson, John B. "Emancipation and Impeachment." *Century Magazine,* LXXXV (Dec. 1912), 196–209.

Hoar, George F. *Autobiography of Seventy Years.* 2 vols. N.Y.: Charles Scribner's Sons, 1908.

Holden, William W. *Memoirs of W.W. Holden.* The John Lawson Monographs of the Trinity College Historical Society. Durham, N.C.: The Seeman Printery, 1911.

Howard, Oliver Otis. *Autobiography of Oliver Otis Howard.* 2 vols. N.Y.: Baker and Taylor, 1908.

Howells, William Dean. *Years of My Youth.* N.Y.: Harper & Bros., 1916.

Hudson, William C. *Random Recollections of an Old Political Reporter.* N.Y.: Cupples and Leon Co., 1911.

Julian, George W. "George W. Julian's Journal—Assassination of Lincoln." *Indiana Magazine of History,* XI (Dec. 1915), 324–37.

—————. *Political Recollections, 1840–1872.* Chicago: Jansen, McClurg and Co., 1884.

—————. *Speeches on Political Questions* [1850–1868], N.Y.: Hurd and Houghton; Cambridge, Mass.: Riverside Press, 1872.

Koerner, Gustave. *Memoirs of Gustave Koerner, 1809–1896: Life-sketches Written at the Suggestion of his Children.* Ed. by Thomas J. McCormack. 2 vols. Cedar Rapids, Iowa: Torch Press, 1909.

Lincoln, Abraham. *The Collected Works of Abraham Lincoln.* Ed. by Roy P. Basler. 9 vols. New Brunswick, N.J.: Rutgers University Press, 1953.

Lodge, Henry Cabot. *Early Memories.* N.Y.: Charles Scribner's Sons, 1913.

Lowell, James Russell. *The Complete Writings of James Russell Lowell.* 16 vols. Cambridge, Mass.: Riverside Press, 1904.

—————. *Letters of James Russell Lowell.* Ed. by Charles Eliot Norton. N.Y.: Harper and Brothers, 1895 [1893].

Lynch, John R. *The Facts of Reconstruction.* The American Negro: His History and Literature. N.Y.: Arno Press and the N.Y. Times, 1968.

McClure, A[lexander] K. *Abraham Lincoln and Men of War-Times: Some Personal Recollections of War and Politics During the Lincoln Administration.* 3rd edn. Philadelphia: Times Publishing Company, 1892.

—————. *Colonel Alexander K. McClure's Recollections of Half a Century.* Salem, Mass.: Salem Press Company, 1902.

McCulloch, Hugh. *Addresses, Speeches, Lectures, and Letters Upon Various Subjects.* Washington: William H. Lepley, 1891.

—————. *Men and Measures of Half a Century.* N.Y.: Charles Scribner's Sons, 1888.

McDonald, David. "Hoosier Justice: The Journal of David McDonald, 1864–68."

Ed. by Donald O. Dewey. *Indiana Magazine of History,* LXII (Sept. 1966), 175–232.

Moore, William G. "Notes of Colonel W.G. Moore, Private Secretary to President Johnson, 1866–1868." *American Historical Review,* XIX (Oct. 1913), 98–132.

Norton, Charles Eliot. *Letters of Charles Eliot Norton.* Ed. by Sara Morton and Mark A. DeWolfe Howe. 2 vols. Boston and N.Y.: Houghton Mifflin Company, 1913.

Owen, Robert Dale. "Political Results from the Varioloid." *Atlantic Monthly,* XXXV (June, 1875), 660–70.

Palmer, John M. *Personal Recollections of John M. Palmer: The Story of an Earnest Life.* Cincinnati: Clarke Co., 1901.

Pierce, Edward L. *Enfranchisement and Citizenship: Addresses and Papers.* Ed. by A.W. Stevens. Boston: Roberts Bros., 1896.

Platt, Thomas Collier. *The Autobiography of Thomas Collier Platt.* Ed. by Louis J. Lang. N.Y.: B.W. Dodge and Co., 1910.

Poore, Ben Perley. *Perley's Reminiscences of Sixty Years in the National Metropolis.* 2 vols. Philadelphia, Chicago, Kansas City: Hubbard Brothers, 1886.

Pruyn, John V.L. "The Impeachment of Andrew Johnson: A Contemporary View." Ed. by Jerome Mushkat. *New York History,* XLVIII (July 1967), 275–86.

Raymond, Henry J. "Extracts the Journal of Henry J. Raymond." *Scribner's Monthly,* XIX (Nov. 1879), 57–61, (Jan. 1880), 419–24, (March 1880), 703–10, XX (June 1880), 275–80.

———. "Henry J. Raymond on the Republican Caucuses of July 1866." Ed. by John A. Krout. *American Historical Review,* XXXIII (July 1928), 835–42.

Rice, Allen Thorndike (ed). *Reminiscences of Abraham Lincoln by Distinguished Men of His Time.* N.Y.: North American Publishing Company, 1888.

Riddle, Albert Gallatin. *Recollections of War Times: Reminiscences of Men and Events in Washington, 1860–1865.* Cleveland: W. Williams, 1887.

Ross, Edmund G. *History of the Impeachment of Andrew Johnson, President of the United States, by the House of Representatives, and His Trial by the Senate for High Crimes and Misdemeanors in Office, 1868.* Santa Fe, N.M.: New Mexican Printing Company, 1896.

Schofield, John. *Forty-Six Years in the Army.* N.Y.: The Century Company, 1897.

Schurz, Carl. *Intimate Letters of Carl Schurz, 1841–1869.* Ed. by Joseph Schafer. Publications of the State Historical Society of Wisconsin, XXX. Madison: Wisconsin State Historical Society, 1928.

———. *Reminiscences of Carl Schurz.* 3 vols. N.Y.: Doubleday, Page Co., 1908–1909; N.Y.: McClure, 1908.

———. *Speeches, Correspondence, and Political Papers of Carl Schurz,* Ed. by Frederic Bancroft. 6 vols. N.Y.: G.P. Putnam's Sons, 1913.

Seward, William H. *The Works of William H. Seward.* Ed. by George E. Baker. 5 vols. Boston: Houghton Mifflin Company, 1884.

Sheridan, Philip H. *Personal Memoirs of P.H. Sheridan.* 2 vols. N.Y.: Charles L. Webster and Co., 1888.

Sherman, John. *Recollections of Forty Years in the House, Senate, and Cabinet: An Autobiography.* 2 vols. N.Y.: The Werner Company, 1895.

Sherman, John and William Tecumseh Sherman. *The Sherman Letters: Correspondence Between General and Senator Sherman from 1837 to 1891.* Ed. by Rachel Sherman Thorndike. N.Y.: Charles Scribner's Sons, 1894.

Sherman, William Tecumseh. *Home Letters of General Sherman.* Ed. by Mark A. DeWolfe Howe. N.Y.: Charles Scribner's Sons, 1909.

Strong, George Templeton. *Diary of George Templeton Strong.* Ed. by Allan Nevins and Milton Halsey Thomas. 4 vols. N.Y.: The Macmillan Company, 1952.

Sumner, Charles. *The Works of Charles Sumner.* 15 vols. Boston: Lee and Shepard, 1870–83.

Tourgée, Albion W. *A Fool's Errand* N.Y.: Fords, Howard and Hulbert, 1880.

Warmoth, Henry Clay. *War, Politics and Reconstruction: Stormy Days in Louisiana.* N.Y.: The Macmillan Company, 1930.

Weed, Thurlow. *Autobiography of Thurlow Weed*. Ed. by Harriet A. Weed. Boston: Houghton Mifflin Company, 1883.

Welles, Gideon. *Civil War and Reconstruction: Selected Essays*. Comp. by Albert Mordell. N.Y.: Twyne Publishers, 1959.

——. *Diary of Gideon Welles—Secretary of the Navy Under Lincoln and Johnson*. 3 vols. Boston and N.Y.: Houghton Mifflin Company, 1911.

Wilson, James. *The Works of James Wilson*. Ed. by Robert Green McCloskey. The John Harvard Library. 2 vols. Cambridge Mass.: The Belknap Press of Harvard University Press, 1967.

ARTICLES, BOOKS, PAMPHLETS, AND SPEECHES

ON CONTEMPORARY POLITICS

Agnew, Daniel. *Our National Constitution: Its Adaption to a State of War or Insurrection*. 2nd edn. Philadelphia: C. Sherman and Son, 1863.

The American Annual Cyclopedia and Register of Important Events. N.Y.: D. Appleton and Co., 1863–1870.

Andrew, John A. *Valedictory Address to the Two Branches of the Legislature of Massachusetts, Jan. 4, 1866*. Boston: Wright and Potter, 1866.

Banks, Nathaniel P. *An Address Delivered at the Customhouse, New Orleans, on the Fourth of July, 1865*. New Orleans: n.p. [1865].

"The Conspiracy at Washington." *Atlantic Monthly*, XX (Nov. 1867), 633–38.

Blaine, James G. *et al.* "Ought the Negro to be Disfranchised? Ought He to Have Been Enfranchised?" *North American Review*, CXXVIII (March 1879), 225–83.

Boutwell, George S. "The Impeachment of Andrew Johnson. From the Standpoint of One of the Managers of the Impeachment Trial." *McClure's Magazine*, XIV (Dec. 1899), 171–82.

Brown, B[enjamin] Gratz. *Freedom and Franchise Inseparable: Letter of Hon. B. Gratz Brown*. Washington: Gideon and Bros. [1864].

Brownson, Orestes A. *The American Republic: Its Constitution, Tendencies, and Destiny*. N.Y.: O'Shea, 1865.

Carpenter, Matthew H. *Letter on Martial Law*. N.p., [1865].

——. *The Powers of Congress: The Constitutionality of Its Acts on Reconstruction. Speech of Hon. Matt. H. Carpenter, at Chicago, Ill., Aug. 12, 1868*. Washington: Union Republican National Committee, 1868.

Carroll, Anna Ella. *The Relation of the National Government to the Revolted Citizens Defined. . . .* Washington: Henry Polkinhorn, 1862.

——. *The War Powers of the General Government*. Washington: Henry Polkinhorn, 1862.

Cincinnati *Commercial* (ed.). *Speeches of the Campaign of 1866, in the States of Ohio, Indiana and Kentucky*. Cincinnati: Cincinnati *Commercial*, 1866.

Clemenceau, Georges Eugène Benjamin. *American Reconstruction*. Ed. by Fernand Baldensperger. Trans. by Margaret Mac Veagh. N.Y. and Toronto: L. Mac Veagh, Dial Press, and Longmans, Green, and Company, 1926.

Conkling, Alfred. *The Powers of the Executive Department of the Government of the United States*. Albany, N.Y.: Weare C. Little, 1866.

Conkling, Roscoe. *Congress and the President: The Political Problem of 1866. Speech of Hon. Roscoe Conkling Delivered at Mechanic's Hall, Utica, Sept. 13, 1866*. [Utica, N.Y.: Roberts, 1866].

Cox, Jacob D. *Speech of Jacob Cox at Columbus, Ohio, August 21, 1866*. Columbus: Glenn & Heide, 1866.

Crosby, Alpheus. *The Present Position of the Seceded States, and the Rights and Duties of the General Government in Respect to Them: An Address to the Phi Beta Kappa Society of Dartmouth College, July 19, 1865*. Boston: Geo. C. Rand and Avery, 1865.

Curtis, B[enjamin] R. *Executive Power*. Boston: Little, Brown and Company, 1862.

Davis, Woodbury. "Political Problems, and Conditions of Peace." *Atlantic Monthly*, XII (Aug. 1863), 252–59.

Drake, Charles Daniel. *Radicalism Vindicated. Letter of Senator Drake, of Missouri, to Senator Johnson, of Maryland*. Washington: Union Republican Congressional Committee, 1867.

Dwight, Theodore. "Trial by Impeachment." *American Law Register*, XV, old series (March 1867), 257–83.

Ellis, Charles Mayo. "The Causes for Which a President Can Be Impeached." *Atlantic Monthly*, XIX (Jan. 1867), 88–92.

R.F.F. "Right to Confiscate and Emancipate." *Monthly Law Reporter*, XXIV (Sept. 1862), 645–56.

Fisher, Sidney George. *Trial of the Constitution*. Philadelphia: J.B. Lippincott, 1862.

Friedel, Frank (ed.). *Union Pamphlets of the Civil War, 1861–1865*. 2 vols. Cambridge, Mass.: Belknap Press of Harvard University Press, 1967.

Gasparin, Count A. de. *Reconstruction, A Letter to President Johnson*. N.Y.: Loyal Publishing Society, 1865.

Grosvenor, William M. "The Law of Conquest the True Basis of Reconstruction." *New Englander*, XXIV (Jan., 1865), 111–35.

Higginson, Thomas Wentworth. "Fair Play the Best Policy." *Atlantic Monthly*, XV (May 1865), 623–31.

Home Reception for Governor Yates, Jacksonville, [Ill.] *Jan. 17, 1865*. Springfield, Ill.: Baker and Phillips, 1865.

Howe, Timothy Otis. *An Address Delivered Before the Wisconsin State Teachers' Association, at its Thirteenth Annual Meeting at Whitewater, Wednesday Evening, Aug. 2, 1865*. Madison: C.M. Campbell, 1865.

Hurd, John C. "Theories of Reconstruction." *American Law Review*, I (Jan. 1867), 238–64.

———. *The Theory of Our National Existence as Shown by the Action of the Government of the United States Since 1861*. Boston: Little, Brown and Company, 1881.

Johnson, Andrew. *Life and Speeches of President Andrew Johnson*. Ed. by G.W. Bacon. London: n.p., n.d.

[Johnson, Reverdy]. *The Dangerous Condition of the Country, the Causes Which Have Led to It, and the Duty of the People. By a Marylander*. Baltimore: The Sun Book and Job Printing Establishment, 1867.

———. *A Further Consideration of the Dangerous Condition of the Country, the Causes Which Have Led to It, and the Duty of the People. By a Marylander*. Baltimore: The Sun Job Printing Establishment, 1867.

L.C.K. "The Power of the President to Grant a General Amnesty." *American Law Register*, VIII, new series (Sept. 1869), 513–32, (Oct. 1869), 577–89.

Kelley, William D. *Speeches, Addresses, and Letters on Industrial and Financial Questions*. Philadelphia: H.C. Baird, 1872.

Larned, Edwin Channing. *The Great Conflict, What Has Been Gained, & What Remains to be Done: Oration at Aurora, Ill., on the 4th of July, 1865*. Chicago: H.A. Newcombe and Co., 1865.

Lawrence, William. "Law of Impeachment." *American Law Register*, XV, old series (Sept. 1867), 641–80.

[Lieber, Francis]. *Amendments of the Constitution, Submitted to the Consideration of the American People*. N.Y.: Loyal Publication Society, 1865.

———. *What Is Our Constitution,—League, Pact, or Government?: Two Lectures on the Constitution of the United States Concluding a Discourse on the Modern State, Delivered in the Law School of Columbia College, During the Winter of 1860 and 1861*. N.Y.: Board of Trustees of Columbia University, 1861.

Loring, George Bailey. *The Present Crisis: Speech . . . at Lyceum Hall, Salem, April 26, 1865; Dr. Loring's Letter to the Salem Gazette, on Reconstruction*. South Danvers, Mass.: Wizard, 1865.

Lothrop, S.K. *Oration Delivered Before the City Authorities of Boston, on the Fourth of July, 1866*. Boston: Alfred Mudge and Son, 1866.

Lowrey, Grosvenor P. *The Commander-in-Chief; A Defence Upon Legal Grounds of the Proclamation of Emancipation; and an Answer to Ex-Judge Curtis' Pamphlet, Entitled "Executive Power."* N.Y.: G.P. Putnam, 1862.

"The Moral Significance of the Republican Triumph." *Atlantic Monthly*, XXIII (Jan. 1869), 124–28.

Morgan, Edwin D. *Remarks of the Hon. Edwin D. Morgan, on Being Called to Preside at the Meeting Held at Cooper Institute, N.Y. City, on the Evening of Oct. 16th, 1867, to Ratify the Republican State Nominations*. Washington: Union Republican Congressional Committee, 1867.

Morse, Sidney H. "Impeachment." *The Radical*, II (Feb. 1867), 373–75.

Morton, Oliver P. *Speech of Governor Oliver P. Morton at the Union State Convention Held at Indianapolis, Ind., February 23, 1864*. N.p. [1864].

Parker, Joel. *Habeas Corpus and Martial Law: A Review of the Opinion of Chief Justice Taney, in the Case of John Merryman*. Philadelphia: John Campbell, 1862.

――――. *Revolution and Reconstruction: Two Lectures Delivered in the Law School of Harvard College in Jan., 1865, and Jan., 1866*. N.Y.: Hurd and Houghton, 1866.

――――. *The Right of Secession: A Review of the Message of Jefferson Davis to the Congress of the Confederate States*. Cambridge, Mass.: Welch, Bigelow and Company, 1861.

――――. *The Three Powers of Government. The Origin of the United States; and the Status of the Southern States, on the Suppression of the Rebellion. The Three Dangers of the Republic*. N.Y.: Hurd and Houghton, 1869.

――――. *The War Powers of Congress, and of the President: An Address Delivered Before the National Club of Salem, March 13, 1863*. Cambridge, Mass.: H.O. Houghton, 1863.

Phillips, Wendell. *Speeches, Lectures, and Letters*. Boston: Lee and Shepard, 1900.

Rickoff, Andrew Jackson. "A National Bureau of Education." *American Journal of Education*, XVI (June 1866), 299–310.

"The Rightful Power of Congress to Confiscate and Emancipate." *Monthly Law Reporter*, XXIV (May 1862), 469–93.

Schurz, Carl. "The True Problem." *Atlantic Monthly*, XIX (March 1867), 371–78.

Smith, Gerrit. *No More Punishment of the South. A Letter to Professor Taylor Lewis, Nov. 6, 1866*. Petersboro, N. Y.: n.p., 1866.

[Stearns, George Luther (comp.)]. *The Equality of All Men Before the Law Claimed and Defended; in Speeches by William D. Kelley, Wendell Phillips, and Frederick Douglass, and Letters from Elizur Wright and Wm. Heighton*. Boston: Rand and Avery, 1865.

Stevens, Thaddeus. *Reconstruction: Speech of the Hon. Thaddeus Stevens, Delivered in the City of Lancaster, Sept. 7, 1865*. Lancaster, Pa.: Examiner and Herald Print Co., 1865.

Stewart, William M. *Reminiscences of Senator William M. Stewart*. Ed. by George Rothwell Brown. N.Y.: Neale Publishing Company, 1908.

Truman, Benjamin Cummings. "Anecdotes of Andrew Johnson." *Century Magazine*, LXXV (Jan. 1913), 435–40.

Trumbull, Lyman. *Argument of Hon. Lyman Trumbull in the Supreme Court of the United States, Mar. 4, 1868, in the Matter of* Ex Parte WILLIAM H. McCARDLE, *Appellant*. Washington: Government Printing Office, 1868.

Union Congressional Executive Committee. *Review of the Decision of the U.S. Supreme Court in the Cases of Lambdin P. Milligan and Others, the Indiana Conspirators*. Washington, Chronicle Printing, 1867.

Vaughan, D.W. "Conservatism." *The Radical*, I (April 1866), 474–78.

Washburne, Israel, Jr. "Power and Duty of Congress on Suffrage." *Universalist Quarterly Review*, XXVI (Jan. 1869), 46–64.

Whipple, E.P. "The President and His Accomplices." *Atlantic Monthly*, XVI (Nov. 1866), 634–43.

——. "The President and Congress." *Atlantic Monthly,* XVI (April 1866), 500–509.

——. "Reconstruction and Negro Suffrage." *Atlantic Monthly,* XVI (Aug. 1865), 238–47.

White, E.B. "National Bureau of Education." *American Journal of Education,* XVI (March 1866), 177–86.

Whiting, William. *Address of Hon. William Whiting, Before the Boston Highlands Grant Club, August 5, 1868.* Boston: Wright and Potter, 1868.

——. *The Return of Rebellious States to the Union: A Letter from Hon. Wm. Whiting to the Union League of Philadelphia.* Philadelphia: C. Sherman, Son and Company, 1864.

——. *The War Powers of the President and the Legislative Powers of Congress, in Relation to Rebellion, Treason, and Slavery.* 4th edn. Boston: Shorey, 1863.

——. *War Powers Under the Constitution of the United States.* 43rd edn. Boston: Little, Brown and Company, 1871.

Wickersham, J.P. "Education as an Element in Reconstruction." *American Journal of Education,* XVI (June 1866), 283–97.

Yates, Richard. *Address of the Hon. Richard Yates, Delivered at the Grand Ovation Tendered Him by the Citizens of Jacksonville, In Approval of His Course in the 39th Congress. Sept. 15, 1866.* Jacksonville: Journal Steam Power Press, 1866.

——. *Speech of the Hon. Richard Yates delivered at Elgin, Ill. on the 4th of July, A.D. 1865.* Jacksonville: Ironmonger and Mendenhall, [1865].

——. *Speech of Senator Yates at Springfield, Illinois, August 22, 1868.* N.p. [1868].

NEWSPAPERS

Boston *Commonwealth*
Boston *Daily Advertiser*
Boston *Evening Journal*
The Liberator (Boston)
The Right Way (Boston)
Boston *Traveller*
Buffalo *Morning Express*
Centreville *Indiana True Republican*
Chicago Tribune
Cincinnati *Commercial*
Cincinnati *Gazette*
Indianapolis *Daily Journal*
Indianapolis *Indiana State Herald*
Madison *Wisconsin State Journal*
New York *Herald*
The Independent (New York)

The Nation (New York)
New York *National Anti-Slavery Standard*
New York Times
New York Tribune
New York *World*
Philadelphia *North American*
Springfield *Illinois State Journal*
Springfield (Massachusetts) *Daily Republican*
San Francisco *Alta California*
The Free American (San Francisco)
Toledo *Blade*
Washington *Daily Morning Chronicle*
Washington *National Intelligencer*
Washington *New (National) Era*

PERIODICALS

American Journal of Education
American Law Register
American Law Review
Atlantic Monthly
Monthly Law Reporter

The New Englander
North American Review
The Radical
The Reporter

SECONDAY SOURCES

UNPUBLISHED DISSERTATIONS, THESES, AND PAPERS

Ashley, Margaret. "An Ohio Congressman in Reconstruction." Unpublished M.A. thesis, Columbia University, 1916.

Bowen, Nancy. "The Top of An Iceberg: Quantitative Analysis Applied to the Finance and Judiciary Committees of the 39th Congress." Unpublished seminar paper, Rice University, 1969).

Bowersox, Laverne Kenneth. "The Reconstruction of the Republican Party in the West, 1865–1870." Unpublished Ph.D. dissertation, Ohio State University, 1931.

Callette, Les. "Lyman Trumbull and the Democratic Tradition." Unpublished Ph.D. dissertation, University of Maryland, 1962.

Clark, Charles B. "Politics in Maryland During the Civil War." Unpublished Ph.D. dissertation, University of North Carolina, 1941.

Cohen, William. "James Miller McKim." Unpublished Ph.D. dissertation, New York University, 1968.

Dante, Harris L. "Reconstruction Politics in Illinois, 1860–1872." Unpublished Ph.D. dissertation, University of Chicago, 1950.

Dew, Lee Allen. "The Racial Ideas of the Authors of the Fourteenth Amendment." Unpublished Ph.D. dissertation, Louisiana State University, 1960.

Dinunzio, Mario. "Lyman Trumbull, United States Senator." Unpublished Ph.D. dissertation, Clark University, 1964.

Dodd, Dorothy. "Henry J. Raymond and the N.Y. Times During Reconstruction." Unpublished Ph.D. dissertation, University of Chicago, 1933.

Downey, Matthew T. "The Rebirth of Reform: A Study of Liberal Reform Movements, 1865–1871." Unpublished Ph.D. dissertation, Princeton University, 1963.

George, Sister Mary Karl. "Zachariah Chandler: Radical Revisited." Unpublished Ph.D. dissertation, St. Louis University, 1965.

Hare, John S. "Allen G. Thurman: A Political Study." Unpublished Ph.D. dissertation, Ohio State University, 1933.

Haugland, John C. "Alexander Ramsey and the Republican Party, 1855–1875: A Study of Personal Politics." Unpublished Ph.D. dissertation, University of Minnesota, 1961.

Henry, George Selden Jr. "Radical Republican Policy Toward the Negro During Reconstruction (1862–1872)." Unpublished Ph.D. dissertation, Yale University, 1963.

Hodnett, Mary Patricia. "Civil War Issues in New York State Politics." Unpublished Ph.D. dissertation, St. John's University, 1971.

Hughes, David F. "Salmon P. Chase, Chief Justice." Unpublished Ph.D. dissertation, Princeton University, 1963.

Kincaid, Larry George. "The Legislative Origins of the Military Reconstruction Act, 1865–1867." Unpublished Ph.D. dissertation, John Hopkins University, 1968.

Kirkland, J.R. "The Army as a Conservative Influence on the Reconstruction of the South." Paper presented at the annual convention of the Southern Historical Association, New Orleans, Louisiana, 1968.

Kleinpell, Eugene H. "James M. Comly, Journalist-Politician." Unpublished Ph.D. dissertation, Ohio State University, 1936.

Leach, R.H. "Benjamin R. Curtis." Unpublished Ph.D. dissertation, Princeton University, 1951.

Lewis, Martin Deming. "Lumberman from Flint: The Michigan Career of Henry H. Crapo, 1855–1869." Unpublished Ph.D. dissertation, University of Chicago, 1957.

Linden, Glenn M. "Congressmen, 'Radicalism,' and Economic Issues." Unpublished Ph.D. dissertation, University of Washington, 1963.

Logsdon, Joseph. "Horace White: Nineteenth Century Liberal." Unpublished Ph.D. dissertation, University of Wisconsin, 1966.

McCarthy, John L. "Reconstruction Legislation and Voting Alignments in the House of Representatives, 1863–1869." Unpublished Ph.D. dissertation, Yale University, 1970.

Mawhinney, Eugene Alberto. "The Development of the Concept of Liberty in the Fourteenth Amendment." Unpublished Ph.D. dissertation, University of Illinois, 1956.

Meador, John A. "Florida Political Parties, 1865–1877." Unpublished Ph.D. dissertation, University of Florida, 1964.

Messamor, F. "John A. Logan." Unpublished Ph.D. dissertation, University of Kentucky, 1939.

Miller, Ernest Paul. "Preston King: A Political Biography." Unpublished Ph.D. dissertation, Columbia University, 1957.

Murphy, Arthur F. "The Political Personality of Chauncey Mitchell Depew." Unpublished Ph.D. dissertation, Fordham University, 1959.

Nelson, Russell K. "Early Life and Congressional Career of Elihu B. Washburne." Unpublished Ph.D. dissertation, University of North Dakota, 1953.

Nortrup, Jack Jr. "Richard Yates: Civil War Governor of Illinois." Unpublished Ph.D. dissertation, University of Illinois, 1960.

Oxford, James L. "John W. Forney, the Washington *Chronicle,* and the Civil War Era." Unpublished Ph.D. dissertation, University of New Mexico, 1952.

Robertson, John Bruce. "Lincoln and Congress." Unpublished Ph.D. dissertation, University of Wisconsin, 1966.

Russell, William A. "A Biography of Alexander K. McClure." Unpublished Ph.D. dissertation, University of Wisconsin, 1953.

Silvestro, Clement Mario. "None but Patriots: The Union Leagues in Civil War and Reconstruction." Unpublished Ph.D. dissertation, University of Wisconsin, 1959.

Smith, James Douglas. "Virginia During Reconstruction, 1865–1870—A Political, Economic and Social Study." Unpublished Ph.D. dissertation, University of Virginia, 1960.

Stroud, Virgil C. "Congressional Investigations of the Conduct of War." Unpublished Ph.D. dissertation, New York University, 1954.

Therry, James R. "The Life of General Robert Cummings Schenck." Unpublished Ph.D. dissertation, Georgetown University, 1968.

Trefousse, Hans L. "The Radical Republicans, Reconstruction, and the Executive and the Impeachment of Andrew Johnson." Paper presented at the annual convention of the American Historical Association, New York, N.Y., 1968.

Ulrich, William John. "The Northern Military Mind in Regard to Reconstruction, 1865–1872: The Attitudes of Ten Leading Union Generals." Unpublished Ph.D. dissertation, Ohio State University, 1959.

PUBLISHED MONOGRAPHS, BIOGRAPHIES, AND SYNTHETIC WORKS

Abbott, Martin. "Free Land, Free Labor, and the Freedmen's Bureau," *Agricultural History,* XXX (Oct. 1956), 150–56.

———. *The Freedmen's Bureau in South Carolina, 1865–1872.* Chapel Hill: North Carolina University Press, 1967.

Abbott, Richard H. *Cobbler in Congress: The Life of Henry Wilson, 1812–1875.* Lexington: University of Kentucky Press, 1972.

Adams, Charles Francis. *Richard Henry Dana: A Biography.* Boston and N.Y.: Houghton Mifflin Company, 1891.

Adler, Selig. *The Senatorial Career of George Franklin Edmunds, 1866–1891.* Urbana: University of Illinois Press, 1934.

Alexander, Thomas Benjamin. *Political Reconstruction in Tennessee.* N.Y.: Russell and Russell, 1968.

Ambler, Charles H. *Francis H. Pierpont: Union War Governor of Virginia and Father of West Virginia*. Chapel Hill: University of North Carolina Press, 1937.

————. *A History of West Virginia*. N.Y. Prentice-Hall, Inc., 1933.

————. *Waitman Thomas Willey*. Huntington, W.Va.: Standard Printing and Publishing Company, 1954.

Avins, Alfred, "The Civil Rights Act of 1866 and the Civil Rights Bill of 1966, and the Right to Buy Property." *Southern California Law Review*, XL (1967), 274–306.

————. "Fourteenth Amendment Limitations on Banning Racial Discrimination: The Original Understanding." *Arizona Law Review*, VIII (Spring 1967), 236–59.

Badeau, Adam. *Grant in Peace: From Appamatox to Mount McGregor—A Personal Memoir*. Hartford, Conn.: S.S. Scranton and Company, 1887.

Baker, Jean H. *The Politics of Continuity: Maryland Political Parties from 1858 to 1870*. Baltimore: Johns Hopkins University Press, 1973.

Barker, James H. *Lives of the Governors of Minnesota*. Volume XIII of the Minnesota Historical Society Collections. St. Paul: Minnesota Historical Society, 1908.

Barnes, Thurlow Weed. *Memoir of Thurlow Weed*. Boston: Houghton, Mifflin Company, 1884.

Barrows, Chester L. *William M. Evarts: Lawyer, Diplomat, Statesman*. Chapel Hill: University of North Carolina Press, 1941.

Bartlett, Irving H. *Wendell Phillips: Brahmin Radical*. Boston: Beacon Press, 1961.

Bauer, Elizabeth Kelly. *Commentaries on the Constitution, 1790–1860*. Volume DLXXV of the Studies in History, Economics and Public Law Edited by the Faculty of Political Science of Columbia University. N.Y.: Columbia University Press, 1952.

Bayles. R.W. "Peter G. Van Winkle and Waitman T. Willey in the Impeachment Trial of Andrew Johnson." *West Virginia History*, XII (Jan. 1952), 75–89.

Beale, Howard K. *The Critical Year: A Study of Andrew Johnson and Reconstruction*. N.Y.: Frederick Ungar Publishing Company, 1930.

Belden, Thomas Graham and Marva Robins Belden. *So Fell the Angels*. Boston: Little, Brown and Company, 1956.

Bellows, Henry Whitney. *Historical Sketch of the Union League Club of New York: Its Origin, Organization, and Work, 1863–1879*. N.Y.: G.P. Putnam's Sons, 1879.

Belz, Herman. "Henry Winter Davis and the Origins of Congressional Reconstruction." *Maryland Historical Magazine*, LXVII (Summer 1972), 129–43.

————. *Reconstructing the Union: Theory and Policy During the Civil War*. Ithaca, N.Y.: Cornell University Press, 1969.

Benedict, Michael Les. *The Impeachment and Trial of Andrew Johnson*. N.Y.: W.W. Norton and Co., 1973.

————. "A New Look at the Impeachment of Andrew Johnson." *Political Science Quarterly*, LXXXVIII (Sept. 1973), 349–67.

————. "The Rout of Radicalism: Republicans and the Elections of 1867." *Civil War History*, XVIII (Nov. 1972), 334–44.

Bentley, George R. *A History of the Freedmen's Bureau*. Philadelphia: University of Pennsylvania Press, 1955.

Berrier, G. Galen. "The Negro Suffrage Issue in Iowa—1865–1868." *Annals of Iowa*, XXXIX (Spring, 1968), 241–61.

Bestor, Arthur. "The American Civil War as a Constitutional Crisis." *American Historical Review*, LXIX (Jan. 1964), 327–52.

Boeck, Georg A. "Senator Grimes and the Iowa Press, 1867–1868." *Mid-America*, XLVIII (July 1966), 147–61.

Bonadio, Felice A. *North of Reconstruction: Ohio Politics, 1865–1870*. N.Y.: New York University Press, 1970.

Bowers, Claude G. *The Tragic Era: The Revolution After Lincoln*. Boston: Houghton Mifflin Company, 1929.

Bradley, Erwin Stanley. *Simon Cameron: A Political Biography.* Philadelphia: University of Pennsylvania Press, 1966.

———. *The Triumph of Militant Republicanism: A Study of Pennsylvania and Presidential Politics.* Philadelphia: University of Pennsylvania Press, 1964.

Brant, Irving. *Impeachment: Trials and Errors.* N.Y.: Alfred A. Knopf, 1972.

Brigham, Johnson. *James Harlan.* Iowa Biographical Series. Iowa City: State Historical Society of Iowa, 1913.

Brock, W.R. *An American Crisis: Congress and Reconstruction, 1865–1867.* N.Y.: St. Martin's Press, 1963.

Brodie, Fawn. *Thaddeus Stevens: Scourge of the South.* N.Y.: W.W. Norton and Company, 1959.

Brown, Bernard Edward. *American Conservatives: The Political Thought of Francis Lieber and John W. Burgess.* N.Y.: Columbia University Press, 1951.

Brown, Francis. *Raymond of the "Times."* N.Y.: W.W. Norton and Company, 1951.

Brown, Ira V. "Pennsylvania and the Rights of the Negro." *Pennsylvania History,* XXVIII (Jan. 1961), 45–57.

———. "William D. Kelley and Radical Reconstruction." *Pennsylvania Magazine of History & Biography,* LXXXV (July 1961), 316–29.

Brummer, Sidney D. *Political History of New York State during the Period of the Civil War.* Volume XXXIX of the Studies in History, Economics and Public Law Edited by the Faculty of Political Science of Columbia University. N.Y.: Longmans, Green and Company, 1911.

Burgess, John W. *Reconstruction and the Constitution, 1866–1876.* The American History Series. N.Y.: Charles Scribner's Sons, 1902.

Cain, Marvin R. *Linicoln's Attorney General, Edward Bates of Missouri.* Columbia: University of Missouri Press, 1965.

Capers, Gerald M. *Occupied City: New Orleans Under the Federals, 1862–1865.* Lexington: University of Kentucky Press, 1965.

Carman, Harry J. and Reinhard H. Luthin. *Lincoln and the Patronage.* N.Y.: Columbia University Press, 1943.

Carpenter, John A. *The Sword and the Olive Branch: Oliver Otis Howard.* Pittsburgh: University of Pittsburgh Press, 1964.

Cashdollar, Charles D. "Andrew Johnson and the Philadelphia Election of 1866." *Pennsylvania Magazine of History and Biography,* XCII (July 1968), 365–83.

Caskey, Willie Malvin. *Secession and Restoration of Louisiana.* Louisiana State University Studies, Number 36. Baton Rouge: Louisiana State University Press, 1938.

Chadsey, Charles Ernest. *The Struggle Between President Johnson and Congress Over Reconstruction.* Volume VIII of the Studies in History, Economics and Public Law Edited by the Faculty of Political Science of Columbia University. N.Y.: Columbia University Press, 1896.

Chamburn, Adolphe de. *The Executive Power in the United States: A Study of the Constitutional Law.* Lancaster, Pa.: Inquirer Printing and Publishing Company, 1874.

Chidsey, Donald Barr. *The Gentleman from New York: A Life of Roscoe Conkling.* New Haven: Yale University Press, 1935.

Clark, Dan Elbert. *History of Senatorial Elections in Iowa.* Iowa City: State Historical Society of Iowa, 1912.

Clarke, Grace [Julian]. *George Julian.* Indianapolis: Indiana Historical Commission, 1932.

Cleaves, Freeman. *Rock of Chickamauga: The Life of George H. Thomas.* Norman: University of Oklahoma Press, 1948.

Coben, Stanley, "Northeastern Business and Radical Reconstruction: A Re-examination." *Mississippi Valley Historical Review,* XLVI (June 1959), 67–90.

Cole, Arthur Charles. *The Era of the Civil War, 1848–1870.* Volume III of *The Centennial History of Illinois.* Springfield: Illinois Centennial Commission, 1919.

———. "President Lincoln and the Illinois Radical Republicans." *Mississippi Valley Historical Review,* IV (March 1918), 417–36.

Coleman, Charles H. *The Election of 1868: The Democratic Effort to Regain Control*. Volume CCCXCII of the Studies in History, Economics and Public Law Edited by the Faculty of Political Science of Columbia University. N.Y.: Columbia University Press, 1933.

Conkling, Alfred. *Life and Letters of Roscoe Conkling, Orator, Statesman, Advocate*. N.Y.: C.C. Webster, 1889.

Cooley, Thomas McIntyre. *The General Principles of Constitutional Law in the United States of America*. Ed. by Alexis C. Angell. 2nd edn. Boston: Little, Brown and Company, 1891.

Conway, Alan. *The Reconstruction of Georgia*. Minneapolis: University of Minnesota Press, 1967.

Corwin, Edwin S. (ed.). *The Constitution of the United States of America: Analysis and Interpretation*. Washington: Government Printing Office, 1952.

————. *The President—Office and Powers, 1787–1957: History and Analysis of Practice and Opinion*. 4th rev. edn. N.Y.: New York University Press, 1957.

————. *The President's Removal Power Under the Constitution*. N.Y.: National Municipal League, 1927.

Cox, LaWanda. "The Promise of Land to the Freedmen." *Mississippi Valley Historical Review*, XLV (Dec. 1958), 413–40.

———— and John H. Cox. "Andrew Johnson and His Ghost Writers: An Analysis of the Freedmen's Bureau and Civil Rights Veto Messages." *Mississippi Valley Historical Review*, XLVIII (Dec. 1961), 460–79.

————. "Negro Suffrage and Republican Politics: The Problem of Motivation in Reconstruction Historiography." *Journal of Southern History*, XXXIII (Aug. 1967), 303–30.

————. *Politics, Principle, and Prejudice, 1865–1866: Dilemma of Reconstruction America*. N.Y.: Free Press of Glencoe, 1963.

Cox, Merlin G. "Military Reconstruction in Florida." *Florida Historical Quarterly*, XLVI (Jan. 1968), 219–33.

Craven, Avery. *Reconstruction: The Ending of the Civil War*. N.Y.: Holt, Rinehart and Winston, 1969.

Current, Richard N. *Old Thad Stevens: A Story of Ambition*. Madison: University of Wisconsin Press, 1942.

Currie, James T. "The Beginnings of Congressional Reconstruction in Mississippi." *Journal of Mississippi History*, XXXV (Aug. 1973), 267–86.

Curry, Leonard P. *Blueprint for Modern America: Non-Military Legislation of the First Civil War Congress*. Nashville: Vanderbilt University Press, 1968.

Curry, Richard O. "The Abolitionists and Reconstruction: A Critical Reappraisal." *Journal of Southern History*, XXXIV (Nov. 1968), 527–45.

————. *Radicalism, Racism, and Party Realignment: The Border States during Reconstruction*. Baltimore and London: Johns Hopkins Press, 1969.

Dancy, John C. "The Negro People in Michigan." *Michigan History Magazine*, XXIV (Winter 1940), 221–42.

Davis, Allen F. "Why Jacob Collamer?" *Vermont History*, XXVII, series 2 (Jan. 1959), 41–53.

Davis, William Watson. *The Civil War and Reconstruction In Florida*. Volume LIII of the Studies in History, Economics and Public Law Edited by the Faculty of Political Science of Columbia University. N.Y.: Columbia University Press, 1913.

Dawson, George Francis. *Life and Services of General John A. Logan as Soldier and Statesman*. Chicago and N.Y.: Bedford, Clarke and Co., 1887.

Detroit *Post and Tribune. Zachariah Chandler: An Outline Sketch of his Life and Public Services*. Detroit: Post and Tribune Co., 1880.

Dew, Lee A. "The Reluctant Radicals of 1866." *Midwest Quarterly*, VIII (Spring 1967), 261–76.

DeWitt, David Miller. *The Impeachment and Trial of Andrew Johnson, Seventeenth President of the United States: A History*. N.Y. and London: The Macmillan Company, 1903.

Dilla, Harriet M. *The Politics of Michigan, 1865–1878*. Volume XLVII of the Studies in History, Economics and Public Law Edited by the Faculty of Political Science of Columbia University. N.Y.: Columbia University Press, 1912.

Donald, David. *Charles Sumner and the Coming of the Civil War.* N.Y.: Alfred A. Knopf, 1960.

———. *Charles Sumner and the Rights of Man.* N.Y.: Alfred A. Knopf, 1970.

———. *Lincoln Reconsidered: Essays on the Civil War Era.* N.Y.: Vintage Books, 1961.

———. *The Politics of Reconstruction, 1863–1867.* The Walter Lynwood Fleming Lectures in Southern History. Baton Rouge: Louisiana State University Press, 1965.

———. "Why They Impeached Andrew Johnson." *American Heritage,* VIII (Dec. 1956), 21–25, 102–103.

Dorris, Jonathan T. *Pardon and Amnesty Under Lincoln and Johnson: The Restoration of the Confederates to Their Rights and Privileges.* Chapel Hill: University of North Carolina Press, 1953.

Doyle, Elisabeth J. "New Orleans Under Military Occupation, 1861–1865." *Mid-America,* XLII (July 1960), 185–92.

Duer, William Alexander. *A Course of Lectures on the Constitutional Jurisprudence of the United States.* N.Y.: Harper and Bros., 1843.

———. *Outlines of the Constitutional Jurisprudence of the United States.* N.Y.: Collins and Hennaway, 1833.

Dunning, William Archibald. *Essays on the Civil War and Reconstruction, and Related Topics.* N.Y.: The Macmillan Company, 1898.

———. *Reconstruction, Political and Economic: 1865–1877.* Volume XXII of *The American Nation: A History.* N.Y. and London: Harper and Bros., 1907.

Dusinberre, William. *Civil War Issues in Philadelphia, 1856–1865.* Philadelphia: University of Pennsylvania Press, 1965.

Eckenrode, Hamilton James. *The Political History of Virginia During the Reconstruction.* Series XXII of the Johns Hopkins University Studies in Historical and Political Science. Baltimore: Johns Hopkins University Press, 1904.

Egle, William H. *Andrew Gregg Curtin: His Life and Services.* Philadelphia: Avil Printing Company, 1895.

Erbe, Carl H. "Constitutional Provisions for the Suffrage in Iowa." *Iowa Journal of History and Politics,* XXII (April 1924), 163–216.

Fahrney, Ralph Lee. *Horace Greeley and the Tribune in the Civil War.* Cedar Rapids, Iowa: Torch Press, 1936.

Fairman, Charles. "Does the Fourteenth Amendment Incorporate the Bill of Rights?: The Original Understanding." *Stanford Law Review,* II (Dec. 1949), 5–139.

———. *Mr. Justice Miller and the Supreme Court, 1862–1890.* Cambridge, Mass.: Harvard University Press, 1939.

———. *Reconstruction and Reunion, 1864–88: Part One.* Volume VI of *History of the Supreme Court of the United States.* N.Y.: The Macmillan Company, 1971.

Farrar, Timothy. *Manual of the Constitution of the United States of America.* Boston: Little, Brown and Company, 1867.

Fehrenbacher, Don Edward. *Chicago Giant: A Biography of "Long John" Wentworth.* Madison: American History Research Center, 1957.

Fessenden, Francis. *Life and Public Services of William Pitt Fessenden.* 2 vols. Boston and N.Y.: Houghton, Mifflin Company, 1907.

Ficklen, John Rose. *History of Reconstruction in Louisiana (Through 1868).* Series XXVIII of the Johns Hopkins University Studies in Historical and Political Science. Baltimore: Johns Hopkins University Press, 1910.

Fishel, Leslie H. Jr. "Wisconsin and Negro Suffrage." *Wisconsin Magazine of History,* XLVI (Spring 1963), 180–96.

Fleming, Walter L. *Civil War and Reconstruction in Alabama.* N.Y.: Columbia University Press, 1905.

Flower, Frank A. *Edwin McMasters Stanton: The Autocrat of Rebellion, Emancipation, and Reconstruction.* Akron, Ohio, N.Y., and Chicago: The Saalfield Publishing Co., 1905.

Folwell, William Watts. *A History of Minnesota*. 4 vols. St. Paul: Minnesota Historical Society, 1926.

Foner, Eric. *Free Soil, Free Labor, Free Men: The Ideology of the Republican Party Before the Civil War*. N.Y.: Oxford University Press, 1970.

Foner, Philip S. *The Life and Writings of Frederick Douglass*. 4 vols. N.Y.: International Press, 1950–55.

Foulke, William Dudley. *Life of Oliver P. Morton, Including his Important Speeches*. 2 vols. Indianapolis and Kansas City: Bowen-Merrill, 1899.

Frank, John P. and Robert F. Munro. "The Original Understanding of 'Equal Protection of the Laws.' " *Columbia Law Review*, L (Feb. 1950), 131–69.

Franklin, John Hope. *Reconstruction: After the Civil War*. Chicago: University of Chicago Press, 1961.

Frederickson, George M. *The Inner Civil War: Northern Intellectuals and the Crisis of the Union*. N.Y.: Harper and Row, 1965.

Freidel, Frank. *Francis Lieber, Nineteenth Century Liberal*. Baton Rouge: Louisiana State University Press, 1947.

Feuss, Claude Moore. *Carl Schurz: Reformer (1829–1906)*. N.Y.: Dodd, Mead and Company, 1932.

Gambill, Edward L. "Who Were the Senate Radicals?" *Civil War History*, XI (June 1965), 237–43.

Gates, Paul W. "Federal Land Policy in the South, 1866–1888." *Journal of Southern History*, VI (Aug. 1940), 303–30.

Gerofsky, Milton. "Reconstruction in West Virginia." *West Virginia History*, VI (July 1945), 295–360.

Gerteis, Louis S. "Salmon P. Chase, Radicalism, and the Politics of Emancipation, 1861–1864." *Journal of American History*, LX (June 1973), 42–62.

Gillette, Wililam. *The Right to Vote: Politics and the Passage of the Fifteenth Amendment*. Series LXXXIII, Johns Hopkins University Studies in Historical and Political Science. Baltimore: Johns Hopkins Press, 1965.

Gilman, Rhoda R. "Ramsey, Donnelly, and the Congressional Campaign of 1868." *Minnesota History*, XXXVI (Dec. 1959), 300–308.

Gorham, George C. *Life and Public Services of Edwin M. Stanton*. 2 vols. Boston and N.Y.: Houghton Mifflin Company, 1899.

Graham, Howard Jay. *Everyman's Constitution: Historical Essays on the Fourteenth Amendment, the "Conspiracy Theory," and American Constitutionalism*. Madison: State Historical Society of Wisconsin, 1968.

Gresham, Matilda. *Life of Walter Quintin Gresham, 1832–1895*. 2 vols. Chicago: Rand McNally and Company, 1919.

Hamilton, Alexander and James Madison and John Jay. *The Federalist, on the New Constitution, Written in the Year 1788, . . . with an Appendix*. Washington: Jacob Gideon, Jr., 1818.

Hamilton, H.G. de Roulhac. *Reconstruction in North Carolina*. Volume LVIII of the Studies in History, Economics and Public Law Edited by the Faculty of Political Science of Columbia University. N.Y.: Columbia University Press, 1914.

Hamlin, Charles Eugene. *The Life and Times of Hannibal Hamlin*. Cambridge, Mass.: Riverside Press, 1899.

Hantke, Richard W. "Elisha W. Keyes and the Radical Republicans." *Wisconsin Magazine of History*, XXXV (Spring 1952), 203–208.

Harbison, Winfred A. "Indiana Republicans and the Re-election of President Lincoln." *Indiana Magazine of History*, XXXIV (March 1938), 42–64.

Harrington, Fred Harvey. *Fighting Politician: Major General N.P. Banks*. Philadelphia: University of Pennsylvania Press, 1948.

Harris, William C. *Presidential Reconstruction in Mississippi*. Baton Rouge: Louisiana State University Press, 1967.

Hart, James. *Tenure of Office Under the Constitution: A Study in Law and Public Policy*. Series IX of the Johns Hopkins University Studies in Historical and Political Science. Baltimore: Johns Hopkins University Press, 1930.

Hesseltine, William B. *Lincoln's Plan of Reconstruction*. Number XIII of the Confederate Centennial Studies. Tuscaloosa, Alabama: Confederate Publishing Company, 1960.

——. *Ulysses S. Grant, Politician.* N.Y.: Dodd, Mead and Company, 1935.

Heyman, Max L., Jr. " 'The Great Reconstructor': General E.R.S. Canby and the Second Military District." *North Carolina Historical Review,* XXXII (Jan. 1955), 52–80.

Hicks, John D. "The Political Career of Ignatius Donnelly." *Mississippi Valley Historical Review,* VIII (June–Sept. 1921), 80–132.

Higsmith, William E. "Some Aspects of Reconstruction in the Heart of Louisiana." *Journal of Southern History,* XIII (Nov. 1947), 460–91.

Hirshson, Stanley P. *Grenville M. Dodge: Soldier, Politician, Railroad Pioneer.* Bloomington: Indiana University Press, 1967.

Hixson, William B. Jr. "Moorfield Storey and the Struggle for Equality." *Journal of American History,* LV (Dec. 1968), 533–54.

Hollister, O.J. *The Life of Schuyler Colfax.* N.Y. and London: Funk and Wagnalls, 1886.

Holst, H. von. *The Constitutional Law of the United States of America.* Trans. by Alfred Bishop Mason. Chicago: Callaghan and Company, 1887.

Hughes, David F. "Chief Justice Chase at the Impeachment Trial of Andrew Johnson." *New York State Bar Journal,* XLI (April 1969), 218–33.

Hunt, Gaillard. *Israel, Elihu and Cadwallader Washburn The: A Chapter in American Biography.* N.Y.: The Macmillan Company, 1925.

——. "The President's Defense: His Side of the Case, As Told by His Correspondence." *Century Magazine,* LXXXV (Jan. 1913), 422–34.

Hunt, H. Draper. *Hannibal Hamlin of Maine: Lincoln's First Vice President.* Syracuse, N.Y.: Syracuse University Press, 1969.

Hyman, Harold M. "Deceit in Dixie: Southerners' Evasions of Union Loyalty Tests." *Civil War History,* III (March 1957), 65–82.

——. *The Era of the Oath: Northern Loyalty Tests During the Civil War and Reconstruction.* Philadelphia: University of Pennsylvania Press, 1954.

——. "Johnson, Stanton and Grant: A Reconsideration of the Army's Role in the Events Leading to Impeachment." *American Historical Review,* LXVI (Oct. 1960), 85–100.

——. "Lincoln and Equal Rights for Negroes: The Irrelevancy of the 'Wadsworth Letter.' " *Civil War History,* XII (Sept. 1966), 258–66.

——. *A More Perfect Union: The Impact of the Civil War and Reconstruction on the Constitution.* N. Y.: Alfred A. Knopf, 1973.

—— (ed.). *The Radical Republicans and Reconstruction 1861–1870.* The American Heritage Series. Indianapolis and N.Y.: Bobbs-Merrill, 1967.

Isely, Jeter Allen, *Horace Greeley and the Republican Party, 1853–1861: A Study of the New York Tribune.* Volume III of Princeton Studies in History. [Princeton, N.J.]: Princeton University Press, 1947.

Jaffa, Harry V. *Crisis of the House Divided: An Interpretation of the Issues in the Lincoln-Douglas Debates.* Garden City, N.J.: Doubleday and Company, 1959.

James, Joseph B. *The Framing of the Fourteenth Amendment.* Volume XXXVII of the Illinois Studies in the Social Sciences. Urbana: University of Illinois Press, 1956.

——. "Southern Reaction to the Proposal of the Fourteenth Amendment." *Journal of Southern History,* XXII (Nov. 1956), 477–97.

Jellison, Charles A. *Fessenden of Maine: Civil War Senator.* Syracuse, N.Y.: Syracuse University Press, 1962.

Katz, Irving. *August Belmont: A Political Biography.* N.Y.: Columbia University Press, 1968.

Kelley, Alfred H. "The Congressional Controversy over School Desegregation, 1867–1875." *American Historical Review,* LXIV (April 1959), 537–63.

——. "The Fourteenth Amendment Reconsidered: The Segregation Question." *Michigan Law Review,* LIV (June 1956), 1049–86.

Kent, James. *Commentaries on American Law.* 4 vols. 2nd edn. New York: O. Holsted, 1826–30.

————. *Commentaries on American Law.* Ed. by George F. Comstock. 3 vols. 11th edn. Boston: Little, Brown and Company, 1867.

Kincaid, Larry G. "Victims of Circumstance: An Interpretation of Changing Attitudes Toward Republican Policy Makers and Reconstruction." *Journal of American History,* LVII (June 1970), 48–66.

King, Willard Leroy. *Lincoln's Manager, David Davis.* Cambridge, Mass.: Harvard University Press, 1960.

Knapp, Charles Merriam. *New Jersey Politics During the Civil War and Reconstruction.* Geneva, N.Y.: W.F. Humphrey, 1924.

Knight, Wesley B. "Forty Acres and a Mule and a Speller." *History of Education Journal,* VIII (Summer 1957), 113–27.

Koenig, Louis W. *The Chief Executive.* N.Y.: Harcourt, Brace and World, 1964.

Kohl, Robert L. "The Civil Rights Act of 1866, Its Hour Come Round at Last: *Jones v. Alfred H. Mayer Co.*" *Virginia Law Review,* LV (March 1969), 272–300.

Kolchin, Peter. "The Business Press and Reconstruction, 1865–1868." *Journal of Southern History,* XXXIII (May 1967), 183–96.

Krug, Mark. *Lyman Trumbull: Conservative Radical.* N.Y.: A.S. Barnes & Co., 1965.

Kutler, Stanley I. "Reconstruction and the Supreme Court: The Numbers Game Reconsidered." *Journal of Southern History,* XXXII (Feb. 1966). 42–58.

————. *The Supreme Court and Reconstruction: Politics and Judicial Power.* Chicago: University of Chicago Press, 1968.

Lane, Brother J. Robert. *A Political History of Connecticut During the Civil War.* Washington: Catholic University of America Press, 1941.

Lerche, Charles O. "Congressional Interpretations of the Guarantee of a Republican Form of Government During Reconstruction." *Journal of Southern History,* XV (May 1949), 192–211.

Lewellen, Fred B. "Political Ideas of James W. Grimes." *Iowa Journal of History and Politics,* XLII (Oct. 1944), 339–404.

Lieber, Francis. *On Civil Liberty and Self-Government.* 2d ed. Philadelphia: J.B. Lippincott, 1859.

Linden, Glenn M. "A Note on Negro Suffrage and Republican Politics." *Journal of Southern History,* XXXVI (Aug. 1970), 411–20.

————. " 'Radicals' and Economic Policies: The House of Representatives, 1861–1873." *Civil War History,* XIII (March 1967), 51–65.

————. " 'Radicals' and Economic Policies: The Senate, 1861–1873." *Journal of Southern History,* XXXII (May 1966), 189–99.

Lindsey, David. *"Sunset" Cox: Irrepressible Democrat.* Detroit: Wayne State University Press, 1959.

Lomask, Milton. *Andrew Johnson: President on Trial.* N.Y.: Farrar, Strauss and Co., 1960.

Luthin, Reinhard H. "A Discordant Chapter in the Lincoln Administration: The Davis-Blair Controversy." *Maryland Historical Magazine,* XXXIX (March 1944), 25–48.

————. "Pennsylvania and Lincoln's Rise to the Presidency." *Pennsylvania Magazine of History and Biography,* LXVII (Jan. 1943), 61–82.

McCarthy, Charles H. *Lincoln's Plan of Reconstruction.* N.Y.: AMS Press, 1966.

McDonough, James L. "John Schofield as Military Dictator of Reconstruction in Virginia." *Civil War History,* XV (Sept. 1969), 237–56.

————. *Schofield: Union General in the Civil War and Reconstruction.* Tallahassee: Florida State University Press, 1972.

McDougall, H.C. "A Decade of Missouri Politics—1860 to 1870—from a Republican Viewpoint." *Missouri Historical Review,* III (Jan. 1909), 126–53.

McFeely, William S. *Yankee Stepfather: General O.O. Howard and the Freedmen.* New Haven and London: Yale University Press, 1968.

McJimsey, George T. *Genteel Partisan: Manton Marble, 1834–1917.* Ames: Iowa State University Press, 1971.

McKitrick, Eric L. *Andrew Johnson and Reconstruction.* Chicago and London: University of Chicago Press, 1960.

McPherson, Edward (ed.). *The Political History of the United States of America, During the Period of Reconstruction* . . . . 3rd edn. Washington: James J. Chapman, 1880.

McPherson, James M. *The Struggle for Equality: Abolitionists and the Negro in the Civil War and Reconstruction*. Princeton, N.J.: Princeton University Press, 1964.

McWhiney, Grady (ed.). *Grant, Lee, Lincoln and the Radicals: Essays on Civil War Leadership*. [Evanston, Ill.]: Northwestern University Press, 1964.

Maddex, Jack P. Jr. *The Virginia Conservatives, 1867–1879: A Study in Reconstruction Politics*. Chapel Hill: University of North Carolina Press, 1970.

Mallam, William D. "The Grant-Butler Relationship." *Mississippi Valley Historical Review,* XLI (Sept. 1954), 259–76.

———. "Lincoln and the Conservatives." *Journal of Southern History,* XXVIII (Feb. 1962), 31–45.

Mantell, Martin E. *Johnson, Grant, and the Politics of Reconstruction*. N.Y. and London: Columbia University Press, 1973.

Merrill, Walter M. *Against Wind and Tide: A Biography of William Lloyd Garrison*. Cambridge, Mass.: Harvard University Press, 1963.

Milton, George F. *The Age of Hate: Andrew Johnson and the Radicals*. New York: Coward, McCann, 1930.

Moore, Clifford H. "Ohio in National Politics, 1865–1896." *Ohio Archaeological and Historical Publications,* XXXVII (1928), 220–427.

Moore, Frederick W. "Representation in the National Congress from the Seceding States, 1861–1865." *American Historical Review,* II (Jan. 1897), 279–93, (April 1897), 461–71.

Morrill, James Roy III. "North Carolina and the Administration of Brevet Major General Sickles." *North Carolina Historical Review,* XLII (Sumner 1965), 291–305.

Morris, Robert L. "The Lincoln-Johnson Plan for Reconstruction and the Republican Convention of 1864." *Lincoln Herald,* LXXI (Spring 1969), 33–40.

Muzzey, David Saville. *James G. Blaine: A Political Idol of Other Days*. N.Y.: Dodd, Mead and Company, 1934.

Myers, William Starr. *The Self-Reconstruction of Maryland, 1864–1867*. Volume XXVII of the Johns Hopkins University Studies in Historical and Political Science. Baltimore: Johns Hopkins University Press, 1909.

Naroll, Raoul S. "Lincoln and the Sherman Peace Fiasco—Another Fable?" *Journal of Southern History,* XX (Nov. 1954), 459–83.

Nathans, Elizabeth Studley. *Losing the Peace: Georgia Republicans and Reconstruction, 1865–1871*. Baton Rouge: Louisiana State University Press, 1968.

Neilson, James Warren, *Shelby M. Cullom, Prairie State Republican*. Urbana: University of Illinois Press, 1962.

Nevins, Allan. *The New York Post: A Century of Journalism*. New York: Russell and Russell, 1968.

Nicolay, John G. and John Hay. *Abraham Lincoln: A History*. 10 vols. New York: The Century Co., 1890.

Ogden, Rollo. *Life and Letters of Edward Lawrence Godkin*. 2 vols. New York: The Macmillan Company, 1907.

Palmer, George Thomas. *A Conscientious Turncoat: The Story of John M. Palmer, 1817–1900*. New Haven: Yale University Press, 1941.

Porter, Kirk H. and Donald Bruce Johnson (eds.). *National Party Platforms, 1840–1956*. Urbana: University of Illinois Press, 1956.

Parker, William Belmont. *The Life and Public Services of Justin Smith Morrill*. Boston and New York: Houghton Mifflin Co., 1924.

Parrish, William E. *Missouri Under Radical Rule, 1865–1870*. Columbia: University of Missouri Press, 1965.

Patton, James Welch. *Unionism and Reconstruction in Tennessee, 1860–1869*. Chapel Hill: University of North Carolina Press, 1934.

Patrick, Rembert W. *The Reconstruction of the Nation*. New York: Oxford University Press, 1967.

Pearson, Henry Greenleaf. *The Life of John A. Andrew: Governor of Massachusetts, 1861–1865.* 2 vols. Boston and New York: Houghton Mifflin Company, 1904.

Peck, Ralph L. "Military Reconstruction and the Growth of Anti-Negro Sentiment in Florida, 1867." *Florida Historical Quarterly,* XLVII (April 1969), 380–400.

Perdue, M. Kathleen. "Salmon P. Chase and the Impeachment Trial of Andrew Johnson." *Historian,* XXIX (Nov. 1964), 75–92.

Perman, Michael. *Reunion Without Compromise: The South and Reconstruction, 1865–1868.* Cambridge, England: Cambridge University Press, 1973.

————. "The South and Congress's Reconstruction Policy, 1866–67." *American Studies,* IV (Feb. 1971), 181–200.

Perry, Thomas Sargent. *Life and Letters of Francis Lieber.* Boston: J.K. Osgood and Company, 1882.

Peterson, Norman L. *Freedom and Franchise: The Political Career of B. Gratz Brown.* Columbia: University of Missouri Press, 1965.

Phinney, Chester Squire. *Francis Lieber's Influence on American Thought and Some of His Unpublished Letters.* Philadelphia: International Printing Company, 1918.

Piatt, Donn. *Memories of the Men Who Saved the Union.* New York and Chicago: Belford Clarke and Company, 1887.

Pierce, Edward L. *Memoir and Letters of Charles Sumner.* 4 vols. Boston: Roberts Brothers, 1893.

Plummer, Mark A. "Governor Crawford's Appointment of Edmund G. Ross to the United States Senate." *Kansas Historical Quarterly,* XXVIII (Summer 1962), 145–53.

Pomeroy, John Norton. *An Introduction to the Constitutional Law of the United States.* New York: Hurd and Houghton, 1870.

Pope, Christie Farnham. "Southern Homesteads for Negroes." *Agricultural History,* XLIV (April 1970), 201–12.

Porter, George H. *Ohio Politics During the Civil War Period.* Volume CV of the Studies in History, Economics and Public Law Edited by the Faculty of Political Science of Columbia University. N.Y.: Longmans, Green and Company, 1911.

Powell, Lawrence N. "Rejected Republican Incumbants in the 1866 Congressional Nominating Conventions: A Study in Reconstruction Politics." *Civil War History,* XIX (Sept. 1973), 218–37.

Quarles, Benjamin. *Frederick Douglass.* N.Y.: Atheneum, 1967.

————. *Lincoln and the Negro.* N.Y. Oxford University Press, 1962.

Ramsdell, Charles William. *Reconstruction in Texas.* Volume XCV of the Studies in History, Economics and Public Law Edited by the Faculty of Political Science of Columbia University. N.Y.: Columbia University Press, 1910.

Randall, James G. *Constitutional Problems Under Lincoln.* N.Y.: D. Appleton and Company, 1926.

————. *Lincoln the President.* 3 vols. N.Y.: Dodd, Mead and Company, 1945–52.

————. "The 'Rule of Law' Under the Lincoln Administration." *Historical Outlook,* XVII (Oct. 1926), 272–78.

———— and David Donald. *The Civil War and Reconstruction.* Boston: D.C. Heath and Company, 1937.

Rawle, William. *A View of the Constitution of the United States of America.* 2d edn. Philadelphia: Philip H. Nicklin, 1829.

Rawley, James A. *Edwin D. Morgan, 1811–1883: Merchant in Politics.* Volume DLXXXII of the Studies in History, Economics and Public Law Edited by the Faculty of Political Science of Columbia University. N.Y.: Columbia University Press, 1956.

Reed, Emily Hazen. *Life of A.P. Dostie; or, The Conflict in New Orleans.* N.Y.: Wm. P. Tomlinson, 1868.

Rhodes, James Ford. *History of the United States from the Compromise of 1850 to the Final Restoration of Home Rule at the South in 1877.* 7 vols. N.Y.: The Macmillan Company, 1907–10.

Richardson, Leon Burr. *William E. Chandler: Republican.* N.Y.: Dodd, Mead and Company, 1940.

Richter, William L. "James Longstreet: From Rebel to Scalawag." *Louisiana History,* XI (Summer 1970), 215–30.

Riddle, Albert Gallatin. *The Life of Benjamin F. Wade.* Cleveland: W.W. Williams, 1886.

Riddleberger, Patrick W. "The Break in the Radical Ranks: Liberals vs. Stalwarts in the Election of 1872." *Journal of Negro History,* XLIV (April 1959), 136–57.

———. *George Washington Julian, Radical Republican: A Study in Nineteenth Century Politics and Reform.* Volume XLV of the Indiana Historical Collections. Indianapolis: Indiana Historical Bureau, 1966.

———. "The Radical Abandonment of the Negro During Reconstruction." *Journal of Negro History,* XLV (April 1960), 88–102.

Ridge, Martin. *Ignatius Donnelly: Portrait of a Politician.* Chicago: University of Chicago Press, 1962.

Rose, Willie Lee. *Rehearsal for Reconstruction: The Port Royal Experiment.* N.Y.: Bobbs-Merrill Company, 1964.

Roseboom, Eugene H. *The Civil War Era, 1850–1873. The History of the State of Ohio.* Ed. by Carl Wittke. Columbus: Ohio State Archaeological and Historical Association, 1944.

Roske, Ralph J. "The Seven Martyrs?" *American Historical Review,* LXIV (Jan. 1959), 323–30.

Ross, Earle Dudley. *The Liberal Republican Movement.* N.Y.: Rumford Press, 1919.

Russ, William A. Jr. "Was There Danger of a Second Civil War During Reconstruction?" *Mississippi Valley Historical Review,* XXV (June 1938), 39–58.

Russell, Charles Edward. *Blaine of Maine: His Life and Times.* N.Y.: Cosmopolitan Book Corporation, 1931.

Russell, William H. "Timothy Otis Howe, Stalwart Republican." *Wisconsin Magazine of History,* XXXV (Winter 1951), 90–99.

Rutland, Robert. "Iowans and the Fourteenth Amendment." *Iowa Journal of History and Politics,* LI (Oct. 1953), 289–300.

Sage, Leland. "William B. Allison and Iowa Senatorial Politics, 1865–1870." *Iowa Journal of History and Politics,* LII (April 1954), 97–128.

———. "William Boyd Allison's First Term in Congress." *Iowa Journal of History and Politics,* L (Oct. 1952), 315–44.

———. *William Boyd Allison: A Study in Practical Politics.* Iowa City: State Historical Society of Iowa, 1956.

Salter, William. *The Life of James W. Grimes, Governor of Iowa, 1854–1858; Senator of the United States, 1859–1869.* N.Y.: D. Appleton Company, 1876.

Sansing, David G. "The Failure of Johnsonian Reconstruction in Mississippi, 1865–1866." *Journal of Mississippi History,* XXXIV (Nov. 1972), 373–90.

Schell, Herbert S. "Hugh McCulloch and the Treasury Department, 1865–1869." *Mississippi Valley Historical Review,* XVII (Dec. 1930), 404–21.

Schlegel, Marvin W. "The Dawes Plan: The Origin of the Joint Committee on Reconstruction." *Virginia Social Science Journal,* VI (Nov. 1971), 134–42.

Schmiel, Eugene D. "The Oberlin Letter: The Post-Civil War Northern Voter and the Freedman." *Northwest Ohio Quarterly,* XLIII (Fall 1971), 75–86.

Schuckers, Jacob William. *The Life and Public Services of Salmon P. Chase, U.S. Senator and Governor of Ohio.* N.Y.: D. Appleton Company, 1874.

Schurz, Carl. *Charles Sumner: An Essay by Carl Schurz.* Ed. by Arthur Reed Hogue. Urbana: University of Illinois Press, 1951.

Scroggs, Jack B. "Southern Reconstruction: A Radical View." *Journal of Southern History,* XXIV (Nov. 1958), 407–29.

Sefton, James E. "The Impeachment of Andrew Johnson: A Century of Writing." *Civil War History,* XIV (June 1968), 120–47.

———. *The United States Army and Reconstruction.* Baton Rouge: Louisiana University Press, 1965.

Seitz, Don C. *Horace Greeley: Founder of the New York Tribune.* Indianapolis: Bobbs-Merrill Company, 1926.

Sellers, James L. "James R. Doolittle." *Wisconsin Magazine of History,* XVII (Dec. 1933), 168–78; (March 1934), 277–306; (June 1934), 393–401; XVIII (Sept. 1934), 20–41; (Dec. 1934), 178–87.

Sewell, Richard H. *John P. Hale and the Politics of Abolition.* Cambridge, Mass.: Harvard University Press, 1965.

Shapiro, Samuel. *Richard Henry Dana, Jr., 1815–1882.* East Lansing: Michigan State University Press, 1961.

Sharkey, Robert P. *Money, Class, and Party: An Economic Study of Civil War and Reconstruction.* Johns Hopkins University Studies in Historical and Political Science. Baltimore: Johns Hopkins Press, 1959.

Shofner, Jerrel H. "Political Reconstruction in Florida." *Florida Historical Quarterly,* XLV (Oct. 1966), 145–70.

Shook, Robert W. "The Federal Military in Texas, 1865–1870." *Texas Military History,* VI (Spring 1967), 3–53.

Shover, Kenneth B. "Maverick at Bay: Ben Wade's Senate Re-election Campaign, 1862–1863." *Civil War History,* XII (March 1966), 23–42.

Simkins, Francis Butler and Robert Hilliard Woody. *South Carolina During Reconstruction.* Chapel Hill: University of North Carolina Press, 1932.

Sinkler, George. "Benjamin Harrison and the Matter of Race." *Indiana Magazine of History,* LXV (Sept. 1969), 197–213.

Smith, Donnal V. *Chase and Civil War Politics.* Volume II of the Ohio Historical Collections. Columbus: F.J. Heer Printing Company, 1931.

Smith, E.B. "Abraham Lincoln: Realist." *Wisconsin Magazine of History,* LII (Winter 1968–69), 158–68.

Smith, George P. "Republican Reconstruction and Section Two of the Fourteenth Amendment." *Western Political Quarterly,* XXIII (Dec. 1970), 829–53.

Smith, Theodore Clarke. *The Life and Letters of James Abram Garfield.* 2 vols. New Haven: Yale University Press, 1925.

Smith, Willard H. "The Colfax-Turpee Congressional Campaigns, 1862–1866." *Indiana Magazine of History,* XXXVIII (June 1942), 123–42.

———. *Schuyler Colfax: The Changing Fortunes of a Political Idol.* Volume XXXIII of the Indiana Historical Collections. Indianapolis: Indiana Historical Bureau, 1952.

Smith, William E. *The Francis Preston Blair Family in Politics.* 2 vols. N.Y.: The Macmillan Company, 1933.

Smith, William Henry. *A Political History of Slavery.* 2 vols. New York and London: G.P. Putnam's Sons, 1903.

Sproat, John G. "Blueprint for Radical Reconstruction." *Journal of Southern History,* XXIII (Feb. 1957), 25–44.

Stackpole, Everett S. *History of New Hampshire.* 4 vols. New York: American Historical Society, 1916.

Stampp, Kenneth M. *The Era of Reconstruction, 1865–1877.* New York: Alfred A. Knopf, 1965.

———. *Indiana Politics During the Civil War.* Volume XXXI of the Indiana Historical Collections. Indianapolis: Indiana Historical Bureau, 1949.

Staples, Thomas S. *Reconstruction in Arkansas, 1862–1874.* Volume CIX of the Studies in History, Economics and Public Law Edited by the Faculty of Political Science of Columbia University. New York: Columbia University Press, 1923.

Stearns, Frank Preston. *The Life and Public Services of George Luther Stearns.* Philadelphia and London: J.B. Lippincott Company, 1907.

Stebbins, Homer Adolph. *A Political History of the State of New York, 1865–1869.* Volume LV of Studies in History, Economics and Public Law Edited by the Faculty of Political Science of Columbia University. New York: Columbia University Press, 1913.

Steiner, Bernard Christian. *Life of Reverdy Johnson.* Baltimore: The Norman, Remington Company, 1914.

Stephenson, Wendell Holmes. *The Political Career of General James H. Lane.* Volume III of the publications of the Kansas State Historical Society. Topeka: Kansas State Historical Society, 1930.

Stewart, John D. II. "The Great Winnebago Chieftain: Simon Cameron's Rise to Power, 1860–1867." *Pennsylvania History,* XXXIX (Jan. 1972), 20–39.

Storey, Moorfield. *Charles Sumner. American Statesmen.* Ed. by John T. Morse, Jr. Boston and N.Y.: Houghton Mifflin Company, 1900.

——— and Edward W. Emerson. *Ebenezer Rockwood Hear: A Memoir.* Boston and N.Y.: Houghton Mifflin Company, 1911.

Story, Joseph. *Commentaries on the Constitution of the United States.* 2 vols. 2nd edn. Boston: Little, Brown and Company, 1851.

Stryker, Lloyd Paul. *Andrew Johnson: Profile in Courage.* N.Y.: The Macmillan Company, 1929.

Swanberg, W.A. *Sickles the Incredible.* N.Y.: Charles Scribner's Sons, 1956.

Swift, Donald C. "John A. Bingham and Reconstruction: The Dilemma of a Moderate." *Ohio History,* LXXVII (Winter, Spring, and Summer 1968), 76–94, 192–94.

Swinney, Everette. "Enforcing the Fifteenth Amendment, 1870–1877." *Journal of Southern History,* XXVIII (May 1962), 202–18.

Tansill, Charles Callan. *The Congressional Career of Thomas F. Bayard, 1869–1885.* Washington: Georgetown University Press, 1946.

Taylor, Alrutheus Ambush. *The Negro in the Reconstruction of Virginia.* N.Y.: Russell and Russell, 1969.

TenBroek, Jacobus. *The Antislavery Origins of the Fourteenth Amendment.* Berkeley and Los Angeles: University of California Press, 1951.

Thach, Charles C., Jr. *The Creation of the Presidency, 1775–1789: A Study in Constitutional History.* Series Number XL of the Johns Hopkins University Studies in Historical and Political Science. Baltimore: Johns Hopkins Press, 1922.

Thayer, William Roscoe. *The Life and Letters of John Hay.* 2 vols. Boston and N.Y.: Houghton Mifflin Company, 1915.

Thomas, Benjamin P. and Harold M. Hyman. *Stanton: The Life and Times of Lincoln's Secretary of War.* N.Y.: Alfred A. Knopf, 1962.

Thompson, Edwin Bruce. *Matthew Hale Carpenter Webster of the West.* Madison: State Historical Society of Wisconsin, 1954.

Thornbrough, Emma Lou. *Indiana in the Civil War Era, 1860–1880. The History of Indiana,* Vol. III. Indianapolis: Indiana Historical Bureau, 1965.

Tilton, Theodore. *Sanctum Sanctorum; or Proof-Sheets from an Editor's Table.* N.Y.: Sheldon and Company, 1870.

Trefousse, Hans L. "The Acquittal of Andrew Johnson and the Decline of the Radicals." *Civil War History,* XIV (June 1968), 148–61.

———. *Ben Butler: The South Called Him Beast!* N.Y.: Twayne Publishers, 1957.

———. "Ben Wade and the Failure of the Impeachment of Johnson." *Bulletin of the Historical and Philosophical Society of Ohio,* XVII (Oct. 1960), 241–52.

———. *Benjamin Franklin Wade: Radical Republican from Ohio.* N.Y.: Twayne Publishers, 1963.

———. "Ben Wade and the Negro." *Ohio Historical Quarterly,* LXVIII (April 1959), 161–76.

———. *The Radical Republicans: Lincoln's Vanguard for Racial Justice.* N.Y.: Alfred A. Knopf, 1968.

———. "Zachariah Chandler and the Withdrawal of Fremont in 1864: New Answers to an Old Riddle." *Lincoln Herald,* LXX (Winter 1968), 181–88.

Trelease, Allen W. *Reconstruction: The Great Experiment.* N.Y.: Harper and Row, 1972.

———. *White Terror: The Ku Klux Klan Conspiracy and Southern Reconstruction.* New York: Harper and Row, 1971.

Tucker, St. John (ed). *Blackstone's Commentaries: with Notes of Reference, to the Constitution and Laws, of the Federal Government of the United States; and of the Common Wealth of Virginia.* 5 vols. Philadelphia: Birch and Small, 1803.

Unger, Irwin. *The Greenback Era: A Social and Political History of American Finance, 1865–1879.* Princeton: Princeton University Press, 1964.

Uzee, Philip D. "The Beginnings of the Louisiana Republican Party." *Louisiana History,* XII (Summer, 1971), 197–211.

Van Deusen, Glyndon G. *Horace Greeley: Nineteenth Century Crusader.* American Century Series. N.Y.: Hill and Wang, 1964.

———. *Thurlow Weed: Wizard of the Lobby.* Boston: Little, Brown and Company, 1947.

———. *William Henry Seward.* N.Y.: Oxford University Press, 1967.

Voegeli, V. Jacque. *Free but Not Equal: The Midwest and the Negro During the Civil War.* Chicago: University of Chicago Press, 1967.

Waller, John L. *Collossal Hamilton of Texas: A Biography of Andrew Jackson Hamilton, Militant Unionist and Reconstruction Governor.* El Paso, Texas: Texas Western Press, 1968.

Warden, Robert Bruce. *An Account of the Private Life and Public Services of Salmon P. Chase.* Cincinnati: Wilstach, Baldwin and Company, 1874.

Ware, Edith Ellen. *Political Opinion in Massachusetts during Civil War and Reconstruction.* Volume LXXIV of the Studies in History, Economics and Public Law Edited by the Faculty of Political Science of Columbia University. N.Y.: Columbia University Press, 1916.

Weaver, Samuel P. *Constitutional Law and Its Administration.* Chicago: Callaghan and Co., 1946.

Webb, Ross A. "Benjamin Bristow: Civil Rights Champion, 1866–1872." *Civil War History,* XV (March 1969), 39–53.

Weisberger, Bernard. "The Dark and Bloody Ground of Reconstruction Historiagraphy." *Journal of Southern History,* XXV (Nov. 1957), 427–47.

Wheeler, Kenneth W. (ed). *For the Union: Ohio Leaders in the Civil War.* Columbus: Ohio State University Press, 1968.

White, Horace. *The Life of Lyman Trumbull.* Boston and N.Y.: Houghton Mifflin Company, 1913.

Wiggins, Sarah Woolfolk. "Unionist Efforts to Control Alabama Reconstruction, 1865–1867." *Alabama Historical Quarterly,* XXX (Spring 1968), 51–64.

Williams, Helen J. and Harry Williams. "Wisconsin Republicans and Reconstruction." *Wisconsin Magazine of History,* XXIII (Sept. 1939), 17–39.

Williams, T. Harry. *Lincoln and the Radicals.* Madison: University of Wisconsin Press, 1941.

Williamson, Joel. *After Slavery: The Negro in South Carolina During Reconstruction, 1861–1877.* Chapel Hill: University of North Carolina Press, 1965.

Wilson, Charles Jay. "The Negro in Early Ohio." *Ohio Archaeological and Historical Society Publications,* XXXIX (1930), 717–68.

Wilson, James Harrison. *The Life of John A. Rawlins: Lawyer, Assistant Adjutant-General, Chief of Staff, Major General of Volunteers, and Secretary of War.* N.Y.: Neale Publishing Company, 1916.

Wilson, Woodrow. *Congressional Government: A Study in American Politics.* Boston and N.Y.: Houghton Mifflin Company, 1913.

Winston, Robert W. *Andrew Johnson: Plebeian and Patriot.* N.Y.: Henry Holt, 1928.

Wood, Forrest G. *Black Scare: The Racist Response to Emancipation and Reconstruction.* Berkeley and Los Angeles: University of California Press, 1968.

———. "On Revising Reconstruction History: Negro Suffrage, White Disfranchisement and Common Sense." *Journal of Negro History,* LI (April 1966), 98–113.

Woodburn, James Albert. *The Life of Thaddeus Stevens.* Indianapolis: Bobbs-Merrill Company, 1913.

Woodley, Thomas Frederick. *Thaddeus Stevens.* Harrisburg, Pa.: Telegraph Press, 1934.

Yates, Richard and Pickering Catharine Yates. *Richard Yates: Civil War Governor.* Ed. by John H. Krenkel. Danville, Ill.: Interstate Printers and Publishers, 1966.

Zornow, William Frank. "The Kansas Senators and the Re-election of Lincoln." *Kansas History Quarterly,* XIX (May 1951), 133–44.

———. *Kansas: A History of the Jayhawk State.* Norman: University of Oklahoma Press, 1957.

———. *Lincoln & the Party Divided.* Norman: University of Oklahoma Press, 1954.

Index

Page numbers in *italics* refer to footnotes; those in **boldface** refer to illustrations.